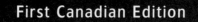

First Canadian Edition

D0094280

Perspectives on Contemporary Issues

Readings Across the Disciplines

Katherine Anne Ackley
University of Wisconsin at Stevens Point

G. Kim Blank
University of Victoria, British Columbia

Stephen Eaton Hume
University of Victoria, British Columbia

THOMSON
NELSON

Australia   Canada   Mexico   Singapore   Spain   United Kingdom   United States

THOMSON

NELSON ™

Perspectives on Contemporary Issues: Readings Across the Disciplines, First Canadian Edition

by Katherine Anne Ackley, G. Kim Blank, and Stephen Eaton Hume

Associate Vice President, Editorial Director:
Evelyn Veitch

Editor-in-Chief, Higher Education:
Anne Williams

Executive Editor:
Laura Macleod

Marketing Manager:
Shelley Collacutt Miller

Developmental Editor:
Theresa Fitzgerald

Photo Researcher and Permissions Coordinator:
Sandra Mark

Senior Content Production Manager:
Natalia Denesiuk Harris

Copy Editor:
Mariko Obokata

Proofreader:
June Trusty

Indexer:
Belle Wong

Production Coordinator:
Ferial Suleman

Design Director:
Ken Phipps

Interior Design:
Hearthside Publishing Services

Cover Design and Interior Design Modifications:
Dianna Little

Cover Image:
© Sylvaine Thomas/ Shutterstock

Compositor:
ICC Macmillan Inc.

Printer:
Thomson/West

Library and Archives Canada Cataloguing in Publication Data

Perspectives on contemporary issues : readings across the disciplines / [compiled and edited by] Katherine Anne Ackley, G. Kim Blank, Stephen Eaton Hume. — 1st Canadian ed.

Includes bibliographical references and index.
ISBN 978-0-17-610328-6

1. College readers.
2. Interdisciplinary approach in education—Problems, exercises, etc. 3. English language—Rhetoric—Problems, exercises, etc. 4. Academic writing—Problems, exercises, etc. 5. Current events—Problems, exercises, etc. 6. Readers—Current events.
I. Ackley, Katherine Anne
II. Blank, G. Kim, 1952– III. Hume, Stephen Eaton, 1947–

PE1417.P4592 2007
808'.0427   C2007-905234-7

ISBN-13: 978-0-17-610328-6
ISBN-10: 0-17-610328-7

CONTENTS

PREFACE

In the Canadian edition of this text, we have tried to bring together diverse voices that represent some of the perspectives that circulate in our complex world. Maybe that's the thing about Canada—we are all over the map when it comes to expressing ourselves and considering the views of others. In this collection are some lesser known Canadians as well as some more familiar names who have risen to the occasion as international and innovative thinkers; for example, Stephen Lewis (on AIDS), Margaret Atwood (on our relationship with the United States), and David Suzuki (on genetics and science). This volume also presents the views of politicians, poets, artists, soldiers, hockey players, football players, activists, academics, journalists, novelists, naturalists, and feminists. Some dead, some alive, but all, we feel, part of our culture. Our hope is that these voices matter, and that, at the very least, they challenge you to think and respond.

Part 1 of this book contains guidelines and checklists for writing and conducting research for an academic paper. Parts 2–4 contain the essays. In each chapter of Parts 2–4, you will find an introduction and, for each essay, a brief biography of the author, a "Personal Response" question that asks you to reflect on the implications of what you have read, and more specific questions for class or small groups that may give you ideas for topics and inspire your writing.

One common culture we share is our love of, and interest in, movies. And so, at the end of each chapter, we have included a section called "For Further Viewing." Here you will find a list of 10 or so movies that relate to the subjects of the essays. These movies may broaden your understanding of the words you have just read. You can rent these films, borrow them from a public library or school library, or download them. Your instructor may want to use some of these movies to amplify class discussion. We hope that these sections emphasize the natural linkage between the art of film and the art of writing, and that they help reflect the diverse ways in which we come to know our world.

ACKNOWLEDGMENTS

We would like to thank the following people for their ideas, support, and inspiration: Sikata Banerjee, Acia Blank, Jenner Blank, Misao Dean, Theresa Fitzgerald, Elizabeth Grove-White, Georgia Hume, Natalie Hume, Laura Macleod, Tara Ney, Mariko Obokata, Laura Parisi, June Trusty, and Madeline Walker. We also thank the three reviewers: Theresa Hyland, Huron University College; Therese Khimasia, The University of Western Ontario; and Susan Lieberman, Grant MacEwan College. Special thanks to Inba Kehoe of the McPherson Library at the University of Victoria.

G. Kim Blank
Stephen Eaton Hume
March 2007

PART ONE

WRITING CRITICALLY AND CONDUCTING RESEARCH

CHAPTER ONE

READING CRITICALLY

READING CRITICALLY IN PREPARATION FOR WRITING CRITICALLY

Critical reading does not necessarily mean that you object to what someone has written or that you view it negatively. Rather, it means that you read something carefully, thoughtfully, and thoroughly for two reasons: first, to understand it, and second, to assess it. You read for meaning first because, obviously, you must understand what you read before it can be examined. Once you develop a clear understanding of a piece of writing, you have a solid basis for moving beyond comprehension to evaluation.

Reading critically involves examining an author's ideas and the evidence the author has supplied in support of those ideas. It means that you try to recognize the difference between reasonable, logical assertions and those that are unreasonable or lack credibility. It requires you to distinguish between fact and opinion, to sort out the evidence an author cites, and to evaluate that evidence in terms of its relevance, accuracy, and importance. Thus, reading critically means that you actively engage in what you read, that you analyze it, and that you evaluate it. Learning to be a critical reader also helps to make you a better writer. If you pay attention to the ways in which professional writers and scholars use language, structure their essays, and develop their ideas, you will learn some valuable lessons for your own writing.

The following guidelines are not ironclad rules for reading critically, but they are useful suggestions to help you get the most from your reading. These reading guidelines will also be very helpful for any kind of writing required in your college or university courses, especially the one for which you are using this textbook. Certainly, reading critically is a necessity for any of the varieties of writing discussed in the remaining chapters in Part 1: summary, critique, argument, synthesis, and research paper.

Read the Title.   Before you read, consider the title. A title often not only reveals the subject of the piece, but it can also tell you something about the way in which the subject will be treated. It may reflect the tone of the piece and sometimes indicates the author's position on the subject. A number of essays in this textbook have revealing titles. For instance, the title "Marilyn Monroe: The Woman Who Died Too Soon," in Chapter 15, indicates that its author, Gloria Steinem, has poignant feelings about Monroe. Similarly, the title "Kill 'Em! Crush 'Em! Eat 'Em Raw!," also in Chapter 15, indicates that the subject will be violence—in this case, violence in football and, by extension, in society.

Find Out About the Author.   If information about the author is provided, read it. Knowing something about the author gives you an idea of the authority and point of view. The headnote is the information located between the title and the beginning of the essay, usually highlighted or set off from the body of the essay itself.

Determine the Purpose.   Good writers have clear purposes in mind as they plan and draft their writing. Most nonfiction writing falls into the category of either persuasive, expository, or expressive writing. These forms of writing are used to achieve different goals, and they adopt different strategies for achieving those goals. In persuasive writing, the emphasis is on the reader: The writer's purpose is to convince the reader of the validity of his or her position on an issue and sometimes even to move the reader to action. In expository writing, the goal is to inform or present an objective explanation. The emphasis is on ideas, events, or objects themselves, not on how the writer feels about them. Much of the writing in textbooks is expository, as are newspaper, magazine, and professional journal articles, and nonfiction books. Expository writing can take many forms, including cause–effect analysis, comparison/contrast, definition, and classification. Expressive writing emphasizes the writer's feelings and subjective view of the world. The writer's focus is on personal feelings about, or attitude toward, the subject. A journal or diary includes expressive writing. Persuasive, expository, and expressive writing often overlap, but usually a writer has one main purpose. From the opening paragraphs of a written work, you should be able to determine its general purpose or aim. A clearly implied or stated purpose helps the writer to shape the writing, and it helps the reader to understand and evaluate the work.

Determine the Intended Audience.   Writers make assumptions about the people they are writing for, and these assumptions influence the tone they use; the evidence they select; the way in which they organize and develop their writing; and even their sentence structure, word choices, and diction level. Knowing whom the writer is addressing helps you to understand the writer's point of view and to explain the choices the writer has made in writing the piece. When writing for college or university courses, or for that matter in any writing you do, you usually assume a general audience of people who are reasonably intelligent and interested in what you have to say. However, professional writers or scholars often write for specific audiences, depending on the publications in which their writing appears. Writers want to know if their audiences will be sympathetic or opposed to their positions. Knowing the likely positions of readers helps the writer to make decisions about what tone to use and what details to include.

Knowing whether an audience is familiar with a subject or whether the audience is specialized or general also governs what kind of evidence to offer and how much to include.

Locate the Thesis Statement or Main Idea.

The thesis states the main idea of the entire essay. Sometimes it is embodied in a single sentence—the thesis statement—and sometimes it is stated in several sentences. If the main idea is not explicitly stated, it should be clearly implied. The thesis statement answers the question, What is the main point of this essay? Whether the thesis is explicit or implicit, it is a necessary component of a clearly written work. A thesis helps the writer to focus the writing and guides the organization and development of key ideas. It also helps to provide direction to the reader and assists in the reader's understanding of the piece. Sometimes, however, the point of what you are reading or viewing can be subtle, complex, or even confusing. That is, it challenges you to think. Also, some pieces, especially if they are nontraditional, such as the Franke James environmental piece, in Chapter 21, or the "My Name is Joe" TV ad, in Chapter 8, leave the meaning up to you. But you still have to ask, What is the point being made? What is the big idea?

Locate Key Ideas and Supporting Evidence or Details.

For this step in your critical reading, you should underline or highlight the major points of the essay. One important tool for an active, critical reader is a pen or pencil. As you read, take time to underline, star, or in some way highlight major points of development. Look for topic sentences of paragraphs. The thesis statement answers the question, What is this essay about? In the same way, the topic sentence answers the question, What is this paragraph about? If a topic sentence is not clearly stated, it should be clearly implied.

Make Marginal Notes as You Read.

In the margins, write your response to a passage, or make note of words, phrases, or entire passages you think are important to the piece. Make notes about the evidence or details that support major points. If you have a question about something the author says, write it in the margin for later consideration. If you are not sure of the meaning of a word, circle it and look it up in a dictionary. Finally, if you are struck by the beauty, logic, or peculiarity of a passage, make comments in the margins.

Summarize What You Have Read.

This is the point at which you test your understanding of what you have read. Go back now and look at your underlinings and notations. Then try to state in your own words what the writing is about and the main points the writer made. If you can accurately summarize a piece of writing, then you probably have a good idea of its meaning. Summarizing also helps you to recall the piece later, perhaps in class or in small-group discussions. Incidentally, summarizing is also a good strategy for your own study habits. After reading an assignment for any of your courses, try to write or tell someone a summary of your reading. If you cannot express in your own words the major ideas of what you have just read, you should reread it.

GUIDELINES FOR READING CRITICALLY

- Consider what the title tells you about the essay.
- Try to learn something about the author.
- Determine the purpose of the writing.
- Determine the audience for whom the piece was written.
- Locate the thesis statement or main idea.
- Locate key ideas and supporting evidence or details.
- Make marginal notes as you read, including not only a summary of key ideas but also your questions about the content.
- Summarize what you have read.
- Evaluate what you have read.
- Evaluate what you feel.

Evaluate What You Have Read.   When you are sure that you understand what you have read and can summarize it objectively, you are ready to respond. You can evaluate something in a number of ways, depending on its purpose. First, consider whether the author achieves the stated or implied purpose and whether the thesis or main idea is thoroughly explained, developed, or argued. Has the writer supplied enough details, examples, or other evidence? If you are evaluating an argument or persuasion essay, is the evidence convincing? Does the piece make a logical and reasonable argument? Are you persuaded to the writer's position? What questions do you have about any of the writer's assertions? Do you wish to challenge the writer on any points? If the purpose of the essay is to describe, has the writer conveyed to you the essence of the subject with appropriately vivid language? For any piece of writing, you can assess how well-written it is. Is it organized? Is the writing clear to you? Does the introduction give you enough information to lead you easily into the essay, and does the conclusion leave you satisfied that the writer has accomplished the purpose of the essay?

Evaluate What You Feel.   Often our first response to something we read, view, or hear works on an emotional level. You might feel, for example, uneasy, mad, sad, skeptical, or enthusiastic. Examining your emotional response can often lead to critical insights. Further, you might also discover something about your own beliefs and values, which is an important step toward becoming a critical reader.

ORGANIZING AND DEVELOPING IDEAS

It is helpful in both your own writing and in evaluating the writing of others to be familiar with common kinds of writing and the strategies writers use for organizing and developing their ideas. If you understand what strategies are available to a writer and what elements make those strategies work, you can better evaluate how well a selection is written. Writers use many different strategies or rhetorical methods to organize and develop their ideas, depending on their purposes and their audience. Whether they pursue persuasive, expository, or expressive purposes, writers must be focused and clear if they want to engage their readers.

Your first draft and early drafts will require rewriting to sharpen your focus. In other words, you might not know what you think until you write it down—so write it down. Writers often refine what they want to express through the act of writing; rewriting your sentences is a key element in the composition process. They can achieve clarity or coherence with good organization and logical development of ideas. Writers seldom use any one method exclusively, or even think about any particular pattern or mode of development. Instead, they first decide what their purpose for writing is, and then they use whatever combination of patterns best achieves that purpose.

In your college or university courses, you will often be given written assignments. No matter what the course, whether it is art history, communications, economics, anthropology, or business, the instructor may require a paper on a subject relevant to the course. Furthermore, students are very likely to encounter essay questions on exams, since instructors seem to agree that one of the best tests of understanding is to ask students to write about course material in some detail on quizzes or exams. Whether it is economics or English, students may be asked to argue a position on a controversial issue. An art professor may ask students to write a description of a painting, or a math professor may test understanding by asking students to explain in writing how to solve a problem. Whatever a writer's purpose, some fairly standard models can help to organize written work. But remember: Seldom will a writer use just one of these rhetorical modes in isolation; they are almost always used in combinations of two or more. The important consideration is how a writer can organize and develop the material for the best effect, in a way that best suits the purpose of the assignment.

Argument/Persuasion. The goal of argument is to convince readers of the validity of the writer's position (argument) or to move readers to accept the author's view and even act on it (persuasion). In argument, a writer sets forth an assertion (often called a proposition) about a debatable topic and offers proof intended to convince readers that the assertion is valid or true. In persuasion, a writer goes a step further and offers a course of action, with the ultimate goal of motivating readers to take action. The supporting evidence or proof must be so convincing that readers cannot help but agree with the validity of the author's position. The reasoning process must be so logical that readers inevitably draw the same conclusions as the author from the evidence presented.

Cause–Effect Analysis. A writer who wants to explain why something happened or show what happened as a result of something—or perhaps both—is doing cause-and-effect analysis. This type of analysis is used frequently in news broadcasts and magazine and newspaper articles to explain phenomena, such as the chain of events that led to a particular action, the effects of a particular event or crisis, or both causes and effects of a specific situation. Cause-and-effect analysis is also used frequently to argue. A writer might use the strategy of causal analysis to argue that offering sex education in schools or making contraceptives readily available to high-school students would be more effective in reducing the number of teenage pregnancies than prohibiting explicit sex scenes on prime-time television. The writer would have to sort out possible causes to explain the rate of teenage pregnancies, determine which causes are likely most responsible and which are contributing factors, and then conjecture likely results if the recommendation were followed.

Comparison/Contrast.   Another strategy for developing ideas is to show similarities and differences between two elements. Comparison and contrast can be useful in an argument piece in which the writer supports one of two possible choices and needs to explain reasons for that choice. In an expository essay—that is, one with the purpose of explaining something—comparison and contrast can be useful to demonstrate a thorough understanding of the subject. Comparing or contrasting usually promotes one of two purposes: to show each of two subjects distinctly by considering both side by side, or to evaluate or judge two things. An analogy is a useful kind of comparison when seeking to explain a complicated or unfamiliar subject by showing its similarities to a less complicated or more familiar subject.

Classification/Division.   Classification is sorting information and ideas into categories or groups; division is breaking information, ideas, or concepts into parts in order to better understand them. A writer may use classification to explain how a particular class of people, things, or ideas can be separated into groups and labelled according to common characteristics that distinguish them from other groups. A writer may use division to make a large, complex subject easier to understand by dividing it into smaller, more manageable parts.

Definition.   Writers often need to define while they inform or argue. Definition is the process of making clear a precise meaning or significance. In definition, a writer conveys the essential characteristics of something by distinguishing it from all other things in its class. You are familiar with dictionary definitions of words. Writers employ a similar technique to clarify or to explain, but usually in more detail than dictionaries. In addition to providing brief definitions of terms, a writer may provide an extended definition—that is, take the meaning of a word beyond its dictionary definition or beyond the limits of a simple definition. An extended definition may take a paragraph or two or even the length of an entire essay. A writer using abstract terms or concepts unfamiliar to an audience will find the extended definition a useful tool. In her highly personal essay on living in poverty as a child, Melanie Scheller defines both the condition of poverty and the emotion of shame in "On the Meaning of Plumbing and Poverty," in Chapter 13.

Exemplification.   Examples and illustrations are crucial to writing, no matter what the primary purpose. Without examples, writing remains at the general or abstract level and leaves readers only vaguely understanding what the writer means. Examples make meaning clear and help to make writing more interesting, livelier, and more engaging than in an essay without details. Examples may be brief and numerous or extended and limited in number, and they may take the form of narratives. It would be difficult to find an effective piece of writing that does not use examples of some sort. For example, notice how Margaret Atwood uses vivid examples to strengthen her argument in "Letter to America" in Chapter 11.

Narration. Narration is the re-creation of an experience for a specific purpose. It may be a brief anecdote, a story, or a case history. Writers use narration for a variety of purposes: to explain, to illustrate a particular point, to report information, to entertain, or to persuade. Often a narrative is only one part of a written work, but occasionally it may be the entire means of development. Journalists are accustomed to asking themselves a series of questions when they write their stories to ensure they give complete narratives: What happened? To whom did it happen? When did it happen? Where did it happen? Why did it happen? How did it happen—that is, under what circumstances or in what way did it happen? Narration is often combined with description. In the process of defining what poverty and shame meant to her, Melanie Scheller uses narration in "On the Meaning of Plumbing and Poverty," in Chapter 13.

Description. Description depicts in words a person, place, or thing by appealing to the senses—that is, by evoking through words certain sights, smells, sounds, or tactile sensations. Description is an almost indispensable part of writing; it is certainly inextricably linked with narration. As with narration and all other kinds of writing, description has a purpose. The purpose of description may be objective: to convey information without bias—or it may be subjective: to express feelings, impressions, or attitudes about a person, place, or thing. We can see how a writer combines description and narration in Jane Smiley's "You Can Never Have Too Many," in Chapter 15.

Keep in mind that these various rhetorical methods—ways of organizing and developing ideas—are almost never used in isolation. Seldom will you find a piece of writing that does not combine two or more of these strategies, which are all equally useful depending on your purpose for writing, the audience you are writing to, and the context you are writing in. For instance, in addition to narration and description, Jane Smiley, in the essay just mentioned, also uses exemplification and comparison/contrast as she examines the effects of Barbie dolls on her daughters' development. You will notice as you read the essays in this textbook that all of the writers employ a variety of strategies to achieve their purpose.

CHAPTER TWO

WRITING A SUMMARY

Students often must write both informal exercises and formal papers based on readings in their textbooks. When writing assignments for the course using this textbook, for instance, you will find frequent use for information or ideas discussed in the readings. For formal writing assignments, you may be instructed to develop a topic from the Personal Response or Questions for Class or Small-Group Discussion sections that follow the essays. You may choose to argue in favour of or against a position another author takes; you may use information from one or more of the readings to write an essay suggested by a particular chapter; you may decide to compare and contrast two or more essays in a chapter or explain various perspectives on an issue. At some point, you may want to use some of the readings from this or another textbook in combination with other print and Internet resources in a research paper.

This and the next three chapters introduce several specific types of assignments and provide guidelines for writing them. This chapter focuses on the summary, Chapter 3 on writing a critique, Chapter 4 on writing an argument, and Chapter 5 on writing a synthesis with documentation. In all of these assignments, you may be called on to paraphrase, quote, and document material you are writing. The guidelines for paraphrasing, quoting, and documenting sources are explained in Chapter 5. All illustrations of handling source material follow MLA (Modern Language Association) documentation style. (Note: If your instructor prefers that you use APA (American Psychological Association) style or gives you a choice of styles, guidelines for APA documentation style appear in Chapter 6.) For tips on formatting course papers, see Appendix 1 (pages 449–450). The terms associated with researching and writing papers are defined in Appendix 2 (pages 451–452).

WRITING A SUMMARY

Summarizing produces an objective restatement of a written passage in your own words in a much shorter version than the original. The purpose of a summary is to highlight both the central idea or ideas and the major points of a work. A summary does not attempt to restate the entire reading. You might summarize an entire book in the space of a paragraph or perhaps even a sentence, although you will not do full justice to a lengthy work that way. Many reasons call for summarizing. Your instructor may ask you to write a summary of an essay, or a passage from an essay, to gauge your understanding. Such an assignment may be informal, something that you write in class as a quiz or an ungraded journal entry; or you may be assigned a formal summary, a longer piece that you write out of class, in detail and with care. Many kinds of writing include summaries as part of the development of their main ideas. For instance, if you are asked to report on an individual or group research project for a science class, you will probably summarize your purpose, methodology, data, and conclusions. If you write an argumentative paper, you may need to summarize either opposing viewpoints or your own supporting evidence. A research paper often includes summaries of information from source materials, and the research process itself necessitates summarizing portions of what you read. Reviews of books or articles almost always include summaries of the works under discussion. Similarly, essay questions on an examination often require summaries of information or data. Across the curriculum, no matter what course you are taking, you will probably be asked to summarize.

Summaries serve useful purposes. Professors summarize as they lecture in order to convey information in a condensed way when a detailed review would take far too much time. Textbook chapters often present summaries of chapter contents as part of chapter introductions. In this textbook, some of the questions for small-group and class discussion following the readings ask you to summarize major points or portions of readings, in order to facilitate your understanding of the text. That process, in turn, enhances the quality of your classroom experience and develops your abilities to follow the discussion intelligently and to make useful contributions to the discussion yourself. Your instructor may ask you to write a summary of a piece you have read as a formal assignment. Summarizing is also an excellent strategy to enhance your own study habits. After reading an assignment for any of your courses, try to write a summary of the reading. If you cannot put into your own words the major ideas of what you have just read, you may need to go back and reread the material.

Outside the classroom and the academic environment, summaries routinely provide brief introductions, overviews, and conclusions of subjects at hand. In business, economics, industry, law, medicine, scientific research, government, journalism, or any other field, both managers and workers often need quick summaries to familiarize themselves with the high points or essence of information. Knowing how to summarize accurately is a skill that you will find useful in both your academic writing and in your profession or job.

A Summary Is Not a Substitute for Analysis.   Do not mistakenly assume that putting another person's words into your own words is an analysis. Instead, a summary is a brief, concise, objective restatement of the important elements of a piece of writing of any length, from a paragraph to an entire book. A summary may be brief, as in a one-paragraph abstract that precedes a report or long paper and provides a very short overview of it, or it may be several paragraphs or even pages in length, depending on the length of the writing or writings being summarized. You may summarize as an informal exercise for your own purposes or as a formal assignment that you hand in to your instructor for evaluation.

Abstract.   An abstract, like all summaries, is a condensed, objective restatement of the essential points of a text. Its distinguishing characteristic is its brevity. Abstracts are usually quite short, perhaps 100 to 200 words, whereas summaries may be much longer, depending on the length of the piece being summarized. As with all summaries, an abstract helps readers determine quickly whether an article or book will be of interest or use. It can also serve as a brief guide to the key points before reading an article or as an aid in recalling the contents of the article after reading it.

Formal and Informal Summaries.   The trick in summarizing accurately is knowing what is important, and therefore must be included, and what is secondary, and therefore should be omitted. Here you see the usefulness of the guidelines for critical reading. When you read critically, you identify the main idea or thesis of the selection, and you highlight the major points. A summary must include the main idea of what you are summarizing, and it should include major points, and only major points. Thus, if you learn to read critically, you can write a summary.

Although the process is the same for both an assignment that you will hand in to your instructor and a summary for your own use, a formal summary requires the kind of care that you give to longer writing assignments. Begin by carefully reading the work. Make a mental note of its thesis or main idea but do not write anything in the margins yet. If you try to highlight for a summary on your first reading, you might end up underlining or noting too many things. Wait until you have read through the entire selection once before writing anything. After your first reading, write in your own words the thesis or central idea as you understand it. Then go back to the article, locate the thesis or main idea, underline it, and compare it with the sentence you wrote. If your sentence differs from the sentence(s) you underlined, rephrase your own sentence. Next, read the article again, this time looking for major points of development or illustration of the thesis. As you reread, make marginal notes and underline, circle, or in some way mark the key supporting points or major ideas in the development of the thesis. After you have finished reading, look at your notes and state in one sentence, in your own words, the thesis and each major point. Do not include details or minor supporting evidence unless leaving them out would misrepresent or unfairly represent what you are summarizing. If the writing you are summarizing comes to any important conclusions, note them as well in one sentence, in your own words. If you are still unclear about which are major and which are minor points, give the piece another reading. The more you read it, the better you understand its purpose, method of development, and major points.

GUIDELINES FOR WRITING A SUMMARY

- On your first reading, mentally note the thesis or central idea of the work or passage you are summarizing without writing anything down.
- After your first reading, write down your understanding of the thesis, locate the thesis in the work, underline it, check what you have written against it, and adjust your own sentence if necessary.
- Now reread the work, noting key points in the margin, by highlighting, or on a separate piece of paper.
- When you have finished your second reading, once again write in your own words a one-sentence summary of the thesis or central idea. Use the author's name and title of the reading in that sentence.
- Write in your own words a one-sentence summary of each major point the author has used to develop, illustrate, or support the thesis or central idea. State only essential details related to each major point.
- Do not include minor points unless you believe their omission would give an unfair representation of what you are summarizing.
- Where appropriate, write in your own words a one-sentence summary of any conclusion from the piece.
- Keep your summary short, succinct, and focused on the central idea and major points of the piece you are summarizing.
- Edit for grammar, punctuation, and spelling before handing in your assignment.

Now you are ready to write your summary. In your opening sentence, state the author's full name, the title of the work, and the thesis or main idea. Write in complete sentences, whether your summary is 100 words or 500 words long. Use the author's last name when referring to what the author says in the article or when quoting the author directly. Do not use the exact words of the author unless you use quotation marks around those words. (Some summaries avoid all exact language, including quotations.) The summary must use your own wording unless you use a key term or concept. Use direct quotations sparingly, and only for a significant word, phrase, or sentence, and make sure that anything you put in quotation marks uses the exact wording of the original article. Provide clear transitions from point to point, just as you would in a longer assignment, and write in clear, coherent language. Edit what you have written before turning it in to your instructor.

WRITING A SYNTHESIS

A synthesis draws conclusions from, makes observations on, or shows connections between two or more sources. In writing a synthesis, you attempt to make sense of the ideas of two or more sources by extracting information that is relevant to your purpose. The ability to synthesize is an important skill, since people are continuously bombarded with a dizzying variety of information and opinions that need sorting out and assessment. To understand your own thinking on a subject, it is always useful to know what others have to say about it. You can see the importance of reading and thinking critically when synthesizing the ideas of others. The sources for a synthesis may be essays, books, editorials, lectures, movies, group discussions, or any of the myriad forms of communication that inform academic and personal lives. At minimum, you will be required in a synthesis to reflect on the ideas of two writers or other sources, assess them, make connections between them, and arrive at your own conclusions on the basis of your analysis. Often you will work with more than two sources; certainly you will do so in a research paper.

Your purpose for writing a synthesis will be determined by the nature of your assignment, although syntheses are most commonly used to either explain or argue. Perhaps you want to explain how something works or show the causes or effects of a particular event. You may argue a particular point, using the arguments of others as supporting evidence or as subjects for disagreement in your own argument. You

GUIDELINES FOR WRITING A SYNTHESIS

- **Determine your purpose for writing by asking yourself what you want to do in your essay.** Without a clear purpose, your synthesis will be a loosely organized, incoherent jumble of words. Although your purpose is often governed by the way in which the assignment is worded, make sure you understand exactly what you intend to do.

- **Consider how best to accomplish your purpose.** Will you argue, explain, compare and contrast, illustrate, show causes and effects, describe, or narrate? How will you use your sources to accomplish your purpose?

- **Read each source carefully and understand its central purpose and major points.** If you are unclear about the meaning of an essay, reread it carefully, noting passages that give you trouble. Discuss these passages with a classmate or with your instructor if you still lack a clear understanding.

- **Write a one-sentence statement of the central idea or thesis and a brief summary of each source you will use in your paper.** This process will help clarify your understanding of your sources and assist in formulating your own central idea. These statements or summaries can then be incorporated appropriately into your synthesis.

- **Write a one-sentence statement of your own thesis or central purpose for writing the synthesis.** This statement should be a complete sentence, usually in the first paragraph of your essay. The thesis statement helps you focus your thoughts as you plan your essay by limiting the nature and scope of what you intend to accomplish. It also is a crucial aid to your readers, because it is essentially a succinct summary of what you intend to do.

- **Develop or illustrate your thesis by incorporating the ideas of your sources into the body of your paper, either by paraphrasing or directly quoting.** Part of your purpose in writing a synthesis is to demonstrate familiarity with your sources and to draw on them in your own essay. This goal requires that you make reference to key ideas of the sources.

- **Document your sources.** Keep in mind the guidelines for documenting all borrowed material.

may want to compare or contrast the positions of other writers for the purpose of stating your own opinion on the subject. When you write a research paper, you most certainly must synthesize the ideas and words of others. Whether your research paper is a report or an argument, you must sort through and make sense of what your sources say. Sometimes you will want to read many sources to find out what a number of people have to say about a particular subject in order to discover your own position.

Synthesis, then, involves not only understanding what others have to say on a given subject but also making connections between them, analyzing their arguments or examples, and/or drawing conclusions from them. These are processes you routinely employ in both your everyday life and in your courses whenever you consider the words, ideas, or opinions of two or more people or writers on a topic.

CHAPTER THREE

WRITING A CRITIQUE

THE CONNECTION BETWEEN READING CRITICALLY AND WRITING A CRITIQUE

A critique is the written form of an evaluation of a passage or an entire work. Reading critically is the biggest aid to writing a critique; applying the guidelines for reading critically is a crucial part of preparing to write a critique. You will need to understand not only the purpose of the piece and its central idea but also the main points the writer makes. Reading critically enriches your understanding of a work and its components, enabling you to focus your critique. So, the first step in writing a critique is to read critically and, in the process, to determine your opinion of the piece. Apply the guidelines detailed in Chapter 1, but especially read for an understanding of the thesis and purpose of the writing, the likely intended audience, the key ideas or supporting evidence for the thesis, the author's use of language, the organization of the piece in relation to the subject matter, and whether the piece has successfully achieved its stated or implied goal. You may need to read the piece several times before you are clear on your own viewpoint and therefore prepared to write your critique.

WRITING A CRITIQUE

When you write a critique, your goal is to make a formal analysis of and response to a piece of writing, whether a selected passage or an entire essay. Your purpose encompasses both explaining and evaluating a piece of writing. In general, a written critique includes five components: (1) an introduction; (2) an objective, concise summary of the work or passage; (3) an objective analysis of the author's presentation; (4) a subjective response detailing your opinion of the author's views; and (5) a conclusion. *A critique differs from a summary, which is an objective restatement in your own words of the original material. When you summarize, you leave out your personal or subjective viewpoint. In a critique, you begin objectively then add your own subjective response to the work.*

A Note on Verb Tense.   Whenever you write about or refer to another person's work, use the present tense: "David Suzuki argues. . . ." or "Suzuki asserts that. . . ." Use the past tense only to refer to something that happened before the time span of the essay: "Suzuki says Josef Mengele, the infamous Nazi doctor, was in the news when forensic scientists discovered his bones in Brazil."

Determining Your Position.   To convince an audience that your analysis and response are reasonable or valid, you must convey your views confidently. Thus, before you even begin writing your critique, you must have a clear idea of your own viewpoint on the work. A firm conviction of your own position will help persuade an audience that your critique is sensible and fair. How do you arrive at your position? You do so by carefully reading and rereading the piece you are to critique, by thinking seriously about what the piece says and how it says it, and by assessing how persuaded you are as a reader by what the author has said. This stage in the writing process is crucial for helping you formulate and make concrete the points you want to make in the formal assignment.

   Any number of tools for generating writing ideas can be used to help you arrive at your position when writing a critique. The following suggestions are no doubt familiar to you from other writing classes, but here they are worded specifically for discovering your response to a piece of writing that you are to critique.

Free Writing.   As soon as you have read or reread the work, write for 10 minutes any impressions of any aspect of the piece that occur to you. Write down everything that comes to mind, no matter how jumbled. When your time is up, select a phrase or word that seems important to your purpose, no matter how vaguely, and write a sentence with the phrase or word in it. Put that sentence at the top of another blank piece of paper and repeat the process of writing for 10 minutes without thinking very deeply or very long about what you are writing. If you do this exercise several times, you should end up with a fairly good idea of the position you want to take in the analysis/assessment part of your paper.

Listing.   Another way to discover your viewpoint is to simply list terms or phrases describing your response to the piece you are critiquing. Then study your list and group related ideas together. Do you see a pattern? Does one dominant viewpoint emerge from these groupings? If so, write a statement reflecting that pattern or viewpoint. This exercise should give you a sense of your position when it comes to writing your assessment of and response to the work.

Asking Questions.   Asking questions is a very useful tool for generating ideas, perhaps most useful when thinking about and drafting your response to a piece of writing. These questions will help you arrive at your overall response to the work and discover your own position in relation to that of the writer whose work you are critiquing.

However, because the response section of a critique expresses your personal, subjective reaction to the work, you will want to ask additional questions:

- Do you agree with the writer's position on the subject? Why or why not?
- What reasons can you give for supporting or disagreeing with the writer?
- Are you convinced by the writer's logic, evidence, and language? Why or why not?
- If you are not convinced, can you give other evidence to counter the arguments or evidence of the writer?

You do not need to go into great detail in the response section of your paper, but you do need to explain your reasons for your response. Give careful thought, then, to not only what you think of the piece of writing but also why you think that way. What specific elements of the work influence your reaction to the work? As with free writing and listing, write your questions and answers. Review what you have written and consider whether you have left anything unasked or unanswered.

When you are satisfied with your pre-writing activities and feel that you have generated enough ideas to write your critique confidently, you are ready to write your first draft. As with all writing assignments, you will likely write several drafts of a paper before you reach the final version. The following section lists the components of a formal critique and gives directions for writing each component.

Introduction.   The first paragraph of your critique should name the author and title of the work that you are critiquing. Do not neglect this information, since it immediately tells readers the subject of your critique. Next, give a very brief overview of the piece in two to four sentences. Your intent in the introduction is not to summarize the piece but to tell readers its purpose. Generally, stating the thesis or central idea of the piece along with a highlight or two and/or its major conclusion(s) will be enough to convey its essence and provide background for the rest of your paper. Finally, your introduction should state your own thesis. In one sentence, indicate your assessment of the passage or work that you examined. Your thesis statement should be worded to reveal your position to readers before they begin reading the body of your paper.

Summary.   The first section in the body of your critique should offer an objective summary of the piece. This summary states the original author's purpose and includes key ideas and major points. Where appropriate, include direct quotations that are particularly important to the development of the piece. Do not write anything evaluative or subjective at this point. Your purpose here is to give a fair and accurate summary of the intent and main points of the work you are analyzing.

Analysis.   Once you have summarized the work by stating its purpose and key points, begin to analyze the work. Your goal is to examine how well the author has achieved the purpose and consider the validity or significance of the author's information. Do not try to look at every point the author makes; rather, limit your focus to several important aspects of the piece. Remain as objective as possible in this section, saving your personal opinion of the author's position for the response section of your critique. Different purposes for writing—persuasive, expository, and expressive—require different criteria to judge a writer's success in achieving the intended purpose. In general, however, certain considerations help in the assessment of any piece of writing. Questions about validity, accuracy, significance, and fairness help you to evaluate any author's success or failure.

Assessing Persuasive Writing.   Chapter 1 defines argumentative writing as a mode of persuasion in which the goal is either to convince readers of the validity of the writer's position (argument) or to move readers to accept the author's view and perhaps even act on it (persuasion). In other words, writers must supply evidence or proof to support their position in such a way as to convince readers that the position is valid, whether readers agree with the position or not. If the purpose is to persuade, the supporting evidence or proof must be so convincing that readers adopt the position themselves. Chapter 4 is devoted to a full discussion of writing an argument, so you may want to look at its section on structuring an argument. In any event, when assessing the success of another writer's argument, you should gauge how well that writer has used the standard strategies for argumentation. Furthermore, pay attention to the writer's use of language. Finally, assess the validity of the argument by examining the evidence presented to support the writer's position and the logic of the conclusions.

Examining a Writer's Language.   In particular, make sure that the writer defines any words or terms that may be unclear, abstract, or ambiguous. Ask yourself whether the writer's language seems intended to intimidate or confuse readers or whether the writer attempts to manipulate readers by relying on emotionally loaded words. Does the writer make sarcastic remarks or personal attacks? Ultimately, examine a writer's evidence, to evaluate credibility and fairness. Good writers do not rely on manipulative language, unclear terms, or loaded or sarcastic words to achieve their purposes.

Examining a Writer's Evidence.   A writer should support any generalizations or claims with ample, relevant evidence. As a critical reader, consider the value or significance of that evidence. Evidence may be supplied in the form of statistics, facts, examples, or appeals to authorities. Keep in mind that statistics can be manipulated to conform to the needs of the person using them, so make sure that they are based on a large and representative sample, that the method of gathering the statistics yields accurate results, and that the statistics come from reliable sources. Look closely at statements of facts, as well; they should give accurate, complete, and trustworthy information. Examples are specific instances or illustrations that reveal a whole type, and they should provide believable, relevant, reliable, and representative support for an author's thesis. Finally, authorities are people who have the training or experience needed to make trustworthy and reliable observations on matters relating to their areas of expertise. In completing a critique, make sure, as far as possible, that the piece under study appeals to believable and credible authorities.

Judging a Writer's Logic.   Argumentative or persuasive writing must portray a logical, reasonable, and accurate reasoning process supplemented by relevant, sensible supporting proofs. You will be in a good position to evaluate a writer's reasoning process if you are mindful of any pitfalls that undermine the success of the argument. Evaluating the writer's logic is part of the process of critiquing a work. The following list is a summary of some flaws in logic that you should look for when writing your critique:

- **Hasty or faulty generalization.** The drawing of a broad conclusion on the basis of very little evidence. Example: Assuming that all rock musicians use hard drugs before performances because of the highly publicized behaviour of a few musicians is an example of faulty generalization.
- **Oversimplification.** Offering a solution or an explanation that is too simple for the problem or issue being argued. This fault in logic overlooks the complexity of an issue. Example: Arguing that the crime rate will go down if we just outlaw handguns overlooks such important considerations as crimes committed with weapons other than handguns and the likely probability that the criminal underworld would continue to have access to guns, illegal or not.
- **Stereotyping.** A form of generalization or oversimplification in which an entire group is narrowly labelled or perceived on the basis of a few in the group. Example: Arguing that women are not suited for combat because women are weaker than men is a stereotype based on the fact that the average woman is weaker than the average man. Not all women are weaker than men, and not all forms of combat involve brute strength.
- **False analogy.** Falsely claiming that, because something resembles something else in one way, it resembles it in all ways. Example: Arguing that anti-abortionists cannot favour the death penalty because they view abortion as murder is a false analogy.
- **Non sequitur.** Drawing inferences or conclusions that do not follow logically from available evidence. Example: Reminding a child who will not eat her food of all the starving children in the world is a line of reasoning that does not follow: If the child eats her food, will that lessen the starvation of other children? If the child does not eat the food, can the food itself somehow aid those starving children?
- **Ad hominem arguments.** Attacking the character of the arguer rather than the argument itself. Example: Arguing that because someone has been in prison, you shouldn't believe anything she says.
- **Circular reasoning or begging the question.** Making a claim that simply rephrases another claim in other words. It assumes as proof the very claim it is meant to support. Example: A parent replying "because I said so" when a child asks why he must do something.
- **Emotionally charged language.** Relying on language guaranteed to appeal to an audience on an emotional rather than an intellectual level. Example: Invoking images of dirty homeless children in rags living on dangerous streets and eating scraps of garbage when arguing for increased funds for child services is an appeal to the emotions. This appeal is all right to use sparingly, but it becomes a fault in logic when the argument is based entirely on such language.
- **Either/or reasoning.** Admitting only two sides to an issue and asserting that the writer's view is the only possible correct one. Example: Arguing that if

you do not support your country's involvement in war as I do, you are not patriotic. The implication is that "either you are for your country or you are against it and the right way is my way."

- **Red herring.** Diverting the audience's attention from the main issue at hand to an irrelevant issue. Example: Just because a hockey player has been charged with spousal abuse doesn't support the argument for getting rid of violence in hockey.

- **Post hoc, ergo propter hoc reasoning.** Assuming that something happened simply because it followed something else without evidence of a causal relationship. Example: Arguing that an airline is faulty because of flight delays at an airport assumes that the airline caused the delays, when a more important factor might be weather conditions that prevented airplanes from flying.

Response.   In this part of your critique, express your own position relative to that of the writer of the piece and give reasons why you believe as you do. You may find yourself in total agreement or absolutely opposed to the author's position, or you may place yourself somewhere in between. You may agree with some points the author makes but disagree with others. No matter what position you take, you must state your viewpoint clearly and provide reasons for your position. These reasons may be closely linked to your assessment of key elements of the paper, as laid out in your assessment section, or they may spring from ideas that you generated in your pre-writing activities.

WRITING A CRITIQUE: PREPARATION AND EVALUATION

First, read the text critically by
- determining the main point, the chief purpose, and the intended audience;
- identifying arguments that support or develop the main point;
- locating evidence used to support the arguments; and
- determining any underlying biases or unexamined assumptions.

Then evaluate the text by asking
- Has the author clearly stated or implied a thesis, main idea, or position?
- Has the author written to a clearly identifiable audience?
- What rhetorical strategies in the development and organization of the essay does the writer use? Is the development appropriate to the purpose? Is the essay logically and clearly organized?
- If the writing is an argument, does the author use verifiable facts or convincing evidence? If the essay seeks to explain, define, describe, or accomplish some other purpose, has the writer supplied enough details to clearly achieve the stated or implied purpose?
- Are language and word choice accurate, imaginative, correct, and/or appropriate?
- Does the text leave any unanswered questions?

GUIDELINES FOR WRITING A CRITIQUE

- Begin with an introduction. The introduction familiarizes readers with the work under discussion, provides a context for the piece, and states your thesis.
- Summarize the main points. The summary tells readers what major points the writer makes to support the stated position.
- Analyze how well the writer has achieved the purpose of the work. The analysis tells readers what aspects of the work you have examined, depending on the kind of writing you are considering. In general, assess the overall presentation of evidence, judging its validity, accuracy, significance, and fairness.
- Explain your response to the piece. The response section tells readers your personal viewpoint by explaining the extent to which you agree or disagree with the author.
- Conclude with your observations of the overall effectiveness of the piece and your personal views on the subject. The conclusion summarizes for readers the results of your analysis and your overall judgment of the piece.

Conclusion.   The final paragraph of your critique should reiterate in several sentences your overall assessment of the piece, the conclusions you have drawn from your analysis, and your personal response to the work. This section is not the place to introduce new material; rather, it is an opportunity to provide an overall summary of your paper. You want your readers to feel that you have given them a thorough and thoughtful analysis of the work under consideration, and that you have brought your comments to a satisfying close.

Evaluation and Editing.   Kim Blank's *Marking Grid and Writing Checklist* (see Appendix 3, page 453) is designed to help you self-evaluate your work, but, more importantly, it is designed to play a role in peer editing and in the peer evaluation process. If followed, the checklist forces you to pay attention to the range of particular components in both your own writing and the writing of others. In short, it answers the question, What should I be looking for when I read the work of others? Following the checklist carefully, and taking responsibility for reading the papers of your peers carefully, is, then, an integral part of your assignment. Instructors can, of course, fine-tune this checklist depending on the assignment or the intended learning outcomes.

Also helpful is *Blank's Really Annoying Quirk List* (see Appendix 4, pages 454–457), which evolved originally to rid the world of wordiness, and then expanded to include some of the most common writing errors that need to be avoided. The idea is simple: If a phrase or grouping of words seems familiar, either drop those words or find a new way to convey what it is you want to say. Get rid of the clutter in your writing.

CHAPTER FOUR

WRITING AN ARGUMENT

Argumentation is a reasoning process that seeks to provide evidence or proof that a proposition is valid or true. An argument sets forth a claim and presents a coherent, organized set of reasons why that claim is reasonable. A typical way of viewing argumentation is to see it in terms of *premises* and a *conclusion*. The conclusion is the statement being argued for, and the premises are the statements of proof. When you make a statement about something that you believe is logical or right and then offer reasons why you believe that way in order to convince someone, you are making an argument. An argument may have several goals or purposes, either singly or in combination, such as to show relationships between things (a causal argument), to explain or define something (a definition argument), to evaluate something or support a position on it (an evaluative argument), or to sway an audience to take action on something (a persuasive argument). In actuality, much of the writing you do in college or university is a form of argument. Argumentation is a useful tool for developing critical thinking because arguing well requires close analysis of our own ideas as well as those of others.

NARROWING YOUR FOCUS AND DISCOVERING YOUR POSITION

All arguments begin with a position, claim, or proposition that is both debatable and has opposing viewpoints. Statements of fact are not debatable; abstract generalizations are too vague. If your position is not debatable, there is no argument. Furthermore, in an argument, your goal is to convince those opposed to your position that yours is valid or true. You might even want to persuade your audience to abandon their position and adopt yours. Your first step, then, is to select a controversial subject or issue that you have a strong interest in. This step begins the process that will ultimately lead you to the position you will take.

One way to approach this step in the process of writing an argument is to ask questions about a controversial or debatable subject or issue. Should it be illegal for women to drink alcohol during pregnancy? Should marijuana or heroin be legalized? Should gay couples be allowed to marry? Although such questions seldom have absolutely right or wrong answers, it is useful to frame your position by saying (or implying), "Yes, women should be allowed to drink alcohol during pregnancy," or, "No, heroin should not be legalized." But making up your mind about how you feel about an issue is only the beginning. You must also convince others that your position is logical, reasonable, or valid. You do that by providing strong evidence or reasons to support your position and by anticipating and addressing the arguments of those who do not agree with you.

A good starting point for discovering a topic to argue is to make a list of controversial issues currently in the news or issues being discussed and debated either publicly or among your friends or family. ***Remember that this step is only a starting point.*** These general topics are far too broad for a short paper, but they give you a beginning from which to start narrowing your focus. From your list, select the subjects that interest you most or that you feel strongly about and develop a series of questions that you might ask about them. When contemplating a topic you would like to argue, this process of considering a variety of views helps you to solidify your position.

Examples

1. Suppose you are interested in the subject of downloading music from the Internet. Is downloading a form of file sharing or does it constitute a violation of copyright law? Should people who wish to download music from the Internet have to pay for that service? People will disagree on how these questions should be answered; thus, these questions are legitimate subjects for argumentation. Suppose you believe that, no, downloading music from the Internet should not be regarded as a criminal act. What other questions does that position lead to? Should downloading music be free and open to anyone who wants to do it? If so, what is the fairest way to treat artists whose music is being downloaded from the Internet? Do they not have the right to profit from the use of their music?

2. Consider the suggestion that the grading system at the college and university level be abolished. You might wonder: Should the grading system be abolished? Why should the grading system be abolished? Why should the grading system not be abolished? What would replace the grading system if it were abolished? How would abolishing the grading system affect students and instructors? Would it change the dynamics of the learning process?

The following list of potentially controversial subjects may give you an idea of the kinds of general topics that can be narrowed for an argumentative paper. To this list, add others that appeal to you as potential topics for an argument. Then, select those subjects that you have the strongest interest in or hold opinions about and, taking each in turn, spend some time writing down questions that come to mind about that subject, related issues that you are aware of, and/or your preliminary position on the subject: What do you think should be done? Why do you believe it should it be done? Which is the best solution to the problem?

At this stage, you are simply brainstorming or free writing to see what you know about subjects that you would be comfortable developing into an argument paper. When you have finished, examine the results of your brainstorming session and narrow your list to the one or two topics that you have the most to say about or feel most strongly about. Brainstorm further on those issues by framing questions about the subject or trying to identify the problem associated with it. Keep in mind that you not only want to find an issue or issues that you have a strong interest in, but you also must consider the implications of the position you take on that issue.

POSSIBLE SUBJECTS FOR ARGUMENTATION

Aboriginal rights	Global warming	Racial profiling
Advertising images	Global insurgency	Restorative justice versus criminal justice
AIDS treatment or prevention	Gun control	Same-sex marriages
Animal rights	Homelessness	Science: Objective truth or cultural construct?
Arts funding	Human cloning	Space exploration
Bilingual education	Human rights	Stem cell research
Binge drinking	Immigration	Steroids and athletes
Canada–U.S. relations	Imperialism	Sweatshops
Canadian identity	Land claims	Television commercials
Capital punishment	Legalization of marijuana	Terrorism
Censorship	Media objectivity	Tobacco use
Child labour	Movies and values	Transfer payments and fiscal federalism
Computer games	The North: Indigenous rights, the environment, or global warming	Universal health care versus privatization
Downloading music from the Internet	Nuclear proliferation	Violence in film
Drugs and drug abuse	Obsession with celebrities	Violence and sexist language in rap lyrics
Drunk driving penalties	Outsourcing jobs	Violence in hockey
Eating disorders	Pay inequity	Violence on television
Eliminating the grading system	Peacekeeping	War: Is there such a thing as a just war?
The environment	Pornography and the Internet	Workplace discrimination
Euthanasia and assisted suicide	Post-colonialism	
Gender issues	Publishing images of war	
Genetic engineering	Quebec separatism	

NARROWING YOUR FOCUS AND DISCOVERING YOUR POSITION

- Make a list of controversial or arguable subjects that you have an opinion about or that you are strongly interested in.
- Ask questions about each subject from as many angles as you can think of.
- Keep narrowing your focus as often as possible.
- Write down ideas that occur to you as you ask your questions.
- Select one or two topics that seem most promising to you.
- Repeat the brainstorming process by asking more questions and writing more thoughts as they occur. At this stage, you are working toward a defensible position on a fairly narrow topic.
- Consider how you might defend your position, how you would counter arguments against it, and what evidence you might need.
- Select the topic that emerges as your strongest and begin the process of thinking about, researching, and writing your paper on that narrow topic.

How will you convince your audience that your position is reasonable or logical? How can you best defend your position? How can you best meet the arguments of those opposed to you?

You are looking for a topic that poses a question or problem you believe you know the answer or solution to. This is your position. Once you know your position, you are ready to commit time to thinking about and researching the best evidence or proof to support your position.

STRUCTURING AN ARGUMENT

The modern essay of argument has its roots in ancient Greek and Roman rhetoric. The essential steps are based on classical counterparts: the introduction, or *exordium,* catches the reader's attention with a statement of the case using evidence, statistics, or an anecdote, and it often proceeds from the general to the specific; *narratio* clearly states the thesis or position to be argued; *divisio* outlines the main point or points to be covered; *confirmatio* defends the writer's arguments using as many examples as necessary to be convincing (for some writers, three examples seems to be the magic number); *confutatio* anticipates and refutes opposing argument or arguments; and *peroratio,* the summation or conclusion of the argument, can be a restatement of the thesis, a call to action, or a revitalization of the trenchant points. It's not necessary to memorize the Latin terms. It's more important that you know that effective arguments often adapt or follow this pattern or contain these elements.

STRATEGIES FOR CONSTRUCTING A CONVINCING ARGUMENT

- Know your audience. Your understanding of the audience helps you to know what evidence you need to make your argument convincing.
- Establish an appropriate tone. Your attitude toward your subject is important in making your argument convincing. Using the appropriate tone strengthens your argument.
- Follow a logical line of reasoning. Whether formal or informal, your argument must be reasonable and sound.
- Use appeals effectively. Appeals to logic, ethics, emotions, or shared values all help develop your argument. Be cautious when appealing to emotions; such appeals are all right in small measure, but your main appeals should be to logic and/or ethics.
- Assess the evidence. Examine carefully the evidence you use for your argument. Weak or flawed evidence weakens your own argument.
- Look for flaws in your own and others' reasoning process. Avoid fallacies or errors in reasoning in your own writing, and examine the arguments of others for such flaws.
- Anticipate the arguments of those opposed to you. Anticipating and countering others' arguments strengthens your own position. Make sure you use the strongest arguments of your opponents, not the weakest ones, and avoid name-calling, accusations, or any belittling statements.
- Make concessions where necessary. Acknowledging truths in the arguments of others reveals that you are aware of those truths but are still committed to your own position. Follow such concessions with your own even stronger evidence, proof, or support.

CHAPTER FIVE

DOCUMENTING SOURCES USING MLA STYLE

The guidelines, in this chapter and in Chapter 6, on citing and documenting sources are based on the sixth edition of Joseph Gibaldi's *MLA Handbook for Writers of Research Papers* (often referred to as the *MLA Handbook*). The main feature of the MLA (Modern Language Association) citation style is that after you quote or refer to a source, you insert the author's last name and the page number of the source in parentheses. This information corresponds with the complete list of works cited at the end of your paper. However, if the author's name is used in a signal phrase that introduces the quotation, only the page number is used in the parenthetical citation. This citation style is generally used in the humanities. Many academic disciplines have their own documentation styles. For example, essays in the social sciences generally use APA (American Psychological Association) style.

Always check with your instructor to confirm the citation style you should use. If you need additional help after reading the next two chapters, consult the *MLA Handbook* or another style guide in your library, bookstore, writing lab, or at a trusted Internet source. Using the rules in the *MLA Handbook* will help give your formal writing credibility. It will also help you avoid plagiarism—the copying of someone else's words or ideas without appropriate credit. The MLA citation style helps readers find your sources easily from the full citations in the Works Cited list that you place at the end of your text. The principle is simple: You want to show your reader that your idea or information is from a specific source, and where the source can be found. Accuracy, then, is very important.

MLA STYLE

As mentioned above, the MLA style of documentation requires that any borrowed material is followed by a brief reference to its source, shown in a parenthetical note. The parenthetical citation is placed within the sentence, after the quotation or paraphrase, and before the period. If punctuation appears at the end of the words you are quoting, ignore a comma, period, or semicolon but include a question mark or exclamation mark within the quotation. In all cases, the period for your sentence follows the parenthetical citation.

The name or title that appears in the parenthetical citation in your text corresponds to an entry in the Works Cited page at the end of your paper. This Works Cited entry contains complete bibliographic information for the work you reference, including the full name of the author, the complete title, the place of publication, name of the publisher, and the date of publication. In some cases, page numbers are included.

Italics and Underlining.   In the papers you write, every letter and punctuation mark (in your Works Cited page, for example) must be easily recognizable; you can avoid ambiguity by using underlining when you intend italics.

Treat Internet Sources as You Do Printed Works.   Because many Internet sources do not have page numbers, use paragraph numbers if available. When composing in HTML (HyperText Markup Language, the most common language for creating website documents), it's a good idea not to substitute underlining for italics because the underlined text may show as an active hypertext link. Check with your instructor for the preferred style.

Illustration: In-Text Citations

- **Book or article with one author.** Name the author followed by the page number:

  (Ueda 15)

GUIDELINES FOR IN-TEXT CITATIONS AND DOCUMENTING SOURCES

- Provide a citation every time you paraphrase or quote directly from a source.
- Add the citation in parentheses following the quotation or paraphrase.
- In the parentheses, list the author's last name and the page number or numbers from which you took the words or ideas. Do not insert any punctuation between the author's last name and the page number.
- If you name the author as you introduce the words or ideas, the parentheses will include only the page number or numbers.
- At the end of your paper, provide an alphabetical list of the authors you quoted or paraphrased with complete bibliographic information, including the author, title, and where you found the material. This list is the Works Cited page.

- **Book or article with two or three authors.** Name the authors followed by the page number:

   (Allis and Chalmers 78)   (Fletcher, Franks, and Jacks 78)
- **Book or article with more than three authors.** Name just the first author followed by "et al." (Latin for "and others") and then the page number:

   (Wang et al. 29)

   Note: List the names in the order in which they appear on the title page. If they are not listed alphabetically, do not change their order.
- **Article or other publication with no author named.** Give a short title followed by the page number:

   ("Teaching" 10)

   Note: If you cite two anonymous articles beginning with the same word, use the full title of each to distinguish one from the other.

   ("Classrooms Without Walls" 45) ("Classrooms in the 21st Century" 96)
- **Two works by the same author.** Give the author's name followed by a comma, a short title, and the page number:

   (Heilbrun, *Hamlet's Mother* 123) (Heilbrun, *Writing a Woman's Life* 35)
- **Works by authors with the same last name.** If your list of cited works has works by authors with the same last name, include the first name of the author in the parenthetical citation and then the page number or numbers.

   (Gregory Smith 16)

PARAPHRASING

Paraphrasing is similar to summarizing in that you restate in your own words something someone else has written, but a paraphrase restates everything in the passage rather than highlighting just the key points. Summaries give useful presentations of the major points or ideas of long passages or entire works, whereas paraphrases are most useful in clarifying or emphasizing the main points of short passages.

GUIDELINES FOR PARAPHRASING

- Restate in your own words the important ideas or essence of a passage.
- Do not repeat more than two or three exact words of any part of the original, unless you enclose them in quotation marks.
- If you must repeat a phrase, clause, or sentence exactly as it appears in the original, put quotation marks around those words.
- Keep the paraphrase about the same length as the original source.
- Give the source of the paraphrased information either in your text or in parentheses immediately after the paraphrase.
- As often as possible, try to paraphrase rather than quote, saving direct quotations for crucial wording to which you need to refer.

COMMENT

Even when you put material into your own words, you must cite the source, including the page number where the paraphrased material is located. When it is clear that you are paraphrasing from the same source in two or more consecutive sentences *and* you have named the author or source in the first sentence, you need only one parenthetical citation at the end of the series of sentences.

To paraphrase, express the ideas of the author in your own words, being careful not to use phrases or key words of the original. Paraphrases are sometimes as long as the original passages, though often they are slightly shorter. Paraphrasing conveys the essence of a sentence or passage in an accurate, fair manner and without the distraction of quotation marks. If your paraphrase repeats the exact words of the original, then you are quoting, and you must put quotation marks around those words and provide a citation. A paper will be more interesting and more readable if you paraphrase more often than you quote. Think of your own response when you read something that contains quotations. Perhaps, like many readers, you will read with interest a paraphrase or short quotation, but you may skip over or skim quickly long passages set off by quotation marks. Readers generally are more interested in the ideas of the author than the author's skill at quoting others.

Illustration: Paraphrasing

Source: Dahl, Ronald. "Burned Out and Bored." *Newsweek* 15 Dec. 1997: 8.
Original (page 8): What really worries me is the intensity of the stimulation. I watch my eleven-year-old daughter's face as she absorbs the powerful onslaught of arousing visuals and gory special effects. Although my son is prohibited from playing violent video games, I have seen some of his third-grade friends at an arcade inflicting blood-splattering, dismembering blows upon on-screen opponents in distressingly realistic games.... Why do children immersed in this much excitement seem starved for more? That was, I realized, the point.
Paraphrase: Dahl believes that the overstimulation of today's youth has resulted in a generation with a previously unprecedented threshold for excitement. It takes increasingly more violent, more shocking, and more thrilling events to stimulate young people (8).

COMMENT

For Internet sources or other electronic sources without pagination, many instructors recommend that you repeat the author's name in parentheses after all paraphrases and direct quotations, even if the name is already included in the text.

QUOTING

When you want to include the words of another writer, but it is not appropriate to either paraphrase or summarize, you will want to quote. Quoting requires that you repeat the exact words of another, placing quotation marks before and after the material being quoted. Be selective in the material you choose to quote directly. How do you know when to quote rather than paraphrase? You should quote only words, phrases, or sentences that are especially striking, significant, or that must be reproduced exactly because you cannot convey them in your own words without weakening their effect or changing their intent. Otherwise, rely on paraphrasing to refer to the ideas of others. In either case, document your source by identifying the original source and the location of your information within that source.

GUIDELINES FOR QUOTING

- Be selective: Quote directly only words, phrases, or sentences that are particularly striking or significant, or whose beauty, originality, or drama would be lost in a paraphrase.
- Quote directly passages that are so succinct that paraphrasing them would be more complicated or take more words than a direct quotation would require.
- Enclose between quotation marks the exact words you are quoting.
- Do not change one word of the original unless you indicate with brackets (also known as square brackets), ellipses, or other conventions that you have done so.
- Provide the source of your quoted material either in your text or in parentheses following the material.

COMMENTS

- Place double quotation marks before and after words taken directly from the original. Do not use single quotation marks, except when you have a quotation within a quotation, in which case single quotation marks enclose the material in the quotation.
- When the quoted material is an integral part of your sentence, especially when preceded by the word *that*, do not capitalize the first letter of the first word.
- Where possible, name the author whose ideas or words you are quoting or paraphrasing.
- In parentheses after the quotation, give the page number in the source where the quotation is located (hence the phrase *parenthetical citation*).

COMMENTS

- When a quotation preceded by *that* forms an integral part of your sentence, do not capitalize the first word in the quotation, even when it is capitalized in the original. If the *t* in *the* is capitalized in the original, place a bracket around the lower-cased *t* in the quotation to indicate that the letter has been changed. Use ellipsis points (three spaced periods) to indicate the omission of text from the original.
- If some text is italicized in the original, you must italicize it in your quotation.
- You do not need brackets around ellipsis points—spaced periods—to indicate that they are your addition. The bracketed ellipsis points in MLA style are no longer used. Even if you use ellipsis points, your writing and the quotation that you have integrated into your paper must be grammatically correct.

COMMENTS

- If your direct quotation is preceded by introductory text and a colon or comma, capitalize the first letter of the first word of the quotation.
- If you quote something that appears in quotation marks in the original source, use single quotation marks within the double quotes.
- If your quotation appears to be a complete sentence but the actual sentence you quote continues in the original, you must use ellipsis points at the end of your quotation to indicate that the original sentence continues.
- If an ellipsis comes at the end of a quotation, the closing quotation mark follows the third period, with no space between the period and quotation mark. The parenthetical citation follows as usual.

Combination of Paraphrase and Direct Quotation. The following two examples illustrate how to combine paraphrasing and quoting for a balanced handling of source material.

> Jack Santino in "Rock and Roll as Music; Rock and Roll as Culture" maintains that "[s]uch things as suicide, drugs, sex, and violence *are* teenage concerns" and that, "while artists have a responsibility not to glamorize them, that does not mean these themes should not be explored" (196).

> In "Rock and Roll as Music; Rock and Roll as Culture," Jack Santino observes: "Furthermore, such things as suicide, drugs, sex, and violence *are* teenage concerns. While artists have a responsibility not to glamorize them, that does not mean these themes should not be explored" (196).

COMMENT

Notice the difference between the two examples. The first integrates the quoted material into the sentence with the word *that,* so the first words in each of the quoted passages do not require a capital first letter. In the second example, the quotation is introduced and set off as a separate sentence, so the first word after the quotation mark begins with a capital letter.

CAUTION

Never incorporate a quotation without in some way introducing or commenting on it. A quotation that is neither introduced nor followed by some concluding comment, referred to as a "bald" or "dropped" quotation, detracts from the smooth flow of your paper.

INTEGRATING SOURCE MATERIAL INTO YOUR PAPER

When quoting or paraphrasing material, pay special attention to your treatment of source materials. Authors have developed many ways of skillfully integrating the words and ideas of others with their own words. Your paper should not read as if you simply cut out the words of someone else and pasted them in your paper. You can achieve smooth integration of source materials into your text if you keep the following suggestions in mind:

- **Mention the cited author's name in the text of your paper to signal the beginning of a paraphrase or quotation.** The first time you mention the name, give both first and last names. After the first mention, give only the last name: **David Frum** argues in "Reaping What We Sow" that Canada's crime problem is spreading out, and that "[i]t's true too that you are now more likely to be mugged in Toronto than in New York City." **Frum** asserts: "While American cities and states are adopting anti-crime policies proved to work, Canadian cities and provinces are adopting policies proved to fail" (233).
- **Mention the source if no author is named.** This practice gives credit to the source while providing an introduction to the borrowed material:

  A *U.S. News & World Report* **article** notes that, although no genes determine what occupation one will go into, groups of genes produce certain tendencies—risk-taking, for instance—that might predispose one to select a particular kind of work ("How Genes Shape Personality" 64).

- **Give citations for all borrowed material.** State the authority's name, use quotation marks as appropriate, reference the source and page number in a parenthetical citation, add some sort of general information, and/or use a pronoun to refer to the authority mentioned in the previous sentence. *Do not rely on one parenthetical citation at the end of several sentences or an entire paragraph.*
- **Vary introductory phrases and clauses.** Avoid excessive reliance on such standard introductory clauses as "Smith says," or "Jones writes." For instance, vary your verbs and/or provide explanatory information about sources, as in the following examples:

  > **David Suzuki** notes the following:

  > **Stephen Lewis** argues this point convincingly:

  > According to **Marshall McLuhan,** the grandfather guru of the media,

  > As **Franke James** illustrates,

- The first mention of an authority in your text (as opposed to the parenthetical citation) should include the author's first name and last name. The second and subsequent references should give the last name only (never the first name alone).

  > **First use of author's name in your paper: Ellen Ullman** correctly observes that . . .

  > **Second and subsequent mentions of that author: Ullman** contends elsewhere that . . .

- **Combine quotations and paraphrases.** A combination provides a smoother style than quoting directly all of the time.
- For **long quotations** (more than four typed lines in your paper), set the quoted material off from the text (referred to as a *block quotation*). Write your introduction to the quotation, generally followed by a colon. Then begin a new line indented 10 spaces from the left margin, and type the quotation, double-spaced as usual.
- **Do not add quotation marks to block quotations indented and set off from the text.** If quotation marks appear in the original, use double quotation marks, not single quotation marks. If you quote a single paragraph or part of a paragraph, do not indent the first line any more than the rest of the quotation.
- For **block quotations,** reverse the style of a normal in-text citation: place the parenthetical citation after the final punctuation of the quotation. See the following example of a block quotation:

  > Northrop Frye writes:

  > His sense of design . . . derived from the trail and the canoe, is the exact opposite of the academic "establishing of foreground." He is primarily a

painter of linear distance. Snowed-over paths wind endlessly through trees, rivers reach nearly to the horizon before they bend and disappear, rocks sink inch by inch under water, and the longest stretch of mountains dips somewhere and reveals the sky beyond. What is furthest in distance is often nearest in intensity. (167)

(Note: If you had cited Frye's article earlier in your paper, you would use only his last name when introducing the block quotation. Also note the ellipsis points to indicate that words were omitted between the words *design* and *derived*.)

USING ELLIPSIS POINTS, BRACKETS, SINGLE QUOTATION MARKS, AND "QTD. IN"

This section offers some additional guidelines on the mechanics of handling source materials and incorporating them into your paper.

Ellipsis Points

- If you want to omit original words, phrases, or sentences from your quotation of source material, use ellipsis points to indicate the omission. Ellipsis points consist of three spaced periods, with spaces before, between, and after the periods. In quotations, ellipses most frequently occur within sentences, almost never at the beginning or the end. In every case, the quoted material must form a grammatically complete sentence, either by itself or in combination with your own words.

Use ellipsis points to indicate that you have left words out of an otherwise direct quotation:

Original: A picture is worth a thousand words—but only sometimes: It depends on which picture and which thousand words.

Quotation with ellipses in the middle: Arnold Keller claims, "A picture is worth a thousand words . . . [i]t depends on which picture and which thousand words" (66).

Use ellipsis points at the end of a quotation only if you have dropped some words from the end of the final sentence quoted. In that case, include four periods, with no space between the last word of the quote and the first ellipsis point.

Quotation with ellipses at the end: You know the old saying, "Eat, drink, and be merry. . . ."

When, at the end of a sentence, the parenthetical reference follows the ellipsis, leave a space before the first ellipsis point; immediately follow with the second and third ellipsis points, the closing quotation mark, a space, the parenthetical reference, and the sentence period.

According to recent studies, "Statistics show that Chinese women's status has improved . . ." (*Chinese Women* 46).

- **Ellipsis points are not necessary** if you are quoting a fragment of a sentence, that is, a few words or a subordinate clause, because context will clearly indicate the omission of some of the original sentence.

  > Sociobiologists add that social and nurturing experiences can "intensify, diminish, or modify" personality traits (Wood and Wood 272).

Brackets

- **The *MLA Handbook for Writers of Research Papers*, sixth edition, says that "[u]nless indicated in brackets or parentheses . . . , changes must not be made in the spelling, capitalization, or interior punctuation of the source" (109).** Although you should look for ways to integrate source material into your text that avoid overuse of brackets, the following guidelines apply when changing source material is unavoidable.
- **If you want to change a word or phrase to conform to your own sentence or add words to make your sentence grammatically correct, use brackets to indicate the change.** The brackets enclose only the changed portion of the original.

  > **Original:** If there is any problem in Toronto, the Mayor insists, it is traceable to the United States: "The U.S. is exporting its problem of violence to the streets of Toronto," David Miller complained on Dec. 27.

  > **Quotation:** "If there is any problem in Toronto, the Mayor insists, it is traceable to the United States: 'The U.S. is exporting [the] problem of violence to . . . Toronto,' David Miller complained on Dec. 27" (232).

  Note: This example illustrates the use not only of brackets but also of ellipsis points and single and double quotation marks.

- Use brackets if you add some explanatory information or editorial comment, or use them to indicate that you have changed the capitalization in the quoted material.

  > **Original:** Traditional marriage is another dying institution in Canada . . . "If we live together," the attitude goes, "why should I commit myself to any one lifestyle? Why should I assume responsibility?"

  > **Quotation:** Even the perspective toward marriage carries the attitude, " '[W]hy should I commit myself? Why should I assume responsibility?' " (Barrett and Rowe 346).

  > **Original:** Then, magically, the fairy godmother appears. She comes from nowhere, summoned, we suppose, by Cinderella's wishes.

  > **Quotation:** Louise Bernikow points out that "[s]he [the fairy godmother] comes from nowhere, summoned . . . by Cinderella's wishes" (19).

- The Latin word *sic* (meaning "thus" or "so") in parentheses indicates that the quotation is accurate although some type of error, spelling, for example, has been made in the original source. Because you are not at liberty to change words when quoting word for word, reproduce the error but use (sic) to indicate that the error is not yours.

  Original: Thrills have less to do with speed then changes in speed.

  Quotation: Dahl makes this observation: "Thrills have less to do with speed then (sic) changes in speed" (18).

Single Quotation Marks

- If you quote text that itself appears in quotation marks in the original, use single marks within the double marks that enclose your own quotation.

  Original: This set me pondering the obvious question: "How can it be so hard for kids to find something to do when there's never been such a range of stimulating entertainment available to them?"

  Quotation: Dahl is led to ask this question: " 'How can it be so hard for kids to find something to do when there's never been such a range of stimulating entertainment available to them?' " (18–19).

- **Occasionally you will have to quote something that is already a quotation within a quotation,** where the original contains single quotation marks within double quotes. In that case, use double quotation marks within single within double:

  Original: In my interviews with the chief witness, he swears he heard Smith say: " 'It wasn't me! I didn't do it!' "

  Quotation: Johnson records an interview with a chief witness in the case. Smith is said to have proclaimed, " ' "It wasn't me! I didn't do it!" ' " (23).

"Qtd. in"

- **If you quote or paraphrase material that is already quoted, use the abbreviation *qtd. in,*** which means "quoted in." Use *qtd. in* whenever you quote or paraphrase the published account of someone else's words or ideas. The Works Cited list will include not the original source of the material you quoted or paraphrased but rather the indirect source, the one where you found the material. You will likely be using the single quotation marks within the double because you are quoting what someone else has quoted.

  Original: Francis Crick makes us think of writers typing away when he talks about amino acids: "A protein is like a paragraph written in a twenty-letter

GUIDELINES FOR INTEGRATING SOURCE MATERIALS INTO YOUR PAPER

- Avoid "bald" or "dropped" quotations by introducing all direct quotations.
- Use the author's name, where appropriate, to signal the beginning of a paraphrase or quotation.
- Cite sources for all borrowed material.
- Name a source if the article does not list an author's name.
- Vary the way you introduce source material.
- Try combining direct quotations and paraphrases in the same sentence.
- Become familiar with appropriate uses of ellipsis points, brackets, single quotation marks, and "qtd. in."

language, the exact nature of the protein being determined by the exact order of the letters."

Quotation: Francis Crick observed of the amino acid: "A protein is like a paragraph written in a twenty-letter language, the exact nature of the protein being determined by the exact order of the letters" (qtd. in Keller 240).

DOCUMENTING SOURCES IN A COLLECTION OF ESSAYS

You have been reading about and looking at examples of the first of two important components of source documentation: in-text citations. The other component, appearing at the end of your paper, is the alphabetical list of all the works you quoted from or paraphrased. This list of works cited typically appears on a new page, titled Works Cited, with no other punctuation, and in the same font and type size as your list of sources and the rest of your paper. Each entry in the list begins with the author's name, last name first, followed by the title of the article, book, or other source and information about where it was published, the name of the publisher, and date of publication. The author's name (or title of the work, if it is published anonymously) in the text's parenthetical citation refers to one item in this list at the end of the paper.

You will find more discussion of documenting sources in Chapter 6, but the brief treatment here gives useful guidelines for short papers using materials reprinted in a collection of essays, such as this textbook.

You or your instructor may prefer an acceptable alternative to constructing a separate page of works cited. Cite bibliographic information about the source parenthetically in your text, just as you do for author and page numbers. If you are writing about one of the readings from this book, or even two or three of them, your instructor may prefer that you provide in parenthetical citations the information that would otherwise appear on a Works Cited page.

A fairly simple difference distinguishes a formal Works Cited page from parenthetical citations of full publication details: The former is more appropriate when the sources are not the focus or subject of the paper but rather provide supporting or illustrative material, as in a synthesis or research paper. The latter is more appropriate when the source is the focus of the paper, its main subject, as in a summary or critique.

Citing One Source.   Suppose your paper quotes or paraphrases a statement from Robert Hughes's essay "Behold the Stone Age." After you write either the exact words of Hughes or your paraphrase of his words, insert a parenthesis, then enter his last name and the page number where you read the words with no punctuation between them, and then close the parenthesis: (Hughes 161). Do not write the word *page* or *pages* or insert a comma between the author's name and the number of the page. If Hughes's piece is the only one you use in your paper, write Work Cited at the end of your paper (or on a separate page, depending on the direction from your instructor) and enter complete bibliographic information for the Hughes article, giving the inclusive pages for the entire Hughes piece, not just the segment you used:

Work Cited

Hughes, Robert. "Behold the Stone Age." *Perspectives on Contemporary Issues.* Ed. Katherine Anne Ackley, G. Kim Blank, and Stephen Eaton Hume. Toronto: Thomson Nelson, 2007. 162–166

CHAPTER SIX

WRITING A RESEARCH PAPER USING MLA STYLE

This chapter presents a brief overview of the key steps in discovering a topic, researching it, and writing a paper incorporating the sources you have used. Keep in mind the discussion in Chapter 5 on paraphrasing, quoting, and documenting sources.

DEFINING YOUR PURPOSE

Your instructor will tell you whether your purpose in the research paper is to argue, explain, analyze, or come to some conclusion about something. Many instructors prefer that students write argumentative papers. In that case, you will make a judgment about your topic on the basis of what you find in your research.

Audience. Whether your instructor tells you the audience to write for or leaves the selection of an audience up to you, having a clear sense of your audience will direct your research and help you to write your paper. If you are writing an argument, address people who are opposed to your position or, at best, uncertain about where they stand on the issue. A good argument seeks to persuade or convince an audience, so anticipating readers who are not already convinced will help sharpen your argument.

Thesis Statement. No matter what your purpose, you will have one central idea, most often articulated early in the paper in the form of a single thesis statement. You will take a position on your topic and defend or illustrate it convincingly with evidence from your source materials.

ASKING QUESTIONS AND DISCOVERING A TOPIC

Ask yourself: Who is my audience? Who are my readers? The answers to these questions will determine your tone, your diction, and your formatting styles. Once you know your purpose and your audience, the next step in writing a research paper is to find a subject you will be comfortable working with for many weeks and then narrow it to a specific topic.

Asking Questions.   One of the best ways to approach the research project is to ask questions about a subject that interests you and seems worth investigating. As you read through the following suggestions for discovering a topic, from brainstorming to generating topics from controversy, think in terms of questions that you might ask about the initial subjects that you think of. Avoid topics that have unanswerable or highly speculative questions. Your goal in the research is to gather evidence, and then to come to the conclusions that your evidence points toward; often enough, the same evidence can be used to come to different conclusions.

Here are examples of questions that would be appropriate to ask when trying to generate ideas for a research paper:

- Should the Canadian Senate be abolished?
- Should high school, college, or university grades be abolished?
- Does Canada need two or more official languages?
- Where should Canadian peacekeeping forces be deployed and why?
- Do advertising images of women set up impossible standards of femininity?
- Is hormone replacement therapy a safe choice for women?
- Which plays a more prominent role in determining behaviour, genes or environment?
- Should smokers pay for their own health care?
- What is the best strategy for combating global terrorism?

Brainstorming.   Most of you are familiar with brainstorming or free writing. To brainstorm or free write, spend five or ten minutes listing all of the subjects you are interested in without stopping to think too hard about what you are doing. Then select one or more of the subjects on your list and brainstorm for another five to ten minutes to write down what you already know about your subject.

Generating a Topic from Personal Interest.   One way to find a topic for your research paper is to begin with subjects you already know well, are interested in, or think you would like to improve your knowledge of. Begin by writing down your hobbies, your favourite sports, issues in your subject major, contemporary social issues that interest you, or topics in classes you are taking.

Narrowing Your Subject to a Specific Topic.   Most research paper assignments are short enough that you must narrow your focus to avoid a treatment of your topic that is too shallow or too hopelessly general. Keep in mind the distinction between **subject** and **topic:** Subject is the general area under investigation, whereas topic is the narrow aspect of that subject that you are investigating. For example, Jack the Ripper is a subject, but entire books have been written on the notorious 1888 murders in the Whitechapel area of London. A suitable topic on the subject would be to explore the controversy surrounding the alleged links of the Duke of Clarence with the murders, taking a position in favour of the theory most plausible to you.

One way to get a sense of how a general topic can be narrowed is to look at the table of contents of a book. Notice the chapter headings, which are subtopics of the broad subject. Chapters are often further subdivided. You want to find a topic that is narrow enough to fully explore without leaving unanswered questions, yet broad enough to say enough about in a reasonably long paper.

To narrow your subject to a topic, take a general subject and go through the brainstorming process again, this time listing everything that comes to mind about that particular subject. What subtopics does your subject have? What questions can you ask about your general subject? How might you narrow your focus on that subject? Ultimately, you want to generate an idea that gives focus to your preliminary library search.

Generating Topics from Personal Opinions.   Virtually any topic can be turned into an argument, but opinions are always subject to debate. One way to generate a research paper topic is to begin with your own strongly held opinions.

Caution: Avoid topics based entirely on opinions. Evaluative statements are especially good for argumentative papers, because they are likely to have differing opinions. Once you say that something is the best, the most significant, the most important, or the greatest, for instance, you have put yourself in the position of defending that statement. You will have to establish your criteria for making your judgment and defend your choice against what others might think. Here are some ideas for this particular approach:

- The most influential person in the 20th century (or in Canada; in the world; or in a particular field, such as education, government, politics, arts, sports, entertainment, or science)
- The most significant battle in World War I or World War II (or the Korean War or the Vietnam War)
- The greatest hockey (or football, tennis, soccer, baseball) player (either now playing or of all time)
- The greatest or worst prime minister
- The best movie, book, or album of all time
- The business or industry with the greatest impact on Canadian life in the last decade (or last 20 years)

Because your conclusion on any of these or similar topics is your opinion, you need to establish criteria for your conclusion, clearly describe the process you used to reach your conclusion, and explain the logical basis for that process.

Generating Topics from Commonly Held Opinions.   Another possibility for a research paper topic is to take a commonly held opinion (though not necessarily one that you share), especially one based on stereotyped assumptions about a group or class of people, and explore the validity of that belief. Your goal is to determine whether the commonly held opinion is a position that is valid, partially valid, or invalid. Even if you cannot arrive at a definitive evaluation of the validity of the statement, you can still present the evidence you find and explain why your research does not reach a conclusion. Here are examples of generally held beliefs:

- Watching violence on television or video games produces violent behaviour.
- Women have more highly evolved verbal skills than men.
- Men naturally perform mechanical tasks better than women.
- Women naturally perform better at nurturing children than men.
- Smoking marijuana leads to the use of hard drugs.
- Rock music promotes violence and apathy.
- People stay on welfare because they are too lazy to work.
- Marriage should only be between people of the opposite sex.
- Homeless people could get off the streets if they really tried.

When determining the validity of a commonly held opinion or belief, your research focuses on gathering evidence without bias. Although you may want to interview people about their opinions on a particular belief, the basis of your conclusion must rest on clearly reliable evidence.

Generating Topics from Controversy.   Yet another way to discover a topic you find intriguing enough to commit many hours of time to is to think of controversial issues that always generate heated debate. These topics may be frequently discussed in newspapers, news magazines, and on television news programs and talk shows:

- Media coverage of celebrity trials should be banned.
- Birth parents should always have a legal right to take back children they have given up for adoption.
- Children whose parents are on welfare should be placed in provincially operated foster homes.
- Women should be barred from participating in combat duty.
- Graphic violence in the movies poses a serious threat to Canadian moral values.
- Ottawa should stop funding projects in the arts and the humanities.
- The federal government should provide unlimited funds to support research to find a cure for AIDS.
- Children who commit murder should be tried as adults no matter what their age.
- Global warming is an invention of the media.

FORMING A PRELIMINARY THESIS

When you believe that you have narrowed your topic sufficiently, you are ready to form your preliminary thesis. This is the position that you believe you want to take on your topic, based on your early thinking about and narrowing down of a subject. Your preliminary or working thesis can be in the form of either a question or a statement. In much the same way as your final thesis gives direction and focus to your paper, your preliminary thesis gives you direction and focus in the research process.

As you review potential sources and read about your topic, you may find yourself changing your preliminary thesis for any number of reasons. Perhaps your topic is too narrow or too new and you simply cannot find enough sources with which to write a fair and balanced research paper. Or you may discover that your topic is too broad to cover in a research paper and that you need to narrow your focus even more. A common reason for changing a preliminary thesis is that, once you actually start reading sources, you discover that you want to change your initial position. You may discover that you were wrong in your assumption or opinion about your topic and that you are persuaded to change your position. Part of the pleasure in researching a topic is discovering new ideas or information, so it makes sense that your early views on your topic may shift as you learn more about it. More than likely, your final thesis will differ in some way from your preliminary thesis.

DEVELOPING A WORKING BIBLIOGRAPHY

With your preliminary thesis in mind, you are ready to start the actual research process. First, you need to locate potential sources. A working bibliography is a list of the sources you might use in your research paper, those that look particularly promising during a preliminary search. At this point, you will not have had time to read or even carefully skim all potential sources, let alone imagine how they fit together to support your hypothesis. Your goal is to find the sources that bear

---

GUIDELINES FOR DEVELOPING A WORKING BIBLIOGRAPHY

- List sources that sound promising for your research, by recording titles and locations as you discover them.
- If the source is a library book, record the title, author, publisher, and call number.
- If the source is an article, write the title of the piece, the name of its author, the title of the magazine or journal, where it appears (e.g., online or print), the date of the issue, and the inclusive pages numbers. You will need all this information to find the article.
- For other sources, such as videotapes, audiotapes, government documents, or pamphlets, write down as much information as you can find to help locate them. Write the location of any source, such as a special collection, government documents, stacks, or periodicals.
- For a source on the Internet, record the URL (Uniform Resource Locator), the name of the site, the name of its creator or author, if available, and the date the source was created, if available. If you use the source in your paper, you will add the date that you accessed the material in the works cited entry. When you are citing a source from a website, make sure that it is the source within the website and not the website itself.
- You may want to retrieve the full-text files of Internet sites that seem promising as you discover them to ensure their availability when you are ready to begin reading and taking notes.

most directly on your topic and select from them the most useful ones to read carefully, taking notes as you read. One obvious place to start looking for sources is the Internet, particularly Internet sources and databases found through your college or university library.

For the working bibliography, some instructors require that you prepare a separate bibliography card for each source that holds promise. Others suggest that you simply make a list of titles and locations of potential sources and wait until you have looked at them more closely before preparing the bibliography cards. If you use your computer to locate sources, you can make a list of potentially useful sources in a special file. Your instructor may have a preference, but most allow students to use the methods that best suit them.

USING THE LIBRARY

Your library has a good number of valuable resources to help you in your search for materials on your research topic. The library is both a virtual and a physical resource. Although the Internet has made searching for research materials easy and quick, libraries have books, periodicals, and other materials that you can hold, leaf through, check out, and read, and many are also accessible online. Furthermore, many libraries have collections on specific subjects and offer databases that are inaccessible from the Internet. Most libraries in colleges and universities have digital resources. However, sometimes just looking through books and journals will give you ideas. Your library may have print copies of sources that you cannot find on the Internet, or you may be able to get material you need through an interlibrary loan.

Online Catalogue.   Begin your library search for sources on your general subject or topic (if you have sufficiently narrowed your focus) by reviewing the online catalogue for titles of potential sources. The catalogue cross-references its collection by author, by title, and by subject heading. In this searching stage, you will probably not know the titles of works or authors, so you will begin by using subject headings or keywords to locate titles that sound relevant to your research subject. The catalogue lists books, audiovisual materials, journals, and government documents housed in the library or accessible online. Jot down the titles and call numbers of materials that look promising and then locate them. One advantage of visiting your library is that you can physically examine a book, flip through its table of contents, check its index, read the author's credentials, and skim some of the text. If it seems to suit your purpose, you can check it out and take it home with you. On the other hand, you can access much of this material from your home computer sitting in your pyjamas and munching granola.

Online Databases and Indexes.   Many libraries provide access to online databases or CD-ROMs that list books and periodical articles related to particular subject areas. You can search these resources by subject heading, author, title, or keyword. In addition to books and other materials listed in the online catalogue, you should look into both general and specialized print indexes and online databases for additional titles of sources. These resources are usually located online or in the reference room. Here are titles of some general indexes/databases:

- *Academic Search Elite* provides abstracts and indexing for more than 3,200 scholarly journals in the social sciences, humanities, education, and other fields. It is available online.
- *Biography Index* lists articles and books on notable people; it also lists the people by profession or occupation.
- *Essay and General Literature Index* focuses on material in the social sciences and humanities, organized according to author, subject, and title.
- *Government of Canada Publications* indexes all government-generated materials.
- *General Science Index* is arranged by subject and lists articles in general science periodicals.
- *JSTOR* holds top economics journals and journals for other disciplines.
- *Periodical Abstracts* provides abstracts of articles from more than 1,600 periodicals, covering the humanities, social sciences, general science, and general interest. It is updated monthly and is available in electronic format.
- *Reader's Guide to Periodical Literature* is a standard research tool for locating articles in popular magazines. It publishes supplements every two weeks, so you can find very recent articles. It is also available online.

Specialized indexes and databases list articles on particular subjects or areas that appear in professional journals, written by and published for specialists in those areas. Indexes cover specific areas of interest in the humanities, fine arts, social sciences, and natural and applied sciences. A look at just a few of the titles of specialized indexes gives you an idea of the resources available in your library's reference room or online:

- *Art Index* collects titles of articles on archaeology, art history, architecture, and the fine arts.
- *Biological Abstracts* gives brief summaries of articles on biology and biomedicine.
- *Business Source Premier* and *ABI Inform* are good sources for current material on business topics.
- *Compendex* indexes journals, conferences, and technical reports in all areas of engineering.
- *EconLit* is the primary index for economics.
- *ERIC* lists journal articles and reports on education topics.
- *Historical Abstracts* contains abstracts of articles on world history.
- *Humanities Index* lists titles of periodical articles on a broad range of topics in the social sciences and humanities.
- *MLA International Bibliography* provides titles of articles on languages and literature, arranged by nationality and literary period.
- *Philosopher's Index* is useful for information on philosophical topics.

- *Psychological Abstracts* (PsycINFO) presents abstracts of articles and books in all areas of the social sciences.
- *Political Science Abstracts* cites sources on a range of topics in political science.

USING ELECTRONIC SOURCES

Although you do not want to miss the pleasure of using the library for sources for your research paper, the Internet can be another valuable tool in your search for potential sources. Most colleges and universities make computers readily available to their students, so even if you do not own a computer, you will likely have access to one in your campus library or computer labs. Although it cannot replace the library, the Internet does offer resources that a library does not. The same could be said of the library, of course. A fair conclusion notes that each offers excellent but different kinds of materials for the researcher.

Locating Material on the Internet.   To find Internet materials, you can use any of a number of equally good search engines. Search engines collect many sites in their data banks; they return sites that match the keywords you enter to begin your search. Search engines gather their information in one of two major ways, either crawler-based technology or human-powered directories, but increasingly they use a combination of both. Crawler-based search engines gather their information automatically by "crawling" or sending "spiders" out to the web, searching the contents of other systems and creating a database of the results. Human-powered directories depend on humans for the listings you receive in response to a search; they manually approve material for inclusion in a database. You can find more about these terms and others related to the Internet at http://www.webopedia.com, an online dictionary and search engine for definitions of computer and Internet terms.

Search Engines.   Be very careful when searching for sources on the Internet. Begin by choosing your search engine from among the best known or most used; they are likely to be the most reliable. For research papers, stick to academic databases or search engines such as Google Scholar.

CREATING A PRELIMINARY BIBLIOGRAPHY

After you have compiled a list of sources to investigate, you can start locating and evaluating them. If you discover that you cannot use a source, cross it off your list or discard the card on which your source information was noted. When you find a source that definitely looks promising for your research topic, record it either on a bibliography card or in a computer file. Make sure you record all pertinent bibliographic information about your source, preferably in the form in which it will appear on your Works Cited page. See the "Documenting Sources" section in this chapter (pages 54–58) for the appropriate formats for various sources.

EVALUATING PRINT SOURCES

Before you begin taking notes from any source, carefully assess the source's reliability. Ideally, your research should rely on unbiased, current, well-documented sources written by people with the authority to discuss the subject. However, you are likely to find a great number of sources that are written from particular perspectives that are out of date or incomplete, that are written by people with no authority whatsoever, or that do not document their own sources. Part of your job as a researcher is to try to discover these aspects of your sources, to reject those that are completely unreliable, and to use with caution sources about which you lack complete confidence. Although you may never know for sure how much to trust a particular source, you can check certain details to help in your assessment.

Check for Bias.   Try to find out whether the author, publication, organization, or person being interviewed is known to give fair coverage. People, organizations, and publications often promote particular perspectives, which you should recognize and take into account. You need not reject sources outright if you know they take particular positions on subjects, especially controversial issues. However, your own paper should be as unbiased as possible, which requires acknowledgment of the known biases of your sources.

Check the Date of Publication.   In general, a more recent publication provides a more reliable source. For many subjects, current information is crucial to accurate analysis. If you are researching issues such as global warming, morality at high governmental levels, or controversial treatments for AIDS victims, you need the most recent available information. However, if you are examining a historical matter, such as the question of Richard III's guilt in his two young cousins' deaths or whether King Arthur of Britain is an entirely mythical figure, you can rely in part on older materials. However, you still want to search out the latest theories, information, or opinions on any subject you research.

Check the Author's Credentials.   Find out whether the author has sufficient education, experience, or expertise to write or speak about your subject. You can learn the author's background in a number of ways. Most books include a short biography of the author, from a sentence or two to several paragraphs, either on the dust jacket or at the beginning or end of the book. This description reveals the author's professional status, other books the author has published, and similar details that help to establish a position of authority.

Check the Reliability of Your Source.   In evaluating a book, determine whether the publishing house is a respectable one. For a magazine, find out whether it is published by a particular interest group. Evaluation of a book could include reading some representative reviews to see how it was received when first published. Both *Book Review Digest* and *Book Review Index* will help you locate reviews.

Check the Thoroughness of Research and Documentation of Sources.   If your source purports to be scholarly, well-informed, or otherwise reliable, check to see how the evidence was gathered. Determine whether the source reports original research or other people's work and the facts or data that support its conclusions. Look for references either at the ends of chapters or in a separate section at the end of the book. Almost all journal articles and scholarly books document sources, whereas few magazine articles and personal accounts do. Also, consider how statistics and other data are used. Statistics are notoriously easy to manipulate, so check how the author uses them and confirm the author's fair interpretation.

EVALUATING INTERNET SOURCES

As with print sources, you must take care to evaluate any material you locate on the Internet. The Internet poses more difficulty because its resources usually offer fewer clues than a book or journal article. However, searching the Internet will turn up many useful sources, such as scholarly projects, reference databases, text files of books, articles in periodicals, and professional sites. You must use your judgment when selecting sources for your research paper. Remember that anyone with some knowledge of the Internet can create a website, so be very cautious about accepting the authority of anything you find on the Internet. In general, personal sites are probably not as reliable as professional sites and those of scholarly projects. Reference databases can be extremely useful tools for locating source materials.

Caution: Wikipedia, an open source website created in 2001, is often the first site on the results page when you enter a term, event, or other information in a search engine. Although Wikipedia often contains useful information, it is not always reliable or objective. Use with caution, and note that some universities are discouraging the use of this resource.

When looking at a website, you must apply the same sort of skills that you bring to any critical reading, particularly when searching for materials for a class assignment. You must ask a number of questions before accepting and using materials that you locate on the Internet. Some key areas to consider are the authority or credentials of the person or persons responsible for the website, the scope, accuracy, timeliness, and nature of the information, and the presentation of the information. The following list of questions will help you evaluate Internet sites:

- What can you tell about the site from its URL (Uniform Record Locator)? Websites exist for a variety of purposes, including the following: to sell a product, to advocate a position, to influence readers, and to inform. They may be sponsored by individuals for personal reasons, by professionals to impart information, by corporations to sell products, by agencies or groups to influence opinion or advocate a specific position. Knowing which domain the abbreviation at the end of the URL represents is your first clue about a website's purpose. The domain is the system for indicating the logical or geographical location of a web page from the Internet. Domains can indicate a country, such as ca (for Canada), uk (for United Kingdom), or au (for Australia). In Canada, the following are common domains:

- Educational websites exist to provide information about educational institutions, including elementary, secondary, and university levels. Their Internet address ends in .ca or .edu.
- Government websites provide information about governmental departments, agencies, and policies. Federal government websites end in gc.ca, whereas provincial government websites use provincial abbreviations followed by ca (e.g., the Government of Nova Scotia is www.gov.ns.ca. U.S. government sites end in .gov).
- Organizational websites advocate the viewpoint of particular groups. The URL for an organizational website typically ends in .org.
- Commercial websites aim to sell products or services. Their URL usually ends in .com.
- News websites exist to provide information about current events. Their Internet address usually ends in .com.
- Personal websites are constructed by individuals about themselves. The address or personal sites end in various ways, most typically .com.
- Entertainment websites exist to amuse, entertain, and provide information about the entertainment industry. Their Internet address usually ends in .com.
- Internet service provider websites exist to provide information about companies and services related to the Internet. Their website addresses end in .net.

- What do you know about the author of the site? Is the author of the website qualified to give information on the subject? Does the site give information about the author's qualifications? Are the author's credentials, such as academic affiliation, professional association, or publications, easily verified? Since anyone can create a web page, you want to determine whether the author of the website is qualified to give the information you are seeking.
- Is the material on the website presented objectively, or do biases or prejudices reveal themselves? The language used may be a clue, but probably the best way to discover a particular bias is to look at a great many sites (and other sources) on the same topic. When you understand the complexity of your topic and the variety of viewpoints on it, you should be able to determine whether a site is objective or subjective.
- Is the information reliable? Can you verify it? How does it compare with information you have learned from other sources? How well does the website compare with other sites on the same topic? Does the site offer unique information or does it repeat information that you can find at other sites?
- How thoroughly does the website cover its topic? Does it provide links to other sites for additional information? Does the site have links to related topics, and do those links work?

- How accurate is the information? The level of accuracy may be difficult to assess when you first begin your research, but the more you read about your topic and examine a variety of sources, the better able you will be to evaluate information accuracy.
- When was the website last updated? Is the information at the site current?

AVOIDING PLAGIARISM

Plagiarism is borrowing another person's words or ideas without giving proper credit. The worst form of plagiarism is deliberately using the words or ideas of someone else without giving any credit to that source. Handing in a paper someone else has written or copying someone else's paper and pretending it is yours are the most blatant and inexcusable forms of plagiarism, crimes that on some campuses carry penalties such as automatic failure in the course or even immediate expulsion from school. Even unintentional plagiarism can result in a failing grade, especially if it appears repeatedly in a paper.

Keep the following standards in mind when you take notes on your source materials and when you write your research paper:

- You commit plagiarism if you use the exact words or ideas of another writer without putting quotation marks around the words or citing a source. The reader of your paper assumes that words without quotation marks or a source citation are your own words.
- You commit plagiarism if you use the exact words of another writer without putting quotation marks around those words, even if the paper cites the source of the material. Readers assume that words followed by a parenthetical citation are paraphrased from the original—that is, that they are your own words and that the general idea was expressed by the author of the source material.
- You commit plagiarism if you paraphrase by changing only a few words of the original or by using the identical sentence structure of the original, with or without a source. Again, readers assume that words without quotation marks followed by a parenthetical citation are your own words, not those of someone else. In a paraphrase, the *idea* is that of another; the *words* are your own.
- You inaccurately handle source material when you use quotation marks around words that are not exactly as they appear in the original. Readers assume that all words within quotation marks are identical to the original.

Accuracy and fairness in note-taking are essential standards. Take great care when you read your source materials and again when you transfer your notes to your final paper.

Keep in mind that your final paper is a synthesis of information you have discovered in your research with your own thoughts on your topic, thoughts that naturally undergo modification, expansion, and/or revision as you read and think about your topic. Probably more than half of the paper will be your own words. These words will usually include all of the introductory and concluding paragraphs, all

GUIDELINES FOR AVOIDING PLAGIARISM

- For direct quotations, write the words exactly as they appear in the original. Add quotation marks before and after the words. Do not change anything.
- For paraphrased material, restate the original thought in your own words, using your own writing style. Do not use the exact sentence pattern of the original, and do not simply rearrange words. You must retain the central idea of the paraphrased material, but express it in your own words.
- When using borrowed material in your paper, whether direct quotations or paraphrases, acknowledge the source by naming either the author or the work when you introduce the material. Doing so not only tells your reader that you are using borrowed material but also often provides a clear transition from your own words and ideas to the borrowed material that illustrates or expands on your ideas.
- Provide an in-text citation for any borrowed material. Give the author's last name if it is not mentioned in the text of the paper, followed by page number(s). If the source material is anonymous, use a shortened version of the title in place of a name.
- Assemble all sources cited in your paper in an alphabetical list at the end of the paper. This is your list of works cited, containing only those works actually used in the paper.

topic sentences and transitional sentences within and between paragraphs, and all introductions to direct quotations. Furthermore, you need no citation for statements of general or common knowledge, such as facts about well-known historical or current events. If you keep running across common information in all of your sources, you can assume it is general knowledge. For example, the date of the Confederation of Canada does not need a citation.

HANDLING SOURCE MATERIAL

Handling source material fairly, accurately, and smoothly is one of your main tasks in writing a successful research paper. More than likely, your instructor will evaluate your research project not only on how successfully you argue, explain, examine, or illustrate your topic, but also on how skillfully you handle source materials. In other words, you must take great care not only when you take notes but also when you transfer those notes to your paper. Always keep in mind—as you are taking notes, when drafting your paper, and when writing its final version—that you must acknowledge the source for all borrowed material. Any information that you take from a source must be properly attributed to its author or, if no author, to its title. Be mindful to provide smooth integration of your source material into your own text. After all, the text is your work: The thesis of paper, the overall organization and development, transitions from point to point, general observations, and the conclusions are all yours. Your source materials serve to support, illustrate, develop, or exemplify your own words. The source materials are central to your paper but must not interrupt the flow of your words.

GUIDELINES FOR HANDLING SOURCE MATERIAL

- Introduce or provide a context for quoted material. "Bald" or "dropped" quotations occur when you fail to integrate quotations smoothly into your text. The abrupt dropping of a quotation disrupts the flow of your text.
- Name your authority or, when no author is named, use the title of the source. Provide this information either in the text itself or in the parenthetical citation. Rely on standard phrases, such as *one writer claims* or *according to one expert,* to introduce quotations or paraphrases.
- In MLA style, use both first and last names of the author at the first mention in your text. After that, use just the last name. Always use the last name only in parenthetical citations (unless you have sources by two authors with the same last name). Check to verify the conventions of other citation styles.
- Acknowledge source material when you first begin paraphrasing. Make sure you give some kind of signal to your reader when you begin paraphrasing borrowed material. This signal is particularly important if you paraphrase more than one sentence from a source. Otherwise, your reader will not know how far back the citation applies.
- Quote sparingly. Quote directly only those passages that are so vividly or memorably phrased that you could not do justice to them by rewording; that require exact wording for accuracy; or that need the authority of your source to lend credibility to what you are saying.
- Integrate source material with your own words. Avoid a cut-and-paste approach to the research process. Remember that source materials serve primarily to support your generalizations. Never run two quotations together without adding a comment or transitional remark.
- Make sure that direct quotations are exact. Do not change words unless you use brackets or ellipses to indicate changes. Otherwise, be exact. For instance, if your source says "$2 million," do not write "two million dollars."
- Make sure that paraphrases or summaries are truly your own words. Do not inadvertently commit plagiarism by failing to paraphrase or summarize fairly.

DOCUMENTING SOURCES

Follow the Appropriate Style Guidelines. The examples of documentation and sample research papers listed first in this chapter all follow MLA (Modern Language Association) documentation style. That style governs because this textbook is often used in English courses, and English is located within the discipline of the humanities. However, your instructor may permit you to choose the style appropriate to the major field you intend to study. APA (American Psychological Association) style is probably as commonly used as MLA in undergraduate course papers. In addition to MLA and APA, other frequently used documentation styles are CBE (Council of Biology Editors) and Chicago (from the University of Chicago Press). Following a summary of the chief differences among these four styles, the chapter lists stylebooks that provide detailed guidelines.

Your college or university library may provide automated citation managers or bibliographic software tools, such as RefWorks and EndNote. If so, try them out. Your reference librarian may be able to help you.

The following are the most common sources you'll use in the Works Cited list of your paper. Pay attention to the alphabetical order of items and the order of material in each entry. Also note punctuation, spacing, and hanging indents.

JOURNAL ARTICLE:

Anthropist, Phil. "How to Give Away Millions." <u>Journal of Eccentric Behaviour</u> 15.3 (2007): 124–29.

JOURNAL ARTICLE FROM AN ELECTRONIC DATABASE:

Bolder, Rollins G. "Caffeine Habituation and the Marking of Student Papers." <u>The Journal of Marks and Marxism</u> 12.6 (2004): 98–116. EBSCO. U. of the Southeast, Toronto. 13 May 2007 <http: www.ebscohost.com>.

MAGAZINE ARTICLE:
(Note: If no author, begin with the title.)

Canuckster, Bertha. "Sex and the Single Hockey Player in Manitoba." <u>McCluhan's Magazine</u> 1 April 2006: 69–70.

BOOK BY ONE AUTHOR:

Blaug, Mark. <u>John Maynard Keynes: Life, Ideas, Legacy</u>. New York: St. Martin's Press, 1990.

BOOK BY TWO AUTHORS:

Wu, Jonathan, and Robert K. Farnsworthy. <u>English Language and the Grammar of the Stampede</u>. Calgary: Kicking Hoof Press, 2005.

EDITED BOOK:

Boarde, William, ed. <u>Advertising and Vegetarianism</u>. Winnipeg: Oxen Book Publishers, 2001.

WORK IN A COLLECTION OF ESSAYS OR AN ANTHOLOGY:

Defoe, Carol. "Birds of Wonder." <u>Winged Creatures of the Gulf Islands</u>. Ed. Robin Cardinal. Montreal: Ortho Press, 1980. 212–18.

BOOK WITH MULTIPLE EDITORS:

Ackley, Katherine Anne, G. Kim Blank, and Stephen Eaton Hume, eds. <u>Perspectives on Contemporary Issues: Readings Across the Disciplines</u>. 1st Canadian ed. Toronto: Thomson Nelson, 2007.

APA

JOURNAL ARTICLE PAGINATED BY ISSUE:

Anthropist, P. (2007). How to give away millions. *Journal of Eccentric Behaviour*, *15*(3), 124–129.

JOURNAL ARTICLE FROM AN ELECTRONIC DATABASE:

Bolder, R. G. (2004). Caffeine habituation and the marking of student papers. *The Journal of Marks and Marxism* 12 (6), 98–116. Retrieved May 13, 2007, from EBSCO.

MAGAZINE ARTICLE:

(Note: If no author, begin with the title.)

Canuckster, B. (2006, April 1). Sex and the single hockey player in Manitoba. *McCluhan's Magazine, 80,* 69–70.

BOOK BY ONE AUTHOR:

Blaug, M. (1990). *John Maynard Keynes: Life, ideas, legacy.* New York: St. Martin's Press.

BOOK BY TWO AUTHORS:

Wu, J., & Farnsworthy, R. K. (2005). *English language and the grammar of the stampede.* Calgary: Kicking Hoof Press.

EDITED BOOK:

Boarde, W. (Ed.). (2001). *Advertising and vegetarianism.* Winnipeg: Oxen Book Publishers.

WORK IN A COLLECTION OF ESSAYS OR AN ANTHOLOGY:

Defoe, C. (1980). Birds of wonder. In R. Cardinal (Ed.), *Winged creatures of the Gulf Islands* (pp. 212–218). Montreal: Ortho Press.

BOOK WITH MULTIPLE EDITORS:

Ackley, K. A., Blank, G. K., & Hume, S. E. (Eds.). (2007). *Perspectives on contemporary issues: Readings across the disciplines.* 1st Canadian ed. Toronto: Thomson Nelson.

Style Guides.   To find full details on a particular documentation style, consult the following style guides:

MLA

Gibaldi, Joseph. *MLA Handbook for Writers of Research Papers.* 6th ed. New York: MLA, 2003.

APA

American Psychological Association. *Publication Manual of the American Psychological Association.* 5th ed. Washington: APA, 2001.

SUMMARY OF DIFFERENCES AMONG DOCUMENTATION STYLES

- **MLA:** Used by writers in many areas of the humanities (English, foreign languages, history, and philosophy); requires parenthetical in-text citations of author and page number that refer to an alphabetical list of works cited at the end of the paper.
- **APA:** Used by writers in the behavioural and social sciences (economics, education, psychology, and sociology); requires parenthetical in-text citations of author and date of publication that refer to an alphabetical list of references at the end of the paper.
- **CBE:** Used by writers in technical fields and the sciences (engineering, biology, physics, geography, chemistry, computer science, and mathematics); requires either a name–year format or a citation-sequence format. The name–year format places the author's last name and the year of publication in parentheses, referring to an alphabetical list of references at the end of the paper.
- **Chicago:** Used by some areas of the humanities, notably history, art, music, and theatre; requires a superscript number (e.g., [1]) for each citation, all of which are numbered sequentially throughout the paper; no number is repeated. Numbers correspond either to footnotes at the bottoms of pages or to a list of notes at the end of the paper.

The first note gives complete information about the source, with shortened information for each subsequent reference to that source. A bibliography follows the notes, giving the same information (except for the page number) as in the first citation of each source. The bibliographic information is also punctuated differently and arranged differently from the note copy.

CBE

CBE Style Manual Committee. *Scientific Style and Format: The CBE Manual for Authors, Editors, and Publishers.* 7th ed. Chicago: Council of Science Editors, 2005.

CHICAGO

The Chicago Manual of Style. 15th ed. Chicago: U of Chicago P, 2003.

Turabian Kate L. *A Manual for Writers of Term Papers, Theses, and Dissertations.* 6th ed. Rev. John Grossman and Alice Bennet. Chicago: University of Chicago Press, 1996.

Internet Citation Guides. Many research resources are available on the Internet, including guides for citing such sources. Your university librarian may have created a website where you will find the names and URLs of sites that give directions for citing electronic sources. Keep in mind that Internet sites constantly change. URLs that were correct when this book was published may no longer be correct, or the sites may have ceased functioning.

GUIDELINES FOR MLA IN-TEXT CITATION

- Name the source for all borrowed material, including both direct quotations and para-phrases, either in your text or in parentheses following the borrowed material.
- Give the citation in parentheses at the end of the sentence containing the quotation or paraphrase.
- In the parentheses, state the author's last name and the page number or numbers from which you took the words or ideas, with no punctuation between the name and the page number.
- For smooth transition to borrowed material, name the author or source when you introduce the words or ideas. In this style, the parentheses will include only the page number or numbers.
- At the first mention of an author in your text, use the author's full name. Thereafter, use the last name only.
- When citing Internet sources that have no page numbers, use the author's last name in parentheses. If you mention the author's name in your text, it is helpful to repeat it in the parenthetical citation as well, to indicate where the borrowed material ends.
- Create a Works Cited page at the end of your paper that lists all sources quoted or paraphrased in the paper. Do not include any works that you consulted but did not directly use in your paper.

PART TWO

THE ARTS, MEDIA STUDIES, AND POPULAR CULTURE

CHAPTER SEVEN

MUSIC AND VIDEO GAMES

INTRODUCTION

What is art, and who decides what is art? Should art be a part of moral education? Is popular music a form of art? Is art just another commodity to be bought and sold? Are the graphics used in video games worthy of being called art?

These topics have particular relevance today when it comes to music and video games. The subject of contemporary music can give rise to heated debate, especially when rock and roll or alternative music is discussed. One extreme view, expressed by Allan Bloom, is that rock music is not just empty of any cultural value, but actually destroys young minds and threatens civilization. Isabelle Leymarie, who wrote "Rock 'n' Revolt" more than a decade ago, addresses an issue that is still hotly discussed: the connection between rock and roll music and actual violence. Some people are firmly convinced that certain lyrics of both mainstream and alternative music actually cause violence by promoting and glorifying it. Others argue just as vehemently that such music simply reflects popular culture, rather than influencing it. As you read about the music that she cites as having been banned or stigmatized, think about the music you like. Have you ever been criticized for the kinds of music you like (or perform)?

Following Leymarie's essay, David Barboza of *The New York Times* reveals the underworld economy of the global video game industry: warehouses in China where gamers work for a few cents a day to babysit the accounts of affluent gamers who do not have the time to play.

MUSIC

ALLAN BLOOM

Allan Bloom (1930–1992) was, for most of his career, an academic philosopher. He held positions at many universities, including the University of Toronto, Yale University, and Cornell University, but was most closely associated with the University of Chicago. Although his scholarly work focused on philosophers such as Plato and Rousseau, he was also interested in politics and education. His most famous and popular work is The Closing of the American Mind *(1987), which proposed that education was in crisis: The curriculum was failing to give students exposure to and knowledge of what he held to be the "best" of Western thought; liberalism and relativism were the causes. The article below is from* The Closing of the American Mind.

Though students do not have books, they most emphatically do have music. Nothing is more singular about this generation than its addiction to music. This is the age of music and the states of soul that accompany it. To find a rival to this enthusiasm, one would have to go back at least a century to Germany and the passion for Wagner's operas. They had the religious sense that Wagner was creating the meaning of life and that they were not merely listening to his works but experiencing that meaning. Today, a very large proportion of young people between the ages of ten and twenty live for music. It is their passion; nothing else excites them as it does; they cannot take seriously anything alien to music. When they are in school and with their families, they are longing to plug themselves back into their music. Nothing surrounding them—school, family, church—has anything to do with their musical world. At best that ordinary life is neutral, but mostly it is an impediment, drained of vital content, even a thing to be rebelled against. Of course, the enthusiasm for Wagner was limited to a small class, could be indulged only rarely and only in a few places, and had to wait on the composer's slow output. The music of the new votaries, on the other hand, knows neither class nor nation. It is available twenty-four hours a day, everywhere. There is the stereo in the home, in the car; there are concerts; there are music videos, with special channels exclusively devoted to them, on the air nonstop; there are the Walkmans so that no place—not public transportation, not the library—prevents students from communing with the Muse, even while studying. And, above all, the musical soil has become tropically rich. No need to wait for unpredictable genius. Now there are many geniuses, producing all the time, two new ones rising to take the place of every fallen hero. There is no dearth of the new and the startling.

The power of music in the soul—described to Jessica marvelously by Lorenzo in the *Merchant of Venice*—has been recovered after a long period of desuetude. And it is rock music alone that has effected this restoration. Classical music is dead among the young. This assertion will, I know, be hotly disputed by many who, unwilling to admit tidal changes, can point to the proliferation on campuses of classes in classical music appreciation and practice, as well as performance groups of all kinds. Their presence is undeniable, but they involve not more than 5 to 10 percent of the students. Classical music is now a special taste, like Greek language or pre-Colombian archaeology, not a common culture of reciprocal communication and psychological shorthand. Thirty years ago, most middle-class families made some of the old European music a part of the home, partly because they liked it, partly because they thought it was good for the kids. University students usually had some early emotive association with Beethoven, Chopin, and Brahms, which was a permanent part of their makeup and to which they were likely to respond throughout their lives. This was probably the only regularly recognizable class distinction between educated and uneducated in America. Many, or even most, of the young people of that generation also swung with Benny Goodman, but with an element of self-consciousness—to be hip, to prove they weren't snobs, to show solidarity with the democratic ideal of a pop culture out of which would grow a new high culture. So there remained a class distinction between high and low, although private taste was beginning to create doubts about whether one really liked the high very much. But all that has changed. Rock music is as unquestioned and unproblematic as the air the students breathe, and very few have any acquaintance at all with classical music. This is a constant surprise to me. And one of the strange aspects of my relations with good students I come to know well is that I frequently introduce them to Mozart. This is a pleasure to me, inasmuch as it is always pleasant to give people gifts that please them. It is interesting to see whether and in what ways their studies are complemented by such music. But this is something utterly new to me as a teacher; formerly my students usually knew much more classical music than I did.

Music was not all that important for the generation of students preceding the current one. The romanticism that had dominated serious music since Beethoven appealed to refinements—perhaps over-refinements—of sentiments that are hardly to be found in the contemporary world. The lives people lead or wish to lead and their prevailing passions are of a different sort than those of the highly educated German and French bourgeoisie, who were avidly reading Rousseau and Baudelaire, Goethe and Heine, for their spiritual satisfaction. The music that had been designed to produce, as well as to please, such exquisite sensibilities had a very tenuous relation to American lives of any kind. So romantic musical culture in America had had for a long time the character of a veneer, as easily susceptible to ridicule as were Margaret Dumont's displays of coquettish chasteness, so aptly exploited by Groucho Marx in *A Night at the Opera*. I noticed this when I first started teaching and lived in a house for gifted students. The "good" ones studied their physics and then listened to classical music. The students who did not fit so easily into the groove, some of them just vulgar and restive under the cultural tyranny, but some of them also serious, were looking for things that really responded to their needs. Almost always they responded to the beat of the newly emerging rock music. They were a bit ashamed of their taste, for it was not respectable. But I instinctively sided with the second group, with real, if coarse, feelings as opposed to artificial and dead ones. Then their musical sans-culotteism won the revolution and reigns unabashed today. No classical music has been produced that can speak to this generation.

Symptomatic of this change is how seriously students now take the famous passages on musical education in Plato's *Republic.* In the past, students, good liberals that they always are, were indignant at the censorship of poetry, as a threat to free inquiry. But they were really thinking of science and politics. They hardly paid attention to the discussion of music itself and, to the extent that they even thought about it, were really puzzled by Plato's devoting time to rhythm and melody in a serious treatise on political philosophy. Their experience of music was an entertainment, a matter of indifference to political and moral life. Students today, on the contrary, know exactly why Plato takes music so seriously. They know it affects life very profoundly and are indignant because Plato seems to want to rob them of their most intimate pleasure. They are drawn into argument with Plato about the experience of music, and the dispute centers on how to evaluate it and deal with it. This encounter not only helps to illuminate the phenomenon of contemporary music, but also provides a model of how contemporary students can profitably engage with a classic text. The very fact of their fury shows how much Plato threatens what is dear and intimate to them. They are little able to defend their experience, which has seemed unquestionable until questioned, and it is most resistant to cool analysis. Yet if a student can—and this is most difficult and unusual—draw back, get a critical distance on what he clings to, come to doubt the ultimate value of what he loves, he has taken the first and most difficult step toward the philosophic conversion. Indignation is the soul's defense against the wound of doubt about its own; it reorders the cosmos to support the justice of its cause. It justifies putting Socrates to death. Recognizing indignation for what it is constitutes knowledge of the soul, and is thus an experience more philosophic than the study of mathematics. It is Plato's teaching that music, by its nature, encompasses all that is today most resistant to philosophy. So it may well be that through the thicket of our greatest corruption runs the path to awareness of the oldest truths.

Plato's teaching about music is, put simply, that rhythm and melody, accompanied by dance, are the barbarous expression of the soul. Barbarous, not animal. Music is the medium of the *human* soul in its most ecstatic condition of wonder and terror. Nietzsche, who in large measure agrees with Plato's analysis, says in *The Birth of Tragedy* (not to be forgotten is the rest of the title, *Out of the Spirit of Music*) that a mixture of cruelty and coarse sensuality characterized this state, which of course was religious, in the service of gods. Music is the soul's primitive and primary speech and it is *alogon*, without articulate speech or reason. It is not only not reasonable, it is hostile to reason. Even when articulate speech is added, it is utterly subordinate to and determined by the music and the passions it expresses.

Civilization or, to say the same thing, education is the taming or domestication of the soul's raw passions—not suppressing or excising them, which would deprive the soul of its energy—but forming and informing them as art. The goal of harmonizing the enthusiastic part of the soul with what develops later, the rational part, is perhaps impossible to attain. But without it, man can never be whole. Music, or poetry, which is what music becomes as reason emerges, always involves a delicate balance between passion and reason, and, even in its highest and most developed forms—religious, warlike, and erotic—that balance is always tipped, if ever so slightly, toward the passionate. Music, as everyone experiences, provides an unquestionable justification and a fulfilling pleasure for the activities it accompanies: the solider who hears the marching band is enthralled and reassured; the religious man is exalted in his prayer by the sound of the organ in the church; and the lover is carried away and his conscience stilled by the romantic guitar. Armed with music, man can damn rational doubt. Out of the music emerge the gods that suit it, and they educate men by their example and their commandments.

Plato's Socrates disciplines the ecstasies and thereby provides little consolation or hope to men. According to the Socratic formula, the lyrics—speech and, hence, reason—must determine the music—harmony and rhythm. Pure music can never endure this constraint. Students are not in a position to know the pleasures of reason; they can only see it as a disciplinary and repressive parent. But they do see, in the case of Plato, that that parent has figured out what they are up to. Plato teaches that, in order to take the spiritual temperature of an individual or a society, one must "mark the music." To Plato and Nietzsche, the history of music is a series of attempts to give form and beauty to the dark, chaotic, premonitory forces in the soul—to make them serve a higher purpose, an ideal, to give man's duties a fullness. Bach's religious intentions and Beethoven's revolutionary and humane ones are clear enough examples. Such cultivation of the soul uses the passions and satisfies them while sublimating them and giving them an artistic unity. A man whose noblest activities are accompanied by a music that expresses them while providing a pleasure extending from the lowest bodily to the highest spiritual, is whole, and there is no tension in him between the pleasant and the good. By contrast a man whose business life is prosaic and unmusical and whose leisure is made up of coarse, intense entertainments, is divided, and each side of his existence is undermined by the other.

Hence, for those who are interested in psychological health, music is at the center of education, both for giving the passions their due and for preparing the soul for the unhampered use of reason. The centrality of such education was recognized by all the ancient educators. It is hardly noticed today that in Aristotle's *Politics* the most important passages about the best regime concern musical education, or that the *Poetics* is an appendix to the *Politics*. Classical philosophy did not censor the singers. It persuaded them. And it gave them a goal, one that was understood by them, until only yesterday. But those who do not notice the role of music in Aristotle and despise Plato went to school with Hobbes, Locke, and Smith, where such considerations have become unnecessary. The triumphant Enlightenment rationalism thought that it had discovered other ways to deal with the irrational part of the soul, and that reason needed less support from it. Only in those great critics of

Enlightenment and rationalism, Rousseau and Nietzsche, does music return, and they were the most musical of philosophers. Both thought that the passions—and along with them their ministerial arts—had become thin under the rule of reason and that, therefore, man *himself* and what he sees in the world have become correspondingly thin. They wanted to cultivate the enthusiastic states of the soul and to reexperience the Corybantic possession deemed a pathology to Plato. Nietzsche, particularly, sought to tap again the irrational sources of vitality, to replenish our dried-up stream from barbaric sources, and thus encouraged the Dionysian and the music derivative from it.

This is the significance of rock music. I do not suggest that it has any high intellectual sources. But it has risen to its current heights in the education of the young on the ashes of classical music, and in an atmosphere in which there is no intellectual resistance to attempts to tap the rawest passions. Modern-day rationalists, such as economists, are indifferent to it and what it represents. The irrationalists are all for it. There is no need to fear that "the blond beasts" are going to come forth from the bland souls of our adolescents. But rock music has one appeal only, a barbaric appeal, to sexual desire—not love, not *eros*, but sexual desire undeveloped and untutored. It acknowledges the first emanations of children's emerging sensuality and addresses them seriously, eliciting them and legitimating them, not as little sprouts that must be carefully tended in order to grow into gorgeous flowers, but as the real thing. Rock gives children, on a silver platter, with all the public authority of the entertainment industry, everything their parents always used to tell them they had to wait for until they grew up and would understand later.

Young people know that rock has the beat of sexual intercourse. That is why Ravel's *Bolero* is the one piece of classical music that is commonly known and liked by them. In alliance with some real art and a lot of pseudo-art, an enormous industry cultivates the taste for the orgiastic state of feeling connected with sex, providing a constant flood of fresh material for voracious appetites. Never was there an art form directed so exclusively to children.

Ministering to and according with the arousing and cathartic music, the lyrics celebrate puppy love as well as polymorphous attractions, and fortify them against traditional ridicule and shame. The words implicitly and explicitly describe bodily acts that satisfy sexual desire and treat them as its only natural and routine culmination for children who do not yet have the slightest imagination of love, marriage, or family. This has a much more powerful effect than does pornography on youngsters, who have no need to watch others do grossly what they can so easily do themselves. Voyeurism is for old perverts; active sexual relations are for the young. All they need is encouragement.

The inevitable corollary of such sexual interest is rebellion against the parental authority that represses it. Selfishness thus becomes indignation and then transforms itself into morality. The sexual revolution must overthrow all the forces of domination, the enemies of nature and happiness. From love comes hate, masquerading as social reform. A worldview is balanced on the sexual fulcrum. What were once unconscious or half-conscious childish resentments become the new Scripture. And then comes the longing for the classless, prejudice-free, conflictless, universal society that necessarily results from liberated consciousness—"We Are the World," a pubescent version of *Alle Menschen werden Brüder*, the fulfillment of which has been inhibited by the political equivalents of Mom and Dad. These are the three great lyrical themes: sex, hate, and a smarmy, hypocritical version of brotherly love. Such polluted sources issue in a muddy stream where only monsters can swim. A glance at the videos that project images on the wall of Plato's cave since MTV took it over suffices to prove this. Hitler's image recurs frequently enough in exciting contexts to give one pause. Nothing noble, sublime, profound, delicate, tasteful, or even decent can find a place in such tableaux. There is room only for the intense, changing, crude, and immediate, which Tocqueville warned us would be the character of democratic art, combined with a pervasiveness, importance, and content beyond Tocqueville's wildest imagination.

Picture a thirteen-year-old boy sitting in the living room of his family home doing his math assignment while wearing his Walkman headphones or watching MTV. He enjoys the liberties hard won over centuries by the alliance of philosophic genius and political heroism, consecrated by the blood of martyrs; he is provided with comfort and leisure by the most productive economy ever known to mankind; science has penetrated the secrets of nature in order to provide him with the marvelous, lifelike electronic sound and image reproduction he is enjoying. And in what does progress culminate? A pubescent child whose body throbs with orgasmic rhythms; whose feelings are made articulate in hymns to the joys of onanism or the killing of parents; whose ambition is to win fame and wealth in imitating the drag-queen who makes the music. In short, life is made into a nonstop, commercially prepackaged masturbational fantasy.

This description may seem exaggerated, but only because some would prefer to regard it as such. The continuing exposure to rock music is a reality, not one confined to a particular class or type of child. One need only ask first-year university students what music they listen to, how much of it, and what it means to them, in order to discover that the phenomenon is universal in America, that it begins in adolescence or a bit before and continues through the college years. It is *the* youth culture and, as I have so often insisted, there is now no other countervailing nourishment for the spirit. Some of this culture's power comes from the fact that it is so loud. It makes conversation impossible, so that much of friendship must be without the shared speech that Aristotle asserts is the essence of friendship and the only true common ground. With rock, illusions of shared feelings, bodily contact and grunted formulas, which are supposed to contain so much meaning beyond speech, are the basis of association. None of this contradicts going about the business of life, attending classes, and doing the assignments for them. But the meaningful inner life is with the music.

This phenomenon is both astounding and indigestible, and is hardly noticed, routine and habitual. But it is of historic proportions that a society's best young and their best energies should be so occupied. People of future civilizations will wonder at this and find it as incomprehensible as we do the caste system, witch-burning, harems, cannibalism, and gladiatorial combats. It may well be that a society's greatest madness seems normal to itself. The child described has parents who have sacrificed to provide him with a good life and who have a great stake in his future happiness. They cannot believe that the musical vocation will contribute very much to that happiness. But there is nothing they can do about it. The family spiritual void has left the field open to rock music, and they cannot possibly forbid their children to listen to it. It is everywhere; all children listen to it; forbidding it would simply cause them to lose their children's affection and obedience. When they turn on the television, they will see President Reagan warmly grasping the daintily proffered gloved hand of Michael Jackson and praising him enthusiastically. Better to set the faculty of denial in motion—avoid noticing what the words say, assume the kid will get over it. If he has early sex, that won't get in the way of his having stable relationships later. His drug use will certainly stop at pot. School is providing real values. And popular historicism provides the final salvation; there are new lifestyles for new situations, and the older generation is there not to impose its values but to help the younger one to find its own. TV, which compared to music plays a comparatively small role in the formation of young people's character and taste, is a consensus monster—the Right monitors its content for sex, the Left for violence, and many other interested sects for many other things. But the music has hardly been touched, and what efforts have been made are both ineffectual and misguided about the nature and extent of the problem.

The result is nothing less than parents' loss of control over their children's moral education at a time when no one else is seriously concerned with it. This has been achieved by the alliance between the strange young males who have the gift of divining the mob's emergent wishes—our versions of Thrasymachus, Socrates' rhetorical adversary—and the record-company executives, the new robber barons, who mine gold out of rock. They discovered a few years back that children are one of the few groups in the country with considerable disposable income, in the form of allowances. Their parents spend all they have providing for the kids. Appealing to them over their parents' heads, creating a world of delight for them, constitutes one of the richest markets in the postwar world. The rock business is perfect capitalism, supplying to demand and helping to create it. It has all the moral dignity of drug trafficking, but it was so totally new and unexpected that nobody thought to control it, and now it is too late. Progress may be made against cigarette smoking because our absence of standards or our relativism does not extend to matters of bodily health. In all other things the market determines the value. (Yoko Ono is among America's small group of billionaires, along with oil and computer magnates, her late husband having produced and sold a commodity of worth comparable to theirs.) Rock is a very big business, bigger than the movies, bigger than professional sports, bigger than television, and this accounts for much of the respectability of the music business. It is difficult to adjust our vision to the changes in the economy and to see what is really important. McDonald's now has more employees than U.S. Steel, and likewise the purveyors of junk food for the soul have supplanted what still seems to be more basic callings.

This change has been happening for some time. In the late fifties, DeGaulle gave Brigitte Bardot one of France's highest honors. I could not understand this, but it turned out that she, along with Peugeot, was France's biggest export item. As

Western nations became more prosperous, leisure, which had been put off for several centuries in favor of the pursuit of property, the means to leisure, finally began to be of primary concern. But, in the meantime, any notion of the serious life of leisure, as well as men's taste and capacity to live it, had disappeared. Leisure became entertainment. The end for which they had labored for so long has turned out to be amusement, a justified conclusion if the means justify the ends. The music business is peculiar only in that it caters almost exclusively to children, treating legally and naturally imperfect human beings as though they were ready to enjoy the final or complete satisfaction. It perhaps thus reveals the nature of all our entertainment and our loss of a clear view of what adulthood or maturity is, and our incapacity to conceive ends. The emptiness of *values* results in the acceptance of the natural *facts* as the ends. In this case infantile sexuality is the end, and I suspect that, in absence of other ends, many adults have to agree that it is.

It is interesting to note that the Left, which prides itself on its critical approach to "late capitalism" and is unrelenting and unsparing in its analysis of our other cultural phenomena, has in general given rock music a free ride. Abstracting from the capitalist element in which it flourishes, they regard it as a people's art, coming from beneath the bourgeoisie's layers of cultural repression. Its antinomianism and its longing for a world without constraint might seem to be the clarion of the proletarian revolution, and Marxists certainly do see that rock music dissolves the beliefs and morals necessary for liberal society and would approve of it for that alone. But the harmony between the young intellectual Left and rock is probably profounder than that. Herbert Marcuse appealed to university students in the sixties with a combination of Marx and Freud. In *Eros and Civilization* and *One Dimensional Man* he promised that the overcoming of capitalism and its false consciousness will result in a society where the greatest satisfactions are sexual, of a sort that the bourgeois moralist Freud called polymorphous and infantile. Rock music touches the same chord in the young. Free sexual expression, anarchism, mining of the irrational unconscious and giving it free rein are what they have in common. The high intellectual life . . . and the low rock world are partners in the same entertainment enterprise. They must both be interpreted as parts of the cultural fabric of late capitalism. Their success comes from the bourgeois's need to feel that he is not bourgeois, to have undangerous experiments with the unlimited. He is willing to pay dearly for them. The Left is better interpreted by Nietzsche than by Marx. The critical theory of late capitalism is at once late capitalism's subtlest and crudest expression. Antibourgeois ire is the opiate of the Last Man.

This strong stimulant, which Nietzsche called Nihiline, was for a very long time, almost fifteen years, epitomized in a single figure, Mick Jagger. A shrewd, middle-class boy, he played the possessed lower-class demon and teen-aged satyr up until he was forty, with one eye on the mobs of children of both sexes whom he stimulated to a sensual frenzy and the other eye winking at the unerotic, commercially motivated adults who handled the money. In his act he was male and female, heterosexual and homosexual; unencumbered by modesty, he could enter everyone's dreams, promising to do everything with everyone; and, above all, he legitimated drugs, which were the real thrill that parents and policemen conspired to deny his

Mick Jagger: Destroying the minds and souls of young people?
Photo Source: CP/Action Press

youthful audience. He was beyond the law, moral and political, and thumbed his nose at it. Along with all this, there were nasty little appeals to the suppressed inclinations toward sexism, racism, and violence, indulgence in which is not now publicly respectable. Nevertheless, he managed not to appear to contradict the rock ideal of a universal classless society founded on love, with the distinction between brotherly and bodily blurred. He was the hero and the model for countless young persons in universities, as well as elsewhere. I discovered that students who boasted of having no heroes secretly had a passion to be like Mick Jagger, to live his life, have his fame. They were ashamed to admit this in a university, although I am not certain that the reason has anything to do with a higher standard of taste. It is probably that they are not supposed to have heroes. Rock music itself and talking about it with infinite seriousness are perfectly respectable. It has proved to be the ultimate leveler of intellectual snobbism. But it is not respectable to think of it as providing weak and ordinary persons with a fashionable behavior, the imitation of which will make others esteem them and boost their own self-esteem. Unaware and unwillingly, however, Mick Jagger played the role in their lives that Napoleon played in the lives of ordinary young Frenchmen throughout the nineteenth century. Everyone else was so boring and unable to charm youthful passions. Jagger caught on.

In the last couple of years, Jagger has begun to fade. Whether Michael Jackson, Prince, or Boy George can take his place is uncertain. They are even weirder than he is, and one wonders what new strata of taste they have discovered. Although each differs from the others, the essential character of musical entertainment is not changing. There is only a constant search for variations on the theme. And this gutter phenomenon is apparently the fulfillment of the promise made by so much psychology and literature that our weak and exhausted Western civilization would find refreshment in the true source, the unconscious, which appeared to the late romantic imagination to be identical to Africa, the dark and unexplored continent. Now all has been explored; light has been cast everywhere; the unconscious has been made conscious, the repressed expressed. And what have we found? Not creative devils, but show business glitz. Mick Jagger tarting it up on the stage is all we brought back from the voyage to the underworld.

My concern here is not with the moral effects of this music—whether it leads to sex, violence, or drugs. The issue here is its effect on education, and I believe it ruins the imagination of young people and makes it very difficult for them to have a passionate relationship to the art and thought that are the substance of liberal education. The first sensuous experiences are decisive in determining the taste for the whole of life, and they are the link between the animal and spiritual in us. The period of nascent sensuality has always been used for sublimation, in the sense of making sublime, for attaching youthful inclinations and longings to music, pictures, and stories that provide the transition to the fulfillment of the human duties and the enjoyment of the human pleasures. Lessing, speaking of Greek sculpture, said "beautiful men made beautiful statues, and the city had beautiful statues in part to thank for beautiful citizens." This formula encapsulates the fundamental principle of the esthetic education of man. Young men and women were attracted by the beauty of heroes whose very bodies expressed their nobility. The deeper understanding of the meaning of nobility comes later, but is prepared for by the sensuous experience and is actually contained in it. What the senses long for as well as what reason later sees as good are thereby not at tension with one another. Education is not sermonizing to children against their instincts and pleasures, but providing a natural continuity between what they feel and what they can and should be. But this is a lost art. Now we have come to exactly the opposite point. Rock music encourages passions and provides models that have no relation to any life the young people who go to universities can possible lead, or to the kinds of admiration encouraged by liberal studies. Without the cooperation of the sentiments, anything other than technical education is a dead letter.

Rock music provides premature ecstasy and, in this respect, is like the drugs with which it is allied. It artificially induces the exaltation naturally attached to the completion of the greatest endeavors—victory in a just war, consummated love, artistic creation, religious devotion, and discovery of the truth. Without effort, without talent, without virtue, without exercise of the faculties, anyone and everyone is accorded the equal right to the enjoyment of their fruits. In my experience, students who have had a serious fling with drugs—and gotten over it—find it difficult to have enthusiasms or great expectations. It is as though the color has been drained out of their lives and they see everything in black and white. The pleasure they experienced in the beginning was so intense that they no longer look for it at the end, or as the end. They may function perfectly well, but dryly, routinely. Their energy has been sapped, and they do not expect their life's activity to produce anything but a living, whereas liberal education is supposed to encourage the belief that the good life is the pleasant life and that the best life is the most pleasant life. I suspect that the rock addiction, particularly in the absence of strong counterattractions, has an effect similar to that of drugs. The students will get over this music, or at least the exclusive passion for it. But they will do so in the same way Freud says that men accept the reality principle—as something harsh, grim, and essentially unattractive, a mere necessity. These students will assiduously study economics or the professions and the Michael Jackson costume will slip off to reveal a Brooks Brothers suit beneath. They will want to get ahead and live comfortably. But this life is as empty and false as the one they left behind. The choice is not between quick fixes and dull calculation. This is what liberal education is meant to show them. But as long as they have the Walkman on, they cannot hear what the great tradition has to say. And, after its prolonged use, when they take it off, they find they are deaf.

PERSONAL RESPONSE

Is Bloom right in saying that rock has a negative effect on your imagination and morals? Is most rock about sexual desire? Should one of civilization's functions be to tame your "raw passions," and can civilization have this effect? Do you agree with Bloom that rock music is like drugs in providing "premature ecstasy"? What role does rock or popular music play in your life?

QUESTIONS FOR CLASS OR SMALL-GROUP DISCUSSION

1. In what ways do the media and technology contribute to creating a passion—or at least a need—for rock music?

2. Bloom suggests that rock music is capable of negatively affecting the consciousness and imagination of young people. Which contemporary rock musicians or groups are currently popular? Discuss their effects on contemporary youth values and behaviour. What kind of message do they present? What is the central message of contemporary rock, or are the messages too varied to be codified?

3. Mick Jagger, lead singer of The Rolling Stones, is singled out by Bloom as being representative of all that is bad about rock music, particularly in the shrewd, "underworld" sexuality he exudes. By far the most famous song by The Rolling Stones is "Satisfaction," which, given the title (and the song's beat), sounds like it must be about sexual gratification ("I can't get no satisfaction"). Examine the lyrics of this song by looking them up on the Internet, and give a close critical reading to what the song is about.

4. Bloom, in writing this piece in the mid-1980s, suggests that "future generations" will show the folly of this preoccupation with rock music. Now, 20 years later, it appears that rock music is more popular than ever. Explain its continuing popularity, and speculate on the future of rock music. How correct is Bloom's prophecy? How relevant is rock music?

5. Examine the relationship between rock music and business in a capitalist or global context.

ROCK 'N' REVOLT

Isabelle Leymarie

Isabelle Leymarie is a Franco-American jazz pianist, dancer, and musicologist who holds a Ph.D. from Columbia University in ethnomusicology. Formerly an assistant professor of African-American Studies at Yale University, she currently resides in Paris. Her study, "Salsa and Migration," appeared in an anthology of writing on Puerto Rico entitled The Commuter Nation *(1992). She has written several books, including* La Salsa et le Latin Jazz *(1993),* Musiques Caraïbes (Caribbean Music) *(1996), and* Cuban Fire: The Saga of Salsa and Latin Jazz *(2003). This essay first appeared in the February 1993 issue of* UNESCO Courier.

Rock, a musical and social phenomenon of unprecedented scope and intensity, raises in acute form the question of the relationship between music and violence. Its history has been fraught with violence. Jim Morrison, leader of The Doors, apostle of sex, alcohol, and LSD, died young, of a heart attack in his bathtub in Paris. Stars Jimi Hendrix and Janis Joplin both died of drug overdoses. Acid rock has become synonymous with punks and English football riots. The fans of Metallica and Guns n' Roses have burned cars, and during a recent concert in Montreal they wrecked a stadium and injured twelve people. The Sex Pistols proclaimed in their song "Anarchy in the UK": "I wanna destroy passers-by, for I wanna be anarchy." John Phillips, a member of The Mamas and The Papas, was reported by musicologist David Tame as claiming that any rock group can whip a crowd into a hysterical frenzy by carefully controlling a sequence of rhythms. In 1967 he went ahead and did just that in Phoenix. When Hell's Angels roughed up spectators during a Rolling Stones concert in California, rocker Mick Jagger remarked that "Something like this happens every time I play that song."

Although physically less conspicuous, violence is also expressed in the lyrics of urban music such as rap (a recent hit by star rapper Ice-T is entitled "Cop Killer") and free jazz ("We are not angry young men, we are enraged!" proclaimed saxophonist Archie Shepp in the late 1960s). Here, violence is palpable in lyrics, song titles, public statements by musicians, and in the music itself: the mega-volumes, "fuzz" effects, and distortions of rock, the hammer beats of rap, the shrieking saxophones and cascading notes of jazz, and the amplified bass of reggae. Violence is also associated with other types of music. In Stanley Kubrick's film *A Clockwork Orange,* the hero, Alex, driven crazy by the sounds of Beethoven, jumps out of a window. In Cuba during the 1920s and 1930s, concerts by rival bands playing the popular music known as *son* degenerated into brawls which had to be broken up by the police.

Violence, in more controlled forms, is present in many musical traditions, old and new: in the wailing of women in the funeral lamentations of Macedonia; in certain Senegalese songs whose lyrics pour out a stream of bitter invective against new wives brought into a household; in the drumbeats of African *griot* storytellers which once stimulated the ardor of warriors and today perform a similar role for the participants in traditional wrestling matches. It is found in martial music, in hunting calls, and in filmed thrillers where it plays a crucial role in setting the mood.

Violence is also present in classical music such as Handel's "Saul," Beethoven's *Eroica Symphony,* in operas generally, such as those of Verdi, who once said that he sought to express "passions above all else" and almost all of whose heroines die tragic deaths, in Mahler's *Fourth Symphony,* in Berlioz's *Symphonie Fantastique,* with its dramatic *Dies irae,* and in Stravinsky's *The Rite of Spring,* in which a virgin, sacrificed to the gods, dances herself to death (a riot broke out during the first performance). One could continue the list indefinitely.

An Extraordinary Power

Is it possible, asks musicologist Gilbert Rouget in his book on music and trance, that music may be endowed with a magical power capable of whipping people into the state of madness which the ancient Greeks called *mania?* Or does it have no objective reality? Rouget cites Timotheus of Miletus, who lived in the fourth century B.C. and once said that music "was capable of tempting Alexander away from a banquet to take up arms, and then of luring him back again to his guests with a lilting harmony." Rouget also quotes Boethius, who claimed that the Dorian mode inspired virtue, whereas the Phrygian mode aroused passion and violence, and refers to Aristotle's theory of the ethos of modes, which was similar to that of Boethius. He concludes that music can induce a trance in some cases and calm in others, and that it "derives its power from its integration into a given set of representations."

It is true that in order to grasp the symbolism in a particular type of music it is essential to be familiar with the set of representations into which it is integrated and the context in which it is performed. In the West, for example, the major modes evoke elation and rejoicing and the minor modes inspire melancholy, while in the

East other modes such as Arab *maqam* and Indian *ragas* evoke totally different emotional moods. Similarly, drums and trumpets are regarded as martial instruments and flutes are associated with pastoral. All this is bound up with mental associations that are to a large extent culturally determined.

Leibniz spoke of the "anxiety-causing effect" of dissonance, and yet today dissonances, which have become commonplace in contemporary music, have lost much of their disquieting character (even Chopin's mazurkas, when first performed, were criticized for their "dissonance"). Verdi's use of double basses to introduce the final scene of *Othello*, Berlioz's use of percussion instruments in the *Symphonie Fantastique*, and Alfred Hitchcock's use of violins to heighten dramatic tension, are all illustrations of the way in which musical choices are both personal and culturally determined.

And yet music, when considered as a group of organized sounds and hence as a purely acoustic phenomenon, is also known to produce certain physiological and psychological effects which have been scientifically documented. Certain rhythms and sound frequencies, for example, can accelerate or slow down the human metabolic rate and even induce hypnosis. John Diamond, a specialist in behavioral physiology, has shown how the relative strength of certain muscles, a function which is easily measurable, varies according to the type of music to which people are listening. Animals and plants are also known to react physically to music. According to studies carried out in India, Russia, and the United States, plants seem to hate "heavy metal" rock music and twist themselves as far away as possible from the offending loudspeaker, while they adore classical violin and will grow even more lushly to the sounds of disco.

Noise engenders violence; it can even drive people to suicide. Some artificial noises, especially those which emanate from continuous-frequency engines, have been found to have a pathological effect on the body's cellular structure, and can sometimes cause cancer, while natural sounds, like those of waves, the warbling of birds, and certain types of classical or African music, can create a sense of wellbeing and even a healing effect by harmonizing with our biorhythms.

In recent years, the practice of music therapy has enjoyed considerable popularity. Members of the Research Group in Pediatric Anaesthesiology at the Hospital for Sick Children in Paris and doctors in many American hospitals have used carefully selected types of music to reduce their patients' dependency on tranquillizers. In *The Burmese Harp* (1956), a fine film by the Japanese director Kon Ichikawa, a soldier-musician saps his comrades' will to fight whenever he plays and sings.

Study of the relationship between music and violence also raises the question of the political aspect of music. In many parts of the world, musicians such as the bards of Nepal, the *griots* or the musicians of Ethiopia are perceived as pariahs or as socially inferior, and are believed to lead dissolute lives and be addicted to drugs and alcohol. Music has often been used as an instrument of domination. In some African societies, *mirliton* reed pipes and other instruments provide a musical accompaniment during the ritual parading of masks, which women and children must not see and which perpetuate male dominance.

The French writer Jacques Attali has observed that in Western societies the upper classes have always encouraged artistic creation, but only in order to maintain the established order and legitimize their own authority. In the 1950s, the

Dominican dictator Rafael Trujillo y Molina encouraged the practice of the *merengue,* a dance closely related to the samba, but gave orders that the musicians should sing his praises and exiled those who opposed him. In many countries, music has become a form of propaganda or been appropriated by the Church, and judgments about music have been an endorsement of manipulation and intolerance.

Authoritarian colonial regimes arbitrarily associated drums with violence and debauchery, and long banned black music. The "New Age" writer Corinne Hélène claims that jazz and juvenile delinquency go hand in hand. But this baseless claim is fraught with prejudice, for how can the beautiful and expressive phrasing of a Sarah Vaughan or an Ella Fitzgerald be associated with juvenile delinquency? Why should jazz as a whole be connected with this social problem when most young jazz musicians are now graduates of music conservatories and universities and the overwhelming majority of jazz fans are intellectuals? How indeed, when music, for many deprived black and Hispanic adolescents of America's urban ghettos, far from leading to delinquency, is often a lifeline?

In the United States, moral-majority pressure groups have stigmatized some rock records as "obscene," in the hope of getting them withdrawn from the market, but they also tried to ban the Robert Mapplethorpe photo exhibition and other artistic events which did not correspond with their ideals. On the other hand, some kinds of music such as "Muzak," which supposedly increase consumer sales and induce people in restaurants to eat more but are actually a form of audio-brainwashing and noise pollution, are broadcast all day long in shopping centres and other public areas.

Jacques Attali has also remarked that "show business, the star system, and the hit parade are signs of deep-rooted institutional and cultural colonization." In this context music, through a sometimes violent protest against official art and the mechanization of society, becomes a means of fighting authority. "Music exists," adds Jacques Attali, "to help us hear the sound of change. It forces us to invent new categories, to come up with a new momentum capable of rejuvenating a view of society that has become ossified, trapped, moribund." This is partly true of rock and its rebellious anti-establishment stance, and of jazz, rap, and reggae—all musical forms which proclaim their black identity and have rejected old models along with the hypocrisy and inhumanity of materialism. In certain ritualized settings, notably during festivals, subversive songs are often used to express grievances against the establishment.

A Yearning for Harmony

Does music engender violence or does it express violence? And if it does express violence, does it, by sublimating violent impulses and dissipating tensions, play a cathartic role and "soothe the savage breast"? Music, for Attali, is the "audible tape of society's vibrations and signs." It is undeniably deeply rooted in the collective psychology: rock, rap, free jazz, and reggae all express the violence of the cultures which have bred them. But people and their environment are inseparable: the pent-up violence in the individual affects society and vice versa. While music reflects the collective *gestalt* of a society, its particular form of expression also reflects the emotions of the musician.

In China, Egypt, India, and ancient Greece, music was believed to possess a certain ethical value and the power to uplift or debase the soul. In ancient China, the imperial government existed in harmony with the twelve celestial tones, and during the Confucian Chin dynasty, certain "virtuous" songs and musical instruments were reputed to temper the harshness of the regime. Classical music is also imbued with spirituality: Mozart's Don Giovanni brings down divine vengeance upon himself by assassinating a nobleman and burns in hell for it. Liszt aspired to compose inspirational works, and although Wagner's *Tetralogy* (the four-opera *Ring* cycle) expresses both the fall of humanity cut adrift from the gods and the distress of the artist faced with the world's misfortunes, Wagner had a deeply moral view of art.

The French sociologist Jean Duvignaud has written that art expresses "nostalgia for a lost form of communication in the shape of a forbidden dream that is continually revived by the irrepressible desire of the human emotional impulse." He goes on to say that a successful work of art "rebuilds behind the self a unity which pieces together the shards of a divided humanity." Now that idealism has been demolished and the philosophy of music has become a thing of the past, while the media (which tend to put the visual image before the musical message) bombard us with vulgar and iconoclastic music, it is more than ever incumbent on musicians and artists in general to adopt an ethical position. The most influential creators of the twentieth century, notably the film-makers whose art is one of our era's most powerful forms of expression—artists such as Kurosawa, Ozu, and Satyajit Ray—have been passionate humanists.

Musical eurhythmics presupposes both inner and outer harmony, peace with oneself and with the universe. Violence, in its latent form, is an intrinsic part of human nature and of the universe generally. But when violence is unleashed and expressed, often in a paroxysm, in music or other art forms, it is a symptom either of social unrest or of inner imbalance or torment, emotional deprivation, and arrested development. And just as the wind can rise from a gentle breeze to a raging hurricane, so music can enchant or destroy us. It is for musicians to create works which enrich life, which contribute to the harmony of humanity, without compromising the quality of their art (some forms of therapeutic music, such as "New Age" music, do not really have any aesthetic value).

However, when music achieves perfection, it allows us to catch a glimpse of the divine; it becomes, according to a Buddhist belief, the most refined art, the path to enlightenment. According to the Taoist sage, Zhuangzi, "Music allows man to remain pure, simple, sincere, and in this way to rediscover his primitive emotions." (A few centuries later, Wagner would also use music to explore primitive forms of expression.) The great violinist Yehudi Menuhin once observed that "music creates order out of chaos." Nietzsche's humorous conclusion was that "Without music, life would be a mistake."

PERSONAL RESPONSE

Describe your favourite kind of music and why it appeals to you. Are you ever criticized for listening to it? What characteristic of this music do you think produces negative or even hostile reactions in some people? Is there a clear generation gap between having and not having an affinity to rock music?

QUESTIONS FOR CLASS OR SMALL-GROUP DISCUSSION

1. Leymarie gives examples of the ways certain mental associations with music "are to a large extent culturally determined." Can you give other examples of the point she makes in this section of her essay?

2. Give examples of musicians or musical groups that have made political statements through their music, especially those who use music as "a means of fighting authority." Discuss the effects, if any, of their music.

3. How would you answer Leymarie's question, "Does music engender violence or does it express violence?"? Discuss whether music creates violent behaviour or simply reflects the culture that produces it.

4. Leymarie discusses her subject objectively for the most part, but she offers her own opinions from time to time. Find examples of such subjectivity and consider how it influences her case.

OGRE TO SLAY? OUTSOURCE IT TO CHINESE

DAVID BARBOZA

David Barboza was a freelance writer and a research assistant for The New York Times *before being hired in 1997 as a staff writer. Since November 2004, he has been a Shanghai-based correspondent writing on art, film, television, and dance for the business and culture sections of* The New York Times. *Barboza covered the Enron scandal and was part of the team that was a finalist for a Pulitzer Prize in 2002.*

FUZHOU, China—One of China's newest factories operates here in the basement of an old warehouse. Posters of World of Warcraft and Magic Land hang above a corps of young people glued to their computer screens, pounding away at their keyboards in the latest hustle for money.

The people working at this clandestine locale are "gold farmers." Every day, in 12-hour shifts, they "play" computer games by killing onscreen monsters and winning battles, harvesting artificial gold coins and other virtual goods as rewards that, as it turns out, can be transformed into real cash.

That is because, from Seoul to San Francisco, affluent online gamers who lack the time and patience to work their way up to the higher levels of gamedom are willing to pay the young Chinese here to play the early rounds for them.

"For 12 hours a day, 7 days a week, my colleagues and I are killing monsters," said a 23-year-old gamer who works here in this makeshift factory and goes by the online code name Wandering. "I make about $250 a month, which is pretty good compared with the other jobs I've had. And I can play games all day."

He and his comrades have created yet another new business out of cheap Chinese labor. They are tapping into the fast-growing world of "massively multiplayer online games," which involve role playing and often revolve around fantasy or warfare in medieval kingdoms or distant galaxies.

With more than 100 million people worldwide logging on every month to play interactive computer games, game companies are already generating revenues of $3.6 billion a year from subscriptions, according to DFC Intelligence, which tracks the computer gaming market.

For the Chinese in game-playing factories like these, though, it is not all fun and games. These workers have strict quotas and are supervised by bosses who equip them with computers, software and Internet connections to thrash online trolls, gnomes and ogres.

As they grind through the games, they accumulate virtual currency that is valuable to game players around the world. The games allow players to trade currency to other players, who can then use it to buy better armor, amulets, magic spells and other accoutrements to climb to higher levels or create more powerful characters.

The Internet is now filled with classified advertisements from small companies—many of them here in China—auctioning for real money their powerful figures, called avatars. These ventures join individual gamers who started marketing such virtual weapons and wares a few years ago to help support their hobby.

"I'm selling an account with a level-60 Shaman," says one ad from a player code-named Silver Fire, who uses QQ, the popular Chinese instant messaging service here in China. "If you want to know more details, let's chat on QQ."

This virtual economy is blurring the line between fantasy and reality. A few years ago, online subscribers started competing with other players from around the world. And before long, many casual gamers started asking other people to baby-sit for their accounts, or play while they were away.

That has spawned the creation of hundreds—perhaps thousands—of online gaming factories here in China. By some estimates, there are well over 100,000 young people working in China as full-time gamers, toiling away in dark Internet cafes, abandoned warehouses, small offices and private homes.

Most of the players here actually make less than a quarter an hour, but they often get room, board and free computer game play in these "virtual sweatshops."

"It's unimaginable how big this is," says Chen Yu, 27, who employs 20 full-time gamers here in Fuzhou. "They say that in some of these popular games, 40 or 50 percent of the players are actually Chinese farmers."

For many online gamers, the point is no longer simply to play. Instead they hunt for the fanciest sword or the most potent charm, or seek a shortcut to the thrill of sparring at the highest level. And all of that is available—for a price.

"What we're seeing here is the emergence of virtual currencies and virtual economies," says Peter Ludlow, a longtime gamer and a professor of philosophy at the University of Michigan, Ann Arbor. "People are making real money here, so these games are becoming like real economies."

The Chinese government estimates that there are 24 million online gamers in China, meaning that nearly one in four Internet users here play online games.

And many online gaming factories have come to resemble the thousands of textile mills and toy factories that have moved here from Taiwan, Hong Kong and other parts of the world to take advantage of China's vast pool of cheap labor.

"They're exploiting the wage difference between the U.S. and China for unskilled labor," says Edward Castronova, a professor of telecommunications at Indiana University and the author of "Synthetic Worlds," a study of the economy of online games. "The cost of someone's time is much bigger in America than in China."

But gold farming is controversial. Many hard-core gamers say the factories are distorting the games. What is more, the big gaming companies say the factories are violating the terms of use of the games, which forbid players to sell their virtual goods for real money. They have vowed to crack down on those suspected of being small businesses rather than individual gamers.

"We know that such business exists, and we are against it," says Guolong Jin, a spokesman for N-Sina, a Chinese joint venture with NC Soft, the Korean creator of Lineage, one of the most popular online games. "Playing games should be fun and entertaining. It's not a way to trade and make money."

Blizzard Entertainment, a division of Vivendi Universal and the creator of World of Warcraft, one of the world's most popular games with more than 4.5 million online subscribers, has also called the trading illegal.

But little has been done to halt the mushrooming black market in virtual goods, many available for sale on eBay, Yahoo and other online sites.

On eBay, for example, 100 grams of World of Warcraft gold is available for $9.99 or two über characters from EverQuest for $35.50. It costs $269 to be transported to Level 60 in Warcraft, and it typically takes 15 days to get the account back at the higher level.

In fact, the trading of virtual property is so lucrative that some big online gaming companies have jumped into the business, creating their own online marketplaces.

Sony Online Entertainment, the creator of EverQuest, a popular medieval war and fantasy game, recently created Station Exchange. Sony calls the site an alternative to "crooked sellers in unsanctioned auctions."

Other start-up companies are also rushing in, acting as international brokers to match buyers and sellers in different countries, and contracting out business to Chinese gold-farming factories.

"We're like a stock exchange. You can buy and sell with us," says Alan Qiu, a founder of the Shanghai-based Ucdao.com. "We farm out the different jobs. Some people say, 'I want to get from Level 1 to 60,' so we find someone to do that."

Now there are factories all over China. In central Henan Province, one factory has 300 computers. At another factory in western Gansu Province, the workers log up to 18 hours a day.

The operators are mostly young men like Luo Gang, a 28-year-old college graduate who borrowed $25,000 from his father to start an Internet cafe that morphed into a gold farm on the outskirts of Chongqing in central China.

Mr. Luo has 23 workers, who each earn about $75 a month.

"If they didn't work here they'd probably be working as waiters in hot pot restaurants," he said, "or go back to help their parents farm the land—or more likely, hang out on the streets with no job at all."

Here in coastal Fujian Province, several gold farm operators offered access to their underground facilities recently, on the condition that their names not be disclosed because the legal and tax status of some of the operations is in question.

One huge site here in Fuzhou has over 100 computers in a series of large, dark rooms. About 70 players could be seen playing quietly one weekday afternoon, while some players slept by the keyboard.

"We recruit through newspaper ads," said the 30-something owner, whose workers range from 18 to 25 years old. "They all know how to play online games, but they're not willing to do hard labor."

Another operation here has about 40 computers lined up in the basement of an old dilapidated building, all playing the same game. Upstairs were unkempt, closet-size dormitory rooms where several gamers slept on bunk beds; the floors were strewn with hot pots.

The owners concede that the risks are enormous. The global gaming companies regularly shut accounts they suspect are engaged in farming. And the government here is cracking down on Internet addiction now, monitoring more closely how much time each player spends online.

To survive, the factories employ sophisticated gaming strategies. They hide their identities online, hire hackers to seek out new strategies, and create automatic keys to bolster winnings.

But at some point, says Mr. Yu, the Fuzhou factory operator who started out selling computer supplies and now has an army of gamers outside his office here, he knows he will have to move on.

"My ultimate goal is to do Internet-based foreign trade," he says, sitting in a bare office with a solid steel safe under his desk. "Online games are just my first step into the business."

PERSONAL RESPONSE

The world of online gaming generates nearly $4 billion a year. About 100 million people go online every month to play multiplayer role-playing games set in fantasy worlds. Online subscribers compete with other people around the world, but many affluent players now hire young Chinese gamers to babysit their accounts while they eat, sleep, or go to work. Do you see anything unethical or unusual about this practice? Or is this just the union of the online gaming market with capitalism? Explain your view.

QUESTIONS FOR CLASS OR SMALL-GROUP DISCUSSION

1. Online gaming is the latest global industry to use cheap Chinese labour. What other Chinese-made products do you use or wear? Is this form of trade a good or bad thing? Explain your answer.

2. Imagine you are a "gold farmer," a young Chinese individual who works in one of China's newest factories, your eyes staring at a computer. A World of Warcraft poster is on the wall. Every day you work a 12-hour shift

killing monsters and harvesting virtual money. You have quotas to meet and you make less than 25 cents an hour—but the pay is better than your last job and you get free room and board in a dormitory with other gamers. Describe what your attitude might be toward the factory owner and the gamers you support.

3. Once a Marxist–Leninist state, China is now considered a market–Leninist state that combines elements of raw capitalism with an authoritarian, central Communist government. China has made huge strides in economic development and modernization in the last few years, especially in the cities, which have become a magnet for workers. It appears that online factory gamers are part of that story. In your opinion, what are the differences or similarities between underground online gaming factories in China and factories that produce socks, cookware, textiles, toys, or athletic footwear. Discuss the differences between a virtual sweatshop and a traditional sweatshop where people work for low wages at long hours in poor conditions.

4. The use of Chinese labour to service Western needs is a form of colonization or cultural imperialism. Discuss.

5. Have you or any of your friends been obsessed with any online games? If so, how do you account for this fixation?

FOR FURTHER VIEWING: MUSIC AND VIDEO GAMES

This Is Spinal Tap (1984); *Scratch* (2001); *Gimme Shelter* (1970); *Some Kind of Monster* (2004); *Shine* (1996); *Almost Famous* (2000); *The Commitments* (1991); *A Hard Day's Night* (1964); *Jailhouse Rock* (1957); *Bird* (1988); *Tomb Raider* (2001); *War Games* (1982); *Stay Alive* (2006).

CHAPTER EIGHT

MEDIA STUDIES

INTRODUCTION

One of the big issues in cultural studies is the impact of the media on our lives. Here we contend with Marshall McLuhan, who is clearly one of the first and one of the most influential media analysts. The interview with McLuhan reflects some of his most important and, for their time, most radical conclusions. His work points out that the media are more than just whatever gives us information. For McLuhan, the media are necessarily an extension of our body and our senses; the technologies (the media) we use to receive or experience information, and even the technologies that just light a room for us, are themselves integral to the content; in fact, he suggests these technologies (i.e., these media) are the content in that they define what we do. What is prophetic about his observations, made more than 40 years ago, is that he foresaw how new technologies were increasingly transforming human behaviour and society, what he calls "the total cultural environment." For example, is there any doubt that the computer chip and the Internet have altered how we construct ourselves, our identities, how we see the world, and what we do? McLuhan would suggest that we need to look at such changes closely and in historical and psychological contexts.

Media analysts have long been interested in one particular aspect of popular culture: violence in the media and its influence on people, especially young people. The first reading in this chapter provides an overview of the issue by Sissela Bok, one of the most well-known contributors in the debate on the role that media violence plays in forming children's characters and values. Bok's "Aggression: The Impact of Media Violence" discusses a topic that is often volatile. As you read her essay, consider your own position on this controversial issue.

Media analysts are interested in whether the media are biased in the way they select the information they report. Many people believe the media are biased toward a liberal-leaning social and political position. Although many think the media too liberal, others think them too conservative. Indeed, liberals often accuse the media of being too conservative while conservatives accuse them of being too liberal. P. J. O'Rourke, who identifies himself as a conservative "a little to the right of Rush Limbaugh," explains in "I Agree with Me" that he has little patience with conservative news programs and books, though he does not think much of liberal media either.

The text of "My Name Is Joe," taken from a celebrated Canadian television commercial, provides an example of how advertising, as a form of media within media, can have a social, cultural, and political impact far beyond a mandate to sell a product—in this case, a particular brand of beer. The ad reminds us of the powerful effect of the media even when their purposes are clear. As in the case of all media studies, these influences need to be examined carefully in ways ranging from individual psychology to global concerns.

AGGRESSION: THE IMPACT OF MEDIA VIOLENCE

Sissela Bok

Born in Sweden and educated in Switzerland, France, and the United States, Sissela Bok earned a Ph.D. in philosophy from Harvard University. She has been a professor of philosophy at Brandeis University and is currently a Distinguished Fellow at the Harvard Center for Population and Development Studies. Widely known for her writings on topics in bioethics, applied ethics, biography and autobiography, and public affairs, her books include Lying: Moral Choice in Public and Private Life *(1978),* Secrets: On the Ethics of Concealment and Revelation *(1983),* A Strategy for Peace: Human Values and the Threat of War *(1989),* Alva Myrdal: A Daughter's Memoir

(1991), Common Values *(1995), and* Mayhem: Violence as Public Entertainment *(1998), from which the following is taken.*

Even if media violence were linked to no other debilitating effects, it would remain at the center of public debate so long as the widespread belief persists that it glamor-izes aggressive conduct, removes inhibitions toward such conduct, arouses viewers, and invites imitation. It is only natural that the links of media violence to aggres-sion should be of special concern to families and communities. Whereas increased fear, desensitization, and appetite primarily affect the viewers themselves, aggres-sion directly injures others and represents a more clear-cut violation of standards of behavior. From the point of view of public policy, therefore, curbing aggression has priority over alleviating subtler psychological and moral damage.

Public concern about a possible link between media violence and societal vio-lence has further intensified in the past decade, as violent crime reached a peak in the early 1990s, yet has shown no sign of downturn, even after crime rates began dropping in 1992. Media coverage of violence, far from declining, has escalated since then, devoting ever more attention to celebrity homicides and copycat crimes. The latter, explicitly modeled on videos or films and sometimes carried out with meticu-lous fidelity to detail, are never more relentlessly covered in the media than when they are committed by children and adolescents. Undocumented claims that violent copycat crimes are mounting in number contribute further to the ominous sense of threat that these crimes generate. Their dramatic nature drains away the public's attention from other, more mundane forms of aggression that are much more com-monplace, and from . . . other . . . harmful effects of media violence.

Media analyst Ken Auletta reports that, in 1992, a mother in France sued the head of a state TV channel that carried the American series *MacGyver,* claiming that her son was accidentally injured as a result of having copied MacGyver's recipe for making a bomb. At the time, Auletta predicted that similar lawsuits were bound to become a weapon against media violence in America's litigious culture. By 1996, novelist John Grisham had sparked a debate about director Oliver Stone's film *Natural Born Killers,* which is reputedly linked to more copycat assaults and mur-ders than any other movie to date. Grisham wrote in protest against the film after learning that a friend of his, Bill Savage, had been killed by nineteen-year-old Sarah Edmondson and her boyfriend Benjamin Darras, eighteen: after repeated viewings of Stone's film on video, the two had gone on a killing spree with the film's mur-derous, gleeful heroes expressly in mind. Characterizing the film as "a horrific movie that glamorized casual mayhem and bloodlust," Grisham proposed legal action:

> Think of a film as a product, something created and brought to market, not too dis-
> similar from breast implants. Though the law has yet to declare movies to be prod-
> ucts, it is only a small step away. If something goes wrong with the product, either
> by design or defect, and injury ensues, then its makers are held responsible. . . .
> It will take only one large verdict against the like of Oliver Stone, and his production
> company, and perhaps the screenwriter, and the studio itself, and then the party will be
> over. The verdict will come from the heartland, far away from Southern California, in

some small courtroom with no cameras. A jury will finally say enough is enough; that the demons placed in Sarah Edmondson's mind were not solely of her own making.

As a producer of books made into lucrative movies—themselves hardly devoid of violence—and as a veteran of contract negotiations within the entertainment industry, Grisham may have become accustomed to thinking of films in industry terms as "products." As a seasoned courtroom lawyer, he may have found the analogy between such products and breast implants useful for invoking product liability to pin personal responsibility on movie producers and directors for the lethal consequences that their work might help unleash.

Oliver Stone retorted that Grisham was drawing "upon the superstition about the magical power of pictures to conjure up the undead spectre of censorship." In dismissing concerns about the "magical power of pictures" as merely superstitious, Stone sidestepped the larger question of responsibility fully as much as Grisham had sidestepped that of causation when he attributed liability to filmmakers for anything that "goes wrong" with their products so that "injury ensues." Because aggression is the most prominent effect associated with media violence in the public's mind, it is natural that it should also remain the primary focus of scholars in the field. The "aggressor effect" has been studied both to identify the short term, immediate impact on viewers after exposure to TV violence, and the long-term influences. . . . There is near-unanimity by now among investigators that exposure to media violence contributes to lowering barriers to aggression among some viewers. This lowering of barriers may be assisted by the failure of empathy that comes with growing desensitization, and intensified to the extent that viewers develop an appetite for violence—something that may lead to still greater desire for violent programs and, in turn, even greater desensitization.

When it comes to viewing violent pornography, levels of aggression toward women have been shown to go up among male subjects who view sexualized violence against women. "In explicit depictions of sexual violence," a report by the American Psychological Association's Commission on Youth and Violence concludes after surveying available research data, "it is the message about violence more than the sexual nature of the materials that appears to affect the attitudes of adolescents about rape and violence toward women." Psychologist Edward Donnerstein and colleagues have shown that if investigators tell subjects that aggression is legitimate, then show them violent pornography, their aggression toward women increases. In slasher films, the speed and ease with which "one's feelings can be transformed from sensuality into viciousness may surprise even those quite conversant with the links between sexual and violent urges."

Viewers who become accustomed to seeing violence as an acceptable, common, attractive way of dealing with problems find it easier to identify with aggressors and to suppress any sense of pity or respect for victims of violence. Media violence has been found to have stronger effects of this kind when carried out by heroic, impressive, or otherwise exciting figures, especially when they are shown as invulnerable and are rewarded or not punished for what they do. The same is true when the violence is shown as justifiable, when viewers identify with the aggressors rather than with their victims, when violence is routinely resorted to, and when the programs have links to how viewers perceive their own environment.

While the consensus that such influences exist grows among investigators as research accumulates, there is no consensus whatsoever about the size of the correlations involved. Most investigators agree that it will always be difficult to disentangle the precise effects of exposure to media violence from the many other factors contributing to societal violence. No reputable scholar accepts the view expressed by 21 percent of the American public in 1995, blaming television more than any other factor for teenage violence. Such tentative estimates as have been made suggest that the media account for between 5 and 15 percent of societal violence. Even these estimates are rarely specific enough to indicate whether what is at issue is all violent crime, or such crimes along with bullying and aggression more generally.

One frequently cited investigator proposes a dramatically higher and more specific estimate than others. Psychiatrist Brandon S. Centerwall has concluded from large-scale epidemiological studies of "white homicide" in the United States, Canada, and South Africa in the period from 1945 to 1974, that it escalated in these societies within ten to fifteen years of the introduction of television, and that one can therefore deduce that television has brought a doubling of violent societal crime:

> Of course, there are many factors other than television that influence the amount of violent crime. Every violent act is the result of a variety of forces coming together—poverty, crime, alcohol and drug abuse, stress—of which childhood TV exposure is just one. Nevertheless, the evidence indicates that if hypothetically, television technology had never been developed, there would today be 10,000 fewer homicides each year in the United States, 70,000 fewer rapes, and 700,000 fewer injurious assaults. Violent crime would be half of what it now is.

Centerwall's study, published in 1989, includes controls for such variables as firearm possession and economic growth. But his conclusions have been criticized for not taking into account other factors, such as population changes during the time period studied, that might also play a role in changing crime rates. Shifts in policy and length of prison terms clearly affect these levels as well. By now, the decline in levels of violent crime in the United States since Centerwall's study was conducted, even though television viewing did not decline ten to fifteen years before, does not square with his extrapolations. As for "white homicide" in South Africa under apartheid, each year brings more severe challenges to official statistics from that period.

Even the lower estimates, however, of around 5 to 10 percent of violence as correlated with television exposure, point to substantial numbers of violent crimes in a population as large as America's. But if such estimates are to be used in discussions of policy decisions, more research will be needed to distinguish between the effects of television in general and those of particular types of violent programming, and to indicate specifically what sorts of images increase the aggressor effect and by what means; and throughout to be clearer about the nature of the aggressive acts studied.

Media representatives naturally request proof of such effects before they are asked to undertake substantial changes in programming. In considering possible remedies for a problem, inquiring into the reasons for claims about risks is entirely appropriate. It is clearly valid to scrutinize the research designs, sampling methods, and possible biases of studies supporting such claims, and to ask about the reasoning leading from particular research findings to conclusions. But to ask for some demonstrable pinpointing of just when and how exposure to media violence affects levels of aggression sets a dangerously high threshold for establishing risk factors.

We may never be able to trace, retrospectively, the specific set of television programs that contributed to a particular person's aggressive conduct. The same is true when it comes to the links between tobacco smoking and cancer, between drunk driving and automobile accidents, and many other risk factors presenting public health hazards. Only recently have scientists identified the specific channels through which tobacco generates its carcinogenic effects. Both precise causative mechanisms and documented occurrences in individuals remain elusive. Too often, media representatives formulate their requests in what appear to be strictly polemical terms, raising dismissive questions familiar from debates over the effects of tobacco: "How can anyone definitively pinpoint the link between media violence and acts of real-life violence? If not, how can we know if exposure to media violence constitutes a risk factor in the first place?"

Yet the difficulty in carrying out such pinpointing has not stood in the way of discussing and promoting efforts to curtail cigarette smoking and drunk driving. It is not clear, therefore, why a similar difficulty should block such efforts when it comes to media violence. The perspective of "probabilistic causation" . . . is crucial to public debate about the risk factors in media violence. The television industry has already been persuaded to curtail the glamorization of smoking and drunk driving on its programs, despite the lack of conclusive documentation of the correlation between TV viewing and higher incidence of such conduct. Why should the industry not take analogous precautions with respect to violent programming?

Americans have special reasons to inquire into the causes of societal violence. While we are in no sense uniquely violent, we need to ask about all possible reasons why our levels of violent crime are higher than in all other stable industrialized democracies. Our homicide rate would be higher still if we did not imprison more of our citizens than any society in the world, and if emergency medical care had not improved so greatly in recent decades that a larger proportion of shooting victims survive than in the past. Even so, we have seen an unprecedented rise not only in child and adolescent violence, but in levels of rape, child abuse, domestic violence, and every other form of assault.

Although America's homicide rate has declined in the 1990s, the rates for suicide, rape, and murder involving children and adolescents in many regions have too rarely followed suit. For Americans aged 15 to 35 years, homicide is the second leading cause of death, and for young African Americans, 15 to 24 years, it is *the* leading cause of death. In the decade following the mid-1980s, the rate of murder committed by teenagers 14 to 17 more than doubled. The rates of injury suffered by small children are skyrocketing, with the number of seriously injured children nearly quadrupling from 1986 to 1993; and a proportion of these injuries are inflicted by children upon one another. Even homicides by children, once next to unknown, have escalated in recent decades.

America may be the only society on earth to have experienced what has been called an "epidemic of children killing children," which is ravaging some of its communities today. As in any epidemic, it is urgent to ask what it is that makes so many capable of such violence, victimizes so many others, and causes countless more to live in fear. Whatever role the media are found to play in this respect, to be sure, is but part of the problem. Obviously, not even the total elimination of media violence would wipe out the problem of violence in the United States or any other society. The same can be said for the proliferation and easy access to guns, or for poverty, drug addiction, and other risk factors. As Dr. Deborah Prothrow-Stith puts it, "It's not an either or. It's not guns or media or parents or poverty."

We have all witnessed the four effects that I have discussed . . . —fearfulness, numbing, appetite, and aggressive impulses—in the context of many influences apart from the media. Maturing involves learning to resist the dominion that these effects can gain over us; and to strive, instead, for greater resilience, empathy, self control, and respect for self and others. The process of maturation and growth in these respects is never completed for any of us; but it is most easily thwarted in childhood, before it has had chance to take root. Such learning calls for nurturing and education at first; then for increasing autonomy in making personal decisions about how best to confront the realities of violence.

Today, the sights and sounds of violence on the screen affect this learning process from infancy on, in many homes. The television screen is the lens through which most children learn about violence. Through the magnifying power of this lens, their everyday life becomes suffused by images of shootings, family violence, gang warfare, kidnappings, and everything else that contributes to violence in our society. It shapes their experiences long before they have had the opportunity to consent to such shaping or developed the ability to cope adequately with this knowledge. The basic nurturing and protection to prevent the impairment of this ability ought to be the birthright of every child.

PERSONAL RESPONSE

Has this essay in any way changed your views on the question of how media violence affects young people? Select a statement or passage that especially interests you, either positively or negatively, and write down three of your responses.

QUESTIONS FOR CLASS OR SMALL-GROUP DISCUSSION

1. Summarize the viewpoints of both John Grisham and Oliver Stone on the matter of copycat killings. Why does Bok think both men sidestep their arguments? What do you think of Grisham's and Stone's arguments? Do you agree with either of them? Does Bok present valid points in her comments on their arguments?

2. Explain what you understand Bok to mean by the term *aggressor effect*. What do investigators have to say about violent pornography and the aggressor effect?

3. Critically respond to this statement: "No reputable scholar accepts the view expressed by 21 percent of the American public in 1995, blaming television

more than any other factor for teenage violence." What does Bok say about the studies conducted by Brandon S. Centerwall?

4. Bok notes the difficulty of showing the precise causal relationships between tobacco smoking and cancer, and between drunk driving and automobile accidents, even though most people seem to accept that smoking causes cancer and that drunk driving is a chief cause of automobile accidents. What do you think of her application of the "probabilistic causation" factor to the matter of media violence? That is, how valid do you find her logic? Are you convinced that even though we cannot precisely pinpoint the direct causes of societal violence, we can still discuss and propose "efforts to curtail" the "risk factors in media violence"?

5. According to Bok, what might be the effects on children of early and ongoing exposure to media violence? What would it take to persuade you that these causal links between exposure to media violence and violent behaviour must continue?

I AGREE WITH ME

P. J. O'ROURKE

P. J. O'Rourke, born in 1947, was editor-in-chief of the National Lampoon *from 1978 to 1981, when he left to become a freelance writer. A gonzo journalist whose credentials include foreign affairs writer at* Rolling Stone *magazine, his work has been widely published, and he is the author of eleven books, including* Republican Party Reptile *(1987),* Modern Manners: An Etiquette Book for Rude People *(1990),* Parliament of Whores *(1991),* Give War a Chance: Eyewitness Accounts of Mankind's Struggle Against Tyranny, Injustice, and Alcohol-free Beer *(1992),* All the Trouble in the World: The Lighter Side of Overpopulation, Famine, Ecological Disaster, Ethnic Hatred, Plague, and Poverty *(1995),* The Bachelor Home Companion: A Practical Guide to Keeping House Like a Pig *(1997),* Eat the Rich: A Treatise on Economics *(1999), and* Peace Kills: America's Fun New Imperialism *(2004). "I Agree with Me" was published in the July/August 2004 issue of* The Atlantic Monthly.

Last year, on a long car trip, I was listening to Rush Limbaugh shout. I usually agree with Rush Limbaugh; therefore I usually don't listen to him. I listen to NPR: "World to end—poor and minorities hardest hit." I like to argue with the radio. Of course, if I had kept listening to Limbaugh, whose OxyContin addiction was about to be revealed, I could have argued with him about drugs. I don't think drugs are bad. I used to be a hippie. I think drugs are fun. Now I'm a conservative. I think fun is bad. I would agree all the more with Limbaugh if, after he returned from rehab, he'd shouted (as most Americans ought to), "I'm sorry I had fun! I promise not to have any more!"

Anyway, I couldn't get NPR on the car radio, so I was listening to Rush Limbaugh shout about Wesley Clark, who had just entered the Democratic presidential-primary race. Was Clark a stalking horse for Hillary Clinton?! Was Clark a DNC-sponsored Howard Dean spoiler?! "He's somebody's sock puppet!" Limbaugh bellowed. I agreed; but a thought began to form. Limbaugh wasn't shouting at Clark, who I doubt tunes in to AM talk radio the way I tune in to NPR. And "Shari Lewis and Lamb Chop!" was not a call calculated to lure Democratic voters to the Bush camp. Rush Limbaugh was shouting at me.

Me. I am a little to the right of . . . Why is the Attila comparison used? Fifth-century Hunnish depredations on the Roman Empire were the work of an over-powerful executive pursuing a policy of economic redistribution in an atmosphere of permissive social mores. I am a little to the right of Rush Limbaugh. I'm so conservative that I approve of San Francisco City Hall marriages, adoption by same-sex couples, and New Hampshire's recently ordained Episcopal bishop. Gays want to get married, have children, and go to church. Next they'll be advocating school vouchers, boycotting HBO, and voting Republican.

I suppose I should be arguing with my fellow right-wingers about that, and drugs, and many other things. But I won't be. Arguing, in the sense of attempting to convince others, has gone out of fashion with conservatives. The formats of their radio and television programs allow for little measured debate, and to the extent that evidence is marshaled to support conservative ideas, the tone is less trial of Socrates than Johnnie Cochran summation to the O.J. jury. Except the jury—with a clever marketing strategy—has been rigged. I wonder, when was the last time a conservative talk show changed a mind?

This is an argument I have with my father-in-law, an avid fan of such programs. Although again, I don't actually argue, because I usually agree with my father-in-law. Also, he's a retired FBI agent, and at seventy-eight is still a licensed private investigator with a concealed-weapon permit. But I say to him, "What do you get out of these shows? You already agree with everything they say."

"They bring up some good points," he says.

"That you're going to use on whom? Do some of your retired-FBI-agent golf buddies feel shocked by the absence of WMDs in Iraq and want to give Saddam Hussein a mulligan and let him take his tee shot over?"

And he looks at me with an FBI-agent look, and I shut up. But the number and popularity of conservative talk shows have grown apace since the Reagan Administration. The effect, as best I can measure it, is nil. In 1988 George Bush won the presidency with 53.4 percent of the popular vote. In 2000 Bush's arguably more conservative son won the presidency with a Supreme Court ruling.

A generation ago there wasn't much conservatism on the airwaves. For the most part it was lonely Bill Buckley moderating *Firing Line.* But from 1964 to 1980 we went from Barry Goldwater's defeat with 38.5 percent of the popular vote to Ronald Reagan's victory with 50.8 percent of the popular vote. Perhaps there was something efficacious in Buckley's—if he'll pardon the word—moderation.

I tried watching *The O'Reilly Factor.* I tried watching Hannity shout about Colmes. I tried listening to conservative talk radio. But my frustration at concurrence would build, mounting from exasperation with like-mindedness to a fury of accord, and I'd hit the OFF button.

I resorted to books. You can slam a book shut in irritation and then go back to the irritant without having to plumb the mysteries of TiVo.

My selection method was unscientific. Ann Coulter, on the cover of *Treason*, has the look of a soon-to-be-ex wife who has just finished shouting. And Bill O'Reilly is wearing a loud shirt on the cover of *Who's Looking Out for You?*

Coulter begins her book thus:

> Liberals have a preternatural gift for striking a position on the side of treason. You could be talking about Scrabble and they would instantly leap to the anti-American position. Everyone says liberals love America, too. No they don't. Whenever the nation is under attack, from within or without, liberals side with the enemy.

Now, there's a certain truth in what she says. But it's what's called a "poetic truth." And it's the kind of poetic truth best conveyed late in the evening after six or eight drinks while pounding the bar. I wasn't in a bar. I was in my office. It was the middle of the day. And I was getting a headache.

Who's Looking Out for You? is not as loud as *Treason*. But there's something of the halftime harangue at the team just in the use of the second-person pronoun.

The answer to O'Reilly's title question could be condensed in the following manner: "Nobody, that's who. The fat cats aren't. The bigwigs aren't. The politicos aren't. Nobody's looking out for you except me, and I can't be everywhere. You've got to look out for yourself. How do you do that? You look out for your friends and family. That's how. And they look out for you. And that's the truth, Bud."

We've all backed away from this fellow while vigorously nodding our heads in agreement. Often the fellow we were backing away from was our own dad.

O'Reilly casts his net wide in search of a nodding, agreeing audience. He embraces people driving poky economy cars ("not imposing gas mileage standards hurts every single American except those making and driving SUVs") and people with romantic memories of the liberalism of yore ("the gold standard for public service was the tenure of Robert Kennedy as attorney general"). He positions himself as a populist worried about illegal aliens' getting across the border and taking our jobs. (I'm worried about illegal aliens' *not* getting across the border and *leaving* us with jobs, such as mowing the lawn and painting the house.) And O'Reilly reaches out to the young by prefacing each chapter with lyrics from pop music groups that are, as far as I know, very up-to-date, such as Spandau Ballet. But the person that O'Reilly's shouting at is still, basically, me: "If President Hillary becomes a reality, the United States will be a polarized, thief-ridden nanny state. . . ."

Does the left have this problem? Do some liberals feel as if they're guarding the net while their teammates make a furious rush at their own goal? NPR seems more whiny than hectoring, except at fundraising time. There's supposed to be a lot of liberal advocacy on TV. I looked for things that debased freedom, promoted license, ridiculed responsibility, and denigrated man and God—but that was *all* of TV. How do you tell the liberal parts from the car ads? Once more I resorted to books.

To answer my question I didn't even have to open Al Franken's *Lies and the Lying Liars Who Tell Them: A Fair and Balanced Look at the Right.* But having done so, I found these chapter headings: "Ann Coulter: Nutcase," "You Know Who I Don't Like? Ann Coulter," and "Bill O'Reilly: Lying Splotchy Bully."

Michael Moore's previous book was *Stupid White Men,* titled in a spirit of gentle persuasion unmatched since Martin Luther, that original Antinomian, wrote *Against the Murderous and Thieving Hordes of Peasants.* Moore's new book, *Dude, Where's My Country?,* contains ten chapters of fulminations convincing the convinced. However, Moore does include one chapter on how to argue with a conservative. As if. Approached by someone like Michael Moore, a conservative would drop a quarter in Moore's Starbucks cup and hurriedly walk away. Also, Moore makes this suggestion: "Tell him how dependable conservatives are. When you need something fixed, you call your redneck brother-in-law, don't you?"

Arguing, in the sense of attempting to convince others, seems to have gone out of fashion with everyone. I'm reduced to arguing with the radio. The distaste for political argument certainly hasn't made politics friendlier—or quieter, given the amount of shouting being done by people who think one thing at people who think the same thing.

But I believe I know why this shouting is popular. Today's Americans are working harder than ever, trying to balance increasing personal, family, and career demands. We just don't have time to make ourselves obnoxious. We need professional help.

PERSONAL RESPONSE

Do you listen to or view talk shows that reinforce your political or social views? Why or why not? From where do you get your political and social views? Is it possible to get beyond personal bias? Values and beliefs have to come from somewhere. Reflect on the sources of your values and beliefs.

QUESTIONS FOR CLASS OR SMALL-GROUP DISCUSSION

1. What do you understand by the terms *conservative* and *liberal*? Which term would you use to categorize O'Rourke?

2. What is O'Rourke's point about argument in the context of radio and television programs? Explain how the example of his father-in-law serves to illustrate his point.

3. Describe the television programs, radio programs, and books that O'Rourke mentions. Have you watched, listened to, or read any of them? How do they illustrate or support his main point?

PLAYBOY INTERVIEW WITH MARSHALL McLUHAN

*A candid conversation with the high priest of popcult and metaphysician of media. In 1961, the name of Marshall McLuhan (1911–1980) was unknown to everyone but his English students at the University of Toronto—and a coterie of academic admirers who followed his abstruse articles in small-circulation quarterlies. But then came two remarkable books—*The Gutenberg Galaxy *(1962) and* Understanding Media *(1964)—and the graying professor from Canada's western hinterlands soon found himself characterized by the* San Francisco Chronicle *as "the hottest academic property around." He has since won a world-wide following for his brilliant—and frequently baffling—theories about the impact of the media on man; and his name has entered the French language as mucluhanisme, a synonym for the world of pop culture.*

Though his books are written in a difficult style—at once enigmatic, epigrammatic and overgrown with arcane literary and historic allusions—the revolutionary ideas lurking in them have made McLuhan a best-selling author. Despite protests from a legion of outraged scholastics and old-guard humanists who claim that McLuhan's ideas range from demented to dangerous, his free-for-all theorizing has attracted the attention of top executives at General Motors (who paid him a handsome fee to inform them that automobiles were a thing of the past), Bell Telephone (to whom he explained that they didn't really understand the function of the telephone) and a leading package-design house (which was told that packages will soon be obsolete). Anteing up $5000, another huge corporation asked him to predict—via closed-circuit television—what their own products will be used for in the future; and Canada's turned-on Prime Minister Pierre Trudeau engages him in monthly bull sessions designed to improve his television image.

McLuhan's observations—"probes," he prefers to call them—are riddled with such flamboyantly undecipherable aphorisms as "The electric light is pure information" and "People don't actually read newspapers—they get into them every morning like a hot bath." Of his own work, McLuhan has remarked: "I don't pretend to understand it. After all, my stuff is very difficult." Despite his convoluted syntax, flashy metaphors and word-playful one-liners, however, McLuhan's basic thesis is relatively simple.

McLuhan contends that all media—in and of themselves and regardless of the messages they communicate—exert a compelling influence on man and society. Prehistoric, or tribal, man existed in a harmonious balance of the senses, perceiving the world equally through hearing, smell, touch, sight and taste. But technological innovations are extensions of human abilities and senses that alter this sensory balance—an alteration that, in turn, inexorably reshapes the society that created the technology. According to McLuhan, there have been three basic technological innovations: the invention of the phonetic alphabet, which jolted tribal man out of his sensory balance and gave dominance to the eye; the introduction of movable type in the 16th Century, which accelerated this process; and the invention of the telegraph in 1844, which heralded an electronics revolution that will ultimately retribalize man

Marshall McLuhan: Oracle of the Electronic Age
Photo Source: AP Images

by restoring his sensory balance. McLuhan has made it his business to explain and extrapolate the repercussions of this electronic revolution.

For his efforts, critics have dubbed him "the Dr. Spock of pop culture," "the guru of the boob tube," a "Canadian Nkrumah who has joined the assault on reason," a "metaphysical wizard possessed by a spatial sense of madness," and "the high priest of popthink who conducts a Black Mass for dilettantes before the altar of historical determinism." Amherst professor Benjamin DeMott observed: "He's swinging, switched on, with it and NOW. And wrong."

But as Tom Wolfe has aptly inquired, "What if he is *right*? Suppose he *is* what he sounds like—the most important thinker since Newton, Darwin, Freud, Einstein and Pavlov?" Social historian Richard Kostelanetz contends that "the most extraordinary quality of McLuhan's mind is that it discerns significance where others see only data, or nothing; he tells us how to measure phenomena previously unmeasurable."

The unperturbed subject of this controversy was born in Edmonton, Alberta, on July 21, 1911. The son of a former actress and a real-estate salesman, McLuhan entered the University of Manitoba intending to become an engineer, but matriculated in 1934 with an M.A. in English literature. Next came a stint as an oarsman and graduate student at Cambridge, followed by McLuhan's first teaching job—at the University of Wisconsin. It was a pivotal experience. "I was confronted with young Americans I was incapable of understanding," he has since remarked. "I felt an urgent need to study their popular culture in order to get through." With the seeds sown, McLuhan let them germinate while earning a Ph.D., then taught at Catholic universities. (He is a devout Roman Catholic convert.)

His publishing career began with a number of articles on standard academic fare; but by the mid-Forties, his interest in popular culture surfaced, and true McLuhan efforts such as "The Psychopathology of *Time* and *Life*" began to appear. They hit book length for the first time in 1951 with the publication of *The Mechanical Bride*—an analysis of the social and psychological pressures generated by the press, radio, movies and advertising—and McLuhan was on his way. Though the book attracted little public notice, it won him the chairmanship of a Ford Foundation seminar on culture and communications and a $40,000 grant, with part of which he started *Explorations,* a small periodical outlet for the seminar's findings. By the late Fifties, his reputation had trickled down to Washington: In 1959, he became director of the Media Project of the National Association of Educational Broadcasters and the United States Office of Education, and the report resulting from this post became the first draft of *Understanding Media.* Since 1963, McLuhan has headed the University of Toronto's Center for Culture and Technology, which until recently consisted entirely of McLuhan's office, but now includes a six-room campus building.

Apart from his teaching, lecturing and administrative duties, McLuhan has become a sort of minor communication industry unto himself. Each month he issues to subscribers a mixed-media report called *The McLuhan Dew-Line;* and, punning on that title, he has also originated a series of recordings called "The Marshall McLuhan Dew-Line Plattertudes." McLuhan contributed a characteristically mind-expanding essay about the media—"The Reversal of the Overheated-Image"—to our December 1968 issue. Also a compulsive collaborator, his literary efforts in tandem with colleagues have included a high school textbook and an analysis of the function of space in poetry and painting. *Counterblast,* his next book, is a manically graphic trip through the land of his theories.

In order to provide our readers with a map of this labyrinthine terra incognita, *Playboy* assigned interviewer Eric Norden to visit McLuhan at his spacious new home in the wealthy Toronto suburb of Wychwood Park, where he lives with his wife, Corinne, and five of his six children. (His eldest son lives in New York, where he is completing a book on James Joyce, one of his father's heroes.) Norden reports: "Tall, gray and gangly, with a thin but mobile mouth and an otherwise eminently forgettable face, McLuhan was dressed in an ill-fitting brown tweed suit, black shoes, and a clip-on necktie. As we talked on into the night before a crackling fire, McLuhan expressed his reservations about the interview—indeed, about the printed word itself—as a means of communication, suggesting that the question-and-answer format might impede the in-depth flow of his ideas. I assured him that he would have as much time—and space—as he wished to develop his thoughts."

The result has considerably more lucidity and clarity than McLuhan's readers are accustomed to—perhaps because the Q. and A. format serves to pin him down by counteracting his habit of mercurially changing the subject in mid-stream of consciousness. It is also, we think, a protean and provocative distillation not only of McLuhan's original theories about human progress and social institutions but of his almost immobilizingly intricate style—described by novelist George P. Elliott as "deliberately anti-logical, circular, repetitious, unqualified, gnomic, outrageous" and, even less charitably, by critic Christopher Ricks as "a viscous fog through which loom stumbling metaphors." But other authorities contend that McLuhan's stylistic medium is part and parcel of his message—that the tightly structured "linear" modes of traditional thought and discourse are obsolescent in the new "postliterate" age of the electric media. Norden began the interview with an allusion to McLuhan's favorite electric medium: television.

PLAYBOY: To borrow Henry Gibson's oft-repeated one-line poem on Rowan and Martin's *Laugh-In*—"Marshall McLuhan, what are you doin'?"

McLUHAN: Sometimes I wonder. I'm making explorations. I don't know where they're going to take me. My work is designed for the pragmatic purpose of trying to understand our technological environment and its psychic and social consequences. But my books constitute the *process* rather than the completed product of discovery; my purpose is to employ facts as tentative probes, as means of insight, of pattern recognition, rather than to use them in the traditional and sterile sense of classi-fied data, categories, containers. I want to map new terrain rather than chart old landmarks.

But I've never presented such explorations as revealed truth. As an investigator, I have no fixed point of view, no commitment to any theory—my own or anyone else's. As a matter of fact, I'm completely ready to junk any statement I've ever made about any subject if events don't bear me out, or if I discover it isn't contributing to an understanding of the problem. The better part of my work on media is actually somewhat like a safe-cracker's. I don't know what's inside; maybe it's nothing. I just sit down and start to work. I grope, I listen, I test, I accept and discard; I try out different sequences—until the tumblers fall and the doors spring open.

PLAYBOY: Isn't such a methodology somewhat erratic and inconsistent—if not, as your critics would maintain, eccentric?

McLUHAN: Any approach to environmental problems must be sufficiently flexible and adaptable to encompass the entire environmental matrix, which is in constant flux. I consider myself a generalist, not a specialist who has staked out a tiny plot of study as his intellectual turf and is oblivious to everything else. Actually, my work is a depth operation, the accepted practice in most modern disciplines from psychiatry to metallurgy and structural analysis. Effective study of the media deals not only with the content of the media but with the media themselves and the total cultural environment within which the media function. Only by standing aside from any phenomenon and taking an overview can you discover its operative principles and lines of force. There's really nothing inherently startling or radical about this study—except that for some reason few have had the vision to undertake it. For the past 3500 years of the Western world, the effects of media—whether it's speech, writing, printing, photography, radio or television—have been systematically overlooked by social observers. Even in today's revolutionary electronic age, scholars evidence few signs of modifying this traditional stance of ostrichlike disregard.

PLAYBOY: Why?

McLUHAN: Because all media, from the phonetic alphabet to the computer, are extensions of man that cause deep and lasting changes in him and transform his environment. Such an extension is an intensification, an amplification of an organ, sense or function, and whenever it takes place, the central nervous system appears to institute a self-protective *numbing* of the affected area, insulating and anesthetizing it from conscious awareness of what's happening to it. It's a process rather like that which occurs to the body under shock or stress conditions, or to the mind in line with the Freudian concept of repression. I call this peculiar form of self-hypnosis Narcissus narcosis, a syndrome whereby man remains as unaware of the psychic and social effects of his new technology as a fish of the water it swims in. As a result, precisely at the point where a new media-induced environment becomes all pervasive and transmogrifies our sensory balance, it also becomes invisible.

This problem is doubly acute today because man must, as a simple survival strategy, become aware of what is happening to him, despite the attendant pain of such comprehension. The fact that he has not done so in this age of electronics is what has made this also the age of anxiety, which in turn has been transformed into its *Doppelgänger*—the therapeutically reactive age of *anomie* and apathy. But despite our self-protective escape mechanisms, the total-field awareness engendered by electronic media is enabling us—indeed, compelling us—to grope toward a consciousness of the unconscious, toward a realization that technology is an extension of our own bodies. We live in the first age when change occurs sufficiently rapidly to make such pattern recognition possible for society at large. Until the present era, this awareness has always been reflected first by the artist, who has had the power—and courage—of the seer to read the language of the outer world and relate it to the inner world.

PLAYBOY: Why should it be the artist rather than the scientist who perceives these relationships and foresees these trends?

McLUHAN: Because inherent in the artist's creative inspiration is the process of subliminally sniffing out environmental change. It's always been the artist who perceives the alterations in man caused by a new medium, who recognizes that the future is the present, and uses his work to prepare the ground for it. But most people, from truck drivers to the literary Brahmins, are still blissfully ignorant of what the media do to them; unaware that because of their pervasive effects on man, it is the medium itself that is the message, *not* the content, and unaware that the medium is also the *massage*—that, all puns aside, it literally works over and saturates and molds and transforms every sense ratio. The content or message of any particular medium has about as much importance as the stenciling on the casing of an atomic bomb. But the ability to perceive media-induced extensions of man, once the province of the artist, is now being expanded as the new environment of electric information makes possible a new degree of perception and critical awareness by nonartists.

PLAYBOY: Is the public, then, at last beginning to perceive the "invisible" contours of these new technological environments

McLUHAN: People are beginning to understand the nature of their new technology, but not yet nearly enough of them—and not nearly well enough. Most people, as I indicated, still cling to what I call the rearview-mirror view of their world. By this I mean to say that because of the invisibility of any environment during the period of its innovation, man is only consciously aware of the environment that has *preceded* it; in other words, an environment becomes fully visible only when it has been superseded by a new environment; thus we are always one step behind in our view of the world. Because we are benumbed by any new technology—which in turn creates a totally new environment—we tend to make the old environment more visible; we do so by turning it into an art form and by attaching ourselves to the objects and atmosphere that characterized it, just as we've done with jazz, and as we're now doing with the garbage of the mechanical environment via pop art.

The present is always invisible because it's environmental and saturates the whole field of attention so overwhelmingly; thus everyone but the artist, the man of integral awareness, is alive in an earlier day. In the midst of the electronic age of software, of instant information movement, we still believe we're living in the mechanical age of hardware. At the height of the mechanical age, man turned back to earlier centuries in search of "pastoral" values. The Renaissance and the Middle Ages were completely oriented toward Rome; Rome was oriented toward Greece, and the Greeks were oriented toward the pre-Homeric primitives. We reverse the old educational dictum of learning by proceeding from the familiar to the unfamiliar by going from the unfamiliar to the familiar, which is nothing more or less than the numbing mechanism that takes place whenever new media drastically extend our senses.

PLAYBOY: If this "numbing" effect performs a beneficial role by protecting man from the psychic pain caused by the extensions of his nervous system that you attribute to the media, why are you attempting to dispel it and alert man to the changes in his environment?

McLUHAN: In the past, the effects of media were experienced more gradually, allowing the individual and society to absorb and cushion their impact to some degree. Today, in the electronic age of instantaneous communication, I believe that our survival, and at the very least our comfort and happiness, is predicated on understanding the nature of our new environment because unlike previous environmental changes, the electric media constitute a total and near-instantaneous transformation of culture, values and attitudes. This upheaval generates great pain and identity loss, which can be ameliorated only through a conscious awareness of its dynamics. If we understand the revolutionary transformations caused by new media, we can anticipate and control them; but if we continue in our self-induced subliminal trance, we will be their slaves.

Because of today's terrific speed-up of information moving, we have a chance to apprehend, predict and influence the environmental forces shaping us—and thus win back control of our own destinies. The new extensions of man and the environment they generate are the central manifestations of the evolutionary process, and yet we still cannot free ourselves of the delusion that it is how a medium is used that counts, rather than what it does to us and with us. This is the zombie stance of the technological idiot. It's to escape this Narcissus trance that I've tried to trace and reveal the impact of media on man, from the beginning of recorded time to the present.

PLAYBOY: Will you trace that impact for us—in condensed form?

McLUHAN: It's difficult to condense into the format of an interview such as this, but I'll try to give you a brief rundown of the basic media breakthroughs. You've got to remember that my definition of media is broad: it includes any technology whatever that creates extensions of the human body and senses, from clothing to the computer. And a vital point I must stress again is that societies have always been shaped more by the nature of the media with which men communicate than by the content of the communication. All technology has the property of the Midas touch; whenever a society develops an extension of itself, all other functions of that society tend to be transmuted to accommodate that new form; once any new technology penetrates a society, it saturates every institution of that society. New technology is thus a revolutionizing agent. We see this today with the electric media and we saw it several thousand years ago with the invention of the phonetic alphabet, which was just as far-reaching an innovation—and had just as profound consequences for man.

PLAYBOY: What were they?

McLUHAN: Before the invention of the phonetic alphabet, man lived in a world where all the senses were balanced and simultaneous, a closed world of tribal depth and resonance, an oral culture structured by a dominant auditory sense of life. The ear, as opposed to the cool and neutral eye, is sensitive, hyperaesthetic and all-inclusive, and contributes to the seamless web of tribal kinship and interdependence in which all members of the group existed in harmony. The primary medium of communication was speech, and thus no man knew appreciably more or less than any other—which meant that there was little individualism and specialization, the hallmarks of "civilized" Western man. Tribal cultures even today simply cannot comprehend the concept of the individual or of the separate and independent citizen. Oral cultures act and react simultaneously, whereas the capacity to act without reacting, without involvement, is the special gift of "detached" literate man. Another basic characteristic distinguishing tribal man from his literate successors is that he lived in a world of *acoustic* space, which gave him a radically different concept of time-space relationships.

PLAYBOY: What do you mean by "acoustic space"?

McLUHAN: I mean space that has no center and no margin, unlike strictly visual space, which is an extension and intensification of the eye. Acoustic space is organic and integral, perceived through the simultaneous interplay of all the senses; whereas "rational" or pictorial space is uniform, sequential and continuous and creates a closed world with none of the rich resonance of the tribal echoland. Our own Western time-space concepts derive from the environment created by the discovery of phonetic writing, as does our entire concept of Western civilization. The man of the tribal world led a complex, kaleidoscopic life precisely because the ear, unlike the eye, cannot be focused and is synaesthetic rather than analytical and linear. Speech is an utterance, or more precisely, an *outering*, of all our senses at once; the auditory field is simultaneous, the visual successive. The modes of life of nonliterate people were implicit, simultaneous and discontinuous, and also far richer than those of literate man. By their dependence on the spoken word for information, people were drawn together into a tribal mesh; and since the spoken word is more emotionally laden than the written—conveying by intonation such rich emotions as anger, joy, sorrow, fear—tribal man was more spontaneous and passionately volatile. Audile-tactile tribal man partook of the collective unconscious, lived in a magical integral world patterned by myth and ritual, its values divine and unchallenged, whereas literate or visual man creates an environment that is strongly fragmented, individualistic, explicit, logical, specialized and detached.

PLAYBOY: Was it phonetic literacy alone that precipitated this profound shift of values from tribal involvement to "civilized" detachment?

McLUHAN: Yes, it was. Any culture is an order of sensory preferences, and in the tribal world, the senses of touch, taste, hearing and smell were developed, for very practical reasons, to a much higher level than the strictly visual. Into this world, the phonetic alphabet fell like a bombshell, installing sight at the head of the hierarchy of senses. Literacy propelled man from the tribe, gave him an eye for an ear and replaced his integral in-depth communal interplay with visual linear values and fragmented consciousness. As an intensification and amplification of the visual function, the phonetic alphabet diminished the role of the senses of hearing and touch and taste and smell, permeating the discontinuous culture of tribal man and translating its organic harmony and complex synaesthesia into the uniform, connected and visual mode that we still consider the norm of "rational" existence. The whole man became fragmented man; the alphabet shattered the charmed circle and resonating magic of the tribal world, exploding man into an agglomeration of specialized and psychically impoverished "individuals," or units, functioning in a world of linear time and Euclidean space.

PLAYBOY: But literate societies existed in the ancient world long before the phonetic alphabet. Why weren't *they* detribalized?

McLUHAN: The phonetic alphabet did not change or extend man so drastically just because it enabled him to read; as you point out, tribal culture had already coexisted with other written languages for thousands of years. But the phonetic alphabet was radically different from the older and richer hieroglyphic or ideogrammic cultures. The writings of Egyptian, Babylonian, Mayan and Chinese cultures were an extension of the senses in that they gave pictorial expression to reality, and they demanded many signs to cover the wide range of data in their societies—unlike phonetic writing, which uses semantically meaningless letters to correspond to semantically meaningless sounds and is able, with only a handful of letters, to encompass all meanings and all languages. This achievement demanded the separation of both sights and sounds from their semantic and dramatic meanings in order to render visible the actual sound of speech, thus placing a barrier between men and objects and creating a dualism between sight and sound. It divorced the visual function from the interplay with the other senses and thus led to the rejection from consciousness of vital areas of our sensory experience and to the resultant atrophy of the unconscious. The balance of the sensorium—or *Gestalt* interplay of all the senses—and the psychic and social harmony it engendered was disrupted, and the visual function was overdeveloped. This was true of no other writing system.

PLAYBOY: How can you be so sure that this all occurred solely because of phonetic literacy—or, in fact, if it occurred at all?

McLUHAN: You don't have to go back 3000 or 4000 years to see this process at work; in Africa today, a single generation of alphabetic literacy is enough to wrench the individual from the tribal web. When tribal man becomes phonetically literate, he may have an improved abstract intellectual grasp of the world, but most of the deeply emotional corporate family feeling is excised from his relationship with his social milieu. This division of sight and sound and meaning causes deep psychological effects, and he suffers a corresponding separation and impoverishment of his imaginative, emotional and sensory life. He begins reasoning in a sequential linear fashion; he begins categorizing and classifying data. As knowledge is extended in alphabetic form, it is localized and fragmented into specialties, creating division of function, of social classes, of nations and of knowledge—and in the process, the rich interplay of all the senses that characterized the tribal society is sacrificed.

PLAYBOY: But aren't there corresponding gains in insight, understanding and cultural diversity to compensate detribalized man for the loss of his communal values?

McLUHAN: Your question reflects all the institutionalized biases of literate man. Literacy, contrary to the popular view of the "civilizing" process you've just echoed, creates people who are much less complex and diverse than those who develop in the intricate web of oral-tribal societies. Tribal man, unlike homogenized Western man, was not differentiated by his specialist talents or his visible characteristics, but by his unique emotional blends. The internal world of the tribal man was a creative mix of complex emotions and feelings that literate men of the Western world have allowed to wither or have suppressed in the name of efficiency and practicality. The alphabet served to neutralize all these rich divergencies of tribal cultures by translating their complexities into simple visual forms; and the visual sense, remember, is the only one that allows us to *detach;* all other senses involve us, but the detachment bred by literacy disinvolves and detribalizes man. He separates from the tribe as a predominantly visual man who shares standardized attitudes, habits and rights with other civilized men. But he is also given a tremendous advantage over the nonliterate tribal man who, today as in ancient times, is hamstrung by cultural pluralism, uniqueness and discontinuity—values that make the African as easy prey for the European colonialist as the barbarian was for the Greeks and Romans. Only alphabetic cultures have ever succeeded in mastering connected linear sequences as a means of social and psychic organization; the separation of all kinds of experiences into uniform and continuous units in order to generate accelerated action and alteration of form—in other words, applied knowledge—has been the secret of Western man's ascendancy over other men as well as over his environment.

PLAYBOY: Isn't the thrust of your argument, then, that the introduction of the phonetic alphabet was not progress, as has generally been assumed, but a psychic and social disaster?

McLUHAN: It was both. I try to avoid value judgments in these areas, but there is much evidence to suggest that man may have paid too dear a price for his new environment of specialist technology and values. Schizophrenia and alienation may be the inevitable consequences of phonetic literacy. It's metaphorically significant, I suspect, that the old Greek myth has Cadmus, who brought the alphabet to man, sowing dragon's teeth that sprang up from the earth as armed men. Whenever the dragon's teeth of technological change are sown, we reap a whirlwind of violence. We saw this clearly in classical times, although it was somewhat moderated because phonetic literacy did not win an overnight victory over primitive values and institutions; rather, it permeated ancient society in a gradual, if inexorable, evolutionary process.

PLAYBOY: How long did the old tribal culture endure?

McLUHAN: In isolated pockets, it held on until the invention of printing in the 16th Century, which was a vastly important qualitative extension of phonetic literacy. If the phonetic alphabet fell like a bombshell on tribal man, the printing press hit him like a 100-megaton H-bomb. The printing press was the ultimate extension of phonetic literacy: Books could be reproduced in infinite numbers; universal literacy was at last fully possible, if gradually realized; and books became portable individual possessions. Type, the prototype of all machines, ensured the primacy of the visual bias and finally sealed the doom of tribal man. The new medium of linear, uniform, repeatable type reproduced information in unlimited quantities and at hitherto-impossible speeds, thus assuring the eye a position of total predominance in man's sensorium. As a drastic extension of man, it shaped and transformed his entire environment, psychic and social, and was directly responsible for the rise of such disparate phenomena as nationalism, the Reformation, the assembly line and its offspring, the Industrial Revolution, the whole concept of causality, Cartesian and Newtonian concepts of the universe, perspective in art, narrative chronology in literature and a psychological mode of introspection or inner direction that greatly intensified the tendencies toward individualism and specialization engendered 2000 years before by phonetic literacy. The schism between thought and action was institutionalized, and fragmented man, first sundered by the alphabet, was at last diced into bite-sized tidbits. From that point on, Western man was Gutenberg man.

PLAYBOY: Even accepting the principle that technological innovations generate far-reaching environmental changes, many of your readers find it difficult to understand how you can hold the development of printing responsible for such apparently unrelated phenomena as nationalism and industrialism.

McLUHAN: The key word is "apparently." Look a bit closer at both nationalism and industrialism and you'll see that both derived directly from the explosion of print technology in the 16th Century. Nationalism didn't exist in Europe until the Renaissance, when typography enabled every literate man to *see* his mother tongue analytically as a uniform entity. The printing press, by spreading mass-produced books and printed matter across Europe, turned the vernacular regional languages of the day into uniform closed systems of national languages—just another variant of what we call mass media—and gave birth to the entire concept of nationalism.

The individual newly homogenized by print saw the nation concept as an intense and beguiling image of group destiny and status. With print, the homogeneity of money, markets and transport also became possible for the first time, thus creating economic as well as political unity and triggering all the dynamic centralizing energies of contemporary nationalism. By creating a speed of information movement unthinkable before printing, the Gutenberg revolution thus produced a new type of visual centralized national entity that was gradually merged with commercial expansion until Europe was a network of states.

By fostering continuity and competition within homogeneous and contiguous territory, nationalism not only forged new nations but sealed the doom of the old corporate, noncompetitive and discontinuous medieval order of guilds and family-structured social organization; print demanded both personal fragmentation and social uniformity, the natural expression of which was the nation-state. Literate nationalism's tremendous speed-up of information movement accelerated the specialist function that was nurtured by phonetic literacy and nourished by Gutenberg, and rendered obsolete such generalist encyclopedic figures as Benvenuto Cellini, the goldsmith-*cum-condottiere-cum*-painter-*cum*-sculptor-*cum*-writer; it was the Renaissance that destroyed Renaissance Man.

PLAYBOY: Why do you feel that Gutenberg also laid the groundwork for the Industrial Revolution?

McLUHAN: The two go hand in hand. Printing, remember, was the first mechanization of a complex handicraft; by creating an analytic sequence of step-by-step processes, it became the blueprint of all mechanization to follow. The most important quality of print is its repeatability; it is a visual statement that can be reproduced indefinitely, and repeatability is the root of the mechanical principle that has transformed the world since Gutenberg. Typography, by producing the first uniformly repeatable commodity, also created Henry Ford, the first assembly line and the first mass production. Movable type was archetype and prototype for all subsequent industrial development. Without phonetic literacy and the printing press, modern industrialism would be impossible. It is necessary to recognize literacy as typographic technology, shaping not only production and marketing procedures but all other areas of life, from education to city planning.

PLAYBOY: You seem to be contending that practically every aspect of modern life is a direct consequence of Gutenberg's invention of the printing press.

McLUHAN: Every aspect of Western *mechanical* culture was shaped by print technology, but the modern age is the age of the *electric* media, which forge environments and cultures antithetical to the mechanical consumer society derived from print.

Print tore man out of his traditional cultural matrix while showing him how to pile individual upon individual into a massive agglomeration of national and industrial power, and the typographic trance of the West has endured until today, when the electronic media are at last demesmerizing us. The Gutenberg Galaxy is being eclipsed by the constellation of Marconi.

PLAYBOY: You've discussed that constellation in general terms, but what precisely are the electric media that you contend have supplanted the old mechanical technology?

McLUHAN: The electric media are the telegraph, radio, films, telephone, computer and television, all of which have not only extended a single sense or function as the old mechanical media did—i.e., the wheel as an extension of the foot, clothing as an extension of the skin, the phonetic alphabet as an extension of the eye—but have enhanced and externalized our entire central nervous systems, thus transforming all aspects of our social and psychic existence. The use of the electronic media constitutes a break boundary between fragmented Gutenberg man and integral man, just as phonetic literacy was a break boundary between oral-tribal man and visual man.

In fact, today we can look back at 3000 years of differing degrees of visualization, atomization and mechanization and at last recognize the mechanical age as an interlude between two great organic eras of culture. The age of print, which held sway from approximately 1500 to 1900, had its obituary tapped out by the telegraph, the first of the new electric media, and further obsequies were registered by the perception of "curved space" and non-Euclidean mathematics in the early years of the century, which revived tribal man's discontinuous time-space concepts—and which even Spengler dimly perceived as the death-knell of Western literate values. The development of telephone, radio, film, television and the computer have driven further nails into the coffin. Today, television is the most significant of the electric media because it permeates nearly every home in the country, extending the central nervous system of every viewer as it works over and molds the entire sensorium with the ultimate message. It is television that is primarily responsible for ending the visual supremacy that characterized all mechanical technology, although each of the other electric media have played contributing roles.

PLAYBOY: But isn't television itself a primarily visual medium?

McLUHAN: No, it's quite the opposite, although the idea that TV is a visual extension is an understandable mistake. Unlike film or photograph, television is primarily an extension of the sense of touch rather than of sight, and it is the tactile sense that demands the greatest interplay of all the senses. The secret of TV's tactile power is that the video image is one of low intensity or definition and thus, unlike either photograph or film, offers no detailed information about specific objects but instead involves the active participation of the viewer. The TV image is a mosaic mesh not only of horizontal lines but of millions of tiny dots, of which the viewer is physiologically able to pick up only 50 or 60 from which he shapes the image; thus he is constantly filling in vague and blurry images, bringing himself into in-depth involvement with the screen and acting out a constant creative dialog with the iconoscope. The contours of the resultant cartoonlike image are fleshed out within the imagination of the viewer, which necessitates great personal involvement and participation;

the viewer, in fact, becomes the screen, whereas in film he becomes the camera. By requiring us to constantly fill in the spaces of the mosaic mesh, the iconoscope is tattooing its message directly on our skins. Each viewer is thus an unconscious pointillist painter like Seurat, limning new shapes and images as the iconoscope washes over his entire body. Since the point of focus for a TV set is the viewer, television is Orientalizing us by causing us all to begin to look within ourselves. The essence of TV viewing is, in short, intense participation and low definition—what I call a "cool" experience, as opposed to an essentially "hot," or high definition–low participation, medium like radio.

PLAYBOY: A good deal of the perplexity surrounding your theories is related to this postulation of hot and cool media. Could you give us a brief definition of each?

McLUHAN: Basically, a hot medium *ex*cludes and a cool medium *in*cludes; hot media are low in participation, or completion, by the audience and cool media are high in participation. A hot medium is one that extends a single sense with high definition. High definition means a complete filling in of data by the medium without intense audience participation. A photograph, for example, is high definition or hot; whereas a cartoon is low definition or cool, because the rough outline drawing provides very little visual data and requires the viewer to fill in or complete the image himself. The telephone, which gives the ear relatively little data, is thus cool, as is speech; both demand considerable filling in by the listener. On the other hand, radio is a hot medium because it sharply and intensely provides great amounts of high-definition auditory information that leaves little or nothing to be filled in by the audience. A lecture, by the same token, is hot, but a seminar is cool; a book is hot, but a conversation or bull session is cool.

In a cool medium, the audience is an active constituent of the viewing or listening experience. A girl wearing open-mesh silk stockings or glasses is inherently cool and sensual because the eye acts as a surrogate hand in filling in the low-definition image thus engendered. Which is why boys make passes at girls who wear glasses. In any case, the overwhelming majority of our technologies and entertainments since the introduction of print technology have been hot, fragmented and exclusive, but in the age of television we see a return to cool values and the inclusive in-depth involvement and participation they engender. This is, of course, just one more reason why the medium is the message, rather than the content; it is the participatory nature of the TV experience itself that is important, rather than the content of the particular TV image that is being invisibly and indelibly inscribed on our skins.

PLAYBOY: Even if, as you contend, the medium is the ultimate message, how can you entirely discount the importance of content? Didn't the content of Hitler's radio speeches, for example, have some effect on the Germans?

McLUHAN: By stressing that the medium is the message rather than the content, I'm not suggesting that content plays *no* role—merely that it plays a distinctly subordinate role. Even if Hitler had delivered botany lectures, some other demagog would have used the radio to retribalize the Germans and rekindle the dark atavistic side of the tribal nature that created European fascism in the Twenties and Thirties. By placing all the stress on content and practically none on the medium, we lose all chance of perceiving and influencing the impact of new technologies on man, and thus we are always dumfounded by—and unprepared for—the revolutionary environmental transformations induced by new media. Buffeted by environmental changes he cannot comprehend, man echoes the last plaintive cry of his tribal ancestor, Tarzan, as he plummeted to earth: "Who greased my vine?" The German Jew victimized by the Nazis because his old tribalism clashed with their new tribalism could no more understand why his world was turned upside down than the American today can understand the reconfiguration of social and political institutions caused by the electric media in general and television in particular.

PLAYBOY: How is television reshaping our political institutions?

McLUHAN: TV is revolutionizing every political system in the Western world. For one thing, it's creating a totally new type of national leader, a man who is much more of a tribal chieftain than a politician. Castro is a good example of the new tribal chieftain who rules his country by a mass-participational TV dialog and feedback; he governs his country on camera, by giving the Cuban people the experience of being directly and intimately involved in the process of collective decision making. Castro's adroit blend of political education, propaganda and avuncular guidance is the pattern for tribal chieftains in other countries. The new political showman has to literally as well as figuratively put on his audience as he would a suit of clothes and become a corporate tribal image—like Mussolini, Hitler and F.D.R. in the days of radio, and Jack Kennedy in the television era. All these men were tribal emperors on a scale theretofore unknown in the world, because they all mastered their media.

PLAYBOY: How did Kennedy use TV in a manner different from his predecessors—or successors?

McLUHAN: Kennedy was the first TV President because he was the first prominent American politician to ever understand the dynamics and lines of force of the television iconoscope. As I've explained, TV is an inherently cool medium, and Kennedy had a compatible coolness and indifference to power, bred of personal wealth, which allowed him to adapt fully to TV. Any political candidate who doesn't have such cool, low definition qualities, which allow the viewer to fill in the gaps with his own personal identification, simply electrocutes himself on television—as Richard Nixon did in his disastrous debates with Kennedy in the 1960 campaign. Nixon was essentially hot; he presented a high-definition, sharply-defined image and action on the TV screen that contributed to his reputation as a phony—the "Tricky Dicky" syndrome that has dogged his footsteps for years. "Would you buy a used car from this man?" the political cartoon asked—and the answer was "no," because he didn't project the cool aura of disinterest and objectivity that Kennedy emanated so effortlessly and engagingly.

PLAYBOY: Did Nixon take any lessons from you the last time around?

McLUHAN: He certainly took lessons from somebody, because in the recent election it was Nixon who was cool and Humphrey who was hot. I had noticed the change in Nixon as far back as 1963 when I saw him on *The Jack Paar Show*. No longer the slick, glib, aggressive Nixon of 1960, he had been toned down, polished, programed and packaged into the new Nixon we saw in 1968: earnest, modest, quietly sincere—in a word, cool. I realized then that if Nixon maintained this mask, he could be elected President, and apparently the American electorate agreed last November.

PLAYBOY: How did Lyndon Johnson make use of television?

McLUHAN: He botched it the same way Nixon did in 1960. He was too intense, too obsessed with making his audience love and revere him as father and teacher, and too classifiable. Would people feel any safer buying a used car from L.B.J. than from the old Nixon? The answer is, obviously, "no." Johnson became a stereotype—even a parody—of himself, and earned the same reputation as a phony that plagued Nixon for so long. The people wouldn't have cared if John Kennedy lied to them on TV, but they couldn't stomach L.B.J. even when he told the truth. The credibility gap was really a communications gap. The political candidate who understands TV—whatever his party, goals or beliefs—can gain power unknown in history. How he uses that power is, of course, quite another question. But the basic thing to remember about the electric media is that they inexorably transform every sense ratio and thus recondition and restructure all our values and institutions. The overhauling of our traditional political system is only one manifestation of the retribalizing process wrought by the electric media, which is turning the planet into a global village.

PLAYBOY: Would you describe this retribalizing process in more detail?

McLUHAN: The electronically induced technological extensions of our central nervous system, which I spoke of earlier, are immersing us in a world-pool of information movement and are thus enabling man to incorporate within himself the whole of mankind. The aloof and dissociated role of the literate man of the Western world is succumbing to the new, intense depth participation engendered by the electronic media and bringing us back in touch with ourselves as well as with one another. But the instant nature of electric-information movement is decentralizing—rather than enlarging—the family of man into a new state of multitudinous tribal existences. Particularly in countries where literate values are deeply institutionalized, this is a highly traumatic process, since the clash of the old segmented visual culture and the new integral electronic culture creates a crisis of identity, a vacuum of the self, which generates tremendous violence—violence that is simply an identity quest, private or corporate, social or commercial.

PLAYBOY: Do you relate this identity crisis to the current social unrest and violence in the United States?

McLUHAN: Yes, and to the booming business psychiatrists are doing. All our alienation and atomization are reflected in the crumbling of such time-honored social values as the right of privacy and the sanctity of the individual; as they yield to the intensities of the new technology's electric circus, it seems to the average citizen that the sky is falling in. As man is tribally metamorphosed by the electric media, we all become Chicken Littles, scurrying around frantically in search of our former identities, and in the process unleash tremendous violence. As the preliterate confronts the literate in the postliterate arena, as new information patterns inundate and uproot the old, mental breakdowns of varying degrees—including the collective nervous breakdowns of whole societies unable to resolve their crises of identity—will become very common.

It is not an easy period in which to live, especially for the television-conditioned young who, unlike their literate elders, cannot take refuge in the zombie trance of Narcissus narcosis that numbs the state of psychic shock induced by the impact of the new media. From Tokyo to Paris to Columbia, youth mindlessly acts out its identity quest in the theater of the streets, searching not for goals but for roles, striving for an identity that eludes them.

PLAYBOY: Why do you think they aren't finding it within the educational system?

McLUHAN: Because education, which should be helping youth to understand and adapt to their revolutionary new environments, is instead being used merely as an instrument of cultural aggression, imposing upon retribalized youth the obsolescent visual values of the dying literate age. Our entire educational system is reactionary, oriented to past values and past technologies, and will likely continue so until the old generation relinquishes power. The generation gap is actually a chasm, separating not two age groups but two vastly divergent cultures. I can understand the ferment in our schools, because our educational system is totally rearview mirror. It's a dying and outdated system founded on literate values and fragmented and classified data totally unsuited to the needs of the first television generation.

PLAYBOY: How do you think the educational system can be adapted to accommodate the needs of this television generation?

McLUHAN: Well, before we can start doing things the right way, we've got to recognize that we've been doing them the wrong way—which most pedagogs and administrators and even most parents still refuse to accept. Today's child is growing up absurd because he is suspended between two worlds and two value systems, neither of which inclines him to maturity because he belongs wholly to neither but exists in a hybrid limbo of constantly conflicting values. The challenge of the new era is simply the total creative process of *growing up*—and mere teaching and repetition of facts are as irrelevant to this process as a dowser to a nuclear power plant. To expect a "turned on" child of the electric age to respond to the old education modes is rather like expecting an eagle to swim. It's simply not within his environment, and therefore incomprehensible.

The TV child finds it difficult if not impossible to adjust to the fragmented, visual goals of our education after having had all his senses involved by the electric media; he craves in-depth involvement, not linear detachment and uniform sequential patterns. But suddenly and without preparation, he is snatched from the cool, inclusive womb of television and exposed—within a vast bureaucratic structure of courses and credits—to the hot medium of print. His natural instinct, conditioned by the electric media, is to bring all his senses to bear on the book he's instructed to read, and print resolutely rejects that approach, demanding an isolated visual attitude to learning rather than the *Gestalt* approach of the unified sensorium. The reading postures of children in elementary school are a pathetic testimonial to the effects of television; children of the TV generation separate book from eye by an average distance of four and a half inches, attempting psychomimetically to bring to the printed page the all-inclusive sensory experience of TV. They are becoming Cyclops, desperately seeking to wallow in the book as they do in the TV screen.

PLAYBOY: Might it be possible for the "TV child" to make the adjustment to his educational environment by synthesizing traditional literate-visual forms with the insights of his own electric culture—or must the medium of print be totally unassimilable for him?

McLUHAN: Such a synthesis is entirely possible, and could create a creative blend of the two cultures—if the educational establishment was aware that there *is* an electric culture. In the absence of such elementary awareness, I'm afraid that the television child has no future in our schools. You must remember that the TV child has been relentlessly exposed to all the "adult" news of the modern world—war, racial discrimination, rioting, crime, inflation, sexual revolution. The war in Vietnam has written its bloody message on his skin; he has witnessed the assassinations and funerals of the nation's leaders; he's been orbited through the TV screen into the astronaut's dance in space, been inundated by information transmitted via radio, telephone, films, recordings and other people. His parents plopped him down in front of a TV set at the age of two to tranquilize him, and by the time he enters kindergarten, he's clocked as much as 4000 hours of television. As an IBM executive told me, "My children had lived several lifetimes compared to their grandparents when they began grade one."

PLAYBOY: If you had children young enough to belong to the TV generation, how would you educate them?

McLUHAN: Certainly not in our current schools, which are intellectual penal institutions. In today's world, to paraphrase Jefferson, the least education is the best education, since very few young minds can survive the intellectual tortures of our educational system. The mosaic image of the TV screen generates a depth-involving *nowness* and simultaneity in the lives of children that makes them scorn the distant visualized goals of traditional education as unreal, irrelevant and puerile. Another basic problem is that in our schools there is simply too much to learn by the traditional analytic methods; this is an age of information overload. The only way to make the schools other than prisons without bars is to start fresh with new techniques and values.

PLAYBOY: A number of experimental projects are bringing both TV and computers directly into the classrooms. Do you consider this sort of electronic educational aid a step in the right direction?

McLUHAN: It's not really too important if there is ever a TV set in each classroom across the country, since the sensory and attitudinal revolution has already taken place at home before the child ever reaches school, altering his sensory existence and his mental processes in profound ways. Book learning is no longer sufficient in any subject; the children all say now, "Let's *talk* Spanish," or "Let the Bard be *heard*," reflecting their rejection of the old sterile system where education begins and ends in a book. What we need now is educational crash programing in depth to first understand and then meet the new challenges. Just putting the present classroom on TV, with its archaic values and methods, won't change anything; it would be just like running movies on television; the result would be a hybrid that is neither. We have to ask what TV can do, in the instruction of English or physics or any other subject, that the classroom cannot do as presently constituted. The answer is that TV can deeply involve youth in the process of learning, illustrating graphically the complex interplay of people and events, the development of forms, the multileveled interrelationships between and among such arbitrarily segregated subjects as biology, geography, mathematics, anthropology, history, literature and languages.

If education is to become relevant to the young of this electric age, we must also supplant the stifling, impersonal and dehumanizing multiversity with a multiplicity of autonomous colleges devoted to an in-depth approach to learning. This must be done immediately, for few adults really comprehend the intensity of youth's alienation from the fragmented mechanical world and its fossilized educational system, which is designed in their minds solely to fit them into classified slots in bureaucratic society. To them, both draft card and degree are passports to psychic, if not physical, oblivion, and they accept neither. A new generation is alienated from its own 3000-year heritage of literacy and visual culture, and the celebration of literate values in home and school only intensifies that alienation. If we don't adapt our educational system to their needs and values, we will see only more dropouts and more chaos.

PLAYBOY: Do you think the surviving hippie subculture is a reflection of youth's rejection of the values of our mechanical society?

McLUHAN: Of course. These kids are fed up with jobs and goals, and are determined to forget their own roles and involvement in society. They want nothing to do with our fragmented and specialist consumer society. Living in the transitional identity vacuum between two great antithetical cultures, they are desperately trying to discover themselves and fashion a mode of existence attuned to their new values; thus the stress on developing an "alternate life style." We can see the results of this retribalization process whenever we look at *any* of our youth—not just at hippies. Take the field of fashion, for example, which now finds boys and girls dressing alike and wearing their hair alike, reflecting the unisexuality deriving from the shift from visual to tactile. The younger generation's whole orientation is toward a return to the native, as reflected by their costumes, their music, their long hair and their sociosexual behavior. Our teenage generation is already becoming part of a jungle clan. As youth enters this clan world and all their senses are electrically extended and intensified, there is a corresponding amplification of their sexual sensibilities. Nudity and unabashed sexuality are growing in the electric age because as TV tattoos its message directly on our skins, it renders clothing obsolescent and a barrier, and the new tactility makes it natural for kids to constantly touch one another—as reflected by the button sold in the psychedelic shops: IF IT MOVES, FONDLE IT. The electric media, by stimulating all the senses simultaneously, also give a new and richer sensual dimension to everyday sexuality that makes Henry Miller's style of randy rutting old-fashioned and obsolete. Once a society enters the all-involving tribal mode, it is inevitable that our attitudes toward sexuality change. We see, for example, the ease with which young people live guiltlessly with one another, or, as among the hippies, in communal ménages. This is completely tribal.

PLAYBOY: But aren't most tribal societies sexually restrictive rather than permissive?

McLUHAN: Actually, they're both. Virginity is not, with a few exceptions, the tribal style in most primitive societies; young people tend to have total sexual access to one another until marriage. But after marriage, the wife becomes a jealously guarded possession and adultery a paramount sin. It's paradoxical that in the transition to a retribalized society, there is inevitably a great explosion of sexual energy and freedom; but when that society is fully realized, moral values will be extremely tight. In an integrated tribal society, the young will have free rein to experiment, but marriage and the family will become inviolate institutions, and infidelity and divorce will constitute serious violations of the social bond, not a private deviation but a collective insult and loss of face to the entire tribe. Tribal societies, unlike detribalized, fragmented cultures with their stress on individualist values, are extremely austere morally, and do not hesitate to destroy or banish those who offend the tribal values. This is rather harsh, of course, but at the same time, sexuality can take on new and richer dimensions of depth involvement in a tribalized society.

Today, meanwhile, as the old values collapse and we see an exhilarating release of pent-up sexual frustrations, we are all inundated by a tidal wave of emphasis on sex. Far from liberating the libido, however, such onslaughts seem to have induced jaded attitudes and a kind of psychosexual *Weltschmerz*. No sensitivity of sensual response can survive such an assault, which stimulates the mechanical view of the body as capable of experiencing specific thrills, but not total sexual-emotional involvement and transcendence. It contributes to the schism between sexual enjoyment and reproduction that is so prevalent, and also strengthens the case for homosexuality. Projecting current trends, the love machine would appear a natural development in the near future—not just the current computerized datefinder, but a machine whereby ultimate orgasm is achieved by direct mechanical stimulation of the pleasure circuits of the brain.

PLAYBOY: Do we detect a note of disapproval in your analysis of the growing sexual freedom?

McLUHAN: No, I neither approve nor disapprove. I merely try to understand. Sexual freedom is as natural to newly tribalized youth as drugs.

PLAYBOY: What's natural about drugs?

McLUHAN: They're natural means of smoothing cultural transitions, and also a short cut into the electric vortex. The upsurge in drug taking is intimately related to the impact of the electric media. Look at the metaphor for getting high: turning on. One turns on his consciousness through drugs just as he opens up all his senses to a total depth involvement by turning on the TV dial. Drug taking is stimulated by today's pervasive environment of instant information, with its feedback mechanism of the inner trip. The inner trip is not the sole prerogative of the LSD traveler; it's the universal experience of TV watchers. LSD is a way of miming the invisible electronic world; it releases a person from acquired verbal and visual habits and reactions, and gives the potential of instant and total involvement, both all-at-onceness and all-at-oneness, which are the basic needs of people translated by electric extensions of their central nervous systems out of the old rational, sequential value system. The attraction to hallucinogenic drugs is a means of achieving empathy with our penetrating electric environment, an environment that in itself is a drugless inner trip.

Drug taking is also a means of expressing rejection of the obsolescent mechanical world and values. And drugs often stimulate a fresh interest in artistic expression, which is primarily of the audile-tactile world. The hallucinogenic drugs, as chemical simulations of our electric environment, thus revive senses long atrophied by the overwhelmingly visual orientation of the mechanical culture. LSD and related hallucinogenic drugs, furthermore, breed a highly tribal and communally oriented subculture, so it's understandable why the retribalized young take to drugs like a duck to water.

PLAYBOY: A Columbia coed was recently quoted in *Newsweek* as equating you and LSD. "LSD doesn't mean anything until you consume it," she said. "Likewise McLuhan." Do you see any similarities?

McLUHAN: I'm flattered to hear my work described as hallucinogenic, but I suspect that some of my academic critics find me a bad trip.

PLAYBOY: Have you ever taken LSD yourself?

McLUHAN: No, I never have. I'm an observer in these matters, not a participant. I had an operation last year to remove a tumor that was expanding my brain in a less pleasant manner, and during my prolonged convalescence I'm not allowed any stimulant stronger than coffee. Alas! A few months ago, however, I was almost "busted" on a drug charge. On a plane returning from Vancouver, where a university had awarded me an honorary degree, I ran into a colleague who asked me where I'd been. "To Vancouver to pick up my LL.D.," I told him. I noticed a fellow passenger looking at me with a strange expression, and when I got off the plane at Toronto Airport, two customs guards pulled me into a little room and started going over my luggage. "Do you know Timothy Leary?" one asked. I replied I did and that seemed to wrap it up for him. "All right," he said. "Where's the stuff? We know you told somebody you'd gone to Vancouver to pick up some LL.D." After a laborious dialog, I persuaded him that an LL.D. has nothing to do with consciousness expansion—just the opposite, in fact—and I was released. Of course, in light of the present educational crisis, I'm not sure there isn't something to be said for making possession of an LL.D. a felony.

PLAYBOY: Are you in favor of legalizing marijuana and hallucinogenic drugs?

McLUHAN: My personal point of view is irrelevant, since all such legal restrictions are futile and will inevitably wither away. You could as easily ban drugs in a retribalized society as outlaw clocks in a mechanical culture. The young will continue turning on no matter how many of them are turned off into prisons, and such legal restrictions only reflect the cultural aggression and revenge of a dying culture against its successor.

Speaking of dying cultures, it's no accident that drugs first were widely used in America by the Indians and then by the Negroes, both of whom have the great cultural advantage in this transitional age of remaining close to their tribal roots. The cultural aggression of white America against Negroes and Indians is not based on skin color and belief in racial superiority, whatever ideological clothing may be used to rationalize it, but on the white man's inchoate awareness that the Negro and Indian—as men with deep roots in the resonating echo chamber of the discontinuous, interrelated tribal world—are actually psychically and socially superior to the fragmented, alienated and dissociated man of Western civilization. Such a recognition, which stabs at the heart of the white man's entire social value system, inevitably generates violence and genocide. It has been the sad fate of the Negro and the Indian to be tribal men in a fragmented culture—men born ahead of rather than behind their time.

PLAYBOY: How do you mean?

McLUHAN: I mean that at precisely the time when the white younger generation is retribalizing and generalizing, the Negro and the Indian are under tremendous social and economic pressure to go in the opposite direction: to detribalize and specialize, to tear out their tribal roots when the rest of society is rediscovering theirs. Long held in a totally subordinate socioeconomic position, they are now impelled to acquire literacy as a prerequisite to employment in the old mechanical service environment of hardware, rather than adapt themselves to the new tribal environment of software, or electric information, as the middle-class white young are doing. Needless to say, this generates great psychic pain, which in turn is translated into bitterness and violence. This can be seen in the microcosmic drug culture; psychological studies show that the Negro and the Indian who are turned on by marijuana, unlike the white, are frequently engulfed with rage; they have a low high. They are angry because they understand under the influence of the drug that the source of their psychic and social degradation lies in the mechanical technology that is now being repudiated by the very white overculture that developed it—a repudiation that the majority of Negroes and Indians cannot, literally, afford because of their inferior economic position.

This is both ironic and tragic, and lessens the chances for an across-the-board racial *détente* and reconciliation, because rather than diminishing and eventually closing the sociopsychic differences between the races, it widens them. The Negro and the Indian seem to always get a bad deal; they suffered first because they were tribal men in a mechanical world, and now as they try to detribalize and structure themselves within the values of the mechanical culture, they find the gulf between them and a suddenly retribalizing society widening rather than narrowing. The future, I fear, is not too bright for either—but particularly for the Negro.

PLAYBOY: What, specifically, do you think will happen to him?

McLUHAN: At best, he will have to make a painful adjustment to two conflicting cultures and technologies, the visual-mechanical and the electric world; at worst, he will be exterminated.

PLAYBOY: Exterminated?

McLUHAN: I seriously fear the possibility, though God knows I hope I'm proved wrong. As I've tried to point out, the one inexorable consequence of any identity quest generated by environmental upheaval is tremendous violence. This violence has traditionally been directed at the tribal man who challenged visual-mechanical culture, as with the genocide against the Indian and the institutionalized dehumanization of the Negro. Today, the process is reversed and the violence is being meted out, during this transitional period, to those who are nonassimilable into the new tribe. Not because of his skin color but because he is in a limbo between mechanical and electric cultures, the Negro is a threat, a rival tribe that cannot be digested by the new order. The fate of such tribes is often extermination.

PLAYBOY: What can we do to prevent this from happening to America's Negro population?

McLUHAN: I think a valuable first step would be to alert the Negro, as well as the rest of society, to the nature of the new electric technology and the reasons it is so inexorably transforming our social and psychic values. The Negro should understand that the aspects of himself he has been conditioned to think of as inferior or "backward" are actually *superior* attributes in the new environment. Western man is obsessed by the forward-motion folly of step-by-step "progress," and always views the discontinuous synaesthetic interrelationships of the tribe as primitive. If the Negro realizes the great advantages of his heritage, he will cease his lemming leap into the senescent mechanical world.

There are encouraging signs that the new black-power movement—with its emphasis on Negritude and a return to the tribal pride of African cultural and social roots—is recognizing this, but unfortunately a majority of Negro Americans are still determined to join the mechanical culture. But if they can be persuaded to follow the lead of those who wish to rekindle their sparks of tribal awareness, they will be strategically placed to make an easy transition to the new technology, using their own enduring tribal values as environmental survival aids. They should take pride in these tribal values, for they are rainbow-hued in comparison with the pallid literate culture of their traditional masters.

But as I said, the Negro arouses hostility in whites precisely because they subliminally recognize that he is closest to that tribal depth involvement and simultaneity and harmony that is the richest and most highly developed expression of human consciousness. This is why the white political and economic institutions mobilize to exclude and oppress Negroes, from semiliterate unions to semiliterate politicians, whose slim visual culture makes them hang on with unremitting fanaticism to their antiquated hardware and the specialized skills and classifications and compartmentalized neighborhoods and life styles deriving from it. The lowest intellectual stratum of whites view literacy and its hardware environment as a novelty, still fresh and still status symbols of achievement, and thus will be the last to retribalize and the first to initiate what could easily become a full-blown racial civil war. The United States as a nation is doomed, in any case, to break up into a series of regional and racial ministates, and such a civil war would merely accelerate that process.

PLAYBOY: On what do you base your prediction that the United States will disintegrate?

McLUHAN: Actually, in this case as in most of my work, I'm "predicting" what has already happened and merely extrapolating a current process to its logical conclusion. The Balkanization of the United States as a continental political structure has been going on for some years now, and racial chaos is merely one of several catalysts for change. This isn't a peculiarly American phenomenon; as I pointed out earlier, the electric media always produce psychically integrating and socially decentralizing effects, and this affects not only political institutions within the existing state but the national entities themselves.

All over the world, we can see how the electric media are stimulating the rise of ministates: in Great Britain, Welsh and Scottish nationalism are recrudescing powerfully; in Spain, the Basques are demanding autonomy; in Belgium, the Flemings insist on separation from the Walloons; in my own country, the *Quebecois* are in the first stages of a war of independence; and in Africa, we've witnessed the germination of several ministates and the collapse of several ambitiously unrealistic schemes for regional confederation. These ministates are just the opposite of the traditional centralizing nationalisms of the past that forged mass states that homogenized disparate ethnic and linguistic groups within one national boundary. The new ministates are decentralized tribal agglomerates of those same ethnic and linguistic groups. Though their creation may be accompanied by violence, they will not remain hostile or competitive armed camps but will eventually discover that their tribal bonds transcend their differences and will thereafter live in harmony and cultural cross-fertilization with one another.

This pattern of decentralized ministates will be repeated in the United States, although I realize that most Americans still find the thought of the Union's dissolution inconceivable. The U.S., which was the first nation in history to begin its national existence as a centralized and literate political entity, will now play the historical film backward, reeling into a multiplicity of decentralized Negro states, Indian states, regional states, linguistic and ethnic states, etc. Decentralism is today the burning issue in the 50 states, from the school crisis in New York City to the demands of the retribalized young that the oppressive multiversities be reduced to a human scale and the mass state be debureaucratized. The tribes and the bureaucracy are antithetical means of social organization and can never coexist peacefully; one must destroy and supplant the other, or neither will survive.

PLAYBOY: Accepting, for the moment, your contention that the United States will be "Balkanized" into an assortment of ethnic and linguistic ministates, isn't it likely that the results would be social chaos and internecine warfare?

McLUHAN: Not necessarily. Violence can be avoided if we comprehend the process of decentralism and retribalization, and accept its outcome while moving to control and modify the dynamics of change. In any case, the day of the super state is over; as men not only in the U.S. but throughout the world are united into a single tribe, they will forge a diversity of viable decentralized political and social institutions.

PLAYBOY: Along what lines?

McLUHAN: It will be a totally retribalized world of depth involvements. Through radio, TV and the computer, we are already entering a global theater in which the entire world is a Happening. Our whole cultural habitat, which we once viewed as a mere container of people, is being transformed by these media and by space satellites into a living organism, itself contained within a new macrocosm or connubium of a supraterrestrial nature. The day of the individualist, of privacy, of fragmented or "applied" knowledge, of "points of view" and specialist goals is being replaced by the over-all awareness of a mosaic world in which space and time are overcome by television, jets and computers—a simultaneous, "all-at-once" world in which everything resonates with everything else as in a total electrical field, a world in which energy is generated and perceived not by the traditional connections that create linear, causative thought processes, but by the intervals, or gaps, which Linus Pauling grasps as the languages of cells, and which create synaesthetic discontinuous integral consciousness.

The open society, the visual offspring of phonetic literacy, is irrelevant to today's retribalized youth; and the closed society, the product of speech, drum and ear technologies, is thus being reborn. After centuries of dissociated sensibilities, modern awareness is once more becoming integral and inclusive, as the entire human family is sealed to a single universal membrane. The compressional, implosive nature of the new electric technology is retrogressing Western man back from the open plateaus of literate values and into the heart of tribal darkness, into what Joseph Conrad termed "the Africa within."

PLAYBOY: Many critics feel that your own "Africa within" promises to be a rigidly conformist hive world in which the individual is totally subordinate to the group and personal freedom is unknown.

McLUHAN: Individual talents and perspectives don't have to shrivel within a retribalized society; they merely interact within a group consciousness that has the potential for releasing far more creativity than the old atomized culture. Literate man is alienated, impoverished man; retribalized man can lead a far richer and more fulfilling life—not the life of a mindless drone but of the participant in a seamless web of interdependence and harmony. The implosion of electric technology is transmogrifying literate, fragmented man into a complex and depth-structured human being with a deep emotional awareness of his complete interdependence with all of humanity. The old "individualistic" print society was one where the individual was "free" only to be alienated and dissociated, a rootless outsider bereft of tribal dreams; our new electronic environment compels commitment and participation, and fulfills man's psychic and social needs at profound levels.

The tribe, you see, is not conformist just because it's inclusive; after all, there is far more diversity and less conformity within a family group than there is within an urban conglomerate housing thousands of families. It's in the village where eccentricity lingers, in the big city where uniformity and impersonality are the milieu. The global-village conditions being forged by the electric technology stimulate more discontinuity and diversity and division than the old mechanical, standardized society; in fact, the global village makes maximum disagreement and creative dialog inevitable. Uniformity and tranquillity are not hallmarks of the global village; far more likely are conflict and discord as well as love and harmony—the customary life mode of any tribal people.

PLAYBOY: Despite what you've said, haven't literate cultures been the only ones to value the concepts of individual freedom, and haven't tribal societies traditionally imposed rigid social taboos—as you suggested earlier in regard to sexual behavior—and ruthlessly punished all who do not conform to tribal values?

McLUHAN: We confront a basic paradox whenever we discuss personal freedom in literate and tribal cultures. Literate mechanical society separated the individual from the group in space, engendering privacy; in thought, engendering point of view; and in work, engendering specialism—thus forging all the values associated with individualism. But at the same time, print technology has homogenized man, creating mass militarism, mass mind and mass uniformity; print gave man private habits of individualism and a public role of absolute conformity. That is why the young today welcome their retribalization, however dimly they perceive it, as a release from

118   CHAPTER 8   Media Studies

the uniformity, alienation and dehumanization of literate society. Print centralizes socially and fragments psychically, whereas the electric media bring man together in a tribal village that is a rich and creative mix, where there is actually *more* room for creative diversity than within the homogenized mass urban society of Western man.

PLAYBOY: Are you claiming, now, that there will be no taboos in the world tribal society you envision?

McLUHAN: No, I'm not saying that, and I'm not claiming that freedom will be absolute—merely that it will be less restricted than your question implies. The world tribe will be essentially conservative, it's true, like all iconic and inclusive societies; a mythic environment lives beyond time and space and thus generates little radical social change. All technology becomes part of a shared ritual that the tribe desperately strives to keep stabilized and permanent; by its very nature, an oral-tribal society—such as Pharaonic Egypt—is far more stable and enduring than any fragmented visual society. The oral and auditory tribal society is patterned by acoustic space, a total and simultaneous field of relations alien to the visual world, in which points of view and goals make social change an inevitable and constant by product. An electrically imploded tribal society discards the linear forward-motion of "progress." We can see in our own time how, as we begin to react in depth to the challenges of the global village, we all become reactionaries.

PLAYBOY: That can hardly be said of the young, whom you claim are leading the process of retribalization, and according to most estimates are also the most radical generation in our history.

McLUHAN: Ah, but you're talking about politics, about goals and issues, which are really quite irrelevant. I'm saying that the result, not the current process, of retribalization makes us reactionary in our basic attitudes and values. Once we are enmeshed in the magical resonance of the tribal echo chamber, the debunking of myths and legends is replaced by their religious study. Within the consensual framework of tribal values, there will be unending diversity—but there will be few if any rebels who challenge the tribe itself.

The instant involvement that accompanies instant technologies triggers a conservative, stabilizing, gyroscopic function in man, as reflected by the second-grader who, when requested by her teacher to compose a poem after the first Sputnik was launched into orbit, wrote: "The stars are so big / The earth is so small / Stay as you are." The little girl who wrote those lines is part of the new tribal society; she lives in a world infinitely more complex, vast and eternal than any scientist has instruments to measure or imagination to describe.

PLAYBOY: If personal freedom will still exist—although restricted by certain consensual taboos—in this new tribal world, what about the political system most closely associated with individual freedom: democracy? Will it, too, survive the transition to your global village?

McLUHAN: No, it will not. The day of political democracy as we know it today is finished. Let me stress again that individual freedom itself will not be submerged in the new tribal society, but it will certainly assume different and more complex dimensions. The ballot box, for example, is the product of literate Western culture—a hot box in a cool world—and thus obsolescent. The tribal will is consensually expressed

NEL

through the simultaneous interplay of all members of a community that is deeply interrelated and involved, and would thus consider the casting of a "private" ballot in a shrouded polling booth a ludicrous anachronism. The TV networks' computers, by "projecting" a victor in a Presidential race while the polls are still open, have already rendered the traditional electoral process obsolescent.

In our software world of instant electric communications movement, politics is shifting from the old patterns of political representation by electoral delegation to a new form of spontaneous and instantaneous communal involvement in all areas of decision making. In a tribal all-at-once culture, the idea of the "public" as a differentiated agglomerate of fragmented individuals, all dissimilar but all capable of acting in basically the same way, like interchangeable mechanical cogs in a production line, is supplanted by a mass society in which personal diversity is encouraged while at the same time everybody reacts and interacts simultaneously to every stimulus. The election as we know it today will be meaningless in such a society.

PLAYBOY: How will the popular will be registered in the new tribal society if elections are passé?

McLUHAN: The electric media open up totally new means of registering popular opinion. The old concept of the plebiscite, for example, may take on new relevance; TV could conduct daily plebiscites by presenting facts to 200,000,000 people and providing a computerized feedback of the popular will. But voting, in the traditional sense, is through as we leave the age of political parties, political issues and political goals, and enter an age where the collective tribal image and the iconic image of the tribal chieftain is the overriding political reality. But that's only one of countless new realities we'll be confronted with in the tribal village. We must understand that a totally new society is coming into being, one that rejects *all* our old values, conditioned responses, attitudes and institutions. If you have difficulty envisioning something as trivial as the imminent end of elections, you'll be totally unprepared to cope with the prospect of the forthcoming demise of spoken language and its replacement by a global consciousness.

PLAYBOY: You're right.

McLUHAN: Let me help you. Tribal man is tightly sealed in an integral collective awareness that transcends conventional boundaries of time and space. As such, the new society will be one mythic integration, a resonating world akin to the old tribal echo chamber where magic will live again: a world of ESP. The current interest of youth in astrology, clairvoyance and the occult is no coincidence. Electric technology, you see, does not require words any more than a digital computer requires numbers. Electricity makes possible—and not in the distant future, either—an amplification of human consciousness on a world scale, without any verbalization at all.

PLAYBOY: Are you talking about global telepathy?

McLUHAN: Precisely. Already, computers offer the potential of instantaneous translation of any code or language into any other code or language. If a data feedback is possible through the computer, why not a feed-*forward* of thought whereby a world consciousness links into a world computer? Via the computer, we could logically proceed from translating languages to bypassing them entirely in favor of an integral cosmic unconsciousness somewhat similar to the collective unconscious envisioned by Bergson. The computer thus holds out the promise of a technologically engendered state of universal understanding and unity, a state of absorption in the logos that could knit mankind into one family and create a perpetuity of collective harmony and peace. This is the *real* use of the computer, not to expedite marketing or solve technical problems but to speed the process of discovery and orchestrate terrestrial—and eventually galactic—environments and energies. Psychic communal integration, made possible at last by the electronic media, could create the universality of consciousness foreseen by Dante when he predicted that men would continue as no more than broken fragments until they were unified into an inclusive consciousness. In a Christian sense, this is merely a new interpretation of the mystical body of Christ; and Christ, after all, is the ultimate extension of man.

PLAYBOY: Isn't this projection of an electronically induced world consciousness more mystical than technological?

McLUHAN: Yes—as mystical as the most advanced theories of modern nuclear physics. Mysticism is just tomorrow's science dreamed today.

PLAYBOY: You said a few minutes ago that *all* of contemporary man's traditional values, attitudes and institutions are going to be destroyed and replaced in and by the new electric age. That's a pretty sweeping generalization. Apart from the complex psychosocial metamorphoses you've mentioned, would you explain in more detail some of the specific changes you foresee?

McLUHAN: The transformations are taking place everywhere around us. As the old value systems crumble, so do all the institutional clothing and garbage they fashioned. The cities, corporate extensions of our physical organs, are withering and being translated along with all other such extensions into information systems, as television and the jet—by compressing time and space—make all the world one village and destroy the old city-country dichotomy. New York, Chicago, Los Angeles—all will disappear like the dinosaur. The automobile, too, will soon be as obsolete as the cities it is currently strangling, replaced by new antigravitational technology. The marketing systems and the stock market as we know them today will soon be dead as the dodo, and automation will end the traditional concept of the job, replacing it with a *role,* and giving men the breath of leisure. The electric media will create a world of dropouts from the old fragmented society, with its neatly compartmentalized analytic functions, and cause people to drop *in* to the new integrated global-village community.

All these convulsive changes, as I've already noted, carry with them attendant pain, violence and war—the normal stigmata of the identity quest—but the new society is springing so quickly from the ashes of the old that I believe it will be possible to avoid the transitional anarchy many predict. Automation and cybernation can play an essential role in smoothing the transition to the new society.

PLAYBOY: How?

McLUHAN: The computer can be used to direct a network of global thermostats to pattern life in ways that will optimize human awareness. Already, it's technologically feasible to employ the computer to program societies in beneficial ways.

PLAYBOY: How do you program an entire society—beneficially or otherwise?

McLUHAN: There's nothing at all difficult about putting computers in the position where they will be able to conduct carefully orchestrated programing of the sensory life of whole populations. I know it sounds rather science-fictional, but if you understood cybernetics you'd realize we could do it today. The computer could program the media to determine the given messages a people should hear in terms of their over-all needs, creating a total media experience absorbed and patterned by all the senses. We could program five hours less of TV in Italy to promote the reading of newspapers during an election, or lay on an additional 25 hours of TV in Venezuela to cool down the tribal temperature raised by radio the preceding month. By such orchestrated interplay of all media, whole cultures could now be programed in order to improve and stabilize their emotional climate, just as we are beginning to learn how to maintain equilibrium among the world's competing economies.

PLAYBOY: How does such environmental programing, however enlightened in intent, differ from Pavlovian brainwashing?

McLUHAN: Your question reflects the usual panic of people confronted with unexplored technologies. I'm not saying such panic isn't justified, or that such environmental programing couldn't be brainwashing, or far worse—merely that such reactions are useless and distracting. Though I think the programing of societies could actually be conducted quite constructively and humanistically, I don't want to be in the position of a Hiroshima physicist extolling the potential of nuclear energy in the first days of August 1945. But an understanding of media's effects constitutes a civil defense against media fallout.

The alarm of so many people, however, at the prospect of corporate programing's creation of a complete service environment on this planet is rather like fearing that a municipal lighting system will deprive the individual of the right to adjust each light to his own favorite level of intensity. Computer technology can—and doubtless will—program entire environments to fulfill the social needs and sensory preferences of communities and nations. The *content* of that programing, however, depends on the nature of future societies—but that is in our own hands.

PLAYBOY: Is it really in our hands—or, by seeming to advocate the use of computers to manipulate the future of entire cultures, aren't you actually encouraging man to abdicate control over his destiny?

McLUHAN: First of all—and I'm sorry to have to repeat this disclaimer—I'm not advocating *anything;* I'm merely probing and predicting trends. Even if I opposed them or thought them disastrous, I couldn't stop them, so why waste my time lamenting? As Carlyle said of author Margaret Fuller after she remarked, "I accept the Universe": "She'd better." I see no possibility of a world-wide Luddite rebellion that will smash all machinery to bits, so we might as well sit back and see what is happening and what will happen to us in a cybernetic world. Resenting a new technology will not halt its progress.

The point to remember here is that whenever we use or perceive any technological extension of ourselves, we necessarily embrace it. Whenever we watch a TV screen or read a book, we are absorbing these extensions of ourselves into our individual system and experiencing an automatic "closure" or displacement of perception; we can't escape this perpetual embrace of our daily technology unless we escape the technology itself and flee to a hermit's cave. By consistently embracing all these technologies, we inevitably relate ourselves to them as servomechanisms. Thus, in order to make use of them at all, we must serve them as we do gods. The Eskimo is a servomechanism of his kayak, the cowboy of his horse, the businessman of his clock, the cyberneticist—and soon the entire world—of his computer. In other words, to the spoils belongs the victor. This continuous modification of man by his own technology stimulates him to find continuous means of modifying it; man thus becomes the sex organs of the machine world just as the bee is of the plant world, permitting it to reproduce and constantly evolve to higher forms. The machine world reciprocates man's devotion by rewarding him with goods and services and bounty. Man's relationship with his machinery is thus inherently symbiotic. This has always been the case; it's only in the electric age that man has an opportunity to *recognize* this marriage to his own technology. Electric technology is a qualitative extension of this age-old man-machine relationship; 20th Century man's relationship to the computer is not by nature very different from prehistoric man's relationship to his boat or to his wheel—with the important difference that all previous technologies or extensions of man were partial and fragmentary, whereas the electric is total and inclusive. Now man is beginning to wear his brain outside his skull and his nerves outside his skin; new technology breeds new man. A recent cartoon portrayed a little boy telling his nonplused mother: "I'm going to be a computer when I grow up." Humor is often prophecy.

PLAYBOY: If man can't prevent this transformation of himself by technology—or *into* technology—how can he control and direct the process of change?

McLUHAN: The first and most vital step of all, as I said at the outset, is simply to understand media and their revolutionary effects on all psychic and social values and institutions. Understanding is half the battle. The central purpose of all my work is to convey this message, that by understanding media as they extend man, we gain a measure of control over them. And this is a vital task, because the immediate interface between audile-tactile and visual perception is taking place everywhere around us. No civilian can escape this environmental blitzkrieg, for there is, quite literally, no place to hide. But if we diagnose what is happening to us, we can reduce the ferocity of the winds of change and bring the best elements of the old visual culture, during this transitional period, into peaceful coexistence with the new retribalized society.

If we persist, however, in our conventional rearview-mirror approach to these cataclysmic developments, all of Western culture will be destroyed and swept into the dustbin of history. If literate Western man were really interested in preserving the most creative aspects of his civilization, he would not cower in his ivory tower bemoaning change but would plunge himself into the vortex of electric technology and, by understanding it, dictate his new environment—turn ivory tower into control tower. But I can understand his hostile attitude, because I once shared his visual bias.

PLAYBOY: What changed your mind?

McLUHAN: Experience. For many years, until I wrote my first book, *The Mechanical Bride,* I adopted an extremely moralistic approach to all environmental technology. I loathed machinery, I abominated cities, I equated the Industrial Revolution with original sin and mass media with the Fall. In short, I rejected almost every element of modern life in favor of a Rousseauvian utopianism. But gradually I perceived how sterile and useless this attitude was, and I began to realize that the greatest artists of the 20th Century—Yeats, Pound, Joyce, Eliot—had discovered a totally different approach, based on the identity of the processes of cognition and creation. I realized that artistic creation is the playback of ordinary experience—from trash to treasures. I ceased being a moralist and became a student.

As someone committed to literature and the traditions of literacy, I began to study the new environment that imperiled literary values, and I soon realized that they could not be dismissed by moral outrage or pious indignation. Study showed that a totally new approach was required, both to save what deserved saving in our Western heritage and to help man adopt a new survival strategy. I adapted some of this new approach in *The Mechanical Bride* by attempting to immerse myself in the advertising media in order to apprehend their impact on man, but even there some of my old literate "point of view" bias crept in. The book, in any case, appeared just as television was making all its major points irrelevant.

I soon realized that recognizing the symptoms of change was not enough; one must understand the *cause* of change, for without comprehending causes, the social and psychic effects of new technology cannot be counteracted or modified. But I recognized also that one individual cannot accomplish these self-protective modifications; they must be the collective effort of society, because they affect all of society; the individual is helpless against the pervasiveness of environmental change: the new garbage—or message—induced by new technologies. Only the social organism, united and recognizing the challenge, can move to meet it.

Unfortunately, no society in history has ever known enough about the forces that shape and transform it to take action to control and direct new technologies as they extend and transform man. But today, change proceeds so instantaneously through the new media that it may be possible to institute a global education program that will enable us to seize the reins of our destiny—but to do this we must first recognize the kind of therapy that's needed for the effects of the new media. In such an effort, indignation against those who perceive the nature of those effects is no substitute for awareness and insight.

PLAYBOY: Are you referring to the critical attacks to which you've been subjected for some of your theories and predictions?

McLUHAN: I am. But I don't want to sound uncharitable about my critics. Indeed, I appreciate their attention. After all, a man's detractors work for him tirelessly and for free. It's as good as being banned in Boston. But as I've said, I can understand their hostile attitude toward environmental change, having once shared it. Theirs is the customary human reaction when confronted with innovation: to flounder about attempting to adapt old responses to new situations or to simply condemn or ignore the harbingers of change—a practice refined by the Chinese emperors, who used to execute messengers bringing bad news. The new technological environments generate the most pain among those least prepared to alter their old value structures. The literati find the new electronic environment far more threatening than do those less committed to literacy as a way of life. When an individual or social group feels that its whole identity is jeopardized by social or psychic change, its natural reaction is to lash out in defensive fury. But for all their lamentations, the revolution has already taken place.

PLAYBOY: You've explained why you avoid approving or disapproving of this revolution in your work, but you must have a private opinion. What is it?

McLUHAN: I don't like to tell people what I think is good or bad about the social and psychic changes caused by new media, but if you insist on pinning me down about my own subjective reactions as I observe the reprimitivization of our culture, I would have to say that I view such upheavals with total personal dislike and dissatisfaction. I do see the prospect of a rich and creative retribalized society—free of the fragmentation and alienation of the mechanical age—emerging from this traumatic period of culture clash; but I have nothing but distaste for the *process* of change. As a man molded within the literate Western tradition, I do not personally cheer the dissolution of that tradition through the electric involvement of all the senses: I don't enjoy the destruction of neighborhoods by high-rises or revel in the pain of identity quest. No one could be less enthusiastic about these radical changes than myself. I am not, by temperament or conviction, a revolutionary; I would prefer a stable, changeless environment of modest services and human scale. TV and all the electric media are unraveling the entire fabric of our society, and as a man who is forced by circumstances to live within that society, I do not take delight in its disintegration.

You see, I am not a crusader; I imagine I would be most happy living in a secure preliterate environment; I would never attempt to change my world, for better or worse. Thus I derive no joy from observing the traumatic effects of media on man, although I do obtain satisfaction from grasping their modes of operation. Such comprehension is inherently cool, since it is simultaneously involvement and detachment. This posture is essential in studying media. One must begin by becoming extraenvironmental, putting oneself beyond the battle in order to study and understand the configuration of forces. It's vital to adopt a posture of arrogant superiority; instead of scurrying into a corner and wailing about what media are doing to us, one should charge straight ahead and kick them in the electrodes. They respond beautifully to such resolute treatment and soon become servants rather than masters. But without this detached involvement, I could never objectively observe media; it would be like an octopus grappling with the Empire State Building. So I employ the greatest boon of literate culture: the power of man to act without reaction—the sort of specialization by dissociation that has been the driving motive force behind Western civilization.

The Western world is being revolutionized by the electric media as rapidly as the East is being Westernized, and although the society that eventually emerges may be superior to our own, the process of change is agonizing. I must move through this pain-wracked transitional era as a scientist would move through a world of disease; once a surgeon becomes personally involved and disturbed about the condition of his patient, he loses the power to help that patient. Clinical detachment is not some kind of haughty pose I affect—nor does it reflect any lack of compassion on my part; it's simply a survival strategy. The world we are living in is not one I would have created on my own drawing board, but it's the one in which I must live, and in which the students I teach must live. If nothing else, I owe it to them to avoid the luxury of moral indignation or the troglodytic security of the ivory tower and to get down into the junk yard of environmental change and steam-shovel my way through to a comprehension of its contents and its lines of force—in order to understand how and why it is metamorphosing man.

PLAYBOY: Despite your personal distaste for the upheavals induced by the new electric technology, you seem to feel that if we understand and influence its effects on us, a less alienated and fragmented society may emerge from it. Is it thus accurate to say that you are essentially optimistic about the future?

McLUHAN: There are grounds for both optimism and pessimism. The extensions of man's consciousness induced by the electric media could conceivably usher in the millennium, but it also holds the potential for realizing the Anti-Christ—Yeats' rough beast, its hour come round at last, slouching toward Bethlehem to be born. Cataclysmic environmental changes such as these are, in and of themselves, morally neutral; it is how we perceive them and react to them that will determine their ultimate psychic and social consequences. If we refuse to see them at all, we will become their servants. It's inevitable that the world-pool of electronic information movement will toss us all about like corks on a stormy sea, but if we keep our cool during the descent into the maelstrom, studying the process as it happens to us and what we can do about it, we can come through.

Personally, I have a great faith in the resiliency and adaptability of man, and I tend to look to our tomorrows with a surge of excitement and hope. I feel that we're standing on the threshold of a liberating and exhilarating world in which the human tribe can become truly one family and man's consciousness can be freed from the shackles of mechanical culture and enabled to roam the cosmos. I have a deep and abiding belief in man's potential to grow and learn, to plumb the depths of his own being and to learn the secret songs that orchestrate the universe. We live in a transitional era of profound pain and tragic identity quest, but the agony of our age is the labor pain of rebirth.

I expect to see the coming decades transform the planet into an art form; the new man, linked in a cosmic harmony that transcends time and space, will sensuously caress and mold and pattern every facet of the terrestrial artifact as if it were a work of art, and man himself will become an organic art form. There is a long road ahead, and the stars are only way stations, but we have begun the journey. To be born in this age is a precious gift, and I regret the prospect of my own death only because I will leave so many pages of man's destiny—if you will excuse the Gutenbergian image—tantalizingly unread. But perhaps, as I've tried to demonstrate in my examination of the postliterate culture, the story begins only when the book closes.

PERSONAL RESPONSE

Had you heard of Marshall McLuhan before you read this interview? Considering McLuhan's impact on our way of thinking, and on the philosophy of thought, why do you think he is not very well known today in Canada?

QUESTIONS FOR CLASS OR SMALL-GROUP DISCUSSION

1. Explain how the world can be seen as a "global village." What does this term mean, and how does it influence your world view?

2. From a McLuhanesque perspective, in what ways does a portable MP3 player, as a technological extension of the self, affect or change social behaviour? What is the effect of these changes?

3. McLuhan suggests that when a new technology becomes "all-pervasive," that is, when we are completely used to it and it seems to be everywhere, it also becomes "invisible." In this way, we are subject to it, rather than subjects just using it. McLuhan calls this being "blissfully ignorant" of the media's power. Consider the consequences of the Internet as an invisible presence, and the lasting changes it may be having on our behaviour and environment.

4. List all the technologies that you use on a regular basis. What senses, needs, behaviours, or parts of your anatomy are they an extension of? Do these technologies begin to "control" your behaviours?

SELLING SUDS [THE TEXT OF THE AD, "MY NAME IS JOE, AND I AM CANADIAN!"]

Hey.
I'm not a lumberjack,
or a fur trader . . .
and I don't live in an igloo
or eat blubber, or own a dogsled . . .
and I don't know Jimmy, Sally or Suzy from Canada,
although I'm certain they're really, really nice.

I have a Prime Minister,
not a President.
I speak English and French,
NOT American.
and I pronounce it ABOUT,
NOT A BOOT.
I can proudly sew my country's flag on my backpack.
I believe in peace keeping, NOT policing.
DIVERSITY, NOT assimilation,
AND THAT THE BEAVER IS A TRULY PROUD AND NOBLE ANIMAL.
A TOQUE IS A HAT,
A CHESTERFIELD IS A COUCH,
AND IT IS PRONOUCED 'ZED' NOT 'ZEE', 'ZED'!

CANADA IS THE SECOND LARGEST LANDMASS!
THE FIRST NATION OF HOCKEY!
AND THE BEST PART OF NORTH AMERICA!

MY NAME IS JOE!
AND I AM CANADIAN!

PERSONAL RESPONSE

Does Joe's speech make you proud or does it make you cringe? Discuss your emotional response to Joe's speech and the source of your response. If you were told that this commercial is sometimes referred to as "The Rant," does knowing this change your response to it?

QUESTIONS FOR CLASS OR SMALL-GROUP DISCUSSION

1. What do you think constitutes Canadian identity? Does Joe's speech fit with your conception of Canadian identity, or does it suggest a kind of stereotype? If so, what kind of stereotype? Look up the commercial on your computer (search under "My Name Is Joe"), and examine how the words are said, the images and music that are used, and what the speaker is like. Comment on these.

2. How might someone else from another country, particularly the United States, react to this speech? Are national stereotypes, which are often the product of the media (particularly television, music, and movies), a good or a bad thing? What are some other national stereotypes you have come across in the media?

3. List and categorize the kinds of things that do or do not construct Canadian identity in the text. Would you say these are neutral, positive, or negative?

4. Take a very close look at Canadian money—paper and coinage—and the images and words used on the various denominations. How do these contribute to or construct Canadian identity?

5. Research the relationship between media, consumerism, and national identity. Analyze how advertising media cross over into politics, nationality, and patriotism.

6. Explore the term *jingoism*, and discuss how this might be applied to the "My Name Is Joe" ad or any other particular advertisements.

FOR FURTHER VIEWING: MEDIA STUDIES

Broadcast News (1987); *The Front Page* (1974); *Good Night, and Good Luck* (2005); *Natural Born Killers* (1994); *Talk Radio* (1988); *Wag the Dog* (1997); *Manufacturing Consent: Noam Chomsky and the Media* (1992); *All the President's Men* (1976); *The Insider* (1999); *Citizen Kane* (1941); *A Face in the Crowd* (1957).

THE NATIONAL GAME

INTRODUCTION

Hockey is "The Game." Ice hockey, that is. It's "Our Game"—our National (Winter) Game. Other nations may sometimes beat us at international hockey events, and there may be more National Hockey League teams in the United States than in Canada, but we expect to be the best, and we expect most NHL teams to have a strong Canadian contingent. It's just the way it is. Clearly no other nation has such passion for the sport; no other nation has its identity wrapped around people skating around on frozen water, wielding sticks, and chasing a frozen disk of rubber.

For many Canadians, every night is hockey night in Canada. Look at the sports pages in Canadian newspapers, or the stories that lead off the television sports news, during the playing season. Look what happens in Calgary when the Flames make the finals of the Stanley Cup, which is Canada's real Holy Grail. Look at the country's love–hate relationship with the Toronto Maple Leafs. Look at the mythology built up around the Montreal Canadiens—"Les Canadiens de Montréal," "The

Flying Frenchmen," Les Habs—the team that won all those championships in the 1950s. Look at how Wayne Gretzky and the Edmonton Oilers are our equivalent to Jason and the Argonauts. And think, too, about all those early mornings across the country when little boys—and, increasingly, little girls—lace 'em up. Look at the beer commercials! In short, we are a little hockey crazed, and it's a Canadian thing, like Tim Hortons coffee—which is appropriate given that Tim Horton was a legendary hockey player for those darn Maple Leafs.

What is worth exploring is not just the history of how hockey evolved to be so important in Canada, but what exactly hockey means, and how it intersects in personal, cultural, political, economic, business, and international realms—playing it, watching it, talking about it, thinking about it. The pieces in this chapter cover just a little of this. Google the words *hockey* and *Canada* together (without quotation marks), and you are likely to receive about 28.3 million hits, which is twice as many results than when you Google *wine* and *cheese*.

Since 2000, "Hockey Day in Canada" (usually in January or February) has cele-brated the game, with the CBC devoting a whole day to broadcasting hockey-related special events, often from a small Canadian town. Momentum for the celebration has grown, and in 2006, when held in Stephenville, Newfoundland and Labrador, it was said that the event was "bigger than Santa." Only in Canada, eh.

THE GAME IS AT CANADA'S CORE, AND NO LABOR DISPUTE CAN DISLODGE IT

Doug Beardsley

Doug Beardsley is a writer, critic, and poet who for many years worked at the University of Victoria, though his hockey roots go back to his hometown of Montreal. Among many other books, he has written about hockey in Country on Ice *(1987) and* Our Game: An All-Star Collection of Hockey Fiction *(1997).*

Ken Dryden, the former goaltender of the Montreal Canadiens, recently spoke about whether Canadians' love of hockey was a passion or a habit. His remarks, made during the lockout but before the cancellation of the National Hockey League's 2004–5 season, caused Canadians to reflect once more on what the game means to them.

I believe it is passion that makes the game synonymous with Canadian life, though the reasons lie buried deep in the snowdrift of the Canadian psyche. Why is our national pride so closely identified with what we call our game?

When we are seen in the world, we are seen as international peacekeepers, bankers, business entrepreneurs—however mistakenly. We are polite, reserved, tolerant, multicultural. Some might say repressed.

In Canada, hockey isn't a matter of life and death; it's more important than that.
Photo Source: CP/Tom Hanson

Then there is hockey, the legal mayhem we invented. I've long felt that the game represents the dark or demonic side of the collective Canadian psyche, our alter ego. The line between passion and violence on ice is a thin red line.

It has often been said that we have never been united as a country because we never experienced a civil war. But I'm convinced that we experienced a series of regional civil wars in the bitter rivalries the game has fostered over the years: between the Montreal Maroons and the Montreal Canadiens of the 1920's; later between Montreal and Toronto; the current battle for the supremacy of Ontario between Toronto and Ottawa; and the Battle of Alberta, which takes place between Edmonton and Calgary. The whole country participates in this seasonal ritual so that, paradoxically, the game becomes a unifying force for all Canadians; we feel our national pride through our hockey teams.

Yet the game also serves as a way out of small-town Canada, "a passport to another place" as the novelist Richard Wright has called it, a passport to a "mythical, enchanted land." It also serves to define us vis-à-vis the United States.

Deep in the collective unconscious, the game is a metaphor for our desperate need to survive in the frozen landscape that is our country. We skate to keep our blood circulating; we skate through winter, we skate to stay alive. As the journalist Rex Murphy put it, "If you can survive the winter, you can survive anything." The game should be played only in places cold enough to generate ice and snow.

Hockey's value as an essential aspect of the Canadian mythos is because "that's where the roots of a people lie," the playwright Thomson Highway said. We articulate ourselves through the game, our game, which is the very lifeblood of what it means to be Canadian.

In my country, the selling of Wayne Gretzky to the Los Angeles Kings in 1988 was considered a traitorous act. Americans have adopted a more clinical response to the game. As Dryden once wrote, in the United States "it is all seen as a fascinating problem in political science."

We played the game before we were a country. The true origins of hockey are not found in European masters like Pieter Brueghel the Elder or our own first tentative strides in Halifax, Nova Scotia; Montreal; or Kingston, Ontario; but, rather, in the early game of lacrosse, or baggataway, as the native Indians called it. In the 17th century, French settlers were attracted to the rugged masculinity and bravado displayed by Canada's native peoples. In the last century, hockey was well served by Catholic schools across our country, which, with their concept of muscular Christianity, fostered and developed hundreds of players for the N.H.L.

When we hear hockey on the radio, we re-create the game in our imaginations, and, in doing so, we re-create ourselves as individuals, and as a people. Even when we watch it on television, or attend an N.H.L. game, we become one with the players on the ice; we feel an intrinsic part of the game, our game.

And what will happen now that the N.H.L. has taken the unprecedented step of canceling a season because of a labor dispute? Canadians may deny that we care, but our national pride is deeply wounded because the Stanley Cup, the Holy Grail, won't be awarded this season. We bleed, and our sense of self suffers accordingly.

As a former recreational player once said: "When we played the game, we played it to the best of our abilities. But when we watch the N.H.L., we get to see the game as it was meant to be played, and we feel graced by the miracle."

The N.H.L. is on thin ice, yet the game itself is alive and well and living north of the border. I have no fear for the future of the game in Canada—or in any place where the climate is cold enough to create ice and snow.

PERSONAL RESPONSE

Do you, or does anyone close to you, support a professional hockey team? Which one, and why? Does this support originate in family history, geography, or for other reasons? Does this team have a collective "character"?

If you are uninterested in hockey, what do you think of it as a national obsession? How have you managed to avoid "The Game"? Are there things you dislike about hockey?

What do you think about the role of violence and fighting in hockey? Is it just part of the game?

What do you think about women's hockey, which has gained popularity and respect in recent years with the success of national teams? The rules for body checking are different in men's and women's hockey. In your opinion, should these rules be the same? Why?

QUESTIONS FOR CLASS OR SMALL-GROUP DISCUSSION

1. Beardsley mentions that "passion" is behind our connection with hockey. What range of factors contribute to this passion?
2. You might think that rivalries create conflict or division within a country or province. Is this the case in hockey? Has it ever happened? Or does the game bring the country together? At what point does the love of the game become an obsession?
3. Beardsley claims that hockey goes deep into our "psyche" and cultural history. What is the "psyche"? What is it about the game that might contribute to this range and depth of feelings?
4. Discuss reasons for Canada's passion for hockey. Try to organize these reasons from least important to most significant.
5. Discuss what you think is wrong with modern professional hockey. Is it good for culture? Is it good for nationalism? Is nationalism good? Is the game economically viable and good for business?
6. Compare hockey to other sports in terms of popularity and style of game.

THE GAME

Ken Dryden

Ken Dryden, born in Hamilton, Ontario, in 1947, is known both as a leading politician with the Liberal Party of Canada and as a former goaltender for the Montreal Canadiens, winning six Stanley Cups with them in the 1970s. He is also known for being a member of the legendary 1972 Team Canada. He is currently the Member of Parliament for York Centre. He is the author of Home Game: Hockey and Life

In Canada (1990), The Moved and the Shaken: The Story of One Man's Life (1993), and The Game (1983), from which the following piece is taken.

Once I used to wait in line like everyone else. Then one day a bank teller motioned me out of the line, and I haven't been back in one since. I feel no small guilt each time; nonetheless I continue to accept such favours. For the tellers and me, it has become normal and routine. They treat me the way they think people like me expect to be treated. And I accept.

It is the kind of special treatment professional athletes have grown accustomed to, and enjoy. It began with hockey, with teenage names and faces in local papers, with hockey jackets that only the best players on the best teams wore, with parents who competed not so quietly on the side; and it will end with hockey. In between, the longer and better we play the more all-encompassing the treatment becomes. People give, easily and naturally. And we accept. Slippers, sweaters, plant holders, mitts, baby blankets, baby clothes sent in the mail. Paintings, carvings, etchings, sculptures in clay, metal, papier-mâché. Shirts, slacks, coats, suits, ties, underwear; cars, carpets, sofas, chairs, refrigerators, beds, washers, dryers, stoves, TV's, stereos, at cost or no cost at all. After all, a special person deserves a special price. A hundred letters a week, more than 3,000 a year—"You're the best," all but a few of them say. On the street, in restaurants and theatres, we're pointed at, talked about like the weather. "There he is, the famous hockey player," your own kids announce to their friends. In other homes, your picture is on a boy's bedroom wall. Magazines, newspapers, radio, TV; hockey cards, posters, T-shirts, and curios, anywhere, everywhere, name, face, thousands of times.

And we love it. We say we don't, but we do. We hate the nuisance and inconvenience, the bother of untimely, unending autographs, handshakes, and smiles, living out an image of ourselves that isn't quite real, abused if we fail to, feeling encircled and trapped, never able to get away. But we also feel special—head-turning, chin-dropping, forget-your-name special. What others buy Rolls-Royces and votes and hockey teams for, what others take off their clothes for, what others kill for, we have. All we have to do is play.

If exposure is the vehicle of celebrity, attention is what separates one celebrity from another. Guy Lafleur and Yvon Lambert are both celebrities, yet on the same ice, the same screen, Lafleur is noticed, Lambert is not. Lambert, methodical and unspectacular, has nothing readily distinctive about him. His image is passed over, his name unheard. Lafleur *is* distinctive. The way he skates, the sound of the crowd he carries with him, the goals he scores.

And so, too, others, for other reasons. Mario Tremblay, for his fiery, untamed spirit; Bob Gainey, for his relentless, almost palpable will; Tiger Williams, Eddie Shack, Ron Duguay, each colourful and exciting; and Dave Schultz, once king of the mountain. As sports coverage proliferates beyond games, as it becomes entertainment and moves to prime time, as we look for the story behind the story, off-ice performance becomes important. And so personas are born, and sometimes made, and cameras and microphones are there as it happens. The crazies, the clowns, the "sports intellectuals," the anti-jock rebels (Jim Bouton, Bill "Spaceman" Lee), the playboys

(Joe Namath, Derek Sanderson), each a distinctive personality, each a bigger celebrity because of what he does away from the game.

TV has given us a new minimum off-ice standard. The modern player must be articulate (or engagingly inarticulate, especially southern style). It's not enough to score a goal and have it picked apart by the all-seeing eyes of replay cameras. A player must be able to put it in his own eloquent words. How did you do it? How did you feel? Live, on camera words that cannot be edited for the morning paper.

Celebrity is a full, integrated life, earned on-ice, performed, sustained, strengthened, re-earned off-ice. As Roger Angell once put it, we want our athletes to be "good at life." Role models for children, people we want to believe earned what they have, every bit as good at things off the ice as on. If they're inarticulate, harsh and pejorative, they're suddenly just jocks. Merely lucky, less likable, less good at life, less celebrated; finally, they even seem less good *on* the ice.

At its extreme, the process creates the category of professional celebrity, people "famous for being famous," so accomplished at being celebrities that their original source of deity is forgotten. At the least, it encourages all celebrities to learn the *skills* of the public person. How to look good, how to sound modest and intelligent, funny and self-deprecatory, anything you want. It's a celebrity's short-cut to the real thing, but it works. Walter Cronkite *looks* trustworthy, Ronald Reagan *seems* like a nice guy, Denis Potvin *sounds* intelligent; or is he only articulate? Good enough at something to be a public person, or simply a good public person? You'll never get close enough long enough to know.

All around us are people anxious to help us look better. Not just flacks and PR types but a whole industry of journalists, commentators, biographers, award-givers. Ghost-writers who put well-paid words under our names, then disappear; charity organizers, volunteers who give time and effort so that "honorary presidents," and "honorary directors" may look even better. Children in hospitals, old folks in old folks' homes—we autograph their casts, shake their hands, make them props to our generosity and compassion. And never far away, photographers and cameramen record the event. It is the bandwagon momentum of celebrityhood.

In the end, for us, is an image. After thousands of confused messages, we cut through what is complex and render it simple. One image, concrete and disembodied. What agents call "Ken Dryden."

Recently, I asked an executive at an advertising agency to pretend he was trying to persuade a client to use me as a commercial spokesman for his company. We'd met two or three times, several years before, so he knew me mostly as others do. He wrote the following memo to his client: "Historically I know you have had some concerns about using an athlete . . . either because of potential problems developing out of their careers and public life, or due to simply their lack of availability. I think Ken is quite different from the rest. He is known as a thoughtful, articulate and concerned individual. I think it would go without saying he would not participate in any endorsation unless he was fully committed to and satisfied with the product.

(His Ralph Nader exposures would assure that.) He is serious, respected and appears to be very much his own man. I don't think we could ever consider using him in humorous or light approaches (like Eddie Shack) unless it would be by juxtaposition with another . . . actor or player. He has good media presence. . . . His physical presence is also commanding. He is quite tall and impressive. . . . Other encouraging things would be his intelligence and educational background. He would be more in tune with our target audience with his credentials as a college graduate (Cornell) and a fledgling professional person (law). Also, during production, I think this intelligence and coolness would help in case of commercial production as well as helping to keep costs under control due to mental errors. . . ."

So that's my image. Is it accurate? It doesn't matter. It's what people think, it presupposes how they'll react to me. And for the ad man and his client, how people will react is what matters.

If I don't like my image, I can do something about it. I can do things that are "good for my image." I can stop doing things that are "bad for my image." As actors remind us casually and often, I can do things to change my image. Is it too serious? If I run around the dressing room throwing water at the right moment, someone is bound to notice. A journalist with a deadline to meet and space to fill, a new angle, news—"Dryden misunderstood."

Want to be known as an antique collector? Collect an antique. A theatre-goer? Go. Once is enough. Tell a journalist, sound enthusiastic, and, above all, play well. Then stand back and watch what happens. Clipped and filed, the new spreads like a chain letter, to other journalists who don't have time to check it out. Presto, it's part of your standard bio. And your image.

If you substitute the word "reputation" for "image," as you might have done a few years ago, you'd have something quite different. A reputation is nothing so trifling or cynical. Like an old barge, it takes time to get it going. It's slow and relentless, difficult to manoeuvre, even harder to stop. An image is nothing so solemn. It is merely a commercial asset, a package of all the rights and good-will associated with "Ken Dryden"—something I can sell to whomever I want.

But it's a sticky matter. For the image I'm selling is *your* image of me. The good-will, though it relates to me, is your good-will. Whatever commercial value there is in my name, my image, it's you who puts it there. You like me or trust me, and any prospective buyer of my image, anxious to put my name alongside his product, knows that and counts on it to make you buy his product. And you might, even though it may not be in your best interest. So by selling my name, I have perhaps taken your trust and turned it against you.

I did a commercial once, six years ago. I'd decided I never would, but this one was different enough to start a web of rationalizations until I forgot the point and accepted. A fast-food chain was looking for a winter promotion; Hockey Canada, the advisory and promotional body, wanted a fundraiser and a way to deliver the message to kids and their parents that minor hockey can be approached and played differently. The idea was a mini-book done by Hockey Canada, then sold through the restaurant chain. I was to be a collaborator on the book, and its public spokesman. But after doing the TV and radio ads (for the book, but with a corporate jingle at the end), and seeing the point-of-purchase cardboard likenesses of me in the restaurant, I realized my mistake.

Since then, I have turned down endorsements for, among other things, a candy bar ("The way I see it, a full body shot of you in the net, mask up, talking, then we draw in tight on your catching glove, you open it, the bar's inside. . . ."), a credit card company ("You may not know me without my mask, but. . . ."), and a roll-on deodorant that would also be promoted by several other people whose names begin with the sound "dry."

It's a game—an ad game, an image game, a celebrity game—that no one really loses. Everyone needs someone to talk about—why not about us? Everyone needs heroes and villains. We earn a little money, get some exposure. The commercials are going to be done anyway. Besides, it doesn't last long. A few years and images change, celebrity cools, it's over. It all evens out.

But it doesn't. We all lose, at least a little. We lose because you think I'm better than I am. Brighter than I am, kinder, more compassionate, capable of more things, as good at life as I am at the game. I'm not. Off the ice I struggle as you do, but off the ice you never see me, even when you think you do. I appear good at other things because I'm good at being a goalie; because I'm a celebrity; because there's always someone around to say I'm good. Because in the cozy glow of success, of good news, you want me to be good. It's my angle, and so long as I play well the angle won't change. I appear bright and articulate because I'm an athlete, and many athletes are not bright and articulate. "Like a dog's walking on his hind legs," as Dr. Johnson once put it, "it is not done well; but you are surprised to find it done at all."

But you don't believe that, just as I don't believe it about celebrities I don't know. They're taller, more talented, more compassionate. They glitter into cameras and microphones, give each other awards for talent and compassion, "great human beings" every one. Wet-eyed I applaud, and believe. And all of us lose. You, because you feel less worthy than you are. Me, because once, when I was twenty-three years old and trying to learn about myself, I wanted to believe I was, or soon would be, everything others said I was. Instead, having learned much and grown older, I feel co-conspirator to a fraud.

Professional athletes do exciting, sometimes courageous, sometimes ennobling things, as heroes do, but no more than you do. Blown up on a TV screen or a page, hyped by distance and imagination, we seem more heroic, but we're not. Our achievement seems grander, but it isn't. Our cause, our commitment, is no different from yours. We are no more than examples, metaphors, because we enter every home; we're models for the young because their world is small and we do what they do.

A few years ago, Joe McGinniss, author of *The Selling of the President, 1968*, wrote a book called *Heroes*. It sketches McGinniss's own tormented trail from being *the youngest*, to *the highly acclaimed*, to *the former*—all before he was thirty. At the same time, he ostensibly searches for the vanished American hero. He talks to George McGovern and Teddy Kennedy, General William Westmoreland, John Glenn, Eugene McCarthy, author William Styron, playwright Arthur Miller—some of them heroes of his, all of them heroes to many.

But it's like chasing a rainbow. He finds that, as he gets closer, his heroes disappear. In homes and bar, on campaign trails, they're distinctly, disappointingly normal. Not wonderfully, triumphantly, down-to-earth normal, but up-close, drinking-too-much, sweating, stinking, unheroically normal. And for heroes, normal isn't enough. We are allowed one image; everything must fit.

The Greeks give their gods human imperfections. In the modern hero, however, every flaw is a fatal flaw. It has only to be found, and it *will* be. Moving from celebrity to hero is like moving from a city to a small town. It a city, the camera's eye, though always present, is distant. In a small town, there isn't that distance. There's no place to hide.

"Whom the gods would destroy," Wilfrid Sheed wrote in *Transatlantic Blues,* "they first oversell." Superficially created, superficially destroyed—for the hero, for the celebrity, it all evens out. Except a heavy price is paid along the way. We all lose again. You, because, saddened and hurt by heroes who turn out not to be heroes at all, you become cynical and stop believing. Me, because I'm in a box. What is my responsibility? Is it, as I'm often told, to be the hero that children think I am? Or is it to live what is real, to be something else.

Recently, a friend asked me to speak to his college seminar. Near the end of two hours, we began to talk about many of these questions. A girl raised her hand. She said that a year or two earlier, on the Academy Awards, she had seen Charlton Heston receive an award for his "humanitarian" work. Heston had made the point, the girl said, that thousands of volunteers had done far more than he, that they deserved the award.

I asked the class what that story told them about Charlton Heston. That he's even modest, they decided. A few of the students laughed; then, one by one, several others joined in.

PERSONAL RESPONSE

What do you think of Dryden's attitude toward "celebrityhood"? He says that he doesn't really care if the image presented of him is accurate. Why do you think he doesn't care? Do you believe him? What is he trying to say?

QUESTIONS FOR CLASS OR SMALL-GROUP DISCUSSION

1. The "game" is hockey, but, according to this piece, what might also be the game? Does Dryden want to play it? Discuss.

2. How is the idea of celebrity constructed? Name all the stakeholders in the establishing of celebrity.

3. At moments, Dryden seems uneasy with the idea of celebrity. Describe this uneasiness. Does it change your view of what celebrity is all about and what its function is?

4. How, in Canada, is celebrity associated with hockey? Describe the popular image of the Canadian professional hockey player. Where does this image come from? Do you think it is accurate? Does it tell us anything about what being Canadian might be?

CHAPTER ONE FROM *HOCKEY DREAMS*

DAVID ADAMS RICHARDS

David Adams Richards, born in 1950, in Newcastle, New Brunswick, is an award-winning Canadian poet, fiction writer, playwright, and screenwriter whose work often circles back to his origins in the Maritimes. His books include Hockey Dreams: Memories of a Man Who Couldn't Play *(1996),* Lines on the Water: A Fisherman's Life on the Miramichi *(1998),* The Bay of Love and Sorrows *(1998), and* Mercy Among the Children *(2000). He now lives in Toronto.*

I was five thousand miles away from home, in the middle of the mountains of British Columbia, in the middle of winter. On a reading tour, in 1989, I was going from town to town while the snow fell, covering up the small roads along the mountain passes.

I was billeted at different houses, and would often find myself in a strange little village, at a stranger's house at midnight. And since I'm a night person I found myself sitting in uncomfortable positions reading cookbooks at one o'clock in the morning.

One of the people who billeted me, I did become quite fond of. He was a man who had moved here with his wife from the United States a number of years before, during the "back to the land" movement. He was very kind to me, although I disagreed with him on the back to the land movement itself. And nothing he told me did anything but reinforce my bias.

But I gave him the greatest compliment I could. I told him he reminded me of my friend Stafford Foley—a boy I grew up with, way back in the Maritimes. Both of them were quite small men, with a great kind-heartedness.

I left his house on a Thursday morning to go to another village, some 40 miles away where I had a reading.

"If you ever need a place to stay again—" he said, "at any time—look me up." He handed me his telephone number.

I told him I would.

It had been snowing for four days. The snowflakes were as big as sugar cookies.

By Thursday night I found myself in an untenable position. It was one of those nights when I wanted to be anywhere but where I was. I had been with my new host fifteen minutes, and already a tense discussion had taken place.

I was honour bred. I knew I could no longer stay in his house. But where would I go? It was after ten at night. The roads were all blocked.

I telephoned my little back-to-the-land friend some 40 miles away. "You have to come and get me," I whispered.

"Now?" he said.

"If you don't mind. You wouldn't have a skidoo or something?"

"No, I have no skidoo—I'd have to take the car."

"Car is fine—I like a car—"

"But it's snowing—"

"Yes."

"What happened?"

"It would be better if you just came and got me as quickly as possible—" I said.

"If I go over the mountain pass—I won't be found until next spring—"

(long pause)

"I know, I know, but desperate circumstances call for desperate measures. That's a chance I'm willing that you take." I sighed.

I said my goodbye to the host, and stood outside the house with my suitcase. The man looked out the window at me now and again, as I waited for my friend, and closed the curtains when I glanced back at him.

Snowstorms were different in this part of Canada. But it was still Canada, dark and gloomy.

It had all started because of a thought I shared that evening. I had thought at supper, that from this part of the world—at this very time of year, in 1961 the Trail Smoke Eaters had left for their long and famous journey. This is what I had told my host. I had happened to mention that journey. The trip to Europe. The idea of hockey versus the dratted ice hockey.

He had come here from Britain in 1969. He had read my books. He thought we'd be kindred spirits, bred of the same bone. And he said, "My good God man— that sounds a bit nationalistic."

It wasn't so much Trail, it was the World Juniors. I was talking about their fight against the Russians at suppertime.

"Didya see when the lad from Big Cove smucked the Russian in the head—set him on his ass?" I asked.

He looked at me as if I might be rather subhuman.

Well, it wasn't so much the World Juniors—it was Team Canada. It was the Summit Series of '72. It was—

"Good God man. I thought you were a novelist," he said.

"Novelist shmovelist—" I said.

So here I was outside waiting, as the snow poured down out of the gloom. But it was too late to turn back.

After an hour I saw the headlights of my friend's compact car coming down the street.

My heart leaped with joy. And in I got.

We turned about and started back into the gloomy night, the windshield wipers on high and visibility almost zero. And besides that my ears popping off every time we went up and down a hill.

"What happened?" he said, finally. "Didn't the reading go as planned?"

"No no—it went all right—for a stormy night. Some showed up—well three or four snowshoed in. I gave a pretty good reading—got to know them all on a first-name basis."

(silence)

"Well—what was the problem?"

"An age old problem," I said seriously.

"Oh yes," he said, looking at me and not understanding, "an age old problem." He smiled gently. "What age old problem is that, David?"

(I know when people finally address me as "David" I am about to make a fool of myself. That I have once again crossed the line from rational human being to something else. So I knew I had to answer him as impassioned and as sincerely as possible. So he would know he had not risked his life for nothing.)

"That son of a bitch doesn't like hockey," I said.

I began to think then that I would go back home, to my childhood home, and see the place again where we went sliding. Where we played hockey on the river. I would make the pilgrimage, for it had to be made.

I would smell the flat ice and the smoke over the dark, stunted trees again. I would visit the place where Michael grew up, and poor Tobias, and see the old lanes we all played road hockey on. Paul and Stafford and Darren and all of us.

But they would be ghosts to me now. Almost everyone was gone. The laughter against the frigid, blue skies would have all disappeared, evaporated like the slush under our boots in 1961.

I found myself somewhere in Northern Ontario, later in the month. I forget the name of the town. It was one of those reading tours where somehow you no longer know where you are.

Again I was billeted. The woman kept a bed-and-breakfast of some kind. I was given a small room at the back of the house. There was a hockey game that night. I don't remember who was playing—it may have been Montreal. It may have been Edmonton. It may have been anyone.

I could hear, far away, the shouts of the crowd, the sound of the announcer. And I left my room and began to look for the TV.

The woman met me in the kitchen.

"Are you hungry?"

"No—I can hear a game coming from somewhere—I just thought someone might be watching it."

"Oh," the woman said. "That's Burl."

"Burl?"

"My husband," she said. "We don't live together anymore—he lives downstairs and I live upstairs. He's downstairs."

"Oh," I said. "Downstairs."

"So if you want to go on downstairs and watch the game—"

"Well—I don't want to intrude."

"Burl? Intrude on Burl? Burl don't mind."

I went back into my room and sat on the edge of the bed fidgeting. There was a great roar. Perhaps Roy had made a fantabulous save. Maybe Burl wouldn't mind.

The wind howled. I could see a streetlight far away from the small window next to my bed.

Things in hockey were changing every day. Canadians and Russians were now playing on the same lines, in arenas all across the United States. The two greatest Canada Cups had already taken place—and within six years it would be called "the World Cup." (I didn't know that then of course.)

Everything was changing. But not so much for *our* benefit—yet we pretended that it was. We still pretended that the NHL was ours. It was always one way to get along. That's what Canadians were like.

Suddenly I felt nostalgic. It would be good to catch the last few periods of a game. I left my room, opened the basement door and tiptoed down.

Then I caught myself. What would I do if I was sitting watching a hockey game and a stranger came tiptoeing around the corner?

I knocked on the side of the wall. No one answered. I hesitated and then walked into the room.

Sideways to me was a man, sitting on the leather couch in his underwear, with a pint of beer between his legs, staring at the television.

"G'day?"

I thought he looked over at me, and nodded.

So I sat down on the chair near the couch and began to watch the game.

It seemed as if Burl had been relegated to a kind of subterranean prison life. There were no windows in the basement, but he had curtains up. He had a huge bar, with two barstools, and a clock that told the time backwards. Above the bar was a picture of himself with a tiny bass, and under the picture his signature, and the words *bass master*. In the picture he was smiling as if he knew in his heart he wasn't a real bass master.

I was beginning to get comfortable. It seemed as if Burl and I would get along.

Suddenly something happened in the game, and we both started yelling at the television. Then roared at the obvious cheap shot someone made.

Burl shook his head. I shook my head. Burl got up and went to the fridge and taking out a beer, opened it. He turned about and started back. I was watching the television and grinning. Suddenly, he stopped. He turned. He looked down. He stared at me as if he had never seen me before.

"Who the Christ are you?"

"David," I said.

"David—David who?—what are you doing here?"

"You know—watching the game here—if you don't mind?"

"Where in hell are you from?"

"The Maritimes—"

"The *Maritimes*—what in the living name of God gives you the right to travel up from the Maritimes?"

"I don't know—"

I began to get a little flustered. He was standing in his underwear with a pint of Molson, and his little bass master photograph on the wall. He turned about, and there in his chair was a man from the Maritimes watching the game.

However, he could understand one thing. He could understand *why* I wanted to watch it. It was only a shock initially because I was watching it in *his* house.

Once I explained why that had to be, he was satisfied. Although, he did not offer me a beer.

Later, I even got to talk about my feelings on the game. How there are two *theirs* in the game, and how *our* game doesn't seem to count anymore. How one *their* is the product of business interests in the States—how we think it is *their* game; and how the second *their* is one that is strangely joined to the first *their*. The second *their* is the European *their*. How European ice hockey is supposedly more *moral* and *refined* then *our game* is. How we need European ice hockey to teach us a lesson. And that both of these *theirs* are linked in trying to defeat the *our* in hockey.

How probably this has already been done. How the huge arenas in the States and the lack of hockey in Hamilton attest to this, more than any of the false promises, or our pretence of still controlling our game does.

Maybe he didn't understand what I said. But he probably did. He probably already knew all of what I was saying before I said it. He understood Henderson's goal and what it meant. He understood when I spoke about my childhood friends, Michael and Tobias, and Stafford, and the game we played on the river in 1961. Because he himself had played those games too.

And of course I always spoke of Stafford Foley when I spoke of hockey. I thought of him on September 28, 1972. I thought of him twenty years later to the day.

September 28, 1992, I was at home in Saint John watching the news when they announced the anniversary of Henderson's goal. It put the hosts at a loss. They did not know how to approach it—as a human interest story or a noteworthy date in history. Finally it seemed that the best way to acknowledge to their audience that it was an anniversary of perhaps the most famous goal ever scored by a Canadian was to be whimsical and remote about its significance.

They laughed as if they didn't want to be known as the ones to credit this as serious historical information. What relevance would Canadians attach to it "now"? one of the announcers asked. And then added that her sport was baseball. You see, she was only pretending to be indifferent. But no one is indifferent to hockey in our country, and so it was a self congratulatory indifference—one that looked out at her audience and said, "I have risen above the game you wish me to celebrate as mine."

Without a doubt in my mind, the franchises in the United States need this reaction from us to exist. If they did not have it—if it was for one moment decided that the game was ours—there would be no lights on in St. Louis before there were lights on at Copps Colosseum. Winnipeg would not be going the way of Quebec.

It was 1984 and I was writer-in-residence at a university in New Brunswick. The Canada Cup was on. The night before, Team Canada had beaten the Russians in overtime to advance to the finals.

In the former Soviet Union, the game against the Russians was on tape delay. All night, all day long, the phone was ringing at the Canadian Embassy in Moscow to ask what the final score was, who won the game. I knew who had won the game. I had watched it live. I wanted to celebrate. I wanted to talk about how exciting it was. I knew no one in Fredericton, however, except for certain English professors. And, as admirable as English professors tend to be, they were a different breed than I.

I went into the common room and poured myself a coffee and sat down—waiting for the arrival of someone to talk to. A young female professor from Newcastle Creek entered the room. She was a nice lady, and had met me once at the president's house. She'd once made the remark that she didn't see how anyone would be able to live without reading Henry James.

As she sat there I glanced at her. Go on, I said to myself, Ask her—she's from Newcastle Creek—Newcastle Creek for God's sake. She'd have cut her teeth on hockey.

I made a stab at my coffee with a stir-stick and looked about. Twice I went to the door and looked down the hall to see if anyone else was coming.

Finally I could stand it no longer. Turning to her I ventured, "Did you see the game last night?"

"Pardon?"

"Did you see the hockey game?"

"We don't have a television," she said.

"Oh, what's wrong?" I said. "Is it broken?"

Then I thought that maybe she and her husband had a fight over a program and someone had thrown the television through the wall—I know people who do that, so I thought—well she was from Newcastle Creek, so I'd better be discreet.

"We don't approve of television," she said.

There was an awkward silence.

I looked about, mumbled something to myself. "Right in front of the net—they score."

I too was from New Brunswick, I too had cut my teeth on hockey. I too remember sitting in front of an ancient black-and-white television watching the small figures of men gliding up and down the ice. I remembered the Richard riot, and how even then I thought it was ugly.

But I had entered, for the first time, another realm, where a woman from Newcastle Creek who may or may not have grown up on salt cod and moose meat could tell me that she disapproved of television and not be a fundamentalist. Could tell me that I wasn't alive until I read Henry James and believe it.

"My husband was up early—to listen to the radio so he could hear the score," she said.

"Oh," I said. I smiled. I had misjudged her. Forever I would be sorry for it.

"Yes," I said. "Did he find out?"

"Yes—he's heartbroken."

"No," I said, "not heartbroken—we won—Canada won 3–2."

She looked at me, as if I really was such a country bumpkin. And I suppose when considering it, I have been looked at like this almost all my life over something or other.

"But we were going for the Russians," she said.

"No," I said.

I had the same tone as a man might who had just learned that the *Titanic* had sunk or Passchendaele had cost us thousands of men for 50 yards of mud.

Hearing my tone, the tone of a person bleeding, maybe she felt as if she had won a moral victory.

"Well, we both hate Gretzky you see." Her accent now turned slightly British.

"Why?"

"Oh, he's just such a Canadian." She smiled.

"You hate greatness or just Canadian greatness?" I asked.

In a way, Canadians have been asking this question all of their lives. And while asking this question they have been running to outsiders for the answer.

In a way my learned friend's stance embodies the notion of the intelligentsia that hockey is a part of what is wrong with our country.

Of course I know this about my country. I have known it since Stafford Foley used to debate the merits of Alex Delvecchio in a room at the tavern, as if he could turn back the clock and make, with the original six, everything right with the world again and with himself.

It was, by some rascals, rather smart-alecky to cheer for the Russians. I remember this all to well.

It was December 31, 1975—all day I waited. Red Army was playing Montreal. I was in Victoria with an acquaintance. He was extremely adept (or he thought he was) at taking the opposite position—the educated, therefore contrived, outrageous part. And so he "wished" to cheer for the Russians. He felt *no one else* would be doing this. (He would only have to listen to one CBC commentary to realize how Canadians bent over backwards to kiss the Russian behinds in order to be fair.)

I shouted at him, told him if he had only known the dozens of minutes of unrecognizable penalties that were given to our amateurs in Sweden and Czechoslovakia over the years he'd feel different. Or if he had only known the hundreds of thousands of dollars that Hockey Canada had given to the Russians to help their sport, he may change his mind.

He stared at me, as if I had not just said something wrong. It went well beyond this. It was as if I had demonstrated the kind of unfair sportsmanship he was ridiculing. "My Good God man—get a hold of yourself; it's only a game—you're frightening the house guests."

What was under attack was simply fear of a lack of Canadian identity. And he, a learned man whose father was a poet, connected to a university, did not wish to have anything to do with the sport that could make us feel—even man-handle us into feeling—Canadian. It was supposed to be done another way; I suppose a more *civilized* way. (Also it was the elitist idea that the ideal of Soviet life was one that hinged on working-class fairness.)

For most people who talk this polemic against hockey as a point of identity there is a certain degree of cant, of wrong-headedness. Besides, part of this kind of conceit hinges on the identity crisis itself. Because some of us continue to believe that Canadians are famous for nothing except hockey. Therefore they argue that Canadians must be greater than what they are famous for.

My answer to that has always been yes and no. And hockey, when you know what it says about us as a people, proves it.

So we sat in silence, he and I, in a little room on that long ago New Year's Eve. Montreal did not win that game as we all know. They tied Red Army 3–3, after outplaying them and outshooting them by a margin of 4–1. Tretiak, who the Czechs always seemed mystified by our inability to score against, saved them—and Dryden was in net for us.

Dryden never played that well against the Soviets, but all in all, well enough.

I remember at one point during that game Guy Lafleur stickhandling at centre ice, and mystifying three Russian players. It comes back to me time and again when I am lectured, usually by university professors, on how the Europeans taught us finesse, and how shameful I am not to record that. I will and do record the Russians' greatness. But, my son, they did not teach us finesse.

Finesse in the age of Orr and Lafleur?

Finesse in the age of Lemieux and Gretzky? In the age of Savard (Denis) or a hundred others?

I was in Australia in 1993, at a literary festival. It is a wonderful country and has a rugby league and Australian rules. In some way (this is exaggerated) the difference between these two kinds of rugby is the same as the difference between ice hockey and hockey.

I was sitting with a writer from the Czech Republic and a woman who worked for Penguin Books. The writer from the Czech Republic and I had an interesting conversation about Australia and how it compared to our countries. All of a sudden he gave a start, and he said, "Oh—you are *Canadian*—I thought you were an American—so mister Canadianman tell me—who is the greatest hockey player in the world today?"

"Gretzky or Lemieux—I'm not sure which," I replied.

"Gretzky or Lemieux—Gretzky or Lemieux—bahhh! What about Jagr—?"

"Who?" the young woman from Penguin asked.

"Jagr—Jagr—the greatest to ever exist."

"Great, no doubt," I said. "Definitely a great asset to the Penguins—but not the greatest who ever lived—he isn't even the greatest of his era—he isn't even the greatest for the Penguins."

"Pardon me?" the woman from Penguin said.

"The Penguins would be nothing without him," my Czech acquaintance said.

"I agree—he is great—but Lemieux is far greater—anyway the Penguins might get rid of them both within the next few years. I am very cynical about it."

"Who are they?" the woman from Penguin said.

She made a stab. "So what do you think of Kundera?" she said to the Czech gentleman after a moment's silence.

"Kundera—what team does he play for?" the Czech writer asked, and winked my way.

The sales representative from Penguin excused herself and did not come back to the table. Her meal got cold. This is true, and I feel badly about this now (a little).

Earlier that day in Melbourne, I needed a pair of shoes for this particular dinner. I went with my wife and son to a shoe store near our hotel. In this store one of the salesmen was a young Russian immigrant. He was fairly new to his job, and new to Australia.

He told me that the one thing he missed was hockey. He mentioned Larionov and Fetisov—he asked me if Fetisov had retired. I was never a big fan of Fetisov (except when he got punched in the head by Clarke) but I understood that his hockey talk was more than a sales pitch. And even if it were only a sales pitch *it worked*. For how many customers could he have used it on in Melbourne?

Years before, in my home town I got drunk one night with a boxer off a Russian ship. We liked each other very much. We talked two things—hockey and boxing. The only thing I can say is that all through the evening this partisan Russian who lived fifteen miles from Leningrad never once mentioned hockey as "ice hockey."

Ah but the game is lost boys, the game is lost. To go on about it, at times, is like a farm boy kicking a dead horse to get up out of a puddle.

But still, some horses are worth a kick or two. And if it is good and even noble to have sport, and if hockey is *our* sport, and if we can make the claim that we play hockey better than any other country—if we can make that claim, without having to listen to apologies about why we made it—then who speaks for *us,* as a HOCKEY nation, when three-quarters of our NHL teams are in the States, and 324 of our players as well?

It is not America's fault, maybe not even ours. Perhaps it is just the nature of the economic beast. And a few years back—in the dark age of Mulroney, when we spoke about selling out our culture, what great ballet were we thinking of—what great ballet had we already let go?

I remember an American friend laughing when she asked where Canada got its baseball players. It was the year Toronto lost to Kansas City and it had put a scare into many Americans. In fact, this lady's hair stood on end the entire time I spoke to her.

I was in New Orleans for a reading tour when the lady asked me this. I stated, "They come from the States or Puerto Rico or the Dominican Republic I believe."

She burst out laughing.

The laugh was insulting. And I countered it. I told her that most NHL players were from Canada.

But she did not respond to this. For hockey had no meaning for her. She stared at me as if I was being flippant. I suppose I was. It has always been a part of my nature. Half pathologically shy, and half flippant. Even when I was little.

PERSONAL RESPONSE

Nostalgia is a kind of warm reflection when we look back on something with glossy, or even glassy, eyes. In this piece by Adams, there is a looking-back upon a certain feeling, or mixed feelings, that circle around the meaning of hockey. What are those feelings, where do they come from, and do you share or even understand his passion for hockey? For what things do you feel nostalgic, and do any of these have associations with what it means to be Canadian?

QUESTIONS FOR CLASS OR SMALL-GROUP DISCUSSION

1. There are a few places when single sentences jump out of this text. Try to locate a couple of these, and discuss why they jump out, and how they affect your reading of the text.

2. At one point Richards writes, "Everything was changing." What, exactly, are the things that "Everything" refers to? What are Richards' concerns, and where do they come from?

3. How would you describe Richards' tone (his attitude toward his subject) in the piece? Does it change? Is it consistent? What is achieved using this tone?

4. What do you think Richards is trying to say through all the little sub-stories and characters in this piece? Summarize what hockey means for Richards.

5. In Canada is hockey "only a game"? If not, what else is it, or what does it represent? How did it become, for many, a national obsession? Is this obsession a good or bad thing? Discuss.

6. Richards goes back and forth across the country, and even to other places in the world, to come up with his rambling contemplations of "the game." What do you think he might be looking for?

7. In your group, have everyone write one sentence about what hockey means, if anything. Separate those who love the game, those who think the game is okay, and those who don't really care. Now debate your point of view so that the others will be convinced to think like you. Take note of what happens in the discussion.

FOR FURTHER VIEWING: THE NATIONAL GAME

The Sweater [animation] (1980); *Net Worth* (1995); *The Rocket* (2005); *Gross Misconduct* (1993); *Slap Shot* (1977); *Rhino Brothers* (2001).

CHAPTER TEN

FILM AND TELEVISION

INTRODUCTION

The movie industry has survived the emergence of television in the mid-20th century and the proliferation of videos, computers, DVDs, widescreen TVs, and downloadable movies in the 21st century. But how has technology changed movies—and the way we see movies? According to Susan Sontag, cinema, once heralded as the art of the 20th century, has become a derivative art that tries to copy past successes. Television is seen as a vast, mindless wasteland. But how will computers change television in the future? Despite new viewing technology appearing almost daily, film and television still must rely on a good story—on the written word. Although special effects, famous actors, and exotic locations can woo viewers, does all good television and cinema depend, more than anything else, on a good story?

NEW AGE DAYDREAMS

Pauline Kael

Pauline Kael (1919–2001) was the film critic at The New Yorker *from 1967 to 1991. She is considered one of the most influential film critics ever and was known for her biting and incisive reviews. She encouraged audiences to see lesser-known movies and was notable for her research into the making of Orson Welles's classic,* Citizen Kane. *Her film criticism has been collected in several best-selling editions.*

A friend of mine broke up with his woman friend after they went to see *Field of Dreams:* she liked it. As soon as I got home from *Dances With Wolves,* I ran to the phone and warned him not to go to it with his new woman friend. Set during the Civil War, this new big Indians-versus-Cavalry epic is about how the white men drove the Native Americans from their land. But Kevin Costner, who directed *Dances With Wolves* and stars in it, is not a man who lets himself be ripped apart by the violent cruelty of what happened. He's no extremist: it's a middle-of-the-road epic. Lieutenant Dunbar (Costner), a Union officer, sees that the Sioux have a superior culture—they're held up as models for the rest of us—and he changes sides. Costner must have heard Joseph Campbell on PBS advising people to "follow your bliss." This is a nature-boy movie, a kid's daydream of being an Indian. When Dunbar has become a Sioux named Dances With Wolves, he writes in his journal that he knows for the first time who he really is. Costner has feathers in his hair and feathers in his head.

Once our hero has become an Indian, we don't have to feel torn or divided. We can see that the white men are foulmouthed, dirty louts. The movie—Costner's début as a director—is childishly naïve. When Lieutenant Dunbar is alone with his pet wolf, he's like Robinson Crusoe on Mars. When he tries to get to know the Sioux, and he and they are feeling each other out, it's like a sci-fi film that has the hero trying to communicate with an alien race. But in this movie it's the white men who are the aliens: the smelly brutes are even killing each other, in the war between the North and the South. Luckily, we Indians are part of a harmonious community. Dances With Wolves has never seen people "so dedicated to their families." And he loves their humor.

At the beginning, there's a bizarre Civil War battle sequence with the wounded Lieutenant Dunbar riding on horseback between rows of Union and Confederate soldiers, his arms outstretched, welcoming bullets in a Christlike embrace, and throughout the movie he is brutalized, seems dead, but rises again. (Does getting beaten give Costner a self-righteous feeling? Even when it's as unconvincingly staged as it is here?) There's nothing really campy or shamelessly flamboyant after the opening. There isn't even anything with narrative power or bite to it. This Western is like a New Age social-studies lesson. It isn't really revisionist; it's the old stuff toned down and sensitized.

Costner and his friend Michael Blake, who worked up the material with him in mind and then wrote the novel and the screenplay, are full of good will. They're trying to show the last years of the Sioux as an independent nation from the Sioux point of view. And it's that sympathy for the Indians that (I think) the audience is responding to. But Costner and Blake are moviemaking novices. Instead of helping us understand the Sioux, they simply make the Sioux like genial versions of us. The film provides the groovy wisdom of the Sioux on the subjects of peace and togetherness: you never fight among yourselves—you negotiate. Each of the Indian characters is given a trait or two; they all come across as simple-minded, but so does the hero. Even the villains are endearingly dumb, the way they are in stories children write.

There's nothing affected about Costner's acting or directing. You hear his laid-back, surfer accent; you see his deliberate goofy faints and falls, and all the close-ups of his handsomeness. This epic was made by a bland megalomaniac. (The Indians should have named him Plays with Camera.) You look at that untroubled face and know he can make everything lightweight. How is he as a director? Well, he has moments of competence. And the movie has an authentic vastness. The wide-screen cinematography, by Dean Semler, features the ridges, horizons, and golden sunsets of South Dakota; it is pictorial rather than emotionally expressive, but it is spacious and open at times, and there are fine images of buffalo pounding by.

Mostly, the action is sluggish and the scenes are poorly shaped. Crowds of moviegoers love the movie, though—maybe partly because the issues have been made so simple. As soon as you see the Indians, amused, watch the hero frolicking with his wolf, you know that the white men will kill it. Maybe, also, crowds love this epic because it is so innocent: Costner shows us his bare ass like a kid at camp feeling one with the great outdoors. He is the boyish man of the hour: the Sioux onscreen revere him, because he is heroic and modest, too. TV interviewers acclaim him for the same qualities. He is the Orson Welles that everybody wants—Orson Welles with no belly.

PERSONAL RESPONSE

How did Kael's review make you feel? Did you want to rent a copy of Costner's movie after reading the review? How does she persuade the reader—what techniques does she use? Her review seems to be a belittling attack on the protagonist and director of the movie, Kevin Costner; she compares him to a surfer. Why? To what effect? After seeing the movie, which uses the Lakota language with English subtitles, do you agree with her assessment of the film?

QUESTIONS FOR CLASS OR SMALL-GROUP DISCUSSION

1. How does Kael communicate her dislike of Costner's movie? Give some examples of the distinctive language she uses to try to persuade the reader of her point of view. How would you describe her tone?

2. What does Kael mean by "Robinson Crusoe on Mars"? Is she referring to the 1964 science-fiction movie of the same name, or does she intend something else?

3. Despite Kael's criticism, she admits the movie was popular. Why do you think people were attracted to the movie and its themes? What does the movie say about war? How does the movie compare to a traditional western or the stereotypical "cowboy and Indian" movies that were produced in Hollywood in the 1940s and 1950s?

4. Canadian actor Graham Greene played Kicking Bird and was nominated for an Academy Award for Best Supporting Actor. He was born on the Six Nations Reserve in Ontario. Make a list of other major Canadian actors, singers, or comedians who had or have careers in American show business. What has made them so successful south of the border? Can you name any other First Nations celebrities from Canada?

5. What is the worst movie you have recently seen? What made it so bad? Be specific and convincing.

A CENTURY OF CINEMA

Susan Sontag

Susan Sontag, one of the twentieth century's pre-eminent thinkers and human rights activists, was born in New York City in 1933. She grew up in Tucson, Arizona, and attended high school in Los Angeles. She received her B.A. from the University of Chicago and did graduate work in philosophy, literature, and theology at Harvard University and Saint Anne's College, Oxford. Her books include four novels; a collection of short stories; several plays; and eight works of nonfiction, starting with Against Interpretation *and including* On Photography, Illness as Metaphor, Where the Stress Falls, *and* Regarding the Pain of Others. *She also wrote and directed four feature-length films. Her books have been translated into thirty-two languages. She died in 2004.*

Cinema's hundred years appear to have the shape of a life cycle: an inevitable birth, the steady accumulation of glories, and the onset in the last decade of an ignominious, irreversible decline. This doesn't mean that there won't be any more new films one can admire. But such films will not simply be exceptions; that's true of great achievement in any art. They will have to be heroic violations of the norms and practices which now govern moviemaking everywhere in the capitalist and would-be capitalist world— which is to say, everywhere. And ordinary films, films made purely for entertainment (that is, commercial) purposes, will continue to be astonishingly witless; already the vast majority fail resoundingly to appeal to their cynically targeted audiences. While the point of a great film is now, more than ever, to be a one-of-a-kind achievement, the commercial cinema has settled for a policy of bloated, derivative filmmaking, a brazen combinatory or re-combinatory art, in the hope of reproducing past successes. Every film that hopes to reach the largest possible audience is designed as some kind of remake. Cinema, once heralded as *the* art of the twentieth century, seems now, as the century closes numerically, to be a decadent art.

Perhaps it is not cinema which has ended but only cinephilia—the name of the distinctive kind of love that cinema inspired. Each art breeds its fanatics. The love movies aroused was more imperial. It was born of the conviction that cinema was an art unlike any other: quintessentially modern; distinctively accessible; poetic and mysterious and erotic and moral—all at the same time. Cinema had apostles (it was like religion). Cinema was a crusade. Cinema was a world view. Lovers of poetry or opera or dance don't think there is *only* poetry or opera or dance. But lovers of cinema could think there was only cinema. That the movies encapsulated everything—and they did. It was both the book of art and the book of life.

As many have noted, the start of moviemaking a hundred years ago was, conveniently, a double start. In that first year, 1895, two kinds of films were made, proposing two modes of what cinema could be: cinema as the transcription of real, unstaged life (the Lumière brothers) and cinema as invention, artifice, illusion, fantasy (Méliès). But this was never a true opposition. For those first audiences watching the Lumière brothers' *The Arrival of a Train at La Ciotat Station*, the camera's transmission of a banal sight was a fantastic experience. Cinema began in wonder, the wonder that reality can be transcribed with such magical immediacy. All of cinema is an attempt to perpetrate and to reinvent the sense of wonder.

Everything begins with that moment, one hundred years ago, when the train pulled into the station. People took movies into themselves, just as the public cried out with excitement, actually ducked, as the train seemed to move toward *them*. Until the advent of television emptied the movie theatres, it was from a weekly visit to the cinema that you learned (or tried to learn) how to strut, to smoke, to kiss, to fight, to grieve. Movies gave you tips about how to be attractive, such as . . . it looks good to wear a raincoat even when it isn't raining. But whatever you took home from the movies was only a part of the larger experience of losing yourself in faces, in lives that were *not* yours—which is the more inclusive form of desire embodied in the movie experience. The strongest experience was simply to surrender to, to be transported by, what was on the screen. You wanted to be kidnapped by the movie.

The prerequisite of being kidnapped was to be overwhelmed by the physical presence of the image. And the conditions of "going to the movies" secured that experience. To see a great film only on television isn't to have really seen that film. (This is equally true of those made for TV, like Fassbinder's *Berlin Alexanderplatz*, and the two *Heimat* films of Edgar Reitz.) It's not only the difference of dimensions: the superiority of the larger-than-you image in the theater to the little image on the box at home. The conditions of paying attention in a domestic space are radically disrespectful of film. Since film no longer has a standard size, home screens can be as big as living room or bedroom walls. But you are still in a living room or a bedroom, alone or with familiars. To be kidnapped, you have to be in a movie theater, seated in the dark among anonymous strangers.

No amount of mourning will revive the vanished rituals—erotic, ruminative—of the darkened theater. The reduction of cinema to assaultive images, and the unprincipled manipulation of images (faster and faster cutting) to be more attention-grabbing, have produced a disincarnated, lightweight cinema that doesn't demand anyone's full attention. Images now appear in any size and on a variety of surfaces: on a screen in a theater, on home screens as small as the palm of your hand or as big as a wall, on disco walls and mega-screens hanging above sports arenas and the outsides of tall public buildings. The sheer ubiquity of moving images has steadily undermined the standards people once had both for cinema as art at its most serious and for cinema as popular entertainment.

In the first years there was, essentially, no difference between cinema as art and cinema as entertainment. And *all* films of the silent era—from the master-pieces of Feuillade, D. W. Griffith, Dziga Vertov, Pabst, Murnau and King Vidor to the most formula-ridden melodramas and comedies—look, are, better than most what was to follow. With the coming of sound, the image-making lost much of its brilliance and poetry, and commercial standards tightened. This way of making movies—the Hollywood system—dominated filmmaking for about twenty-five years (roughly from 1930 to 1955). The most original directors, like Erich von Stroheim and Orson Welles, were defeated by the system and eventually went into artistic exile in Europe—where more or less the same quality-defeating system was in place with lower budgets; only in France were a large number of superb films produced throughout this period. Then, in the mid-1950s, vanguard ideas took hold again, rooted in the idea of cinema as a craft pioneered by the Italian films of the early postwar era. A dazzling number of original, passionate films of the highest seriousness got made with new actors and tiny crews, went to film festivals (of which there were more and more), and from there, garlanded with festival prizes, into movie theaters around the world. This golden age actually lasted as long as twenty years.

It was at this specific moment in the hundred-year history of cinema that going to movies, thinking about movies, talking about movies became a passion among university students and other young people. You fell in love not just with actors but with cinema itself. Cinephilia had first become visible in the 1950s in France: its forum was the legendary film magazine *Cahiers du Cinéma* (followed by similarly fervent magazines in Germany, Italy, Great Britain, Sweden, the United States and Canada). Its temples, as it spread throughout Europe and the Americas, were the cinematheques and film clubs specializing in films from the past and directors' retro-spectives. The 1960s and early 1970s were the age of feverish moviegoing, with the full-time cinephile always hoping to find a seat as close as possible to the big screen, ideally the third row center. "One can't live without Rossellini," declares a character in Bertolucci's *Before the Revolution* (1964)—and means it.

Cinephilia—a source of exultation in the films of Godard and Truffaut and the early Bertolucci and Syberberg; a morose lament in the recent films of Nani Moretti—was mostly a Western European affair. The great directors of "the other Europe" (Zanussi in Poland, Angelopoulos in Greece, Tarkovsky and Sokurov in Russia, Jancsó and Tarr in Hungary) and the great Japanese directors (Ozu, Mizoguchi, Kurosawa, Naruse, Oshima, Imamura) have tended not to be cinephiles, perhaps because in Budapest or Moscow or Tokyo or Warsaw or Athens there wasn't a chance to get a cinematheque education. The distinctive thing about cinephile taste

Kurosawa's Seven Samurai: *Heroes from another culture*
Photo Source: CP/Everett

was that it embraced both "art" films and popular films. Thus, European cinephilia had a romantic relation to the films of certain directors of Hollywood at the apogee of the studio system: Godard for Howard Hawks, Fassbinder for Douglas Sirk. Of course, this moment—when cinephilia emerged—was also the moment when the Hollywood studio system was breaking up. It seemed that moviemaking had re-won the right to experiment; cinephiles could *afford* to be passionate (or sentimental) about the old Hollywood genre films. A host of new people came into cinema, including a generation of young film critics from *Cahiers du Cinéma;* the towering figure of that generation, indeed of several decades of filmmaking anywhere, was Jean-Luc Godard. A few writers turned out to be wildly talented filmmakers: Alexander Kluge in Germany, Pier Paolo Pasolini in Italy. (The model for the writer who turns to filmmaking actually emerged earlier, in France, with Pagnol in the 1930s and Cocteau in the 1940s; but it was not until the 1960s that this seemed, at least in Europe, normal.) Cinema appeared to be reborn.

For some fifteen years there was a profusion of masterpieces, and one allowed oneself to imagine that this would go on forever. To be sure, there was always a conflict between cinema as an industry and cinema as an art, cinema as routine and cinema as experiment. But the conflict was not such as to make impossible the making of wonderful films, sometimes within and sometimes outside of mainstream cinema. Now the balance has tipped decisively in favor of cinema as an industry. The great cinema of the 1960s and 1970s has been thoroughly repudiated. Already in the 1970s Hollywood was plagiarizing and banalizing the innovations in narrative method and editing of successful new European and ever-marginal independent American films. Then came the catastrophic rise in production costs in the 1980s, which secured the worldwide reimposition of industry standards of making and distributing films on a far more coercive, this time truly global, scale. The result can be seen in the melancholy fate of some of the greatest directors of the last decades. What place is there today for a maverick like Hans Jürgen Syberberg, who has stopped making films altogether, or for the great Godard, who now makes films about the history of film on video? Consider some other cases. The internationalizing of financing and therefore of casts was a disaster for Andrei Tarkovsky in the last two films of his stupendous, tragically abbreviated career. And these conditions for making films have proved to be as much an artistic disaster for two of the most valuable directors still working: Krzysztof Zanussi (*The Structure of Crystals, Illumination, Spiral, Contract*) and Theo Angelopoulos (*Reconstruction, Days of '36, The Travelling Players*). And what will happen now to Béla Tarr (*Damnation, Satantango*)? And how will Aleksandr Sokurov (*Save and Protect, Days of Eclipse, The Second Circle, Stone, Whispering Pages*) find the money to go on making films, his sublime films, under the rude conditions of Russian capitalism?

Predictably, the love of cinema has waned. People still like going to the movies, and some people still care about and expect something special, necessary from a film. And wonderful films are still being made: Mike Leigh's *Naked*, Gianni Amelio's *Lamerica*, Hou Hsiao-hsien's *Goodbye South, Goodbye*, and Abbas Kiarostami's *Close-Up* and Koker trilogy. But one hardly finds anymore, at least among the young, the distinctive cinephilic love of movies, which is not simply love of but a certain *taste* in films (grounded in a vast appetite for seeing and reseeing as much as possible of cinema's glorious past). Cinephilia itself has come under attack, as something quaint, outmoded, snobbish. For cinephilia implies that films are unique, unrepeatable, magic experiences. Cinephilia tells us that the Hollywood remake of Godard's *Breathless* cannot be as good as the original. Cinephilia has no role in the era of hyperindustrial films. For by the very range and eclecticism of its passions, cinephilia cannot help but sponsor the idea of the film as, first of all, a poetic object; and cannot help but incite those outside the movie industry, like painters and writers, to want to make films, too. It is precisely this that must be defeated. That has been defeated.

If cinephilia is dead, then movies are dead . . . no matter how many movies, even very good ones, go on being made. If cinema can be resurrected, it will only be through the birth of a new kind of cine-love.

PERSONAL RESPONSE

What role does watching movies play in your life? Do you prefer to watch movies at home or in a darkened theatre surrounded by strangers? What are your three favourite movies of all time, and what kind of movies are they?

QUESTIONS FOR CLASS OR SMALL-GROUP DISCUSSION

1. Sontag says that cinema is an attempt to perpetuate or re-invent the sense of wonder that reality can be transcribed with magical immediacy. However, she also says that contemporary film is often "witless" and characterized by pointless rapid cutting between images. Name two contemporary films that illustrate her position. What is the effect of the quick cut on you, the viewer?

2. How have music videos affected commercial cinema?

3. Do you believe that commercial cinema has become a combinatory or re-combinatory art? What exactly does Sontag mean by "combinatory"?

4. Examine the relationship between cinema and capitalism and the effect of showcases such as the Sundance Film Festival on independent filmmaking. What, in your opinion, is the effect of the Toronto International Film Festival on moviegoers' tastes? In what ways does the Toronto festival differ from Cannes?

5. Agree or disagree with Sontag's contention that if cinema can be resurrected, it can only be through a new kind of cine-love.

6. In Sontag's essay, originally published in 1995, in the German newspaper *Frankfurter Rundschau,* she writes that cinema appears to be in an irreversible decline. Do you believe cinema is still declining? Can you give at least three examples that support your point of view?

TRAILER PARK BOYS

DAN BROWN

Dan Brown is the senior arts editor and reporter for the Canadian Broadcasting Corporation (CBC); he was also an editor and senior writer for Newsworld International and helped establish the National Post's *Arts & Life section.*

April may prove to be a decisive month in the life of *Trailer Park Boys.*

On April 11, the series about three Nova Scotia petty criminals shot in the style of a faux documentary returns for a fourth season on Showcase, the Canadian specialty channel on which it originated and developed a loyal audience.

A few days later, on April 15, the show will have the first cross-border test of its appeal. That's when it will debut on BBC America, a digital network available to viewers in the United States.

Will the hard-living characters—who have become Canadian icons in only a few short years on cable—strike a chord with people outside this country? "We're going to find out soon enough," says Mike Volpe, the show's executive producer.

Good ol' Canadian boys?
Photo Source: CP/*Halifax Daily News*/Scott Dunlop

Only one thing is certain: *Trailer Park Boys* will rise or fall based on the trio of foul-mouthed misfits at the heart of the program. As with many successful TV comedies, viewers aren't tuning in to see how the show's plots turn out; story is secondary to character.

"Look at *Seinfeld*. If recent TV history has taught us anything, it's that the premise really isn't that important," explains Sean Davidson, news editor for the trade paper *Playback*.

Ricky (Robb Wells), Bubbles (Mike Smith) and Julian (John Paul Tremblay) are the key to the program's success. The show has lasted this long for the same reason that every comedy lasts—because the audience enjoys spending time with the people who populate a particular imaginary world.

"I think the characters are just really rich," says Volpe, adding that viewers tell him they like the program because they see elements of real people, people who they grew up with or family members, reflected in the denizens of Sunnyvale, the titular trailer park.

What's so interesting about Ricky and his friends is that they seem to represent a paradox. On the one hand, they're quintessentially Canadian; on the other, they embody universal qualities.

"They play road hockey, they're big hockey fans. Bubbles loves Wayne Gretzky and they love Rush. These are all undeniably Canadian things to do," says Volpe, before adding that he doesn't believe the characters are solely defined by their nationality.

Davidson agrees. "I don't mean this in a bad way, but I don't see anything uniquely Canadian about those characters," he says. "The show could be just as easily set in Arkansas or somewhere in the Ozarks or whatnot. You could watch it your whole life and never click into the fact that it's made in the Maritimes."

Which doesn't mean it lacks little touches that are designed to resonate with Canadians. When the season opener begins, for instance, it finds Ricky and Bubbles playing table-top hockey—using a chunk of hashish for a puck. It would be foolish to assume such a hockey game has never taken place in this country.

"You can't invent that stuff," says Volpe. "That's real-life stuff."

Andrew Clark is the closest thing this country has to an expert on homegrown comedy. An instructor at Humber College's School of Comedy in Toronto, he is also the author of *Stand and Deliver,* a history of the humour business in Canada. He says that, more than being Canadian, what's important about the Sunnyvale residents is their standing in society.

"Good comedy characters are generally what you'd call 'low-status,'" he says. "Most people can relate much more easily to a guy who's on the low end trying to get by and make his way or her way, than they can with someone who has everything."

In other words, what matters is that the folks in the trailer park are underdogs. Clark sees them being in the same mold as Wayne Campbell, the goofus created by Mike Myers, or the lovable losers brought to life on the big screen by John Candy. They are part of a tradition that stretches all the way back to Greek comedy.

"You just want to root for these guys because, you know what? They're not trying to hurt anyone. And the folks that they are trying to hurt kind of deserve it: the government, insurance companies—the overdogs, as it were," notes Volpe. "So these guys are just trying to eke out a living. There's a little bit of a Robin Hood thing going on: they steal from the rich to give to the poor, which happens to be themselves."

Clark sees the boys as the latest in a long line of comic characters that started with the CBC Radio duo of Woodhouse and Hawkins, then was later embodied by Charlie Farquharson and Bob and Doug McKenzie. "Rural works in Canada," he says. "We like the idea of the rural bumpkin who says the bad thing but is also being honest."

Volpe points out, however, that it was not the intention of Mike Clattenburg, the show's creator, to consciously mine Canadian comedy history. "It was never set out to be the new hosers, the new Bob and Doug," he says.

In Davidson's view, another important aspect of the show's appeal is the way the stories are presented. According to him, the documentary look of the program stops channel surfers from flipping because they don't know if they've stumbled across an episode of the reality show *Cops,* news footage or a genuine documentary.

The pseudo-documentary feel came about due to budgetary constraints. Volpe says it would be impossible to do a conventional program with the same amount of money as *Trailer Park Boys.* "You have to look for interesting ways of telling stories that you can do for a low budget," he says. "We say 'It's cheap by design,' which works for us."

Davidson believes the decision to eschew a laugh track was also a critical one—it forces viewers to be more engaged in what's going on. He compares *Trailer Park Boys* to Ken Finkleman's *The Newsroom*, saying that a "great hallmark of good Canadian programming right now" is the absence of a laugh track. This helps the characters come into the living rooms of viewers in all their raw glory.

But will it work south of the border? With episode titles like *Fuck Community College, Let's Get Drunk and Eat Chicken Fingers,* the series will be pushing the envelope in the States.

Volpe says only one change has been made to each episode to accommodate more sensitive U.S. viewers: the foul-mouthed characters will have their curse words bleeped out. In the post-Janet Jackson state of U.S. television, Volpe says, it was an inevitable concession.

"It's going to be a lot of bleeps."

PERSONAL RESPONSE

If you have ever watched *Trailer Park Boys,* what do you think of it? What, for you, is the source of humour, or what do you not like about the program? If you have not seen the program, reflect on what kinds of television programs you like to watch on your "down time." If you don't watch television, discuss the power of television with someone who you think is a TV junkie, and try to find out what it is that person likes so much about television.

QUESTIONS FOR CLASS OR SMALL-GROUP DISCUSSION

1. Comedy, and in particular sitcoms, take up a significant portion of prime-time programming on TV. Why? What is it about comedy that tends to attract large viewing audiences? Think of some comedies that have had lasting power on television. What is it that gives them such a long shelf life?

2. *Trailer Park Boys* is clearly a representation of "low-status" persons and their lifestyle. Make a list of successful television comedies, and organize them according to representations of upper-class, middle-class, and lower-class persons and lifestyles. Also consider television comedies that use the conflict between these classes as a source of comedy. Can you draw any conclusions?

3. *Trailer Park Boys* depends quite a bit on its characters. Would you, for example, call the main characters archetypes, stereotypes, or original types? Discuss what makes them similar to other types or what distinguishes them from other types.

4. The argument is posed that *Trailer Park Boys* both is and is not uniquely Canadian. What do you think?

5. Canada is a surprising source of comedians and comic actors that have been successful in the American market. Compile such a list. Can you think of reasons why Canada has produced so many comedians?

6. *Trailer Park Boys* does not have a laugh track. What is the effect of not having a laugh track on your viewing of the show, or of any show, and why?

7. Do you think *Trailer Park Boys* is making any kind of social message?

8. Describe the way that *Trailer Park Boys* is filmed (camera movement, etc.), and discuss how these filming techniques contribute to how you respond to the show.

FOR FURTHER VIEWING: FILM AND TELEVISION

The Truman Show (1998); *Being There* (1979); *Ed Wood* (1994); *The Player* (1992); *Sunset Boulevard* (1950); *Network* (1976); *Hollywood Bollywood* (2002); *Hearts of Darkness: A Filmmaker's Apocalypse* (1991); *Breathless* (1960); *Before the Revolution* (1964); *The Arrival of the Train at La Ciotat Station* [*L'Arrivée d'un train à La Ciotat*] (1895); *Nanook of the North* (1922); *This Film Is Not Yet Rated* (2006); *Modern Times* (1936).

CHAPTER ELEVEN

ARTS AND CULTURE

INTRODUCTION

Robert Hughes, in his discussion of prehistoric cave paintings in "Behold the Stone Age," remarks on the timelessness of the human impulse to create. Because the very nature of artistic expression changes over time, from culture to culture and from generation to generation within each culture, art provides a rich record of the lives of humans and their relationship with their world from the very earliest period of human existence. As you read Hughes's essay, consider whether you agree with him on the implications of the cave paintings.

Can you think of other such discoveries that reveal something of the nature of both prehistoric humans and humans today? Consider, too, how society might be changed without art—or even how your own life might be changed if art were not a part of it. Think, too, of the variety of artistic forms familiar to you. Can any one art form in particular be said to reflect the essence of your culture? Why or why not? Consider also the two very different essays by Northrop Frye and Margaret Atwood. Frye, by analyzing two Canadian painters, draws conclusions about the nature of Canadian identity, whereas

Atwood, in formulating a critique of contemporary American life, also comments on being a Canadian, as well as the benefits and drawbacks of living next door to a global superpower.

BEHOLD THE STONE AGE

ROBERT HUGHES

Robert Hughes has been art critic for Time *magazine for over thirty years and author of at least sixteen books, including* The Art of Australia *(1966),* Heaven and Hell in Western Art *(1969),* The Shock of the New *(1981),* The Fatal Shore *(1987), and* A Jerk on One End: Reflections of a Mediocre Fisherman *(1999). He has made dozens of TV documentaries, mainly for the BBC and other English production companies, since the mid-1960s. He became widely known in 1981 as the creator and host of the much acclaimed television history series on modern art,* The Shock of the New. *Hughes wrote this cover story for the February 13, 1995, issue of* Time.

Not since the Dead Sea Scrolls has anything found in a cave caused so much excitement. The paintings and engravings, more than 300 of them, amount to a sort of Ice Age Noah's ark—images of bison, mammoths, and woolly rhinoceroses, of a panther, an owl, even a hyena. Done on the rock walls with plain earth pigments—red, black, ocher—they are of singular vitality and power, and despite their inscrutability to modern eyes, they will greatly enrich our picture of Cro-Magnon life and culture.

When the French government last month announced that a local official, Jean-Marie Chauvet, had discovered the stunning Paleolithic cave near Avignon, experts swiftly hailed the 20,000-year-old paintings as a trove rivaling—and perhaps surpassing—those of Lascaux and Altamira. "This is a virgin site—it's completely intact. It's great art," exulted Jean Clottes, an adviser to the French Culture Ministry and a leading authority on prehistoric art. It has also reopened some of the oldest and least settled of questions: When, how, and above all why did Homo sapiens start making art?

In the span of human prehistory, the Cro-Magnon people who drew the profusion of animals on the bulging limestone walls of the Chauvet cave were fairly late arrivals. Human technology—the making of tools from stone—had already been in existence for nearly two million years. There are traces of symbolism and ritual in burial sites of Neanderthals, an earlier species, dating back to 100,000 B.P. (before the present). Not only did the placement of the bodies seem meaningful, but so did the surrounding pebbles and bones with fragmentary patterns scratched on them. These, says Clottes, "do indicate that the Neanderthals had some creative capacity."

Though the dates are vastly generalized, most prehistorians seem to agree that art—communication by visual images—came into existence somewhere around 40,000 B.P. That was about the time when Cro-Magnons, Homo sapiens, reached Ice Age Europe, having migrated from the Middle East. Some experts think the Cro-Magnons brought a weapon that made Neanderthals an evolutionary has-been:

a more advanced brain, equipped with a large frontal lobe "wired" for associative thinking. For art, at its root, is association—the power to make one thing stand for and symbolize another, to create the agreements by which some marks on a surface denote, say, an animal, not just to the markmaker but to others.

Among the oldest types of art is personal decoration—ornaments such as beads, bracelets, pendants, and necklaces. The body was certainly one of the first surfaces for symbolic expression. What did such symbols communicate? Presumably the wearer's difference from others, as a member of a distinct group, tribe, or totemic family: that he was a bison-man, say, and not a reindeer-man.

The Cro-Magnons were not the inarticulate Alley Oops of popular myth. They were nomadic hunter-gatherers with a fairly developed technology. They wore animal-skin clothing and moccasins tailored with bone needles, and made beautiful (and highly efficient) laurel-leaf-shaped flint blades. Living in small groups, they constructed tents from skins, and huts from branches and (in what is now Eastern Europe) mammoth bones.

Most striking was their yearning to make art in permanent places—the walls of caves. This expansion from the body to the inert surface was in itself a startling act of lateral thinking, an outward projection of huge cultural consequence, and Homo sapiens did not produce it quickly. As much time elapsed between the first recognizable art and the cave paintings of Lascaux and Altamira, about fifteen to twenty millenniums, as separates Lascaux (or Chauvet) from the first TV broadcasts. But now it was possible to see an objective image in shared space, one that was not the property of particular bodies and had a life of its own; and from this point the whole history of human visual communication unfolds.

We are apt to suppose that Cro-Magnon cave art was rare and exceptional. But wrongly; as New York University anthropologist Randall White points out, more than 200 late–Stone Age caves bearing wall paintings, engravings, bas-relief decorations, and sculptures have been found in southwestern Europe alone. Since the discovery of Lascaux in 1940, French archaeologists have been finding an average of a cave a year—and, says professor Denis Vialou of Paris's Institute of Human Paleontology, "there are certainly many, many more to be discovered, and while many might not prove as spectacular as Lascaux or Chauvet, I'd bet that some will be just as exciting."

No doubt many will never be found. The recently discovered painted cave at Cosquer in the south of France, for instance, can be reached only by scuba divers. Its entrance now lies below the surface of the Mediterranean; in the Upper Paleolithic period, from 70,000 B.P. to 10,000 B.P., so much of Europe's water was locked up in glaciers that the sea level was some 300 feet lower than it is today.

Why the profuseness of Cro-Magnon art? Why did these people, of whom so little is known, need images so intensely? Why the preponderance of animals over human images? Archaeologists are not much closer to answering such questions than they were a half-century ago, when Lascaux was discovered.

Part of the difficulty lies in the very definition of art. As anthropologist Margaret Conkey of the University of California, Berkeley puts it, "Many cultures don't really produce art, or even have any concept of it. They have spirits, kinship, group identity. If people from highland New Guinea looked at some of the Cro-Magnon cave art, they wouldn't see anything recognizable"—and not just because there are no woolly rhinos in New Guinea either. Today we can see almost anything as an aesthetic configuration and pull it into the eclectic orbit of late-Western "art experience"; museums have trained us to do that. The paintings of Chauvet strike us as aesthetically impressive in their power and economy of line, their combination of the sculptural and the graphic—for the artists used the natural bulges and bosses of the rock wall to flesh out the forms of the animals' rumps and bellies. But it may be that aesthetic pleasure, in our sense, was the last thing the Ice Age painters were after.

These were functional images; they were meant to produce results. But what results? To represent something, to capture its image on a wall in colored earths and animal fat, is in some sense to capture and master it; to have power over it. Lascaux is full of nonthreatening animals, including wild cattle, bison, and horses, but Chauvet pullulates with dangerous ones—cave bears, a panther, and no fewer than fifty woolly rhinos. Such creatures, to paraphrase Claude Lévi-Strauss, were good to think with, not good to eat. We can assume they had a symbolic value, maybe even a religious value, to those who drew them, that they supplied a framework of images in which needs, values, and fears—in short, a network of social consciousness—could be expressed. But we have no idea what this framework was, and merely to call it *animistic* does not say much.

Some animals have more than four legs, or grotesquely exaggerated horns; is that just style, or does it argue a state of ritual trance or hallucination in the artists? No answer, though some naturally occurring manganese oxides, the base of some of the blacks used in cave paintings, are known to be toxic and to act on the central nervous system. And the main technique of Cro-Magnon art, according to prehistorian Michel Lorblanchet, director of France's National Center of Scientific Research, involved not brushes but a kind of oral spray-painting—blowing pigment dissolved in saliva on the wall. Lorblanchet, who has re-created cave paintings with uncanny accuracy, suggests that the technique may have had a spiritual dimension: "Spitting is a way of projecting yourself onto the wall, becoming one with the horse you are painting. Thus the action melds with the myth. Perhaps the shamans did this as a way of passing into the world beyond."

Different hands (and mouths) were involved in the production, but whose hands? Did the whole Cro-Magnon group at Chauvet paint, or did it have an élite of artists, to be viewed by nonartists as something like priests or professionals? Or does the joining of many hands in a collaborative work express a kind of treaty between rival groups? Or were the paintings added to over generations, producing the crowded, palimpsest-like effect suggested by some of the photos? And so on.

A mere picture of a bison or a woolly rhino tells us nothing much. Suppose, France's Clottes suggests, that 20,000 years from now, after a global cataclysm in which all books perished and the word vanished from the face of the earth, some excavators dig up the shell of a building. It has pointy ogival arches and a long axial hall at the end of which is a painting of a man nailed to a cross. In the absence of written evidence, what could this effigy mean? No more than the bison or rhino on the rock at Chauvet. Representation and symbolism have parted company.

Chauvet cave could be viewed as a religious site—a Paleolithic cathedral. Some have even suggested that a bear's skull found perched on a rock was an "altar." Says Henry de Lumley, director of France's National Museum of Natural History: "The fact that the iconography is relatively consistent, that it seems to obey certain rules about placement and even the way animals are drawn . . . is evidence of something sacred." Yet nobody lived in the cave, and no one in his right mind could imagine doing so; the first analyses of the contents have yielded no signs of human habitation, beyond the traces of animal-fat lamps and torches used by temporary visitors, and some mounds of pigmented earth left behind by the artists.

Modern artists make art to be seen by a public, the larger (usually) the better. The history of public art as we know it, across the past 1,000 years and more, is one of increasing access—beginning with the church open to the worshippers and ending with the pack-'em-in ethos of the modern museum, with its support-system of orientation courses, lectures, films, outreach programs, and souvenir shops. Cro-Magnon cave art was probably meant to be seen by very few people, under conditions of extreme difficulty and dread. The caves may have been places of initiation and trial, in which consciousness was tested to an extent that we can only dimly imagine, so utterly different is our grasp of the world from that of the Cro-Magnons.

Try to imagine an art gallery that could be entered only by crawling on your belly through a hole in the earth; that ramified into dark tunnels, a fearful maze in the earth's bowels in which the gallerygoer could, at any moment, disturb one of the bears whose claw marks can still be seen on the walls; where the only light came from flickering torches, and the bones of animals littered the uneven floor. These are the archaic conditions that, one may surmise, produced the array of cave fears implanted in the human brain—fears that became absorbed into a later, more developed culture in such narratives as that of the mythical Cretan labyrinth in whose core the terrible Minotaur waited. Further metabolized, and more basically misunderstood, these sacred terrors of the deep earth undergird the Christian myth of hell. Which may, in fact, be the strongest Cro-Magnon element left in modern life.

PERSONAL RESPONSE

Describe your own interests in the visual arts by explaining whether you like art in general. Who, if any, are your favourite artists, and which are your favourite works of art? What exactly do you consider art? Make sure you go online and look at some Paleolithic and Neanderthal art.

QUESTIONS FOR CLASS OR SMALL-GROUP DISCUSSION

1. This essay raises a number of questions about the purpose and nature of Cro-Magnon art. What implications do you think those questions have for art today? Explain your answer.

2. What impact, if any, do you think the discovery of the paintings in a Paleolithic cave in France will have on people today? What do you think modern humans can learn from them?

3. In what ways has art remained essentially the same since the period that Hughes describes in this essay? What significant changes do you see? Be as specific as possible in your answer.

4. Hughes describes the paintings in the French cave and theorizes why they were created. Can you offer any other plausible reasons for the cave paintings? Explain your answer in detail.

CANADIAN AND COLONIAL PAINTING

NORTHROP FRYE

Northrop Frye's book Fearful Symmetry: A Study of William Blake *appeared in 1947 to great acclaim, and many influential books appeared over the next four-and-a-half decades, including* Anatomy of Criticism *(1957),* The Educated Imagination *(1963),* The Bush Garden *(1971),* The Great Code *(1982), and* Words with Power *(1990). He won the Governor General's Literary Award for Non-Fiction for his book* Northrop Frye on Shakespeare *(1986). As a teacher and educator, Frye's impact continues to be profound, and his* Anatomy of Criticism *has been considered a bible in many English departments across North America. Frye was born in Sherbrooke, Quebec, in 1912, and died in Toronto in 1991. For most of his life, he taught at the University of Toronto, where his lectures became legendary. He had a particular habit of reciting pages of poetry or prose from memory, a feat that always astounded his students.*

The countries men live in feed their minds as much as their bodies: the bodily food they provide is absorbed in farms and cities: the mental, in religion and arts. In all communities this process of material and imaginative digestion goes on. Thus a large tract of vacant land may well affect the people living near it as too much cake does a small boy: an unknown but quite possibly horrible Something stares at them in the dark: hide under the bedclothes as long as they will, sooner or later they must stare back. Explorers, tormented by a sense of the unreality of the unseen, are first: pioneers and traders follow. But the land is still not imaginatively absorbed, and moves on to haunt the artist. This is a very real incubus. It glares through the sirens, gorgons, centaurs, griffins, cyclops, pygmies and chimeras of the poems which followed the Greek colonies: there the historical defeat which left a world of mystery outside the Greek clearing increased the imaginative triumph. In our own day the exploration and settlement has been far more thorough and the artistic achievement proportionately less: the latter is typified in the novels of Conrad which are so often concerned with finding a dreary commonplace at the centre of the unknown. All of which is an elaborate prologue to the fact that I propose to compare Tom Thomson with Horatio Walker, as suggested by a recent showing of them at the Art Gallery of Toronto; still, when in Canadian history the sphinx of the unknown land takes its riddle from Frazer and Mackenzie to Tom Thomson, no one can say that there has been an anti-climax.

Griffins and gorgons have no place in Thomson certainly, but the incubus is there, in the twisted stumps and sprawling rocks, the strident colouring, the scarecrow evergreens. In several pictures one has the feeling of something not quite emerging which is all the more sinister for its concealment. The metamorphic stratum is too old: the mind cannot contemplate the azoic without turning it into the monstrous. But that is of minor importance. What is essential in Thomson is the imaginative instability, the emotional unrest and dissatisfaction one feels about a country which has not been lived in: the tension between the mind and a surrounding not integrated with it. This is the key to both his colour and his design. His underlying "colour harmony" is not a concord but a minor ninth. Sumachs and red maples are conceived, quite correctly, as a *surcharge* of colour: flaming reds and yellows are squeezed straight out of the tube on to an already brilliant background: in softer light ambers and pinks and blue-greens carry on a subdued cats' chorus. This in itself is mere fidelity to the subject, but is not all. Thomson has a marked preference for the transitional over the full season: he likes the delicate pink and green tints on the birches in early spring and the irresolute sifting of the first snow through the spruces; and his autumnal studies are sometimes a Shelleyan hectic decay in high winds and spinning leaves, sometimes a Keatsian opulence and glut. His sense of design, which, of course, is derived from the trail and the canoe, is the exact opposite of the academic "establishing of foreground." He is primarily a painter of linear distance. Snowed-over paths wind endlessly through trees, rivers reach nearly to the horizon before they bend and disappear, rocks sink inch by inch under water, and the longest stretch of mountains dips somewhere and reveals the sky beyond. What is furthest in distance is often nearest in intensity. Or else we peer through a curtain of trees to a pool and an opposite shore. Even when there is no vista a long tree-trunk will lean away from us and the whole picture will be shattered by a straining and pointing diagonal.

This focusing on the farthest distance makes the foreground, of course, a shadowy blur: a foreground tree—even the tree in *West Wind*—may be only a green blob to be looked past, not at. Foreground leaves and flowers, even when carefully painted, are usually thought of as obstructing the vision and the eye comes back to them with a start. Thomson looks on a flat area with a naive Rousseauish stare (see the "decorative panels"). In fact, of all important Canadian painters, only David Milne seems to have a consistent foreground focus, and even he is fond of the obstructive blur.

Thomson's snow: In Canada, the outdoors is where we get our meaning.

Photo Source: Ernest Mayer, The Winnipeg Art Gallery

When the Canadian sphinx brought her riddle of unvisualized land to Thomson it did not occur to him to hide under the bedclothes, though she did not promise him money, fame, happiness or even self-confidence, and when she was through with him she scattered his bones in the wilderness. Horatio Walker, one of those wise and prudent men from whom the greater knowledges are concealed, felt differently. It was safety and bedclothes for him. He looked round wildly for some spot in Canada that had been thoroughly lived in, that had no ugly riddles and plenty of picturesque cliches. He found it in the Ile d'Orléans. That was a Fortunate Isle with rainbows and full moons instead of stumps and rocks: it had been cosily inhabited for centuries, and suggested relaxed easy-going narratives rather than inhuman landscapes. Pictures here were ready-made. There was Honest Toil with the plough and the quaint Patient Oxen; there were pastoral epigrams of sheep-shearing and farmers trying to gather in hay before the storm broke; there was the note of Tender Humour supplied by small pigs and heraldic turkeys; there was the Simple Piety which bowed in Childlike Reverence before a roadside *calvaire*. Why, it was as good as Europe, and had novelty besides. And for all Canadians and Americans under the bedclothes who wanted, not new problems of form and outlines, but the predigested picturesque, who preferred dreamy association-responses to detached efforts of organized vision, and who found in a queasy and maudlin nostalgia the deepest appeal of art, Horatio Walker was just the thing. He sold and sold and sold.

PERSONAL RESPONSE

After reading Frye's essay, what do you think about Thomson and Walker? Since his death, Thomson's work has grown more valuable and popular. In 2002, the National Gallery of Canada staged a major exhibition of his work, giving Thomson the same level of prominence afforded, in previous years, to Picasso, Renoir, and the Group of Seven.

Consider why Walker was far more commercially famous during his lifetime. Search online to view paintings by Thomson and Walker—what do you think of them?

QUESTIONS FOR CLASS OR SMALL-GROUP DISCUSSION

1. Why do you think Thomson captures the spirit of the Canadian identity, whereas Walker, who at the time of his death was more commercially successful, does not?

2. What is an incubus? What does Frye mean when he says "the incubus is there" in Thomson's twisted stumps and sprawling rocks, the "scarecrow evergreens"? On the Internet, look up a painting by Henry Fuseli called "The Incubus."

3. The essential thing about Thomson is his "emotional instability, the emotional unrest one feels about a country which has not been lived in: the tension between the mind and a surrounding not integrated with it." What

does this passage say about the Canadian identity and the land in which Canadians live?

4. Thomson's autumn studies are sometimes Shelleyan, sometime Keatsian. Discuss poems by Shelley and Keats that amplify Frye's comments.

5. Thomson looks with a naïve "Rousseauish stare." Some texts say Frye is referring to the philosopher Jean-Jacques Rousseau. However, some make an argument that he is referring instead to the painter Henri Rousseau. In what way were Rousseau's paintings similar to Thomson's?

6. What does Frye means when he says the "Canadian sphinx ... scattered his [Thomson's] bones in the wilderness?" Have you ever canoed in the wilderness of Algonquin Park or spent the night by one of this park's lakes? How exactly did Tom Thomson die?

LETTER TO AMERICA

MARGARET ATWOOD

Margaret Atwood is one of Canada's most honoured and famous writers—and she has published in just about every genre. She was born in 1939 in Ottawa, though many of her early years were spent in northern Quebec. She is best known for her many novels, including The Edible Woman *(1969),* Surfacing *(1972),* Lady Oracle *(1976),* The Handmaid's Tale *(1985),* Alias Grace *(1996), and* The Blind Assassin *(2000).*

Dear America:

This is a difficult letter to write, because I'm no longer sure who you are. Some of you may be having the same trouble.

I thought I knew you: we'd become well acquainted over the past fifty-five years. You were the Mickey Mouse and Donald Duck comic books I read in the late 1940s. You were the radio shows—Jack Benny, *Our Miss Brooks.* You were the music I sang and danced to: the Andrews Sisters, Ella Fitzgerald, the Platters, Elvis. You were a ton of fun.

You wrote some of my favourite books. You created Huckleberry Finn, and Hawkeye, and Beth and Jo in *Little Women,* courageous in their different ways. Later, you were my beloved Thoreau, father of environmentalism, witness to individual conscience; and Walt Whitman, singer of the great Republic; and Emily Dickinson, keeper of the private soul. You were Hammett and Chandler, heroic walkers of mean streets; even later, you were the amazing trio, Hemingway, Fitzgerald, and Faulkner, who traced the dark labyrinths of your hidden heart. You were Sinclair Lewis and Arthur Miller, who, in their own American idealism, went after the sham in you, because they thought you could do better.

You were Marlon Brando in *On the Waterfront,* Humphrey Bogart in *Key Largo,* you were Lillian Gish in *The Night of the Hunter.* You stood up for freedom, honesty, and justice; you protected the innocent. I believed most of that. I think you did, too. It seemed true at the time.

You put God on the money, though, even then. You had a way of thinking that the things of Caesar were the same as the things of God: that gave you self-confidence. You have always wanted to be a city upon a hill, a light to all nations, and for a while you were. Give me your tired, your poor, you sang, and for a while you meant it.

We've always been close, you and us. History, that old entangler, has twisted us together since the early seventeenth century. Some of us used to be you; some of us want to be you; some of you used to be us. You are not only our neighbours: In many cases—mine, for instance—you are also our blood relations, our colleagues, and our personal friends. But although we've had a ringside seat, we've never understood you completely, up here north of the 49th parallel. We're like Romanized Gauls—look like Romans, dress like Romans, but aren't Romans—peering over the wall at the real Romans. What are they doing? Why? What are they doing now? Why is the haruspex eyeballing the sheep's liver? Why is the soothsayer wholesaling the Bewares?

Perhaps that's been my difficulty in writing you this letter: I'm not sure I know what's really going on. Anyway, you have a huge posse of experienced entrail sifters who do nothing but analyze your every vein and lobe. What can I tell you about yourself that you don't already know?

This might be the reason for my hesitation: embarrassment, brought on by a becoming modesty. But it is more likely to be embarrassment of another sort. When my grandmother—from a New England background—was confronted with an unsavoury topic, she would change the subject and gaze out the window. And that is my own inclination: keep your mouth shut, mind your own business.

But I'll take the plunge, because your business is no longer merely your business. To paraphrase Marley's ghost, who figured it out too late, mankind is your business. And vice versa: when the Jolly Green Giant goes on the rampage, many lesser plants and animals get trampled underfoot. As for us, you're our biggest trading partner: We know perfectly well that if you go down the plughole, we're going with you. We have every reason to wish you well.

I won't go into the reasons why I think your recent Iraqi adventures have been—taking the long view—an ill-advised tactical error. By the time you read this, Baghdad may or may not be a pancake, and many more sheep entrails will have been examined. Let's talk, then, not about what you're doing to other people but about what you're doing to yourselves.

You're gutting the Constitution. Already your home can be entered without your knowledge or permission, you can be snatched away and incarcerated without cause, your mail can be spied on, your private records searched. Why isn't this a recipe for widespread business theft, political intimidation, and fraud? I know you've been told that all this is for your own safety and protection, but think about it for a minute. Anyway, when did you get so scared? You didn't used to be easily frightened.

You're running up a record level of debt. Keep spending at this rate and pretty soon you won't be able to afford any big military adventures. Either that or you'll go the way of the USSR: lots of tanks, but no air conditioning. That will make folks very cross. They'll be even crosser when they can't take a shower because your shortsighted bulldozing of environmental protections has dirtied most of the water and dried up the rest. Then things will get hot and dirty indeed.

You're torching the American economy. How soon before the answer to that will be not to produce anything yourselves but to grab stuff other people produce, at gunboat-diplomacy prices? Is the world going to consist of a few mega-rich King Midases, with the rest being serfs, both inside and outside your country? Will the biggest business sector in the United States be the prison system? Let's hope not.

If you proceed much further down the slippery slope, people around the world will stop admiring the good things about you. They'll decide that your city upon the hill is a slum and your democracy a sham, and therefore you have no business trying to impose your sullied vision on them. They'll think you've abandoned the rule of law. They'll think you've fouled your own nest.

The British used to have a myth about King Arthur. He wasn't dead, but sleeping in a cave, it was said; and in the country's hour of greatest peril, he would return. You too have great spirits of the past you may call upon: men and women of courage, of conscience, of prescience. Summon them now, to stand with you, to inspire you, to defend the best in you. You need them.

PERSONAL RESPONSE

If you were to write a personal letter to America, what would you say, and what tone would you take? What are the things you like about America, and what are the things you don't like?

QUESTIONS FOR CLASS OR SMALL-GROUP DISCUSSION

1. Although there is a political issue behind this letter, it is clear that Atwood has an affinity to American culture. Describe that affinity. Do you think most Canadians feel a closeness to American culture? Describe that closeness and where it comes from.

2. Are there qualities in this letter that seem to be distinctly Canadian? Describe them.

3. What is Atwood's overriding attitude toward America? Is it simple or complex, confused or confusing, clear or ambivalent?

4. Describe the letter that someone from another culture might write to America.

5. It is sometimes hard to say where art—or high culture—ends and where low culture, or popular culture, begins. How do you make this distinction when it comes to what America gives to the rest of the world, and perhaps

to Canada, more so than any other country? Does being next door to the most influential country in the world make us culturally vulnerable? How do we combat and cope with a country with this much influence? Discuss.

6. This piece was written in the spring of 2003, in response to America's presence in Iraq. How has history played out since that time? Would you write a different letter today?

FOR FURTHER VIEWING: ARTS AND CULTURE

Jésus de Montréal (1988); *Lust for Life* (1956); *Pollock* (2000); *Sister Wendy's Story of Painting* (1997); *The Agony and the Ecstasy* (1965); *La Belle Noiseuse* (1991); *The Moon and Sixpence* (1942); *Crumb* (1994); *Fantasia* (1940); *Black Orpheus* (1959); *Orphée* (1950); *Thirty Two Short Films About Glenn Gould* (1993); *Fantasia* [animated] (1940); *Steamboat Willie* [animated] (1928).

PART THREE

SOCIETY AND ECONOMICS

THE MARKETPLACE

INTRODUCTION

Fifty years ago, Canadian thinker Marshall McLuhan said that the world was becoming a global village connected by an inclusive network of technology and communications. His observation seemed quaint in the 1960s, but in this section it is clear that his prophecy has come true. The world is interconnected now in a way it never was before. Thomas Friedman writes about the controversial outsourcing of jobs to developing countries by looking at the problem from a different direction. He compares Indians who have call centre jobs to a group of young Palestinians he met on the West Bank who saw themselves as suicide bombers in waiting, and he asks the reader to see outsourcing as more than just economics. Kofi Annan, the former United Nations secretary-general, advocates activism and new thinking when he writes about the elimination of world poverty. And Sharon LaFraniere looks at the hidden world of forced child labour. Some may argue that child labour is an economic necessity in parts of the globe, but who would argue that child slavery is justified?

30 LITTLE TURTLES

Thomas Friedman

Thomas Friedman, born in 1953, is the author of The World Is Flat *(2005) and other books. He joined* The New York Times *in 1981 as a financial reporter specializing in OPEC- and oil-related news. He later served as the chief diplomatic correspondent, the chief White House correspondent, and the international economics correspondent. His foreign affairs column, which appears twice a week in* The New York Times, *is syndicated to seven hundred other newspapers worldwide. He has served as a visiting professor at Harvard University, has been awarded honorary degrees from several universities, and has won three Pulitzer Prizes for his writing.*

BANGALORE, India

Indians are so hospitable. I got an ovation the other day from a roomful of Indian 20-year-olds just for reading perfectly the following paragraph: "A bottle of bottled water held 30 little turtles. It didn't matter that each turtle had to rattle a metal ladle in order to get a little bit of noodles, a total turtle delicacy. The problem was that there were many turtle battles for less than oodles of noodles."

I was sitting in on an "accent neutralization" class at the Indian call center 24/7 Customer. The instructor was teaching the would-be Indian call center operators to suppress their native Indian accents and speak with a Canadian one—she teaches British and U.S. accents as well, but these youths will be serving the Canadian market. Since I'm originally from Minnesota, near Canada, and still speak like someone out of the movie "Fargo," I gave these young Indians an authentic rendition of "30 Little Turtles," which is designed to teach them the proper Canadian pronunciations. Hence the rousing applause.

Watching these incredibly enthusiastic young Indians preparing for their call center jobs—earnestly trying to soften their t's and roll their r's—is an uplifting experience, especially when you hear from their friends already working these jobs how they have transformed their lives. Most of them still live at home and turn over part of their salaries to their parents, so the whole family benefits. Many have credit cards and have become real consumers, including of U.S. goods, for the first time. All of them seem to have gained self-confidence and self-worth

A lot of these Indian young men and women have college degrees, but would never get a local job that starts at $200 to $300 a month were it not for the call centers. Some do "outbound" calls, selling things from credit cards to phone services to Americans and Europeans. Others deal with "inbound" calls—everything from tracing lost luggage for U.S. airline passengers to solving computer problems for U.S. customers. The calls are transferred here by satellite or fiber optic cable.

I was most taken by a young Indian engineer doing tech support for a U.S. software giant, who spoke with pride about how cool it is to tell his friends that he just spent the day helping Americans navigate their software. A majority of these call center workers are young women, who not only have been liberated by earning a decent local wage (and therefore have more choice in whom they marry), but are using the job to get M.B.A.'s and other degrees on the side.

I gathered a group together, and here's what they sound like: M. Dinesh, who does tech support, says his day is made when some American calls in with a problem and is actually happy to hear an Indian voice: "They say you people are really good at what you do. I am glad I reached an Indian." Kiran Menon, when asked who his role model was, shot back: "Bill Gates—[I dream of] starting my own company and making it that big." I asked C. M. Meghna what she got most out of the work: "Self-confidence," she said, "a lot of self-confidence, when people come to you with a problem and you can solve it—and having a lot of independence." Because the call center teams work through India's night—which corresponds to America's day—"your biological clock goes haywire," she added. "Besides that, it's great."

There is nothing more positive than the self-confidence, dignity and optimism that comes from a society knowing it is producing wealth by tapping its own brains—men's and women's—as opposed to one just tapping its own oil, let alone one that is so lost it can find dignity only through suicide and "martyrdom."

Indeed, listening to these Indian young people, I had a déjà vu. Five months ago, I was in Ramallah, on the West Bank, talking to three young Palestinian men, also in their 20's, one of whom was studying engineering. Their hero was Yasir Arafat. They talked about having no hope, no jobs and no dignity, and they each nodded when one of them said they were all "suicide bombers in waiting."

What am I saying here? That it's more important for young Indians to have jobs than Americans? Never. But I am saying that there is more to outsourcing than just economics. There's also geopolitics. It is inevitable in a networked world that our economy is going to shed certain low-wage, low-prestige jobs. To the extent that they go to places like India or Pakistan—where they are viewed as high-wage, high-prestige jobs—we make not only a more prosperous world, but a safer world for our own 20-year-olds.

PERSONAL RESPONSE

Friedman asks you to consider geopolitics and not just economics when you think about the problem of outsourcing. But what if you or someone in your family had just lost a job that went overseas to someone else who was willing to do the job for less? What if your computer had crashed in the middle of the night, and you phoned a help number and got someone on the line who worked from India or Puerto Rico? What if this person did not have a command of English? Would you still see Friedman's point? Consider whether you agree or disagree with Friedman's position that we must make a safer world for young people—and that outsourcing is one way to do it.

QUESTIONS FOR CLASS OR SMALL-GROUP DISCUSSION

1. What is geopolitics? What is outsourcing? What is offshoring? Why at this time in history have these three terms become so important?

2. What do you make of Friedman's opening sentence? Is he being ironic?

3. Why are call centre operators in India being taught to speak with Canadian accents?

4. Friedman says a majority of call centre workers are young women who are earning a decent wage, enabling them to have more choice in whom they marry, and allowing them to get university degrees on the side. Does this influence your position on outsourcing?

5. How does outsourcing relate to the concept of globalization?

DEVELOPMENT WITHOUT BORDERS

KOFI ANNAN

Kofi Annan, born in Ghana in 1938, was the seventh secretary-general of the United Nations. He began his first term in 1997, and his second term ended on December 31, 2006. He was a reformist who pleaded with powerful nations, such as the United States, to pay attention to the economies of weaker countries. For example, he said global warming was caused by a lack of leadership in industrialized countries and that the poorest people in the world, who do not create significant pollution, carry the burden of rising temperatures, pollution-induced climate change, and droughts. Annan and the United Nations were awarded the 2001 Nobel Peace Prize. This paper was published in the Summer 2001 issue of Harvard International Review.

What is globalization? More than ever before, groups and individuals are interacting directly across borders without involving the state. This happens partly due to new technology and partly because states have found that prosperity is better secured by releasing the creative energies of their people than by restricting them.

The benefits of globalization are obvious: faster growth, higher standards of living, and new opportunities. However, globalization's benefits are very unequally distributed; the global market is not yet underpinned by shared social objectives, and if all of today's poor follow the same path that brought the rich to prosperity, the earth's resources will soon be exhausted. The challenge we face is to ensure that globalization becomes a positive force for all people instead of leaving billions in squalor.

If we are to get the most out of globalization, we must learn how to provide better governance at the local, national, and international levels. We must think afresh about how we manage our joint activities and our shared interests, since so many challenges that we confront today are beyond the reach of any state acting on its own.

This should not be seen as a future of world government or the eclipse of nation states. On the contrary, states will draw strength from each other by acting together within the framework of common institutions based on shared rules and values. Governments must work together to make these changes possible, but governments alone cannot make them happen. Much of the heavy lifting will be done by private investment and charitable foundations.

The best ideas, however, will come from nongovernmental sources: from academic researchers, nonprofit organizations, business, the media, and the arts. These elements compose civil society, and they have a vital role to play.

At the UN Millennium Summit in September 2000, world leaders resolved to halve three figures: the number of people whose income is less than one US dollar a day, the proportion of people who suffer from hunger, and the proportion of people who are unable to reach or afford safe drinking water. They resolved to accomplish these goals by 2015. History will judge this generation by what it did to fulfill that pledge.

Success in achieving sustained growth depends on expanding access to the opportunities of globalization. That in turn depends in large measure on the quality of governance a country enjoys. Countries can only compete in the global market if their people benefit from the rule of law, effective state institutions, transparency and accountability in the management of public affairs, and respect for human rights. Their people must have a say in the decisions that affect their lives.

If developing countries succeed in creating the right economic and social environment, new technology can put many opportunities within their reach. That is especially true of information technology, which does not require vast amounts of hardware, financial capital, or even energy, and which is relatively environment-friendly. What information technology does require is brain power—the one commodity that is equally distributed among the peoples of the world. So for a relatively small investment—for example, an investment in basic education—we can bring all kinds of knowledge within reach of the world's poor and enable poor countries to leapfrog some of the long and painful stages of development that other nations had to go through.

In short, there is much that poor countries can do to help themselves. But rich countries have an indispensable role to play. For wealthy nations to preach the virtues of open markets to developing countries is mere hypocrisy if they do not open their own markets to those countries' products or stem the flooding of the world market with subsidized food exports that make it impossible for farmers in developing countries to compete. Nor can they expect developing countries to protect the global environment, unless they are ready to alter their own irresponsible patterns of production and consumption.

Developing countries must be helped to export their way to prosperity. Everyone now agrees that the burden of debt must be lifted from the poorest countries, but developed countries have not yet come forward with sufficient resources to alleviate this burden. Nations, whether in debt or not, need help to reach the stage where they can produce goods and services that the rest of the world wants to buy. Many also need help in resolving destructive conflicts and rebuilding a peaceful, productive society.

Long ago, all members of the Organization for Economic Cooperation and Development committed 0.7 percent of their gross domestic product to development aid. Very few made good on that commitment. Private companies, as well as governments, have an obligation to consider the interests of the poor when making investment choices and when pricing their products. Companies are the largest beneficiaries of globalization; it is in their interest to make this trend sustainable, by helping it work for all.

Only when the lives of ordinary men, women, and children in cities and villages around the world are made better will we know that globalization is becoming inclusive, allowing everyone to share in its opportunities. This is the key to eliminating world poverty.

PERSONAL RESPONSE

Do you agree with Annan that rich countries have an obligation to help developing countries? Annan asks private companies to consider the poor when making investment choices because companies are the largest beneficiaries of globalization. Is that a useful or persuasive tactic? What if Annan had instead urged companies to behave in a compassionate manner?

QUESTIONS FOR CLASS OR SMALL-GROUP DISCUSSION

1. Do you think it possible for world leaders to achieve the goals resolved upon at the UN Millennium Summit? What will they have to do to accomplish these goals?

2. Discuss ways in which rich or strong nations could help poor or developing countries enhance their schools and economies.

3. To what extent do you agree with this statement: "Private companies, as well as governments, have an obligation to consider the interests of the poor when making investment choices and when pricing their products"?

4. Suggest some possible results of rich countries not helping poor countries.

AFRICA'S WORLD OF FORCED LABOR, IN A 6-YEAR-OLD'S EYES

Sharon LaFraniere

Sharon LaFraniere is an award-winning journalist for The New York Times. *In covering southern Africa for the* Times, *she has specialized in writing on the challenges facing the region's women and children. Reporting from both war zones and disaster areas, she has been praised for the way she looks at everyday life in ways that are both respectful and unflinching.*

KETE KRACHI, Ghana—Just before 5 a.m., with the sky still dark over Lake Volta, Mark Kwadwo was rousted from his spot on the damp dirt floor. It was time for work.

Shivering in the predawn chill, he helped paddle a canoe a mile out from shore. For five more hours, as his coworkers yanked up a fishing net, inch by inch, Mark bailed water to keep the canoe from swamping.

He last ate the day before. His broken wooden paddle was so heavy he could barely lift it. But he raptly followed each command from Kwadwo Takyi, the powerfully built 31-year-old in the back of the canoe who freely deals out beatings.

"I don't like it here," he whispered, out of Mr. Takyi's earshot.

Mark Kwadwo is 6 years old. About 30 pounds, dressed in a pair of blue and red underpants and a Little Mermaid T-shirt, he looks more like an oversized toddler than a boat hand. He is too little to understand why he has wound up in this fishing village, a two-day trek from his home.

But the three older boys who work with him know why. Like Mark, they are indentured servants, leased by their parents to Mr. Takyi for as little as $20 a year.

Until their servitude ends in three or four years, they are as trapped as the fish in their nets, forced to work up to 14 hours a day, seven days a week, in a trade that even adult fishermen here call punishing and, at times, dangerous.

Mr. Takyi's boys—conscripts in a miniature labor camp, deprived of schooling, basic necessities and freedom—are part of a vast traffic in children that supports West and Central African fisheries, quarries, cocoa and rice plantations and street markets. The girls are domestic servants, bread bakers, prostitutes. The boys are field workers, cart pushers, scavengers in abandoned gem and gold mines.

By no means is the child trafficking trade uniquely African. Children are forced to race camels in the Middle East, weave carpets in India, and fill brothels all over the developing world.

The International Labor Organization, a United Nations agency, estimates that 1.2 million are sold into servitude every year in an illicit trade that generates as much as $10 billion annually.

Studies show they are most vulnerable in Asia, Latin America and Africa.

Africa's children, the world's poorest, account for roughly one-sixth of the trade, according to the labor organization. Data is notoriously scarce, but it suggests victimization of African children on a huge scale.

A 2002 study supervised by the labor organization estimated that nearly 12,000 trafficked children toiled in the cocoa fields of Ivory Coast alone. The children, who had no relatives in the area, cleared fields with machetes, applied pesticides and sliced open cocoa pods for beans.

In an analysis in February, Unicef says child trafficking is growing in West and Central Africa, driven by huge profits and partly controlled by organized networks that transport children both within and between countries.

"We know it is a huge problem in Africa," said Pamela Shifman, a child protection officer at the New York headquarters of Unicef. "A lot of it is visible. You see the kids being exploited. You watch it happen. Somebody brought the kids to the place where they are. Somebody exploited their vulnerability."

Building the global economy?
Photo Source: UN/DPI Photo

Otherwise, she asked, "How did they get there?"

John R. Miller, the director of the State Department Office to Monitor and Combat Trafficking in Persons, said the term trafficking failed to convey the brutality of what was occurring.

"A child does not consent," he said. "The loss of choice, the deception, the use of frauds, the keeping of someone at work with little or no pay, the threats if they leave—it is slavery."

Some West African families see it more as a survival strategy. In a region where nearly two-thirds of the population lives on less than $1 a day, the compensation for the temporary loss of a child keeps the rest of the family from going hungry. Some parents argue that their children are better off learning a trade than starving at home.

Indeed, the notion that children should be in the care of their parents is not a given in much of African society.

Parents frequently hand off children to even distant relatives if it appears they will have a chance at education and more opportunity.

Only in the past six years or so has it become clear how traffickers take advantage of this custom to buy and sell children, sometimes with no more ceremony than a goat deal.

In 2001, 35 children, half of them under age 15, were discovered aboard a vessel in a Benin port. They said they were being shipped to Gabon to work.

In 2003, Nigerian police rescued 194 malnourished children from stone quarries north of Lagos. At least 13 other children had died and been buried near the pits, the police said.

Last year, Nigerian police stumbled upon 64 girls aged 14 and younger, packed inside a refrigerated truck built to haul frozen fish. They had traveled hundreds of miles from central Nigeria, the police said, and were destined for work as housemaids in Lagos.

In response to such reports, African nations have passed a raft of legislation against trafficking, adopting or strengthening a dozen laws last year alone.

There were nearly 200 prosecutions of traffickers on the continent last year, four times as many as in 2003, according to the State Department's trafficking office.

Some countries are encouraging villages to form their own surveillance committees. In Burkina Faso, the government reported, such committees, together with the police, freed 640 children from traffickers in 2003. Still, government officials in the region say, only a tiny fraction of victims are detected.

Ghana, an Oregon-size nation of 21 million people, has yet to prosecute anyone under the new antitrafficking law it adopted last December. But the government had taken other steps—including eliminating school fees that forced youngsters out of classrooms, increasing birth registrations so that children have legal identities and extending small loans to about 1,200 mothers to give them alternatives to leasing out their children.

The International Organization for Migration, an intergovernmental agency set up after World War II to help refugees, has also mounted a United States-financed program to rescue children from the fishing industry.

Since 2003, the organization says, 587 children have been freed from Ghana's Lake Volta region, taken to shelters for counseling and medical treatment, then reunited with parents or relatives.

"We sign a social contract with the fishermen," said Eric Peasah, the agency's Ghana field representative. "If they have 10 children, we say, 'Release four, and you can't get more, or you will be prosecuted.' Once they sign that, we come back and say we want to release more."

To reduce child trafficking significantly, said Marilyn Amponsah Annan, who is in charge of children's issues for the Ghanaian government, adults must be convinced that children have the right to be educated, to be protected, and to be spared adult burdens—in short, the right to a childhood.

"You see so many children with so many fishermen," she said. "Those little hands, those little bodies. It is always very sad, because this is the world of adults.

"We have to educate these communities because they do not know any other way of existence. They believe this is what they need to do to survive."

That is the fishermen's favorite defense in Kete Krachi, a day's drive through dense forests from Ghana's capital, Accra. For the area's roughly 9,000 residents, fishing is their lifeblood. Children keep it going.

Nearly every canoe here holds at least a few of them, some no older than 5 or 6, often supervised by a teenager. A dozen boys, interviewed in their canoes or as they sewed up ratty nets ashore, spoke of backbreaking toil, 100-hour workweeks and frequent beatings. They bore a pervasive fear of diving into the lake's murky waters to free a tangled net, and never resurfacing.

One 10-year-old said he was sometimes so exhausted that he fell asleep as he paddled. Asked when he rested, another boy paused from his net mending, seemingly confused. "This is what you see now," he said.

They never see the pittance they earn. The fishermen say they pay parents or relatives each December, typically on trips to the families' villages during the December holidays.

The children's sole comfort seems to be the shared nature of their misery, a camaraderie of lost boys who have not seen their families in years, have no say in their fate and, in some cases, were lured by false promises of schooling or a quick homecoming.

On Nkomi, a grassy island in the lake, Kwasi Tweranim, in his mid to late teens, and Kwadwo Seaako, perhaps 12 or 13, seemed united by fear and resentment of their boss. Both bear inchlong scars on their scalps where, they said, he struck them with a wooden paddle.

"I went down to disentangle the net, and when I came up, my master said that I had left part of it down there," Kwasi said. "Then I saw black, and woke up in another boat. Only the grace of God saved me."

Kwadwo, stammering badly, said he had been punished when the net rolled in the water.

Not every fisherman is so pitiless. Christian Lissah employs eight children under 13, mostly distant relatives. He said he knew many children who were treated no better than workhorses, and some who had drowned.

"In general, this is not a good practice because people mishandle the children," he said. Yet he said he could not imagine how he would fish profitably without child workers, and depends on friends and acquaintances to keep him supplied—for a commission.

"You must get people who are a very low background who need money," he said. "Some of them are eager to release their children."

Mark Kwadwo's parents, Joe Obrenu and his wife, Ama, were an easy sell. Mr. Obrenu fished the seas off Aboadzi, a hilly, sun-drenched town on the Gulf of Guinea, and his wife dried the catch for sale. But the two often ran short of food, said Mark's aunt, Adwoa Awotwe. Over the years, they sold five of their children into labor, she said, including Mark's 9-year-old sister Hagar, who performs domestic chores for Mr. Takyi.

Mr. Obrenu drummed up other recruits from neighbors, sometimes to their lasting regret. "It was hunger, to get a little money; the whole today, I have not eaten," said Efua Mansah, whose 7-year-old son, Kwabena, boarded a small blue bus with Mr. Takyi four years ago for the 250-mile trip to Kete Krachi.

She has seen him only twice since then. In all that time, Mr. Takyi has paid her $66, she said, a third of which she spent on buses and ferries to pick up the money.

In her one-room hut decorated with empty plastic bottles, she forced back tears. "I want to bring my son home," she said.

Mark also cried when his turn to leave came this year, his aunt said, so his mother told him that Mr. Takyi would take him to his father. Instead he was brought to Mr. Takyi's compound of caked mud huts, to a dark six-foot-square cubicle with a single tiny window. He shares it with five other children, buzzing flies and a few buckets of fish bait.

In two days, a smile never creased Mark's delicate features. He seldom offered more than a nod or a shake of the head, with a few telling exceptions: "I was beaten in the house. I can't remember what I did, but he caned me," he said of Mr. Takyi.

Mr. Takyi, who sleeps and works in the same gray T-shirt, is disarmingly frank about his household. He can afford to feed the children only twice a day, he said, and cannot clothe them adequately. He himself has been paddling the lake since age 8.

"I can understand how the children feel," he said. "Because I didn't go to school, this is work I must do. I also find it difficult."

Yet he does not hesitate to break a branch from the nearest tree to wake the boys for the midnight shift.

"Almost all the boys are very troublesome," he complained. "I want them to be humble children but they don't obey my orders."

One recent morning, his young crew, wrapped in thin bedsheets for warmth, hiked in the darkness down to the shore.

They paddled out in two leaky but stable canoes, searching the water for a piece of foam that marked where their net was snagged on submerged tree stumps. Kwabena, 11, stripped off his cutoff shorts and dived in with an 18-year-old to free it, yanking it at one point with his teeth.

Mark has not mastered the rhythm of paddling. Mr. Takyi said the boy cries when the water is rough or he is cold. He cannot swim a stroke. If the canoe capsizes, Mr. Takyi said, he will save him.

"I can't pay what is asked for older boys," Mr. Takyi said, as Mark bailed out the canoe with the sawed-off bottom of a plastic cooking oil container. "That is why I go for this. When I get money, I go to get another one."

In the other canoe, Kwame Akuban and Kofi Quarshie plucked fish from the net with the air of prisoners waiting for their terms to end.

Kofi, 10, said his mother had told him his earnings would feed their family. But he suspects another motive. "They didn't like me," he said softly.

Kwame, 12, said his parents had promised to retrieve him in a year's time and send him to school.

"I have been here three years and I am not going home, and I am not happy," he said quietly.

As if on cue, Mr. Takyi shouted: "Remove the fish faster, or I will cane you."

Running away is a common fantasy among the boys. Kofi Nyankom, who came from Mark's hometown three years ago, at age 9, was one of the few to actually try it.

Last December, he ran to town half-naked, his back a mass of bruises. He said Mr. Takyi had tied up him and whipped him.

George Achibra, a school district official, demanded that the police intervene, and Mr. Takyi was forced to let Kofi go.

But before many weeks passed, he had brought in a replacement—younger, more helpless, more submissive. It was Mark Kwadwo.

PERSONAL RESPONSE

How did you feel when you read about parents who, for a few dollars a year, give up their children to be indentured servants? What would you do about this if you were a federal politician in Canada or a United Nations official?

QUESTIONS FOR CLASS OR SMALL-GROUP DISCUSSION

1. According to this article, forced child labour is not unique to Africa. Children are forced to race camels in the Middle East, weave carpets in India, and fill brothels all over the developing world. Is it elitist for people in the West to want to change other cultures and eliminate these practices? Is it a just cause? Discuss.

2. The International Labor Organization, a United Nations agency, estimates that 1.2 million children are sold into servitude every year in an illicit trade that generates as much as $10 billion annually. Studies show that children are most vulnerable in Asia, Latin America, and Africa. Why doesn't LaFraniere begin her piece with these statistics—why does she begin and end her article with the example of a boy who must work as a deckhand?

3. Get a group of people together to watch the documentary *Born into Brothels* (2004) and relate it to this essay. Discuss your response to the film.

FOR FURTHER VIEWING: THE MARKETPLACE

Goin' Down the Road (1970); *Wall Street* (1987); *Roger and Me* (1989); *Enron: The Smartest Guys in the Room* (2005); *The Corporation* (2003); *Children Who Labor* (1912); *Supersize Me* (2004).

CHAPTER THIRTEEN

POVERTY AND HOMELESSNESS

INTRODUCTION

Poverty, like the sea, is all around us. It makes no difference where you live—in a small town or in a big city—poverty is visible. Many families whose incomes provide just enough for shelter and food are only a paycheque away from living on the streets. Compounding these difficulties are certain stereotyped beliefs about people on welfare and those living on the streets. Charges of laziness and fraud are often levelled at welfare recipients, despite studies that demonstrate that the vast majority of people on welfare want to work and live independent lives.

The essays in this chapter examine some of the issues associated with poverty and homelessness. The first is a classic satire by Jonathan Swift in which he offers a unique solution to the problem of poverty in early 18th-century Ireland. Written when Ireland was a far poorer country than England, its population largely Catholic, and its primary occupation agricultural, "A Modest Proposal" takes a satiric look at ways to solve the very serious problem of poverty and its attendant woes. In its structure and use of logic, the essay is also a model of persuasion and economic discourse. Next, Melanie Scheller's highly personal essay, "On the Meaning of Plumbing and Poverty," presents graphic, painful details and a very real sense not only of the experience of a child living in poverty but also of the shame and diminished self-esteem she carried with her as a result of living in homes without indoor plumbing. Lars Eighner's classic tale, "On Dumpster Diving," casts a cold eye on one individual's experience of living on the streets. After reading these essays, you may ask yourself whether it is possible to eliminate global poverty—or poverty in your own community. What would it take?

A MODEST PROPOSAL

For preventing the children of poor people in Ireland from being a burden to their parents or country, and for making them beneficial to the public

JONATHAN SWIFT

Jonathan Swift (1667–1745) was an Irish author and journalist, widely regarded as the foremost prose satirist in the English language. He is perhaps best known for Gulliver's Travels *(1726), which, in its bowdlerized form (i.e., minus the mature content), is often published as a children's book. Published as a pamphlet in 1729, "A Modest Proposal" mocked the language and conventions of early economists.*

It is a melancholy object to those who walk through this great town[1] or travel in the country, when they see the streets, the roads, and cabin doors, crowded with beggars of the female sex, followed by three, four, or six children, all in rags and importuning every passenger for an alms. These mothers, instead of being able to work for their honest livelihood, are forced to employ all their time in strolling to beg sustenance for their helpless infants, who, as they grow up, either turn thieves for want of work, or leave their dear native country to fight for the Pretender[2] in Spain, or sell themselves to the Barbadoes.[3]

I think it is agreed by all parties that this prodigious number of children in the arms, or on the backs, or at the heels of their mothers, and frequently of their fathers, is in the present deplorable state of the kingdom a very great additional grievance; and therefore whoever could find out a fair, cheap, and easy method of making these children sound, useful members of the commonwealth would deserve so well of the public as to have his statue set up for a preserver of the nation.

But my intention is very far from being confined to provide only for the children of professed beggars; it is of a much greater extent, and shall take in the whole number of infants at a certain age who are born of parents in effect as little able to support them as those who demand our charity in the streets.

As to my own part, having turned my thoughts for many years upon this important subject, and maturely weighed the several schemes of other projectors, I have always found them grossly mistaken in their computation. It is true, a child just dropped from its dam may be supported by her milk for a solar year, with little other nourishment; at most not above the value of two shillings,[4] which the mother may certainly get, or the value in scraps, by her lawful occupation of begging; and it is exactly at one year old that I propose to provide for them in such a manner as instead of being a charge upon their parents or the parish, or wanting food and raiment for the rest of their lives, they shall on the contrary contribute to the feeding, and partly to the clothing, of many thousands.

There is likewise another great advantage in my scheme, that it will prevent those voluntary abortions, and that horrid practice of women murdering their bastard children, alas, too frequent among us, sacrificing the poor innocent babies, I doubt,[5] more to avoid the expense than the shame, which would move tears and pity in the most savage and inhuman breast.

The number of souls in this kingdom being usually reckoned one million and a half, of these I calculate there may be about two hundred thousand couple whose wives are breeders; from which number I subtract thirty thousand couples who are able to maintain their own children, although I apprehend there cannot be so many under the present distresses of the kingdom; but this being granted, there will remain an hundred and seventy thousand breeders. I again subtract fifty thousand for those women who miscarry, or whose children die by accident or disease within the year. There only remain an hundred and twenty thousand children of poor parents annually born. The question therefore is, how this number shall be reared and provided for, which, as I have already said, under the present situation of affairs, is utterly impossible by all the methods hitherto proposed. For we can neither employ them in handicraft or agriculture; we neither build houses (I mean in the country) nor cultivate land. They can very seldom pick up a livelihood by stealing till they arrive at six years old, except where they are of towardly parts;[6] although I confess they learn the rudiments much earlier, during which time they can however be looked upon only as probationers, as I have been informed by a principal gentleman in the county of Cavan, who protested to me that he never knew above one or two instances under the age of six, even in a part of the kingdom so renowned for the quickest proficiency in that art.

I am assured by our merchants that a boy or a girl before twelve years old is no salable commodity; and even when they come to this age they will not yield above three pounds, or three pounds and half a crown[7] at most on the Exchange; which cannot turn to account either to the parents or the kingdom, the charge of nutriment and rags having been at least four times that value.

I shall now therefore humbly propose my own thoughts, which I hope will not be liable to the least objection.

I have been assured by a very knowing American of my acquaintance in London, that a young healthy child well nursed is at a year old a most delicious, nourishing, and wholesome food, whether stewed, roasted, baked, or boiled; and I make no doubt that it will equally serve in a fricassee or a ragout.

I do therefore humbly offer it to public consideration that of the hundred and twenty thousand children, already computed, twenty thousand may be reserved for breed, whereof only one fourth part to be males, which is more than we allow to sheep, black cattle, or swine; and my reason is that these children are seldom the fruits of marriage, a circumstance not much regarded by our savages, therefore one male will be sufficient to serve four females. That the remaining hundred thousand may at a year old be offered in sale to the persons of quality and fortune through the kingdom, always advising the mother to let them suck plentifully in the last month, so as to render them plump and fat for a good table. A child will make two dishes at an entertainment for friends; and when the family dines alone, the fore or hind quarter will make a reasonable dish, and seasoned with a little pepper or salt will be very good boiled on the fourth day, especially in winter.

I have reckoned upon a medium that a child just born will weigh twelve pounds, and in a solar year if tolerably nursed increaseth to twenty-eight pounds.

I grant this food will be somewhat dear, and therefore very proper for landlords, who, as they have already devoured most of the parents, seem to have the best title to the children.

Infant's flesh will be in season throughout the year, but more plentiful in March, and a little before and after. For we are told by a grave author, an eminent French physician,[8] that fish being a prolific diet, there are more children born in Roman Catholic countries about nine months after Lent than at any other season; therefore, reckoning a year after Lent, the markets will be more glutted than usual, because the number of popish infants is at least three to one in this kingdom; and therefore it will have one other collateral advantage, by lessening the number of Papists among us.[9]

I have already computed the charge of nursing a beggar's child (in which list I reckon all cottagers, laborers, and four fifths of the farmers) to be about two shillings per annum, rags included; and I believe no gentleman would repine to give ten shillings for the carcass of a good fat child, which, as I have said, will make four dishes of excellent nutritive meat, when he hath only some particular friend or his own family to dine with him. Thus the squire will learn to be a good landlord, and grow popular among the tenants; the mother will have eight shillings net profit, and be fit for work till she produces another child.

Those who are more thrifty (as I must confess the times require) may flay the carcass; the skin of which artificially[10] dressed will make admirable gloves for ladies, and summer boots for fine gentlemen.

As to our city of Dublin, shambles[11] may be appointed for this purpose in the most convenient parts of it, and butchers we may be assured will not be wanting; although I rather recommend buying the children alive, and dressing them hot from the knife as we do roasting pigs.

A very worthy person, a true lover of his country, and whose virtues I highly esteem, was lately pleased in discoursing on this matter to offer a refinement upon my scheme. He said that many gentlemen of this kingdom, having of late destroyed their deer, he conceived that the want of venison might well be supplied by the bodies of young lads and maidens, not exceeding fourteen years or age nor under twelve, so great a number of both sexes in every county being now ready to starve for want of work and service; and these to be disposed of by their parents, if alive, or otherwise by their nearest relations. But with due deference to so excellent a friend and so deserving a patriot, I cannot be altogether in his sentiments; for as to the males, my American acquaintance assured me from frequent experience that their flesh was generally touch and lean, like that of our schoolboys, by continual exercise, and their taste disagreeable; and to fatten them would not answer the charge. Then as to the females, it would, I think with humble submission, be a loss to the public, because they soon would become breeders themselves: and besides, it is not improbable that some scrupulous people might be apt to censure such a practice (although indeed very unjustly) as a little bordering on cruelty; which, I confess, hath always been with me the strongest objection against any project, how well soever intended.

But in order to justify my friend, he confessed that this expedient was put into his head by the famous Psalmanazar, a native of the island of Formosa,[12] who came from thence to London above twenty years ago, and in conversation told my friend that in his country when any young person happened to be put to death, the executioner sold the carcass to persons of quality as a prime dainty; and that in his time the body of a plump girl of fifteen, who was crucified for an attempt to poison the emperor, was sold to his Imperial Majesty's prime minister of state, and other great mandarins of the court, in joints from the gibbet, at four hundred crowns. Neither indeed can I deny that if the same use were made of several plump young girls in this town, who without one single groat[13] to their fortunes cannot stir abroad without a chair,[14] and appear at the playhouse and assemblies in foreign fineries which they never will pay for, the kingdom would not be the worse.

Some persons of a desponding spirit are in great concern about that vast number of poor people who are aged, diseased, or maimed, and I have been desired to employ my thoughts what course may be taken to ease the nation of so grievous an encumbrance. But I am not in the least pain upon that matter, because it is very well known that they are every day dying and rotting by cold and famine, and filth and vermin, as fast as can be reasonably expected. And as to the younger laborers, they are now in almost as hopeful a condition. They cannot get work, and consequently pine away for want of nourishment to a degree that if at any time they are accidentally hired to common labor, they have not strength to perform it; and thus the country and themselves are happily delivered from the evils to come.

I have too long digressed, and therefore shall return to my subject. I think the advantages by the proposal which I have made are obvious and many, as well as of the highest importance.

For first, as I have already observed, it would greatly lessen the number of Papists, with whom we are yearly overrun, being the principal breeders of the nation as well as our most dangerous enemies; and who stay at home on purpose to deliver the kingdom to the Pretender, hoping to take their advantage by the absence of so many good Protestants, who have chosen rather to leave their country than to stay at home and pay tithes against their conscience to an Episcopal curate.

Secondly, the poorer tenants will have something valuable of their own, which by law may be made liable to distress,[15] and help to pay their landlord's rent, their corn and cattle being already seized and money a thing unknown.

Thirdly, whereas the maintenance of an hundred thousand children, from two years old and upwards, cannot be computed at less than ten shillings a piece per annum, the nation's stock will be thereby increased fifty thousand pounds per annum, besides the profit of a new dish introduced to the tables of all gentlemen of fortune in the kingdom who have any refinement in taste. And the money will circulate among ourselves, the goods being entirely of our own growth and manufacture.

Fourthly, the constant breeders, besides the gain of eight shillings sterling per annum by the sale of their children, will be rid of the charge of maintaining them after the first year.

Fifthly, this food would likewise bring great custom to taverns, where the vintners will certainly be so prudent as to procure the best receipts[16] for dressing it to perfection, and consequently have their houses frequented by all the fine gentlemen, who justly value themselves upon their knowledge in good eating; and a skilful cook, who understands how to oblige his guests, will contrive to make it as expensive as they please.

Sixthly, this would be a great inducement to marriage, which all wise nations have either encouraged by rewards or enforced by laws and penalties. It would increase the care and tenderness of mothers toward their children, when they were sure of a settlement for life to the poor babes, provided in some sort by the public, to their annual profit instead of expense. We should see an honest emulation among the married women, which of them could bring the fattest child to the market. Men would become as fond of their wives during the time of their pregnancy as they are now of their mares in foal, their cows in calf, or sows when they are ready to farrow; nor offer to beat or kick them (as is too frequent a practice) for fear of a miscarriage.

Many other advantages might be enumerated. For instance, the addition of some thousand carcasses in our exportation of barreled beef, the propagation of swine's flesh, and improvement in the art of making good bacon, so much wanted among us by the great destruction of pigs, too frequent at our tables, which are no way comparable in taste or magnificence to a well-grown, fat, yearling child, which roasted whole will make a considerable figure at a lord mayor's feast or any other public entertainment. But this and many others I omit, being studious of brevity.

Supposing that one thousand families in this city would be constant customers for infants' flesh, besides others who might have it at merry meetings, particularly weddings and christenings, I compute that Dublin would take off annually about twenty thousand carcasses, and the rest of the kingdom (where probably they will be sold somewhat cheaper) the remaining eighty thousand.

I can think of no one objection that will possibly be raised against this proposal, unless it should be urged that the number of people will be thereby much lessened in the kingdom. This I freely own, and it was indeed one principal design in offering it to the world. I desire the reader will observe, that I calculate my remedy for this one individual kingdom of Ireland and for no other that ever was, is, or I think ever can be upon earth. Therefore let no man talk to me of other expedients: of taxing our absentees at five shillings a pound: of using neither clothes nor household furniture except what is of our own growth and manufacture: of utterly rejecting the materials and instruments that promote foreign luxury: of curing the expensiveness of pride, vanity, idleness, and gaming in our women: of introducing a vein of parsimony, prudence, and temperance: of learning to love our country, in the want of which we differ even from Laplanders and the inhabitants of Topinamboo[17]: of quitting our animosities and factions, nor acting any longer like the Jews, who were murdering one another at the very moment their city was taken: of being a little cautious not to sell our country and conscience for nothing: of teaching landlords to have at least one degree of mercy toward their tenants: lastly, of putting a spirit of honesty, industry, and skill into our shopkeepers; who, if a resolution could now be taken to buy only our native goods, would immediately unite to cheat and exact upon us in the price, the measure, and the goodness, nor could ever yet be brought to make one fair proposal of just dealing, though often and earnestly invited to it.

Therefore I repeat, let no man talk to me of these and the like expedients, till he hath at least some glimpse of hope that there will ever be some hearty and sincere attempt to put them in practice.

But as to myself, having been wearied out for many years with offering vain, idle, visionary thoughts, and at length utterly despairing of success, I fortunately fell upon this proposal, which, as it is wholly new, so it hath something solid and real, of no expense and little trouble, full in our own power, and whereby we can incur no danger in disobliging England. For this kind of commodity will not bear exportation, the flesh being of too tender a consistence to admit a long continuance in salt, although perhaps I could name a country[18] which would be glad to eat up our whole nation without it.

After all, I am not so violently bent upon my own opinion as to reject any offer proposed by wise men, which shall be found equally innocent, cheap, easy, and effectual. But before something of that kind shall be advanced in contradiction to my scheme, and offering a better, I desire the author or authors will be pleased maturely to consider two points. First, as things now stand, how they will be able to find food and raiment for an hundred thousand useless mouths and backs. And secondly, there being a round million of creatures in human figure throughout this kingdom, whose sole subsistence put into a common stock would leave them in debt two millions of pounds sterling, adding those who are beggars by profession to the bulk of farmers, cottagers, and laborers, with their wives and children who are beggars in effect; I desire those politicians who dislike my overture, and may perhaps be so bold to attempt an answer, that they will first ask the parents of these mortals whether they would not at this day think it a great happiness to have been sold for food at a year old in the manner I prescribe, and thereby have avoided such a perpetual scene of misfortunes as they have since gone through by the oppression of landlords, the impossibility of paying rent without money or trade, the want of common sustenance, with neither house nor clothes to cover them from the inclemencies of the weather, and the most inevitable prospect of entailing the like or greater miseries upon their breed forever.

I profess, in the sincerity of my heart, that I have not the least personal interest in endeavoring to promote this necessary work, having no other motive than the public good of my country, by advancing our trade, providing for infants, relieving the poor, and giving some pleasure to the rich. I have no children by which I can propose to get a single penny; the youngest being nine years old, and my wife past childbearing.

NOTES

1. Dublin.
2. The Pretender, son of King James II, who was dethroned in a Protestant revolution, was barred from succeeding to the British crown; many Irish Catholics supported his claim as rightful heir, joined him in exile, and tried to further his unsuccessful efforts at counterrevolution.
3. Many of the poor in Ireland emigrated as indentured servants, for they were unable to pay for their own passage. Such bargains made them virtual slaves for a fixed period of time, usually about seven years.
4. There were twelve shillings to the British pound, and a pound in 1729 would have bought approximately one hundred and fifty dollars' worth of goods in today's money.
5. "Expect" or "believe."
6. Show talent.
7. A crown was one-fourth of a pound.
8. François Rabelais (1483–1553), a comic writer.
9. Swift's audience would have been Anglo-Irish Protestants. Papists are Roman Catholics.
1. Skillfully.
2. Slaughterhouses.
3. George Psalmanazar, a Frenchman who pretended to be from Formosa (now Taiwan), had written a book about his supposed homeland that described human sacrifice and cannibalism.
4. Worth about four English pence; there were 240 pence to the pound in 1729.
5. A chair, often covered, carried on poles by two people; akin to a taxi.
6. Seizure in payment of debts.
7. Recipes.
8. In Brazil.
9. England.
10. Skillfully.
11. Slaughterhouses.
12. George Psalmanazar, a Frenchman who pretended to be from Formosa (now Taiwan), had written a book about his supposed homeland that described human sacrifice and cannibalism.
13. Worth about four English pence; there were 240 pence to the pound in 1729.
14. A chair, often covered, carried on poles by two people; akin to a taxi.
15. Seizure in payment of debts.
16. Recipes.
17. In Brazil.
18. England.

PERSONAL RESPONSE

At what point did you realize that Swift is not serious in his proposal to use toddlers for food? Do you think his rather unusual suggestion stirs sympathy for the deplorable condition of the people of Ireland?

QUESTIONS FOR CLASS OR SMALL-GROUP DISCUSSION

1. Where does Swift state his thesis? What are the main points of his argument? Where does he offer counterarguments?

2. When Swift wrote "A Modest Proposal," the word *modest* meant simple, easy to achieve, and not likely to be met with opposition. Does that meaning accurately describe what he says? Locate other words that are unfamiliar or whose historic references you may not know, search out their meanings, and share your findings with the class.

3. Where does Swift use irony (saying one thing but meaning the opposite), understatement (saying less than he means), and overstatement (saying more than he means)?

4. Readers are often shocked at the use of toddlers as food in Swift's satire. What are some of the other proposed economic uses of toddlers?

5. What do you imagine are the politics behind Swift's essay?

ON THE MEANING OF PLUMBING AND POVERTY

MELANIE SCHELLER

Melanie Scheller's essay, "On the Meaning of Plumbing and Poverty," first appeared in the North Carolina Independent Weekly *in 1990.*

Several years ago I spent some time as a volunteer on the geriatric ward of a psychiatric hospital. I was fascinated by the behavior of one of the patients, an elderly woman who shuffled at regular intervals to the bathroom, where she methodically flushed the toilet. Again and again she carried out her sacred mission as if summoned by some supernatural force, until the flush of the toilet became a rhythmic counterpoint for the ward's activity. If someone blocked her path or if, God forbid, the bathroom was in use when she reached it, she became agitated and confused.

Obviously, that elderly patient was a sick woman. And yet I felt a certain kinship with her, for I too have suffered from an obsession with toilets. I spent much of my childhood living in houses without indoor plumbing and, while I don't feel compelled to flush a toilet at regular intervals, I sometimes feel that toilets, or the lack there of, have shaped my identity in ways that are painful to admit.

I'm not a child of the Depression, but I grew up in an area of the South that had changed little since the days of the New Deal. My mother was a widow with six children to support, not an easy task under any circumstances, but especially difficult in rural North Carolina during the 1960s. To her credit, we were never seriously in danger of going hungry. Our vegetable garden kept us stocked with tomatoes and string beans. We kept a few chickens and sometimes a cow. Blackberries were free for the picking in the fields nearby. Neighbors did their good Christian duty by bringing us donations of fresh fruit and candy at Christmastime. But a roof over our heads—that wasn't so easily improvised.

Like rural Southern gypsies, we moved from one dilapidated Southern farm-house to another in a constant search for a decent place to live. Sometimes we moved when the rent increased beyond the $30 or $40 my mother could afford. Or the house burned down, not an unusual occurrence in substandard housing. One year, when we were gathered together for Thanksgiving dinner, a stranger walked in without knocking and announced that we were being evicted. The house had been sold without our knowledge and the new owner wanted to start remodeling immediately. We tried to finish our meal with an attitude of thanksgiving while he worked around us with his tape measure.

Usually, we rented from farm families who'd moved from the old home place to one of the brick boxes that are now the standard in rural Southern architecture. The old farmhouse wasn't worth fixing up with a septic tank and flush toilet, but it was good enough to rent for a few dollars a month to families like mine. The idea of tenants' rights hadn't trickled down yet from the far reaches of the liberal North. It never occurred to us to demand improvements in the facilities. The ethic of the land said we should take what we could get and be grateful for it.

Without indoor plumbing, getting clean is a tiring and time-consuming ritual. At one point, I lived in a five-room house with six or more people, all of whom congregated in the one heated room to eat, do homework, watch television, dress and undress, argue, wash dishes. During cold weather we dragged mattresses from the unheated rooms and slept huddled together on the floor by the woodstove. For my bathing routine, I first pinned a sheet to a piece of twine strung across the kitchen. That gave me some degree of privacy from the six other people in the room. At that time, our house had an indoor cold-water faucet, from which I filled a pot of water to heat on the kitchen stove. It took several pots of hot water to fill the metal washtub we used.

Since I was a teenager and prone to sulkiness if I didn't get special treatment, I got to take the first bath while the water was still clean. The others used the water I left behind, freshened up with hot water from the pot on the stove. Then the tub had to be dragged to the door and the bath water dumped outside. I longed to be like the woman in the Calgon bath oil commercials, luxuriating in a marble tub full of scented water with bubbles piled high and stacks of thick, clean towels nearby.

People raised in the land of the bath-and-a-half may wonder why I make such a fuss about plumbing. Maybe they spent a year in the Peace Corps, or they back-packed across India, or they worked at a summer camp and, gosh, using a latrine isn't all that bad. And of course it's *not* that bad. Not when you can catch the next plane out of the country, or pick up your duffel bag and head for home, or call mom and dad to come and get you when things get too tedious. A sojourn in a Third World country, where everyone shares the same primitive facilities, may cause some temporary discomfort, but the experience is soon converted into amusing anecdotes for cocktail-party conversation. It doesn't corrode your self-esteem with a sense of shame the way a childhood spent in chronic, unrelenting poverty can.

In the South of my childhood, not having indoor plumbing was the indelible mark of poor white trash. The phrase "so poor they didn't have a pot to piss in" said it all. Poor white trash were viciously stereotyped, and never more viciously than on the playground. White-trash children had cooties—everybody knew that. They had ringworm and pink-eye—don't get near them or you might catch it. They picked their noses. They messed in their pants. If a white-trash child made the mistake of catching a softball during recess, the other children made an elaborate show of wiping it clean before they would touch it.

Once a story circulated at school about a family whose infant daughter had fallen into the "slop jar" and drowned. When I saw the smirks and heard the laughter with which the story was told, I felt sick and afraid in the pit of my stomach. A little girl had died, but people were laughing. What had she done to deserve that laughter? I could only assume that using a chamber pot was something so disgusting, so shameful, that it made a person less than human.

My family was visibly and undeniably poor. My clothes were obviously hand-me-downs. I got free lunches at school. I went to the health department for immunizations. Surely it was equally obvious that we didn't have a flush toilet. But, like an alcoholic who believes no one will know he has a problem as long as he doesn't drink in public, I convinced myself that no one knew my family's little secret. It was a form of denial that would color my relationships with the outside world for years to come.

Having a friend from school spend the night at my house was out of the question. Better to be friendless than to have my classmates know my shameful secret. Home visits from teachers or ministers left me in a dither of anticipatory anxiety. As they chattered on and on with Southern small talk about tomato plants and relish recipes, I sat on the edge of my seat, tensed against the dreaded words, "May I use your bathroom, please?" When I began dating in high school, I'd lie in wait behind the front door, ready to dash out as soon as my date pulled in the driveway, never giving him a chance to hear the call of nature while on our property.

With the help of a scholarship I was able to go away to college, where I could choose from dozens of dormitory toilets and take as many hot showers as I wanted, but I could never openly express my joy in using the facilities. My roommates, each a pampered only child from a well-to-do family, whined and complained about having to share a bathroom. I knew that if I expressed delight in simply having a bathroom, I would immediately be labeled as a hick. The need to conceal my real self by stifling my emotions created a barrier around me and I spent my college years in a vacuum of isolation.

Almost twenty years have passed since I first tried to leave my family's chamber pot behind. For many of those years, it followed behind me—the ghost of chamber pots past—clanging and banging and threatening to spill its humiliating contents at any moment. I was convinced that everyone could see it, could smell it even. No college degree or job title seemed capable of banishing it.

If finances had permitted, I might have become an Elvis Presley or a Tammy Faye Baker, easing the pain of remembered poverty with gold-plated bathtub fixtures and leopard-skinned toilet seats. I feel blessed that gradually, ever so gradually, the shame of poverty has begun to fade. The pleasures of the present now take priority over where a long-ago bowel movement did or did not take place. But, for many Southerners, chamber pots and outhouses are more than just memories.

In North Carolina alone, 200,000 people still live without indoor plumbing. People who haul their drinking water home from a neighbor's house or catch rainwater in barrels. People who can't wash their hands before handling food, the way restaurant employees are required by state law to do. People who sneak into public restrooms every day to wash, shave, and brush their teeth before going to work or to school. People who sacrifice their dignity and self-respect when forced to choose between going homeless and going to an outhouse. People whose children think they deserve the conditions in which they live and hold their heads low to hide the shame. But they're not the ones who should feel ashamed. No, they're not the ones who should feel ashamed.

PERSONAL RESPONSE

What do you think of Scheller's experiences growing up in poverty? Can you sympathize with her? Have you ever been so poor that you felt helpless and vulnerable? Do you recall a particular period or occasion in your life when you felt a similar sense of shame or acute awareness of yourself in relation to others?

QUESTIONS FOR CLASS OR SMALL-GROUP DISCUSSION

1. Summarize in your own words the effects of poverty on Scheller, and then discuss your own reactions to what she describes.
2. Scheller says that people wonder why she "make[s] such a fuss about plumbing." Indeed, she writes about a subject that people seldom discuss in either conversation or writing. How well do you think she has handled her subject? Does she convince you of her reasons for making the fuss?
3. Scheller concludes by repeating "they're not the ones who should feel ashamed." Who does she imply should feel ashamed? Do you agree with her on this point? Why?
4. Compare Scheller's description of her environment with Canadian neighbourhoods that you consider to be poor.

ON DUMPSTER DIVING

LARS EIGHNER

Lars Eighner, born in 1948, in Corpus Christi, Texas, is known for his best-selling memoir, Travels with Lizbeth, *in which he recounts his three years of living homeless on the streets with his dog.*

Long before I began Dumpster diving I was impressed with Dumpsters, enough so that I wrote the Merriam-Webster[1] research service to discover what I could about the word *Dumpster*. I learned from them that it is a proprietary word belonging to the Dempster Dumpster company. Since then I have dutifully capitalized the word,

One man's garbage is another man's survival.
Photo Source: © Stephen McSweeny/Shutterstock

although it was lowercased in almost all the citations Merriam-Webster photo-copied for me. Dempster's word is too apt. I have never heard these things called anything but Dumpsters. I do not know anyone who knows the generic name for these objects. From time to time I have heard a wino or hobo give some corrupted credit to the original and call them Dipsy Dumpsters.

I began Dumpster diving about a year before I became homeless.

I prefer the word *scavenging* and use the word *scrounging* when I mean to be obscure. I have heard people, evidently meaning to be polite, use the word *foraging*, but I prefer to reserve that word for gathering nuts and berries and such, which I do also according to the season and the opportunity. *Dumpster diving* seems to me to be a little too cute and, in my case, inaccurate because I lack the athletic ability to lower myself into the Dumpsters as the true divers do, much to their increased profit.

I like the frankness of the word *scavenging*, which I can hardly think of without picturing a big black snail on an aquarium wall. I live from the refuse of others. I am a scavenger. I think it a sound and honorable niche, although if I could I would natu-rally prefer to live the comfortable consumer life, perhaps—and only perhaps—as a slightly less wasteful consumer, owing to what I have learned as a scavenger.

While Lizbeth[2] and I were still living in the shack on Avenue B as my savings ran out, I put almost all my sporadic income into rent. The necessities of daily life I began to extract from Dumpsters. Yes, we ate from them. Except for jeans, all my clothes came from Dumpsters. Boom boxes, candles, bedding, toilet paper, a virgin male love doll, medicine, books, a typewriter, dishes, furnishings, and change, some-times amounting to many dollars—I acquired many things from the Dumpsters. I have learned much as scavenger. I mean to put some of what I have learned down here, beginning with the practical art of Dumpster diving and proceeding to the abstract.

What is safe to eat?

After all, the finding of objects is becoming something of an urban art. Even respectable employed people will sometimes find something tempting sticking out of a Dumpster or standing beside one. Quite a number of people, not all of them of the bohemian type, are willing to brag that they found this or that piece in the trash. But eating from Dumpsters is what separates the dilettanti from the pro-fessionals. Eating safely from the Dumpsters involves three principles: using the senses and common sense to evaluate the condition of the found materials, knowing the Dumpsters of a given area and checking them regularly, and seeking always to answer the question, "Why was this discarded?"

Perhaps everyone who has a kitchen and a regular supply of groceries has, at one time or another, made a sandwich and eaten half of it before discovering mold on the bread or got a mouthful of milk before realizing the milk had turned. Nothing of the sort is likely to happen to a Dumpster diver because he is constantly reminded that most food is discarded for a reason. Yet a lot of perfectly good food can be found in Dumpsters.

Canned goods, for example, turn up fairly often in the Dumpsters I frequent. All except the most phobic people would be willing to eat from a can, even if it came from a Dumpster. Canned goods are among the safest of foods to be found in Dumpsters but are not utterly foolproof.

Although very rare with modern canning methods, botulism is a possibility. Most other forms of food poisoning seldom do lasting harm to a healthy person, but botulism is almost certainly fatal and often the first symptom is death. Except for carbonated beverages, all canned goods should contain a slight vacuum and suck air when first punctured. Bulging, rusty, and dented cans and cans that spew when punctured should be avoided, especially when the contents are not very acidic or syrupy.

Heat can break down the botulin, but this requires much more cooking than most people do to canned goods. To the extent that botulism occurs at all, of course, it can occur in cans on pantry shelves as well as in cans from Dumpsters. Need I say that home-canned goods are simply too risky to be recommended.

From time to time one of my companions, aware of the source of my provisions, will ask, "Do you think these crackers are really safe to eat?" For some reason it is most often the crackers they ask about.

This question has always made me angry. Of course I would not offer my com-panion anything I had doubts about. But more than that, I wonder why he cannot evaluate the condition of the crackers for himself. I have no special knowledge and I have been wrong before. Since he knows where the food comes from, it seems to me he ought to assume some of the responsibility for deciding what he will put in his mouth. For myself I have few qualms about dry foods such as crackers, cookies, cereal, chips, and pasta if they are free of visible contaminates and still dry and crisp. Most often such things are found in the original packaging, which is not so much a positive sign as it is the absence of a negative one.

Raw fruits and vegetables with intact skins seem perfectly safe to me, excluding of course the obviously rotten. Many are discarded for minor imperfections that can be pared away. Leafy vegetables, grapes, cauliflower, broccoli, and similar things may be contaminated by liquids and may be impractical to wash.

Candy, especially hard candy, is usually safe if it has not drawn ants. Chocolate is often discarded only because it has become discolored as the cocoa butter de-emulsified. Candying, after all, is one method of food preservation because pathogens do not like very sugary substances.

All of these foods might be found in any Dumpster and can be evaluated with some confidence largely on the basis of appearance. Beyond these are foods that cannot be correctly evaluated without additional information.

I began scavenging by pulling pizzas out of the Dumpster behind a pizza delivery shop. In general, prepared food requires caution, but in this case I knew when the shop closed and went to the Dumpster as soon as the last of the help left.

Such shops often get prank orders; both the orders and the products made to fill them are called *bogus*. Because help seldom stays long at these places, pizzas are often made with the wrong topping, refused on delivery for being cold, or baked incorrectly. The products to be discarded are boxed up because inventory is kept by counting boxes. A boxed pizza can be written off; an unboxed pizza does not exist.

I never placed a bogus order to increase the supply of pizzas and I believe no one else was scavenging in this Dumpster. But the people in the shop became suspicious and began to retain their garbage in the shop overnight. While it lasted I had a steady supply of fresh, sometimes warm pizza. Because I knew the Dumpster I knew the source of the pizza, and because I visited the Dumpster regularly I knew what was fresh and what was yesterday's.

The area I frequent is inhabited by many affluent college students. I am not here by chance; the Dumpsters in this area are very rich. Students throw out many good things, including food. In particular they tend to throw everything out when they move at the end of a semester, before and after breaks, and around midterm, when many of them despair of college. So I find it advantageous to keep an eye on the academic calendar.

Students throw food away around breaks because they do not know whether it has spoiled or will spoil before they return. A typical discard is a half jar of peanut butter. In fact, nonorganic peanut butter does not require refrigeration and is unlikely to spoil in any reasonable time. The student does not know that, and since it is Daddy's money, the student decides not to take a chance. Opened containers require caution and some attention to the question, "Why was this discarded?" But in the case of discards from student apartments, the answer may be that the item was thrown out through carelessness, ignorance, or wastefulness. This can sometimes be deduced when the item is found with many others, including some that are obviously perfectly good.

Some students, and others, approach defrosting a freezer by chucking out the whole lot. Not only do the circumstances of such a find tell the story, but also the mass of frozen goods stays cold for a long time and items may be found still frozen or freshly thawed.

Yogurt, cheese, and sour cream are items that are often thrown out while they are still good. Occasionally I find a cheese with a spot of mold, which of course I just pare off, and because it is obvious why such a cheese was discarded, I treat it with less suspicion than an apparently perfect cheese found in similar circumstances. Yogurt is often discarded, still sealed, only because the expiration date on the carton had passed. This is one of my favourite finds because yogurt will keep for several days, even in warm weather.

Students throw out canned goods and staples at the end of semesters and when they give up college at midterm. Drugs, pornography, spirits, and the like are often discarded when parents are expected—Dad's Day, for example. And spirits also turn up after big party weekends, presumably discarded by the newly reformed. Wine and spirits, of course, keep perfectly well even once opened, but the same cannot be said of beer.

My test for carbonated soft drinks is whether they still fizz vigorously. Many juices or other beverages are too acidic or too syrupy to cause much concern, provided they are not visibly contaminated. I have discovered nasty molds in vegetable juices, even when the product was found under its original seal; I recommend that such products be decanted slowly into a clear glass. Liquids always require some care. One hot day I found a large jug of Pat O'Brien's Hurricane mix. The jug had been opened but was still ice cold. I drank three large glasses before it became apparent to me that someone had added the rum to the mix, and not a little rum. I never tasted the rum, and by the time I began to feel the effects I had already ingested a very large quantity of the beverage. Some divers would have considered this a boon, but being suddenly intoxicated in a public place in the early afternoon is not my idea of a good time.

I have heard of people maliciously contaminating discarded food and even handouts, but mostly I have heard of this from people with vivid imaginations who have had no experience with the Dumpsters themselves. Just before the pizza shop stopped discarding its garbage at night, jalapeños began showing up on most of the thrown-out pizzas. If indeed this was meant to discourage me, it was a wasted effort because I am a native Texan.

For myself, I avoid game, poultry, pork, and egg-based foods, whether I find them raw or cooked. I seldom have the means to cook what I find, but when I do I avail myself of plentiful supplies of beef, which is often in very good condition. I suppose fish becomes disagreeable before it becomes dangerous. Lizbeth is happy to have any such thing that is past its prime and, in fact, does not recognize fish as food until it is quite strong.

Home leftovers, as opposed to surpluses from restaurants, are very often bad. Evidently, especially among students, there is a common type of personality that carefully wraps up even the smallest leftover and shoves it into the back of the refrigerator for six months or so before discarding it. Characteristic of this type are the reused jars and margarine tubs to which the remains are committed. I avoid ethnic foods I am unfamiliar with. If I do not know what it is supposed to look like when it is good, I cannot be certain I will be able to tell if it is bad.

No matter how careful I am I still get dysentery at least once a month, oftener in warm weather. I do not want to paint too romantic a picture. Dumpster diving has serious drawbacks as a way of life.

I learned to scavenge gradually, on my own. Since then I have initiated several companions into the trade. I have learned that there is a predictable series of stages a person goes through in learning to scavenge.

At first the new scavenger is filled with disgust and self-loathing. He is ashamed of being seen and may lurk around, trying to duck behind things, or he may try to dive at night. (In fact, most people instinctively look away from a scavenger. By skulking around, the novice calls attention to himself and arouses suspicion. Diving at night is ineffective and needlessly messy.)

Every grain of rice seems to be a maggot. Everything seems to stink. He can wipe the egg yolk off the found can, but he cannot erase from his mind the stigma of eating garbage.

That stage passes with experience. The scavenger finds a pair of running shoes that fit and look and smell brand-new. He finds a pocket calculator in perfect working order. He finds pristine ice cream, still frozen, more than he can eat or keep. He begins to understand: People throw away perfectly good stuff, a lot of perfectly good stuff.

At this stage, Dumpster shyness begins to dissipate. The diver, after all, has the last laugh. He is finding all manner of good things that are his for the taking. Those who disparage his profession are the fools, not he.

He may begin to hang on to some perfectly good things for which he has neither a use nor a market. Then he begins to take note of the things that are not perfectly good but are nearly so. He mates a Walkman with broken earphones and one that is missing a battery cover. He picks up things that he can repair.

At this stage he may become lost and never recover. Dumpsters are full of things of some potential value to someone and also of things that never have much intrinsic value but are interesting. All the Dumpster divers I have known come to the point of trying to acquire everything they touch. Why not take it, they reason, since it is all free? This is, of course, hopeless. Most divers come to realize that they must restrict themselves to items of relatively immediate utility. But in some cases the diver simply cannot control himself. I have met several of these pack-rat types. Their ideas of the values of various pieces of junk verge on the psychotic. Every bit of glass may be a diamond, they think, and all that glistens, gold.

I tend to gain weight when I am scavenging. Partly this is because I always find far more pizza and doughnuts than water-packed tuna, nonfat yogurt, and fresh vegetables. Also I have not developed much faith in the reliability of Dumpsters as a food source, although it has been proven to me many times. I tend to eat as if I have no idea where my next meal is coming from. But mostly I just hate to see food go to waste and so I eat much more than I should. Something like this drives the obsession to collect junk.

As for collecting objects, I usually restrict myself to collecting one kind of small object at a time, such as pocket calculators, sunglasses, or campaign buttons. To live on the street I must anticipate my needs to a certain extent: I must pick up and save warm bedding I find in August because it will not be found in Dumpsters in November. As I have no access to health care, I often hoard essential drugs, such as antibiotics and antihistamines. (This course can be recommended only to those with some grounding in pharmacology. Antibiotics, for example, even when indicated are worse than useless if taken in insufficient amounts.) But even if I had a home with extensive storage space, I could not save everything that might be valuable in some contingency.

I have proprietary feelings about my Dumpsters. As I have mentioned, it is no accident that I scavenge from ones where good finds are common. But my limited experience with Dumpsters in other areas suggests to me that even in poorer areas, Dumpsters, if attended with sufficient diligence, can be made to yield a livelihood. The rich students discard perfectly good kiwifruit; poorer people discard perfectly good apples. Slacks and Polo shirts are found in the one place; jeans and T-shirts in the other. The population of competitors rather than the affluence of the dumpers most affects the feasibility of survival by scavenging. The large number of competitors is what puts me off the idea of trying to scavenge in places like Los Angeles.

Curiously, I do not mind my direct competition, other scavengers, so much as I hate the can scroungers.

People scrounge cans because they have to have a little cash. I have tried scrounging cans with an able-bodied companion. Afoot a can scrounger simply cannot make more than a few dollars a day. One can extract the necessities of life from the Dumpsters directly with far less effort than would be required to accumulate the equivalent value in cans. (These observations may not hold in places with container redemption laws.)

Can scroungers, then, are people who must have small amounts of cash. These are drug addicts and winos, mostly the latter because the amounts of cash are so small. Spirits and drugs do, like all other commodities, turn up in Dumpsters and the scavenger will from time to time have a half bottle of a rather good wine with his dinner. But the wino cannot survive on these occasional finds; he must have his daily dose to stave off the DTs. All the cans he can carry will buy about three bottles of Wild Irish Rose.

I do not begrudge them the cans, but can scroungers tend to tear up the Dumpsters, mixing the contents and littering the area. They become so specialized that they can see only cans. They earn my contempt by passing up change, canned goods, and readily hockable items.

There are precious few courtesies among scavengers. But it is common practice to set aside surplus items: pairs of shoes, clothing, canned goods, and such. A true scavenger hates to see good stuff go to waste, and what he cannot use he leaves in good condition in plain sight.

Can scroungers lay waste to everything in their path and will stir one of a pair of good shoes to the bottom of a Dumpster, to be lost or ruined in the muck. Can scroungers will even go through individual garbage cans, something I have never seen a scavenger do.

Individual garbage cans are set out on the public easement only on garbage days. On other days going through them requires trespassing close to a dwelling. Going through individual garbage cans without scattering litter is almost impossible. Litter is likely to reduce the public's tolerance of scavenging. Individual cans are simply not as productive as Dumpsters; people in houses and duplexes do not move so often and for some reason do not tend to discard as much useful material. Moreover, the time required to go through one garbage can that serves one household is not much less than the time required to go through a Dumpster that contains the refuse of twenty apartments.

But my strongest reservation about going through individual garbage cans is that this seems to me a very personal kind of invasion to which I would object if I were a householder. Although many things in Dumpsters are obviously meant never to come to light, a Dumpster is somehow less personal.

I avoid trying to draw conclusions about the people who dump in the Dumpsters I frequent. I think it would be unethical to do so, although I know many people will find the idea of scavenger ethics too funny for words.

Dumpsters contain bank statements, correspondence, and other documents, just as anyone might expect. But there are also less obvious sources of information. Pill bottles, for example. The labels bear the name of the patient, the name of the doctor, and the name of the drug. AIDS drugs and anti-psychotic medicines, to name but two groups, are specific and are seldom prescribed for any other disorders. The plastic compacts for birth-control pills usually have complete label information.

Despite all of this sensitive information, I have had only one apartment resident object to my going through the Dumpster. In that case it turned out the resident was a university athlete who was taking bets and who was afraid I would turn up his wager slips.

Occasionally a find tells a story. I once found a small paper bag containing some unused condoms, several partial tubes of flavored sexual lubricants, a partially used compact of birth-control pills, and the torn pieces of a picture of a young man. Clearly she was through with him and planning to give up sex altogether.

Dumpster things are often sad—abandoned teddy bears, shredded wedding books, despaired-of sales kits. I find many pets lying in state in Dumpsters. Although I hope to get off the streets so that Lizbeth can have a long and comfortable old age, I know this hope is not very realistic. So I suppose when her time comes she too will go into a Dumpster. I will have no better place for her. And after all, it is fitting, since for most of her life her livelihood has come from the Dumpster. When she finds something I think is safe that has been spilled from a Dumpster, I let her have it. She already knows the route around the best ones. I like to think that if she survives me she will have a chance of evading the dog catcher and of finding her sustenance on the route.

Silly vanities also come to rest in the Dumpsters. I am a rather accomplished needleworker. I get a lot of material from the Dumpsters. Evidently sorority girls, hoping to impress someone, perhaps themselves, with their mastery of a womanly art, buy a lot of embroider-by-number kits, work a few stitches horribly, and eventually discard the whole mess. I pull out their stitches, turn the canvas over, and work an original design. Do not think I refrain from chuckling as I make gifts from these kits.

I find diaries and journals. I have often thought of compiling a book of literary found objects. And perhaps I will one day. But what I find is hopelessly commonplace and bad without being, even unconsciously, camp. College students also discard their papers. I am horrified to discover the kind of paper that now merits an A in an undergraduate course. I am grateful, however, for the number of good books and magazines the students throw out.

In the area I know best I have never discovered vermin in the Dumpsters, but there are two kinds of kitty surprise. One is alley cats whom I meet as they leap, claws first, out of Dumpsters. This is especially thrilling when I have Lizbeth in tow. The other kind of kitty surprise is a plastic garbage bag filled with some ponderous, amorphous mass. This always proves to be used cat litter.

City bees harvest doughnut glaze and this makes the Dumpster at the doughnut shop more interesting. My faith in the instinctive wisdom of animals is always shaken whenever I see Lizbeth attempt to catch a bee in her mouth, which she does whenever bees are present. Evidently some birds find Dumpsters profitable, for birdie surprise is almost as common as kitty surprise of the first kind. In hunting season all kinds of small game turn up in Dumpsters, some of it, sadly, not entirely dead. Curiously, summer and winter, maggots are uncommon.

The worst of the living and near-living hazards of the Dumpsters are the fire ants. The food they claim is not much of a loss, but they are vicious and aggressive. It is very easy to brush some surface of the Dumpster and pick up half a dozen or more fire ants, usually in some sensitive area such as the underarm. One advantage of bringing Lizbeth along as I make Dumpster rounds is that, for obvious reasons, she is very alert to ground-based fire ants. When Lizbeth recognizes a fire-ant infestation around her feet, she does the Dance of the Zillion Fire Ants. I have learned not to ignore this warning from Lizbeth, whether I perceive the tiny ants or not, but to remove ourselves at Lizbeth's first pas de bourée. All the more so because the ants are the worst in the summer months when I wear flip-flops if I have them. (Perhaps someone will misunderstand this. Lizbeth does the Dance of the Zillion Fire Ants when she recognizes more fire ants than she cares to eat, not when she is being bitten. Since I have learned to react promptly, she does not get bitten at all. It is the isolated patrol of fire ants that falls in Lizbeth's range that deserves pity. She finds them quite tasty.)

By far the best way to go through a Dumpster is to lower yourself into it. Most of the good stuff tends to settle at the bottom because it is usually weightier than the rubbish. My more athletic companions have often demonstrated to me that they can extract much good material from a Dumpster I have already been over.

To those psychologically or physically unprepared to enter a Dumpster, I recommend a stout stick, preferably with some barb or hook at one end. The hook can be used to grab plastic garbage bags. When I find canned goods or other objects loose at the bottom of a Dumpster, I lower a bag into it, roll the desired object into the bag, and then hoist the bag out—a procedure more easily described than executed. Much Dumpster diving is a matter of experience for which nothing will do except practice.

Dumpster diving is outdoor work, often surprisingly pleasant. It is not entirely predictable; things of interest turn up every day and some days there are finds of great value. I am always very pleased when I can turn up exactly the thing I most wanted to find. Yet in spite of the element of chance, scavenging more than most other pursuits tends to yield returns in some proportion to the effort and intelligence brought to bear. It is very sweet to turn up a few dollars in change from a Dumpster that has just been gone over by a wino.

The land is now covered with cities. The cities are full of Dumpsters. If a member of the canine race is ever able to know what it is doing, then Lizbeth knows that when we go around to the Dumpsters, we are hunting. I think of scavenging as a modern form of self-reliance. In any event, after having survived nearly ten years of government service, where everything is geared to the lowest common denominator, I find it refreshing to have work that rewards initiative and effort. Certainly I would be happy to have a sinecure again, but I am no longer heartbroken that I left one.

I find from the experience of scavenging two rather deep lessons. The first is to take what you can use and let the rest go. I have come to think that there is no value in the abstract. A thing I cannot use or make useful, perhaps by trading, has no value however rare or fine it may be. I mean useful in a broad sense—some art I would find useful and some otherwise.

I was shocked to realize that some things are not worth acquiring, but now I think it is so. Some material things are white elephants that eat up the possessor's substance. The second lesson is the transience of material being. This has not quite converted me to a dualist, but it has made some headway in that direction. I do not suppose that ideas are immortal, but certainly mental things are longer lived than other material things.

Once I was the sort of person who invests objects with sentimental value. Now I no longer have those objects, but I have the sentiments yet.

Many times in our travels I have lost everything but the clothes I was wearing and Lizbeth. The things I find in Dumpsters, the love letters and rag dolls of so many lives, remind me of this lesson. Now I hardly pick up a thing without envisioning the time I will cast it aside. This I think is a healthy state of mind. Almost everything I have now has already been cast out at least once, proving that what I own is valueless to someone.

Anyway, I find my desire to grab for the gaudy bauble has been largely sated. I think this is an attitude I share with the very wealthy—we both know there is plenty more where what we have came from. Between us are the rat-race millions who nightly scavenge the cable channels looking for they know not what.

I am sorry for them.

NOTES

1. A large publisher of dictionaries.
2. The author's dog.

PERSONAL RESPONSE

Have you ever "dived" in a dumpster for food or anything else, either out of necessity or just because you were curious? Check out your local dumpster on any given day—what are some of the things you find besides food? When you walk past a destitute street person, what feelings or reactions surface? Do you find it easy or hard to make eye contact?

QUESTIONS FOR CLASS OR SMALL-GROUP DISCUSSION

1. "Dumpster diving" is part of the language of Freeganism, a movement dedicated to the minimal consumption of resources. "Freegans" avoid buying anything (http://freegan.info). Why do you think this movement does or does not make sense?

2. Why does Eighner feel sorry for the "rat-race millions" who scavenge for unknown things on the cable channels?

3. What does garbage tell you about a culture?

4. Ask a friend if you can go through his or her garbage. What can you find out about your friend from looking through the garbage? What conclusions can you make about your culture by examining this garbage? Were there things in the garbage that could have been recycled or even eaten?

FOR FURTHER VIEWING: POVERTY AND HOMELESSNESS

The Grapes of Wrath (1940); *Born into Brothels: Calcutta's Red Light Kids* (2004); *Leaving Las Vegas* (1995); *Titicut Follies* (1967); *Mother Theresa* (1986); *Of Mice and Men* (1939); *City of Joy* (1992); *Les Misérables* (1998); *Angela's Ashes* (1999); *Seven Samurai* (1954).

CHAPTER FOURTEEN

CRIMINAL BEHAVIOUR

INTRODUCTION

Our neighbours to the south have the highest rate of violent crime in the world, or, at least, unlike some countries, they track it and have publicly available statistics to prove it. Much media attention—via television, newspapers, magazines, and Internet news services—is spent on covering crime. It gets bold headlines right beside war, sports, politics, economics, and the weather. Then there is the obsession with crime in popular culture—in comic books, novels, movies, and countless (and we mean *countless*!) television shows. No doubt we are fascinated with criminal behaviour. It sells. Representations of anti-social, non-civilized, dangerous behaviour are a commodity to be sold, as are the representations of catching and punishing anti-social, non-civilized, dangerous behaviour; that is, the only thing better than watching the bad guy is watching the bad guy get caught.

There are lots of questions. Why are we interested in criminal behaviour? What range of activities constitutes criminal behaviour? Who, or what, determines what criminal behaviour is? How much power should law enforcement officers have? Who is most likely to be involved in criminal behaviour, and why? How should criminal behaviour be dealt with and punished? How effective is prison? Why are crime rates among Aboriginals so high (in Canada, Aboriginals make up about 3 percent of the population but 20 percent of the prison population)? Are there effective alternatives to the criminal justice system, and when should they be used? Does the media glorify criminal behaviour and criminals? But there is one thing true of criminal behaviour: Everyone has an opinion.

This chapter's essays deal with some of the most wrenching, difficult issues of our time. In "There Are No Lessons to Be Learned from Littleton," Gary Kleck writes about the massacre at a high school in Littleton, Colorado, that tragically served as a copycat crime for other deranged shooters in Canada and the United States. The Littleton massacre eventually became the subject of Michael Moore's award-winning documentary, *Bowling for Columbine,* which examines America's marketing of fear and obsessive tendency toward gun violence. In "Homeboy," we learn about the life of one of the world's most famous activists—Malcolm X—who began a life of crime, but was "saved" through his conversion to the Nation of Islam and later to Sunni Islam. Some critics have complained that director Spike Lee's movie version of *The Autobiography of Malcolm X* overemphasized his life of crime, ignoring, for the most part, his series of religious conversions that followed. In Mike Royko's essay on guns, we come face to face with the dance of death—and the drum beat of statistics—that has become part of our life in this and the last century. And finally, David Frum, a noteworthy Canadian writer, zeroes in on Canada's crime rate, which, he says, is higher than the crime rate in the United States.

THERE ARE NO LESSONS TO BE LEARNED FROM LITTLETON

Gary Kleck

Gary Kleck, author of Point Blank: Guns and Violence in America *(1991) and* Targeting Guns: Firearms and Their Control *(1997), is a professor in the School of Criminology and Criminal Justice at Florida State University. This essay was first published in the winter/ spring 1999 issue of* Criminal Justice Ethics.

On April 21, 1999, two young men armed with guns and explosives murdered 13 people, wounded 31 others, and then committed suicide in a high school in Littleton, Colorado. This mass shooting had been preceded by three other highly publicized mass shootings in schools involving adolescent boys in the preceding year-and-a-half in Pearl, Mississippi; West Paducah, Kentucky; and Jonesboro,

Arkansas (and there had been at least seven other multi-victim school shootings in the six years before that), and was followed by two more occurring within a month in Springfield, Oregon, and Conyers, Georgia.

In the aftermath of this spate of murders, a wave of commentary followed, in which journalists and other writers of every ideological stripe explained to their readers what lessons were to be learned from Littleton or, more broadly, from this cluster of massacres. In a typical commentary, a writer would diagnose one or more key problems that supposedly contributed to the killings, and then prescribe one or more solutions. The diagnoses and solutions generally fitted remarkably well with preexisting news media themes, reflecting either an impressive ability of news providers to identify causes and solutions in advance or a tendency to exclude the solutions that do not easily fit the themes.

A partial list of the problems that have been blamed for the recent mass killings in schools would include: guns, "assault weapons," large-capacity ammunition magazines, lax regulation of gun shows; the failure of parents to secure guns, school cliques, and the exclusion of "outsiders"; bullying and taunting in schools, especially by high school athletes; inadequate school security, especially a lack of metal detectors, armed guards, locker searches, and so forth; excessively large high schools; inadequate monitoring of potentially violent students by schools; lazy, uninvolved Baby Boomer parents and correspondingly inadequate supervision of their children; young killers not being eligible for the death penalty; a lack of religion, especially in schools; violent movies and television; violent video games; violent material and communications on the World Wide Web/Internet (including bomb-making instructions); anti-Semitism, neo-Nazi sentiments, and Hitler worship; "Industrial" music, Marilyn Manson's music, and other "dark" variants of rock music; Satanism; "Goth" culture among adolescents; and Southern culture.

The purpose of this essay is not to sort out which diagnoses are correct. Many of them are plausible, and some are probably even accurate. Likewise, some of the proposed preventive measures may well be effective. Rather, my main point is that it is generally a mistake to diagnose the causes of violence and crime, or to identify effective ways to reduce violence and crime, via a focus on unusual, heavily publicized violent events, because diagnoses and prescriptions developed or promoted in the immediate aftermath of such events are especially likely to be irrelevant or even counterproductive.

A casual consumer of the flood of news coverage of these shootings could easily draw the conclusion that violence in schools is a growing problem or that youth violence, gun violence, or violence in general has been increasing. In fact, these are the recent trends in violence:

- the homicide rate dropped by a third from 1991 to 1998,
- the juvenile share of arrests for violent crime has been declining since 1992,
- gun violence, and the gun share of violent crimes, has been declining since 1993,
- the lethality of gun crime (the share ending in death) has been declining since the mid-1970s,

- mass murder has been declining for decades (the share of homicide victims killed in incidents with four or more victims dropped in half between 1976 and 1994), and
- school gun violence has generally declined since national statistics were first gathered for the 1992–1993 school year.

In sum, the cluster of mass shootings in schools that occurred in the late 1990s may well be one of the few forms of violence that have been increasing in recent years. Even gun homicides in schools have generally been declining in recent years, despite the massacres. Indeed, excluding the Littleton killings, U.S. schools experienced just two gun homicides during the 1998–1999 school year, which would have been the lowest total since national statistics were first compiled. While some of these facts were mentioned occasionally in news stories about these events, many writers nevertheless offered explanations for the nonexistent "trend" in youth/school/gun violence.

Misdescription of the phenomenon to be explained leads to misdiagnosis of its causes. If there is no increase in youth/school/gun violence, it is fruitless to search for contributing factors that have been increasing in recent years. The only kind of violence that did increase was mass shootings in schools, (so far) only for a very short period of time. Thus, long-term or significant social trends may be irrelevant to these murders, however relevant some of them may be to more commonplace forms of violence. Rather, this short-term clustering may largely reflect an endogenous process by which each new act is triggered by news media accounts of the previous ones. Adolescent boys, faced with powerlessness and anonymity, and otherwise unhappy for a multitude of diverse reasons, recognize that fame, importance, and a sort of immortality have been the rewards for previous mass killers and realistically anticipate the same rewards for themselves if they copy their actions. This process can perpetuate itself until the news media loses interest or competing stories push schoolyard massacres off the front pages.

A tragedy that has already occurred obviously cannot be prevented by any actions taken now. Therefore, actions will prevent harm only to the extent that the events they can effectively head off are likely to be repeated in the future. Yet, the more bizarre an event, the less likely it is to be repeated. Thus, because bizarre events are unlikely to be repeated in quite the same way in the future, the more narrowly a preventive measure is tailored to the specifics of such events, the less likely it is to save lives.

One might argue that while commentary on these media-heavy tragedies might not successfully identify measures that could prevent such events in the future, analysis of the extraordinary events might identify measures that could prevent more commonplace kinds of violence. This might make sense if the heavily publicized events closely resembled more ordinary acts of violence, but in many important ways they do not.

Particular violent events are heavily covered by the news media precisely because they are unusual and thus unrepresentative of broader categories of crime and violence. For example, violent incidents with many victims are the ones most likely to be covered heavily. Yet less than one percent of Americans who are murdered are killed in incidents with four or more dead victims (often regarded by experts as the admittedly arbitrary cutoff between mass killings and "ordinary" homicides). Only two percent are killed in incidents with more than two victims, and these are most commonly killings within families. Their high body count itself makes mass killings unusual and unrepresentative of murder or violence in general.

This would not be problematic if the causes of, and likely solutions to, mass killings matched closely with likely causes and solutions to "ordinary" violence, but mass killings differ from ordinary violence in crucial ways. For example, mass killings are almost invariably planned, while other homicides and assaults are rarely planned. Likewise, firearms are virtually a necessity to killing large numbers of people in a single incident, but far less essential for killing a single person. Further, mass killers often come from middle-class backgrounds and have little prior record of criminal behavior, while these things are rarely true of "ordinary" killers.

A particularly worrisome implication is that a focus on mass murders tends to distract attention from the role of underclass poverty in generating the "ordinary" violence that accounts for almost all of its casualties. There really was a recent increase in juvenile violence, especially with guns, but it was confined to the period from 1985 to 1991, and it had little to do with middle class–linked causes, and everything to do with the collapse of the legitimate economy in America's inner city ghettoes and the resultant rise of the crack economy to fill the vacuum.

Just as few homicides involve large numbers of victims, very few occur in schools. Schools continue to be the safe havens that they were traditionally perceived to be, however much media coverage of these killings has eroded that perception. While there is serious violence in a few schools, and considerable gun violence outside of schools, gun violence in schools is extremely rare. In the 1996–97 school year, 90 percent of public schools did not experience a single serious violent crime (murder, rape, sexual battery, robbery, or attack with a weapon) regardless of gun involvement, and over 99.99 percent have never had a homicide. The violence that does occur in schools is mostly unarmed fighting (including a good deal of bullying), while gun violence, even among adolescents, is almost entirely confined to places other than schools. Less than one in 400 adolescent gun homicides in 1994 occurred in a school or on school grounds.

The school shootings triggered a barrage of transparently irrelevant proposed solutions, tossed out without regard to their relevance to the events that supposedly occasioned the proposals. Mississippi responded to the Pearl shootings by making murder on school property a capital offense, even though premeditated murder, regardless of location, was already a capital offense in Mississippi. The killers in this incident, moreover, were ineligible for the death penalty because of their ages, eleven and thirteen; the minimum age for the death penalty was left unchanged.

Following the first four of these shootings, members of Congress were pushing a bill that would "crack down" on dealers who sell firearms to children even though none of these cases involved a dealer selling a gun to a child. After the shooting in West Paducah, in which the killer was armed with five firearms and shot eight different people in the school lobby, newspapers reported that the school system was considering installing metal detectors. The stories did not explain how metal detectors could prevent attacks by those willing to shoot their way into a school.

After it was found that such transfers were involved in the Littleton case, some analysts proposed restricting sales at gun shows. Gun show sales, however, had nothing at all to do with any of the other high-profile school shootings. The most common modes of acquisition of guns by shooters were theft (the West Paducah, Jonesboro, and Conyers shootings, as well as a somewhat less prominent case in Edinboro, Pennsylvania), while the Springfield shooter was given his guns by his father. Further, even in the Littleton case the three longguns that accounted for all of the deaths were purchased on the killers' behalf by the eighteen-year-old girlfriend of one of the shooters. Under both Colorado and federal law, she would have been eligible to purchase the same guns from any gun store. Further, one of the two killers turned eighteen before the shootings and was likewise eligible to buy longguns from any gun store.

Consequently, regulation of gun shows was totally irrelevant to preventing any of these massacres. One irony of addressing such proposals in the context of mass killings, however, is that some of them make sense, but not in connection with mass killings. As a result, some people will reject the value of a measure with regard to ordinary violence because it is irrelevant to the unusual events at hand. A prime example is extending background checks to private gun transfers at gun shows. The Littleton and other mass shootings are the worst possible examples of cases in which the background checks could succeed since determined killers who plan their murders over a long period of time are the people least likely to be blocked from getting a gun by background checks. As a long-time advocate of extending background checks to all private transfers of guns, not just the few that take place at gun shows, I worry that the real merits of such a step will be obscured by the inane debate over the nonexistent link between gun shows and the Littleton massacre. More broadly, mass killings and other premeditated murders are the very worst examples for buttressing a case in favor of gun control because they involve the perpetrators most strongly motivated and able to evade the controls.

Even under the best of circumstances, the lessons one could derive from the examination of individual violent events are inherently ambiguous. The fact that violence did occur necessarily means that all existing preventive measures failed. This can lead to any of a number of very different conclusions: (1) we need different preventive measures, (2) we need more of the existing measures, or (3) nothing can be done. The ongoing issue most frequently linked to the school shootings was gun control, and reactions by those on both sides of that issue were predictable. Pro-gun people concluded that despite the existence of laws completely prohibiting the purchase and carrying of guns by minors, youthful killers got guns anyway; therefore gun control is ineffective. Meanwhile, pro-control people concluded that if existing gun controls failed, it showed that stronger measures were called for—anything from tougher controls over gun shows and laws requiring guns to be kept locked to lawsuits against gun companies supposedly marketing guns to juveniles.

Assessments of preventive measures based on a narrow focus on violent events that did occur, however, are inherently misleading because they necessarily focus only on the failures of preventive efforts. One cannot infer how much success a policy has had by counting its failures. Successes of preventive measures, unlike failures, usually cannot be observed directly. Instead, they can be detected only indirectly through careful comparison of persons, places, and times subject to the preventive measures with those not subject to them.

Diagnosis of the causes of violence is similarly distorted by a narrow focus on the attributes of a few violent actors, distracting attention from violent actors who lacked the attributes, and from the even larger number of people who had the attributes but were not violent.

Those who propose preventive measures in the context of these mass shootings can plausibly assert that the irrelevance of their proposals to these incidents does not matter because the proposals are meritorious with respect to more common sorts of violence. If that is the case, however, honest advocates should show why their proposals are relevant to more ordinary violence and not coast dishonestly on the emotional momentum created by extraordinary violent events that their policies could not prevent. It would, however, be naive to expect those playing hard-ball politics to follow the intellectually honest path since they will be loathe to forego exploiting the emotional power that comes from tying their recommendations to the most horrific and frightening crimes.

One might justify drawing lessons from high-profile tragedies by arguing that one should make use of the temporarily elevated level of concern about violence to advance worthy solutions that might not prevent unusual events like those that just occurred, but would be effective in the long run with more mundane crimes.

This argument, however, would seem to depend on the dubious premise that people make wise choices in times of fear and hysteria (sometimes euphemistically referred to as "intense public concern"). Unfortunately, frightened people often favor actions that make them feel better over those that would actually make them safer, if the actions can be implemented quickly and easily and are touted as producing results immediately.

People are less likely to be in a logical or critical frame of mind in the aftermath of the most ghastly crimes, a situation that smart advocates exploit. In such a context, people are more willing to believe that "something must be done," and not look too closely at the details and full set of consequences of proposed solutions. Decisions about serious matters should not be made in the sort of overheated aftermath in which demagoguery flourishes. Such an atmosphere is more conducive to lynch mob justice and empty, politically easy gestures than to wise public policy.

Littleton and the other school shootings do raise serious issues, some largely ignored by the news media, and others only briefly mentioned and obscured by the noisy debates over the irrelevancies. These issues might include school bullying and taunting, male-on-female teen dating violence, and violence-saturated entertainment disseminated by profit-hungry corporations. But we will be best able to separate the issues that matter from the ones that do not if we learn our lessons from careful analysis of "ordinary" crime and violence rather than from the freakish events chosen for our attention by the news media.

PERSONAL RESPONSE

Do you agree with the author that "there are no lessons to be learned from Littleton"? If you disagree, what lessons do you think can be learned from Littleton and other school shootings? How do you feel when you hear about a school shooting, such as the 2007 Virginia Tech massacre, in which 32 people were shot and killed? What, in your opinion, went wrong for the Virginia Tech massacre to happen, or was it a random, inexplicable act? What lesson, if any, can be learned from the massacre of 14 women at Montreal's École Polytechnique on December 6, 1989?

QUESTIONS FOR CLASS OR SMALL-GROUP DISCUSSION

1. We tend to think of school shootings as predominantly American. Clearly they are not. Discuss the differences between the American and Canadian portrayals of these massacres by comparing media stories.

2. Kleck seems to say that gun homicides have been decreasing, but that gun massacres in schools are a kind of freakish anomaly. Do you agree? How does his argument stand up in light of recent events?

3. Kleck blames the news media for ignoring statistics on violence that would indicate a drop in violent crime. If you worked for a news outlet, how would you treat such statistics if you were covering the story of a school massacre?

4. Write the headlines you would use in a newspaper story based on any of the shootings described in the introduction of this piece. What element does your headline emphasize and why?

5. We are clearly searching for answers to why these shootings happen. Which theories do you think are most viable? Guns? Culture? Evil? Violence in popular culture? Bad parenting? Music? Emotional imbalance? Social alienation? Try to come up with your own explanations.

HOMEBOY

MALCOLM X (AS TOLD TO ALEX HALEY)

Malcolm X (1925–1965) was one of the most influential and coura-geous men of the twentieth century. Born Malcolm Little in Omaha, Nebraska, he went from being a hoodlum, thief, and drug dealer to a world-famous activist for human rights. In 1946, after committing a series of crimes, he was arrested on burglary charges and sent to prison. By the time he was paroled in 1952, he had become a follower of the Nation of Islam, which taught that white society was evil and worked to undermine African Americans. He also took the name "X" to signify his lost tribal name; "Little" was considered a slave name. Malcolm X became the national spokesperson for the Nation of Islam and spread its

message in newspaper columns, on the radio, and in public gatherings.
Malcolm X eventually suspected corruption within the organization,
and became disenchanted with its leader, Elijah Muhammad. In 1965,
during a speaking engagement in Manhattan, armed members of the
Nation of Islam assassinated Malcolm X.

I looked like Li'l Abner. Mason, Michigan, was written all over me. My kinky reddish hair was cut hick style, and I didn't even use grease on it. My green suit's coat sleeves stopped just above my wrists, the pant legs showed three inches of socks. Just a shade lighter green than the suit was my narrow-collared, three-quarter length Lansing department store topcoat. My appearance was too much for even Ella. But she told me later she had seen countrified members of the Little family come up from Georgia in even worse shape than I was.

Ella had fixed up a nice little upstairs room for me. And she was truly a Georgia Negro woman when she got into the kitchen with her pots and pans. She was the kind of cook who would heap up your plate with such as ham hock, greens, black-eyed peas, fried fish, cabbage, sweet potatoes, grits and gravy, and cornbread. And the more you put away, the better she felt. I worked out at Ella's kitchen table like there was no tomorrow.

Ella still seemed to me as big, black, outspoken and impressive a woman as she had been in Mason and Lansing. Only about two weeks before I arrived, she had split up with her second husband—the soldier, Frank, whom I had met there the previous summer; but she was taking it right in stride. I could see, though I didn't say, how any average man would find it almost impossible to live for very long with a woman whose every instinct was to run everything and everybody she had anything to do with—including me. About my second day there in Roxbury, Ella told me that she didn't want me to start hunting for a job right away, like most newcomer Negroes did. She said that she had told all those she'd brought North to take their time, to walk around, to travel the buses and the subway, and get the feel of Boston, before they tied themselves down working somewhere, because they would never again have the time to really see and get to know anything about the city they were living in. Ella said she'd help me find a job when it was time for me to go to work.

So I went gawking around the neighborhood—the Waumbeck and Humboldt Avenue Hill section of Roxbury, which is something like Harlem's Sugar Hill, where I'd later live. I saw those Roxbury Negroes acting and living differently from any black people I'd ever dreamed of in my life. This was the snooty-black neighborhood; they called themselves the "Four Hundred," and looked down their noses at the Negroes of the black ghetto, or so-called "town" section where Mary, my other half-sister, lived.

What I thought I was seeing there in Roxbury were high-class, educated, important Negroes, living well, working in big jobs and positions. Their quiet homes sat back in their mowed yards. These Negroes walked along the sidewalks looking haughty and dignified, on their way to work, to shop, to visit, to church. I know now, of course, that what I was really seeing was only a big-city version of those "successful" Negro bootblacks and janitors back in Lansing. The only difference was that the ones in Boston had been brainwashed even more thoroughly. They prided themselves on being incomparably more "cultured," "cultivated," "dignified," and better off than their black brethren down in the ghetto, which was no further away than you could throw a rock. Under the pitiful misapprehension that it would make them "better," these Hill Negroes were breaking their backs trying to imitate white people.

Any black family that had been around Boston long enough to own the home they lived in was considered among the Hill elite. It didn't make any difference that they had to rent out rooms to make ends meet. Then the native-born New Englanders among them looked down upon recently migrated Southerner home-owners who lived next door, like Ella. And a big percentage of the Hill dwellers were in Ella's category—Southern strivers and scramblers, and West Indian Negroes, whom both the New Englanders and the Southerners called "Black Jews." Usually it was the Southerners and the West Indians who not only managed to own the places where they lived, but also at least one other house which they rented as income property. The snooty New Englanders usually owned less than they.

In those days on the Hill, any who could claim "professional" status—teachers, preachers, practical nurses—also considered themselves superior. Foreign diplomats could have modeled their conduct on the way the Negro postmen, Pullman porters, and dining car waiters of Roxbury acted, striding around as if they were wearing top hats and cutaways.

I'd guess that eight out of ten of the Hill Negroes of Roxbury, despite the impressive-sounding job titles they affected, actually worked as menials and servants. "He's in banking," or "He's in securities." It sounded as though they were discussing a Rockefeller or a Mellon—and not some grayheaded, dignity-posturing bank janitor, or bond-house messenger. "I'm with an old family" was the euphemism used to dignify the professions of white folks' cooks and maids who talked so affectedly among their own kind in Roxbury that you couldn't even understand them. I don't know how many forty- and fifty-year-old errand boys went down the Hill dressed like ambassadors in black suits and white collars, to downtown jobs "in government," "in finance," or "in law." It has never ceased to amaze me how so many Negroes, then and now, could stand the indignity of that kind of self-delusion.

Soon I ranged out of Roxbury and began to explore Boston proper. Historic buildings everywhere I turned, and plaques and markers and statues for famous events and men. One statue in the Boston Commons astonished me: a Negro named Crispus Attucks, who had been the first man to fall in the Boston Massacre. I had never known anything like that.

I roamed everywhere. In one direction, I walked as far as Boston University. Another day, I took my first subway ride. When most of the people got off, I followed. It was Cambridge, and I circled all around in the Harvard University campus. Somewhere, I had already heard of Harvard—though I didn't know much more about it. Nobody that day could have told me I would give an address before the Harvard Law School Forum some twenty years later.

I also did a lot of exploring downtown. Why a city would have two big railroad stations—North Station and South Station—I couldn't understand. At both of the stations, I stood around and watched people arrive and leave. And I did the same thing at the bus station where Ella had met me. My wanderings even led me down along the piers and docks where I read plaques telling about the old sailing ships that used to put into port there.

In a letter to Wilfred, Hilda, Philbert, and Reginald back in Lansing, I told them about all this, and about the winding, narrow, cobblestoned streets, and the houses that jammed up against each other. Downtown Boston, I wrote them, had the biggest stores I'd ever seen, and white people's restaurants and hotels. I made up my mind that I was going to see every movie that came to the fine, air-conditioned theaters.

On Massachusetts Avenue, next door to one of them, the Loew's State Theater, was the huge, exciting Roseland State Ballroom. Big posters out in front advertised the nationally famous bands, white and Negro, that had played there. "COMING NEXT WEEK," when I went by that first time, was Glenn Miller. I remember thinking how nearly the whole evening's music at Mason High School dances had been Glenn Miller's records. What wouldn't that crowd have given, I wondered, to be standing where Glenn Miller's band was actually going to play? I didn't know how familiar with Roseland I was going to become.

Ella began to grow concerned, because even when I had finally had enough sight-seeing, I didn't stick around very much on the Hill. She kept dropping hints that I ought to mingle with the "nice young people my age" who were to be seen in the Townsend Drugstore two blocks from her house, and a couple of other places. But even before I came to Boston, I had always felt and acted toward anyone my age as if they were in the "kid" class, like my younger brother Reginald. They had always looked up to me as if I were considerably older. On weekends back in Lansing where I'd go to get away from the white people in Mason, I'd hung around in the Negro part of town with Wilfred's and Philbert's set. Though all of them were several years older than me, I was bigger, and I actually looked older than most of them.

I didn't want to disappoint or upset Ella, but despite her advice, I began going down into the town ghetto section. That world of grocery stores, walk-up flats, cheap restaurants, poolrooms, bars, storefront churches, and pawnshops seemed to hold a natural lure for me.

Not only was this part of Roxbury much more exciting, but I felt more relaxed among Negroes who were being their natural selves and not putting on airs. Even though I did live on the Hill, my instincts were never—and still aren't—to feel myself any better than any other Negro.

I spent my first month in town with my mouth hanging open. The sharp-dressed young "cats" who hung on the corners and in the poolrooms, bars and restaurants, and who obviously didn't work anywhere, completely entranced me. I couldn't get over marvelling at how their hair was straight and shiny like white men's hair; Ella told me this was called a "conk." I had never tasted a sip of liquor, never even smoked a cigarette, and here I saw little black children, ten and twelve years old, shooting craps, playing cards, fighting, getting grown-ups to put a penny or a nickel on their number for them, things like that. And these children threw around swear words I'd never heard before, even, and slang expressions that were just as new to me, such as "stud" and "cat" and "chick" and "cool" and "hip." Every night as I lay in bed I turned these new words over in my mind. It was shocking to me that in town, especially after dark, you'd occasionally see a white girl and a Negro man strolling arm in arm along the sidewalk, and mixed couples drinking in the neon-lighted bars—not slipping off to some dark corner, as in Lansing. I wrote Wilfred and Philbert about that, too.

I wanted to find a job myself, to surprise Ella. One afternoon, something told me to go inside a poolroom whose window I was looking through. I had looked through that window many times. I wasn't yearning to play pool; in fact, I had never held a cue stick. But I was drawn by the sight of the cool-looking "cats" standing around inside, bending over the big, green, felt-topped tables, making bets and shooting the bright-colored balls into the holes. As I stared through the window this particular afternoon, something made me decide to venture inside and talk to a dark, stubby, conk-headed fellow who racked up balls for the pool-players, whom I'd heard called "Shorty." One day he had come outside and seen me standing there and said, "Hi, Red," so that made me figure he was friendly.

As inconspicuously as I could, I slipped inside the door and around the side of the poolroom, avoiding people, and on to the back, where Shorty was filling an aluminum can with the powder that pool players dust on their hands. He looked up at me. Later on, Shorty would enjoy teasing me about how with that first glance he knew my whole story. "Man, that cat still *smelled* country!" he'd say, laughing. "Cat's legs was so long and his pants so short his knees showed—an' his head looked like a briar patch!"

But that afternoon Shorty didn't let it show in his face how "country" I appeared when I told him I'd appreciate it if he'd tell me how could somebody go about getting a job like his.

"If you mean racking up balls," said Shorty, "I don't know of no pool joints around here needing anybody. You mean you just want any slave you can find?" A "slave" meant work, a job.

He asked what kind of work I had done. I told him that I'd washed restaurant dishes in Mason, Michigan. He nearly dropped the powder can. "My homeboy! Man, gimme some skin! I'm from Lansing!"

I never told Shorty—and he never suspected—that he was about ten years older than I. He took us to be about the same age. At first I would have been embarrassed to tell him, later I just never bothered. Shorty had dropped out of first-year high school in Lansing, lived a while with an uncle and aunt in Detroit, and had spent the last six years living with his cousin in Roxbury. But when I mentioned the names of Lansing people and places, he remembered many, and pretty soon we sounded as if we had been raised in the same block. I could sense Shorty's genuine gladness, and I don't have to say how lucky I felt to find a friend as hip as he obviously was.

"Man, this is a swinging town if you dig it," Shorty said. "You're my homeboy—I'm going to school you to the happenings." I stood there and grinned like a fool. "You got to go anywhere now? Well, stick around until I get off."

One thing I liked immediately about Shorty was his frankness. When I told him where I lived, he said what I already knew—that nobody in town could stand the Hill Negroes. But he thought a sister who gave me a "pad," not charging me rent, not even running me out to find "some slave," couldn't be all bad. Shorty's slave in the poolroom, he said, was just to keep ends together while he learned his horn. A couple of years before, he'd hit the numbers and bought a saxophone. "Got it right in there in the closet now, for my lesson tonight." Shorty was taking lessons "with some other studs," and he intended one day to organize his own small band. "There's a lot of bread to be made gigging right around here in Roxbury," Shorty explained to me. "I didn't dig joining some big band, one-nighting all over just to say I played with Count or Duke or somebody." I thought that was smart. I wished I had studied a horn; but I never had been exposed to one.

All afternoon, between trips up front to rack balls, Shorty talked to me out of the corner of his mouth: which hustlers—standing around, or playing at this or that table—sold "reefers," or had just come out of prison, or were "second-story men." Shorty told me that he played at least a dollar a day on the numbers. He said as soon as he hit a number, he would use the winnings to organize his band.

I was ashamed to have to admit that I had never played the numbers. "Well, you ain't never had nothing to play with," he said, excusing me, "but you start when you get a slave, and if you hit, you got a stake for something."

He pointed out some gamblers and some pimps. Some of them had white whores, he whispered. "I ain't going to lie—I dig them two-dollar white chicks," Shorty said. "There's a lot of that action around here, nights; you'll see it." I said I already had seen some. "You ever had one?" he asked.

My embarrassment at my inexperience showed. "Hell, man," he said, "don't be ashamed. I had a few before I left Lansing—them Polack chicks that used to come over the bridge. Here, they're mostly Italians and Irish. But it don't matter what kind, they're something else! Ain't no different nowhere—there's nothing they love better than a black stud."

Through the afternoon, Shorty introduced me to players and loungers. "My homeboy," he'd say, "he's looking for a slave if you hear anything." They all said they'd look out.

At seven o'clock, when the night ball-racker came on, Shorty told me he had to hurry to his saxophone lesson. But before he left, he held out to me the six or seven dollars he had collected that day in nickel and dime tips. "You got enough bread, homeboy?"

I was okay, I told him—I had two dollars. But Shorty made me take three more. "Little fattening for your pocket," he said. Before we went out, he opened his saxophone case and showed me the horn. It was gleaming brass against the green velvet, an alto sax. He said, "Keep cool, homeboy, and come back tomorrow. Some of the cats will turn you up a slave."

When I got home, Ella said there had been a telephone call from somebody named Shorty. He had left a message that over at the Roseland State Ballroom, the shoeshine boy was quitting that night, and Shorty had told him to hold the job for me.

"Malcolm, you haven't had any experience shining shoes," Ella said. Her expression and tone of voice told me she wasn't happy about my taking that job. I didn't particularly care, because I was already speechless thinking about being somewhere close to the greatest bands in the world. I didn't even wait to eat any dinner.

The ballroom was all lighted when I got there. A man at the front door was letting in members of Benny Goodman's band. I told him I wanted to see the shoeshine boy, Freddie.

"You're going to be the new one?" he asked. I said I thought I was, and he laughed. "Well, maybe you'll hit the numbers and get a Cadillac, too." He told me that I'd find Freddie upstairs in the men's room on the second floor.

But downstairs before I went up, I stepped over and snatched a glimpse inside the ballroom. I just couldn't believe the size of that waxed floor! At the far end, under the soft, rose-colored lights, was the bandstand with the Benny Goodman musicians moving around, laughing and talking, arranging their horns and stands.

A wiry, brown-skinned, conked fellow upstairs in the men's room greeted me. "You Shorty's homeboy?" I said I was, and he said he was Freddie. "Good old boy," he said. "He called me, he just heard I hit the big number, and he figured right I'd be quitting." I told Freddie what the man at the front door had said about a Cadillac. He laughed and said, "Burns them white cats up when you get yourself something. Yeah, I told them I was going to get me one—just to bug them."

Freddie then said for me to pay close attention, that he was going to be busy and for me to watch but not get in the way, and he'd try to get me ready to take over at the next dance, a couple of nights later.

As Freddie busied himself setting up the shoeshine stand, he told me, "Get here early . . . your shoeshine rags and brushes by this footstand . . . your polish bottles, paste wax, suede brushes over here . . . everything in place, you get rushed, you never need to waste motion. . . ."

While you shined shoes, I learned, you also kept watch on customers inside, leaving the urinals. You darted over and offered a small white hand towel. "A lot of cats who ain't planning to wash their hands, sometimes you can run up with a towel and shame them. Your towels are really your best hustle in here. Cost you a penny a piece to launder—you always get at least a nickel tip."

The shoeshine customers, and any from the inside rest room who took a towel, you whiskbroomed a couple of licks. "A nickel or a dime tip, just give 'em that," Freddie said. "But for two bits, Uncle Tom a little—white cats especially like that. I've had them to come back two, three times a dance."

From down below, the sound of the music had begun floating up. I guess I stood transfixed. "You never seen a big dance?" asked Freddie. "Run on awhile, and watch."

There were a few couples already dancing under the rose-colored lights. But even more exciting to me was the crowd thronging in. The most glamorous-looking white women I'd ever seen—young ones, old ones, white cats buying tickets at the window, sticking big wads of green bills back into their pockets, checking the women's coats, and taking their arms and squiring them inside.

Freddie had some early customers when I got back upstairs. Between the shoeshine stand and thrusting towels to men just as they approached the wash basin, Freddie seemed to doing four things at once. "Here, you can take over the whiskbroom," he said, "just two or three licks—but let 'em feel it."

When things slowed a little, he said, "You ain't seen nothing tonight. You wait until you see a spooks' dance! Man, our own people carry *on!*" Whenever he had a moment, he kept schooling me. "Shoelaces, this drawer here. You just starting out, I'm going to make these to you as a present. Buy them for a nickel a pair, tell cats they need laces if they do, and charge two bits."

Every Benny Goodman record I'd ever heard in my life, it seemed, was filtering faintly into where we were. During another customer lull, Freddie let me slip back outside again to listen. Peggy Lee was at the mike singing. Beautiful! She had just joined the band and she was from North Dakota and had been singing with a group in Chicago when Mrs. Benny Goodman discovered her, we had heard some customers say. She finished the song and the crowd burst into applause. She was a big hit.

"It knocked me out, too, when I first broke in here," Freddie said, grinning, when I went back in there. "But, look, you ever shined any shoes?" He laughed when I said I hadn't, excepting my own. "Well, let's get to work. I never had neither." Freddie got on the stand and went to work on his own shoes. Brush, liquid polish, brush, paste wax, shine rag, lacquer sole dressing . . . step by step, Freddie showed me what to do.

"But you got to get a whole lot faster. You can't waste time!" Freddie showed me how fast on my own shoes. Then, because business was tapering off, he had time to give me a demonstration of how to make the shine rag pop like a firecracker. "Dig the action?" he asked. He did it in slow motion. I got down and tried it on his shoes. I had the principle of it. "Just got to do it faster," Freddie said. "It's a jive noise, that's all. Cats tip better, they figure you're knocking yourself out!"

By the end of the dance, Freddie had let me shine the shoes of three or four stray drunks he talked into having shines, and I had practiced picking up my speed on Freddie's shoes until they looked like mirrors. After we had helped the janitors to clean up the ballroom after the dance, throwing out all the paper and cigarette butts and empty liquor bottles, Freddie was nice enough to drive me all the way home to Ella's on the Hill in the second-hand maroon Buick he said he was going to trade in on his Cadillac. He talked to me all the way. "I guess it's all right if I tell you, pick up a couple of dozen packs of rubbers, two-bits apiece. You notice some of those cats that came up to me around the end of the dance? Well, when some have new chicks going right, they'll come asking you for rubbers. Charge a dollar, generally you'll get an extra tip."

He looked across at me. "Some hustles you're too new for. Cats will ask you for liquor, some will want reefers. But you don't need to have nothing except rubbers— until you can dig who's a cop."

"You can make ten, twelve dollars a dance for yourself if you work everything right," Freddie said, before I got out of the car in front of Ella's. "The main thing you got to remember is that everything in the world is a hustle. So long, Red."

The next time I ran into Freddie I was downtown one night a few weeks later. He was parked in his pearl gray Cadillac, sharp as a tack, "cooling it."

"Man, you sure schooled me!" I said, and he laughed; he knew what I meant. It hadn't taken me long on the job to find out that Freddie had done less shoe-shining and towel-hustling than selling liquor and reefers, and putting white "Johns" in touch with Negro whores. I also learned that white girls always flocked to the Negro dances—some of them whores whose pimps brought them to mix business and pleasure, others who came with their black boy friends, and some who came in alone, for a little freelance lusting among a plentiful availability of enthusiastic Negro men.

At the white dances, of course, nothing black was allowed, and that's where the black whores' pimps soon showed a new shoeshine boy what he could pick up on the side by slipping a phone number or address to the white Johns who came around the end of the dance looking for "black chicks."

Most of the Roseland dances were for whites only, and they had white bands only. But the only white band ever to play there at a Negro dance to my recollection, was Charlie Barnet's. The fact is that very few white bands could have satisfied the Negro dancers. But I know that Charlie Barnet's "Cherokee" and his "Redskin Rhumba" drove those Negroes wild. They'd jampack that ballroom, the black girls in way-out silk and satin dresses and shoes, their hair done in all kinds of styles, the men sharp in their zoot suits and crazy conks, and everybody grinning and greased and gassed.

Some of the bandsmen would come up to the men's room at about eight o'clock and get shoeshines before they went to work. Duke Ellington, Count Basie, Lionel Hampton, Cootie Williams, Jimmie Lunceford were just a few of those who sat in my chair. I would really make my shine rag sound like someone had set off Chinese firecrackers. Duke's great alto saxman, Johnny Hodges—he was Shorty's idol—still owes me for a shoeshine I gave him. He was in the chair one night, having a friendly argument with the drummer, Sonny Greer, who was standing there, when I tapped the bottom of his shoes to signal that I was finished. Hodges stepped down, reaching his hand in his pocket to pay me, but then snatched his hand out to gesture, and just forgot me, and walked away. I wouldn't have dared to bother the man who could do what he did with "Daydream" by asking him for fifteen cents.

I remember that I struck up a little shoeshine-stand conversation with Count Basie's great blues singer, Jimmie Rushing. (He's the one famous for "Sent For You Yesterday, Here You Come Today" and things like that.) Rushing's feet, I remember, were big and funny-shaped—not long like most big feet, but they were round and roly-poly like Rushing. Anyhow, he even introduced me to some of the other Basie cats, like Lester Young, Harry Edison, Buddy Tate, Don Byas, Dickie Wells, and Buck Clayton. They'd walk in the rest room later, by themselves. "Hi, Red." They'd be up there in my chair, and my shine rag was popping to the beat of all of their records, spinning in my head. Musicians never have had, anywhere, a greater shoeshine-boy fan than I was. I would write to Wilfred and Hilda and Philbert and Reginald back in Lansing trying to describe it.

I never got any decent tips until the middle of the Negro dances, which is when the dancers started feeling good and getting generous. After the white dances, when I helped to clean out the ballroom, we would throw out perhaps a dozen empty liquor bottles. But after the Negro dances, we would have to throw out cartons full of empty fifth bottles—not rotgut, either, but the best brands, and especially Scotch.

During lulls up there in the men's room, sometimes I'd get in five minutes of watching the dancing. The white people danced as though somebody had trained them—left, one, two; right, three, four—the same steps and patterns over and over, as though somebody had wound them up. But those Negroes—nobody in the world could have choreographed the way they did whatever they felt—just grabbing partners, even the white chicks who came to the Negro dances. And my black brethren today may hate me for saying it, but a lot of black girls nearly got run over by some of those Negro males scrambling to get at those white women; you would have thought God had lowered some of his angels. Times have sure changed; if it happened today, those same black girls would go after those Negro men—and the white women, too.

Anyway, some couples were so abandoned—flinging high and wide, improvising steps and movements—that you couldn't believe it. I could feel the beat in my bones, even though I had never danced.

"*Showtime!*" people would start hollering about the last hour of the dance. Then a couple of dozen really wild couples would stay on the floor, the girls changing to low white sneakers. The band now would really be blasting, and all the other dancers would form a clapping, shouting circle to watch that wild competition as it began, covering only a quarter or so of the ballroom floor. The band, the spectators and the dancers, would be making the Roseland Ballroom feel like a big rocking ship. The spotlight would be turning pink, yellow, green, and blue, picking up the couples lindy-hopping as if they had gone mad. "*Wail, man, wail!*" people would be shouting at the band; and it *would* be wailing, until first one and then another couple just ran out of strength and stumbled off toward the crowd, exhausted and soaked with sweat. Sometimes I would be down there standing inside the door jumping up and down in my gray jacket with the whiskbroom in the pocket, and the manager would have to come and shout at me that I had customers upstairs.

The first liquor I drank, my first cigarettes, even my first reefers, I can't specifically remember. But I know they were all mixed together with my first shooting craps, playing cards, and betting my dollar a day on the numbers, as I started hanging out at night with Shorty and his friends. Shorty's jokes about how country I had been made us all laugh. I still was country, I know now, but it all felt so great because I was accepted. All of us would be in somebody's place, usually one of the girls', and we'd be turning on, the reefers making everybody's head light, or the whisky aglow in our middles. Everybody understood that my head had to stay kinky a while longer, to grow long enough for Shorty to conk it for me. One of these nights, I remarked that I had saved about half enough to get a zoot.

"*Save?*" Shorty couldn't believe it. "Homeboy, you never heard of credit?" He told me he'd call a neighborhood clothing store the first thing in the morning, and that I should be there early.

A salesman, a young Jew, met me when I came in. "You're Shorty's friend?" I said I was; it amazed me—all of Shorty's contacts. The salesman wrote my name on a form, and the Roseland as where I worked, and Ella's address as where I lived. Shorty's name was put down as recommending me. The salesman said, "Shorty's one of our best customers."

I was measured, and the young salesman picked off a rack a zoot suit that was just wild: sky-blue pants thirty inches in the knee and angle-narrowed down to twelve inches at the bottom, and a long coat that pinched my waist and flared out below my knees.

As a gift, the salesman said, the store would give me a narrow leather belt with my initial "L" on it. Then he said I ought to also buy a hat, and I did—blue, with a feather in the four-inch brim. Then the store gave me another present: a long, thick-linked, gold-plated chain that swung down lower than my coat hem. I was sold forever on credit.

When I modeled the zoot for Ella, she took a long look and said, "Well, I guess it had to happen." I took three of those twenty-five-cent sepia-toned, while-you-wait pictures of myself, posed the way "hipsters" wearing their zoots would "cool it"—hat angled, knees drawn close together, feet wide apart, both index fingers jabbed toward the floor. The long coat and swinging chain and the Punjab pants were much more dramatic if you stood that way. One picture, I autographed and airmailed to my brothers and sisters in Lansing, to let them see how well I was doing. I gave another one to Ella, and the third to Shorty, who was really moved: I could tell by the way he said, "Thanks, homeboy." It was part of our "hip" code not to show that kind of affection.

Shorty soon decided that my hair was finally long enough to be conked. He had promised to school me in how to beat the barbershops' three- and four-dollar price by making up congolene, and then conking ourselves.

I took the little list of ingredients he had printed out for me, and went to a grocery store, where I got a can of Red Devil lye, two eggs, and two medium-sized white potatoes. Then at a drugstore near the poolroom, I asked for a large jar of vaseline, a large bar of soap, a large-toothed comb and a fine-toothed comb, one of those rubber hoses with a metal spray-head, a rubber apron and a pair of gloves.

"Going to lay on that first conk?" the drugstore man asked me. I proudly told him, grinning, "Right!"

Shorty paid six dollars a week for a room in his cousin's shabby apartment. His cousin wasn't at home. "It's like the pad's mine, he spends so much time with his woman," Shorty said. "Now, you watch me—"

He peeled the potatoes and thin-sliced them into a quart-sized Mason fruit jar, then started stirring them with a wooden spoon as he gradually poured in a little over half the can of lye. "Never use a metal spoon; the lye will turn it black," he told me.

A jelly-like, starchy-looking glop resulted from the lye and potatoes, and Shorty broke in the two eggs, stirring real fast—his own conk and dark face bent down close. The congolene turned pale-yellowish. "Feel the jar," Shorty said. I cupped my hand against the outside, and snatched it away. "Damn right, it's hot, that's the lye," he said. "So you know it's going to burn when I comb it in—it burns *bad*. But the longer you can stand it, the straighter the hair."

He made me sit down, and he tied the string of the new rubber apron tightly around my neck, and combed up my bush of hair. Then, from the big vaseline jar, he took a handful and massaged it hard all through my hair and into the scalp. He also thickly vaselined my neck, ears and forehead. "When I get to washing out your head, be sure to tell me anywhere you feel any little stinging," Shorty warned me, washing his hands, then pulling on the rubber gloves, and tying on his own rubber apron. "You always got to remember that any congolene left in burns a sore into your head."

The congolene just felt warm when Shorty started combing it in. But then my head caught fire.

I gritted my teeth and tried to pull the sides of the kitchen table together. The comb felt as if it was raking my skin off.

My eyes watered, my nose was running. I couldn't stand it any longer; I bolted to the washbasin. I was cursing Shorty with every name I could think of when he got the spray going and started soap-lathering my head.

He lathered and spray-rinsed, lathered and spray-rinsed, maybe ten or twelve times, each time gradually closing the hot-water faucet, until the rinse was cold, and that helped some.

"You feel any stinging spots?"

"No," I managed to say. My knees were trembling.

"Sit back down, then. I think we got it all out okay."

The flame came back as Shorty, with a thick towel, started drying my head, rubbing hard. "*Easy,* man, *easy!*" I kept shouting.

"The first time's always worst. You get used to it better before long. You took it real good, homeboy. You got a good conk."

When Shorty let me stand up and see in the mirror, my hair hung down in limp, damp strings. My scalp still flamed, but not as badly; I could bear it. He draped the towel around my shoulders, over my rubber apron, and began again vaselining my hair.

I could feel him combing, straight back, first the big comb, then the fine-toothed one.

Then, he was using a razor, very delicately, on the back of my neck. Then, finally, shaping the sideburns.

My first view in the mirror blotted out the hurting. I'd seen some pretty conks, but when it's the first time, on your *own* head, the transformation, after the lifetime of kinks, is staggering.

The mirror reflected Shorty behind me. We both were grinning and sweating. And on top of my head was this thick, smooth sheen of shining red hair—real red—as straight as any white man's.

How ridiculous I was! Stupid enough to stand there simply lost in admiration of my hair now looking "white," reflected in the mirror in Shorty's room. I vowed that I'd never again be without a conk, and I never was for many years.

This was my first really big step toward self-degradation: when I endured all of that pain, literally burning my flesh with lye, in order to cook my natural hair until it was limp, to have it look like a white man's hair. I had joined that multitude of Negro men and women in America who are brainwashed into believing that the black people are "inferior"—and white people "superior"—that they will even violate and mutilate their God-created bodies to try to look "pretty" by white standards.

Look around today, in every small town and big city, from two-bit catfish and soda-pop joints into the "integrated" lobby of the Waldorf-Astoria, and you'll see conks on black men. And you'll see black women wearing these green and pink and purple and red and platinum-blonde wigs. They're all more ridiculous than a slapstick comedy. It makes you wonder if the Negro has completely lost his sense of identity, lost touch with himself.

You'll see the conk worn by many, many so-called "upper class" Negroes, and, as much as I hate to say it about them, on all too many Negro entertainers. One of the reasons I've especially admired some of them, like Lionel Hampton and Sidney Poitier, among others, is that they have kept their natural hair and fought to the top. I admire any Negro man who has never had himself conked, or who has had the sense to get rid of it—as I finally did.

I don't know which kind of self-defacing conk is the greater shame—the one you'll see on the heads of the black so-called "middle class" and "upper class," who ought to know better, or the one you'll see on the heads of the poorest, most down-trodden, ignorant black men. I mean the legal-minimum-wage ghetto-dwelling kind of Negro, as I was when I got my first one. It's generally among these poor fools that you'll see a black kerchief over the man's head, like Aunt Jemima; he's trying to make his conk last longer, between trips to the barbershop. Only for special occasions is this kerchief-protected conk exposed—to show off how "sharp" and "hip" its owner is. The ironic thing is that I have never heard any woman, white or black, express any admiration for a conk. Of course, any white woman with a black man isn't thinking about his hair. But I don't see how on earth a black woman with any race pride could walk down the street with any black man wearing a conk—the emblem of his shame that he is black.

To my own shame, when I say all of this I'm talking first of all about myself—because you can't show me any Negro who ever conked more faithfully than I did. I'm speaking from personal experience when I say of any black man who conks today, or any white-wigged black woman, that if they gave the brains in their heads just half as much attention as they do their hair, they would be a thousand times better off.

PERSONAL RESPONSE

Malcolm X talks about degrading oneself to try to be like someone else, or to be like the members of another race who are considered superior. Have you had any experiences where you wanted to be like someone else at the expense of your own pride and self-esteem? What made you want to efface yourself to be like another?

QUESTIONS FOR CLASS OR SMALL-GROUP DISCUSSION

1. Look up and define the term *Jim Crow*. What are its origins, and is *Jim Crow* a relevant term in contemporary culture? Can this term be applied to Canada or Canadian history? Discuss.

2. Although Malcolm X will later revile his time as a homeboy on the streets of Roxbury and Harlem, some see the homeboy stage in his life as a

celebratory, black way of resisting white capitalism: making money from hustling white people, avoiding the white boss and work ethic, wearing the zoot suit and thus defying wartime austerity, and making his own rules even under the tyranny of Jim Crow laws. Compare the events in this essay with minority subcultures in today's urban centres, for example, with black rappers.

3. This essay portrays Roxbury, Massachusetts (a Boston neighbourhood), in the early 1940s, during a time of legalized racism and segregation. Describe, using specific examples from the text, ways in which racism created opportunities and contexts for criminal activity. In what ways does contemporary racism have similar effects? In general, how are poverty and racism linked to crime?

4. What other significant African American leaders emerged at this time in history, and what was their contribution to the civil rights movement?

ANOTHER ACCOLADE FOR CHARTER ARMS CORP.

Mike Royko

Mike Royko (1932–1997) was a journalist who worked in Chicago, his hometown. In 1972, he was awarded the Pulitzer Prize for commentary journalism. His work was noted for its plain and direct honesty.

I was pleased to see that the stories reporting the death of John Lennon were specific and accurate about the kind of gun that was used to murder the world-renowned musician.

It was a .38 calibre pistol made by Charter Arms Corp. of Bridgeport, Conn.

You might ask: What difference does it make what kind of gun was used?

It makes a great deal of difference. Especially to Charter Arms Corp.

There are guns and then there are guns. Cheap guns, ordinary guns, and finely crafted guns.

And when people become emotional about guns, as many do when somebody famous is killed, they tend to lump all guns together. They don't show proper respect for an excellent gun, such as the Charter .38.

It happens this is not the first time a famous person has been shot by this make of weapon. When former Alabama Gov. George C. Wallace was shot and paralyzed for life by another deranged person in 1974, the bullet that tore into his spine came from a Charter .38.

If I'm not mistaken, this makes the Charter .38 the first gun in modern times to have two famous people to its credit. The weapons used to blast President Kennedy, the Rev. Dr. Martin Luther King, Jr., and Sen. Robert F. Kennedy were all of different manufacture.

When Wallace was shot, a CBS reporter made it obvious that he didn't know a fine gun from a cheap gun.

The reporter went on network TV and said that Wallace had been wounded by a "cheap handgun." He obviously had in mind the kind of Saturday Night Special that is so popular among the criminal riffraff who have no respect for quality and workmanship.

When the proud executives of Charter Arms Corp. heard the reporter, they became indignant.

They contacted the CBS and demanded an apology. The incident was described in an editorial in the company magazine of the Charter Corp.

The editorial, which was headlined "An Apology from CBS," said:

"We are too dedicated to high quality in American-made handguns and have poured too much of ourselves into our products to have one of them even casually referred to as a 'cheap handgun'."

"That was exactly the phrase used in a broadcast description of the handgun used by Arthur Bremer in his assassination attempt on Gov. Wallace, which happened to be one of our Undercover .38 Specials.

"The broadcast emanated from CBS . . . and our public relations people were immediately instructed to bring the error to their attention."

The editorial went on to say that an apology was indeed received from CBS network vice-president, who contritely told Charter Arms Corp., "I am sending a copy of your letter to all our TV producers. In the event that we make reference to the Undercover .38 special used by Arthur Bremer, we will certainly avoid characterizing it as a 'Saturday Night Special' or any other term which labels it as a 'cheap weapon'."

Presumably that soothed the wounded pride of the gunmakers at Charter Arms Corp., since no further public protests were heard.

And you can't blame them for having felt hurt at such a slur on their product. When Wallace was shot, a Charter .38 cost $105. Today, with rising prices, the gun costs about $180 or $190, depending on where you do your gun shopping.

That is not a cheap gun, especially when compared to the trashy weapons that some gunmen, to whom quality is unimportant, arm themselves with.

Now I don't know if it was mere coincidence that both Bremer, who shot Wallace, and Mark David Chapman, who apparently shot Lennon, used the same weapon. Or if it was that they both recognized quality when they saw it, and were willing to spend money to get the best.

But the fact is, both opted for quality and they got what they paid for. There was no misfiring, no jamming, no bullet flying off line, and no gun exploding in their hands—all of which can happen when one uses a cheap gun.

True, Wallace wasn't killed. That was the fault of Bremer, not the Charter gun. Bremer shot Wallace in the stomach, which isn't the best place to shoot a person if you want to kill him.

But even in that case, the gun did its job—blowing a terrible hole in Wallace's gut and putting him into a wheelchair for good.

In the case of Lennon, you couldn't ask for a better performance from a gun. Lennon was shot several times, but according to the doctor who pronounced him dead, the first bullet hit him in the chest and killed him on the spot. The other shots weren't even necessary.

You can never be sure of getting those kinds of results from a Saturday Night Special.

Now the Charter Arms Corp. has the unique distinction of having two famous people shot by one of their products, I wonder if they have considered using it in their advertising. Something simple and tasteful like: "The .38 that got George Wallace AND John Lennon. See it all at your gun dealer now."

If so, they shouldn't wait. With so many handguns—both cheap and of high quality—easily available to Americans, it could be just a matter of time until another manufacturer moves into the lead in the famous-person derby. All it would take would be a few pop-pop-pops from say, a Colt—maybe a politician or two and another rock star or two—and they would have the lead.

On the other hand, maybe Charter Arms Corp. doesn't want recognition—just the kind of pride one feels in a job of fine craftsmanship.

If so, they have a right to feel proud.

Once again, your product really did the job, gents.

PERSONAL RESPONSE

In some free societies, the right to bear arms is important. It represents one kind of individual freedom. What are your views on the right to bear arms? What exactly do Canada's laws say regarding handguns and bearing arms? Draw some comparisons with American laws and attitudes. Do you think individuals should have the right to carry arms?

QUESTIONS FOR CLASS OR SMALL-GROUP DISCUSSION

1. How would you describe Royko's tone, and what effect does it have on how you respond? Do you think this tone masks other, more personal attitudes? In the second-to-last paragraph, Royko writes, "If so, they have the right to feel proud." How would you say this out loud to capture Royko's tone?

2. Describe the tensions (or disconnect) between the quality of the Charter .38 and what it does or is meant for, and who might use such a weapon? What kind of reaction do you get from this?

3. Discuss whether you think this piece, written more than 25 years ago, is still relevant, or if it is dated. Does this essay have any relevance to Canadian attitudes toward gun control? Discuss.

4. Consider and describe the role that the media (in this case, CBS) played in this story. Also describe the role that the media, in a larger sense, play in the cultural presentation of crime. What does the media report on, how do they report on it, and why?

REAPING WHAT WE SOW

David Frum

Born in Toronto in 1960, and having earned degrees from Yale University and Harvard University, David Frum is a frequent television and radio guest consultant on American policy, and is often considered one of the most influential minds in the United States. His recent books include An End to Evil: What's Next in the War on Terror, *co-authored with Richard Perle (2004) and* The Right Man: The Surprise Presidency of George W. Bush *(2003). He presently has an appointment at the American Enterprise Institute, and he frequently writes columns for prominent American, British, and Canadian newspapers. He has also worked as a speechwriter and special assistant for American president George W. Bush.*

Tuesday, January 03, 2006

After a spasm of heart-rending, frightening violence, Toronto's Mayor, David Miller, and its news media want Torontonians to remember one thing: The city is very, very safe. Really.

"Chicago: 445 homicides. Washington D.C.: 195 homicides. Baltimore: 268 homicides. Toronto: 78 homicides." So opened a story in Sunday's *Toronto Star*.

If there is any problem in Toronto, the Mayor insists, it is traceable to the United States: "The U.S. is exporting its problem of violence to the streets of Toronto," David Miller complained on Dec. 27.

And naturally Prime Minister Paul Martin agreed. "What we saw yesterday is a stark reminder of the challenge that governments, police forces and communities face to ensure that Canadian cities do not descend into the kind of rampant gun violence we have seen elsewhere."

Feel better now? Well, don't. The Prime Minister, the Mayor and the media are hiding crucial facts. Here are three:

1) America's crime problem has dramatically improved, while Canada's is becoming seriously worse. Toronto's 78 homicides in 2005 appears to compare favorably to the homicide totals of the three American cities cited by the *Star*. But those 78 Toronto homicides in 2005 represent a 28% increase over the 61 homicides recorded in Toronto in 1995. Meanwhile, the three U.S. cities cited by the *Star* each achieved dramatic decreases over the past decade. Chicago down 46% from 823, Washington down 46% from 365, Baltimore down 17% from 322.

More broadly: Canada's overall crime rate is now 50% higher than the crime rate in the United States. Read that again slowly—it seems incredible, but it's true. It's true too that you are now more likely to be mugged in Toronto than in New York City.

2) America's crime problem is becoming concentrated in ever fewer places, while Canada's is spreading out to ever more places.

The United States is a huge country, and it will always be possible to find a jurisdiction with shocking crime numbers. The overwhelming majority of Americans,

Crime in Canada: You're under arrest.
Photo Source: © Jack Dagley Photography/Shutterstock

however, live in places that are becoming steadily safer. Since the early 1990s, crime rates have dropped in 48 of the 50 states and 80% of American cities. Over that same period, crime rates have risen in six of the 10 Canadian provinces and in seven of Canada's 10 biggest cities.

3) While American cities and states are adopting anti-crime policies proved to work, Canadian cities and provinces are adopting policies proved to fail.

Over a decade of successful crime-fighting in the U.S., criminologists and police departments have learned some important lessons.

Bluntly: prison works. Criminals do not commit crimes while they are held in prison. Yet a Canadian criminal is 80% less likely to go to jail than his American counterpart.

Putting police on the street works. Yet Canada employs 25% fewer police officers per capita than the United States.

Enforcing laws against vagrancy, prostitution and drug dealing works. Yet Canada is either decriminalizing or tolerating all three. The right kinds of gun laws work too: for example, extending the sentence of any criminal who commits any crime—down to jaywalking—while in possession of a gun.

Gun registries and gun bans on the other hand do not work. Youth programs do not work. Counselling does not work. Grants to community activists, peer counsellors and after-school facilities do not work. The $50-million Paul Martin has just announced for local crime-prevention will be directed to individuals and groups connected to the Liberal party's patronage machine. That money will do nothing to enhance the safety of the City of Toronto. And if it finds its way to individuals or groups who lobby against effective law-enforcement, that money will actually make the problem worse.

It is not guns from across the border that threaten Canadians. It is the weak and cynical policies of home-grown politicians, and especially the Chretien/Martin Liberals. The $2-billion wasted on the gun registry could have paid for more cops, more prisons, more of everything that would protect the lives and security of Canadians. It is the federal Liberal government that released young offenders back into the community, the federal Liberals who appoint the judges who refuse to punish, the federal Liberals who run the prison system as if it were a summer camp, the federal Liberals who refuse to deport immigrants who break the law, the federal Liberals who have subordinated public safety to ethnic politics.

And then it is the federal Liberals who have the gross and extreme indecency to try to exploit for their own selfish political ends the crime and grief and suffering for which they bear so much of the blame.

PERSONAL RESPONSE

Do you think of Canada as a relatively peaceful country? How would you compare Canada to other countries in terms of its handling of crime? How closely aligned are most Canadians to American beliefs and values? Would you have any problem living in the United States?

QUESTIONS FOR CLASS OR SMALL-GROUP DISCUSSION

1. Frum is usually labelled as a neo-conservative. What does this term mean? Discuss how the term *neo-conservative* might or might not be applied to the views or politics behind this piece.

2. This kind of writing is often referred to as an opinion column or an editorial. What, exactly, is Frum's opinion, and whom is he trying to convince?

3. What evidence does Frum use? Is it compelling? Why or why not?

4. Describe Frum's tone, and locate words and phrases that appear to be emotional or non-objective. Does the use of emotional words and phrases help or hinder his case? Why or why not?

5. If we were to follow Frum's views, what, presumably, should Canada be trying to do?

6. Frum worked as a speechwriter for U.S. president George W. Bush. What do you think of Canadians who are helping to create U.S. foreign and domestic policies?

FOR FURTHER VIEWING: CRIMINAL BEHAVIOUR

Cool Hand Luke (1967); *The Thin Blue Line* (1988); *A Clockwork Orange* (1971); *Capturing the Friedmans* (2003); *Bowling for Columbine* (2002); *Scarface* (1983) and *Scarface* (1932); *Cocaine Cowboys* (2006); *The Godfather,* Parts I and II (1972, 1974); *Pulp Fiction* (1994); *Strangers on a Train* (1951); *Yojimbo* (1961); *City of God [Cidade de Deus]* (2002); *M* (1931).

GENDER AND SEX ROLES

INTRODUCTION

"Men and women, women and men. It will never work," wrote Erica Jong. John Berger wrote, "Men act and women appear. Men look at women. Women watch themselves being looked at." And Andrea Dworkin wrote, "Men are distinguished from women by their commitment to do violence rather than to be victimized by it." And we've all heard, "Boys will be boys, and girls will be girls." There is the nursery rhyme:

> What are little boys made of?
> Hammers and nails, and puppy dog tails,
> That's what little boys are made of.
> What are little girls made of?
> Sugar and spice, and everything nice,
> That's what little girls are made of.

There is no bottom line to the gender issue, to resolving sexual politics, and to the basic fact that human beings generally, and initially, come mainly in two biological varieties—male and female—and in an infinite variety of behaviours that play off and around the male–female preferences.

The most controversial issue in studying gender may have to do with the old nature versus nurture issue: How much of our behaviour is wired according to our gender (biological destiny), and how much if it is cultured (i.e., socially constructed)? Despite the gains of DNA research and the neurosciences, we are not likely to get to the bottom of that one. Then there is the politics of gender, and how much society privileges men: the patriarchy, the phallocentric stance, the male gaze. Here much feminist work, especially in the last 50 years, has exposed clear sexist discrimination and forced progressive changes to counter stereotyping. This work has also brought attention to gay rights and issues. But you only need to look at who runs things in politics, government, and business to see that men still hugely rule the roost. The question remains: Why?

YOU CAN NEVER HAVE TOO MANY

JANE SMILEY

Jane Smiley is the author of many novels, including The Greenlanders *(1988),* A Thousand Acres *(1991),* Moo *(1995),* The All-True Travels and Adventures of Lidie Newton *(1998),* Horse Heaven *(2000), and* Good Faith *(2003). She published a memoir,* A Year at the Races: Reflections on Horses, Humans, Love, Money, and Luck, *in 2004. This essay was first published in a collection of essays entitled* The Barbie Chronicles, *edited by Yona Zeldis McDonough (1999).*

For my daughter's sixteenth birthday, my six-year-old son wanted to give her a Barbie. I greatly guided him toward the Rapunzel Barbie, whose hair was so long that her head was cocked backward on her neck, or the Birthday Wishes Barbie, in a massive organdy skirt. The one he finally chose was Baywatch Barbie. Okay, she had a dolphin with her. I am willing to admit that that might have been the draw. But you know, Barbies are all right with me. I may have had more Barbies pass through my house than anyone. I like to think so.

I was slightly too old for Barbie myself when they first came out in 1959—I was more of a stuffed-animal girl, anyway—so my first real Barbie experience came when my now–twenty-year-old daughter was three. My First Barbie came home, and was disrobed. The clothes were lost. I spent the required amount of time deploring Barbie's proportions and coloring and the fact that her feet can wear only high heels. Barbie could not have been shaped more differently from me, or have a more different *weltanschauung* from mine, but, hey, here she came with all her stuff.

The one I still remember most fondly was Twirly Curls Barbie. Like Rapunzel Barbie, Twirly Curls Barbie had a serious neck problem because of the weight of her hair. But she came with an intriguing pink-and-cream machine that attached to the ends of a couple of hanks of hair and twisted them together in a chignon. The catch was that the hair had to be neatly combed for the machine to work, an impossible task for a four-year-old, so I spent a lot of time combing the doll until I gave up. My daughters were not in the habit of shaving their Barbies' heads, but they could have. It's a good idea.

Both my girls went through periods where they would wear only pink and purple. I chalk this up to the Barbie influence. Both of them learned how to put on makeup before kindergarten. Lucy could apply lipstick with her eyes closed by the time she was five.

I don't wear makeup. Nor do I have any gowns, bikinis, pink high heels, floral accessories or feminine furniture (like a dressing table or a pink chaise longue). There are no blonds in my family. I could never wear short shorts or feather boas or halter tops. In other words, if my daughters were to learn certain Hollywood-inspired essentials of American womanhood, it wasn't going to be from me, but from Barbie.

And so the Barbies came through the house in a flood. And I am here to tell you that Doctor Barbie was not one of them. Frilly, sexy, pink, purple, bedizened and bejeweled were the preferred Barbies at my house, the more rhinestones the better. We had dozens, because, frankly, Barbies are cheap in more ways than one. My daughters had three mothers: me; their stepmother, who was not unlike me stylistically; and Barbie.

A friend of mine (male) maintains that Barbies have such staying power because they are the only anatomically adult dolls available, and children can manipulate and control them as they cannot the other adults in their lives. But I think girls like Barbie because through her they can try on a no-holds-barred, all-stops-out model of femininity, and that is something they need to do, especially if their own mothers are more androgynous-looking and sober-dressing than Barbie can be. The more a girl is drawn to Barbie, the less she should be deprived of her, no matter what the child's mother's own values are. Longing is more likely to breed attachment than satisfaction is.

Finally, after seventeen years, the Barbies in my house went the way of all flesh. In their last year with us, they were subject to any number of tragic narratives, at least partly inspired by that disguised Barbie literature, *Sweet Valley High*. I discovered the older girls showing the younger girls how to bandage the Barbies with toilet paper (gruesomely decorated with red nail polish) when they happened to get into alcohol-related car crashes with Ken.

My older daughter wandered in the land of Barbie for many years—after all, Nancy Drew is a Barbie; Elizabeth and Jessica, the *Sweet Valley High* twins, are Barbies; Cinderella, Sleeping Beauty, and Beauty of *Beauty and the Beast* all are Barbies. The prettiest girl in school, always a blond, or so it seems, is a Barbie, too. All the blonds on TV and in the movies are Barbies. A girl has to have a Barbie doll in order to decide whether she herself wants to be a Barbie.

On one hand, she has the ever-present mom, who is wearing jeans, cutting her hair ever shorter, getting glasses at forty if not sooner, driving a dark-colored sedan, going to work or cleaning the house, or, worse, espousing all kinds of selfless values of hard work, charity, civic virtue, environmental responsibility.

On the other hand, she has the ever-present Barbie, a tireless consumer whose favorite color is pink, whose jeans are much harder to get on her than her ballet tutu, whose hair requires constant care, and who has more high heels than any First Lady of the Philippines who ever lived. Barbie represents, in every way, getting what you want when you want it, no matter who objects.

Just after she stopped reading *Sweet Valley High* and passed her Barbies down to her younger sister, my older daughter changed her views on her future. No longer did she plan to be a fashion consultant or a Hollywood movie star. No longer did beauty school attract her. She began to read authors like Sandra Cisneros and books like *Our Bodies, Ourselves*. She began her collection of all the works of U2, a band Barbie would never understand. She became socially conscious. She got to be the editor of her high-school newspaper, not because it was a status position, but because she had views she wanted to air on homophobia, the environment and women's rights.

Now she is planning to go to graduate school and law school and become an expert on women's health issues, perhaps adolescent health issues like anorexia and bulimia. She can go on for hours about women's problems with appearance and self image. Barbie should be proud. My daughter wouldn't have gotten here without her.

Have we ever known a Barbie who, in the end, was cherished? I don't think so. More than all the other dolls in the toy box, perhaps because she isn't cuddly or sweet, Barbie is meant to be fiddled with, thought about, manipulated, done to. All of this aids in a girl's making up her mind about who she is and what she wants. That Barbie is a genius.

PERSONAL RESPONSE

What is your opinion of Barbie dolls? Have you or have any of your friends or family ever owned a Barbie? How many and which ones?

QUESTIONS FOR CLASS OR SMALL-GROUP DISCUSSION

1. What does Smiley mean when she writes: "I spent the required amount of time deploring Barbie's proportions and coloring and the fact that her feet can wear only high heels"?

2. "The more a girl is drawn to Barbie, the less she should be deprived of her, no matter what the child's mother's own values are." Paraphrase this sentence and comment on whether you agree.

3. "A girl has to have a Barbie doll in order to decide whether she herself wants to be a Barbie." Does this statement make sense to you? Is this true for all kinds of imaginative toys? To what extent do imaginative toys influence later behaviour by shaping personality types?

4. Some cultural critics think that Barbie is a positive role model because of the variety of her jobs and roles. She can be anyone and do almost anything! Discuss Barbie as a positive female role model.

MARILYN MONROE: THE WOMAN WHO DIED TOO SOON

Gloria Steinem

Gloria Steinem, born in 1934, is probably the most important American feminist (and women's liberationist) thinker, writer, and activist; she is strongly associated with the New Left movement in the United States. From her journalist beginnings, she eventually became the founding editor of Ms. *magazine. Her books include* Outrageous Acts and Everyday Rebellions (1983), Marilyn: Norma Jean (1986), *and* Revolution from Within *(1992).*

Saturday afternoon movies—no matter how poorly made or incredible the plot, they were a refuge from my neighborhood and all my teenage miseries. Serials that never ended, Doris Day, who never capitulated, cheap travelogues, sci-fi features with zippers in the monster suits: I loved them all, believed them all, and never dreamed of leaving until the screen went sickeningly blank.

But I walked out on Marilyn Monroe. I remember her on the screen, huge as a colossus doll, mincing and whispering and simply hoping her way into total vulnerability. Watching her, I felt angry, even humiliated, but I didn't understand why.

After all, Jane Russell was in the movie, too (a very bad-taste version of *Gentlemen Prefer Blondes*), so it wasn't just the vulnerability that all big-breasted women seem to share. (If women viewers prefer actresses who are smaller, neater—the Audrey Hepburns of the world—it is not because we're jealous of the *zoftig* ones as men suppose. It's just that we would rather identify with a woman we don't have to worry about, someone who doesn't seem in constant danger.) Compared to Marilyn, Jane Russell seemed in control of her body and even of the absurd situations in this movie.

Perhaps it was the uncertainty in the eyes of this big, blond child-woman; the terrible desire for approval that made her different from Jane Russell. How dare she express the neediness that so many women feel, but try so hard to hide? How dare she, a movie star, be just as unconfident as I was?

So I disliked her and avoided her movies, as we avoid that which reflects our fears about ourselves. If there were jokes made on her name and image when I was around, I joined in. I contributed to the laughing, the ridicule, the put-downs, thus proving that I was nothing like her. Nothing at all.

I, too, got out of my neighborhood in later years, just as she had escaped from a much worse life of lovelessness, child abuse, and foster homes. I didn't do it, as she did, through nude calendar photographs and starlet bits. (Even had there been such opportunities for mildly pretty girls in Toledo, Ohio, I would never have had the courage to make myself so vulnerable.) Yes, I was American enough to have show-business dreams. The boys in my neighborhood hoped to get out of a lifetime in the factories through sports; the girls, if we imagined anything other than marrying a few steps up in the world, always dreamed of show-business careers. But after high-school years as dancer on the Toledo show-business circuit, or what passed for show business there, it seemed hopeless even to me. In the end, it was luck and an encouraging

Norma Jean Baker
Photo Source: CP/Everett

mother and a facility with words that got me out; a facility that helped me fake my way through the college entrance exams for which I was totally unprepared.

But there's not much more confidence in girls who scrape past college boards than there is in those who, like Marilyn, parade past beauty-contest judges. But the time I saw her again, I was a respectful student watching the celebrated members of the Actors Studio do scenes from what seemed to me very impressive and highbrow plays (Arthur Miller and Eugene O'Neill were to be served up that day).

She was a student, too, a pupil of Lee Strasberg, leader of the Actors Studio and American guru of the Stanislavski method, but her status as a movie star and sex symbol seemed to keep her from being taken seriously even there. She was allowed to observe, but not to do scenes with her colleagues.

So the two of us sat there, mutually awed, I think, in the presence of such theater people as Ben Gazzara and Rip Torn, mutually insecure in the masculine world of High Culture, mutually trying to fade into the woodwork.

I remember thinking that Strasberg and his actors seemed to take positive pleasure in their power to ignore this great and powerful movie star who had come to learn. Their greetings to her were a little too studiously casual, their whispers to each other about her being there a little too self-conscious and condescending. Though she stayed in the back of the room, her blond head swathed in a black scarf and her body hidden in a shapeless black sweater and slacks, she gradually became a presence, if only because the group was trying so hard *not* to look, to remain oblivious and cool.

As we filed slowly out of the shabby room after the session was over, Marilyn listened eagerly to the professional postmortem being carried on by Ben Gazzara and others who walked ahead of us, her fingers nervously tracing a face that was luminous and without makeup, as if she were trying to hide herself, to apologize for being there. I was suddenly glad she hadn't participated and hadn't been subjected to the criticisms of this rather vulturous group. (Perhaps it was an unschooled reaction, but I hadn't enjoyed watching Strasberg encourage an intimate love scene between an actor and actress, and then pick them apart with humiliating authority.) Summoning my nerve, I did ask the shy, blond woman in front of me if she could imagine playing a scene for this group.

"Oh, no," Marilyn said, her voice childish, but much less whispery than on the screen. "I admire all these people so much. I'm just not good enough." Then, after a few beats of silence: "Lee Strasberg is a genius, you know. I plan to do what he says."

Her marriage to Arthur Miller seemed quite understandable to me and to other women, even those who were threatened by Miller's casting off of a middle-aged wife to take a younger, far more glamorous one. If you can't be taken seriously in your work, if you have an emotional and intellectual insecurity complex, then marry a man who has the seriousness you've been denied. It's a traditional female option far more acceptable than trying to achieve that identity on one's own.

Of course, Marilyn's image didn't really gain seriousness and intellectuality. Women don't gain serious status by sexual association any more easily than they do by hard work. (At least, not unless the serious man dies and we confine ourselves to being keepers of the flame. As Margaret Mead has pointed out, widows are almost the only women this country honors in authority.) Even Marilyn's brave refusal to be intimidated by threats that she would never work in films again if she married Miller, who was then a "subversive" called to testify before the House Un-American Activities Committee, was considered less brave than Miller's refusal to testify. Indeed, it was barely reported at all.

Perhaps she didn't take her own bravery seriously either. She might be giving up her livelihood, the work that meant so much to her, but she was about to give that up for marriage anyway. As Mrs. Arthur Miller, she retired to a Connecticut farm and tried to limit her life to his solitary work habits, his friends, and his two children. Only when they badly needed money did she come out of retirement again, and that was to act in *The Misfits,* a film written by her husband.

On the other hand, the public interpretation was very different. She was an egocentric actress forcing one of America's most important playwrights to tailor a screenplay to her inferior talents: that was the gossip-column story here and in Europe. But her own pattern argues the case for her. In two previous marriages, to an aircraft factory worker at the age of sixteen and later to Joe Di Maggio, she had cut herself off from the world and put all her energies into being a housewife. When it didn't work out, she blamed herself, not the role, and added one more failure to her list of insecurities. "I have too many fantasies to be a housewife," she told a woman friend sadly. And finally, to an interviewer: "I guess I *am* a fantasy."

The Misfits seemed to convey some facets of the real Marilyn: honesty, an innocence and belief that survived all experience to the contrary, kindness toward other women, a respect for the life of plants and animals. Because for the first time she wasn't only a sex object and victim, I was also unembarrassed enough to notice her acting ability. I began to see her earlier movies—those in which, unlike *Gentlemen Prefer Blondes,* she wasn't called upon to act the female impersonator.

For me as for so many people, she was a presence in the world, a life force.

Over the years, I heard other clues to her character. When Ella Fitzgerald, a black artist and perhaps the greatest singer of popular songs, hadn't been able to get a booking at an important Los Angeles nightclub in the fifties, it was Marilyn who called the owner and promised to sit at a front table every night while she sang. The owner hired Ella, Marilyn was faithful to her promise each night, the press went wild, and, as Ella remembers with gratitude," After that, I never had to play a small jazz club again."

Even more movingly, there was her last interview. She pleaded with the reporter to end with "What I really want to say: That what the world really needs is a real feeling of kinship. Everybody: stars, laborers, Negroes, Jews, Arabs. We are all brothers. . . . Please don't make me a joke. End the interview with what I believe."

And then she was gone. I remember being told, in the middle of a chaotic student meeting in Europe, that she was dead. I remember that precise moment on August 5, 1962—the people around me, what the room looked like—and I've discovered that many other people remember that moment of hearing the news, too. It's a phenomenon usually reserved for the death of family and presidents.

She was an actress, a person on whom no one's fate depended, and yet her energy and terrible openness to life had made a connection to strangers. Within days after her body was discovered, eight young and beautiful women took their lives in individual incidents clearly patterned after Marilyn Monroe's death. Some of them left notes to make that connection clear.

Two years later, Arthur Miller's autobiographical play, *After The Fall,* brought Marilyn back to life in the character of Maggie. But somehow that Maggie didn't seem the same. She had Marilyn's pathetic insecurity, the same need to use her sexual self as her only way of getting recognition and feeling alive. But, perhaps naturally, the play was about Miller's suffering, not Marilyn's. He seemed honestly to include some of his own destructive acts. (He had kept a writer's diary of his movie-star wife, for instance, and Marilyn's discovery of it was an emotional blow, the beginning of the end for that marriage. It made her wonder: Was her husband exploiting her, as most men had done, but in a more intellectual way?) Nonetheless, the message of the play was mostly Miller's view of his attempts to shore up a creature of almost endless insecurities; someone doomed beyond his helping by a mysterious lack of confidence.

To women, that lack was less mysterious. Writer Diana Trilling, who had never met Marilyn, wrote an essay just after her death that some of Marilyn's friends praised as a more accurate portrayal than Miller's. She described the public's "mockery of [Marilyn's] wish to be educated"; the sexual awareness that came only from outside, from men's reactions, "leaving a great emptiness where a true sexuality would have supplied her with a sense of herself as a person with connection and content." She questioned whether Marilyn had really wanted to die, or only to be asleep, not to be conscious through the loneliness of that particular Saturday night.

Trilling also recorded that feeling of connection to Marilyn's loneliness felt by so many strangers ("especially women to whose protectiveness her extreme vulnerability spoke so directly"), so much so that we fantasized our ability to save her, if only we had been there. "But we were the friends," as Trilling wrote sadly, "of whom she knew nothing."

"She was an unusual woman—a little ahead of her times," said Ella Fitzgerald. "And she didn't know it."

Now that women's self-vision is changing, we are thinking again about the life of Marilyn Monroe. Might our new confidence in women's existence with or without the approval of men have helped a thirty-six-year-old woman of talent to stand on her own? To resist the insecurity and ridicule? To stop depending on sexual attractiveness as the only proof that she was alive—and therefore to face aging with confidence? Because the ability to bear a child was denied to her, could these new ideas have helped her to know that being a woman included much more? Could she have challenged the Freudian analysts to whom she turned in her suffering?

Most of all, we wonder if the support and friendship of other women could have helped. Her early experiences of men were not good. She was the illegitimate daughter of a man who would not even contribute for her baby clothes; her mother's earliest memory of her own father, Marilyn's grandfather, was his smashing a pet kitten against the fireplace in a fit of anger; Marilyn herself said she was sexually attacked by a foster father while still a child; and she was married off at sixteen because another foster family could not take care of her. Yet she was forced always to depend for her security on the goodwill and recognition of men; even to be interpreted by them in writing because she feared that sexual competition made women dislike her. Even if they had wanted to, the women in her life did not have the power to protect her. In films, photographs, and books, even after her death as well as before, she has been mainly seen through men's eyes.

We are too late. We cannot know whether we could have helped Norma Jean Baker or the Marilyn Monroe she became. But we are not too late to do as she asked. At last, we can take her seriously.

PERSONAL RESPONSE

Are there female actors or celebrities who provoke in you either a strong positive or strong negative reaction? Why? What do these figures represent? Have you ever had dreams of show business? What were those dreams, and where did they come from? Madonna, the rock star, is a version of Monroe. Discuss.

QUESTIONS FOR CLASS OR SMALL-GROUP DISCUSSION

1. What was it about Monroe that Steinem at first didn't like? Does this dislike make sense to you? Why or why not?

2. How aware are you of Marilyn Monroe as a legend, celebrity icon, and personality? Where did this knowledge come from? If you have never heard of her, look her up on the Internet, and try to assess what she represents, and why she remains a subject of considerable interest.

3. What does it mean to be a sex symbol? Does culture need or seek such figures? To what purpose? What values or beliefs are wrapped around the idea of sex symbols? Is a sex symbol an archetype?

4. Steinem: "Women don't gain serious status by sexual association any more easily than they do by hard work." Do you agree? Why or why not?

5. Steinem suggests Monroe represents failure and fear. What kind of failures, and what kind of fears?

6. Discuss Steinem's change in her attitude toward Monroe. How do you account for her about-turn?

7. Monroe is a construction of, and subject to, what is sometimes referred to as *the male gaze*. What do you think this term means? Can you apply it to a larger cultural habit? Are women more likely to be sex objects than men? Discuss.

8. Steinem suggests that women have to stop depending on the approval of men and on sexual attractiveness as ways to achieve identity. Is Steinem's observation correct? Discuss.

CANADA'S NEW PM WORRIES GAY COUPLES

Rebecca Cook Dube

Rebecca Cook Dube is an award-winning journalist. She has written about beer, same-sex marriage, terrorism, child abuse, and global warming for USA Today, The Associated Press, The Christian Science Monitor, MSNBC.com, *and* The Globe and Mail.

TORONTO—As the winter sky darkened over City Hall, Michele Schultz and Christina Chora held hands and read their vows.

Standing before them in a long blue robe, Toronto wedding director Lois Code declared, "I do now, by the virtue of the authority vested in me by the province of Ontario, pronounce you legally married."

Schultz, 37, and Chora, 39, have been together 20 years. Same-sex marriage has been legal in Toronto for almost three years and throughout Canada since July. Why tie the knot now? Schultz has a two-word answer: "Stephen Harper."

Harper, sworn in this month as prime minister, is the first Conservative to lead Canada in 13 years. He has pledged to hold a vote in Parliament on overturning Canada's same-sex marriage law, which was approved last year and made Canada the fourth country in the world to legalize gay and lesbian marriage nationwide.

Gay and lesbian couples have been hurrying to wed ever since Harper started gaining momentum before last month's elections. The rush to marry has continued since Harper and the Conservatives defeated Prime Minister Paul Martin and his Liberal Party on Jan. 23.

"We were just worried that now he's in power, he would take away our legal right to get married," Schultz said after the ceremony. "We always planned to do it, and we thought we'd better do it now."

Shotgun weddings

The law gives same-sex married couples the same rights and benefits as their heterosexual counterparts. If Parliament tosses out the legislation, gay and lesbian couples who haven't wed will lose the opportunity to get those benefits. Harper has said if the law is overturned, he will not try to invalidate same-sex marriages that already have taken place.

Code said her office has been busy marrying other same-sex couples who have the same concern. "A lot of people were going to wait for the summer and decided not to wait," she said. "They refer to it as their shotgun weddings."

Toronto city spokesman Brad Ross said 90 same-sex couples got marriage licenses in January, up from 60 in January 2005. Toronto has issued 3,058 same-sex licenses, including 1,172 for U.S. residents, since Ontario legalized gay marriage in June 2003.

Harper won as a moderate, but he promised social conservatives he would reopen the same-sex marriage debate. As opposition leader last year, Harper proposed civil unions for same-sex couples rather than marriage—a compromise he called "the real Canadian way."

January's election gave Harper's Conservatives a plurality, but his party does not have a majority of seats in the House of Commons. It's unclear whether he has the votes to overturn same-sex marriage legislation. "It could go either way," said Laurie Arron, director of advocacy for Egale Canada, a national gay and lesbian rights organization.

A survey of lawmakers conducted this month by The Globe and Mail newspaper predicted same-sex marriage would narrowly survive a new vote.

Canada's public has given pollsters contradictory opinions. In December, a Leger Marketing Poll conducted for the Canadian Press found 55% of 2,013 Canadians polled said they wanted a new vote in Parliament. A poll of 2,034 Canadians conducted by Environics for the Canadian Broadcasting Corp. before the election found 66% didn't want the government to reopen the issue.

It could be a court matter

Both sides agree that if Parliament overturns the law, the courts will decide the matter. Arron said he believes the Supreme Court will protect same-sex marriage rights. Lower courts have said the constitution guarantees gay marriage. Harper has vowed not to override the Supreme Court (permitted under Canadian law) it if rules same-sex marriage is a fundamental human right.

Reopening the same-sex marriage debate has done damage, Arron said. "A lot of LGBT (lesbian, gay, bisexual and transgender) people felt included and felt like first-class citizens" when the law passed last summer. Harper's victory, he said, "already has taken away that sense of security."

Some business people worry the debate could tarnish Canada's image as a same-sex marriage haven. Ric Tremaine, president of the Gay Toronto Tourism Guild, runs an inn that specializes in gay and lesbian weddings and caters to Americans. "For small businesses and Toronto, it's an economic issue," Tremaine said. He's been telling potential customers, "If you've been thinking about doing it, maybe you ought to do it now."

Canadian same-sex marriages are not legally valid in the USA, although some American employers recognize them for purposes of benefits.

The first gay couple to be legally wed in Canada, Kevin Bourassa and Joe Varnell of Toronto, caution against a rush to the altar. "The biggest squabble about your wedding should be where you're going to put your aunt who's coming from Scotland, it shouldn't be about a political party," Varnell said.

Bourassa said he believes the law will survive: "We are confident that Canada will remain a beacon of equality and justice around the world."

Maybe so, but gay and lesbian couples continue to accelerate their wedding plans. Susan Green and Tiffany Veinot of Toronto are ready to dash to City Hall if their marriage rights look shaky. "There's a real political calculus for us," said Green, 41. "We want a big ceremony with friends, but we have to keep one eye on Stephen Harper."

PERSONAL RESPONSE

What are your feelings about same-sex marriage? Do you think same-sex marriage undermines traditional Canadian values? What are the origins of traditional Canadian values?

QUESTIONS FOR CLASS OR SMALL-GROUP DISCUSSION

1. Do you believe same-sex marriage is a fundamental human right? Why or why not?
2. The term *shotgun wedding* is used. Look up this term in a dictionary that provides etymologies or on the Internet, and explain how and when it came into use. What values and beliefs are associated with the term *shotgun wedding*.

3. The article says Prime Minister Harper opposes same-sex marriage but supports same-sex civil unions as "the Canadian way." What does he mean by "the Canadian way"? Whose way is this, and what kind of values are they?

4. Why did Dube begin the article with a scene of two women exchanging vows? "As the winter sky darkened over City Hall" implies that it is late in the day or a storm is coming—what else does it imply in the context of this article?

KILL 'EM! CRUSH 'EM! EAT 'EM RAW!

John McMurtry

John McMurtry, born in 1939, was formerly a professional football player in the Canadian Football League. He is presently a professor emeritus of philosophy at the University of Guelph; he is active in the anti-globalization movement and monetary reform; his area of expertise includes the value structure of economic theory. Recent works include Value Wars: The Global Market Versus the Life Economy *(2002) and* The Cancer Stage of Capitalism *(1999). The following piece was published in* Maclean's *in 1971.*

A few months ago my neck got a hard crick in it. I couldn't turn my head; to look left or right I'd have to turn my whole body. But I'd had cricks in my neck since I started playing grade-school football and hockey, so I just ignored it. Then I began to notice that when I reached for any sort of large book (which I do pretty often as a philosophy teacher at the University of Guelph) I had trouble lifting it with one hand. I was losing the strength in my left arm, and I had such a steady pain in my back I often had to stretch out on the floor of the room I was in to relieve the pressure.

A few weeks later I mentioned to my brother, an orthopedic surgeon, that I'd lost the power in my arm since my neck began to hurt. Twenty-four hours later I was in a Toronto hospital not sure whether I might end up with a wasted upper limb. Apparently the steady pounding I had received playing college and professional football in the late Fifties and early Sixties had driven my head into my backbone so that the discs had crumpled together at the neck—"acute herniation"—and had cut the nerves to my left arm like a pinched telephone wire (without nerve stimulation, of course, the muscles atrophy, leaving the arm crippled). So I spent my Christmas holidays in the hospital in heavy traction and much of the next three months with my neck in a brace. Today most of the pain has gone, and I've recovered most of the strength in my arm. But from time to time I still have to don the brace, and surgery remains a possibility.

Not much of this will surprise anyone who knows football. It is a sport in which body wreckage is one of the leading conventions. A few days after I went into

A casualty of professional sports—or of masculinity?
Photo Source: CP/Richard Lam

hospital for that crick in my neck, another brother, an outstanding football player in college, was undergoing spinal surgery in the same hospital two floors above me. In his case it was a lower, more massive herniation, which every now and again buckled him so that he was unable to lift himself off his back for days at a time. By the time he entered the hospital for surgery he had already spent several months in bed. The operation was successful, but, as in all such cases, it will take him a year to recover fully.

These aren't isolated experiences. Just about anybody who has ever played football for any length of time, in high school, college or one of the professional leagues, has suffered for it later physically.

Indeed, it is arguable that body shattering is the very *point* of football, as killing and maiming are of war. (In the United States, for example, the game results in 15 to 20 deaths a year and about 50,000 major operations on knees alone.) To grasp some of the more conspicuous similarities between football and war, it is instructive to listen to the imperatives most frequently issued to the players by their coaches, teammates and fans. "Hurt 'em!" "Level 'em!" "Kill 'em!" "Take 'em apart!" Or watch for the plays that are most enthusiastically applauded by the fans. Where someone is "smeared," "knocked silly," "creamed," "nailed," "broken in two," or even "crucified." (One of my coaches when I played corner linebacker with the Calgary Stampeders in 1961 elaborated, often very inventively, on this language of destruction: admonishing us to "unjoin" the opponent, "make 'im remember you" and "stomp 'im like a bug.") Just as in hockey, where a fight will bring fans to their feet more often than a skillful play, so in football the mouth waters most of all for the really crippling block or tackle. For the kill. Thus the good teams are "hungry," the best players are "mean," and "casualties" are as much a part of the game as they are of a war.

The family resemblance between football and war is, indeed, striking. Their languages are similar: "field general," "long bomb," "blitz," "take a shot," "front line," "pursuit," "good hit," "the draft" and so on. Their principles and practices are alike: mass hysteria, the art of intimidation, absolute command and total obedience, territorial aggression, censorship, inflated insignia and propaganda, blackboard maneuvers and strategies, drills, uniforms, formations, marching bands and training camps. And the virtues they celebrate are almost identical: hyper-aggressiveness, coolness under fire and suicidal bravery. All this has been implicitly recognized by such jock-loving Americans as media stars General Patton and President Nixon, who have talked about war as a football game. Patton wanted to make his Second World War tank men look like football players. And Nixon, as we know, was fond of comparing attacks on Vietnam to football plays and drawing coachly diagrams on a blackboard for TV war fans.

One difference between war and football, though, is that there is little or no protest against football. Perhaps the most extraordinary thing about the game is that the systematic infliction of injuries excites in people not concern, as would be the case if they were sustained at, say, a rock festival, but a collective rejoicing and euphoria. Players and fans alike revel in the spectacle of a combatant felled into semiconsciousness, "blindsided," "clotheslined" or "decapitated." I can remember, in fact, being chided by a coach in pro ball for not "getting my hat" injuriously into a player who was already lying helpless on the ground. (On another occasion, after the Stampeders had traded the celebrated Joe Kapp to BC, we were playing the Lions in Vancouver and Kapp was forced on one play to run with the ball. He was coming "down the chute," his bad knee wobbling uncertainly, so I simply dropped on him like a blanket. After I returned to the bench I was reproved for not exploiting the opportunity to unhinge his bad knee.)

After every game, of course, the papers are full of reports on the day's injuries, a sort of post-battle "body count," and the respective teams go to work with doctors and trainers, tape, whirlpool baths, cortisone and morphine to patch and deaden the wounds before the next game. Then the whole drama is reenacted—injured athletes held together by adhesive, braces and drugs—and the days following it are filled with even more feverish activity to put on the show yet again at the end of the next week. (I remember being so taped up in college that I earned the nickname "mummy.") The team that survives this merry-go-round spectacle of skilled masochism with the fewest incapacitating injuries usually wins. It is a sort of victory by ordeal: "We hurt them more than they hurt us."

My own initiation into this brutal circus was typical. I loved the game from the moment I could run with a ball. Played shoeless on a green open field with no one keeping score and in a spirit of reckless abandon and laughter, it's a very different sport. Almost no one gets hurt and it's rugged, open and exciting (it still is for me). But then, like everything else, it starts to be regulated and institutionalized by adult authorities. And the fun is over.

So it was as I began the long march through organized football. Now there was a coach and elders to make it clear by their behavior that beating other people was the only thing to celebrate and that trying to shake someone up every play was the only thing to be really proud of. Now there were severe rule enforcers, audiences, formally recorded victors and losers, and heavy equipment to permit crippling bodily moves and collisions (according to one American survey, more than 80% of all football injuries occur to fully equipped players). And now there was the official "given" that the only way to keep playing was to wear suffocating armor, to play to defeat, to follow orders silently and to renounce spontaneity for joyless drill. The game had been, in short, ruined. But because I loved to play and play skillfully, I stayed. And progressively and inexorably, as I moved through high school, college and pro leagues, my body was dismantled. Piece by piece.

I started off with torn ligaments in my knee at 13. Then, as the organization and the competition increased, the injuries came faster and harder. Broken nose (three times), broken jaw (fractured in the first half and dismissed as a "bad wisdom tooth," so I played with it for the rest of the game), ripped knee ligaments again. Torn ligaments in one ankle and a fracture in the other (which I remember feeling relieved about because it meant I could honorably stop drill-blocking a 270-pound defensive end). Repeated rib fractures and cartilage tears (usually carried, again, through the remainder of the game). More dislocations of the left shoulder than I can remember (the last one I played with because, as the Calgary Stampeder doctor said, it "couldn't be damaged any more"). Occasional broken or dislocated fingers and toes. Chronically hurt lower back (I still can't lift with it or change a tire without worrying about folding). Separated right shoulder (as with many other injuries, like badly bruised hips and legs, needled with morphine for the games). And so on. The last pro game I played—against Winnipeg Blue Bombers in the Western finals in 1961—I had a recently dislocated left shoulder, a more recently wrenched right shoulder and a chronic pain center in one leg. I was so tied up with soreness I couldn't drive my car to the airport. But it never occurred to me or anyone else that I miss a play as a corner linebacker.

By the end of my football career, I had learned that physical injury—giving it and taking it—is the real currency of the sport. And that in the final analysis the "winner" is the man who can hit to kill even if only half his limbs are working. In brief, a warrior game with a warrior ethos into which (like almost everyone else I played with) my original boyish enthusiasm had been relentlessly taunted and conditioned.

In thinking back on how all this happened, though, I can pick out no villains. As with the social system as a whole, the game has a life of its own. Everyone grows up inside it, accepts it and fulfills its dictates as obediently as helots. Far from ever questioning the principles of the activity, people simply concentrate on executing these principles more aggressively than anybody around them. The result is a group of people who, as the leagues become of a higher and higher class, are progressively insensitive to the possibility that things could be otherwise. Thus, in football, anyone who might question the wisdom or enjoyment of putting on heavy equipment on a hot day and running full speed at someone else with the intention of knocking him senseless would be regarded simply as not really a devoted athlete and probably "chicken." The choice is made straightforward. Either you, too, do your very utmost to efficiently smash and be smashed, or you admit incompetence or cowardice and quit. Since neither of these admissions is very pleasant, people generally keep any doubts they have to themselves and carry on.

Of course, it would be a mistake to suppose that there is more blind acceptance of brutal practices in organized football than elsewhere. On the contrary, a recent Harvard study has approvingly argued that football's characteristics of "impersonal acceptance of inflicted injury," an overriding "organization goal," the "ability to turn oneself on and off" and being, above all, "out to win" are of "inestimable value" to big corporations. Clearly, our sort of football is no sicker than the rest of our society. Even its organized destruction of physical well-being is not anomalous. A very large part of our wealth, work and time is, after all, spent in systematically destroying and harming human life. Manufacturing, selling and using weapons that tear opponents to pieces. Making even bigger and faster predator-named cars with which to kill and injure one another by the million every year. And devoting our very lives to outgunning one another for power in an ever more destructive rat race. Yet all these practices are accepted without question by most people, even zealously defended and honored. Competitive, organized injuring is integral to our way of life, and football is simply one of the more intelligible mirrors of the whole process: a sort of colorful morality play showing us how exciting and rewarding it is to Smash Thy Neighbor.

Now it is fashionable to rationalize our collaboration in all this by arguing that, well, man *likes* to fight and injure his fellows and such games as football should be encouraged to discharge this original-sin urge into less harmful channels than, say, war. Public-show football, this line goes, plays the same sort of cathartic role as Aristotle said stage tragedy does: without real blood (or not much), it releases players and audience from unhealthy feelings stored up inside them.

As an ex-player in the seasonal coast-to-coast drama, I see little to recommend such a view. What organized football did to me was make me *suppress* my natural urges and re-express them in an alienating, vicious form. Spontaneous desires for free bodily exuberance and fraternization with competitors were shamed and forced under ("if it ain't hurtin' it ain't helpin'") and in their place were demanded armoured mechanical moves and cool hatred of all opposition. Endless authoritarian drill and dressing-room harangues (ever wonder why competing teams can't prepare for a game in the same dressing room?) were the kinds of mechanisms employed to reconstruct joyful energies into mean and alien shapes. I am quite certain that everyone else around me was being similarly forced into this heavily equipped military prevision and angry antagonism, because there was always a mutinous attitude about full-dress practices, and everybody (the pros included) had to concentrate incredibly hard for days to whip themselves into just one hour's hostility a week against another club. The players never speak of these things, of course, because everyone is so anxious to appear tough.

The claim that men like seriously to battle one another to some sort of finish is a myth. It only endures because it wears one of the oldest and most propagandized of masks—the romantic combatant. I sometimes wonder whether the violence all around us doesn't depend for its survival on the existence and preservation of this tough-guy disguise.

As for the effect of organized football on the spectator, the fan is not released from supposed feelings of violent aggression by watching his athletic heroes perform it so much as encouraged in the view that people-smashing is an admirable mode of self-expression. The most savage attackers, after all, are, by general agreement, the most efficient and worthy players of all (the biggest applause I ever received as a football player occurred when I ran over people or slammed them so hard they couldn't get up). Such circumstances can hardly be said to lessen the spectators' martial tendencies. Indeed it seems likely that the whole show just further develops and titillates the North American addiction for violent self-assertion. . . . Perhaps, as well, it helps explain why the greater the zeal of U.S. political leaders as football fans (Johnson, Nixon, Agnew), the more enthusiastic the commitment to hard-line politics. At any rate there seems to be a strong correlation between people who relish tough football and people who relish intimidating and beating the hell out of commies, hippies, protest marchers and other opposition groups.

Watching well-advertised strong men knock other people around, make them hurt, is in the end like other tastes. It does not weaken with feeding and variation in form. It grows.

I got out of football in 1962. I had asked to be traded after Calgary had offered me a $25-a-week-plus-commissions off-season job as a clothing-store salesman. ("Dear Mr. Finks:" I wrote. [Jim Finks was then the Stampeders' general manager.] "Somehow I do not think the dialectical subtleties of Hegel, Marx and Plato would be suitably oriented amidst the environmental stimuli of jockey shorts and herring-bone suits. I hope you make a profitable sale or trade of my contract to the East.") So the Stampeders traded me to Montreal. In a preseason intersquad game with the Alouettes I ripped the cartilages in my ribs on the hardest block I'd ever thrown.

I had trouble breathing and I had to shuffle-walk with my torso on a tilt. The doctor in the local hospital said three weeks rest, the coach said scrimmage in two days. Three days later I was back home reading philosophy.

PERSONAL RESPONSE

Participating in male contact sports no doubt significantly increases the risk of serious or lifelong injuries. Why do many men nonetheless participate, and even strive to play at the highest levels where the chances for injury are increased? Are the pressures personal or cultural, or are men wired, or predisposed, to want to participate in physically challenging activities? That is, are such activities part of male culture or habit, or is it a gender-neutral desire that both males and females share?

QUESTIONS FOR CLASS OR SMALL-GROUP DISCUSSION

1. Do you think that men—as both players and viewers—like violent contact sports more than women do? Why? Discuss.
2. McMurtry makes a clear connection between football and war, especially in their common lexicon. Do you agree with McMurtry's assessment that the spectacle of football "develops and titillates the North American addiction for violent self-assertion"?
3. McMurtry believes that when a game is regulated and institutionalized, the "fun is over," though he is mainly referring to the fun of childhood sports. What do you think of this idea? What does he mean by *regulated* and *institutionalized*? Who is responsible for the regulations and institutionalization, and what is gained by these practices?
4. List McMurtry's reasons for accepting the violence in football. Which reasons seem most convincing? Why? Accepting violence on a cultural level is more of a male quality than a female quality. Do you agree?
5. Is violence in sport any different from other kinds of male-dominated cultural activities, such as business and politics? In what ways are these activities also rife with forms of violence?

FOR FURTHER VIEWING: GENDER AND SEX ROLES

Le Déclin de l'empire américain (1986); *Killing Us Softly* (1979); *Tootsie* (1982); *Thelma and Louise* (1991); *Gentlemen Prefer Blondes* (1953); *The Crying Game* (1992); *Boys Don't Cry* (1999); *Dreamworlds II: Desire, Sex, Power in Music Video* (1997); *Bend It Like Beckham* (2002); *The Celluloid Closet* (1995); *The Life and Times of Harvey Milk* (1984); *Diary of a Chambermaid* (1964); *Ed Wood* (1994); *Woman in the Dunes* (1964); *When We Were Kings* (1996).

CHAPTER SIXTEEN

THE POLITICS OF ETHNICITY

INTRODUCTION

Some contemporary scholars claim that ethnicity and race are not "real" but are socially constructed—that is, racial differences are invented to categorize and privilege certain groups, mainly for reasons of power. In other words, although the biological difference between groups of people is so small that it is considered scientifically meaningless, race and ethnicity nonetheless lead to profound differences in people's lives. The central negative example of these differences is racism, which fuelled the system of slavery and Jim Crow segregation, and continues today in subtler economic and social forms. We might say that a central positive example is cultural diversity, the celebration of which was enshrined in Canadian law through the Multicultural Act of 1971, though many argue that the Act was in fact a hegemonic and colonial move to silence the dissent of marginal cultures. The topics of race and ethnicity have motivated a wide range of stimulating and passionate writing in North America in the last century. The following essays look at race from a variety of perspectives, demonstrating that this is one of the most engaging and complex issues of our time.

THE ETHICS OF COURAGE

Taiaiake Alfred

Taiaiake Alfred was born of the Mohawk Nation, in Montreal, in 1964. He is presently an academic (Ph.D., Cornell University), and he has also served as a U.S. Marine. He is a frequent consultant to First Nations groups and organizations. His last two books are Wasáse: Indigenous Pathways of Action and Freedom *(2005) and* Peace, Power, Righteousness: An Indigenous Manifesto *(1999). He teaches at the University of Victoria, British Columbia.*

Not all of us have been conquered. There are still strong Onkwehonwe who persevere in their struggle for an authentic existence and who are capable of redefining, regenerating, and reimagining our collective existences. If we are willing to put our words into action and transform our rhetoric into practice, we too can achieve the fundamental goal of the indigenous warrior: to live life as an act of indigeneity, to move across life's landscapes in an indigenous way, as my people say, *Onkwehonweneha.* A warrior confronts colonialism with the truth in order to regenerate authenticity and recreate a life worth living and principles worth dying for. The struggle is to restore connections severed by the colonial machine. The victory is an integrated personality, a cohesive community, and the restoration of respectful and harmonious relationships.

Translating this ethical sense and idea on a way of being into a concise political philosophy is difficult, for it resists institutionalization. I might suggest, as a starting point, conceptualizing *anarcho-indigenism.* Why? And why this term? Conveyance of the indigenous warrior ethic will require its codification in some form—a creed and an ethical framework for thinking through challenges. To take root in people's minds the new ethic will have to capture the spirit of a warrior in battle and bring it to politics. How might this spirit be described in contemporary terms relating to political thought and movement? The two elements that come to my mind are *indigenous,* evoking cultural and spiritual rootedness in this land and the Onkwehonwe struggle for justice and freedom, and the political philosophy and movement that is fundamentally anti-institutional, radically democratic, and committed to taking action to force change: *anarchism.*

This philosophical outlook is close to what Vaclav Havel described as his utopia—in his terms, a decentralized economy, local decision-making, government based on direct election of political leaders, and the elimination of political parties as governing institutions, a sort of a spiritual socialism:

> It's hard to imagine the kind of system I've tried to describe here coming about unless man, as I've said, "comes to his senses." This is something no revolutionary or reformer

can bring about; it can only be the natural expression of a more general state of mind, the state of mind in which man can see beyond the tip of his own nose and prove capable of taking on—under the aspect of eternity—responsibility even for the things that don't immediately concern him, and relinquish something of his private interest in favor of the interest of the community, the general interest. Without such a mentality, even the most carefully considered project aimed at altering systems will be for naught.[1]

There are philosophical connections between indigenous and some strains of anarchist thought on the spirit of freedom and the ideals of a good society. Parallel critical ideas and visions of post-imperial futures have been noted by a few thinkers, but something that may be called anarcho-indigenism has yet to develop into a coherent philosophy.[2] There are also important strategic commonalities between indigenous and anarchist ways of seeing and being in the world: a rejection of alliances with legalized systems of oppression, non-participation in the institutions that structure the colonial relationship, and a belief in bringing about change through direct action, physical resistance, and confrontations with state power. It is on this last point that connections have already been made between Onkwehonwe groups and non-indigenous activist groups, especially in collaborations between anarchists and Onkwehonwe in the anti-globalization movement.

But even before this, and without explicit linkages in theory or politically, resurgences of Onkwehonwe self-determination have been seen by the state in the same way as anarchist challenges to state authority: direct defence of rights and freedoms in a physical sense has been met with extremes of repression by the state.

The so-called "Oka Stand-off" in 1990 saw a surge of indigenous power in the resistance of the Kanien'kehaka communities (located around the city of Montréal) to the Canadian state's attempt to expropriate lands and impose its police authority on them. The determination and disciplined tactics of the *Kahnawakero*:non—people of Kahnawake, women and men alike and together—stymied the Canadian army's efforts to occupy the Kanien'kehaka village, and their ferocious but non-lethal defence of their lands and homes forced the army, trained and equipped only to confront other military forces in conventional armed combat, to withdraw after a prolonged effort. This incident, which happened at the end of a wearying 78-day stand-off between the Kanien'kehaka and Canadian police and military forces, is an unappreciated benchmark of indigenous resistance struggles.[3] Its lessons were reinforced by the so-called "Gustafsen Lake stand-off," where a serious paramilitary force was brought to bear by the Canadian state (this time in interior British Columbia) against a small group of Onkwehonwe who had occupied a sacred ceremonial site and refused to vacate the premises when ordered to do so by the Settler who held legal title to the land. Splitting-the-Sky, one of the defiant Onkwehonwe leaders in the conflict, describes what happened:

We were unarmed. But then they brought in arms, we weren't too far out to get some rifles, because everybody up there in the Cariboo hunts. I mean, everybody has shotguns and it's no big secret. So we ended up with about 17 shotguns to defend ourselves. I was asked at that time, "What should be the stance we make?" "Well," I said, "According to Canadian law, if somebody puts a gun in your face, you have

Our home and native land?
Photo Source: CP/Shaney Komulainen

a right to pick up a gun and defend yourself from being attacked or killed." That is Canadian law. Every citizen has that right according to due process of law—the Canadian law. And so it was a question of self-defence.[4]

These two incidents illustrate how immediate the issue of violence and self-defence is to any serious conception of resurgent indigenous power. The logic of contending with state power is inescapable. If contention is necessary to make change, if contention leads necessarily to confrontation, and if confrontation has an inherent element of potential or real violence, as the experiences in Oka and Gustafsen Lake demonstrate, then we must be prepared to accept violence and to deal with it. To continue advancing, the intelligent course of action is contention. Dogmatically pacifist movements have only succeeded in making change when they are backed by the support of the threat of violence—either explicit in the form of organized armed resistance movements subsumed within the larger non-violent movement or implicit in the fear the state and Settler society have of the potential of unorganized violence coming out of frustration. Thus we must contend, and we must confront, and we must be prepared to shoulder the burden of conflict. But how?

Governments will always use violence, and it is a responsibility to recognize this. How do we resist the power of violence and prevent it from becoming a way of life as it has become in places like Israel, Northern Ireland, and Sri Lanka? In a sense, the question could be framed as: What is our theory of violence?

In treading this ground, we must proceed cautiously. It is crucial to understand the difference between courageously standing up to violence employed in the service of oppression and using violence to advance our own political objectives. We can take sobering insights from the words of suicide bombers from al-Qassam, the military arm of Hamas, the Palestinian Islamist organization. One of the Hamas planners said, in an interview questioning why they had implemented the suicide bomber strategy, "We paid a high price when we used only slingshots and stones. We need to exert more pressure, make the cost of the occupation that much more expensive in human lives, that much more unbearable."[5] They clearly planned the suicide bomber strategy as an effort to draw their oppressors (Israelis) into the world of pain experienced by the Palestinians, to make the price of the Israeli occupation of Palestine high for everyone. But is it possible to use violence and fear to create a new consciousness? Ultimately, the Hamas planner said, they recognize that the "battles for Islam are won not through the gun but by striking fear into the enemy's heart."

This candid exposition of the terrorist logic (which could be applied to the strategies of both sides of the Israeli-Palestinian conflict) illustrates the push, in violent conflicts, to ever-escalating levels and intensities. The rationale is always there, and within the ethical and ideological frame of force as a legitimate strategy, a moral justification can always be found. But our questions must be asked from within the foundations of our spiritual teachings and cultures as Onkwehonwe. Our question centres on an indigenous logic and the struggle for Onkwehonwe strength and freedom. Is it acceptable to move against the aggressor/oppressor using armed resistance? The best way to find an answer to that question is by delving into the experience of other colonized peoples who have contended with imperial power and sought to rid themselves from foreign occupation and who have resisted violent oppression.

In the contemporary era, one of the best known and most instructive cases of anti-colonial resistance is that of Vietnam. In the Onkwehonwe view, what were the underlying reasons for a Vietnamese revolution against French colonial rule? Essentially, it was a rebellion by the Vietnamese against economic exploitation by European and Euroamerican imperialism and for control of their own land and resources. It was not the Europeans' civilizing mission that was intolerable to the Vietnamese; many appreciated the advances in transportation, communication, education, political institutions, and physical infrastructure, all of which they needed and wanted. They had endured, for generations, a corrupt and ineffective "indigenous" government. In the final analysis what made colonial rule intolerable—and what must be seen as the major cause of the revolution—was French racism and abuse towards the Vietnamese people and the French exploitation of the economic resources of that country. Vietnamese intellectuals reacted strongly to the French attempt to undermine indigenous social institutions, and the average person reacted strongly to the imposition of French taxes and the unfair demands by and advantages given to French businesses operating in Vietnam.[6]

But, given the other options that existed then as now, why did the Vietnamese peoples' movements develop and begin to carry out campaigns of armed resistance against the French and, eventually, the United States? The rationale was voiced in different ways by the revolutionary hero of Vietnam, Ho Chi Minh, and Nguyen Thuang Huyen, one of Vietnam's "patriotic scholars." Nguyen Thuang Huyen believed that the *I Ching* defined revolution in reformist terms as dynastic change within an established system of rule; a regime clinging to power would crush any attempt at reform, leaving those who wished for change no choice but to resort to a corresponding violence to defeat and replace their rulers.

Ho Chi Minh believed instead in a more systematic, Western, notion of revolution. Reform, he thought, is what happens *within* an institution; whether it is successful or not, some of the old regime remains. Revolution, on the other hand, *replaces* one system with another. He concluded that there was no accommodating the French regime, which had shown itself unable to accept Vietnamese national independence and to abandon its interests in the colony of "Indochina." Thus, a movement that preserved the imperial system was unacceptable; the only way the Vietnamese people could achieve real change was through an armed revolutionary movement to replace imperial rule with a self-determining Vietnamese state.

> First, you must understand that to gain independence from a great power like France is a formidable task that cannot be achieved without some outside help, not necessarily in things like arms, but in the nature of advice and contracts. One doesn't in fact gain independence by throwing bombs and such. That was the mistake the early revolutionaries all too often made. One must gain it through organization, propaganda, training and discipline. One also needs . . . a set of beliefs, a gospel, a practical analysis, you might even say a bible. Marxism-Leninism gave me that framework.

Thus, Ho's adoption of Marxism/Leninism, with its implicit theory of revolutionary violence, was not simply expedient (in that he could approach the Soviet Union and China for cash and arms and training) but was influenced by considerations of the Vietnamese peoples' necessity of survival in the face of a humbling and divisive colonial power. Imperialism was the oppressor, so an alliance with the anti-capitalist/anti-colonial communist bloc was the answer. Armed struggle was seen in this frame as necessary and unavoidable.

Focusing on the same ideological frame, the thoughts and methods of the Argentinean guerrilla leader, Che Guevara, offer great insights into the practices of armed revolution from an insurgent or minority position.[7] Guevara argued that the colonial enemy will fight to remain in power, that feudalism is globalized and mutually supportive, and that the anti-imperial struggle was continental in nature given the extent of the influence of the United States over North and South America. This prescient analysis is no longer questionable in the age of globalization. His Leninist assessment of imperialism still holds:

> We must bear in mind that imperialism is a world system, the last stages of capitalism—and it must be defeated in a world confrontation. The strategic end of this struggle should be the destruction of imperialism. Our share, the responsibility of the exploited and underdeveloped of the world, is to eliminate the foundations of imperialism: our oppressed nations, from where they extract capitals, raw materials— instruments of domination—arms and all kinds of articles. . . . [8]

However, there is a fundamental problem with Guevara's logic when he makes the shift from diagnosis to prescription: revolutionary struggles using direct armed confrontation have failed to stop capitalism's expansion. Everywhere except in the local struggles in Vietnam and Cuba, armed struggle, peasant uprisings or *foco*, and militant international socialist solidarity have failed to produce long-term or generally successful resistances. The question for us today is: What kind of "world confrontation" is necessary to bring about not the Guevarian military "defeat" (which has proven impossible to achieve) but the transformation of imperialism?

An emblem of the "revolutionary" person and spirit, Guevara was uncompromising in his belief in the necessity of armed struggle and his hatred of imperialists. These are, in fact, the essences of the revolutionary spirit: violence and hatred. But the experience of revolutionary action in world history points to a fatal flaw (aside from the truth of living and dying by the sword): revolution and armed resistance theories with their simplistic materialist notions ignore the inextricable bonds between means and ends.

Even the inspiring Frantz Fanon, whose theory was layered with meaning, combining deep psychological insight with political-economic analysis, did not recognize the inability of a strategy of decolonization based on violence to transcend violence in the society and state which it achieves.[9]

There is also a basic question to be put to the Onkwehonwe contemplating different ways of bringing about change: Are we ready to kill and to die for the cause of self-determination? If the answer is no—and I believe most Onkwehonwe would say no—then our strategy and tactics must be shaped instead to reflect the level of conflict tolerance and willingness to engage in direct action that actually exists among our people. Yet the spirit of resistance of the old revolutionaries is worth emulating. Guevara wrote: "We cannot foresee the future, but we should never give in to the defeatist temptation of being the vanguard of a nation which yearns for freedom, but abhors the struggle it entails and awaits its freedom as a crumb of victory."[10] To honour the spirit and yet have an approach that respects our values and is effective against our adversaries and enemies, we need to define "struggle" in a way that makes sense for us in our circumstances. This means finding a theoretical logic that rejects violence as a means of liberation.

Before that is possible we must recognize the attraction of violence. It is a powerful strategic weapon. Violence gets attention, it consumes state resources, people have a morbid attraction to its effects, and it is perhaps the easiest means of resistance. But the drawbacks to violence are serious. Violence forces people to choose sides, and because it is repugnant to so many people, it causes them to disavow the cause; it limits potential allies; and it is as addictive as a drug—its immediacy and paraphernalia are seductive and intoxicating in the short term, and in the long term, the inevitable cycle of repression creates a situation justifying further violence.[11]

There are arguments in any movement both for and against violence that make sense. Western notions of non-violence are rooted in a counter-historical reading of Jesus' teaching (given that Judeo-Christian societies are among the most violent the world has ever known) and are advocated as a moral choice. But, in fact, this reading is unnecessary; non-violent action coupled with a capacity for physical self-defence is a strategic choice, not a moral choice. It is simply the best way of prevailing in a struggle. In a state context, rather than attempting to destroy or displace state authority, non-violence offers a sound strategic vision that will mobilize a movement to deny rulers control of community life and will undermine the legitimacy of the state both domestically and internationally. Because the practices and theories of politics today are so permeated with the logic of armed force, my argument here will seem counterintuitive to most people. But in fact, non-violent resistance, as the foundation of a movement made up of many different tactics responding to the demands of circumstance, has been historically widespread and effective against all types of repressive regimes.[12]

So resurgence raises the questions of ethics in terms of maintaining a connection to Onkwehonwe values and ways of living while fighting in creative ways and preserving the ideas and values that are the foundation of Onkwehonwe existence.

It is a warrior's definition of courage that most concerns us, as it will be individuals who will contend against the state. Willpower and determination are the elements of courage. They are not a finite reserve and must be nurtured, fed, and developed if Onkwehonwe are to be able to stand up to state authority in any way—whether it be protest, contention, or more aggressive assertions. People who engage in battle in whatever form are not "fearless." Ninety-eight per cent of combat soldiers break down mentally in wartime situations, and for military commanders, the question is not if, but when will the men's well of courage run dry?[13] Onkwehonwe, like all warriors in battle, will realize our collective courage from sharing in others' wells of strength and determination and building up our collective store of mental and emotional strength by supporting each other in struggle and achieving victories along the way to our goals. And it is the warrior's question that is our challenge: How to shore up courage? The answer is that we, like any warrior in battle, need to realize that our collective fortitude consists in sharing in others' courage, as leaders inspire and motivate us to persevere when we feel like quitting the fight, and by building up our collective store of mental and emotional strength through the uplifting and cumulative effects that victory provides a people.

Courage in facing adversity is one part of the ethical question; the other centres on not *suffering* harm but *causing* harm. Being in contention with state power will, without a doubt, cause human harm or some form of suffering due to the strong reaction it will provoke among the conservative defenders of the colonial status quo. This much is undeniable: white society, through the agencies of the state, will use violence in the attempt to suppress any serious threat to the colonial order. Given this fact, some may argue that causing any disruption in society that causes any form of human suffering is wrong in the first instance. This is a false logic on two grounds: first, Onkwehonwe are *already* suffering in the status quo; and secondly, the state does not *have* to respond violently to Onkwehonwe challenges, it *chooses* to do so. The responsibility for violence begins and ends with the state, not with the people who are challenging the inherent injustices perpetrated by the state and who are seeking to alleviate their own present suffering under the state's existing institutions and practices. But behind the logic of this attitude of "I am doing something people don't like, therefore I am a bad person" is the totally misguided rumination of a colonial mentality, the source of the reluctance, fear, and inability of oppressed people to take action in support of their rights.

Change necessitates conflict, but a violent form of conflict is a strategic choice of the state supported by colonial elites and by public opinion as well. We understand the implications of our actions in a rational ethical frame, not on emotion or judged by a Judeo-Christian guilt complex. Some people's interests and property or emotional attachments to evil colonial institutions and symbols may be affected or harmed; there is the potential for wrong to be done in the context of any movement. This is true, but the focus of our ethical reasoning must be in justifying our actions by putting them in context, in focusing on the details and implications of the actions we promote, and in forcing the state and other political actors to justify their actions and the implications of their choices. We can thus work through the ethical dilemma of promoting contention and being responsible for engendering a response from the state that is likely to turn violent. Careful thought—and the mental discipline of a true warrior—leads to the ethical consideration of the consequences, the intent, and the nature of the actions we take in the course of our struggle against the state. Yet these are all less important ethically than the main consideration, which is the motivation we bring to the struggle and the spirit of our actions.

In the case of actions conducted as part of indigenous resurgences, "causing harm" would be an accidental and unintended result of creative engagements with the state and social forces of our oppression. Contrast this with simplistically reasoned Western ethics (which comes out of the proscriptive orders of Judeo-Christianity and which is embedded within the liberal tradition so central to justifying colonialism) where the focus is on acts themselves. Onkwehonwe and other non-Western cultures are not shackled to the monotheistic delusion and put acts in context of a situation. This is at once dangerously liberating ("Thou Shalt Not Kill" provides moral security, even if it is broken with impunity by Jews and Christians, compared to the Onkwehonwe pronouncement "Don't Kill, Unless You Have To and the Circumstance Requires It"), cumbersome, and constraining—because it depends on human reason negotiating the complexity of the real world.

This is an ethics of spiritual and physical courage, of restraint, and of mental discipline. Everything has to be thought through, there are no moral absolutes or set rules for guiding human behaviours either in the personal or political realms. Even in regard to the "Golden Rule" basic principles that transcend moral systems and cultures (do not lie, kill, steal, commit adultery), to which the Buddhist and Onkwehonwe philosophical systems add proscription against alcohol, these should be understood as rational, intelligent guidelines, or the wisdom of the ages, rather than divine orders.

The Dalai Lama, in *Ancient Wisdom, Modern World*, has defined ethics as, "the indispensable interface between my desire to be happy and yours."[14] How do we determine if something we are doing is wrong? We can take our cue from Buddhist teachings: you are wrong when you consciously do something to cause unhappiness and harm to others for selfish ends. So for Onkwehonwe, as for Buddhists, the central question of ethics doesn't involve simply proving something was done and labelling the doer evil or wrong because of his role in conducting an act that has been objectively defined as such. Instead, the crucial process is contextualizing the whole experience and trying to figure out why the act was done and what made the person do it, so as to determine whether the act was evil or not.

For our contentious actions to be properly considered, they must be put into context, and the motivation of the vision driving the act needs to be understood. It is true that in situations of extreme contention there is a deep disregard by some people of the basic human impulse towards care and affection for others—this is the colonialists' position en masse. But the fact that Settler society is "evil" in the sense that it has inherited not rights but wrongs from its forefathers, does not mean that we can justify any action taken against the evil based on an eye-for-an-eye ethic. We want and desire peaceful coexistence, and we must advance our cause against the evil of colonialism accordingly.

The real question facing Onkwehonwe is how to counter the evil of imperialism ethically. Raw anger against the Settler society is potentially a good thing because it is a force capable of driving us to action—altruistic action. Yet anger must be investigated to discover its roots and to discern its appropriate focus. It should not be denied—either suppressed out of fear or for a show of stereotypical stoicism—but it must be restrained and channelled through a deliberate and voluntary discipline. This is "patient forbearance" in Buddhist teachings. In terms of our discussion here, it may be that the most suitable term is *non-violent militancy,* meaning remaining firm in the face of fear, doing what is necessary for what is right, yet not allowing negative thoughts and emotions to control us.

For sure, this is different from do-nothing passivity and the total loss of confidence that is cowardice. The middle path between raging violence and complacency is akin to the Gandhian strategy of non-cooperation.[15]

The Indian mass movement against British colonization was not passive, but militantly pacifist, and it actively confronted power in a strategic, creative, and tactically diverse manner without using violence. It was built on the spiritual strengthening of the people; the development of personal and community capacity for self-sufficiency; non-cooperation with the institutions of domination; and the disruption of oppressive systems by using strategies of militant non-violence, such as civil disobedience, boycotts, strikes, sit-downs and sit-ins of all kinds, protest marches, and rallies. There are, of course, differences between the situation in imperially occupied India and the situations of our peoples, but for cultural, political, and strategic reasons the basic Gandhian approach is a solid conceptual foundation for Onkwehonwe resurgences.

The beauty and strength of this approach to confronting imperialism is that it goes straight to the core of state power in its assault on injustice. The basic structure of the state as a system of power is tripartite: it has power, or force, in a physical or military sense; it has authority, or laws, which it uses to regulate and discipline people to its power; and it has legitimacy, which it manufactures and manipulates to create and maintain support. These facets of power create a reality in which the state's capacity for and use of force is unquestioned. The state cannot be defeated militarily because it has too much physical force at its disposal. To this kind of power we must defer. But the authority of the state is something we *can* contest. The legal and bureaucratic structures that manage the state's power are vulnerable because they rely on people's cooperation in order to function. This kind of power we must defy. And state legitimacy is the most imperceptible yet crucial form of power. It relies on the psychological and social conditioning of people to create an acceptance of the state and the forms of power it normalizes: imperatives to obey the state's offices and authorities and to fear the state's ability to enforce its rules with violent repression of serious dissent and disobedience. The first and most important objective of movements against state power must be to deny the state's legitimacy in theoretical and concrete ways. In the long term, legitimacy is the most important form of power the state possesses. Regimes cannot survive without the legitimation by subjects of their authority and consequent acceptance of their right to use force to maintain the social, political, and economic order represented by the institutions that make up the state.

In colonial relationships, impositions of power and authority can probably be absorbed, tolerated, or accommodated by indigenous populations in various ways over time, but true conquest becomes inevitable when the Settlers' imperial claims to legitimacy are accepted and normalized by Onkwehonwe. Legitimation (acceptance and support for colonial institutions) is the fundamental battlefield. Imperialists and colonial governments know this from their long history of scourge and defilement of non-white countries. This is why, for the colonizers, the most important and immediate imperative is to assimilate indigenous peoples culturally: without an indigenous cultural foundation or root there is no memory store or intellectual base upon which to build a challenge to the empire.

It is the capacity of action premised on indigenous authenticity that is most important and immediately imperative for anti-imperial struggle. Culture exists in communities and in the lives of people; culture is the foundation of indigenous resurgences—contrary to the institutional-organizational approach to confronting state power, which structures resistance in forms of counter-imperial organizations that mimic the state in order to confront it on its own terms.

The Gandhian movement was not formed on organizations at all. It was centred on inspired leadership-by-example, by leaders convincing people to stand up and take action and to coordinate their various and autonomous demonstrations of courage. This is the same leadership model which is the foundation of Onkwehonwe political systems.

So far in this line of thinking, we have the beginnings of a conceptual vocabulary for our movement: the tactics of militant non-violence and anti-institutional strategies are key. Add to these the politics of contention. This brings us to the question of forms of contentious action against the state. What is action? Is it a demonstration of courage to throw out strong words and to oppose the state verbally? Antonio Gramsci coined the term, "contradictory consciousness," for a situation in which the oppressed both reject and accept their subjugation at the same time.[16] This is most definitely a character of aboriginalist mentality and rhetoric; piercing this crippling hypocrisy is the first step to our reawakening as peoples. Words can, in fact, be powerful shocks to the system and are capable of causing people to rethink their identity and their place within colonialism. But if they are to be powerful enough to cause crises in the contradictory consciousness of the colonized individual, the words must be dangerous and must push people outside the bounds of their comfort zone and beyond acceptability. The test of whether one's words are contentious in this sense is this question: How much guts does it take to say what you are thinking and to be who you are?

What separates the warrior from the cooperator is this dangerous engagement with power. Passivity shifts resistance to the less dangerous spheres that the dominant power has designated/created as areas for negotiation or reform—after all, it does not take any courage to *negotiate*, to *advocate*, or to *reform*. Rhetorical power is dangerously contentious when it seeks to provoke a response outside of the accepted, normalized, and sanctioned patterns of interaction that form the colonial status quo. And to be truly dangerous, words and ideas must be convincing in their logic and so grounded in social, cultural, and political reality that there is imminent possibility of their affecting and shaping the actions of people. Overblown rhetoric and fantastic pronouncements that resonate with no one and have no possibility of forming the basis of action are not warrior words at all. They are only small acts of blustery cowardice, rhetorical withdrawals from dangerous realities that are just as condemnable as bodily withdrawals in the face of physical danger.

Some people, no doubt, would consider Gandhi's pacifism as a lesser form of contention than struggles founded on revolutionary materialist theories. Compared to the spirited agitation on Gandhian principles Ward Churchill's "libratory praxis," for example, may seem radical and extremely courageous. He rejects non-violence (specifically, the unwillingness to kill) as an "illness" and argues for the necessity of a violent socialist revolution to supplant the capitalist state. He focuses his approach on efforts to deprogram people's aversions to the tools of violence; therapeutic discussions, spending time with oppressed people as "reality therapy," and hands-on sessions to demystify weaponry are some of the tactical suggestions offered.[17] There are very few, if any, Onkwehonwe (and others) who would even consider adopting his approach and program, so that his ideas appear ludicrous, not dangerous. No one is seriously considering these ideas as a platform for a real movement; they are therefore rendered safe. So Gandhi's more moderate sounding but more attractive and viable ideas can be seen for what they are in comparison: truly dangerous and really revolutionary.

The fact that there are people like Ward Churchill who do fantasize about carrying out acts of violent revolution—and I will admit from personal experience and from many conversations that this fantasy is widespread among Onkwehonwe and harboured by many frustrated warriors—highlights that anger is a very strong force in contemporary Onkwehonwe societies. We must understand that raging violence is always more of a reaction to the internal and external hypocrisy of colonial relations than to injustices in economic or political forms.[18] But for Onkwehonwe resurgences, this path of raging anger is overly emotional, and it replicates the exact wrong that we are trying to confront. Yet it continues to energize young males especially; they are the frustrated warriors acting out against state oppression and not channelling it internally.[19] This is a useless waste of energy. The revolutionary guerrilla model of change is clearly a gendered concept rooted in machismo and valorizations of violence—the common and unexamined male approach to the universal need to prove a strength which comes to women naturally through their capacity to bear pain and especially to endure childbirth (which explains why there is such a mocking distaste for this approach among females).

The joke on the guerrilla mentality is even crueller today than at times when empires were in fact vulnerable to attacks in a physical sense. Oppression has become increasingly invisible; no longer constituted in conventional terms of military occupation, onerous taxation burdens, blatant land thefts, etc. In this post-modern imperial context, rather than engaging in futile (albeit glorious!) military confrontation with the armies of the empire, latter-day armed guerrillas find themselves punching at air, thus compounding the frustration factor. The forces that oppress us today are beyond elusive. The power of empire is not in machines, bayonets, barbed wire, or even soldiers. Its effects have become ever more present and damaging to be sure, but as a military or protest action target, it is almost invisible. Doubly frustrated warriors soon come to realize what the social theorist C. Wright Mills observed in the 1950s, the "movement from authority to manipulation":

> No longer can the problem of power be set forth as the simple one of changing the process of coercion into those of consent. The engineering of consent to authority has moved into the realm of manipulation where the powerful are anonymous. Impersonal manipulation is more insidious than coercion precisely because it is hidden; one cannot locate the enemy and declare war upon him. Targets for aggression are unavailable, and certainty is taken from men.[20]

If this is so, whom do we attack? What building do we capture? At whom do we direct our hatred when the empire is dispersed and more of an infusion that flavours our lives than an obstacle to be overcome? It seems impossible, facing a post-modern imperialist state, to isolate a discrete target for direct resistance actions, so we must continue our struggle by engaging its corrupting power *at all times* and *in all ways,* as perpetual warriors. The only way to do this is in creative contention.

Violence, or at least the guerrilla posture, does remain attractive for emotional and cultural reasons. To prevent people from being drawn to useless strategies of resistance, the Onkwehonwe movement requires discipline. By discipline I mean the development of a resurgent power and culture of resistance that channels our angry and potentially deadly and self-destructive energies into a positive force for change. This strength lies in Onkwehonwe communities and people being decultured and disabused of the colonial mentalities and various colonial myths and recultured to support the resurgence of action against state manipulations of their identity. Strong people and strong, united communities can provide the support and validation for serious actions; we need authentic ideas and intellectual tools drawn from the heritage of Onkwehonwe peoples, physical infrastructure, and reinforcement of community cohesion in communications and media and education. It is a major problem that we are, for the most part, lacking these sources of strength in ourselves and in our Onkwehonwe communities. Outside of the Zapatista army and other indigenous Mexican people currently supporting rebellions of indigenous truth against capitalism,[21] there is no cultural base for mass action, nor is there a crucial mass of strong people to support actions and strategy that have any hope of challenging state power in any form. This must change if we are to survive.

Lacking a resurgent warrior culture, we need to consider the ways in which, outside of futile raging against the symbols of state power, we can effectively act against state power in psychological terms to generate the required strength.

Psychologically, we can cope with battle stress and take action against it in two basic ways: through direct action we can alter the relationships between ourselves and the sources of our stress; and through "palliation," a technical term meaning that there is no change in our relationship with the sources of our stress, we can do things to make us feel better.[22] The choices fall on the continuum between change and palliation. Yet the myriad palliation tactics and processes evident in our communities and politics today are losing their ability to make us feel better about our colonial oppression. This is the psychology of deep denial, using religiosity and chemical aids—drugs, alcohol, sugar, tobacco, and processed junk food—to distance and medicate the pain. There is no fundamental difference between the subversion of pain inherent in alcoholism and the psychological denial of the obvious corruption inherent in the politics of assimilation. If we are concerned about addressing our relationships with the sources of our stress, and not only with medicating the pains caused by that stress, direct action is the only solution.

The target of direct action must be the most immediate danger and cause of our collective stress: the racism that is still rampant in Settler society. Violent, degrading, and belittling white attitudes and behaviours are systematically woven into the fabric of Settler culture. This racism manifests itself in every facet of colonial society. There are intellectually false premises that form the bases for beliefs about national identities. There are denials of truth that are the foundations of colonial politics. There are legal fictions masquerading as justice. And there are economic deprivations rationalized to form capitalist economic theories and policies.

Yet it is the bold and unchallenged white arrogance and racial prejudice against indigenous peoples that is the first and most important target of action. The personal and mundane maintenance of colonialism and colonial power relations through words and behaviours on a one-to-one level, conversationally and socially, must be stopped. Psychological research has conclusively proven that the racism of white society manifest in its most basic form, hostility and aggression, more than anything else assaults the sense of self-control and affects the health and well-being of people who are discriminated against.[23] The constant hostility of white people and lack of acceptance on a societal level has been proven in studies of African-Americans in the United States to have a direct effect on the rates of high blood pressure in that population, for example. So racism is expressed on all levels in many forms as a personal relationship, and it is embedded systemically in colonial relations. This must be acted against if our people are to survive and restrengthen. This is the orienting first goal of the Onkwehonwe struggle for freedom.

There is a real question here on how we would inoculate people from fear to allow them to act with courage against this root cause of Onkwehonwe stress, suffering, and premature death. I believe it must be a primary belief in all of our leaders and peoples' minds that the racism of white society *can* be overcome; our people must be reoriented culturally and politically so that their conscious and subconscious minds learn that stress and hate can be defeated and that they have a responsibility to act against racism. In doing so, they will be truly living the ethic of courage as warriors for the next generations.

NOTES

1. Vaclav Havel, *Disturbing the Peace,* trans. Paul Wilson (New York, NY: Vintage, 1991) 17.
2. See Hakim Bey, *T.A.Z.* (San Francisco, CA: AK Press, 1985) and *Immediatism* (San Francisco, CA: 1994). See also Richard Day, "Who Is This *We* That Gives the Gift? Native American Political Theory and *The Western Tradition,*" *Critical Horizons* 2:2 (2001): 173–201; Richard Day and Tonio Sadik, "The BC Land Questions, Liberal Multiculturalism, and the Spectre of Aboriginal Nationhood," *BC Studies* 143 (Summer 2002): 5–34.
3. Sean M. Maloney, "Domestic Operations: The Canadian Approach," *Parameters,* US Army War College Quarterly (Autumn 1997). See also Sandra Lambertus, *Wartime Images, Peacetime Wounds: The Media and the Gustafsen Lake Standoff* (Toronto, ON: University of Toronto Press, 2004).
4. *Monday Brownbagger,* 25 March 2002, Co-Op Radio, CFRO, Vancouver, BC.
5. Nasra Hassam, "An Arsenal of Believers," *The New Yorker* (19 November 2001). For an interrogation of the notion of non-lethal physical resistance or "limited violence," as well as an excellent analysis of the strategic shift from limited violence to armed struggle as the primary means of resistance to Israeli occupation by Palestinians, see Edy Kaufman, "Limited Violence and the Palestinian Struggle," *Unarmed Forces: Nonviolent Action in Central America and the Middle East*, ed. Graeme MacQueen, Canadian Papers in Peace Studies 1 (Toronto, ON: Science for Peace, 1992).
6. The most authoritative source on the ideological foundations of the Vietnamese revolutionary resistance is Duiker's biography of the communist leader, from which the quotations in the text are drawn. See William J. Duiker, *Ho Chi Minh: A Life* (London, UK: Allen and Unwin, 2000).
7. For an excellent analysis of the life and mythology of Che Guevara, see Jorge Casteñeda, *Compagñero: The Life and Death of Che Guevara* (New York: Random House, 1997).
8. Che Guevara, *Guerrilla Warfare* (New York, NY: Monthly Review Press, 1961) 171.
9. This is most clearly evident in Frantz Fanon, *The Wretched of the Earth* (New York, NY: Grove Press, 1963). For a full explanation and discussion of Frantz Fanon's ideas, see Nigel C. Gibson, *Fanon: The Postcolonial Imagination* (Cambridge, UK: Polity, 2003).
10. Guevara, *Guerrilla Warfare* 171.
11. Sidney Tarrow, *Power in Movement: Social Movements and Contentious Politics,* 2nd ed. (Cambridge, UK: Cambridge University Press, 1998) 93–105.
12. Peter Ackerman and Jack DuVall, *A Force More Powerful: A Century of Nonviolent Conflict* (New York, NY: Palgrave, 2005) 5. Also, for solid arguments for non-violence as a strategic option based on the success of Latin American social movements in forcing change in those societies, see Philip McManus and Gerald Schlabach, eds., *Relentless Persistence: Nonviolent Action in Latin America* (Santa Cruz, CA: New Society Publishers,

1991). And for an argument against the notion that violence is the most powerful means of political action, see Gene Sharp's "Nonviolent Struggle Today," *Unarmed Forces: Nonviolent Action in Central America and the Middle East,* ed., Graeme MacQueen, Canadian Papers in Peace Studies 1 (Toronto, ON: Science for Peace, 1992).

13. Dave Grossman, *On Killing: The Psychological Cost of Learning to Kill in War and Society* (Toronto, ON: Little, Brown and Company, 1995) 83–85.
14. Tenzin Gyatso, the Fourteenth Dali Lama of Tibet, *Ancient Wisdom, Modern World: Ethics for the New Millennium* (Toronto, ON: Little, Brown and Company, 1998) 48.
15. For a description and explanation of the Indian anti-imperial struggle, see Mahatma K. Gandhi, *Non-Violent Resistance, Satyagraha* (New York, NY: Schocken Books, 1961) and his *An Autobiography: The Story of My Experiments with Truth,* trans. M. Desai (1927, 1929; New York, NY: Penguin 2001); also see Krishnalal Shridharani, *War Without Violence* (Belmont, CA: Harcourt Brace, 1939).
16. The Gramscian approach to theorizing indigenous struggles is best developed in Charles R. Hale, *Resistance and Contradiction* (Stanford, CA: Stanford University Press, 1994) 31.
17. Ward Churchill and Mike Ryan, *Pacifism as Pathology* (Winnipeg, MB: Arbeiter Ring Publishing, 1998) 93–101.
18. Hannah Arendt, *On Violence* (Belmont, CA: Harcourt Brace, 1969) 65.
19. The frustrated warrior concept and its link to violence is developed in B. Duran and E. Duran, *Native American Post-Colonial Psychology* (Albany, NY: State University of New York Press, 1995).
20. C. Wright Mills, *White Collar: The American Middle Classes* (New York, NY: Oxford University Press, 1956) 110.
21. See Tom Hayden, ed. *The Zapatista Reader* (New York, NY: Avalon, 2002).
22. Richard Holmes, *Acts of War* (New York, NY: The Free Press, 1985) 29.
23. Grossman, *On Killing* 77–84.

PERSONAL RESPONSE

Here is a point of view to get you thinking about the larger topic behind this essay: *Racism* is a misleading term, since, among humans, there are, in fact, no races, only the human race. There are, of course, variations among groups of people, based on ethnicity, culture, and history; also peoples' appearances differ because of geographical influences and the length of time groups have stayed together in locations over many generations. Why, then, do we think in terms of races? How has history played out because of this thinking? Do you think there are distinct races?

QUESTIONS FOR CLASS OR SMALL-GROUP DISCUSSION

1. This is quite a dense piece of writing with many terms of reference: indigenous, utopia, passive resistance, racism, ethics, self-determination, nationalism, ideology, altruism, and settler culture. Pick three of the terms you feel least familiar with. Define and discuss them in order to help understand Alfred's thesis.

2. According to Alfred, in the process of colonization, what has been lost or destroyed for indigenous people? What can be achieved by re-finding or recovering these things? What kinds of changes are needed? How feasible or realistic are such changes?

3. When you hear the word *anarchism*, what connotations do you have? Are they positive or negative? Discuss the possible use or misuse of anarchism.

4. Would you characterize this piece as descriptive, instructive, or prescriptive—and why? What kind of attitude do you find behind the words? Identify particular instances of this attitude.

5. According to Alfred, what are the pro and cons of armed struggle and violence in order to make social change?

6. What does Alfred mean by the term *non-violent militancy?* Discuss non-violent militancy as a possible means for change.

7. According to Alfred, what are the best ways to avoid being drawn into "useless strategies of resistance"? What does Alfred believe indigenous peoples must do in order to overcome the prejudice of settler culture and white society? Discuss the soundness of his strategies.

LETTER FROM BIRMINGHAM JAIL

Martin Luther King, Jr.

Martin Luther King, Jr. (1929–1968) was one of the most influential spiritual leaders of the twentieth century. Dr. King (he had a Ph.D. in theology from Boston University) drew on the New Testament teachings of Jesus and the passive-resistance techniques of Mahatma Gandhi to help transform society. After Rosa Park's arrest, in 1955, for refusing to give up her bus seat to a white rider, and the subsequent Montgomery, Alabama, bus boycott, King found himself at the centre of the civil rights movement. In 1963, in Birmingham, Alabama, King and nearly 2,500 other civil rights workers were jailed following a battle with police. While imprisoned, he wrote "Letter from Birmingham Jail." In 1964, at the age of 35, he became the youngest person ever to win the Nobel Peace Prize. He was assassinated on April 14, 1968, in Memphis, Tennessee.

April 16, 1963

MY DEAR FELLOW CLERGYMEN:

While confined here in the Birmingham city jail, I came across your recent statement calling my present activities "unwise and untimely." Seldom do I pause to answer criticism of my work and ideas. If I sought to answer all the criticisms that cross my desk, my secretaries would have little time for anything other than such correspondence in the course of the day, and I would have no time for constructive work. But since I feel that you are men of genuine good will and that your criticisms are sincerely set forth, I want to try to answer your statements in what I hope will be patient and reasonable terms.

I think I should indicate why I am here In Birmingham, since you have been influenced by the view which argues against "outsiders coming in." I have the honor of serving as president of the Southern Christian Leadership Conference, an organization operating in every southern state, with headquarters in Atlanta, Georgia. We have some eighty-five affiliated organizations across the South, and one of them is the Alabama Christian Movement for Human Rights. Frequently we share staff, educational and financial resources with our affiliates. Several months ago the affiliate here in Birmingham asked us to be on call to engage in a nonviolent direct-action program if such were deemed necessary. We readily consented, and when the hour came we lived up to our promise. So I, along with several members of my staff, am here because I was invited here I am here because I have organizational ties here.

But more basically, I am in Birmingham because injustice is here. Just as the prophets of the eighth century B.C. left their villages and carried their "thus saith the Lord" far beyond the boundaries of their home towns, and just as the Apostle Paul left his village of Tarsus and carried the gospel of Jesus Christ to the far corners of the Greco-Roman world, so am I. compelled to carry the gospel of freedom beyond my own home town. Like Paul, I must constantly respond to the Macedonian call for aid.

Moreover, I am cognizant of the interrelatedness of all communities and states. I cannot sit idly by in Atlanta and not be concerned about what happens in Birmingham. Injustice anywhere is a threat to justice everywhere. We are caught in an inescapable network of mutuality, tied in a single garment of destiny. Whatever affects one directly, affects all indirectly. Never again can we afford to live with the narrow, provincial "outside agitator" idea. Anyone who lives inside the United States can never be considered an outsider anywhere within its bounds.

You deplore the demonstrations taking place in Birmingham. But your statement, I am sorry to say, fails to express a similar concern for the conditions that brought about the demonstrations. I am sure that none of you would want to rest content with the superficial kind of social analysis that deals merely with effects and does not grapple with underlying causes. It is unfortunate that demonstrations are taking place in Birmingham, but it is even more unfortunate that the city's white power structure left the Negro community with no alternative.

In any nonviolent campaign there are four basic steps: collection of the facts to determine whether injustices exist; negotiation; self-purification; and direct action. We have gone through all these steps in Birmingham. There can be no gainsaying the fact that racial injustice engulfs this community. Birmingham is probably the most thoroughly segregated city in the United States. Its ugly record of brutality is widely known. Negroes have experienced grossly unjust treatment in the courts. There have been more unsolved bombings of Negro homes and churches in Birmingham than in any other city in the nation. These are the hard, brutal facts of the case. On the basis of these conditions, Negro leaders sought to negotiate with the city fathers. But the latter consistently refused to engage in good-faith negotiation.

Then, last September, came the opportunity to talk with leaders of Birmingham's economic community. In the course of the negotiations, certain promises were made by the merchants—for example, to remove the stores humiliating racial signs. On the basis of these promises, the Reverend Fred Shuttlesworth and the leaders of the Alabama Christian Movement for Human Rights agreed to a moratorium on all demonstrations. As the weeks and months went by, we realized that we were the victims of a broken promise. A few signs, briefly removed, returned; the others remained.

As in so many past experiences, our hopes had been blasted, and the shadow of deep disappointment settled upon us. We had no alternative except to prepare for direct action, whereby we would present our very bodies as a means of laying our case before the conscience of the local and the national community. Mindful of the difficulties involved, we decided to undertake a process of self-purification. We began a series of workshops on nonviolence, and we repeatedly asked ourselves: "Are you able to accept blows without retaliating?" "Are you able to endure the ordeal of jail?" We decided to schedule our direct-action program for the Easter season, realizing that except for Christmas, this is the main shopping period of the year. Knowing that a strong economic withdrawal program would be the by-product of direct action, we felt that this would be the best time to bring pressure to bear on the merchants for the needed change.

Then it occurred to us that Birmingham's mayoralty election was coming up in March, and we speedily decided to postpone action until after election day. When we discovered that the Commissioner of Public Safety, Eugene "Bull" Connor, had piled up enough votes to be in the run-off we decided again to postpone action until the day after the run-off so that the demonstrations could not be used to cloud the issues. Like many others, we waited to see Mr. Connor defeated, and to this end we endured postponement after postponement. Having aided in this community need, we felt that our direct-action program could be delayed no longer.

You may well ask: "Why direct action? Why sit-ins, marches and so forth? Isn't negotiation a better path?" You are quite right in calling, for negotiation. Indeed, this is the very purpose of direct action. Nonviolent direct action seeks to create such a crisis and foster such a tension that a community which has constantly refused to negotiate is forced to confront the issue. It seeks so to dramatize the issue that it can no longer be ignored. My citing the creation of tension as part of the work of the nonviolent-resister may sound rather shocking. But I must confess that I am not afraid of the word "tension." I have earnestly opposed violent tension, but there is a type of constructive, nonviolent tension which is necessary for growth. Just as Socrates felt that it was necessary to create a tension in the mind so that individuals could rise from the bondage of myths and half-truths to the unfettered realm of creative analysis and objective appraisal, we must we see the need for nonviolent gadflies to create the kind of tension in society that will help men rise from the dark depths of prejudice and racism to the majestic heights of understanding and brotherhood.

The purpose of our direct-action program is to create a situation so crisis-packed that it will inevitably open the door to negotiation. I therefore concur with you in your call for negotiation. Too long has our beloved Southland been bogged down in a tragic effort to live in monologue rather than dialogue.

One of the basic points in your statement is that the action that I and my associates have taken in Birmingham is untimely. Some have asked: "Why didn't you give the new city administration time to act?" The only answer that I can give to this query is that the new Birmingham administration must be prodded about as much as the outgoing one, before it will act. We are sadly mistaken if we feel that the election of Albert Boutwell as mayor will bring the millennium to Birmingham. While Mr. Boutwell is a much more gentle person than Mr. Connor, they are both segregationists, dedicated to maintenance of the status quo. I have hope that Mr. Boutwell will be reasonable enough to see the futility of massive resistance to desegregation. But he will not see this without pressure from devotees of civil rights. My friends, I must say to you that we have not made a single gain civil rights without determined legal and nonviolent pressure. Lamentably, it is an historical fact that privileged groups seldom give up their privileges voluntarily. Individuals may see the moral light and voluntarily give up their unjust posture; but, as Reinhold Niebuhr has reminded us, groups tend to be more immoral than individuals.

We know through painful experience that freedom is never voluntarily given by the oppressor; it must be demanded by the oppressed. Frankly, I have yet to engage in a direct-action campaign that was "well timed" in the view of those who have not suffered unduly from the disease of segregation. For years now I have heard the word "Wait!" It rings in the ear of every Negro with piercing familiarity. This "Wait" has almost always meant "Never." We must come to see, with one of our distinguished jurists, that "justice too long delayed is justice denied."

We have waited for more than 340 years for our constitutional and God-given rights. The nations of Asia and Africa are moving with jetlike speed toward gaining political independence, but we stiff creep at horse-and-buggy pace toward gaining a cup of coffee at a lunch counter. Perhaps it is easy for those who have never felt the stinging dark of segregation to say, "Wait." But when you have seen vicious mobs lynch your mothers and fathers at will and drown your sisters and brothers at whim; when you have seen hate-filled policemen curse, kick and even kill your black brothers and sisters; when you see the vast majority of your twenty million Negro brothers smothering in an airtight cage of poverty in the midst of an affluent society; when you suddenly find your tongue twisted and your speech stammering as you seek to explain to your six-year-old daughter why she can't go to the public amusement park that has just been advertised on television, and see tears welling up in her eyes when she is told that Funtown is closed to colored children, and see ominous clouds of inferiority beginning to form in her little mental sky, and see her beginning to distort her personality by developing an unconscious bitterness toward white people; when you have to concoct an answer for a five-year-old son who is asking: "Daddy, why do white people treat colored people so mean?"; when you take a cross-county drive and find it necessary to sleep night after night in the uncomfortable corners of your automobile because no motel will accept you; when you are humiliated day in and day out by nagging signs reading "white" and "colored"; when your first name becomes "nigger," your middle name becomes "boy" (however old you are) and your last name becomes "John," and your wife and mother are never given the respected title "Mrs."; when you are harried by day and haunted by night by the fact that you are a Negro, living constantly at tiptoe stance, never quite knowing what to expect next, and are plagued with inner fears and outer resentments; when you are forever fighting a degenerating sense of "nobodiness" then you will understand why we find it difficult to wait. There comes a time when the cup of endurance runs over, and men are no longer willing to be plunged into the abyss of despair. I hope, sirs, you can understand our legitimate and unavoidable impatience.

You express a great deal of anxiety over our willingness to break laws. This is certainly a legitimate concern. Since we so diligently urge people to obey the Supreme Court's decision of 1954 outlawing segregation in the public schools, at first glance it may seem rather paradoxical for us consciously to break laws. One may well ask: "How can you advocate breaking some laws and obeying others?" The answer lies in the fact that there are two types of laws: just and unjust. I would be the Brat to advocate obeying just laws. One has not only a legal but a moral responsibility to obey just laws. Conversely, one has a moral responsibility to disobey unjust laws. I would agree with St. Augustine that "an unjust law is no law at all."

Now, what is the difference between the two? How does one determine whether a law is just or unjust? A just law is a man-made code that squares with the moral law or the law of God. An unjust law is a code that is out of harmony with the moral law. To put it in the terms of St. Thomas Aquinas: An unjust law is a human law that is not rooted in eternal law and natural law. Any law that uplifts human personality is just. Any law that degrades human personality is unjust. All segregation statutes are unjust because segregation distorts the soul and damages the personality. It gives the segregator a false sense of superiority and the segregated a false sense of inferiority. Segregation, to use the terminology of the Jewish philosopher Martin Buber, substitutes an "I-it" relationship for an "I-thou" relationship and ends up relegating persons to the status of things. Hence segregation is not only politically, economically and sociologically unsound, it is morally wrong and awful. Paul Tillich said that sin is separation. Is not segregation an existential expression of man's tragic separation, his awful estrangement, his terrible sinfulness? Thus it is that I can urge men to obey the 1954 decision of the Supreme Court, for it is morally right; and I can urge them to disobey segregation ordinances, for they are morally wrong.

Let us consider a more concrete example of just and unjust laws. An unjust law is a code that a numerical or power majority group compels a minority group to obey but does not make binding on itself. This is difference made legal. By the same token, a just law is a code that a majority compels a minority to follow and that it is willing to follow itself. This is sameness made legal.

Let me give another explanation. A law is unjust if it is inflicted on a minority that, as a result of being denied the right to vote, had no part in enacting or devising the law. Who can say that the legislature of Alabama which set up that state's segregation laws was democratically elected? Throughout Alabama all sorts of devious methods are used to prevent Negroes from becoming registered voters, and there are some counties in which, even though Negroes constitute a majority of the population, not a single Negro is registered. Can any law enacted under such circumstances be considered democratically structured?

Sometimes a law is just on its face and unjust in its application. For instance, I have been arrested on a charge of parading without a permit. Now, there is nothing wrong in having an ordinance which requires a permit for a parade. But such an ordinance becomes unjust when it is used to maintain segregation and to deny citizens the First Amendment privilege of peaceful assembly and protest.

I hope you are able to see the distinction I am trying to point out. In no sense do I advocate evading or defying the law, as would the rabid segregationist. That would lead to anarchy. One who breaks an unjust law must do so openly, lovingly, and with a willingness to accept the penalty. I submit that an individual who breaks a law that conscience tells him is unjust and who willingly accepts the penalty of imprisonment in order to arouse the conscience of the community over its injustice, is in reality expressing the highest respect for law.

Of course, there is nothing new about this kind of civil disobedience. It was evidenced sublimely in the refusal of Shadrach, Meshach and Abednego to obey the laws of Nebuchadnezzar, on the ground that a higher moral law was at stake. It was practiced superbly by the early Christians, who were willing to face hungry lions and the excruciating pain of chopping blocks rather than submit to certain unjust laws of the Roman Empire. To a degree, academic freedom is a reality today because Socrates practiced civil disobedience. In our own nation, the Boston Tea Party represented a massive act of civil disobedience.

We should never forget that everything Adolf Hitler did in Germany was "legal" and everything the Hungarian freedom fighters did in Hungary was "illegal." It was "illegal" to aid and comfort a Jew in Hitler's Germany. Even so, I am sure that, had I lived in Germany at the time, I would have aided and comforted my Jewish brothers. If today I lived in a Communist country where certain principles dear to the Christian faith are suppressed, I would openly advocate disobeying that country's antireligious laws.

I must make two honest confessions to you, my Christian and Jewish brothers. First, I must confess that over the past few years I have been gravely disappointed with the white moderate. I have almost reached the regrettable conclusion that the Negro's great stumbling block in his stride toward freedom is not the White Citizen's Counciler or the Ku Klux Klanner, but the white moderate, who is more devoted to "order" than to justice; who prefers a negative peace which is the absence of tension to a positive peace which is the presence of justice; who constantly says: "I agree with you in the goal you seek, but I cannot agree with your methods of direct action"; who paternalistically believes he can set the timetable for another man's freedom; who lives by a mythical concept of time and who constantly advises the Negro to wait for a "more convenient season." Shallow understanding from people of good will is more frustrating than absolute misunderstanding from people of ill will. Lukewarm acceptance is much more bewildering than outright rejection.

I had hoped that the white moderate would understand that law and order exist for the purpose of establishing justice and that when they fan in this purpose they become the dangerously structured dams that block the flow of social progress. I had hoped that the white moderate would understand that the present tension in the South is a necessary phase of the transition from an obnoxious negative peace, in which the Negro passively accepted his unjust plight, to a substantive and positive peace, in which all men will respect the dignity and worth of human personality. Actually, we who engage in nonviolent direct action are not the creators of tension. We merely bring to the surface the hidden tension that is already alive. We bring it out in the open, where it can be seen and dealt with. Like a boil that can never be cured so long as it is covered up but must be opened with all its ugliness to the natural medicines of air and light, injustice must be exposed, with all the tension its exposure creates, to the light of human conscience and the air of national opinion before it can be cured.

In your statement you assert that our actions, even though peaceful, must be condemned because they precipitate violence. But is this a logical assertion? Isn't this like condemning a robbed man because his possession of money precipitated the evil act of robbery? Isn't this like condemning Socrates because his unswerving commitment to truth and his philosophical inquiries precipitated the act by the misguided populace in which they made him drink hemlock? Isn't this like condemning Jesus because his unique God-consciousness and never-ceasing devotion to God's will precipitated the evil act of crucifixion? We must come to see that, as the federal courts have consistently affirmed, it is wrong to urge an individual to cease his efforts to gain his basic constitutional rights because the quest may precipitate violence. Society must protect the robbed and punish the robber.

I had also hoped that the white moderate would reject the myth concerning time in relation to the struggle for freedom. I have just received a letter from a white brother in Texas. He writes: "All Christians know that the colored people will receive equal rights eventually, but it is possible that you are in too great a religious hurry. It has taken Christianity almost two thousand years to accomplish what it has. The teachings of Christ take time to come to earth." Such an attitude stems from a tragic misconception of time, from the strangely rational notion that there is something in the very flow of time that will inevitably cure all ills. Actually, time itself is neutral; it can be used either destructively or constructively. More and more I feel that the people of ill will have used time much more effectively than have the people of good will. We will have to repent in this generation not merely for the hateful words and actions of the bad people but for the appalling silence of the good people. Human progress never rolls in on wheels of inevitability; it comes through the tireless efforts of men willing to be co-workers with God, and without this hard work, time itself becomes an ally of the forces of social stagnation. We must use time creatively, in the knowledge that the time is always ripe to do right. Now is the time to make real the promise of democracy and transform our pending national elegy into a creative psalm of brotherhood. Now is the time to lift our national policy from the quicksand of racial injustice to the solid rock of human dignity.

You speak of our activity in Birmingham as extreme. At first I was rather disappointed that fellow clergymen would see my nonviolent efforts as those of an extremist. I began thinking about the fact that I stand in the middle of two opposing forces in the Negro community. One is a force of complacency, made up in part of Negroes who, as a result of long years of oppression, are so drained of self-respect and a sense of "somebodiness" that they have adjusted to segregation; and in part of a few middle class Negroes who, because of a degree of academic and economic security and because in some ways they profit by segregation, have become insensitive to the problems of the masses. The other force is one of bitterness and hatred, and it comes perilously close to advocating violence. It is expressed in the various black nationalist groups that are springing up across the nation, the largest and best-known being Elijah Muhammad's Muslim movement. Nourished by the Negro's frustration over the continued existence of racial discrimination, this movement is made up of people who have lost faith in America, who have absolutely repudiated Christianity, and who have concluded that the white man is an incorrigible "devil."

I have tried to stand between these two forces, saying that we need emulate neither the "do-nothingism" of the complacent nor the hatred and despair of the black nationalist. For there is the more excellent way of love and nonviolent protest. I am grateful to God that, through the influence of the Negro church, the way of nonviolence became an integral part of our struggle.

If this philosophy had not emerged, by now many streets of the South would, I am convinced, be flowing with blood. And I am further convinced that if our white brothers dismiss as "rabble-rousers" and "outside agitators" those of us who employ nonviolent direct action, and if they refuse to support our nonviolent efforts, millions of Negroes will, out of frustration and despair, seek solace and security in black-nationalist ideologies a development that would inevitably lead to a frightening racial nightmare.

Oppressed people cannot remain oppressed forever. The yearning for freedom eventually manifests itself, and that is what has happened to the American Negro. Something within has reminded him of his birthright of freedom, and something without has reminded him that it can be gained. Consciously or unconsciously, he has been caught up by the Zeitgeist, and with his black brothers of Africa and his brown and yellow brothers of Asia, South America and the Caribbean, the United States Negro is moving with a sense of great urgency toward the promised land of racial justice. If one recognizes this vital urge that has engulfed the Negro community, one should readily understand why public demonstrations are taking place. The Negro has many pent-up resentments and latent frustrations, and he must release them. So let him march; let him make prayer pilgrimages to the city hall; let him go on freedom rides—and try to understand why he must do so. If his repressed emotions are not released in nonviolent ways, they will seek expression through violence; this is not a threat but a fact of history. So I have not said to my people: "Get rid of your discontent." Rather, I have tried to say that this normal and healthy discontent can be channeled into the creative outlet of nonviolent direct action. And now this approach is being termed extremist.

But though I was initially disappointed at being categorized as an extremist, as I continued to think about the matter I gradually gained a measure of satisfaction from the label. Was not Jesus an extremist for love: "Love your enemies, bless them that curse you, do good to them that hate you, and pray for them which despitefully use you, and persecute you." Was not Amos an extremist for justice: "Let justice roll down like waters and righteousness like an ever-flowing stream." Was not Paul an extremist for the Christian gospel: "I bear in my body the marks of the Lord Jesus." Was not Martin Luther an extremist: "Here I stand; I cannot do otherwise, so help me God." And John Bunyan: "I will stay in jail to the end of my days before I make a butchery of my conscience." And Abraham Lincoln: "This nation cannot survive half slave and half free." And Thomas Jefferson: "We hold these truths to be self-evident, that all men are created equal . . ." So the question is not whether we will be extremists, but what kind of extremists we will be. Will we be extremists for hate or for love? Will we be extremist for the preservation of injustice or for the extension of justice? In that dramatic scene on Calvary's hill three men were crucified. We must never forget that all three were crucified for the same crime—the crime of extremism. Two were extremists for immorality, and thus fell below their environment. The other, Jesus Christ, was an extremist for love, truth and goodness, and thereby rose above his environment. Perhaps the South, the nation and the world are in dire need of creative extremists.

I had hoped that the white moderate would see this need. Perhaps I was too optimistic; perhaps I expected too much. I suppose I should have realized that few members of the oppressor race can understand the deep groans and passionate yearnings of the oppressed race, and still fewer have the vision to see that injustice must be rooted out by strong, persistent and determined action. I am thankful, however, that some of our white brothers in the South have grasped the meaning of this social revolution and committed themselves to it. They are still too few in quantity, but they are big in quality. Some—such as Ralph McGill, Lillian Smith, Harry Golden, James McBride Dabbs, Ann Braden and Sarah Patton Boyle—have written about our struggle in eloquent and prophetic terms. Others have marched with us down nameless streets of the South. They have languished in filthy, roach-infested jails, suffering the abuse and brutality of policemen who view them as "dirty nigger lovers." Unlike so many of their moderate brothers and sisters, they have recognized the urgency of the moment and sensed the need for powerful "action" antidotes to combat the disease of segregation.

Let me take note of my other major disappointment. I have been so greatly disappointed with the white church and its leadership. Of course, there are some notable exceptions. I am not unmindful of the fact that each of you has taken some significant stands on this issue. I commend you, Reverend Stallings, for your Christian stand on this past Sunday, in welcoming Negroes to your worship service on a non segregated basis. I commend the Catholic leaders of this state for integrating Spring Hill College several years ago.

But despite these notable exceptions, I must honestly reiterate that I have been disappointed with the church. I do not say this as one of those negative critics who can always find something wrong with the church. I say this as a minister of the gospel, who loves the church; who was nurtured in its bosom; who has been sustained by its spiritual blessings and who will remain true to it as long as the cord of Rio shall lengthen.

When I was suddenly catapulted into the leadership of the bus protest in Montgomery, Alabama, a few years ago, I felt we would be supported by the white church felt that the white ministers, priests and rabbis of the South would be among our strongest allies. Instead, some have been outright opponents, refusing to understand the freedom movement and misrepresenting its leaders; all too many others have been more cautious than courageous and have remained silent behind the anesthetizing security of stained-glass windows.

In spite of my shattered dreams, I came to Birmingham with the hope that the white religious leadership of this community would see the justice of our cause and, with deep moral concern, would serve as the channel through which our just grievances could reach the power structure. I had hoped that each of you would understand. But again I have been disappointed.

I have heard numerous southern religious leaders admonish their worshipers to comply with a desegregation decision because it is the law, but I have longed to hear white ministers declare: "Follow this decree because integration is morally right and because the Negro is your brother." In the midst of blatant injustices inflicted upon the Negro, I have watched white churchmen stand on the sideline and mouth pious irrelevancies and sanctimonious trivialities. In the midst of a mighty struggle to rid our nation of racial and economic injustice, I have heard many ministers say: "Those are social issues, with which the gospel has no real concern." And I have watched many churches commit themselves to a completely other-worldly religion which makes a strange, un-Biblical distinction between body and soul, between the sacred and the secular.

I have traveled the length and breadth of Alabama, Mississippi and all the other southern states. On sweltering summer days and crisp autumn mornings I have looked at the South's beautiful churches with their lofty spires pointing heavenward. I have beheld the impressive outlines of her massive religious-education buildings. Over and over I have found myself asking: "What kind of people worship here? Who is their God? Where were their voices when the lips of Governor Barnett dripped with words of interposition and nullification? Where were they when Governor Walleye gave a clarion call for defiance and hatred? Where were their voices of support when bruised and weary Negro men and women decided to rise from the dark dungeons of complacency to the bright hills of creative protest?"

Yes, these questions are still in my mind. In deep disappointment I have wept over the laxity of the church. But be assured that my tears have been tears of love. There can be no deep disappointment where there is not deep love. Yes, I love the church. How could I do otherwise? I am in the rather unique position of being the son, the grandson and the great-grandson of preachers. Yes, I see the church as the body of Christ. But, oh! How we have blemished and scarred that body through social neglect and through fear of being nonconformists.

There was a time when the church was very powerful—in the time when the early Christians rejoiced at being deemed worthy to suffer for what they believed. In those days the church was not merely a thermometer that recorded the ideas and principles of popular opinion; it was a thermostat that transformed the mores of society. Whenever the early Christians entered a town, the people in power became disturbed and immediately sought to convict the Christians for being "disturbers of the peace" and "outside agitators" But the Christians pressed on, in the conviction that they were "a colony of heaven," called to obey God rather than man. Small in number, they were big in commitment. They were too God-intoxicated to be "astronomically intimidated." By their effort and example they brought an end to such ancient evils as infanticide and gladiatorial contests.

Things are different now. So often the contemporary church is a weak, ineffectual voice with an uncertain sound. So often it is an archdefender of the status quo. Far from being disturbed by the presence of the church, the power structure of the average community is consoled by the church's silent and often even vocal sanction of things as they are.

But the judgment of God is upon the church as never before. If today's church does not recapture the sacrificial spirit of the early church, it will lose its authenticity, forfeit the loyalty of millions, and be dismissed as an irrelevant social club with no meaning for the twentieth century. Every day I meet young people whose disappointment with the church has turned into outright disgust.

Perhaps I have once again been too optimistic. Is organized religion too inextricably bound to the status quo to save our nation and the world? Perhaps I must turn my faith to the inner spiritual church, the church within the church, as the true *ekklesia* and the hope of the world. But again I am thankful to God that some noble souls from the ranks of organized religion have broken loose from the paralyzing chains of conformity and joined us as active partners in the struggle for freedom, They have left their secure congregations and walked the streets of Albany, Georgia, with us. They have gone down the highways of the South on tortuous rides for freedom. Yes, they have gone to jail with us. Some have been dismissed from their churches, have lost the support of their bishops and fellow ministers. But they have acted in the faith that right defeated is stronger than evil triumphant. Their witness has been the spiritual salt that has preserved the true meaning of the gospel in these troubled times. They have carved a tunnel of hope through the dark mountain of disappointment.

I hope the church as a whole will meet the challenge of this decisive hour. But even if the church does not come to the aid of justice, I have no despair about the future. I have no fear about the outcome of our struggle in Birmingham, even if our motives are at present misunderstood. We will reach the goal of freedom in Birmingham and all over the nation, because the goal of America is freedom. Abused and scorned though we may be, our destiny is tied up with America's destiny. Before the pilgrims landed at Plymouth, we were here. Before the pen of Jefferson etched the majestic words of the Declaration of Independence across the pages of history, we were here. For more than two centuries our forebears labored in this country without wages; they made cotton king; they built the homes of their masters while suffering gross injustice and shameful humiliation—and yet out of a bottomless vitality they continued to thrive and develop. If the inexpressible cruelties of slavery could not stop us, the opposition we now face will surely fail. We will win our freedom because the sacred heritage of our nation and the eternal will of God are embodied in our echoing demands.

Before closing I feel impelled to mention one other point in your statement that has troubled me profoundly. You warmly commended the Birmingham police force for keeping "order" and "preventing violence." I doubt that you would have so warmly commended the police force if you had seen its dogs sinking their teeth into unarmed, nonviolent Negroes. I doubt that you would so quickly commend the policemen if you were to observe their ugly and inhumane treatment of Negroes here in the city jail; if you were to watch them push and curse old Negro women and young Negro girls; if you were to see them slap and kick old Negro men and young boys; if you were to observe them, as they did on two occasions, refuse to give us food because we wanted to sing our grace together. I cannot join you in your praise of the Birmingham police department.

It is true that the police have exercised a degree of discipline in handling the demonstrators. In this sense they have conducted themselves rather "nonviolently" in public. But for what purpose? To preserve the evil system of segregation. Over the past few years I have consistently preached that nonviolence demands that the means we use must be as pure as the ends we seek. I have tried to make clear that it is wrong to use immoral means to attain moral ends. But now I must affirm that it is just as wrong, or perhaps even more so, to use moral means to preserve immoral ends. Perhaps Mr. Connor and his policemen have been rather nonviolent in public, as was Chief Pritchett in Albany, Georgia, but they have used the moral means of nonviolence to maintain the immoral end of racial injustice. As T. S. Eliot has said: "The last temptation is the greatest treason: To do the right deed for the wrong reason."

I wish you had commended the Negro sit-inners and demonstrators of Birmingham for their sublime courage, their willingness to suffer and their amazing discipline in the midst of great provocation. One day the South will recognize its real heroes. They will be the James Merediths, with the noble sense of purpose that enables them to face jeering, and hostile mobs, and with the agonizing loneliness that characterizes the life of the pioneer. They will be old, oppressed, battered Negro women, symbolized in a seventy-two-year-old woman in Montgomery, Alabama, who rose up with a sense of dignity and with her people decided not to ride seg-regated buses, and who responded with ungrammatical profundity to one who inquired about her weariness: "My feets is tired, but my soul is at rest." They will be the young high school and college students, the young ministers of the gospel and a host of their elders, courageously and nonviolently sitting in at lunch counters and willingly going to jail for conscience' sake. One day the South will know that when these disinherited children of God sat down at lunch counters, they were in reality standing up for what is best in the American dream and for the most sacred values in our Judaeo-Christian heritage, thereby bringing our nation back to those great wells of democracy which were dug deep by the founding fathers in their formulation of the Constitution and the Declaration of Independence.

Never before have I written so long a letter. I'm afraid it is much too long to take your precious time. I can assure you that it would have been much shorter if I had been writing from a comfortable desk, but what else can one do when he is alone in a narrow jail cell, other than write long letters, think long thoughts and pray long prayers?

If I have said anything in this letter that overstates the truth and indicates an unreasonable impatience, I beg you to forgive me. If I have said anything that understates the truth and indicates my having a patience that allows me to settle for anything less than brotherhood, I beg God to forgive me.

I hope this letter finds you strong in the faith. I also hope that circumstances will soon make it possible for me to meet each of you, not as an integrationist or a civil rights leader but as a fellow clergyman and a Christian brother. Let us all hope that the dark clouds of racial prejudice will soon pass away and the deep fog of misunderstanding will be lifted from our fear-drenched communities, and in some not too distant tomorrow the radiant stars of love and brotherhood will shine over our great nation with all their scintillating beauty.

Yours for the cause of Peace and Brotherhood,

Martin Luther King, Jr.

PERSONAL RESPONSE

How would you feel about your aggressors if you were beaten and arrested at a human rights demonstration? What would you do? What issues would motivate you to publicly protest?

QUESTIONS FOR CLASS OR SMALL-GROUP DISCUSSION

1. Search online for the names of other men or women who wrote while in prison. What kinds of books or pamphlets did they write and what was the impact of their writing? King wrote some of his letter on scraps of paper. What other materials have jailed writers used?

2. Find documentaries or film clips of the Birmingham clash. Describe what you see and the feelings and thoughts that the images evoke in you.

3. What was King's strategy in writing this letter? Another activist in this chapter, Taiaiake Alfred, writes of "useless strategies" of resistance. How effective would you describe King's non-violent strategy during the civil rights movement? Was that strategy popular with all civil rights leaders and moderates in the white community?

4. Is King's message still relevant in North America and the world? Discuss.

5. Describing Hitler's actions as "legal," King writes of a "higher law" and says he would openly disobey a country's laws if they suppressed Christian principles. Under what circumstances would you disobey Canada's laws—or would you never disobey them?

6. King says he doesn't mind being called an extremist and says the following were extremists: Jesus, St. Paul, Amos, Martin Luther, John Bunyan, Thomas Jefferson, and Abraham Lincoln. Using examples, explain how each of these men was an extremist.

FROM SATCHEL, THROUGH HANK GREENBERG, TO EL DIVINO LOCO

Mordecai Richler

Mordecai Richler was born in Montreal in 1931, and passed away in his home city in 2001. He was a writer of all genres—fiction, journalism, sports, scripts, and essays—but he is best known for his clear style, controversial views, and comical and satirical touch. He won numerous awards and honours, and is considered by many as the most important Canadian writer of his generation. His fiction includes The Apprenticeship of Duddy Kravitz *(1959),* Barney's Version *(1997),* Solomon Gursky Was Here *(1989), and the* Jacob Two-Two *stories. Collections of his writing include* Belling the Cat *(1998),* Oh Canada! Oh Quebec! Requiem for a Divided Country *(1992), and* Dispatches from the Sporting Life *(2000).*

Come spring, I turn hungrily to the sports pages first every morning to ponder the baseball scores, held in the thrall of overgrown boys whose notion of humour is to slip an exploding device into a cigar, drench a phone receiver with shaving cream, or line the inside of a teammate's hat with shoe polish. But, to be fair, a certain corrosive wit is not unknown among some ball players. Asked if he threw spitters, Hall of Fame pitcher Lefty Gomez replied, "Not intentionally, but I sweat easy." Invited to comment on whether he favoured grass over AstroTurf, relief pitcher Tug McGraw said, "I don't know. I never smoked AstroTurf." On another occasion, a reporter asked McGraw how he intended to budget his latest salary increase. "Ninety per cent, I'll spend on good times, women, and Irish whisky," he said. "The other ten per cent I'll probably waste." Then the immortal Leroy "Satchel" Paige once said, "Don't look back. Something might be gaining on you."

Satchel Paige, one of the greatest pitchers the game has ever known, was shamefully confined to the Negro leagues in his prime. Only in 1948, when he was forty-two years old, did he finally get a chance to compete in the majors, signed by Bill Veeck to play for the Cleveland Indians. Paige helped the Indians to win a World Series in 1949, went on to pitch for the St. Louis Browns for a couple of years, and then dropped out of sight.

The film director Robert Parrish once told me a story about Paige that he then included in his memoir, *Hollywood Doesn't Live Here Anymore.* In the early fifties, Parrish was shooting a western in Mexico, *The Wonderful Country,* in which Robert Mitchum was playing the lead. Mitchum suggested that they get Satchel to play a black sergeant in the U.S. Tenth Cavalry.

"Where can we find him?" Parrish asked.

"Why don't you call Bill Veeck?"

Parrish called Veeck and learned that Paige was now with the Miami Marlins in the Southern Association, but he didn't think that Parrish could contact him because he was in jail on a misdemeanour charge and the judge, who was a baseball fan, would let him out only on the days he was to pitch. Parrish called the judge.

"Well," said the judge, "I think we can work it out. Leroy has a sore arm and has lost his last four games. I'll let him out if you'll guarantee he doesn't touch a baseball until he comes back to Miami."

Paige arrived in Durango, Mexico, a week later, accompanied by a beautiful teenaged black girl whom he introduced as Susan. Parrish knew he had a daughter and assumed that's who she was. "Paige . . . stayed with us for six weeks," wrote Parrish in his memoir, "and when it was time to send him back to Miami, Mitchum and I took him to the airport. Susan boarded the small commuter plane, and Mitchum, Paige, and I stood on the tarmac . . . and after a while, Mitchum asked a question that had been bothering both of us since Paige arrived. "Is Susan your daughter?" he asked.

"No," said Paige. "She's my daughter's nurse."

There was a pause and then Mitchum finally said, "But your daughter's not here."

Paige looked at Mitchum and smiled. "How about that?" he said. Then he turned and boarded the plane, still smiling.

The late Hank Greenberg wrote in his autobiography, *Hank Greenberg: The Story of My Life,* of John King, a legendary left-handed slugger who hit .380 in the Texas League but never made it to the bigs because he couldn't cope with southpaw pitching. Once, according to Greenberg, King came out of a restaurant and saw a beggar with a tin cup: "King slipped a quarter into the cup. As he turned around, he saw the beggar pull the quarter out of the cup with his left hand and John went back and grabbed the coin out of his hand, and said, 'No left-handed son of a bitch is going to get any of my money.'"

If my devotion to baseball is an occasional embarrassment to me, I blame it on being a Montrealer. We put up with plenty here. Going into the 1989 season of dubious promise, for instance, Claude Brochu, president of Les Expos and a former Seagrams marketing maven, pronounced that the year would be successful if fans would just increase their consumption and spend $7.25 per game on soggy hot dogs and lukewarm beer rather than the measly $5.50 they grudgingly parted with the previous season. Baseball, once a game of inches, was now a business of pennies. Hank Greenberg's father, a prescient man, understood this as early as 1929, when Hank signed his first pro contract.

"Pop," Hank said, "are you against baseball as a career?"

His father nodded.

"The Tigers offered nine thousand dollars."

His father whistled softly. "Nine thousand dollars," he said. "You mean they would give you that kind of money just to go out and play baseball?"

"That's right."

"And they'll let you finish college first?"

"Yes."

"I thought baseball was a game," his father said, "but it's a business—apparently a very good business. Take the money."

My problem with Montreal baseball is compounded by the fact that in a climate where we are fortunate to reap seven weeks of summer, maybe six, the game is played on a zippered carpet in a concrete container that resembles nothing so much as an outsize toilet bowl—a toilet bowl the cost of which would humble even a Pentagon procurement agent. The ugly Olympic Stadium, more properly known in Montreal as the Big Owe, cost $650 million to build in 1976, *more than the combined cost of all the domed stadiums constructed in North America up to that time.* And this price doesn't include the parking facilities, which set taxpayers back another $70 million. Nor did it take into account the so-called retractable roof, finally put in place in 1988, its reported cost another $80 million. A roof that retracted only erratically come 1989 and already leaked in several places.

Despite these local difficulties, I am not only addicted to the game but also to books that celebrate it: say, George V. Higgins's *The Progress of the Seasons: Forty Years of Baseball in Our Town,* composed in praise of those who came closest to the sun, playing in Boston's Fenway Park. Baseball, writes Higgins, differs from football and basketball in that it is "a game played by generally normal-sized men whose proportions approximate those of the majority of onlookers, and whose feats are therefore plausibly imagined by the spectator as his own acts and deeds."

There is a lot in that, certainly, but also an exception to the rule, the towering six-feet-four Hank Greenberg, who first came up with the Detroit Tigers in 1930 and before he was done, in 1947, had hit 331 home runs in a career that was interrupted by four years of military service in the Second World War. Greenberg, whose lifetime batting average was .313, was twice named MVP. He drove in 1,276 runs and remains tied with Lou Gehrig for highest average of runs batted in per game with .920, or nearly one RBI a game for his career. He is also one of only two Jewish players in the Hall of Fame, the other being Sandy Koufax.

Ira Berkow, who did an admirable job of editing and amending *Hank Greenberg,* an autobiography that remained unfinished when Greenberg died of cancer in 1986, notes that Greenberg's one-time teammate Birdie Tebbets recalled, "There was nobody in the history of the game who took more abuse than Greenberg, unless it was Jackie Robinson." But Greenberg, a man of immense dignity, refused to either Anglicize his name or flaunt his Jewishness. Instead, he put up with the taunts, though on one occasion he did walk over to the Yankee dugout, which was riding him hard, and challenge everybody on the team.

The racial slurs that Jewish players once heard in the majors were not always devoid of wit. Andy Cohen, a New York Giants infielder who came up to the bigs before Greenberg, tells about one Texas League game in 1925. "I made a good catch and the fans gave me a pretty big hand. Then I heard one guy yell out, 'Just like the rest of the Jews. Take everything they can get their hands on.'"

In 1934, Greenberg, a non-observant Jew, decided that it wouldn't be proper for him to play on Yom Kippur, the holiest day of the Jewish calendar, and became the subject of a poem of sorts by Edgar A. Guest, the last stanza of which read:

> Came Yom Kippur—holy fast day world wide
> over the Jew—
> And Hank Greenberg to his teaching and the
> old tradition true

Spent the day among his people and he didn't
    come to play.
Said Murphy to Mulrooney, "We shall lose the
    game today!
We shall miss him on the infield and shall miss
    him at the bat,
But he's true to his religion—and I honor him
    for that!"

Another incident, even more famous, came in 1938, when Greenberg hit fifty-eight home runs, two short of Babe Ruth's record, with five games left to play. When he failed to hit another homer that season, a lot was made of the story that pitchers had thrown him anti-Semitic fastballs, racist sliders, and Jew-baiting curves, but Greenberg would have none of it. "Some people still have it fixed in their minds," he wrote, "that the reason I didn't break Ruth's record was because I was Jewish, that the ball players did everything they could to stop me. That's pure baloney. The fact is quite the opposite: So far as I could tell, the players were mostly rooting for me, aside from the pitchers."

Walter Matthau told Berkow that when he was growing up on the Lower East Side of Manhattan, his idol was Hank Greenberg: "Greenberg for me put a stop to the perpetuation of the myth at the time that all Jews wound up as cutters or pants pressers. Or, if they were lucky, salesmen in the garment center."

Years later Matthau joined the Beverly Hills Tennis Club only because Hank Greenberg was then a member.

"For thirty years," said Matthau, "I told a story which I read in the newspapers about Hank Greenberg at a port of embarkation during the Second World War. The story had it that there was a soldier who had had a little too much to drink, and he was weaving around all the soldiers sitting there. He was quite a big fella. And he said in a very loud voice, 'Anybody here named Goldberg or Ginsburg? I'll kick the livin' daylights out of him.' Or words to that effect. Hank had been sitting on his helmet, and he stood up and said, 'My name is Greenberg, soldier.' The soldier looked at him from head to foot and said, 'Well, I said nothin' about Greenberg, I said Goldberg or Ginsburg.' I told this to Hank when I met him at the club. He said it never happened. I told him I didn't care to hear that. I was going to continue to tell that story because I liked it. He said, 'Okay, whatever you say, Walter.'"

The most original and quirky baseball book I have read in ages, *El Béisbol: Travels through the Pan-American Pastime,* by John Krich, is an antic tour through far fields, where Fan Appreciation Day is "*El Día de Los Fanáticos,*" the Day of the Fanatics; pitchers must beware of a *robador de bases;* and Roberto Clemente is still worshipped above all.

El Béisbol abounds in vivid set pieces, among them a game Krich attended in Puerto Rico with Vic Power, a slugger with the Cleveland Indians in the late fifties, and Rubén Gomez, a.k.a. *El Divino Loco* (the Divine Crazy), who pitched for the Giants in the first game they played after their move to San Francisco. "Oh, baby,"

Power told Krich. "My biggest salary in the major leagues was thirty-eight thousand dollars. Now the average Puerto Rican kid wants that for a signing bonus. The kid's mama, she knows too much!"

PERSONAL RESPONSE

This is a light journalistic piece, with no apparent strong thesis or purpose other than to tell a couple of stories about some old-time baseball players. Why do you think people like to tell (and hear) such sport stories? Have you ever told such stories yourself, or listened to others telling such stories? What kinds of feelings behind these stories make them increasingly fascinating for so many?

QUESTIONS FOR CLASS OR SMALL-GROUP DISCUSSION

1. The three subjects of this piece—Paige, Greenberg, and Clemente—are ethnic minorities. The other subject of this piece is Richler's confessed devotion and addiction to baseball. Try to bring these subjects together to make a kind of thesis for this piece.

2. When Walter Matthau told Greenberg the story that he had been telling for years, the truth of the story did not seem to be important. Why? What possibly could be more important than the truth?

3. Sports, or at least professional sports, is a highly visible cultural activity. How can professional sports be used to understand prejudice, and do you think the sports world is ahead of cultural attitudes or just a reflection of them? Explain your position with some examples.

4. What is the submerged thesis in this piece? Why does Richler find these players so intriguing?

5. Does professional sport provide a viable way for minorities to gain social power? Discuss.

ADDRESS BY THE PRIME MINISTER ON THE CHINESE HEAD TAX REDRESS

STEPHEN HARPER, Prime Minister of Canada

Born in Toronto, in 1959, Stephen Harper was sworn in as Canada's 22nd prime minister on February 6, 2006. He holds a master's degree in economics from the University of Calgary. In June 2006, the Prime Minister issued an official apology for the head tax imposed on Chinese Canadians. This tax was imposed on anyone immigrating to Canada from China between 1885 and 1923. It was replaced in 1923 by the Exclusion Act, which barred all Chinese immigrants from Canada until 1947.

22 June 2006
Ottawa, Ontario
Notes for an Address by
The Right Honourable Stephen Harper
Prime Minister of Canada

Mr. Speaker, I rise today to formally turn the page on an unfortunate period in Canada's past.

One during which a group of people—who only sought to build a better life—was repeatedly and deliberately singled out for unjust treatment.

I speak, of course, of the head tax that was imposed on Chinese immigrants to this country, as well as the other restrictive measures that followed.

The Canada we know today would not exist were it not for the efforts of the Chinese labourers who began to arrive in the mid-nineteenth century.

Almost exclusively young men, these immigrants made the difficult decision to leave their families behind in order to pursue opportunities in a country halfway around the world they called "gold mountain."

Beginning in 1881, over 15,000 of these Chinese pioneers became involved in the most important nation-building enterprise in Canadian history—the construction of the Canadian Pacific Railway.

From the shores of the St. Lawrence, across the seemingly endless expanses of shield and prairie, climbing the majestic Rockies, and cutting through the rugged terrain of British Columbia,

—This transcontinental link was the ribbon of steel that bound our fledgling country together.

It was an engineering feat—one for which the back-breaking toil of Chinese labourers was largely responsible—

—That was instrumental to the settlement of the West and the subsequent development of the Canadian economy.

The conditions under which these men worked were at best harsh, and at times impossible: tragically, some one thousand Chinese labourers died building the CPR.

But in spite of it all, these Chinese immigrants persevered, and in doing so, helped to ensure the future of Canada.

But from the moment that the railway was completed, Canada turned its back on these men.

Beginning with the Chinese Immigration Act of 1885, a head tax of $50 was imposed on Chinese newcomers in an attempt to deter immigration.

Not content with the tax's effect, the government subsequently raised the amount to $100 in 1900, and then to $500—the equivalent of two years' wages—in 1903.

This tax remained in place until 1923, when the government amended the Chinese Immigration Act and effectively banned most Chinese immigrants until 1947.

Similar legislation existed in the Dominion of Newfoundland, which also imposed a head tax between 1906 and 1949, when Newfoundland joined Confederation.

The Government of Canada recognizes the stigma and exclusion experienced by the Chinese as a result.

We acknowledge the high cost of the head tax meant many family members were left behind in China, never to be reunited, or that families lived apart and, in some cases, in poverty, for many years.

We also recognize that our failure to truly acknowledge these historical injustices has led many in the community from seeing themselves as fully Canadian.

Therefore, Mr. Speaker, on behalf of all Canadians and the Government of Canada, we offer a full apology to Chinese Canadians for the head tax and express our deepest sorrow for the subsequent exclusion of Chinese immigrants.

Gar nar dai doe heem.

This apology is not about liability today: it is about reconciliation with those who endured such hardship, and the broader Chinese-Canadian community,

—One that continues to make such an invaluable contribution to our great country.

And while Canadian courts have ruled that the head tax, and immigration prohibition, were legally authorized, we fully accept the moral responsibility to acknowledge these shameful policies of our past.

For over six decades, these race-based financial measures, aimed solely at the Chinese, were implemented with deliberation by the Canadian state.

This was a grave injustice, and one we are morally obligated to acknowledge.

To give substantial meaning to today's apology, the Government of Canada will offer symbolic payments to living head tax payers and living spouses of deceased payers.

In addition, we will establish funds to help finance community projects aimed at acknowledging the impact of past wartime measures and immigration restrictions on ethno-cultural communities.

No country is perfect. Like all countries, Canada has made mistakes in its past, and we realize that.

Canadians, however, are a good and just people, acting when we've committed wrong.

And even though the head tax—a product of a profoundly different time—lies far in our past, we feel compelled to right this historic wrong for the simple reason that it is the decent thing to do, a characteristic to be found at the core of the Canadian soul.

Mr. Speaker, in closing, let me assure the House that this government will continually strive to ensure that similar unjust practices are never allowed to happen again.

We have the collective responsibility to build a country based firmly on the notion of equality of opportunity, regardless of one's race or ethnic origin.

Our deep sorrow over the racist actions of our past will nourish our unwavering commitment to build a better future for all Canadians.

Thank you.

PERSONAL RESPONSE

Do you think that this kind of public apology serves a purpose? When you read Harper's address, do you feel it is a genuine act of reconciliation? As a Canadian, do you feel properly represented by this apology?

QUESTIONS FOR CLASS OR SMALL-GROUP DISCUSSION

1. What is the purpose of a public apology? What are the differences between a private apology made by an individual and a public apology made by a government? How political is such an apology? When the application forms for redress were issued, they were available in French and English but not Chinese. Discuss.

2. How much historical information is contained in this apology? Search in your library or on the Internet for information on the Chinese head tax. Does this apology feel like complete information? Does it feel like a full understanding is expressed? Discuss.

3. We increasingly see apologies that address wrongdoings of the past. What motivates these apologies at this particular point in history? Why did it take so much time to pass before this apology was made? Can history's wrongs be made right by such apologies? Discuss.

4. What function do financial reparations make in an apology like this? Do you think these financial redresses are appropriate? Go online and find a federal government website that gives details of the payments. How was it decided how much would be paid? Keep in mind that the payments were made with taxpayers' money. Discuss.

5. Although Canada brought in Chinese immigrants in the 1880s to build the Canadian Pacific Railway through the mountains of British Columbia, the head tax was imposed to discourage immigration and exclude Chinese immigrants from Canadian jobs. To what extent does this gesture of apology in 2006 turn into a nationalistic action?

FOR FURTHER VIEWING: THE POLITICS OF ETHNICITY

Atanarjuat [*The Fast Runner*] (2002); *Mon oncle Antoine* (1971); *Dances with Wolves* (1990); *Little Big Man* (1970); *To Kill a Mockingbird* (1962); *Gandhi* (1982); *Schindler's List* (1993); *Glory* (1989); *Do the Right Thing* (1989); *Malcolm X* (1992); *The Birth of a Nation* (1915); *The Color Purple* (1985); *Their Eyes Were Watching God* (2005); *Kandahar* [*Safar e Ghandehar*] (2001); *Under the Willow Tree: Chinese Pioneer Women in Canada* (1997).

CHAPTER SEVENTEEN

WAR AND IMPERIALISM

INTRODUCTION

The story is an old one: One group wants to have dominance over another group. What is remarkable is how much human history, and how much humanity, has been used up in playing out this story of conflict. The two world wars of the 20th century alone tallied close to 100 million deaths. Just as remarkable, people continue to willingly sacrifice themselves in defending their group, or at least what they believe are the interests of their group. It is a story, then, filled with tragedy and glory but, as often as not, also a great deal of fog.

History suggests that the reasons for war are often complex and confusing: It may have to do with leaders, with resources, with territory, with religion, with ethnicity, with ideology, with power—any reason or combination of reasons will do. Unfortunately, there seems to be little reason to expect world peace in the future; conflicts like "the war on terrorism" have become in equal measures globalized, random, politicized, and ever-present; conflicts in many developing countries seem unstoppable; the worlds of "the haves" and the "have-nots" seem farther apart than ever; leaders come along who believe that they have various forms of righteousness on their side and their side alone. Hope, though, as the saying goes, is eternal; and as John Lennon suggested, it might be interesting to "give peace a chance."

Theories of war are highly debated. Some would suggest that war is the result of unseen, unpredictable accidents. Others believe that war is always about competition. Some say that aggression is hard-wired (i.e., innate, instinctual) in human—and especially male—behaviour. Some inevitably see war having its root in class and culture differences. But there remains a bigger and more controversial question: Is war necessary and inevitable? The "just war" theory suggests that it is. However, some critiques of the "just war" theory, in particular some feminist critiques, point out that notions of self-preservation acted out violently are either a male characteristic or culturally constructed. Finally, war is held to be about pragmatics, about one side making gains at the expense of another's loss.

Imperialism, which is akin to empire-building, often involves war, with, of course, the invading, victorious side as the imperialists, and the invaded group being colonized. Often, pure economics seems to be the reason: Take over a territory and you can take over whatever that territory has, including its natural resources and human capital; exploitation (sometimes under the banner of civilizing another group of people) is sometimes the name of the game; the imperialists who stay behind are called, in the most banal way, settlers. In the end, the invaded group often becomes dependent upon the invaders, leading to significant problems when the invader leaves or is forced out.

But imperialism does not necessarily need a war or a physically invading force. Sometimes imperialism is more subtle, and can be achieved by invading with ideas, goods, beliefs, and values; if you can get another country to buy into your practices, then it can be said that you have colonized that country or group, and you can exert forms of control over them (sometimes referred to as "cultural imperialism"). In recent history, this type of colonization is also tied to the ideas of neo-colonization (when control over colonies is based on economic control) or globalization (which, when spun in a positive way, suggests economic interdependence and growth among nations). Strong voices on both sides debate whether globalization is a good or bad thing. Some might suggest that modern war is a result of globalization based on the needs and ideology of the so-called American empire.

JAPAN'S KAMIKAZE PILOTS AND CONTEMPORARY SUICIDE BOMBERS: WAR AND TERROR

Yuki Tanaka

Yuki Tanaka is a research professor at the Hiroshima Peace Institute and a coordinator of Japan Focus (www.japanfocus.org). He has a Ph.D. from the University of Western Australia. Tanaka's books include Hidden Horrors: Japanese War Crimes in World War II *(1996) and* Japan's Comfort Women: Sexual Slavery and Prostitution During World War II and the U.S. Occupation *(2002).*

Kamikaze Pilots

It is widely believed that the major source of kamikaze suicide pilots was the Air Force Cadet Officer System in the Japanese Imperial Navy and Army Forces, which recruited university and college students on a voluntary basis. In fact, however, the majority of kamikaze pilots were young noncommissioned or petty officers, that is graduates of Navy and Army junior flight training schools. A total of 708 noncommissioned Army officers died as kamikaze pilots, while the total death toll of Army Air Force officer class kamikaze pilots was 621. In the Navy, 1732 petty officers died as kamikaze pilots compared with 782 officers. Many assume that the majority of kamikaze pilots were former college students, because the letters-home, diaries and wills of these young men, who became kamikaze pilots through the Air Force Cadet Officer System, were compiled and published as books and pamphlets after the war. The best known of these publications is Kike Wadatsumi no Koe (Listen to the Voices from the Sea). Unfortunately similar personal records left behind by noncommissioned and petty officers are not publicly available. It is therefore necessary to rely on private records to gain a fuller understanding of the thoughts and ideas of these kamikaze pilots.

The Navy Air Force Cadet Officer System was introduced in 1934 to assure preparation of well-trained fighter pilots. Until 1942 students were exempt from conscription. However, with the soaring death toll of Japanese soldiers, the conscription of all healthy male university and college students of Humanities and Social Science, who were 20 years of age or older, was introduced in October, 1943. Students were allowed to apply for the position of Navy Air Force cadet, but the selection criteria were stricter than for those of other cadet positions in the Japanese Imperial Forces, both in the Navy and the Army. The Army introduced the Air Force Cadet Officer System in July 1943, but many students chose the Navy which enjoyed the aura of being modern and fashionable.

Between 1934 and 1942, 507 Air Force Cadet Officers were accepted into the Navy Air Force. From September 1943 the numbers increased rapidly, with 14,347 inducted between September 1943 and 1944, and an additional 285 in 1945 for a total of 15,149. Of these, 2,485 (16%) died, of whom 685 died as kamikaze pilots.

The total death toll of Navy kamikaze officer pilots, including 685 former college students, was 782. This means that only 12 percent of those who died among Navy

The universal soldier?
Photo Source: © Reuters

kamikaze officer pilots were professional fighters. The percentage of former students amongst the Navy kamikaze officer pilots who died in the Battle of Okinawa (i.e. in Ten Ichigo Sakusen [Operation Heaven No. 1]) between late March and late July in 1945) was as high as 81.3%. (Or, according to another source, 82.9%.) In the Army, 58 percent of the kamikaze officer pilots who died in the Battle of Okinawa were former students. This statistical data is the main source of the criticism of the leaders of the Japanese Imperial Forces from surviving former student kamikaze pilots and the relatives of those who died on mission towards the end of the war. They claim that the Navy particularly sacrificed former students in order to save professional pilots.

In analyzing private records of the cadet officer kamikaze pilots, the following psychological themes emerged as bases for accepting or responding to a kamikaze attack mission.

1) Rationalizing one's own death to defend one's country and its people

In the final years, the cadets clearly understood that Japan would lose the war. Therefore, they had to rationalize their own deaths in order to believe that their sacrifice would not be a total waste. To this end, some convinced themselves that their determination to fight to the end would save the Japanese people (i.e. the Yamato race) and their country by forcing the Allied Forces to make concessions so as to end the war as quickly as possible to avoid further Allied casualties by kamikaze attack. However, as testimonies of dead and surviving pilots clearly show, their idea of "country" was far from the nationalistic notion of "nation-state." For most of these young students, "country" meant their own "beautiful hometowns" where their beloved families lived. In this context it is interesting to note that there is very little reference in their wills, letters-home, and diaries of their loyalty to the emperor. Occasionally we find some stereotypical militaristic phrases such as "Kokoku Goji (Uphold the Empire)," "Shinshu Fumetsu (the Immortal Divine Land)," "Yukyu no Taigi (the Noble Cause of Eternal Loyalty)," and the like, but these words are usually used rhetorically rather than conveying deep conviction or abiding nationalistic sentiment.

2) The belief that to die for the "country" was [to] show filial piety to one's own parents, particularly to one's mother:

Many wills and last letters convey apology to parents for the inability to return all the favors the kamikaze pilots had received and for causing their parents grief by their premature death. Yet, they also state that their death for the "noble cause" was one way to compensate for the misery caused their parents. This way of thinking is clearly intertwined with the idea of defending the "country," i.e. the "hometown." The announcement of their death as kamikaze pilots in the national press brought praise and honor to their parents, in particular, praise by residents of their local community. Thus, in this way, filial piety ("koo") to parents became identical with "loyalty ("chu") to parents and then to "country." Their loyalty to the emperor invariably emerges as a logical extension of loyalty to parents and hometown, rather than the reverse. To defend one's mother in one's hometown was thus the most basic, almost instinctive, element in rationalizing a cadet's death as a kamikaze pilot. This explains why many intelligent youths accepted their suicidal mission despite feelings among some of deep mistrust and criticism of military leaders and politicians. The majority of cadets viewed their unavoidable duty as defending their mothers no matter how corrupt the society and politics. The strong emotional attachment to mothers is overwhelmingly clear in their private records, a phenomenon perhaps related to the fact that the majority of these youth were not yet involved in sustained relationships.

3) Strong solidarity with their flight-mates who shared their fate as Kamikaze pilots:

This solidarity, which can be termed "a convoy of death," clearly softened the fear of death by making participants feel that others would die with them on the same mission. US pilots flying in formation communicated with each other by radio. Japanese planes were not equipped with radios, but it was common practice for the same flight formation team to be maintained through all stages from training to actual combat in order to create and sustain coordinated team actions. Not surprisingly, unusually strong friendships formed, especially among kamikaze pilots. In cases where pilots in the same team were separated on different missions, many complained bitterly to their commanders, claiming that they had pledged to die together. It seems that, in some cases, their friendship even developed into homosexual relationships.

4) A strong sense of responsibility and contempt for cowardice:

Most of these top university students were sincere and had a strong sense of responsibility. They felt that if they themselves would not carry out the mission nobody else would follow suit. They also saw escape from their "duty," for whatever reason, as an act of cowardice. "To live free from cowardice as a human being" was a strongly expressed desire. It seems that this mentality derived from university life, which had sheltered them from conventional ways of thinking. Clearly, they were naïve and such naïvety and sincerity were encouraged at cadet school where students with similar social background lived and trained together while preparing to die for country. However, some boys, if clearly a minority, resisted orders to complete kamikaze missions by feigning illness or fleeing. (There was even one case in which a kamikaze pilot took off on a mission, but deliberately crashed his plane into a military brothel, killing several "comfort women," including his favorite, as well as himself.)

5) A lack of an image of the enemy:

One of the striking features of these youths' ideas is that they convey no discernible image of their enemy. In their diaries and letters-home there is barely any reference to their adversaries. The enemy did not exist in their mind. Specifically, virtually no sense of "hatred of the enemy" can be found in their writings. Perhaps this was partly due to the fact that these cadets had never experienced actual combat. By contrast, the Allied navy soldiers who encountered kamikaze attacks usually regarded the kamikaze pilots with intense fear and hatred, calling them "crazy, cruel, and inhumane Japs". In the case of these Japanese youths, a concrete mental concept of "the enemy" did not exist at all. Instead they were preoccupied by philosophical ideas such as how to find some spiritual value in their brief lives, how to spend their remaining time meaningfully, and how to philosophically justify their suicidal act. The concept of killing the enemy, as opposed to fighting for "country," was simply lacking in their thinking.

Contemporary Suicide Bombers

In the absence of detailed information on the ideology and psychology of contemporary "terrorist suicide bombers," it is not easy to compare the kamikaze mentality with that of terrorist bombers. One important difference stems from the fact that kamikaze attacks were implemented and legitimized by the military regime of a nation-state, while "terrorist suicide bombing" is generally planned and authorized by organizations outside a state structure. Certain preliminary comparisons are nevertheless still possible.

As surviving former kamikaze pilots correctly point out, in contrast to contemporary terrorist bombers, their targets were always military planes, ships and personnel, never civilians. To be sure, under wartime conditions, particularly in the final months of the Pacific War, military targets were the only ones that the kamikaze could challenge. Had they been closer to American civilians, as Palestinian suicide bombers are to Israeli civilians, they too might have attacked civilian targets. Nevertheless there seem to be some fundamental similarities between the two groups of suicide attackers: in the imbalance of technological power between them and their foes, in the conceptions of those who dispatch them, and in the mentality of those who sacrifice their lives.

The following discussion emphasizes Palestinian suicide bombers, though they are of course not alone in seeking to use this strategy. Anwar Ayam, the brother of a Palestinian suicide bomber, is said to have observed, "It will *destroy their economy*. It causes more casualties than any other type of operation. It will *destroy their social life*. They are scared and nervous, and it will force them to leave the country because they are afraid." (emphasis added) In the eyes of the attackers, the distinction between military and civilian in the ranks of their oppressors is not a real concern. The goal for Palestinian suicide bombers is to shake the foundations of the Israeli establishment by destroying its social and economic life, and above all its sense of security as a means, ultimately of forcing the Israelis to leave their occupied land. The same logic applies to the 9/11 bombings in New York and Washington, and suicide bombings in Iraq. For kamikaze pilots, too, the ultimate aim of their actions was not to kill enemy soldiers or to achieve victory in the war, but to force the Allies to make concessions to end the war by terrorizing them with suicide attack. In both cases, concrete images of the victims may be lacking in the attackers' mind, thus the actions of killing others becomes ritualised. This observation is not, of course, limited to killing by kamikaze or suicide bombers but may extend to other terrains of war.

In this sense there is an important similarity between suicide bombing (including kamikaze attack) and the "strategic bombing." Strategic bombing, i.e., the indiscriminate bombing of civilians, is justified as the most efficient method of destroying the morale of the enemy nation, and thus the most economical way to force surrender. In this concept too, concrete images of victims are absent in the minds of strategists and bombers. This similarity is not surprising. This is because the indiscriminate bombing of civilians conducted by military forces is nothing but state violence against civilians, that is, it is state terrorism. "Terrorist attacks" either by a group or by a state can only be executed when images of victims are abstracted and detached from the minds of attackers and strategists.

Another similarity between kamikaze attack and suicide bombing is the huge technological gap in military capability between suicide attackers and their enemies. To be sure, Japan, in contrast to the Palestinians in particular, had created a powerful army, navy and air force that allowed it to become the dominant power in Asia in the 1920s and 1930s. Nevertheless, the kamikaze strategy, particularly as it emerged in 1944–45, was a direct response to the fact that the Japanese Imperial Navy had lost most of its major battleships and almost all its aircraft carriers, while the Allied Forces had numerous aircraft carriers, hundreds of battleships, and thousands of aircraft with abundant fuel, bombs and ammunition. By 1944, the Imperial Army troops stationed throughout the Asia Pacific were incapacitated and struggling to survive without food and ammunition, indeed, many were cut loose from supplies and left to their own devices.

Bombing of major Japanese cities such as Tokyo, Nagoya, Osaka, Kobe and Fukuoka by B-29 bombers, underway by March 1945, caused hundreds of thousands of civilian casualties. Kamikaze pilots saw their "country" being destroyed and their own families directly targeted by aerial bombardment. In these circumstances, the Japanese military leaders decision to emphasize the suicide kamikaze attack was a desperate strategy whose only possible meaning was to convince the US and its allies to ease surrender terms and prevent a US landing in Japan.

Similarly, Palestinian fighters have no comparable weaponry to directly attack F-16 jet fighters, Apache helicopters, tanks, missiles and the like; before their eyes their homes are blown up, women and children are torn apart, their bodies charred and chewed up by shrapnel, and Palestinian communities are fenced in by Israeli barbed wire that makes them captives in their own land. Moreover, Palestinians have endured decades of torture, humiliation, killing and the robbing of their lands and resources by Israel. In contrast the Israelis have been astonishingly free of reprisal from within the territories during these years. With far fewer strategic options than those available to Japan in the Pacific War, a segment of the Palestinian resistance, in utter despair, has opted for suicide bombing in urban centres as the most effective means to demoralize Israelis. For some young Palestinians who see no future in their life, terminating their own lives is not such a terrifying and difficult matter. It is a natural psychological extension for one who no longer finds meaning in his or her own life to slight the lives of others as well.

In my view, religious or ideological indoctrination is not the decisive factor in turning a young person into a suicide attacker. Rather religion and ideology are used to justify and formalize their cause of self-sacrifice and to rationalize the killing enemies, whether military or civilians. In so doing, they mirror the strategies of their oppressors who likewise, in practice, make no distinction between military and civilian targets. Ritualising killing makes it psychologically easier not only to annihilate enemies but also to terminate one's own life.

Ritualised violence and brutality as exemplified by suicide attack may constitute the most negative manifestations of a human being's desire to let one's own people live by sacrificing one's own life. However, war and violent conflict inevitably brutalize not only suicide attackers, but all human beings. Undoubtedly war is an act of madness, its absurdity clearly shown in the paired (but imbalanced) actions and reactions of World War II: as Japan adopted kamikaze-style suicide attacks, the US used "strategic bombing" to indiscriminately kill hundreds of thousands of civilians, and finally engaged in atomic bombing attacks. Yet, to a great extent, it is the former acts that have borne the opprobrium of history while the latter would come to shape the strategic horizons of subsequent wars. Thus terrorist suicide bombing, which is occurring more and more frequently throughout the world, bears the opprobrium of "lunatic actions by fanatics," while the bombing of civilians, such as those executed by the U.S. and British forces in Afghanistan and Iraq, are widely regarded as "legitimate military operations." It is crucial that we find effective ways to break the vicious cycle of these two types of terrorism.

PERSONAL RESPONSE

When you watch the news, especially TV news, it is easy to think that suicide bombing is either a modern phenomenon that began when terrorists hijacked airliners and flew them into the Twin Towers in New York City, on September 11, 2001, or a phenomenon unique to the last decade. Can suicide bombing be fully understood only in the context of the last century?

QUESTIONS FOR CLASS OR SMALL-GROUP DISCUSSION

1. Note what the author says about Palestine and Israel. Are his comments based on opinion or on fact?

2. World War II saw the indiscriminate killing of civilians. Some of the most prominent examples were the bombings of London, Dresden, Tokyo, Nagasaki, and Hiroshima. Are civilian casualties ever justified in war? Is there such a thing as a just war? Do you believe the media pays too much attention to suicide bombing and not enough to conventional bombing that also kills civilians? What does the author mean by "ritualized" killing?

3. Make a list of conditions that would cause someone to want to become a suicide bomber.

4. In May 2007, CTV and CNN reported that one in four younger U.S. Muslims—those under the age of 30—believed that suicide bombings to defend their religion were acceptable at least in some circumstances, though most American Muslims overwhelmingly rejected the tactic. How do you feel about the results of the survey? Do you feel that suicide bombing can ever be justified as a viable or rational tactic?

INTRODUCTION TO *SHAKE HANDS WITH THE DEVIL: THE FAILURE OF HUMANITY IN RWANDA*

LT.-GEN. ROMÉO DALLAIRE (WITH BRENT BEARDSLEY)

Born in 1946 and brought up in Montreal, Roméo Dallaire was, in 1993, appointed by the United Nations to command an international peacekeeping force to prevent ethnic cleansing in Rwanda, a small

African country. Lieutenant-General Dallaire foresaw and then wit-
nessed the genocide taking place, and though his efforts were genuinely
heroic, he had little on-the-spot support to do much more than act as
a witness to the slaughter of 800,000 people over the period of a few
months. His story and struggle has become well known internationally.

It was an absolutely magnificent day in May 1994. The blue sky was cloudless, and there was a whiff of breeze stirring the trees. It was hard to believe that in the past weeks an unimaginable evil had turned Rwanda's gentle green valleys and mist-capped hills into a stinking nightmare of rotting corpses. A nightmare we all had to negotiate every day. A nightmare that, as commander of the UN peacekeeping force in Rwanda, I could not help but feel deeply responsible for.

In relative terms, that day had been a good one. Under the protection of a limited and fragile ceasefire, my troops had successfully escorted about two hundred civilians—a few of the thousands who had sought refuge with us in Kigali, the capital of Rwanda—through many government- and militia-manned checkpoints to reach safety behind the Rwandese Patriotic Front (RPF) lines. We were seven weeks into the genocide, and the RPF, the disciplined rebel army (composed largely of the sons of Rwandan refugees who had lived over the border in camps in Uganda since being forced out of their homeland at independence), was making a curved sweep toward Kigali from the north, adding civil war to the chaos and butchery in the country.

Having delivered our precious cargo of innocent souls, we were headed back to Kigali in a white UN Land Cruiser with my force commander pennant on the front hood and the blue UN flag on a staff attached to the right rear. My Ghanaian sharpshooter, armed with a new Canadian C-7 rifle, rode behind me, and my new Senegalese aide-de-camp, Captain Ndiaye, sat to my right. We were driving a particularly dangerous stretch of road, open to sniper fire. Most of the people in the surrounding villages had been slaughtered, the few survivors escaping with little more than the clothes on their backs. In a few short weeks, it had become a lonely and forlorn place.

Suddenly up ahead we saw a child wandering across the road. I stopped the vehicle close to the little boy, worried about scaring him off, but he was quite unfazed. He was about three years old, dressed in a filthy, torn T-shirt, the ragged remnants of underwear, little more than a loincloth, drooping from under his distended belly. he was caked in dirt, his hair white and matted with dust, and he was enveloped in a cloud of flies, which were greedily attacking the open sores that covered him. He stared at us silently, sucking on what I realized was a high-protein biscuit. Where had the boy found food in this wasteland?

I got out of the vehicle and walked toward him. Maybe it was the condition I was in, but to me this child had the face of an angel and eyes of pure innocence. I had seen so many children hacked to pieces that this small, whole, bewildered boy was a vision of hope. Surely, he could not have survived all on his own? I motioned for my aide-de-camp to honk the horn, hoping to summon up his parents, but the sound echoed over the empty landscape, startling a few birds and little else. The boy remained transfixed. He did not speak or cry, just stood sucking on his biscuit and staring up at us with his huge, solemn eyes. Still hoping that he wasn't all alone, I sent my aide-de-camp and the sharpshooter to look for signs of life.

We were in a ravine lush with banana trees and bamboo shoots, which created a dense canopy of foliage. A long straggle of deserted huts stood on either side of the road. As I stood alone with the boy, I felt an anxious knot in my stomach: this would be a perfect place to stage an ambush. My colleagues returned, having found no one. Then a rustling in the undergrowth made us jump. I grabbed the boy and held him firmly to my side as we instinctively took up defensive positions around the vehicle and in the ditch. The bushed parted to reveal a well-armed RPF soldier about fifteen years old. He recognized my uniform and gave me a smart salute and introduced himself. He was part of an advance observation post in the nearby hills. I asked him who the boy was and whether there was anyone left alive in the village who could take care of him. The soldier answered that the boy had no name and no family but that he and his buddies were looking after him. That explained the biscuit but did nothing to ally my concerns over the security and health of the boy. I protested that the child needed proper care and that I could give it to him: we were protecting and supporting orphanages in Kigali where he would be much better off. The soldier quietly insisted that the boy stay where he was, among his own people.

I continued to argue, but this child soldier was in no mood to discuss the situation and with haughty finality stated that his unit would care and provide for the child. I could feel my face flush with anger and frustration, but then noticed that the boy himself had slipped away while we had been arguing over him, and God only knew where he had gone. My aide-de-camp spotted him at the entrance to a hut a short distance away, clambering over a log that had fallen across the doorway. I ran after him, closely followed by my aide-de-camp and the RPF child soldier. By the time I had caught up to the boy, he had disappeared inside. The log in the doorway turned out to be the body of a man, obviously dead for some weeks, his flesh rotten with maggots and beginning to fall away from the bones.

As I stumbled over the body and into the hut, a swarm of flies invaded my nose and mouth. It was so dark inside that at first I smelled rather than saw the horror that lay before me. The hut was a two-room affair, one room serving as a kitchen and living room and the other as a communal bedroom; two rough windows had been cut into the mud-and-stick wall. Very little light penetrated the gloom, but as my eyes became accustomed to the dark, I saw strewn around the living room in a rough circle the decayed bodies of a man, a woman and two children, stark white bone poking through the desiccated, leather-like covering that had once been skin. The little boy was crouched beside what was left of his mother, still sucking on his biscuit. I made my way over to him as slowly and quietly as I could and, lifting him into my arms, carried him out of the hut.

The warmth of his tiny body snuggled against mine filled me with a peace and serenity that elevated me above the chaos. This child was alive yet terribly hungry, beautiful but covered in dirt, bewildered but not fearful. I made up my mind: this boy would be the fourth child in the Dallaire family. I couldn't save Rwanda, but I could save this child.

Before I had held this boy, I had agreed with the aid workers and representatives of both the warring armies that I would not permit any exporting of Rwandan orphans to foreign places. When confronted by such requests from humanitarian organizations, I would argue that the money to move a hundred kids by plane to France or Belgium could help build, staff and sustain Rwandan orphanages that could house three thousand children. This one boy eradicated all my arguments. I could see myself arriving at the terminal in Montreal like a latter-day St. Christopher* with the boy cradled in my arms, and my wife, Beth, there ready to embrace him.

That dream was abruptly destroyed when the young soldier, fast as a wolf, yanked the child from my arms and carried him directly into the bush. Not knowing how many members of his unit might already have their gunsights on us, we reluctantly climbed back into the Land Cruiser. As I slowly drove away, I had much on my mind.

By withdrawing, I had undoubtedly done the wise thing: I had avoided risking the lives of my two soldiers in what would have been a fruitless struggle over one small boy. But in that moment, it seemed to me that I had backed away from a fight for what was right, that this failure stood for all our failures in Rwanda.

Whatever happened to that beautiful child? Did he make it to an orphanage deep behind the RPF lines? Did he survive the following battles? Is he dead or is he now a child soldier himself, caught in the seemingly endless conflict that plagues his homeland?

That moment, when the boy, in the arms of a soldier young enough to be his brother, was swallowed whole by the forest, haunts me. It's a memory that never lets me forget how ineffective and irresponsible we were when we promised the Rwandans that we would establish an atmosphere of security that would allow them to achieve a lasting peace. It has been almost nine years since I left Rwanda, but as I write this, the sounds, smells and colours come flooding back in digital clarity. It's as if someone has sliced into my brain and grafted this horror called Rwanda frame by blood-soaked frame directly on my cortex. I could not forget even if I wanted to. For many of these years, I have yearned to return to Rwanda and disappear into the blue-green hills with my ghosts. A simple pilgrim seeking forgiveness and pardon. But as I slowly begin to piece my life back together, I know the time has come for me to make a more difficult pilgrimage: to travel back through all those terrible memories and retrieve my soul.

I did try to write this story soon after I came back from Rwanda in September 1994, hoping to find some respite for myself in sorting out how my own role as Force Commander of UNAMIR interconnected with the international apathy, the complex political manoeuvres, the deep well of hatred and barbarity that resulted in genocide in which over 800,000 people lost their lives. Instead, I plunged into a disastrous mental health spiral that led me to suicide attempts, a medical release from the Armed Forces, the diagnosis of post-traumatic stress disorder, and dozens upon dozens of therapy sessions and extensive medication, which still have a place in my daily life.

It took me seven years to finally have the desire, the willpower and the stamina to begin to describe in detail the events of that year in Rwanda. To recount, from

---

*St. Christopher: a fearless martyr of the third century, patron saint of travellers.

my insider's point of view, how a country moved from the promise of a certain peace to intrigue, the fomenting of racial hatred, assassinations, civil war and genocide. And how the international community, through an inept UN mandate and what can only be described as indifference, self-interest and racism, aided and abetted these crimes against humanity—how we all helped create the mess that has murdered and displaced millions and destabilized the whole central African region.

A growing library of books and articles is exploring the tragic events in Rwanda from many angles: eyewitness accounts, media analyses, assaults on the actions of the American administration at the time, condemnations of the UN's apparent ineptitude. But even in the international and national inquiries launched in the wake of the genocide, the blame somehow slides away from the individual member nations of the UN, and in particular those influential countries with permanent representatives on the Security Council, such as the United States, France and the United Kingdom, who sat back and watched it all happen, who pulled their troops or didn't offer any troops in the first place. A few Belgian officers were brought to court to pay for the sins of Rwanda. When my sector commander in Kigali, Colonel Luc Marchal, was court-martialled in Brussels, the charges against him were clearly designed to deflect any responsibility away from the Belgian government for the deaths of the ten Belgian peacekeepers under my command. The judge eventually threw out all the charges, accepting the fact that Marchal had performed his duties magnificently in a near-impossible situation. But the spotlight never turned to the reasons why he and the rest of the UNAMIR force were in such a dangerous situation in the first place.

It is time that I tell the story from where I stood—literally in the middle of the slaughter for weeks on end. A public account of my actions, my decisions and my failings during that most terrible year may be a crucial missing link for those attempting to understand the tragedy both intellectually and in their hearts. I know that I will never end my mourning for all those Rwandans who placed their faith in us, who thought the UN peacekeeping force was there to stop extremism, to stop the killings and help them through the perilous journey to a lasting peace. That mission, UNAMIR, failed. I know intimately the cost in human lives of the inflexible UN Security Council mandate, the pennypinching financial management of the mission, the UN red tape, the political manipulations and my own personal limitations. What I have come to realize as the root of it all, however, is the fundamental indifference of the world community to the plight of seven to eight million black Africans in a tiny country that had no strategic or resource value to any world power. An overpopulated little country that turned in on itself and destroyed its own people, as the world watched and yet could not manage to find the political will to intervene. Engraved still in my brain is the judgment of a small group of bureaucrats who came to "assess" the situation in the first weeks of the genocide: "We will recommend to our government not to intervene as the risks are high and all that is here are humans."

My story is not a strictly military account nor a clinical, academic study of the breakdown of Rwanda. It is not a simplistic indictment of the many failures of the UN as a force for peace in the world. It is not a story of heroes and villains, although such a work could easily be written. This book is a *cri de coeur* for the slaughtered thousands, a tribute to the souls hacked apart by machetes because of their supposed difference from those who sought to hang on to power. It is the story of a commander who, faced with a challenge that didn't fit the classic Cold War-era peacekeeper's rule book, failed to find an effective solution and witnessed, as if in punishment, the loss of some of his own troops, the attempted annihilation of an ethnicity, the butchery of children barely out of the womb, the stacking of severed limbs like cordwood, the mounds of decomposing bodies being eaten by the sun.

This book is nothing more nor less than the account of a few humans who were entrusted with the role of helping others taste the fruits of peace. Instead, we watched as the devil took control of paradise on earth and fed on the blood of the people we were supposed to protect.

PERSONAL RESPONSE

What feelings do you have when you read Dallaire's account of what happened? How would have you responded in his situation? Is your response to Dallaire coloured by your being a Canadian?

QUESTIONS FOR CLASS OR SMALL-GROUP DISCUSSION

1. What does Dallaire's desire to save the little boy reveal about him and about the real situation in Rwanda?
2. Discuss the various levels of failure, being haunted, and guilt in the piece and in what the piece suggests. Who or what has failed? Who or what is haunted, and by what? Who feels guilt, and why?
3. There are many terms and phrases to describe what happened in Rwanda: war, tribal war, civil war, mass murder, ethnic cleansing, and genocide. Discuss how these different terms make us look at the event differently. Which term do you think is most appropriate, and why?
4. In the writings by Dallaire and Stephen Lewis, the United Nations comes under strong criticism. Research how the UN functions, and offer constructive criticism of how it has handled any one of these issues: genocide, AIDS/HIV, or the environment.

AN UNQUIET AWAKENING

MORDECAI RICHLER

Mordecai Richler was born in Montreal in 1931, and passed away in his home city in 2001. He was a writer of all genres—fiction, journalism, sports, scripts, and essays—but he is best known for his clear style, controversial views, and comical and satirical touch. He won numerous awards and honours, and is considered by many as the most important Canadian writer of his generation. His fiction includes The Apprenticeship of Duddy Kravitz *(1959),* Barney's Version

(1997), Solomon Gursky Was Here *(1989), and the* Jacob Two-Two *stories. Collections of his writing include* Belling the Cat *(1998),* Oh Canada! Oh Quebec! Requiem for a Divided Country*(1992), and* Dispatches from the Sporting Life *(2000).*

Reading was not one of my boyhood passions. Girls, or rather the absence of girls, drove me to it. When I was 13 years old, short for my age, more than somewhat pimply, I was terrified of girls. They made me feel sadly inadequate.

Retreating into high seriousness, I acquired a pipe, which I chewed on ostentatiously, and made it my business to be seen everywhere, even at school basketball games, absorbed by books of daunting significance. The two women who ran the lending library, possibly amused by my pretensions, tried to interest me in fiction.

"I want fact. I can't be bothered with stories," I protested, waving my pipe at them affronted, "I just haven't got the time for such nonsense."

Novels, I knew, were mere romantic make-believe, not as bad as poetry, to be fair, but bad enough.

I fell ill with a childhood disease, I no longer remember which, but obviously I meant it as a rebuke to those girls in tight sweaters who continued to ignore me. Never mind, they would mourn at my funeral, burying me with my pipe. Too late, they would say, "Boy, was he ever an intellectual."

The women from the lending library, concerned, dropped off books for me at our house. The real stuff. Fact-filled. Providing me with the inside dope on Theodore Herzl's childhood and *Brazil Yesterday, Today and Tomorrow.*

One day they brought me a novel: *All Quiet on the Western Front* by Erich Maria Remarque. The painting on the jacket that was taped to the book showed a soldier wearing what was unmistakably a German Army helmet. What was this, I wondered, some sort of bad joke?

Nineteen forty-four that was, and I devoutly wished every German left on the face of the earth an excruciating death. The Allied invasion of France had not yet begun, but I cheered every Russian counterattack, each German city bombed, and—with the help of a map tacked to my bedroom wall—followed the progress of the Canadian troops fighting their way up the Italian boot. Boys from our street had already been among the fallen. Izzy Draper's uncle, Harvey Kegelmass' older brother. The boy who was supposed to marry Gita Holtzman.

All Quiet on the Western Front lay unopened on my bed for two days. Finally, I was driven to picking it up out of boredom. I never expected that a mere novel, a stranger's tale, could actually be dangerous, creating such turbulence in my life, obliging me to question so many received ideas. About Germans. About my own monumental ignorance of the world. About what novels were.

At the age of 13 in 1944, happily as yet untainted by English 104, I couldn't tell you whether Remarque's novel was

a. a slice of life
b. symbolic
c. psychological
d. seminal.

I couldn't even say if it was well or badly written. In fact, as I recall, it didn't seem to be "written" at all. Instead, it just flowed. Now, of course, I understand that writing that doesn't advertise itself is art of a very high order. It doesn't come easily. But at the time I wasn't capable of making such distinctions. I also had no notion of how *All Quiet on the Western Front* rated critically as a war novel. I hadn't read Stendhal or Tolstoy or Crane or Hemingway. I hadn't even heard of them. I didn't know that Thomas Mann, whoever he was, had praised the novel highly. Neither did I know that in 1929 the judges at some outfit called the Book-of-the-Month Club had made it their May selection.

But what I did know is that, hating Germans with a passion, I had read only 20, maybe 30, pages before the author had seduced me into identifying with my enemy, 19-year-old Paul Baumer, thrust into the bloody trenches of the First World War with his schoolmates: Muller, Kemmerich and the reluctant Joseph Behm, one of the first to fall. As if that weren't sufficiently unsettling in itself, the author, having won my love for Paul, my enormous concern for his survival, then betrayed me in the last dreadful paragraphs of his book:

"He fell in October 1918, on a day that was so quiet and still on the whole front, that the army report confined itself to the single sentence: All Quiet on the Western Front.

"He had fallen forward and lay on the earth as though sleeping. Turning him over one saw that he could not have suffered long; his face had an expression of calm, as though almost glad the end had come."

The movies, I knew from experience, never risked letting you down like that. No matter how bloody the battle, how long the odds, Errol Flynn, Robert Taylor, even Humphrey Bogart could be counted on to survive and come home to Ann Sheridan, Lana Turner or—if they were sensitive types—Loretta Young. Only character actors, usually Brooklyn Dodger fans, say George Tobias or William Bendix, were expendable.

Obviously, having waded into the pool of serious fiction by accident, I was not sure I liked or trusted the water. It was too deep. Anything could happen.

There was something else, a minor incident in *All Quiet on the Western Front* that would not have troubled an adult reader but, I'm embarrassed to say, certainly distressed that 13-year-old boy colliding with his first serious novel:

Sent out to guard a village that has been abandoned because it is being shelled too heavily, Katczinsky, the incomparable scrounger, surfaces with suckling pigs and potatoes and carrots for his comrades, a group of eight altogether:

"The suckling pigs are slaughtered, Kat sees to them. We want to make potato cakes to go with the roast. But we cannot find a grater for the potatoes. However, that difficulty is soon over. With a nail we punch a lot of holes in a pot lid and there we have a grater. Three fellows put on thick gloves to protect their fingers against the grater, two others peel the potatoes, and business gets going."

The business, I realized, alarmed—not affronted—was the making of potato latkes, a favorite of mine as well as Paul Baumer's, a dish I had always taken to be Jewish, certainly not a German concoction.

What did I know? Nothing. Or, looked at another way, my real education, my life-long addiction to fiction, began with the trifling discovery that the potato latke was not of Jewish origin, but something borrowed from the German and now a taste that Jew and German shared in spite of everything.

I felt easier about my affection for the German soldier Paul Baumer once I was told by the women from the lending library that when Hitler came to power in 1933 he had burned all of Erich Maria Remarque's books and in 1938 he took away his German citizenship. Obviously Hitler had grasped that novels could be dangerous, something I learned when I was only 13 years old. He burned them; I began to devour them. I started to read at the breakfast table and on streetcars, often missing my stop, and in bed with benefit of a flashlight. It got me into trouble.

I grasped, for the first time, that I didn't live in the centre of the world but had been born into a working-class family in an unimportant country far from the cities of light: London, Paris, New York. Of course this wasn't my fault, it was my inconsiderate parents who were to blame. But there was, I now realized, a larger world out there beyond St. Urbain Street in Montreal.

Preparing myself for the Rive Gauche, I bought a blue beret, but I didn't wear it outside, or even in the house if anybody else was at home. I looked at but lacked the courage to buy a cigarette holder.

As my parents bickered at the supper table, trapped in concerns now far too mundane for the likes of me—what to do if Dworkin raised the rent again, how to manage my brother's college fees—I sat with but actually apart from them in the kitchen, enthralled, reading for the first time, "All happy families are alike but an unhappy family is unhappy after its own fashion."[1]

Erich Maria Remarque, born in Westphalia in 1897, went off to war, directly from school, at the age of 18. He was wounded five times. He lost all his friends. After the war he worked briefly as a schoolteacher, a stonecutter, a test driver for a tire company and an editor of *Sportbild* magazine. His first novel, *Im Westen Nichts Neues*, was turned down by several publishers before it was brought out by the Ullstein Press in Berlin in 1928. *All Quiet on the Western Front* sold 1.2 million copies in Germany and was translated in 29 languages, selling some four million copies throughout the world. The novel has been filmed three times; the first time, memorably by Lewis Milestone in 1930. The Milestone version, with Lew Ayres playing Paul Baumer, won Academy Awards for best picture and best direction.

Since *All Quiet on the Western Front* once meant so much to me, I picked it up again with a certain anxiety. After all this time, I find it difficult to be objective about the novel. Its pages still evoke for me a back bedroom with a cracked ceiling and a sizzling radiator on St. Urbain Street: mice scrabbling in the walls, and a window looking out on the sheets frozen stiff on the laundry line.

Over the years the novel has lost something in shock value. The original jacket copy of the 1929 Little, Brown & Company edition of *All Quiet on the Western Front* warns the reader that it is "at times crude" and "will shock the supersensitive by its outspokenness." Contemporary readers, far from being shocked, will be amused by the novel's discretion, the absence of explicit sex scenes, the unbelievably polite dialogue of the men in the trenches.

The novel also has its poignant moments, both in the trenches and when Paul Baumer goes home on leave, an old man of 19, only to find insufferably pompous schoolmasters still recruiting the young with mindless prattle about the fatherland and the glory of battle. Strong characters are deftly sketched. Himmelstoss, the postman who becomes a crazed drillmaster. Tjaden, the peasant soldier. Kantorek, the schoolmaster.

On the front line the enemy is never the Frogs or the Limeys, but the insanity of the war itself. It is the war, in fact, and not even Paul Baumer, that is the novel's true protagonist. In a brief introduction to the novel Remarque wrote: "This book is to be neither an accusation nor a confession, and least of all an adventure, for death is not an adventure to those who stand face to face with it. It will try simply to tell of a generation of men who, even though they may have escaped its shells, were destroyed by the war."

Since the First World War we have become altogether too familiar with larger horrors. The Holocaust, Hiroshima, the threat of a nuclear winter. Death by numbers, cities obliterated by decree. At peace, as it were, we live the daily dread of the missiles in their silos, ours pointed at them, theirs pointed at us. None of this, however, diminishes the power of *All Quiet on the Western Front*, a novel that will endure because of its humanity, its honor and its refusal to lapse into sentimentality or strike a false note.

NOTE

1. The opening sentence of *Anna Karenina* by Leo Tolstoy.

PERSONAL RESPONSE

Can you recall the first, or one of the first, works of fiction you read that was idea-changing for you? Or maybe a movie? Can you describe your experience? What brought you into the world of that fiction? Did you identify with a character, a feeling, a place, or incident—or was it something else?

QUESTIONS FOR CLASS OR SMALL-GROUP DISCUSSION

1. Describe what Richler finds so important and powerful about fiction. What possibilities does fiction have? Do you agree?
2. Describe the process whereby Richler finds himself slipping into the world of *All Quiet on the Western Front*.
3. What was the big discovery for Richler when he read *All Quiet on the Western Front* years later?
4. What does Richler pass on to be learned about war?

A NEW KIND OF WAR

ERNEST HEMINGWAY

Ernest Hemingway was one of the most important novelists of the twentieth century. His fiction includes The Sun Also Rises *(1926), A* Farewell to Arms *(1929), and* The Old Man and the Sea *(1952), which was instrumental in his winning the Nobel Prize in 1954. He also wrote numerous classic short stories. His writing—terse, compact, and powerful—transformed not only English literature but also screenwriting and cinema. As a young man he worked briefly at the* Toronto Star. *He was an outstanding war reporter and especially noteworthy are his dispatches from the Spanish Civil War (1937–39.)*

MADRID.—The window of the hotel is open and, as you lie in bed, you hear the firing in the front line seventeen blocks away. There is a rifle fire all night long. The rifles go "tacrong, capong, craang, tacrong," and then a machine gun opens up. It has a bigger calibre and is much louder—"rong, cararong, rong, rong." Then there is the incoming boom of a trench mortar shell and a burst of machine-gun fire. You lie and listen to it and it is a great thing to be in bed with your feet stretched out gradually warming the cold foot of the bed and not out there in University City or Carabanchel. A man is singing hard-voiced in the street below, and three drunks are arguing when you fall asleep.

In the morning, before your call comes from the desk, the roaring burst of a high explosive shell wakes you and you go to the window and look out to see a man, his head down, his coat collar up, sprinting desperately across the paved square. There is the acrid smell of high explosive you hoped you'd never smell again, and, in a bathrobe and bedroom slippers, you hurry down the marble stairs and almost into a middle-aged woman, wounded in the abdomen, who is being helped into the hotel entrance by two men in blue workmen's smocks. She has her two hands crossed below her big, old-style Spanish bosom and from between her fingers the blood is spurting in a thin stream. On the corner, twenty yards away, is a heap of rubble, smashed cement and thrown up dirt, a single dead man, his torn clothes dusty, and a great hole in the sidewalk from which the gas from a broken main is rising, looking like a heat mirage in the cold morning air.

"How many dead?" you ask a policeman.

"Only one," he says. "It went through the sidewalk and burst below. If it would have burst on the solid stone of the road there might have been fifty."

A policeman covers the body, from which the head is missing; they send for someone to repair the gas main and you go in to breakfast. A charwoman, her eyes red, is scrubbing the blood off the marble floor of the corridor. The dead man wasn't you nor anyone you know and everyone is very hungry in the morning after a cold night and a long day the day before up at the Guadalajara front.

"Did you see him?" asked someone else at breakfast.

"Sure," you say.

"That's where we pass a dozen times a day. Right on that corner." Someone makes a joke about missing teeth and someone else says not to make that joke. And everyone has the feeling that characterizes war. It wasn't me, see? It wasn't me.

The Italian dead up on the Guadalajara front weren't you, although Italian dead, because of where you had spent your boyhood, always seemed, still, like our dead. No. You went to the front early in the morning in a miserable little car with a more miserable little chauffeur who suffered visibly the closer he came to the fighting. But at night, sometimes late, without lights, the big trucks roaring past, you came on back to sleep in a bed with sheets in a good hotel, paying a dollar a day for the best rooms on the front. The smaller rooms in the back, on the side away from the shelling, were considerably more expensive. After the shell that lit on the sidewalk in front of the hotel you got a beautiful double corner room on that side, twice the size of the one you had had, for less than a dollar. It wasn't me they killed. See? No. Not me. It wasn't me anymore.

Then, in a hospital given by the American Friends of Spanish Democracy, located out behind the Morata front along the road to Valencia, they said, "Raven wants to see you."

"Do I know him?"

"I don't think so," they said, "but he wants to see you."

"Where is he?"

"Upstairs."

In the room upstairs they are giving a blood transfusion to a man with a very gray face who lay on a cot with his arm out, looking away from the gurgling bottle and moaning in a very impersonal way. He moaned mechanically and at regular intervals and it did not seem to be him that made the sound. His lips did not move.

"Where's Raven?" I asked.

"I'm here," said Raven.

The voice came from a high mound covered by a shoddy gray blanket. There were two arms crossed on the top of the mound and at one end there was something that had been a face, but now was a yellow scabby area with a wide bandage across where the eyes had been.

"Who is it?" asked Raven. He didn't have lips, but he talked pretty well without them and with a pleasant voice.

"Hemingway," I said. "I came up to see how you were doing."

"My face was pretty bad," he said. "It got sort of burned from the grenade, but it's peeled a couple of times and it's doing better."

"It looks swell," I said. "It's doing fine."

I wasn't looking at it when I spoke.

"How are things in America?" he asked. "What do they think of us over there?"

"Sentiment's changed a lot," I said. "They're beginning to realize the government is going to win this war."

"Do you think so?"

"Sure," I said.

"I'm awfully glad," he said. "You know, I wouldn't mind any of this if I could just watch what was going on. I don't mind the pain, you know. It never seemed important really. But I was always awfully interested in things and I really wouldn't mind the pain at all if I could just sort of follow things intelligently. I could even be some use. You know, I didn't mind the war at all. I did all right in the war. I got hit once before and I was back and rejoined the battalion in two weeks. I couldn't stand to be away. Then I got this."

He had put his hand in mine. It was not a worker's hand. There were no callouses and the nails on the long, spatulate fingers were smooth and rounded.

"How did you get it?" I asked.

"Well, there were some troops that were routed and we went over to sort of reform them and we did and then we had quite a fight with the fascists and we beat them. It was quite a bad fight, you know, but we beat them and then someone threw this grenade at me."

Holding his hand and hearing him tell it, I did not believe a word of it. What was left of him did not sound like the wreckage of a soldier somehow. I did not know how he had been wounded, but the story did not sound right. It was the sort of way everyone would like to have been wounded. But I wanted him to think I believed it.

"Where did you come from?" I asked.

"From Pittsburgh. I went to the University there."

"What did you do before you joined up here?"

"I was a social worker," he said. Then I knew it couldn't be true and I wondered how he had really been so frightfully wounded and I didn't care. In the war that I had known, men often lied about the manner of their wounding. Not at first; but later. I'd lied a little myself in my time. Especially late in the evening. But I was glad he thought I believed it, and we talked about books, he wanted to be a writer, and I told him about what happened north of Guadalajara and promised to bring some things from Madrid next time we got out that way. I hoped maybe I could get a radio.

"They tell me Dos Passos and Sinclair Lewis are coming over, too," he said.

"Yes," I said. "And when they come I'll bring them up to see you."

"Gee, that will be great, he said. "You don't know what that will mean to me."

"I'll bring them," I said.

"Will they be here pretty soon?"

"Just as soon as they come I'll bring them."

"Good boy, Ernest," he said. "You don't mind if I call you Ernest, do you?"

The voice came very clear and gentle from that face that looked like some hill that had been fought over in muddy weather and then baked in the sun.

"Hell, no," I said. "Please. Listen, old-timer, you're going to be fine. You'll be a lot of good, you know. You can talk on the radio."

"Maybe," he said. "You'll be back?"

"Sure," I said. "Absolutely."

"Goodbye, Ernest," he said.

"Goodbye," I told him.

Downstairs they told me he'd lost both eyes as well as his face and was also badly wounded all through the legs and in the feet.

"He's lost some toes, too," the doctor said, "but he doesn't know that."

"I wonder if he'll ever know it."

"Oh, sure he will," the doctor said. "He's going to get well."

And it still isn't you that gets hit but it is your countryman now. Your countryman from Pennsylvania, where once we fought at Gettysburg.

Then, walking along the road, with his left arm in an airplane splint, walking with the gamecock walk of the professional British soldier that neither ten years of militant party work nor the projecting metal wings of the splint could destroy, I met Raven's commanding officer, Jock Cunningham, who had three fresh rifle wounds through his upper left arm (I looked at them, one was septic) and another rifle bullet under his shoulder blade that had entered his left chest, passed through, and lodged there. He told me, in military terms, the history of the attempt to rally retiring troops on his battalion's right flank, of his bombing raid down a trench which was held at one end by the fascists and at the other end by the government troops, of the taking of this trench and, with six men and a Lewis gun, cutting off a group of some eighty fascists from their own lines, and of the final desperate defense of their impossible position his six men put up until the government groups came up and, attacking, straightened out the line again. He told it clearly, completely convincingly, and with a strong Glasgow accent. He had deep, piercing eyes sheltered like an eagle's, and, hearing him talk, you could tell the sort of soldier he was. For what he had done he would have had a V.C. in the last war. In this war there are no decorations. Wounds are the only decorations and they do not award wound stripes.

"Raven was in the same show," he said. "I didn't know he'd been hit. Ay, he's a good mon. He got his after I got mine. The fascists we'd cut off were very good troops. They never fired a useless shot when we were in that bad spot. They waited in the dark there until they had us located and then opened with volley fire. That's how I got four in the same place."

We talked for a while and he told me many things. They were all important, but nothing was as important as what Jay Raven, the social worker from Pittsburgh with no military training, had told me was true. This is a strange new kind of war where you learn just as much as you are able to believe.

PERSONAL RESPONSE

There is a saying that the first casualty of war is the truth. When you read "A New Kind of War," how do you feel about what Hemingway saw and heard? Would you write about it differently?

QUESTIONS FOR CLASS OR SMALL-GROUP DISCUSSION

1. Why does Hemingway say this is "a new kind of war"? Can you name other wars that can be defined in the same way?
2. Hemingway describes the sounds at night as he tries to fall asleep in a wartorn city. Why is this description an effective way to open his dispatch?

3. What does he mean by "in this war there are no decorations"?

4. Given Hemingway's account, which phrase seems most appropriate: war is glory; war is inevitable; war is hell; war is foolish; war is sad; or war is adventure?

THE UNVEILING OF THE AMERICAN EMPIRE

CHALMERS JOHNSON

Chalmers Johnson, born in 1931, in Phoenix, Arizona, spent much of his career as an academic. He is president of the non-profit organization Japan Policy Research Institute and the author of numerous books, articles, and reviews, including Blowback: The Costs and Consequences of American Empire *(2000) and* The Sorrows of Empire: Militarism, Secrecy, and the End of the Republic *(2004). The piece below is the prologue from the latter.*

Our nation is the greatest force for good in history.
         —President George W. Bush, Crawford, Texas, August 31, 2002

As distinct from other peoples on this earth, most Americans do not recognize—or do not want to recognize—that the United States dominates the world through its military power. Due to government secrecy, they are often ignorant of the fact that their government garrisons the globe. They do not realize that a vast network of American military bases on every continent except Antarctica actually constitutes a new form of empire.

Our country deploys well over half a million soldiers, spies, technicians, teachers, dependents, and civilian contractors in other nations and just under a dozen carrier task forces in all the oceans and seas of the world. We operate numerous secret bases outside our territory to monitor what the people of the world, including our own citizens, are saying, faxing, or e-mailing to one another. Our globe-girding military and intelligence installations bring profits to civilian industries, which design and manufacture weapons for the armed forces or undertake contract services to build and maintain our far-flung outposts. One task of such contractors is to keep uniformed members of the imperium housed in comfortable quarters, well fed, amused, and supplied with enjoyable, affordable vacation facilities. Whole sectors of the American economy have come to rely on the military for sales. On the eve of our second war on Iraq, for example, the Defense Department ordered 273,000 bottles of Native Tan sunblock (SPF 15), almost triple its 1999 order and undoubtedly a boon to the supplier, Control Supply Company of Tulsa, Oklahoma, and its subcontractor, Sun Fun Products of Daytona Beach, Florida.[1]

The new American empire has been a long time in the making. Its roots go back to the early nineteenth century, when the United States declared all of Latin

America its sphere of influence and busily enlarged its own territory at the expense of the indigenous people of North America, as well as British, French, and Spanish colonialists, and neighboring Mexico. Much like their contemporaries in Australia, Algeria, and tsarist Russia, Americans devoted much energy to displacing the original inhabitants of the North American continent and turning over their lands to new settlers. Then, at the edge of the twentieth century, a group of self-conscious imperialists in the government—much like a similar group of conservatives who a century later would seek to implement their own expansive agendas under cover of the "war on terrorism"—used the Spanish-American War to seed military bases in Central America, various islands in the Caribbean, Hawaii, Guam, and the Philippines.

With the Second World War, our nation emerged as the richest and most powerful on earth and a self-designated successor to the British Empire. But as enthusiastic as some of our wartime leaders, particularly President Franklin D. Roosevelt, were for the task, the American people were not. They demanded that the country demobilize its armies and turn the nation's attention to full employment and domestic development. Peace did not last long, however. The Cold War and a growing conviction that vital interests, even national survival, demanded the "containment" of the Soviet Union helped turn an informal empire begun during World War II into hundreds of installations around the world for the largest military we ever maintained in peacetime.

During the almost fifty years of superpower standoff, the United States denied that its activities constituted a form of imperialism. Ours were just reactions to the menace of the "evil empire" of the USSR and its satellites. Only slowly did we Americans become aware that the role of the military was growing in our country and that the executive branch—the "imperial presidency"—was eroding the democratic underpinnings of our constitutional republic. But even at the time of the Vietnam War and the abuses of power known as Watergate, this awareness never gained sufficient traction to reverse a Cold War–driven transfer of power from the representatives of the people to the Pentagon and the various intelligence agencies, especially the Central Intelligence Agency.

By the time the Soviet Union collapsed in 1991, and with it the rationale for American containment policies, our leaders had become so accustomed to dominance over half the globe that the thought of giving it up was inconceivable. Many Americans simply concluded that they had "won" the Cold War and so deserved the imperial fruits of victory. A number of ideologists began to argue that the United States was, in fact, a "good empire" and should act accordingly in a world with only one dominant power. To demobilize and turn our resources to peaceful ends would, they argued, constitute the old-fashioned sin of "isolationism."

In the first post–Cold War decade, we mounted many actions to perpetuate and extend our global power, including wars and "humanitarian" interventions in Panama, the Persian Gulf, Somalia, Haiti, Bosnia, Colombia, and Serbia, while maintaining unchanged our Cold War deployments in East Asia and the Pacific. In the eyes of its own people, the United States remained at worst an informal empire. After all, it had no colonies and its massive military forces were deployed around the world only to maintain "stability," or guarantee "mutual security," or promote a liberal world order based on free elections and American-style "open markets."

Americans like to say that the world changed as a result of the September 11, 2001, terrorist attacks on the World Trade Center and the Pentagon. It would be more accurate to say that the attacks produced a dangerous change in the thinking of some of our leaders, who began to see our republic as a genuine empire, a new Rome, the greatest colossus in history, no longer bound by international law, the concerns of allies, or any constraints on its use of military force. The American people were still largely in the dark about why they had been attacked or why their State Department began warning them against tourism in an ever-growing list of foreign countries. ("Why do they hate us?" was a common plaint heard on talk shows, and the most common answer was "jealousy.") But a growing number finally began to grasp what most non-Americans already knew and had experienced over the previous half century—namely, that the United States was something other than what it professed to be, that it was, in fact, a military juggernaut intent on world domination.

Americans may still prefer to use euphemisms like "lone superpower," but since 9/11, our country has undergone a transformation from republic to empire that may well prove irreversible. It suddenly became "un-American" to question the Bush administration's "war on terrorism," let alone a war on Iraq, or on the whole "axis of evil," or even on the sixty or so countries that the president and his secretary of defense announced contained al-Qaeda cells and so were open targets for unilateral American intervention. The media allowed themselves to be manipulated into using sanitized expressions like "collateral damage," "regime change," "illegal combatants," and "preventive war" as if these somehow explained and justified what the Pentagon was doing. At the same time, the government was making strenuous efforts to prevent the new International Criminal Court from ever having the option of considering war crimes charges against American officials.

This book is a guide to the American empire as it begins openly to spread its imperial wings. Its reach is global: as of September 2001, the Department of Defense acknowledged at least 725 American military bases existed outside the United States. Actually, there are many more, since some bases exist under leaseholds, informal agreements, or disguises of various kinds. And more have been created since the announcement was made. The landscape of this military empire is as unfamiliar and fantastic to most Americans today as Tibet or Timbuktu were to nineteenth-century Europeans. Among its recent additions are the al-Udeid air base in the desert of Qatar, where several thousand American military men and women live in air-conditioned tents, and the al-Masirah Island naval air stations in the Gulf of Oman, where the only diversion is "wadi ball," a cross between volleyball and football. It includes expensive, permanent garrisons built between 1999 and 2001 in such unlikely places as Kosovo, Kyrgyzstan, and Uzbekistan. America's modern empire of bases also has its entertainment and getaway spots, much like those north Indian hill towns the administrators of the British Raj used for rest and recreation in the summer heat. The modern equivalents of Darjeeling, Kalimpong, and Srinagar are the armed forces' ski and vacation center at Garmisch in the Bavarian Alps, its resort hotel in downtown Tokyo, and the 234 military golf courses it operates worldwide, not to mention the seventy-one Learjets, thirteen Gulfstream IIIs, and seventeen Cessna Citation luxury jets used to fly admirals and generals to such spots. At a cost of $50 million apiece, each Gulfstream accommodates twelve passengers plus two pilots, one flight engineer, a communications systems operator, and a flight attendant.

Like empires of old, ours has its proconsuls, in this case high-ranking military officers who enforce extraterritorial "status of forces agreements" on host governments to ensure that American troops are not held responsible for crimes they commit against local residents. Our militarized empire is a physical reality with a distinct way of life but it is also a network of economic and political interests tied in a thousand different ways to American corporations, universities, and communities but kept separate from what passes for everyday life back in what has only recently come to be known as "the homeland." And yet even that sense of separation is disappearing—for the changing nature of the empire is changing our society as well.

For example, slowly but surely the Department of Defense is obscuring and displacing the Department of State as the primary agency for making and administering foreign policy. We now station innumerably more uniformed military officers than civilian diplomats, aid workers, or environmental specialists in foreign countries—a point not lost on the lands to which they are assigned. Our garrisons send a daily message that the United States prefers to deal with other nations through the use or threat of force rather than negotiations, commerce, or cultural interaction and through military-to-military, not civilian-to-civilian, relations. This point was made clear in a speech at the military academy at West Point on June 1, 2002, when President George W. Bush argued that the United States must be prepared to wage a "war on terror" against as many as sixty countries. "We must take that battle to the enemy, disrupt his plans and confront the worst threats before they emerge." Americans must be "ready for preemptive action when necessary to defend our liberty and to defend our lives. . . . In the world we have entered, the only path to safety is the path of action. And this nation will act."

As historian Arthur Schlesinger Jr., adviser to President John F. Kennedy, observed on the first anniversary of the 9/11 attacks, "One of the astonishing events of recent months is the presentation of preventive war as a legitimate and moral instrument of U.S. foreign policy. . . . During the Cold War, advocates of preventive war were dismissed as a crowd of loonies. . . . The policy of containment plus deterrence won the Cold War. After the collapse of the Soviet Union, everyone thanked heaven that the preventive-war loonies had never got into power in any major country. Today, alas, they appear to be in power in the United States."[2] He was referring specifically to the first Bush administration's secretary of defense, Dick Cheney—now, of course, vice president—the second Bush administration's secretary of defense, Donald Rumsfield, and their cronies in the Pentagon. The last time civilian and uniformed militarists even approximated the domination of American political life we see today was when Secretary of Defense Robert McNamara was dictating policy toward Vietnam.

Like most other Americans who are not actively involved with the armed forces, I paid very little attention to our empire of military bases until February 1996, when I made my first visit to our de facto American military colony of Okinawa, a small Japanese island that we have continuously occupied since 1945. My last encounter with the military had ended forty years earlier—when, in the summer of 1955, I left active duty as a naval officer in the western Pacific. In 1996, in the wake of the rape of a twelve-year-old Okinawan girl by two American marines and a sailor, I was invited by the island's governor, Masahide Ota, to speak about the problem of our bases. I visited Kin village—almost totally swallowed by the marines' massive Camp Hansen, where the abduction and rape had occurred—and interviewed local officials. I came away deeply disturbed both by Okinawan hostility and by the fact that no serious American strategy could explain the deployment of thirty-eight separate bases on the choicest 20 percent of the island.

It was apparent from the numerous beaches, golf courses, and other recreational facilities reserved for the use of our military and the duplication involved in separate air force, navy, and Marine Corps airfields that the bases had simply sprouted willy-nilly with the advent of the Cold War. No consideration had been given to equitable land use or the lives of the 1.3 million Okinawans. The military's situation in Okinawa struck me as similar to that of Soviet troops in East Germany after the Berlin Wall came down. In both cases the troops preferred to stay on because the pleasures of life as a legionnaire in an imperial garrison far outstripped those of life back in the "homeland."

The troops and their families were happy with their clubs, apartment, gyms, swimming pools, and shopping malls (known in military argot as "base exchanges") and undoubtedly preferred Okinawa to being stuck in small stateside towns like Oceanside, California, adjacent to the Marine Corps base at Camp Pendleton. If nothing else, the penalty for a rape conviction in California is considerably more onerous than for servicemen convicted of the same felony in Okinawa by the Japanese. Under terms of the Status of Forces Agreement the United States imposed on Japan in 1953, the Japanese are even required to provide special meals for those few American servicemen turned over to Japanese authorities and actually imprisoned. On average there were 2,800 calories in the meals served to Japanese prisoners but 4,000 in those served to the twelve Americans jailed at the end of 2001.[3]

After visiting Okinawa, I began to research, and write about, the history of our military there—from the final bloody battle of World War II against the Japanese army to the attempts of senior U.S. officers and Department of Defense officials to trivialize the rape of September 4, 1995.[4] My perspective was that of an academic. I had spent my life as a university professor studying the politics and economics of Japan and China, not as an analyst of America's global military hegemony. As was true of many Japanese not resident in Okinawa, I tended to see the island's situation as unique and at worst a sad case of Pentagon complacency and neglect. The solution seemed self-evident: close some of the unneeded bases, return substantial ground forces to American territory, lessen the burdens imposed on the Okinawan people, and so begin to reverse some of the hatred of the United States evident everywhere on the island. I thought that if the Pentagon imposed real priorities, it might even be able to preserve some of its facilities there, like Kadena Air Force Base, that might prove useful in a post–Cold War world. Otherwise, it seemed to me that sooner or later the Okinawans would revolt and throw us out, as the Filipinos had done in 1992 and the South Koreans threatened to do in 2003—just as the East Berliners had done to the Soviet Union in 1989.

Only slowly did I come to understand that Okinawa was typical, not unique. The conditions there—expropriations of the island's most valuable land for bases, extraterritorial status for American troops who committed crimes against local civilians, bars and brothels crowding around the main gates of bases, endless accidents, noise, sexual violence, drunk-driving crashes, drug use, and environmental pollution—are replicated anywhere there are American garrisons. Compared with the numerous bases on the Japanese mainland, the more than one hundred installations in South Korea, and the huge deployments in Germany, Britain, Italy, the Balkans, the Persian Gulf, Latin America, and elsewhere, Okinawa in not unusual except in the number of bases given the size of the island. America's military proconsuls being publicity-averse, the American press seldom visits, or reports on, its empire of bases. I had been given a glimpse into an aspect of contemporary American life that most Americans never see.

In light of these experiences, in the late 1990s I devoted myself to writing a book about American foreign policy, which I entitled *Blowback,* using the CIA's term for the unanticipated consequences of unacknowledged actions in other people's countries. My intention was to warn my fellow Americans about the conduct of our foreign policy over the previous half century, focusing particularly on the decade after the demise of the Soviet Union and on the evolving political situation in East Asia. The book appeared in the early spring of 2000. In it I argued that many aspects of what the American government had done abroad virtually invited retaliatory attacks from nations and peoples who had been victimized. The blowback from the second half of the twentieth century has only just begun. In a sense, blowback is simply another way of saying that a nations reaps what it sows. Although individual Americans usually know what they have sown, they rarely have the same knowledge at a national level, since so much of what the managers of our empire have done has been kept secret.

Although I became interested in our overseas bases when I visited Okinawa, I had already gained some insight into the organization of American imperialism and its secret operations. From 1967 to 1973, I served as a consultant to the Office of National Estimates of the Central Intelligence Agency.[5] I had been asked to join a panel of about twenty international relations specialists from outside the agency to read drafts of national intelligence estimates and offer nonbureaucratic critiques of them. Intelligence estimates are formal analyses and conclusions compiled from raw intelligence data that the CIA director is charged with coordinating with other intelligence agencies and then delivering to the president and his advisers. These estimates, which do not indicate the sources of the intelligence under consideration, are written in an inoffensive bureaucratic prose intended to smooth over differences of interpretation between, say, the State Department's intelligence bureau and the Defense Intelligence Agency. I was invited to become a consultant by Richard Helms, the director, who only a few years later would be convicted of lying under oath to Congress for testifying that the agency had nothing to do with the overthrow of President Salvador Allende of Chile. Thus began my introduction to the secret world.

In 1967, I was best known as an academic specialist on China. The agency was interested in my opinions on several major issues of the time—the war in Vietnam, the Sino-Soviet split, and the internal Maoist purge of the Communist Party known as the Cultural Revolution, as well an insurgency and counterinsurgency, what the Chinese called People's War, a subject that then preoccupied Washington. The meetings with us outside consultants were held twice a year in former director Allen Dulles's home on the property of Camp Peary, then a "secret" CIA training base in Virginia.

Although I had been given a very high security clearance, I soon found that I did not have to worry about inadvertently disclosing national secrets. The best reason to keep the national intelligence estimates secret, I once told my wife, was their utter banality. Perhaps they were so highly classified because it would have been embarrassing to have it known that such conventional journalism passed for strategic thought in the Oval Office. The meetings were convivial and stimulating, but only rarely did national estimates wander from the standard militarist wisdom of the Vietnam War era. (On the other hand, CIA analysts who knew Vietnam well privately applauded Daniel Ellsberg's release of "The Pentagon Papers," because they were convinced that the war could not be won.)

There was one perk associated with being a consultant to the Office of National Estimates that I greatly treasured: the library in Dulles's home, filled with the latest CIA reports on subjects not on the agenda, back copies of old intelligence estimates, and classified journals devoted to the tradecraft of spying, was open all night. Those who did not spend the evening playing poker or telling one another tales of Cold War derring-do were welcome to sit in the library and browse through the collected documents for as long as they could stay awake. I recall spending most of one night reading in fascinating detail how the Russians had sprung their spy George Blake from Wormwood Scrubs Prison in London.

In the course of this enlightening nocturnal activity, I slowly realized that, at the CIA, the tail wagged the dog, that America's real business was covert activities, not intelligence collecting and analysis. During World War II, William J. Donovan founded the Office of Strategic Services, the CIA's predecessor. Only later did I learn that "an internal CIA history of Donovan's imprint on the Agency says he saw intelligence analysis as a convenient cover for subversive operations abroad. This subterfuge proved useful down the years."[6] So much for the valuable contributions of my consultancy, an experience that cured me of any tendency to think that the government keeps secrets as a matter of national security. Agencies classify things in order to protect themselves from congressional scrutiny or from political or bureaucratic rivals elsewhere within the government. True secrets need not be classified. They are simply closely held by prudent leaders. Interestingly enough, in September 2002, as the Bush administration was daily terrifying the world with statements about Saddam Hussein's clandestine weapons and the need for a preventive invasion of Iraq, the CIA revealed that there was no national intelligence estimate on Iraq and that it had not thought to prepare one for over two years.[7]

Part and parcel of the growth of militarism in the United States, the CIA has evolved into the president's private army to be used for secret projects he personally wants carried out (as, for example, in Nicaragua and Afghanistan during the 1980s). One begins to understand why John F. Kennedy was such an avid fan of Ian Fleming's James Bond tales. In 1961, Kennedy listed *From Russia with Love* as one of his favorite books. No doubt he envied Dr. No and the head of SMERSH, both of whom had private, semimilitary forces at their disposal to do whatever they wanted. Kennedy found his first in the CIA, until it humiliated him in the failed Bay of Pigs operation in Cuba, and then in the army's Green Berets.

Today the CIA is just one of several secret commando units maintained by our government. In the Afghan war of 2001, the CIA's semimilitary operatives worked so closely with the army Special Operations troops (Green Berets, Delta Force commandos, etc.) that it became impossible to distinguish them. The United States has proudly admitted that its first casualty in the Afghan invasion was a CIA operative. During August 2002, Defense Secretary Donald Rumsfeld revealed plans to expand Special Operations forces within the military and merge them with the CIA's Special Activities Division (its covert operatives). Although it seems unlikely that the numerous private armies of our government can ever fully overcome interservice and bureaucratic rivalries, their story is an integral part of the growth of American militarism and the secrecy that accompanies it.[8]

The present book, *The Sorrows of Empire*, follows from my earlier book *Blowback*. In that book I assumed that the American government still functioned more or less as it had during the Cold War, and I stressed the potential for conflict in East Asia. But I did not focus on the extent of militarism in America or on the vast empire of military bases that had sprung up more or less undetected and that is today a geopolitical fact of life. In the wake of September 11, 2001, it no longer seems necessary to issue warnings; instead a diagnosis, even an autopsy, may be more appropriate. In my opinion, the growth of militarism, official secrecy, and a belief that the United States is no longer bound, as the Declaration of Independence so famously puts it, by "a decent respect for the opinions of mankind" is probably irreversible. A revolution would be required to bring the Pentagon back under democratic control, or to abolish the Central Intelligence Agency, or even to contemplate enforcing article 1, section 9, clause 7 of the Constitution: "No money shall be drawn from the Treasury, but in Consequence of Appropriations made by Law; and a regular Statement and Account of the Receipts and Expenditures of all public Money shall be published from time to time."

This article is one that empowers Congress and makes the United States a democracy. It guarantees that the people's representatives will know what the state apparatus is actually doing and it authorizes full disclosure of these activities. It has not been applied to the Department of Defense or the Central Intelligence Agency since their creation. Instead there has been a permanent policy of "don't ask, don't tell." The White House has always kept the intelligence agencies' budgets secret, and deceptions in the defense budget date back to the Manhattan Project of World War II and the secret decisions to build atomic bombs and use them against the Japanese. In 1997, then Senator Robert Torricelli (D-New Jersey) proposed an amendment to the 1998 Defense Authorization bill requiring that Congress disclose aggregate intelligence expenditures. He lost, but he was able to point out that the intelligence agencies spend more than the combined gross national products of North Korea, Libya, Iran, and Iraq—and they do so in the name of the American people but without any advice or supervision from them.

The subject matter of this book is American militarism, its physical presence in the world, the growth of the "special forces" as a private army of the president, and the secrecy that allows ever more militarized and secret institutions to live and thrive. This is not an optimistic report. As the great sociologist of the modern state, Max Weber, concluded, "Every bureaucracy seeks to increase the superiority of the professionally informed by keeping their knowledge and intentions secret. Bureaucratic administration always tends to be an administration of 'secret sessions': in so far as it can, it hides its knowledge and action from criticism. . . . The concept of 'official secret' is the specific invention of the bureaucracy, and nothing is so fanatically defended by the bureaucracy as this attitude. . . . In facing a parliament the bureaucracy, out of a sure power instinct, fights every attempt of the parliament to gain knowledge by means of its own experts or interest groups. . . . Bureaucracy naturally welcomes a poorly informed and hence a powerless parliament—at least in so far as ignorance somehow agrees with the bureaucracy's interests."[9]

Weber could have been describing America's government today. In the war against Afghanistan the only information available to the public and its representatives came from the Department of Defense. The military has become expert at managing the news. Following the attacks of September 11, government at every level began to restrict information available to the public, including charges it was bringing against people it had picked up in Afghanistan and elsewhere and was holding incommunicado in a Pentagon prison in Cuba. Our newspapers began to read like official gazettes, television news simply gave up and followed the orders of its corporate owners, and the two political parties competed with each other in being obsequious to the White House.

As militarism, the arrogance of power, and the euphemisms required to justify imperialism inevitably conflict with America's democratic structure of government and distort its culture and basic values, I fear that we will lose our country. If I overstate the threat, I am sure to be forgiven because the future generations will be so glad I was wrong. The danger I foresee is that the United States is embarked on a path not unlike that of the former Soviet Union during the 1980s. The USSR collapsed for three basic reasons—internal economic contradictions driven by ideological rigidity, imperial overstretch, and an inability to reform. Because the United States is far wealthier, it may take longer for similar afflictions to do their work. But the similarities are obvious and it is nowhere written that the United States, in its guise as an empire dominating the world, must go on forever.

NOTES

1. Paul Sperry, "Defense Department Orders 273,000 Bottles of Sunblock." *WorldNetDaily,* October 9, 2002 <http://www.worldnetdaily.com/news/article.asp?ARTICLE_ID=29225>.
2. Arthur Schlesinger Jr., "The Immorality of Preventive War," *History News Network,* August 26, 2002. Also see Jimmy Carter, "The Troubling New Face of America," *Washington Post,* September 5, 2002.
3. "U.S. Soldiers in Prison Handled Well Thanks to SOFA; Even Beefsteak Served; 40 Percent More in Calories Taken by Them than Japanese, with Even Desserts Served at Every Supper," *Asahi Shimbun* (Tokyo), October 11, 2002, p. 39.
4. See, e.g., "The Pentagon's Colonial Pretensions Thrive in Asia," *Los Angeles Times,* November 2, 1995; "Fort Okinawa: *Go-Banken-sama,* Go Home!" *Bulletin of the Atomic Scientists* 52:4 (July/August 1996), pp. 22–29; "The Okinawan Rape Incident and the End of the Cold War in East Asia," *California Western International Law Journal* 27:2 (Spring 1997), pp. 389–97; *Okinawa: Cold War Island* (Cardiff, Calif.: Japan Policy Research Institute, 1999) (editor and contributor); "Time to Bring the Troops Home: America's Provocative Military Posture in Asia Makes War with China More Likely," *Nation,* May 14, 2001, pp. 20–22; and "Okinawa between the United States and Japan," in Josef Kreiner, ed., *Ryukyu in World History, JapanArchiv 2* (Bonn: Bier'sche Verlagsanstalt, 2001), pp. 365–94.
5. See Chalmers Johnson, "The CIA and Me," *Bulletin of Concerned Asian Scholars* 29:1 (Jan.–Mar. 1997), pp. 34–37. Also see Willard C. Matthias, *America's Strategic Blunders: Intelligence Analysis and National Security Policy, 1936-1991* (University Park: Pennsylvania State University Press, 2001), pp. 297–98.
6. Tim Weiner, *Blank Check: The Pentagon's Black Budget* (New York: Warner Books, 1990), p. 114.
7. Eric Schmitt and Alison Mitchell, "U.S. Lacks Up-to-Date Review of Iraqi Arms," *New York Times,* September 11, 2002.
8. Tom Bowman, "Special Forces' Role May Expand," *Baltimore Sun,* August 3, 2002; Lawrence J. Korb and Jonathan D. Tepperman, "Soldiers Should Not Be Spying," *New York Times,* August 21, 2002; Rowan Scarborough, "Study Urges Wider Authority for Covert Troops vs. Terror," *Washington Times,* December 12, 2002; Scarborough, "Rumsfeld Bolsters Special Force," *Washington Times,* January 6, 2003; and Douglas Waller, "The CIA's Secret Army," *Time,* January 26, 2004. For an excellent summary of the CIA's record in running "secret wars," see "America's Shadow Warriors," *New York Times,* March 3, 2003.
9. Max Weber, *Economy and Society* (1922), in H. H. Gerth and C. Wright Mills, eds. and trans., *From Max Weber: Essays in Sociology* (New York: Oxford University Press, 1958), pp. 233–34. Also see William Pfaff, "Governments Don't Like to Be Accountable," *International Herald Tribune,* September 2, 2002; and Daniel P. Moynihan, *Secrecy: The American Experience* (New Haven: Yale University Press, 1999).

PERSONAL RESPONSE

Before reading this piece, did you think of the United States as an empire-builder and imperialist nation? Are you convinced by Johnson's argument? What does it feel like living beside a nation as powerful as the United States? Has your attitude toward the United States changed over the last number of years, and if so, why? When you think of what an empire is, what comes to mind? Which empires in history are you familiar with? What does history tell us about empires?

QUESTIONS FOR CLASS OR SMALL-GROUP DISCUSSION

1. This piece was written as a prologue to a book, and, as such, has a personal tone (tone being the attitude toward the subject being addressed). Try to describe the tone of this piece.

2. Who is Johnson writing to? What effect does his choice of audience have on you as a reader?

3. List the evidence or characteristics that, for Johnson, make the United States an "empire."

4. There are many key expressions and terms in this piece: for example, Cold War, Watergate, imperialism, empire, isolationism, imperial presidency, war on terror, axis of evil, collateral damage, regime change, preventative war, foreign policy, militarism, and ideological rigidity. Explore three of the terms you feel least familiar with, and try to come up with an understanding of them.

5. Discuss the possibility that the United States is a "good empire."

WOMEN CONFRONTING WAR

Jennifer Turpin

Jennifer Turpin has served as dean of the College of Arts and Sciences at the University of San Francisco since 2003. She holds an associated faculty position at the European University Center for Peace Studies (UNESCO). Her research examines violence and its relationship to the distribution of power. She is the author of The Gendered New World Order: Militarism, Development, and the Environment *(1996),* The Web of Violence: From Interpersonal to Global *(1997), and she is the co-editor of* The Women in War Reader *(1999).*

War has profound and unique effects on women. Rather than being separate from women's lives, war making relies on women's participation. However, conventional views of the relationship between gender and war suggest that men make war, women make peace. Men, representing their nations or social groups, combat men of another group, while women remain outside the fighting, protected by "their" men. Women do remain invisible in military policy-making, reflecting taken-for-granted international assumptions about the maleness of war. But both feminist scholarship and empirical reality challenge the prevailing assumptions about war's relationship to men and women.

It is important to examine the many faces of women confronting war: the distinct impact that war has on women due to their gender and the various ways that women respond. We should consider the major debates within this field of study and explore gender inequality as a cause of war.

The Impact of War on Women

Women suffer from war in many ways, including, dying, experiencing sexual abuse and torture, and losing loved ones, homes, and communities. Many people assume that women are unlikely to die in wars, since so few women serve in the armed forces worldwide. (But women, as civilians, are more likely to be killed in war than are soldiers.)

Women as Direct Casualties

War's impact on women has changed with the development of increasingly efficient war-making technologies that make war and militarism more and more deadly. The past century has witnessed the killing of about 104 million people in wars—more than three quarters of all war dead recorded since the year 1500. Most people killed in war are civilians. The advent of high-altitude bombing, more powerful bombs, and a strategy of "total war" in practice has ended the distinction between combatants and civilians as targets of war. While 50 percent of World War II's casualties were civilians, in the 1980s this figure rose to 80 percent, and by 1990 it was a staggering 90 percent. Women and their children continue to be the vast majority of these civilian casualties (Hauchler and Kennedy 1994; Vickers 1993).

These deaths are not randomly distributed throughout the world—most of the wars since the 1960s have taken place in the less-developed countries, particularly in Asia and sub-Saharan Africa. Military intervention, on the other hand, is perpetrated primarily by the former colonial powers, mostly by the United States, followed by Britain and then the USSR/Russia, Belgium, South Africa, and India. In addition to their direct intervention, the United States and former Soviet Union have also exported the most arms to the developing world (Hauchler and Kennedy 1994).

Besides analyzing war through the lens of gender, we must also explore the global intersections between gender and class, race, nation, and ethnicity. Women may be more or less vulnerable to the effects of war and militarization depending on their home society, their economic status, and their racial/ethnic identity. Women in developing countries are most likely to experience war, and most likely to be driven from their homelands (Forbes Martin 1992; Hauchler and Kennedy 1994; Sivard 1996).

Women as War Refugees

Women are also most likely to be uprooted by war. More than four-fifths of war refugees are women and young girls, who also experience additional and often sexualized violence during their flight. By the end of 1992 more than 46 million people had lost their homes; about 36 million of these were women and girls. In Africa there were more than 23.6 million external and internal refugees; more than 12.6 million people fled their homes in the Middle East and in South and Central Asia. There are two million displaced persons in Latin America, and about six million refugees in Europe. About two million people fled the former Yugoslavia (Hauchler and Kennedy 1994).

Refugee women often serve as their children's sole caretakers, as many of them are widows or separated from their spouses and other extended family. They must seek food and safety not only for themselves, but also for their children, who also need health care, housing, and an education. Refugee women in exile are often the supporters of an extended family network, playing a central economic role yet still lacking decision-making power in their societies (Forbes Martin 1992).

Wartime Sexual Violence Against Women

The United Nations High Commissioner for Refugees (UNHCR) cites sexual attacks on women and girls by camp guards as a major problem (Vickers 1993). Even those women and girls stationed in camps and refugee settlements, as well as in new societies of residence, frequently suffer sexual abuse, abduction, and forced prostitution. History has demonstrated the link between war and control of women's sexuality and reproduction through rape, sexual harassment, and militarized prostitution.

Rape. John Tenhula relates the stories of women and children who fled Vietnam by boat and were the subjects of attacks by pirates during their flight. He quotes eyewitnesses of these attacks: "Two of the young and pretty girls were taken to the front of the boat and raped. Everyone heard everything, all of the screams. That is what I remember, the screams. After a while the screams stopped, the crying stopped and there was silence" (1991:69).

But being young and pretty has very little to do with becoming a victim of wartime rape. There are numerous accounts of very old women being brutally raped and murdered. These women, who often have limited mobility and live alone, are especially vulnerable to attack by soldiers.

The torture of political prisoners is also gendered. Women imprisoned for their political activities are commonly raped repeatedly by multiple rapists. In the former Yugoslavia, thousands of Muslim women have been forced into camps and raped by Serbian soldiers, and Muslim and Croat soldiers have also committed mass rapes (Stiglmayer 1994). Rape has been used as a weapon for ethnic cleansing, using attacks on women to humiliate and attempt to exterminate another ethnic group.

The idea that genocide could be accomplished by the mass rape of the women of the enemy's ethnic group derives from a patriarchal definition of ethnicity. The child is thought to inherit the ethnicity of her/his father, implying, for example, that if a Serb soldier rapes a Muslim woman and she becomes pregnant, her child would be a Serb. And because women are viewed as symbols of the family, and the family as the basis of society, the humiliation for women of giving birth to the enemy's children symbolizes the destruction of the community.

Vesna Nikolić-Ristanović has interviewed many refugee women from different ethnic groups in the former Yugoslavia. Those women who became pregnant because of wartime rape expressed anguish over carrying a child who was both their own and the enemy's. This form of psychological torture is incomparable to other forms of wartime torture. In addition, raped women are often stigmatized. Women may be shunned by their own families and communities, viewed as tainted, worthless "property."

The horrifying reports of mass, ethnically defined rape have attracted widespread public attention, but they are not unique to the war in the former Yugoslavia (Rejali 1998). Soviet soldiers raped approximately two million women in eastern Germany in 1945. In 1971 Pakistani soldiers raped more than 200,000 Bengali women in the Bangladesh war of independence (Hauchler and Kennedy 1994). One estimate claims that during the war against Kuwait, Iraqi troops raped as many as 3,200 women between August 1990 and February 1991 (Enloe 1993). The link between rape and war has been ignored by many policymakers and scholars, but feminists have identified wartime rape as symptomatic of war's gendered nature.

Even the United Nations peacekeepers—the multilateral forces sent to protect civilian human rights in war-torn areas—have committed rape and sexual abuse against women and young girls. Such cases have been documented in Mozambique, Somalia, Cambodia, and other regions. This suggests that those trained to fight wars are not best suited to protect the human rights of women and children, and that sexual violence is endemic to military culture.

Attitudes of military personnel often support the sexual abuse of women and girls. When the head of the U.N. mission in Cambodia was questioned about the sexual abuse of women and girls by U.N. troops, he responded that he was "not a puritan: eighteen-year-old, hot-blooded soldiers had a right to drink a few beers and chase after young beautiful things of the opposite sex" (Fetherston 1995:22). And in 1995, when three United States Marines were charged with assaulting and raping a twelve-year-old girl on the Japanese island of Okinawa, the commander of the United States Pacific Command told reporters: "I think it was absolutely stupid, as I've said several times. For the price they paid to rent the car, they could have had a girl" (Enloe 1996:15). In addition to implicitly accepting rape as a part of military life, militaries around the world also support and may even enforce prostitution attached to their military installations.

Prostitution. Wartime prostitution may be either physically forced or economically coerced. During World War II the Japanese military set up brothels in eastern and southern Asia, forcing between 100,000 and 200,000 women into prostitution. Cynthia Enloe has pointed out that prostitution relies not only on the "sex worker" and the "client," but rather involves a whole host of characters, mainly men, who contribute to the creation and maintenance of prostitution as an institution around any military base in the world. It includes husbands and lovers, bar and brothel owners, local public health officials, local police and mayors, national and foreign finance ministry and defense officials, male soldiers in the national, local, and foreign forces, and local civilian male prostitution customers.

Militaries may manage and control the lines of women working as prostitutes by implementing curfews, demanding regular checkups for sexually transmitted diseases, and even regulating which customers they have sex with. During World War II, brothels linked to United States military bases generally had two separate entrances: one for men of color and another for whites (Enloe 1993; Riley 1997).

Because militaries may provide huge infusions of capital into the societies where they establish bases, the local government has an incentive to cooperate with demands for women to have sex with the soldiers, and poor women may have little other choice in order to support themselves and their families.

The prostitutes are often young girls endeavoring to support their families, or women who need to support their children. Stories are told of young girls coming down from the mountain around Subic Bay (the recently closed United States military base in the Philippines) when American military ships pull into the harbor. The girls, from poor rural families, come to serve as prostitutes for American servicemen. And girls who are orphaned by war may be sold into domestic and sexual slavery. In societies where women are valued for their virginity, these girls may be permanent outcasts, trapped in a life of prostitution, and if they live to old age, of poverty.

Wartime Domestic Violence

While battering of women is common in most societies in peacetime, recent research indicates that domestic violence increases in wartime. This suggests a link between gendered violence at the micro and macro levels, and calls for an inquiry into the gendered dynamics of power from the household to the international arena. Among the findings of research conducted through a Belgrade agency for domestic violence are the following: an increase in the number of sons who commit violence against their mothers in wartime; an increase in the number of assaults involving weapons, including pistols, grenades, and other weapons from the war; an increase in violence in marriages where the husband and wife's ethnicity differ; an increase in alcohol consumption among men returning from combat; and a link between economic decline, especially refugee status, and wife battering and rape (Nikolić-Ristanović, 1998).

What wartime conditions would lead to an increase in woman battering and rape within the household? Several factors have been postulated. First, in wartime there is an influx of weapons into societies, and those weapons are often not controlled or limited to battlefield use. Research from both criminology and security studies demonstrates that the presence of weapons increases both the likelihood and lethality of violence. Second, former soldiers or soldiers who have contact with their families have been affected by their experiences in combat. They may be frustrated, nervous, intolerant, and aggressive.

State-produced media propaganda that endorses violence as an acceptable means of conflict resolution, combined with hate propaganda against members of other ethnic groups, may also be related to the escalation of domestic violence in wartime. All of these factors, along with a cultural acceptance of violence against women, even at peacetime, put women at greater risk.

REFERENCES

Enloe, Cynthia. 1993. *The Morning After: Sexual Politics at the End of the Cold War.* Berkeley: University of California Press.

———. 1996. "Spoils of War." *Ms. Magazine,* March/April, p. 15.

Fetherston, A. B. 1995. "U.N. Peacekeepers and Cultures of Violence." *Cultural Survival Quarterly* 19:1, 19–23.

Forbes Martin, Susan. 1992. *Refugee Women*. London: Zed Books.

Hauchler, Ingomar, and Paul M. Kennedy. 1994 *Global Trends*. New York: Continuum Publishers.

Nikolić-Ristanović, Vesna. 1998. "War, Nationalism, and Mothers in the Former Yugoslavia." In Lois Ann Lorentzen and Jennifer Turpin (eds.), *The Women and War Reader*. New York and London: New York University Press.

Rejali, Darius. 1998. "After Feminist Analyses of Bosnian Violence." In Lois Ann Lorentzen and Jennifer Turpin (eds.), *The Women and War Reader*. New York and London: New York University Press.

Riley, Robin. 1997. "Practical Warriors: Gender and Militarism." Paper presented at the American Sociological Association Meetings, August 7–13, Toronto, Canada.

Sivard, Ruth Leger. 1996. *World Military and Social Expenditures*. Washington, DC: World Priorities Institute.

Stiglmayer, Alexandra (ed.). 1994. *Mass Rape: The War against Women in Bosnia-Herzegovina*. Lincoln: University of Nebraska Press.

Tenhula, John. 1991. *Voices from Southeast Asia*. New York: Holmes and Meier.

Vickers, Jeanne. 1991. *Women and the World Economic Crisis*. London: Zed Books.

———. 1993. *Women and War*. London: Zed Brooks.

PERSONAL RESPONSE

War has always seemed like a man's business, but of course it is not. Women and children are necessarily affected. When you think of war victims, what images come to mind? Do your grandparents, or perhaps your parents or other relatives, have any stories that describe the impact of war on their lives and that go beyond what took place on the battlefield?

QUESTIONS FOR CLASS OR SMALL-GROUP DISCUSSION

1. What is the point of looking at war through a gender lens? What details or issues do you begin to take note of?

2. This piece suggests that women are victims of war in more than one way. Summarize the kinds of ways in which women are victims of war-time or military behaviour.

3. In more or less every image we see of soldiers and politicians making decisions about war or planning war, only men are featured. Discuss. What does it mean when women are not involved with this kind of decision-making? If women were involved in issues and politics that had to do with military behaviours, there would not be so much conflict or war. Discuss.

4. Can you think of any war movies in which women play significant roles? What kinds of roles are these? Women should be given the same roles as men in battle/war situations. Discuss.

5. In what ways are women "used" to promote war and the participation of men in war?

6. War is a masculine behaviour. Discuss.

FOR FURTHER VIEWING: WAR AND IMPERIALISM

The Fog of War: Eleven Lessons from the Life of Robert S. McNamara (2003); *Flags of Our Fathers* (2006); *Letters from Iwo Jima* (2006); *All Quiet on the Western Front* (1930); *Catch-22* (1970); *Seven Samurai* (1954); *Platoon* (1986); *Hotel Rwanda* (2004); *Why We Fight* (2005); *Dr. Strangelove or: How I Learned to Stop Worrying and Love the Bomb* (1964); *Shake Hands with the Devil: The Journey of Roméo Dallaire* (2004); *La Grande Illusion* (1937); *Paths of Glory* (1957); *The Burmese Harp* (1956); *The Bridge Over the River Kwai* (1957); *Das Boot* (1981); *Lawrence of Arabia* (1962); *Fahrenheit 9/11* (2004); *Les Bons Débarras* (1980); *Obchod na korze* (1965); *Nanjing 1937* (1995); *Une affaire de femmes* (1988); *The Last King of Scotland* (2006); *Blood Diamond* (2006); *Shooting Dogs* (2005); *The Battle of Algiers* (1965).

PART FOUR

SCIENCE AND TECHNOLOGY

DIGITAL TECHNOLOGY AND THE INTERNET

INTRODUCTION

The following essays cover a wide range of topics, but central to all these essays is the computer, which has effected perhaps the most revolutionary change in human behaviour since the invention of the printing press. How was the computer invented? What is the human story behind this invention? How does an enormous country, such as China—which has a "market-Leninist" economy and an authoritarian state—police the Internet? And what, if any, are the dehumanizing effects of our modern world?

THE WILD WEB OF CHINA

DAVID BARBOZA

David Barboza was a freelance writer and a research assistant for The New York Times *before being hired in 1997 as a staff writer. Since November 2004, he has been a Shanghai-based correspondent writing on art, film, television, and dance for the business and culture sections of* The New York Times. *Barboza covered the Enron scandal and was part of the team that was a finalist for a Pulitzer Prize in 2002.*

SHANGHAI—By some estimates, there are more than 30,000 people patrolling the Web in China, helping to form one of the world's far-reaching Internet filtering systems.

But while China's huge Internet police force is busy deleting annoying phrases like "free speech" and "human rights" from online bulletin boards, specialists say that Wild West capitalism has moved from the real economy in China to the virtual one.

Indeed, the unchecked freedoms that exist on the Web, analysts say, are perhaps unwittingly ushering in an age of startling social change. The Web in China is a thriving marketplace for everyone, including scam artists, snake oil salesmen, and hard-core criminals who are only too eager to turn consumers into victims.

China: Surfing the global economy.
Photo Source: © AFP/Getty Images

Chinese entrepreneurs who started out brazenly selling downloadable pirated music and movies from online storefronts have extended their product lines—peddling drugs and sex, stolen cars, firearms, and even organs for transplanting.

Much of this is happening because Internet use has grown so fast, with 100 million Web surfers in China, second only to the United States. Last year, online revenue—which the government defines more broadly than it is in the United States—was valued at $69 billion, up around 58 percent from the year before, according to a survey by the China Internet Development Research Center.

By 2010, Wall Street analysts say China could have the world's leading online commerce, with revenue coming from advertising, e-commerce and subscription fees, as well as illicit services.

The authorities have vowed to crack down on illegal Web sites and say that more than 2,000 sex and gambling sites have been shut down in recent years. But new sites are eluding them every day.

"It's a wild place," Xiao Qiang, director of the China Internet Project at the graduate journalism school of the University of California, Berkeley, said of China's Web. "Outside of politics, China is as free as anywhere. You can find porn just about anywhere on the Internet."

On any of China's leading search engines, enter sensitive political terms like "Tiananmen Square" or "Falun Gong," and the computer is likely to crash or simply offer a list of censored Web sites. But terms like "hot sex" or "illegal drugs" take users to dozens of links to Web sites allowing them to download sex videos, gain entry to online sports gambling dens, or even make purchases of heroin. The scams are flourishing.

A small sampling recently turned up these sites:

A look-alike Web site pretending to be part of the Industrial and Commercial Bank of China asks visitors to enter their account passwords.

A Web site that calls itself Honest Company specializes in deception—selling bugging devices, machines to produce fake credit cards and tools that rig casino slot machines.

A pornographic Web site asks people to pay $2 a month to download sex videos and chat with other online customers in the nude.

A Web site advertises the sale of gamma hydroxybutyrate, a drug that acts as a relaxant and is thought to reduce inhibitions. Sometimes called a "date rape" drug, it is sold on the Web in China with instructions about how to use it to assault women.

Even the official New China News Agency seems to have gotten into the act. While the top of its news pages carries dispatches like "China Aims to Achieve Balance of Payments in 2006," some at the bottom feature links to soft-porn photographs of Chinese movie stars like Gong Li and Zhou Xun.

"The Internet is a reflection of the real world," says Lu Weigang, an analyst at the China Internet Network Information Center in Beijing. "Everything you have in the real world appears on the Internet."

Countless Web sites peddle police weapons, pepper spray, and even machines to siphon electricity from power lines. Earlier this week, an eBay user in China offered to put up for auction his or her kidney and liver for $100,000. Reached on

Monday, eBay said that selling human organs was forbidden on its site and deleted the entry.

And a Web site called the Patriotic Hacker asserts that an instructor "led and initiated attacks on Japanese Web sites more than 10 times." It says he even managed to shut down the official Web site for the Yasukuni Shrine, dedicated to Japan's World War II military heroes.

There are also Web sites here that sell "miracle drugs" promising to cure cancer or AIDS, sites that say they will create fake government ID cards and some that even promise to break into the national education database to change official records.

Most of the sites are forbidden by law. On paper, the government's Internet regulations forbid the display of any information that damages state security, harms the dignity of the state, promotes pornography and gambling, or "spreads evil cults" and "feudal superstitions."

How does all this get by the Internet patrols in a country where violators risk 3 to 10 years in prison, or in some cases even the death penalty? Analysts say that the growth in the Internet has simply created too many sites to patrol.

"The Chinese government launches campaigns on the Internet to crack down on pornography or the sale of illegal goods once or twice a year, but this is not an efficient way," Lu Weigang at the China Internet Network Information Center said.

In the view of Dali L. Yang, a professor of political science at the University of Chicago: "It's truly remarkable. This is fundamentally a social revolution."

PERSONAL RESPONSE

North Americans generally take Internet freedoms for granted. What would be your reaction if you discovered that the federal government planned to patrol the Internet, controlling, for example, what you could Google? If Chinese citizens object to Internet policing, what are their options? What happens in China to political dissenters?

QUESTIONS FOR CLASS OR SMALL-GROUP DISCUSSION

1. Politically and economically, it is correct for the Chinese government to restrict Internet freedoms in China. Do you agree or disagree with this statement? Use specific examples from the essay or from your own experience to help build your argument.

2. According to Barboza, if you "enter sensitive political terms like 'Tiananmen Square' or 'Falun Gong,'" on the Internet in China, "the computer is likely to crash or simply offer a list of censored Web sites. But terms like 'hot sex' or 'illegal drugs' take users to dozens of links to Web sites allowing them to download sex videos, gain entry to online sports gambling dens, or even make purchases of heroin." Compare this experience to the Internet in North America. Discuss the major differences.

3. The economist Milton Friedman once said that the Internet was the world's greatest force for globalization. Discuss his comment in the context of Barboza's article.

4. Is the Internet a force for bringing diverse people together, or might it also be used to generate conflict and to exploit differences?

CODE-BREAKER

JIM HOLT

Jim Holt has written on science, ethics, and philosophy for Slate, The New York Times Magazine, *and* The New Yorker. *He has also hosted a radio show for BBC Wales.*

On June 8, 1954, Alan Turing, a forty-one-year-old research scientist at Manchester University, was found dead by his housekeeper. Before getting into bed the night before, he had taken a few bites out of an apple that was, apparently, laced with cyanide. At an inquest, a few days later, his death was ruled a suicide. Turing was, by necessity rather than by inclination, a man of secrets. One of his secrets had been exposed two years before his death, when he was convicted of "gross indecency" for having a homosexual affair. Another, however, had not yet come to light. It was Turing who was chiefly responsible for breaking the German Enigma code during the Second World War, an achievement that helped save Britain from defeat in the dark days of 1941. Had this been publicly known, he would have been acclaimed a national hero. But the existence of the British code-breaking effort remained closely guarded even after the end of the war; the relevant documents weren't declassified until the nineteen-seventies. And it wasn't until the eighties that Turing got the credit he deserved for a second, and equally formidable, achievement: creating the blueprint for the modern computer.

It is natural to view Turing as a gay martyr, hounded to death for his sexuality despite his great service to humanity. But it is also tempting to speculate about whether he really was a suicide. The flight to Moscow, in 1951, of Guy Burgess and Donald Maclean, British diplomats and rumored lovers who had been covertly working for the Soviets, prompted one London newspaper to editorialize that Britain should adopt the American policy of "weeding out both sexual and political perverts." Turing's role in wartime code-breaking had left him with an intimate knowledge of British intelligence. After his conviction for homosexuality, he may have seemed out of control. He began travelling abroad in search of sex, visiting countries bordering on the Eastern bloc. The coroner at his inquest knew none of this. No one tested the apple found by his bedside for cyanide.

The possibility of clandestine assassination is hinted by the title of David Leavitt's short biography, "The Man Who Knew Too Much: Alan Turing and the Invention of the Computer" (Norton/Atlas; $22.95), borrowed from the Hitchcock thriller. Leavitt, the author of several novels and short-story collections with gay

Alan Turing: Scientist? Victim? Enigma?
Photo Source: NPG x82217 Alan Mathison Turing by Elliott & Fry quarter-plate glass negative, 29 March
1951 National Portrait Gallery, London

protagonists, rings the gay-martyr theme in the book's opening pages by invoking
another film classic, "The Man in the White Suit." In that 1951 comedy, which
Leavitt reads as a gay allegory, a scientist is chased by a mob that feels threatened

by a miraculous invention of his. Then a third film is mentioned, one that evidently made an impression on Turing: the 1937 Disney animation "Snow White and the Seven Dwarfs." Those who knew him said that he was particularly fond of chanting the witch's couplet, "Dip the apple in the brew, / Let the sleeping death seep through." So we're prepared for a life story that, though steeped in logic and mathematics, is part mystery, part parable of sexual politics, part fairy tale.

Alan Mathison Turing was conceived in India, where his father worked in the Indian civil service, and born in 1912 during a visit by his parents to London. Instead of taking their child back to the East, they sent him to live with a retired Army couple in a seaside English town. Alan was a good-looking boy, dreamy, rather clumsy, hopelessly untidy, and not very popular with his classmates. The loneliness of his childhood was finally dispelled when, in his early teens, he met another boy who shared his passion for science. They became inseparable friends, exploring esoterica like Einstein's relativity theory together. When, a year later, the boy died of tuberculosis, Turing seems to have been left with an ideal of romantic love that he spent the rest of his life trying to duplicate.

In 1931, Turing entered Cambridge. His college, King's, "had a very 'gay' reputation," Leavitt notes, and was known for its links to the Bloomsbury group. Turing's unworldliness kept him apart from the aesthetic set; he preferred the more Spartan pleasures of rowing and long-distance running. But Cambridge also had a rich scientific culture, and Turing's talents flourished in it. With the backing of John Maynard Keynes, he was elected a Fellow of King's College in 1935, at the age of twenty-two. When the news reached his old school, the boys celebrated with a clerihew: "Turing / Must have been alluring / To get made a don / So early on." With a stipend, no duties, and High Table dining privileges, he was free to follow his intellectual fancy. That spring, attending lectures in the foundations of mathematics, he was introduced to a deep and unresolved matter known as the "decision problem." A few months later, during one of his habitual runs, he lay down in a meadow and conceived a sort of abstract machine that settled it in an unexpected way.

The decision problem asks, in essence, whether reasoning can be reduced to computation. That was the dream of the seventeenth-century philosopher Gottfried von Leibniz, who imagined a calculus of reason that would permit disagreements to be resolved by taking pen in hand and saying, *Calculemus*—"Let us calculate." Suppose, that is, you have a set of premises and a putative conclusion. Is there some automatic procedure for deciding whether the former entails the latter? Can you determine, in principle, whether a conjecture can be proved true or false? The decision problem calls for a mechanical set of rules for deciding whether such an inference is valid, one that is guaranteed to yield a yes-or-no answer in a finite amount of time. Such a method would be particularly useful to mathematicians, since it would allow them to resolve many of the conundrums in their field—like Fermat's last theorem, or Goldbach's conjecture—by brute force. That is why David Hilbert, who in 1928 challenged the mathematical community to solve the decision problem, called it "the principal problem of mathematical logic."

Turing began by thinking about what happens when a human carries out a computation by means of a pencil, a scratch pad, and a set of mindless instructions. By ruthlessly paring away inessential details, he arrived at an idealized machine that, he was convinced, captured the essence of the process. The machine was somewhat homely in conception: it consists of an unending tape divided into squares (rather like an infinite strip of toilet paper). Over this tape a little scanner travels back and forth, one square at a time, writing and erasing 0's and 1's. The scanner's action at any moment depends on the symbol in the square it is over and the state it is in—its "state of mind," so to speak. There are only a finite number of states, and the way they link up what the scanner sees to what it does constitutes the machine's program. (A typical line in a program would be something like "When the machine is in state A scanning 0, it will replace 0 by 1, move one square to the left, and then go into state B.")

Turing was able to do some amazing things with his abstract devices, which soon became known as "Turing machines." Despite their simple design, he showed, they could be made to perform all sorts of complicated mathematics. Each machine's functioning, moreover, could be encapsulated in a single number (typically, a very long one), so that one machine could be made to operate on another by putting the number of the second machine on the tape of the first. If a machine were fed its own number, then it could operate on itself. Turing was thereby able to exploit something akin to the paradoxes of self-reference ("I am lying") and show that certain sorts of Turing machines could not exist. For instance, there could be no Turing machine that, when fed with the program number of another machine, would decide whether that machine would eventually come to a halt in its computation or would grind on forever. (If there were such a machine, it could be tweaked into a Hamlet-like variant that would decide, in effect, "I will come to a halt if and only if I never come to a halt.") But the halting problem, it turned out, was merely the decision problem in disguise. Turing was able to prove that no computing machine of the kind he envisaged could solve the decision problem. Reasoning could not be reduced to computation after all.

But the death of Leibniz's dream turned out to be the birth of the computer age. The boldest idea to emerge from Turing's analysis was that of a *universal* Turing machine: one that, when furnished with the number describing the mechanism of any particular Turing machine, would perfectly mimic its behavior. In effect, the "hardware" of a special-purpose computer could be translated into "software" and then entered like data into the universal machine, where it would be run as a program—the way, for example, the operating system on your laptop treats a word-processing program as data. What Turing had invented, as a by-product of his advance in logic, was the stored-program computer.

Turing was twenty-three when he dispatched the decision problem. Just as he was finishing his work, discouraging news reached Cambridge from across the Atlantic: a Princeton logician named Alonzo Church had beaten him to the punch. Unlike Turing, however, Church did not arrive at the idea of a universal computing machine; instead, he used a far more arcane construction known as the "lambda calculus." Still, Turing decided that he might profit from studying with the more established logician. So he made his way to America, crossing the Atlantic in steerage and arriving in New York, where, he wrote to his mother, "I had to go through the ceremony of initiation to the U.S.A., consisting of being swindled by a taxi-driver."

At Princeton, Turing took the first steps toward building a working model of his imaginary computer, pondering how to realize its logical design in a network of relay-operated switches; he even managed to get into a machine shop in the physics department and construct some of the relays himself. In addition to his studies with Church, he also had dealings with the formidable John von Neumann, who would later be credited with innovations in computer architecture that Turing himself had pioneered. On the social side, he found the straightforward manners of Americans congenial, with certain exceptions: "Whenever you thank them for anything, they say 'You're welcome.' I rather liked it at first, thinking I was welcome, but now I find it comes back like a ball thrown against a wall, and become positively apprehensive. Another habit they have is to make the sound described by authors as 'Aha.' They use it when they have no suitable reply to a remark."

In 1938, Turing was awarded a Ph.D. in mathematics by Princeton, and, despite the urgings of his father, who worried about imminent war with Germany, decided to return to Britain. Back at Cambridge, he became a regular at Ludwig Wittgenstein's seminar on the foundations of mathematics. Turing and Wittgenstein were remarkably alike: solitary, ascetic, homosexual, drawn to fundamental questions. But they disagreed sharply on philosophical matters, like the relationship between logic and ordinary life. "No one has ever yet got into trouble from a contradiction in logic," Wittgenstein insisted. To which Turing's response was "The real harm will not come in unless there is an application, in which case a bridge may fall down." Before long, Turing would himself demonstrate that contradictions could indeed have life-or-death consequences.

On September 1, 1939, Nazi troops invaded Poland. Three days later, Turing reported to Bletchley Park, a Victorian Tudor-Gothic estate northwest of London where the British cipher service had secretly relocated. He and the other code-breakers arrived at Bletchley under the guise of "Captain Ridley's Shooting Party" (which had some locals grumbling about able-bodied men not doing their bit in the war). The task they faced was daunting. Since the use of radio communications in the First World War, effective cryptography—insuring that private messages could be sent via a public medium—had been critical to the military. The Nazis were convinced that their encryption system—based on a machine that looked like a souped-up typewriter, called the Enigma—would play a vital role in their expected victory.

The Enigma, invented for commercial use in 1918 and soon adopted by the German military, had an alphabetic keyboard and, next to that, a set of twenty-six little lamps, one for each letter. When a letter on the keyboard was pressed, a different letter on the lampboard would light up. If you typed the letters "d-o-g," the letters "r-l-u" might light up on the lampboard. When "rlu" was sent out in Morse code by a radio operator, a recipient would pick it up, type it on the keyboard of his Enigma machine, and the letters "d-o-g" would light up on the lampboard—so long as the settings of the two machines were the same. And that is where things get interesting. Inside the Enigma were a number of rotating wheels that determined the match between entered and coded letters; each time a letter was typed, one of the wheels would turn, altering the wiring. (Thus, if you typed "g-g-g," the coded version might be "q-d-a.") The military version of the Enigma also had something called a "plugboard," by which the connections between letters could be further scrambled. The settings of the wheels and the plugboard were changed each day at midnight. And further layers of complexity were added, increasing the number of possible keys to something like a hundred and fifty quintillion.

The most impenetrable communications were those of the German Navy, which used the Enigma machine with special cunning and discipline. By early 1941, Germany's growing U-boat fleet was devastating British shipping, sinking around sixty ships a month. Unlike Germany, Britain was almost completely reliant on the sea-lanes for sustenance. Unless some counter-strategy could be found, the British Isles faced being starved into submission. When Turing arrived at Bletchley Park, no work was being done on the naval Enigma, which many considered to be unbreakable. Indeed, it has been said, there were only two people who thought the Enigma could be broken: Frank Birch, the head of Bletchley's naval-intelligence division, because it *had* to be broken; and Alan Turing, because it was an interesting problem.

Taking on the naval Enigma, Turing soon detected a weakness. A coded naval message would frequently contain formulaic bits, like WETTER FUER DIE NACHT ("weather for the night"), that might be guessed at. Such a "crib," he realized, could be exploited to yield logical chains, each of which corresponded to billions of possible Enigma settings. When one of these chains led to a contradiction, the billions of settings to which it corresponded could be ruled out. Now the problem was reduced to checking millions of logical chains—daunting, to be sure, but not impossible. Turing set about devising a machine that would automate the search for logical consistency, eliminating contradictory chains rapidly enough for the codebreakers to deduce that day's Enigma settings before the intelligence became stale. The result was the size of several refrigerators, with dozens of rotating drums (which mimicked the Enigma wheels) and massive coils of colored wire suggesting a Fair Isle sweater. In operation, it sounded like thousands of knitting needles clattering away, as its relay switches checked one logical chain after another. In a nod to an earlier, Polish code-breaking machine, which made an ominous ticking sound, the people at Bletchley called the thing a Bombe.

On a good day, a Bombe could yield that day's Enigma key in as little as an hour, and, by 1941, eighteen Bombes were up and running. With the Nazi naval communications rendered transparent, the British could pinpoint the position of the U-boats, steering convoys safely around them and, taking the offensive, sending destroyers to sink them. Even as the Battle of the Atlantic began to shift, the German High Command refused to believe that the Enigma could have been broken, suspecting instead espionage and treachery.

As the Enigma evolved, Turing continued to devise new strategies to defeat it. Known at Bletchley as the Prof, Turing was famed for his harmless eccentricities, like keeping his tea mug chained to the radiator and wearing a gas mask as he rode his bicycle to work (it helped to alleviate his hay fever). He impressed his colleagues as a friendly, approachable genius, always willing to explain his ideas, and he became especially close to a woman he worked with, playing what he called "sleepy chess" with her after their night-shift code-breaking. Having convinced himself that he was in love with her, he proposed marriage, and was eagerly accepted, even after he divulged his "homosexual tendencies" to her. But he later decided it wouldn't work and broke off the engagement. It seems to have been the only time in his life that he contemplated a heterosexual relationship.

By 1942, Turing had mastered most of the theoretical problems posed by the Enigma. Now that the United States was ready to throw its vast resources into the code-breaking effort, he was dispatched as a liaison to Washington, where he helped the Americans get their own Bombe-making and Enigma-monitoring under way. Then he headed to New York, where he was to work on another top-secret project, involving the encryption of speech, at Bell Laboratories, which were then situated near the piers in Greenwich Village. While at Bell Labs, he became engrossed with a question that came to occupy his postwar work: was it possible to build an artificial brain? On one occasion, Turing stunned the entire executive mess at Bell Labs into silence by announcing, in a typically clarion tone, "I'm not interested in developing *a powerful* brain. All I'm after is just a *mediocre* brain, something like the president of the American Telephone and Telegraph Company."

Turing's early work had raised a fascinating possibility: perhaps the human brain is something like a universal Turing machine. Of course, the brain looks more like cold porridge than like a machine. But Turing suspected that what made the brain capable of thought was its logical structure, not its physical embodiment. Building a universal Turing machine might thus be the way to erase the line between the mechanical and the intelligent.

In 1945, Turing wrote up a plan for building a computer which contained every-thing from the abstract structure down to the circuit diagrams and a cost estimate of eleven thousand two hundred pounds. At Britain's National Physical Laboratory, where he worked after the war, he had nothing like the resources of the Americans, and yet he rose to the challenge posed by his straitened circumstances. When it came to the computer's memory, for example, the most obvious storage device was one in which the data took the form of vibrations in liquid mercury. But Turing reckoned that gin would be just as effective, and far cheaper. On one occasion, he noticed a drainpipe lying in a field and had a colleague help him drag it back to the laboratory for use in his computer hardware. Frustrated with the inept administration at the N.P.L., he finally accepted an offer to direct the development of a computer prototype at Manchester University. Arriving in that grim Northern industrial city at the age of thirty-six, he found it "mucky" and noted that the Mancunian male wasn't much to look at.

Despite his immersion in engineering details, Turing's fascination with com-puting was essentially philosophical. "I am more interested in the possibility of producing models of the action of the brain than in the practical applications of computing," he wrote to a friend. Turing conjectured that, initially, at least, com-puters might be suited to purely symbolic tasks, those presupposing no "contact with the outside world," like mathematics, cryptanalysis, and chess-playing (for which he himself worked out the first programs on paper). But he imagined a day when a machine could simulate human mental abilities so well as to raise the question of whether it was actually capable of thought. In a paper published in the philosophy journal *Mind,* he proposed the now classic "Turing test": a computer could be said to be intelligent if it could fool an interrogator—perhaps in the course of a dialogue conducted via teletype—into thinking it was a human being. Turing argued that the only way to know that other people are conscious is by comparing their behavior to one's own, and that there is no reason to treat machines any differently.

To Leavitt, the idea of a computer mimicking a human inevitably suggests that of a gay man "passing" as straight. Here and elsewhere, he shows a rather overdeveloped ability to detect psychosexual significance. (When, in the *Mind* paper, Turing writes of certain human abilities that it is hard to imagine a machine developing, like the ability to "enjoy strawberries and cream," Leavitt sees a "code word for tastes that Turing prefers not to name.") But the book does succeed, on the whole, in giving a poignant depiction of Turing the man. And the bar was set pretty high. Two decades ago, a mathematician named Andrew Hodges published "Alan Turing: The Enigma," which is one of the finest scientific biographies ever written, and has remained an essential resource for all subsequent accounts of Turing's life. In 1987, Hugh Whitemore's superb play about Turing, "Breaking the Code," opened on Broadway, with Derek Jacobi in the starring role. Both of these works not only captured the pathos of Turing's life; they also gave a lucid account of his technical achievement. (Whitemore's play miraculously compressed the decision problem and the Enigma decoding into a couple of brief speeches without any real distortion.)

It is on the technical side that Leavitt falls short. His exposition, full of the sort of excess detail that mathematicians call "hair," is marred by confusions and errors. In trying to describe how Turing resolved the decision problem, Leavitt gets wrong the central idea of a "computable number." Discussing the earlier logical work of Kurt Gödel, Leavitt says that it established that the axiomatic system of Bertrand Russell and Alfred North Whitehead's "Principia Mathematica" was "inconsistent," when Gödel proved no such thing, and a definition of something called Skewes number is precisely backward. Although Leavitt seems to have made a valiant attempt to master this material in preparation for writing the book, his explanatory efforts will leave initiates irritable and beginners perplexed.

Turing lived for the remainder of his life in Manchester. He bought a small house in a suburb and bicycled the ten miles to the university each day, donning a slightly ludicrous yellow oilskin and hat when it rained. Although nominally the deputy director of the computing laboratory (which developed the world's first commercially available electronic computer), he also took on a fundamental mystery in biology: how is it that living things, which start out as a cluster of identical cells, eventually grow into the variety of different forms found in nature? Working out systems of equations to model this process of morphogenesis, he used the prototype computer to find solutions; seated at the console, using the machine's manual controls, Turing looked, in the words of one colleague, as if he were "playing the organ."

Shortly before Christmas, 1951, Turing was walking along Oxford Street in Manchester when his eye was caught by a nineteen-year-old working-class youth named Arnold Murray. The encounter turned into an affair of sorts, with Murray coming to Turing's house on several occasions, having dinner with him, and then spending the night. A month later, Turing was invited by the BBC to take part in a radio debate on the question "Can Automatic Calculating Machines Be Said to Think?" (He had already received some rather breathless publicity on his ideas about artificial intelligence from the British papers.) On one of the days that the program aired, Turing came home to find that his house had been burglarized. The burglar, as he suspected, was an associate of Murray's who was confident that a homosexual would never go to the police. But Turing did go to the police. After some initial dissembling about how he came by his information about the culprit's identity, Turing volunteered the details of his affair to the startled detectives. Turing was charged, under the same 1885 act that led to the prosecution of Oscar Wilde, with "gross indecency." This crime was punishable by up to two years' imprisonment, but the judge, taking into account Turing's intellectual distinction (though knowing nothing of his activities during the war), sentenced him to probation, on the condition that he "submit for treatment by a duly qualified medical practitioner."

The treatment of choice was hormonal. Earlier, American researchers had tried to convert gay men to heterosexuality by injecting them with male hormones, on the theory that they suffered from a masculinity deficit; surprisingly, this only seemed to intensify their homosexual drive. So the opposite approach was tried. By giving homosexuals large doses of female hormones, it was found, their libido could be destroyed in as little as a month. This chemical castration had the side effect of causing temporary breast enlargement, as Turing found to his humiliation, and his lean runner's body took on fat.

The news of Turing's conviction received no national attention. The reaction of his mother, to whom he had grown close over the years, was one of affectionate exasperation. His lab colleagues dismissed it all as "typical Turing." With his criminal record of "moral turpitude," he was barred from the United States. But, once his probation ended, in April of 1953, and the effects of the hormone regimen wore off, he travelled to Europe for romantic liaisons. His position at Manchester was secure: the university created a special Readership in the Theory of Computing for him, which came with a pay raise. He was free to continue with his work on mathematical biology and artificial intelligence, and he enjoyed the growing talk among logicians of "Turing machines."

Why, then, more than two years after the trial, and more than a year after the hormone treatment ended, would he have committed suicide? Leavitt describes Turing's life after his arrest as "a slow, sad descent into grief and madness." That's overly dramatic. Turing did start seeing a Jungian analyst and developed a taste for Tolstoy, but neither is an infallible sign of madness. He also, a few months before his death, sent a friend a series of postcards containing eight "messages from the unseen world." Some were terse aphorisms: "Science is a differential Equation. Religion is a Boundary Condition." Others had a Blakean cast: "Hyperboloids of wondrous Light / Rolling for aye through Space and Time / Harbour those Waves which somehow might / Play out God's wondrous pantomime." Well, it does rhyme.

Turing's death, as Leavitt also notes, occurred in a period of acute anxiety about spies and homosexuals and Soviet entrapment. That week, newspapers announced that the former head of Los Alamos, Robert Oppenheimer, had been judged a security risk. And, as Andrew Hodges wrote, "Had the headline been 'ATOMIC SCIENTIST FOUND DEAD,' the questions would have been immediate and public."

Still, Leavitt concedes that there is no evidence that the death of the Man Who Knew Too Much was anything other than a suicide. Indeed, the only person who seems to have had doubts was Turing's mother, who insisted that her son must have accidentally ingested something from one of the chemical experiments he conducted at home. Turing was rather sloppy, and he was known to eat an apple every night before going to bed. On the other hand, he once wrote a letter to a friend mentioning a method of suicide that "involved an apple and electric wiring."

Was Turing's death a kind of martyrdom? Was it the perfect suicide—one that deceived the person whose feelings he cared most about, his mother—or, more improbably, the perfect murder? Leavitt is the latest to broach these questions without resolving them. Perhaps, he imagines at the end of his book, the message Turing wanted to convey is one that has so far been overlooked: "In the fairy tale the apple into which Snow White bites doesn't kill her; it puts her to sleep until the Prince wakes her up with a kiss." This note of macabre camp doesn't suit a man who eschewed all forms of egoistic fuss as he solved the most important logic problem of his time, saved countless lives by defeating a Nazi code, conceived the computer, and rethought how mind arises from matter.

PERSONAL RESPONSE

Alan Turing broke the German Enigma code in World War Two and created the blueprint for the modern computer. What kind of person do you imagine Turing was?

QUESTIONS FOR CLASS OR SMALL-GROUP DISCUSSION

1. Why does Holt begin his essay with the image of the cyanide-laced apple? In the first paragraph, he mentions the apple, gross indecency, the German Enigma code, and the modern computer. In your opinion, do these terms grab the reader's interest, or should Holt have introduced his subject in another way?
2. Holt describes the medical treatments Turing underwent following his charge of gross indecency. Describe these medical treatments and compare the attitudes toward sexual orientation in the 1950s with contemporary views toward lesbians, gay men, and people who are bisexual.
3. Is this story compelling or interesting? Why or why not? Would it make a good movie? Why or why not?
4. What kind of person was Turing? Was he a hero or a victim? Why?
5. Do you think Turing was today's equivalent of a hacker genius? Explain.

DINING WITH ROBOTS

ELLEN ULLMAN

Ellen Ullman is the author of Close to the Machine *(1997), a memoir about her twenty years of experience as a software engineer. Her essays have appeared in* Harper's, Salon, Wired, *and* The New York Times.

On the first day of the first programming course I ever took, the instructor compared computer programming to creating a recipe. I remember he used the example of baking a cake. First you list the ingredients you'll need—flour, eggs, sugar, butter, yeast—and these, he said, are like the machine resources the program will need in order to run. Then you describe, in sequence, in clear declarative language, the steps you have to perform to turn those ingredients into a cake. Step one: Preheat the oven. Two: Sift together dry ingredients. Three: Beat the eggs. Along the way were decisions he likened to the if/then/else branches of a program: If using a counter-top electric mixer, then beat three minutes; else if using a hand electric mixer, then beat four; else beat five. And there was a reference he described as a sort of subroutine: Go to page 117 for details about varieties of yeast (with "return here" implied). He even drew a flow chart that took the recipe all the way through to the end. Let cool, slice, serve.

I remember nothing, however, about the particulars of the cake itself. Was it angel food? Chocolate? Layered? Frosted? At the time, 1979 or 1980, I had been working as a programmer for more than a year, self-taught, and had yet to cook anything more complicated than poached eggs. So I knew a great deal more about coding than about cakes. It didn't occur to me to question the usefulness of comparing something humans absolutely must do to something machines never do: that is, eat.

In fact, I didn't think seriously about the analogy for another twenty-five years, not until a blustery fall day in San Francisco, when I was confronted with a certain filet of beef. By then I had learned to cook. (It was that or a life of programmer food: pizza, takeout, whatever's stocked in the vending machines.) And the person responsible for the beef encounter was a man named Joe, of Potter Family Farms, who was selling "home-raised and butchered" meat out of a stall in the newly renovated Ferry Building food hall.

The hall, with its soaring, arched windows, is a veritable church of food. The sellers are small, local producers; everything is organic, natural, free-range; the "baby lettuces" are so young one should perhaps call them "fetal"—it's that sort of place. Before shopping, it helps to have a glass of wine, as I had, to prepare yourself for the gasping shock of the prices. Sitting at a counter overlooking the bay, watching ships and ferries ply the choppy waters, I'd sipped down a nice Pinot Grigio, which had left me with lowered sales resistance by the time I wandered over to the Potter Farms meat stall. There Joe greeted me and held out for inspection a large filet—"a beauty," he said. He was not at all moved by my remonstrations that I eat meat but rarely cook it. He stood there as a man who had—personally—fed, slaughtered, and butchered this cow, and all for me, it seemed. I took home the beef.

I don't know what to do with red meat. There is something appalling about meat's sheer corporeality—meat meals are called *fleishidich* in Yiddish, a word that doesn't let you forget that what you are eating is *flesh*. So for help I turned to *The Art of French Cooking*, Volume I, the cookbook Julia Child wrote with Louisette Bertholle and Simone Beck. I had bought this book when I first decided I would learn to cook. But I hadn't been ready for it then. I was scared off by the drawings of steer sides lanced for sirloins, porterhouses, and T-bones. And then there was all that talk of blanching, deglazing, and making a roux. But I had stayed with it, spurred on by my childhood memories of coming across Julia on her TV cooking show, when I'd be zooming around the dial early on weekend mornings and be stopped short at the sight of this big woman taking whacks at red lumps of meat. It was the physicality of her cooking that caught me, something animal and finger-painting-gleeful in her engagement with food.

And now, as rain hatched the windows, I came upon a recipe that Julia and her coauthors introduced as follows:

Sauté de Boeuf à La Parisienne
[Beef Sauté with Cream and Mushroom Sauce]

This sauté of beef is good to know about if you have to entertain important guests in a hurry. It consists of small pieces of filet sautéed quickly to a nice brown outside and a rosy center, and served in a sauce. In the variations at the end of the recipe, all the sauce ingredients may be prepared in advance. If the whole dish is cooked ahead of time, be very careful indeed in its reheating that the beef does not overcook. The cream and mushroom sauce here is a French version of beef Stroganoff, but less tricky as it uses fresh rather than sour cream, so you will not run into the problem of curdled sauce.

Serve the beef in a casserole, or on a platter surrounded with steamed rice, *risotto*, or potato balls sautéed in butter. Buttered green peas or beans could accompany it, and a good red Bordeaux wine.

And it was right then, just after reading the words "a good red Bordeaux wine," that the programming class came back to me: the instructor at the board with his flow chart, his orderly procedural steps, the if/then decision branches, the subroutines, all leading to the final "let cool, slice, serve." And I knew in that moment that my long-ago instructor, like my young self, had been laughably clueless about the whole subject of cooking food.

If you have to entertain important guests.

A nice brown outside.

Rosy center.

Stroganoff.

Curdled.

Risotto.

Potato balls in butter.

A good red Bordeaux.

I tried to imagine the program one might write for this recipe. And immediately each of these phrases exploded in my mind. How to tell a computer what "important guests" are? And how would you explain what it means to "have to" serve them dinner (never mind the yawning depths of "entertain")? A "nice brown," a "rosy center:"; you'd have to have a mouth and eyes to know what these mean, no matter how well you might translate them into temperatures. And what to do about "Stroganoff," which is not just a sauce but a noble family, a name that opens a chain of association that catapults the human mind across seven centuries of Russian history? I forced myself to abandon that line of thought and stay in the smaller realm of sauces made with cream, but this inadvertently opened up the entire subject of the chemistry of lactic proteins, and why milk curdles. Then I wondered how to explain "risotto": the special short-grained rice, the select regions on earth where it grows, opening up endlessly into questions of agriculture, its arrival among humans, the way it changed the earth. Next came the story of potatoes, that Inca food, the brutalities through which it arrives on a particular plate before a particular woman in Europe, before our eponymous Parisienne: how it is converted into a little round ball, and then, of course, buttered. (Then, lord help me, this brought up the whole subject of the French and butter, and how can they possibly get away with eating so much of it?)

But all of this was nothing compared to the cataclysm created by "a good red Bordeaux."

The program of this recipe expanded infinitely. Subroutine opened from subroutine, association led to exploding association. It seemed absurd even to think of describing all this to a machine. The filet, a beauty, was waiting for me.

Right around the time my programming teacher was comparing coding to cakemaking, computer scientists were finding themselves stymied in their quest to create intelligent machines. Almost from the moment computers came into existence, researchers believed that the machines could be made to think. And for the next thirty or so years, their work proceeded with great hope and enthusiasm. In 1967 the influential MIT computer scientist Marvin Minsky declared, "Within a generation the problem of creating 'artificial intelligence' will be substantially solved." But by 1982 he was less sanguine about the prospects, saying, "The AI problem is one of the hardest science has ever undertaken."

Computer scientists had been trying to teach the computer what human beings know about themselves and the world. They wanted to create inside the machine a sort of mirror of our existence, but in a form a computer could manipulate: abstract, symbolic, organized according to one theory or another of how human knowledge is structured in the brain. Variously called "micro worlds," "problem spaces," "knowledge representations," "classes," and "frames," these abstract universes contained systematized arrangements of facts, along with rules for operating upon those— theoretically all that a machine would need to become intelligent. Although it wasn't characterized as such at the time, this quest for a symbolic representation of reality was oddly Platonic in motive, a computer scientist's idea of the pure, unchanging forms that lie behind the jumble of the physical world.

But researchers eventually found themselves in a position like mine when trying to imagine the computer program for my *boeuf à la Parisienne:* the network of associations between one thing and the next simply exploded. The world, the actual world we inhabit, showed itself to be too marvelously varied, too ragged, too linked and interconnected, to be sorted into any set of frames or classes or problem spaces. What we hold in our minds is not abstract, it turned out, not an ideal reflection of existence, but something inseparable from our embodied experience of moving about in a complicated world.

Hubert L. Dreyfus, a philosopher and early critic of artificial intelligence research, explained the problem with the example of a simple object like a chair.

He pointed out the futility of trying to create a symbolic representation of a chair to a computer, which had neither a body to sit in it nor a social context in which to use it. "Chairs would not be equipment for sitting if our knees bent backwards like those of flamingoes, or if we had no tables, as in traditional Japan or the Australian bush," he wrote in his 1979 book *What Computers Can't Do*. Letting flow the myriad associations that radiate from the word *chair*, Dreyfus went on:

> Anyone in our culture understands such things as how to sit on kitchen chairs, swivel chairs, folding chairs; and in arm chairs, rocking chairs, deck chairs, barber's chairs, sedan chairs, dentist's chairs, basket chairs, reclining chairs . . . since there seems to be an indefinitely large variety of chairs and of successful (graceful, comfortable, secure, poised, etc.) ways to sit in them. Moreover, understanding chairs also includes social skills such as being able to sit appropriately (sedately, demurely, naturally, casually, sloppily, provocatively, etc.) at dinners, interviews, desk jobs, lectures, audiences, concerts. . . .

At dinners where one has to entertain important guests . . . at the last minute . . . serving them beef in a French version of Stroganoff . . . with buttered potatoes . . . and a good red Bordeaux.

Several weeks after making Julia's *boeuf*, I was assembling twelve chairs (dining chairs, folding chairs, desk chair) around the dining table, and I was thinking not of Dreyfus but of my mother. In her younger days, my mother had given lavish dinner parties, and it was she who had insisted, indeed commanded, that I have all the necessary equipment for the sort of sit-down dinner I was giving that night. I surveyed the fancy wedding-gift stainless she had persuaded me to register for ("or else you'll get a lot of junk," she said), the Riedel wine glasses, also gifts, and finally the set of china she had given me after my father's death, when she sold their small summer house—"the country dishes" is how I think of them, each one hand-painted in a simple design, blue cornflowers on white.

It wasn't until I started setting the table, beginning with the forks, that I thought of Dreyfus. Salad forks, fish forks, crab forks, entrée forks, dessert forks— at that moment it occurred to me that the paradigm for an intelligent machine had changed, but what remained was the knotty problem of teaching a computer what it needed to know to achieve sentience. In the years since Dreyfus wrote his book, computer scientists had given up on the idea of intelligence as a purely abstract proposition—a knowledge base and a set of rules to operate upon it—and were now building what are called social robots, machines with faces and facial expressions, who are designed to learn about the world the way human beings do: by interacting with other human beings. Instead of being born with a universe already inscribed inside them, these social machines will start life with only basic knowledge and skills. Armed with cute faces and adorable expressions, like babies, they must inspire humans to teach them about the world. And in the spirit of Dreyfus, I asked myself: If such a robot were coming to dinner, how could I, as a good human hostess and teacher, explain everything I would be placing before it tonight?

Besides the multiple forks, there will be an armory of knives: salad knife, fish knife, bread knife, dessert knife. We'll have soup spoons and little caviar spoons made of bone, tea spoons, tiny demitasse spoons, and finally the shovel-shaped ice-cream spoons you can get only in Germany—why it is that only Germans recognize the need for this special ice cream implement? My robot guest could learn in an instant the name and shape and purpose of every piece of silverware, I thought: it would instantly understand the need for bone with caviar because metal reacts chemically with roe. But its mouth isn't functional; the mouth-part is there only to make us humans feel more at ease; my robot guest doesn't eat. So how will it understand the complicated interplay of implement, food, and mouth—how each tool is designed to hold, present, complement the intended fish or vegetable, liquid or grain? And the way each forkful or spoonful finds its perfectly dimensioned way into the moist readiness of the mouth, where the experience evanesces (one hopes) into the delight of taste?

And then there will be the wine glasses: the flutes of champagne, the shorter ones for white wine, the pregnant Burgundy glasses, the large ones for Cabernet blends. How could I tell a machine about the reasons for these different glasses, the way they cup the wine, shape the smell, and deliver it to the human nose? And how to explain wine at all? You could spend the rest of your life tasting wine and still not exhaust its variations, each bottle a little ecosystem of grapes and soils and weather, yeast and bacteria, barrels of wood from trees with their own soil and weather, the variables cross-multiplying until each glassful approaches a singularity, a moment in time on earth. Can a creature that does not drink or taste understand this pleasure? A good red Bordeaux!

I went to the hutch to get out the china. I had to move aside some of the pieces I never use: the pedestaled cigarette holders, the little ashtrays, the relish tray for the carrots, celery, and olives it was once de rigueur to put on the table. Then I came to the coffeepot, whose original purpose was not to brew coffee—that would have been done in a percolator—but to serve it. I remembered my presiding over the many dinners she had given, the moment when the table was scraped clean of crumbs and set for dessert, the coffee cups and saucers stacked beside her as she poured out each cup and passed it down the line. Women used to serve coffee at table, I thought. But my own guests would walk over and retrieve theirs from the automatic drip pot. My mother is now ninety-one; between her time as a hostess and mine, an enormous change had occurred in the lives of women. And, just then, it seemed to me that all that upheaval was contained in the silly fact of how one served coffee to dinner guests. I knew I would never want to go back to Mother's time, but all the same I suddenly missed the world of her dinner parties, the guests waving their cigarettes as they chatted, my mother so dressed up, queenly by the coffee pot, her service a kind of benign rule over the table. I put the pot in the corner of the hutch and thought: It's no good trying to explain all this to my robot guest. The chain of associations from just this one piece of china has led me to regret and nostalgia, feelings I can't explain even to myself.

The real problem with having a robot to dinner is pleasure. What would please my digital guest? Human beings need food to survive, but what drives us to choose one food over another is what I think of as the deliciousness factor. Evolution, that good mother, has seen fit to guide us to the apple instead of the poison berry by our attraction to the happy sweetness of the apple, its fresh crispness, and, in just the right balance, enough tartness to make it complicated in the mouth. There are good and rational reasons why natural selection has made us into creatures with fine taste discernment—we can learn what's good for us and what's not. But this very sensible survival imperative, like the need to have sex to reproduce, works itself out through the not very sensible, wilder part of our nature: desire for pleasure.

Can a robot desire? Can it have pleasure? When trying to decide if we should confer sentience upon another creature, we usually cite the question first posed by the philosopher Jeremy Bentham: Can it suffer? We are willing to ascribe a kind of consciousness to a being whose suffering we can intuit. But now I wanted to look at the opposite end of what drives us, not at pain but at rapture: Can it feel pleasure? Will we be able to look into the face of a robot and understand that some deep, inherent need has driven it to seek a particular delight?

According to Cynthia Breazeal, who teaches as MIT and is perhaps the best known of the new social-robot researchers, future digital creatures will have drives that are analogous to human desires but that will have nothing to do with the biological imperatives of food and sex. Robots will want the sort of things that machines need: to stay in good running order, to maintain physical homeostasis, to get the attention of human beings, upon whom they must rely, at least until they learn to take care of themselves. They will be intelligent and happy the way dolphins are: in their own form, in their own way.

Breazeal is very smart and articulate, and her defense of the eventual beingness of robotic creatures is a deep challenge to the human idea of sentience. She insists that robots will eventually become so lifelike that we will one day have to face the question of their inherent rights and dignity. "We have personhood because it's granted to us by society," she told me. "It's a status granted to one another. It's not innately tied to being a carbon-based life form."

So challenged, I spent a long time thinking about the interior life of a robot. I tried to imagine it: the delicious swallowing of electric current, the connoisseurship of voltages, exquisite sensibilities sensing tiny spikes on the line, the pleasure of a clean, steady flow. Perhaps the current might taste of wires and transistors, capacitors and rheostats, some components better than others, the way soil and water make up the *terroir* of wine, the difference between a good Bordeaux and a middling one. I think robots will delight in discerning patterns, finding mathematical regularities, seeing a world that is not mysterious but beautifully self-organized. What pleasure they will take in being fast and efficient—to run without cease!—humming along by their picosecond clocks, their algorithms compact, elegant, error-free. They will want the interfaces between one part of themselves and another to be defined, standardized, and modular, so that an old part can be unplugged, upgraded, and plugged back in their bodies forever renewed. Fast, efficient, untiring, correct, standardized, organized: the virtues we humans strive for but forever fail to achieve, the reasons we invented our helpmate, the machine.

The dinner part, which of course proceeded without a single robot guest, turned out to be a fine, raucous affair, everyone talking and laughing, eating and drinking to just the right degree of excess. And when each guest rose to pour his or her own cup of coffee, I knew it was one of those nights that had to be topped off with a good brandy. By the time the last friend had left, it was nearly two a.m., the tablecloth was covered with stains, dirty dishes were everywhere, the empty crab shells were beginning to stink, and the kitchen was a mess. Perfect.

Two day later I was wheeling a cart through the aisles of Safeway—food shopping can't always be about fetal lettuces—and I was thinking how neat and regular the food looked. All the packaged, pre-prepared dinners lined up in boxes on the shelves. The meat in plastic-wrapped trays, in standard cuts, arranged in orderly rows. Even the vegetables looked cloned, identical bunches of spinach and broccoli, perfectly green, without an apparent speck of dirt. Despite the influence of Julia Child and California-cuisine guru Alice Waters, despite the movement toward organic, local produce, here it all still was: manufactured, efficient, standardized food.

But of course it was still here, I thought. Not everyone can afford the precious offerings of the food hall. And even if you could, who really has the time to stroll through the market and cook a meal based on what looks fresh that day? I have friends who would love to spend rainy afternoons turning a nice filet into *boeuf à la Parisienne*. But even they find their schedules too pressed these days; it's easier just to pick something up, grab a sauce out of a jar. Working long hours, our work life invading home life through e-mail and mobile phones, we all need our food-gathering trips to be brief and organized, our time in the kitchen efficiently spent, our meals downed in a hurry.

As I picked out six limes, not a bruise or blemish on them, it occurred to me that I was not really worried about robots becoming sentient, human, indistinguishable from us. That long-standing fear—robots who fool us into taking them for humans—suddenly seemed a comic-book peril, born of another age, as obsolete as a twenty-five-year-old computer.

What scared me now were the perfect limes, the five varieties of apples that seemed to have disappeared from the shelves, the dinner I'd make and eat that night in thirty minutes, the increasing rarity of those feasts that turn the dining room into a wreck of sated desire. The lines at the check-out stands were long; neat packages rode along on the conveyor belts; the air was filled with the beep of scanners as the food, labeled and bar-coded, identified itself to the machines. Life is pressuring us to live by the robots' pleasures, I thought. Our appetites have given way to theirs. Robots aren't becoming us, I feared; we are becoming them.

—in memory of Julia Child

PERSONAL RESPONSE

Ullman quotes a social robot researcher who says robots one day will have to face the question of their inherent rights and dignity. Do you think that day will occur in your lifetime? How close are we now?

QUESTIONS FOR CLASS OR SMALL-GROUP DISCUSSION

1. Just when you think that Ullman has gone on too long about the subject of food, it hits you: she's writing about pleasure, something we may have forgotten how to enjoy as our school and work lives flood the sanctuary of our home life. Discuss the reasons why you agree or disagree with this assessment.

2. Robots aren't becoming us—we are becoming them. Do you agree or disagree? Provide clear, vivid examples to back up your position.

3. Technology takes away our time by providing infinite diversions; that is, technology controls us. Discuss.

4. Robots appear frequently in popular culture, especially in movies, including *Metropolis* (a silent film), the *Star Wars* series, *The Terminator* series, and *I, Robot*. Can you think of other movies that feature robots? Discuss our fascination with the idea of robots.

FOR FURTHER VIEWING: DIGITAL TECHNOLOGY AND THE INTERNET

Pulse (2006); *The Net* (1995); *Pirates of Silicon Valley* (1999); *Takedown* (2000); *Hackers* (1995); *The Matrix* (1999); *Tron* (1982); *South Park: When Technology Attacks* (2005); *Metropolis* (1927); *The Stepford Wives* (1975); *Blade Runner* (1982); *Terminator 2: Judgment Day* (1991); *I, Robot* (2004); *Artificial Intelligence: AI* (2001).

CHAPTER NINETEEN

NATURAL SCIENCES

INTRODUCTION

The essays in this chapter demonstrate the skill and art of communicating science to the public. In the last 20 years or so, science writing has become a popular genre. The writers in this chapter are four of the best science writers today. You may also want to look at the writing of other authors; for example, Primo Levi (*The Periodic Table*), Edwin Abbott (*Flatland*), Michio Kaku (*Einstein's Cosmos*), George Gamow (the *Mr. Tompkins* series), Alan Lightman (*Einstein's Dreams*), and Lewis Thomas (*The Lives of a Cell.*) Science writing also plays an important cultural role, especially as science becomes increasingly inaccessible to public understanding. The Internet is a good place to search for science writing and breaking science news. Several excellent sites provide news summaries, links, and blogs, including "Science in the News Daily," which is operated by Sigma Xi, The Scientific Research Society. Also, most online news sites, such as CBC, CNN, and BBC, have science news sections.

GENETICS AFTER AUSCHWITZ

David Suzuki

Born in Vancouver, B.C., in 1936, Suzuki attained a Ph.D. in zoology from the University of Chicago. After gaining prominence as a geneticist, he achieved international recognition as an environmentalist, writer, and prolific broadcaster. His media work includes A Planet for the Taking *and* The Secret of Life. *He has published more than forty books, including* The Sacred Balance *and* From Naked Ape to Superspecies. *He has received countless media and professional awards as well as honorary degrees for his contribution to environmental issues and civil rights activism.*

The best guide we have to help us through the maze of ethical questions that are created by genetic engineering is history; we forget its lesson at the risk of repeating the same mistakes. Consider Josef Mengele, the infamous doctor at the Nazi death camp at Auschwitz. He was in the news again a few years ago when forensic scientists eventually concluded that bones discovered in a grave in Brazil were indeed Mengele's remains. Recalling his activities should give every scientist pause.

Mengele gained his notoriety for his experiments in genetics. I was trained as a geneticist, yet never in all the years of my education or during my entire career as a scientist did I encounter his name except in the popular press. In the field of science, Mengele does not exist.

I went to a liberal arts undergraduate school that is ranked as one of the top in North America. My first genetics professor—my inspiration and hero—was a Jew who had received his Ph.D. from Curt Stern, one of the most important figures in classical genetics. Stern was also a Jew who had fled Nazi Germany and eventually ended up at Berkeley.

I earned a bachelor of arts degree, and though I was enrolled in honors biology, the curriculum stipulated that no more than half my courses be in science. So I had wonderful courses in music, Michelangelo, twentieth-century history, world religion, and literature. It was a marvelous opportunity rarely available to science students today, yet I never did encounter the philosophy or history of science. I was never taught about the excitement geneticists had felt at the turn of the century about the notion of improving the human species through selective breeding.

No one told us that geneticists had made bold claims about the "hereditary basis" for racial inferiority or superiority (which are value judgments, not terms that have any scientific meaning). Some of the leading geneticists in the twenties and thirties wrote of the genetic basis for nomadism in gypsies, criminality, drunkenness, and vagrancy, but we budding scientists did not learn of the important role that our predecessors had played in encouraging laws regulating immigration from certain countries, prohibiting interracial marriage, and sterilizing patients in mental institutions.

During my education in graduate school, I was never taught that being a scientist entailed enormous social responsibilities. We did not learn that the social context and value system within which scientific investigations occur affect the kind of research done and the way results are interpreted. No one told us that there are limits to science, that it provides only a fragmented view of nature that can never encompass the whole. There is no code of ethics governing our activity, nor is there a sense that it is a privilege for a scientist to have public support.

Today's science student has a heavy load of science courses and little opportunity to take others outside the discipline. Science students in my university don't have room among their courses for philosophy, history, religion, or literature. I remember one of the professors in my department during the student protests of the 1970s saying, "Okay, look. We'll keep all the best zoology courses for our honors and majors students and we'll *educate* the rest of them." Needless to say, he was sneering at the term *educate*.

Today, so much is happening in science that it is difficult for a scientist to stay abreast of all developments. Even though more research papers published will turn out to be wrong, trivial, or unimportant in a few years, we feel compelled to emphasize the latest work, thereby ignoring more and more of the classical studies and history. But what a loss that is.

We don't learn that geneticists were the prime movers behind the Nazi Race Purification program and that the voices of opposition to Hitler from scientists and doctors were silent. It was our colleagues, the likes of Mengele, who were carrying out their so-called research in death camps.

I know my fellow scientists find it easy to dismiss the doctors of death like Mengele. We say, "Hell, he was a medical doctor carrying out pseudo-scientific experiments. He wasn't a geneticist at all, he was a nut." But "real" geneticists in Germany didn't say so. Besides, is it enough to write him off as a grotesque caricature of a scientist, a freak who happens once in a generation?

I don't think so. Germany boasted some of the most eminent geneticists and biologists of the day when the Nazi program was set in motion. The history of scientists not only in countries like Nazi Germany but in Fascist Italy, Japan, and during the McCarthy years in the United States is not a proud one. As Cornell University historian Joseph Haberer has written: "What becomes evident is that scientific leaders, when faced with a choice between the imperatives of conscience and power, nationalism and internationalism, justice and patriotism, invariably gravitated toward power, nationalism, and patriotism." It's a sobering indictment and one that can only be avoided in the future if we remember the past.

I do not believe for a minute that Josef Mengele was merely an aberration, who can therefore be lightly dismissed. Scientists are often driven, consumed, focused on the immediate problem at hand, and this is the great joy and strength of involvement in science. But it can also blind *any* of us to wider implications of what we and our peers are doing.

Mengele was one within a vast range of people who call themselves scientists. He was some scientist's student; he was a colleague, a peer of the medical-scientific community. It lets us off the hook too easily to say simply that he was a monster.

The explosion of the atomic bomb smashed the romantic notion of scientific innocence. The brouhaha over recombinant DNA and the vocal objections to the

American Strategic Defense Initiative (Star Wars) are hopeful signs that the horrible silence of the scientific community may not happen again. But unless we acknowledge the likes of Josef Mengele and include him in courses taken by science students, we could quickly forget the lesson of history he provides.

The reluctance of scientists to take an unflinching look at their own history was clear when I was invited in the fall of 1987 to attend a meeting in Toronto of the organizing committee of the Couchiching Conference. Each year experts from various disciplines meet in Couchiching, Ontario, to discuss a specific topic. In 1987 the subject was the Rise and Fall of the American Empire. In 1988 the conference was to look [at] DNA and genetic engineering, a timely topic in view of the tremendous advances in molecular genetics and the proposal to decipher the entire genetic blueprint of a human cell.

The Couchiching committee focused on the technology of the DNA manipulation and its future implications, which are fascinating. But the really important questions have to do with what scientists and people in power will do with the unprecedented ability to alter the genetic makeup of life-forms. And the only way to anticipate that comes from looking backward.

At the Couchiching meeting, I reminded the committee that early in this century a brand new science—genetics—had made spectacular and rapid discoveries about the laws of heredity. Scientists were understandably excited about the potential to apply this knowledge for the benefit of humankind. I pointed out that in prewar Germany, where culture and science were at a peak, doctors and scientists had embraced the possibility of applying the benefits of genetic discovery. By extrapolating from studies of the inheritance of *physical* characteristics in fruit flies and corn plants to *behavior* and *intelligence* in people, they concluded that human beings could be "perfected" through selective breeding and elimination of "defectives." The Nazi Race Purification programs seemed to represent the application of some of the most "progressive" ideas in science.

Thus, I suggested, doctors and scientists—especially geneticists—had, in their intoxication with new findings, popularized the notion of the overriding importance of heredity in human behavior and sold it to Hitler's National Socialists. This emphasis on heredity led inexorably to the horrors of the Holocaust, which scientists must therefore acknowledge some responsibility for. Two of the committee members (one a molecular biologist and both Jews) were outraged. They denied the suggestion that scientists have to bear some of the blame for the excesses of Nazi action and accused me of being "hysterical."

This selective memory of science's history amounts to a coverup and a revisionism that only ensures that the same thing could happen again. Even a suggestion that there is an unpleasant aspect to science's past is interpreted as opposition to science. I once hosted a television series that included a program presenting some history of genetics. In reviewing that show, Stephen Strauss, the *Globe and Mail's* science writer, wrote: "You are of the clergy, a scientist who left the monastery/laboratory to reform the world's understanding of his faith, and who now may well be on the way to becoming a heretic. (Some of your fellow geneticists think that.)" An accusation or even suggestion of heresy powerfully reinforces dogma and threatens dissenters with excommunication from the scientific community. I can understand why scientists are reluctant to face up to the past. Fortunately, a few exceptional ones won't let us forget.

Benno Müller-Hill is a professor of molecular biology in Cologne, West Germany. Few texts in molecular biology and genetics fail to mention his work. While at Harvard University working with Walter Gilbert (who later earned a Nobel Prize), Müller-Hill carried out a classic experiment that allowed the isolation and purification of a protein molecule called a repressor, which controls gene activity. Only a few copies of the repressor are present in each cell, so the Müller-Hill/Gilbert experiment was a scientific tour de force. Müller-Hill's lab went on to collect sufficient quantities of the material to determine the primary structure of the protein. A scientist of world-class stature, he continues to do research. For the past decade, he has also studied the history of genetics in Nazi Germany.

One of Müller-Hill's articles, entitled "Genetics after Auschwitz," appeared in *Holocaust and Genocide Studies*. In a document that is at once chilling and agonizing— an unflinching look by a scientist at the role of scientists in the Holocaust.

The article opens this way: "The past must be recollected and remembered before it can be evaluated. ... It is particularly difficult for scientists. Science is oriented to the present . . . only today's results exist. Only new data or new theories bring glory, honor and money for new research. Reflection on the past almost excludes the reflecting scientist from the ranks of present-day science." He goes on to summarize his studies and his book: "The rise of genetics is characterized by a gigantic process of repression of its history." Later he writes: "[G]eneticists have refused—and even now refuse—to acknowledge their history."

Science transcends national boundaries because it is practiced by an international community sharing knowledge through freely available publications. As governments around the world tie scientific innovation to their economic well-being, scientists are under tremendous pressure to do work that is socially "relevant" or "practical." Most research grants are now awarded and renewed on the basis of these considerations, and the potential economic rewards of an application of new ideas is great. Scientists focus even more than ever on work going on now and in the future. But if scientists, for the most humane of reasons, can participate in work that exceeds ethical lines, then surely it behooves us to pay attention to what has happened in the past. Today most scientists are too busy, or they ignore or selectively recall their history.

When Müller-Hill went to the archives of the German Research Association in 1981 to look at extensive historical records, he was told that he was the first person to do so since the end of the war. He was seeking answers to the questions, Was Auschwitz the result of pure scientific thinking? How does scientific reason change into the greatest unreason? Is this an inevitable process of the growth of pure scientific reason? Even asking such important questions carries the risk of denial and hostility from the scientific profession.

The German biographer P. Fischer illustrates this risk in his biography of Nobel laureate and geneticist Max Delbrück. In 1947, Nobel laureate H.J. Müller, as president of the American Society of Genetics, asked Delbrück, who was returning to his native Germany, "to gather first-hand information about geneticists still in Germany, and to investigate whether any evidence exists that might absolve them from the guilt of having actively supported Nazism and prostituted genetics under the Nazis." Delbrück failed to do so because "he did not have the courage; he considered it improper to inquire which German scientists had related to the National Socialist government. So he failed to fulfill the mission entrusted to him by the American Genetic Commission. . . . Later Delbrück was convinced by one of his closest friends, plant geneticist Georg Melchers, that virtually no German biologist had ever worked towards furthering the race theories, and that biology in general was not guilty of formulating the inhuman ideologies which resulted in inhuman action." Thus, even a scientist as great as Delbrück could not resist the pressures from his peer group and finally accepted the party line.

In the article "Genetics after Auschwitz" Müller-Hill says:

> The number of medical doctors who guided scientific selection in Auschwitz by killing through gas or slave labor was small. Nevertheless nine university professors were actively involved in selecting 70,000 mentally ill persons for the gas chambers. . . . The exact numbers of Jews killed in Auschwitz is unknown. Two-and-a-half million is the number Höss got from Eichmann. . . . Auschwitz was not only a site of destruction and a laboratory of human biology; it was also planned as a place of chemical production. IG-Farben had placed their largest investment during the war near Auschwitz. . . . When one regards the potential for scientific investigation, production and destruction, Auschwitz turns into a monument of modern science and technology. Human biology and technical chemistry should never have been the same again after Auschwitz was liberated, but nothing changed. The human biologists and medical doctors who were not caught in the act escaped by a semantic trick; this was pseudo-science or pseudo-medicine, they said, so they were free to start again with real science and medicine.

Müller-Hill traces the web of German scientists who were connected to the work carried out at Auschwitz. It included some of the leaders of the day. The most infamous of the scientists at Auschwitz was Josef Mengele.

Mengele was not just some scientist from the provinces. He had worked with the foremost German scientists of his time: first with the anthropologist Professor Theodor Mollisson in Munich, then with the human geneticist and specialist in internal medicine, Count Professor Otmar von Verschauer. Mengele was not an amateur who operated outside the established structures of science. Von Verschauer, Mengele's mentor, applied for grants for work at Auschwitz on "human twin studies, human eye defects, human tuberculosis and . . . specific serum proteins." The grants were all approved.

Müller-Hill continues:

> What happened to the twins? They were analysed anthropologically, physiologically and psychologically. Anything that could be measured was measured. Those who had interesting anomalies were killed by Mengele or his helpers. The interesting organs were sent to the K.W.I. for Anthropology at Berlin-Dahlem. . . .

Was Professor von Verschauer a unique case? No, other researchers had already profited from the murder of the insane. . . . Some 70,000 patients of German mental institutions were killed by gas during 1940 and the first half of 1941.

Many of their brains ended up in scientific laboratories.

What is astonishing is that to most geneticists these infamous scientists and events don't exist: they have been expunged from history.

For biologists, Nazi Germany provides important lessons that might temper our rush to exploit new ideas uncritically. But according to Benno Müller-Hill, there has been a systematic suppression and revision of the history of science under the Nazis. Müller-Hill provides an explanation of how this came about:

> Auschwitz had just reached its highest destructive potential when the paper appeared which showed that DNA was the basic genetic material. It took several years until the significance of this discovery was generally understood, but when the double helix was published in 1953, only fools did not realize that genetics had virtually exploded. The speed of this development left no time for looking back or for regrets over the blood and tears that had been spilled in the process. Scientists discuss George Orwell's *Animal Farm* and *1984* and do not see that they themselves have created a universe which is equally frightening. No secret police forces them to forget the past. They obliterate it themselves on the marketplace of science. They have come to believe that they have a beautiful past, or perhaps no past at all. The chapters of textbooks which deal with genetics and society contain only a few token sentences about National Socialism.

If history is not remembered, can the scientific community be involved in horrors like those of Nazi Germany again? Of course, though undoubtedly in a different manifestation. Scientists are, above all else, human beings with all the foibles, idiosyncrasies, and diversity found in any other group of people. Ambition, driving curiosity, desire for power, thirst for financial security, fear—there are many reasons why people do what they do. And in the current scramble to capitalize on the enormous potential of genetic engineering, organ transplants, and a cure for AIDS, individual scientists have not been above cutting corners or compromising on ethical standards.

In part, the very methodology of science itself make this easier, says Müller-Hill:

> Scientists observe and analyse objects. An object is a thing without rights. When a human being becomes an object he is nothing but a slave. What interests the scientist is the answer to the question he asks the object, but not the object's own questions. In general, the scientist never analyses the whole object but only a small part of it. Others dismember the object, he receives only one part of it for his analysis. The answers which he expects from the part he analyses may be numbers, DNA sequences or images. . . . This process of objectivization of the whole world, and finally of oneself as part of science, seems the main interest and pleasure of the scientist's brain. There is little place for other things in the scientist's mind.

But, it is often countered, weren't the people who carried out the atrocities in Nazi Germany second-rate intellectuals, mediocre but ambitious opportunists?

Müller-Hill disagrees: "It was not in the interest of the Nazi elite that the sciences be dominated by a mob of liars and charlatans. The Nazis needed functioning science and technology to assist their wars of robbery and destruction."

But could there be a repetition of what was done by the Nazis?

> The killing of deficient newborn babies as practised in Germany between 1939 and 1945 has simply become anachronistic. Most geneticists sincerely believe that here they have created new values. They do not see that they appeal to the forces of the market which state that cost-efficiency considerations make it advisable, for both parents and state, to destroy the cost-inefficient embryo.

Müller-Hill's ideas are not pleasant, and he has encountered naked hostility from his scientific peers. But unless we hear him out and dig out the bad as well as the good in science's history, we will ensure that scientists will continue to do terrible things for what seem to be the highest reasons—just as their predecessors did. We need to remember that scientists are human too.

Geneticist R. Gold wrote a letter to the *Globe and Mail* to rebut the columns I wrote on Müller-Hill's work, yet Gold's letter itself provides an illustration of how revisionism is enforced by well-meaning scientists.

One tactic of the revisionist is to set up a straw man that can be knocked down. Thus, he writes:

> In his columns, Dr. Suzuki gives intermittent indications that he wants to go further than this to argue that there is a sort of evil inherent in the science of genetics and in geneticists themselves. He seems to imply, that if we are not carefully watched, we will be up to our old tricks again and indeed may already be engaging in nefarious schemes to harm humanity.

He goes on to say that I imply "that evil occurs because scientists are prone to evil."

He infers exactly the *opposite* to what I have written throughout my career in popularizing science. I have constantly emphasized that scientists are *no better or worse* than any other group of people, but it was enthusiasm about new insights in the mechanics of heredity early in this century that led some of the finest scientists to proclaim that human beings could be "improved" through selective breeding. The goals were laudable—to avoid suffering and improve the human condition—yet those ideas were warped into Nazi race purification, again, with the encouragement of some scientists. In our current excitement about the rapidly accumulating manipulative powers of DNA, many of the same claims are again being made.

Gold is a geneticist and surely knows that one of our colleagues at Harvard deliberately violated the federal guidelines on recombinant DNA experiments and, when discovered, quit the university to set up his own private biotechnology company. It was a UCLA doctor who violated federal grant restrictions by administering DNA to children with hereditary diseases. A Montana professor went ahead with prohibited field studies of DNA-engineered organisms in elm trees. There are other deliberate violations of regulations by reputable scientists. It is precisely because they are *not* evil or fanatics, but ordinary human beings who are totally caught up in their own ambitions and beliefs, that we must remember the pitfalls that the past reveals.

As I've mentioned, Müller-Hill pointed out another way that postwar German scientists rationalized what happened during the Holocaust so that the events could be discounted: "This was pseudo-science or pseudo-medicine, they said, so they were free to start again with real science and medicine." That's precisely what Gold does: "The concept of racial purity is not a scientific concept and has no place in genetics. It is simply intellectual rubbish that was dragged in to justify actions undertaken for other reasons." Thus Gold rewrites history.

Early in this century, leading scientists—geneticists and anthropologists—had popularized the idea of scientifically improving the human condition by preventing "inferior" people from reproducing or by encouraging those considered "superior" to have more children. They established the social climate for the adoption of race purification policies by Nazi Germany. Seen today, these ideas are indeed "intellectual rubbish," but in the twenties and thirties they were serious scientific proposals. The important lesson is that we should be very careful about rushing to apply in society or the ecosystem ideas derived in the laboratory. But we won't learn that essential lesson if we persist in papering over the past.

Gold's final accusation is that I have not addressed "what we should do about all this. Should we stop doing the research that will continue to provide us with these choices, and, if not, what advice has he as to the choices we should make?" As a once-practicing scientist, I continue to take enormous vicarious delight in the insights gained by scientists and have long written of the need for better support of good science in this country. But it would be foolhardy to suggest that there are no detrimental or unpredictable negative consequences of the application of science.

Gold seems unwilling to face up to the vast changes that have happened in science and its relationship to society in a few decades. In half a century, human population has more than *doubled,* while the per capita consumption of resources in the highly industrialized nations has increased many times more. In the same period, the scientific community has greatly expanded its numbers, just as the interval between discovery and application has decreased radically. Surely, then, there must be constant reassessment of the changing relationship between science and society, and the best guide that we have is history. Accusations of heresy, neo-Ludditism, or anti-intellectualism become powerful means of discouraging critical dissent or inquiry. In the long run, that does an enormous disservice to the public *and* to science itself.

PERSONAL RESPONSE

Do you think that science should be more concerned with ethics, or should science make the pursuit of scientific truth its priority? What factors determine the relationship between science and society?

QUESTIONS FOR CLASS OR SMALL-GROUP DISCUSSION

1. Discuss Suzuki's views on "the limits of science." He believes that science students miss out on certain aspects of knowledge in their studies. According to Suzuki, what are the effects of such omissions in the education of scientists?

2. What is Suzuki trying to point out about the case of Joseph Mengele? How do you think most scientists would respond to Suzuki's views on Mengele? What can be learned?

3. Besides the scientific discoveries and scientific explorations that Suzuki mentions, can you think of others that have a strong overlap with or influence on politics, beliefs, policies, or economics?

4. What is involved in making decisions to alter the genetic makeup of life-forms? Are some alterations more or less important than others? How should the degrees of importance be determined, and who should determine them? Should nature be left to run its own course?

5. Sum up Suzuki's message to scientists. Sum up his message to non-scientists, like us.

THE DISCUS THROWER

Richard Selzer

The son of a family doctor, Richard Selzer, born in 1928, was practising surgery and teaching at Yale Medical School when, at age 40, he began to write. Selzer has written numerous essays and stories, many of which draw on his experiences as a physician. He is the recipient of many awards and honours for his writing. Now retired from his medical career, he devotes his time to writing.

"Do not go gentle"

I spy on my patients. Ought not a doctor to observe his patients by any means and from any stance, that he might the more fully assemble evidence? So I stand in the doorways of hospital rooms and gaze. Oh, it is not all that furtive an act. Those in bed need only look up to discover me. But they never do.

From the doorway of Room 542 the man in the bed seems deeply tanned. Blue eyes and close-cropped white hair give him the appearance of vigor and good health. But I know that his skin is not brown from the sun. It is rusted, rather, in the last stage of containing the vile repose within. And the blue eyes are frosted, looking inward like the windows of a snowbound cottage. This man is blind. This man is also legless—the right leg missing from midthigh down, the left from just below the knee. It gives him the look of a bonsai, roots and branches pruned into the dwarfed facsimile of a great tree.

Propped on pillows, he cups his right thigh in both hands. Now and then he shakes his head as though acknowledging the intensity of his suffering. In all of this he makes no sound. Is he mute as well as blind?

The room in which he dwells is empty of all possessions—no get-well cards, small, private caches of food, day-old flowers, slippers, all the usual kickshaws of a sickroom. There is only the bed, a chair, a nightstand, and a tray on wheels that can be swung across his lap for meals.

"What time is it?" he asks.

"Three o'clock."

"Morning or afternoon?"

"Afternoon."

He is silent. There is nothing else he wants to know. "How are you? I say.

"Who is it?" he asks.

"It's the doctor. How do you feel?" He does not answer right away.

"Feel?" he says.

"I hope you feel better," I say.

I press the button at the side of the bed.

"Down you go," I say.

"Yes, down," he says.

He falls back upon the bed awkwardly. His stumps, unweighted by legs and feet, rise in the air, presenting themselves. I unwrap the bandages from the stumps, and begin to cut away the black scabs and the dead, glazed fat with scissors and forceps. A shard of white bone comes loose. I pick it away. I wash the wounds with disinfectant and redress the stumps. All this while, he does not speak. What is he thinking behind those lids that do not blink? Is he remembering a time when he was whole? Does he dream of feet? Of when his body was not a rotting log?

He lies solid and inert. In spite of everything, he remains impressive, as though he were a sailor standing athwart a slanting deck.

"Anything more I can do for you?" I ask.

For a long moment he is silent.

"Yes," he says at last and without the least irony. "You can bring me a pair of shoes."

In the corridor, the head nurse is waiting for me.

"We have to do something about him," she says. "Every morning he orders scrambled eggs for breakfast and, instead of eating them, he picks up the plate and throws it against the wall."

"Throws his plate?"

"Nasty. That's what he is. No wonder his family doesn't come to visit. They probably can't stand him any more than we can."

She is waiting for me to do something.

"Well?"

"We'll see," I say.

The next morning I am waiting in the corridor when the kitchen delivers his breakfast. I watch the aide place the tray on the stand and swing it across his lap. She presses the button to raise the head of the bed. Then she leaves.

In time the man reaches to find the rim of the tray, then on to find the dome of the covered dish. He lifts off the cover and places it on the stand. He fingers across the plate until he probes the eggs. He lifts the plate in both hands, sets it on the palm of his right hand, centers it, balances it. He hefts it up and down slightly, getting the feel of it. Abruptly, he draws back his right arm as far as he can.

There is the crack of the plate breaking against the wall at the foot of bed and the small wet sound of the scrambled eggs dropping to the floor.

And then he laughs. It is a sound you have never heard. It is something new under the sun. It could cure cancer.

Out in the corridor, the eyes of the head nurse narrow.

"Laughed, did he?"

She writes something down on her clipboard.

A second aide arrives, brings a second breakfast tray, puts it on the nightstand, out of his reach. She looks over at me shaking her head and making her mouth go. I see that we are to be accomplices.

"I've got to feed you," she says to the man.

"Oh, no you don't" the man says.

"Oh, yes I do," the aide says, "after the way you just did. Nurse says so."

"Get me my shoes," the man says.

"Here's oatmeal," the aide says. "Open." And she touches the spoon to his lower lip.

"I ordered scrambled eggs," says the man.

"That's right," the aide says.

I step forward.

"Is there anything I can do?" I say.

"Who are you?" the man asks.

In the evening I go once more to that ward to make my rounds. The head nurse reports to me that Room 542 is deceased. She has discovered this quite by accident, she says. No, there has been no sound. Nothing. It's a blessing, she says.

I go into his room, a spy looking for secrets. He is still there in his bed. His face is relaxed, grave, dignified. After a while, I turn to leave. My gaze sweeps the wall at the foot of the bed, and I see the place where it has been repeatedly washed, where the wall looks very clean and very white.

PERSONAL RESPONSE

Selzer has said in an interview that the denial of death is the engine that drives modern culture. What does he mean? How do you feel about that?

QUESTIONS FOR CLASS OR SMALL-GROUP DISCUSSION

1. Selzer has said that surgery and writing have taught him about death. What does "The Discus Thrower" teach you about death?
2. The essay has an epigram: "Do not go gentle." What poem is the source of the epigram, and what does the epigram mean in the context of the essay?

3. Why does the patient throw the plate against the wall? How do the nurses respond to his behaviour? Selzer compares the patient to a bonsai and a snowbound cottage. Explain these comparisons in the context of the essay.

EVEN BEES MUST REST THEIR HEADS

Diane Ackerman

A poet, essayist, and naturalist, Diane Ackerman has hosted a PBS TV series based on her best-selling book, A Natural History of the Senses. *Among her many awards and honours are a Guggenheim Fellowship and being named a Literary Lion by the New York Public Library. Her children's book,* Animal Sense, *was illustrated by Peter Sís.*

Atop a fothergilla leaf, a fat bumblebee is slumbering, motionless. A breeze jolts the leaf, but the bee seems to be buttoned in place.

Sometimes foraging bees can't make it back to the hive before dark, and must grab a leaf and wait through night chill for dawn. Many die in the process. On cold nights, they need hive mates to keep warm, and last night was one of those.

Unlike honey bees (and humans, for that matter), bumblebees don't store food and huddle indoors, staying sociable and warm all winter. Instead, most of their family dies, leaving behind only young pregnant females that hibernate below ground, held in suspense until spring.

This is an older female (younger ones stay home to help in the nursery). Is it waiting for the first sunlight? The morning damp to dry?

At last, it tilts its head and stirs. Two feet jut out and back, in a hokey-pokey sort of move, then its wings flex a little without lifting.

Ten minutes later, still not flying, it climbs to the top of the leaf and ambles around. Then it begins working the bellows of its abdomen, rhythmically, in a bee version of calisthenics, to limber up the flight muscles. Still no flashing wings, but lots of quiver.

Bumblebees can twitch their wing muscles fast to create body heat. A neat trick. Monarch butterflies also shiver to stay warm, or use their wings as solar panels, unless the temperature really plunges, and then they're as paralyzed as this bumblebee was, and easy prey.

I remember one chilly morning in California, when a colleague and I held just-tagged monarch butterflies in our open mouths and warmed them with our breath, so that they could fly to safety.

This bumblebee's two leg baskets are bulging with pollen, a heavy load to haul home. It may have misjudged the pollen weight or the flying time.

There is much for even a bumblebee to analyze and decide.

Where is her ground hive, anyway? It's bound to be in a burrow dug by some obliging creature, or maybe a grassy nest stolen from a field mouse.

I'd go looking, but I want to keep the bumblebee company on the ledge of its day. As sun finds the fothergilla, the bumblebee flurries its wings, levitates, and lumbers away at last, buzzing with rich cargo.

PERSONAL RESPONSE

We often think of the natural sciences in global terms or even in economic terms. But sometimes we are reminded that the natural sciences are about the ordinary miracles that happen in everyday life. Think of Ackerman's essay as a poem, or write a short poem yourself, using some of her imagery.

QUESTIONS FOR CLASS OR SMALL-GROUP DISCUSSION

1. Underline any unfamiliar words in Ackerman's essay, and look up their meanings.

2. Give at least three examples of the use of visual language; i.e., language that allows you to actually see what is happening. How does this visual language help with your engagement with the essay?

3. Compare this essay to the work of Annie Dillard. How are these two writers similar? How are they different? Provide examples.

4. What is the role of discovery in our culture? Should science always be outcome-based or should it have applications that are not immediately practical, for the sake of knowledge only? Who should finance scientific discovery?

5. Recently, the media have reported on the massive disappearance of bees in Canada, the United States, South America, and Europe, and the whole-sale collapse of bee colonies. The bees' importance is obvious beyond the fact that they produce honey: they are essential to pollinating crops. Do an Internet search and list the theories that try to explain why bees are disappearing. Which is the most valid theory? How might we, as individuals, take responsibility to address this problem? What will happen to the food supply if bees disappear? Do bees hold a special status in our culture? Describe their status and how it came about. Name some famous people, including writers, who have kept hives and raised bees.

CRANES

Jennifer Ackerman

Jennifer Ackerman is a contributing writer and editor for The New York Times, National Geographic Magazine, *and many other publications. She has written essays and articles on the nature and politics of barrier islands, the origin of birds, parasites as agents of evolutionary change, and the work of Nobel prize-winning molecular biologist Christiane Nusslein-Volhard. Her writing has been collected in several anthologies.*

From a blind overlooking the wetlands of central Wisconsin, I can see a long-legged bird in the distance, a stroke of white curled at the top, like a bright question mark against the emerald green grasses. Then up pops another from the screen of reeds. The birds are yearlings, five feet tall, with snow-white plumage and elegant black wing tips that spread like fingers when they fly. They're quiet now, but from the long trachea coiled in their breastbones may come a wild, singing whoop, harsh and thrilling, that gives their tribe its name.

This would be a primordial scene—big sky, undulations of tall marsh grasses, wild whooping cranes—were it not for a penned area nearby, where several whooper chicks, well camouflaged in tawny feathers, forage in the shallows. In a whisper, crane biologist Richard Urbanek explains that these chicks have been raised in captivity but have never heard a human voice nor seen a human form, except in crane costume. As part of an experimental program to reintroduce a wild migratory population of whooping cranes to the eastern half of North America, these chicks have been fed and tended by crane-costumed people for two months. Now, before they are released to the wild, they are being taught the habits of their ancestors with modern techniques pioneered by Operation Migration, an organization devoted to helping endangered birds learn their traditional migratory routes. Near the pen is a long stretch of open grass, a runway, where the chicks are learning to fly behind an ultralight plane flown by a pilot in crane costume who will guide them from this refuge twelve hundred miles south across seven states to wintering grounds in Florida.

Two cohorts have already made such trips—and returned on their own, the first whooping cranes in perhaps more than a century to fly freely over the eastern United States. After three years of ultralight-led migrations, the new eastern migratory population numbers thirty-six birds, including the yearlings and the chicks. The success of this effort is leading the way for a more ambitious project half a world away in the northern reaches of Russia. In the fall of 2005 an international team plans to lead a flock of young captive-bred Siberian cranes along part of their traditional migratory route, from Russia to Iran, to restore the birds' knowledge of the ancient flyway—not with ultralights but with hang gliders that will soar a difficult path extending more than three thousand miles over four different countries.

These human-guided migratory flights are among the most recent acts of vigorous intervention to rescue from extinction a singular creature—what conservationist Aldo Leopold called "no mere bird" but "wilderness incarnate." For thousands of years cranes have been honored for their beauty, their ancient ancestry, impressive size and flight. In Africa and Europe their image appears in prehistoric art. They figure on Egyptian tombs, in Russian songs, in the totems and clans of Native Americans, in Australian dances, and Greek and Roman myths. In many parts of Asia cranes are held sacred as symbols of happiness, good luck, long life, peace. After the dropping of the bomb that people said was brighter than a thousand suns, a young girl stricken with radiation sickness set out to fold a thousand paper

How can beauty, science, and ethics mix?
Photo Source: © Joel Bauchat Grant/Shutterstock

cranes in the hopes that she would recover. She died before reaching her goal, but other children pursued the task, and now the stone monuments of Peace Memorial Park in Hiroshima are ornamented with millions of the tiny folded cranes.

The esteem in which these birds are held has not spared them destruction. Cranes are among the most endangered families of birds, having been hunted, persecuted, chivied out of their last havens by human pressures. Nine of the planet's fifteen species are threatened with extinction. In East Asia loss of wetlands threatens the red-crowned, the hooded, and the white-naped cranes. The graceful blue crane, the national bird of South Africa, has suffered from predation by wild dogs and the cultivation of tree plantations, which has eliminated great stretches of its unique grassland habitat.

Whoopers, the rarest of cranes, were extirpated from much of their range in North America in the nineteenth century by hunting, egg collecting, and habitat destruction as settlers drained wetlands and plowed prairie for farming. By the early 1940s only twenty-one birds remained. The extreme plight of the whooping crane alerted many people to the high price we may pay for harming the natural world—and the need for extraordinary efforts to recover what is almost lost. With the help of habitat protection, hunting restrictions, and captive-breeding programs begun in the 1960s, the remnant population of whooping cranes began to grow. It now numbers three hundred birds in the wild and more than one hundred in captivity—not anywhere near its original abundance, but a big step on the road to recovery.

One man who had led the strenuous work to save the whooping crane is George Archibald, cofounder of the International Crane Foundation (ICF) in Baraboo, Wisconsin. Now Archibald has a new dream. In a patch of prairie spangled with blooms of butterfly milkweed and *Silphium* not far from the headquarters of the ICF, Archibald sits in the same dark shack where Aldo Leopold wrote his classic essays on conservation. A self-described "craniac," Archibald is considered the world's foremost expert on cranes. He is an unassuming man, committed to rescuing cranes from the abyss of extinction, and forever optimistic about his chances for success. In the past quarter century he has helped to launch crane conservation programs in Japan, China, South Korea, India, Iran, South Africa, Australia, and Russia. He and his team of ICF have created a species bank of captive cranes to guard against extinction. He has carried crane eggs tens of thousands of miles in plywood boxes and delivered them safely to captive-breeding facilities. He has danced with cranes, sung with them, devoted his life to saving them and their habitat.

Why? "Cranes are ambassadors of the ecosystems in which they live and also of international goodwill," he says, "two things we need to conserve. Because these birds require pristine habitat, they act as umbrella species; if you save them, you are also saving the wetland and grassland ecosystems on which they depend. And because their migratory routes don't heed political boundaries, any effort to protect them requires the participation of diverse people in different countries. So they act as vehicles for cooperation between nations that are often politically polarized." He pauses. "Also, I love them."

Archibald's latest goal is to restore a population of migratory Siberian cranes to Central Asia. Sometimes called snow wreaths, the magnificent Siberians are the most highly specialized of cranes, depending exclusively on bogs, marshes, and other wetlands for resting, feeding, and roosting. They are also the most critically endangered, their numbers dwindling from loss of habitat and from hunting during migrations. The Siberians have traditionally migrated more than three thousand miles from the high tundra of Siberia across eleven countries to wintering grounds in China, India, and Iran. The success of the migration depends on the welfare of chains of wetlands across the continent, which serve as stopover points for the birds.

Archibald and an international team are working to secure legislation safeguarding these areas and upgrading their protection. The effort takes patience, as many of these nations are dealing with difficult political situations, limited resources, and skeptical leaders.

In the summer of 2005 the team plans to raise a dozen Siberian chicks in captivity with crane-costumed parents and train them to fly behind hang gliders flown by crane-costumed pilots. Then, sometime that autumn, three hang gliders will launch from Uvat, Russia, soar over western Kazakhstan, stopping at the Volga River's Astrakhan Nature Reserve, then wing south over Azerbaijan, along the western shores of the Caspian Sea, to the flooded fields at Fereydun Kenar and Esbaran, the cranes' wintering grounds in Iran. The birds will follow.

The international effort to find these birds safe passage in such politically trou-bled areas is considered crazy by some and brilliant by others, a way of drawing global attention to the cranes and their world—minnow, bulrush, cattail, river shallow, aura of ancient flyways that unite regions and ignore borders.

PERSONAL RESPONSE

Do you believe that we should try to save species from extinction? What is the purpose of such efforts?

QUESTIONS FOR CLASS OR SMALL-GROUP DISCUSSION

1. What is an umbrella species and in what way do cranes fit that definition?
2. Why are cranes called "ambassadors of goodwill" and "wilderness incarnate"?
3. Compile a list of species that are threatened with extinction. How many of these species are in Canada? What actions should governments take in addressing the problems of species threatened by extinction?
4. Is it culturally responsible to prevent the extinction of a species or is it merely interference with nature or natural outcomes?

FOR FURTHER VIEWING: NATURAL SCIENCES

A Brief History of Time (1991); *Jurassic Park* (1993); *The Incredible Shrinking Man* (1957); *The Incredible Shrinking Woman* (1981); *Godzilla* (1954); *Tarantula* (1955); *Shine* (1996); *A Beautiful Mind* (2001); *Frankenstein* (1931, 1994); *Young Frankenstein* (1974); *The Sterilization of Leilani Muir* (1996); *Gorillas in the Mist: The Story of Dian Fossey* (1988).

CHAPTER TWENTY

GLOBAL HEALTH

INTRODUCTION

Epidemics, pandemics, and plagues have always been with us. Consider such major outbreaks of disease as the bubonic plague in Europe and China; cholera epidemics in various parts of the world from time to time, including up to the present; the smallpox epidemic that swept Sweden in 1764; the typhus epidemic that killed more than 3 million Russians during World War I; and the influenza pandemic of 1918 to 1919 that killed more than 20 million people around the world. More recently, untreatable, deadly viruses have infected populations in certain areas of the world, worrying health officials that these viruses may spread elsewhere. The Ebola virus in Africa, for instance, produces acute suffering in its victims, and most die within days of being infected. Viruses are particularly difficult to contain because they live inside body cells, where antibiotics cannot reach them. Worse, once a person is infected with a virus, it can continue to live in the body's cells, waiting to strike again many years later. Even such previously treatable diseases as herpes, hepatitis, and chicken pox are becoming resistant to treatment. These and other viruses pose a considerable threat to the general population.

HIV/AIDS remains the most pressing and controversial global health problem. Some predictions hold that, unless support is radically increased, as many as 70 million persons in developing countries will, within the next few decades, perish.

In 2006, the United Nations and the World Health Organization reported that, since 1981, AIDS had claimed 25 million persons. Although this rapid spread of AIDS is obviously a human tragedy of the first order, the negative spin-off affects the realms of economics, politics, and international relations. Most nations are struggling to deal with the issues of prevention, responsibility, and assistance. The history of medicine often seems to be a history of human ingenuity versus the ingenuity of bacteria and viruses. AIDS is a modern plague in one sense because it is overpowering, and a cure seems to be beyond the scope of human will or ingenuity.

In the following essays, Stephen Lewis, former Canadian ambassador to the United Nations, writes about the politics and tragedy of AIDS, while Daniel Defoe gives an account of the bubonic plague that attacked 17th-century London. Barbara Tuchman's piece draws a vivid picture of calamities in 14th-century Europe, drawing parallels between that century and the modern world.

PANDEMIC: MY COUNTRY IS ON ITS KNEES

Stephen Lewis

Born in 1937, in Ottawa, Stephen Lewis has been a politician, a broadcaster, the Canadian ambassador to the United Nations, and a special envoy and advisor to the United Nations. He now directs the Stephen Lewis Foundation, which establishes community-based projects to battle the HIV/AIDS pandemic in Africa. In 2005, Time *magazine deemed him one of the most influential people in the world, and in 2003,* Maclean's *magazine named him Canadian of the Year. The piece below is based on one of his CBC Massey Lectures and appears in his book* Race Against Time *(2005).*

It will doubtless become clear, during the course of these lectures, that I have a love affair with Africa. It seems appropriate, therefore, to describe how that affair came about, and how it relates to the Africa of today.

I left the University of Toronto prematurely in the spring of 1960. It was premature because my academic career (a significant abuse of the word "career") was abysmal in the extreme, and when it became clear (it was never really in doubt) that I wouldn't graduate, I flunked out belligerently, and took off for other climes. I don't intend to search the depths of my psyche for an explanation, thus enlisting the bemusement of the Canadian public that may be listening to, or reading, these lectures. Suffice to say that I loved the university environment, feasted at its academic high tables, and read voraciously throughout my undergraduate years. But I just couldn't muster the energy for exams. It turned out to make little difference in life, although, if I may set your collective minds at ease, I don't wander around recommending similar conduct to the post-secondary youth of today.

My first job after university, in the early summer of 1960, was with the Socialist International in London, England. It seemed a perfect fit: it took me away from my hapless university career and allowed me, nonetheless, to follow my ideology. For those of you who may not be familiar with my ancestral political background, I was raised in a social democratic family: my father, David Lewis, was the federal secretary of the Co-operative Commonwealth Federation (CCF), precursor of the New Democratic Party (NDP), of which he eventually became the federal leader. I have a brother and two sisters; we all understood, even when pre-pubescent, that either we were ideological clones of our parents, or we were disinherited.

The Socialist International was a coordinating body of all of the democratic socialist parties in the western and developing world. It was defiantly anti-communist, and most member parties at the time would have described themselves as democrats first and socialists second. I was but a lowly researcher. However, simply being at the Socialist International allowed me a close-up view of both the British Labour Party and the British Trade Union movement. I was in England during the great Clause 4 debate on nationalization, which served me well in future years when I headed a provincial NDP caucus, some of whose members were maniacal public ownership fanatics.

My research role also permitted me to monitor mail on a daily basis. Lo and behold, after only a few weeks on the job, there fell into my hands an invitation, extended to all and sundry, to attend a week-long conference in September, of the World Assembly of Youth in Accra, Ghana. I was utterly intrigued and replied to say that I would be pleased to come to represent the hundreds of thousands of Canadian left-wing youth. (There were eight of us at the time.)

So off I went to Ghana, as thrilled and excited as any twenty-two-year-old would be at the prospect of adventure, however brief, on a new and, for me, unknown continent. Although the conference lasted only seven days, I stayed in Africa for a year; I was crazy about the continent from the moment I set foot on its soil—the music, the energy, the kindness, the generosity, the camaraderie, the purposefulness of everything. Remember, when I was in Ghana it had been independent for only two years; the sense of possibility was everywhere.

I found it all irresistible. The World Assembly of Youth was the best thing that had ever happened to me—so it was rather comical to learn several years later, via the poet-essayist-editor Stephen Spender in the pages of his monthly magazine, *Encounter,* that the World Assembly of Youth was a CIA front. I'm probably the first person you've ever met who's indebted to the CIA.

Ghana was a revelation in a number of ways. I had two jobs: teaching English and history at Accra High School, and "extra-mural studies" at the University of Legon. Just imagine, if you will, having *Merchant of Venice* as the Shakespeare text for a grade ten class, and fifteen minutes into a reading of the play, a bright young girl's hand goes up, and she asks with beatific innocence, "Mr. Lewis, what is a Jew?" I was momentarily stunned by the question. That innocence, that absence of malice, or prejudice, or intolerance (i.e., anti-Semitism) was one of the most heartwarming characteristics of the new Ghana—indeed, of all African countries in the immediate flowering of liberation.

My job at the University of Legon was even better than my daytime teaching job. I travelled three nights a week to villages within a fifty-kilometre radius of Accra, ferrying kerosene lamps and a portable library, teaching the literate elements of the community: the cocoa marketing board employees, the local teachers, the firefighters. It was giddy and exhilarating. They were desperate for learning, faces shining in the oscillating glimmer of the light. I can't remember when I've had such fun or been so excited by students.

But there was more. President Kwame Nkrumah—a pan-Africanist to his core; a man who saw a "United States of Africa" as the ultimate anti-colonial vindication of Africa's destiny—was flying South African dissidents in the dead of night out of what was then Basutoland (now Lesotho), a British protectorate surrounded by South Africa, and into the freedom of Ghana. This was the generation of freedom fighters yet to come, and they stayed in student residences on the Legon campus. I became fast friends with many of them and soaked up the anti-apartheid liberation ideology. It was particularly easy to do because also living on the campus, having recently been thrown out of South Africa by then president Hendrik Verwoerd, was Leslie Rubin. When Alan Paton (the celebrated author of *Cry, the Beloved Country*) was president, Leslie had been vice-president of the Liberal Party, serving as the last elected white person representing Africans of the Cape Province in the South African senate. Those were the grounds for his eviction by Verwoerd.

I worshipped Leslie; we spent a great deal of time together during the few months I was in Ghana. After he left South Africa, he became the first dean of the University of Legon Law School, later authoring the definitive Ghanaian constitution. He was a kind and fatherly figure, a man of great principle and passion in the anti-apartheid struggle. Apart from his natural academic gifts, Leslie was a pamphleteer of extraordinary talent, often writing under the pseudonym of Martin Burger, savaging the apartheid administration. His finest tract, which had great influence outside of South Africa, was titled "This Is Apartheid," and consisted of a remarkably down-to-earth, non-legal, populist exposition of forty apartheid laws. It was a truly blood-chilling document, exposing for all the world to see the madness and brutality of the Nazi-like regime.

One of the bizarre consequences of these varied and valued contacts in Ghana was a phone call my father received in the fall of 1960, out of the blue, from the Canadian Ministry of Foreign Affairs, saying that I had been banned from South Africa. My father couldn't figure out how that had happened when his son was clearly resident in Ghana, but he soon understood: one of the well-known incidental truths about apartheid was its twisted and demented irrationality. I was *persona non grata* by association, and it was particularly absurd because of course I had not the slightest intention of visiting South Africa. However, the encounters with my new South African friends, and their tales of ugly facism at home had an influence on me which lasted for the rest of my life. It was no accident that when I was elected to the Ontario Legislature in 1963, one of my earliest private member's bills was an act designed to ban the import of South African wines and liquors into Ontario. Many of my legislative colleagues were mystified; my Tory friends were derisive. But my views had been well and truly formed.

I had been in Ghana for just a few months when I received a letter from a young man I'd met at the World Assembly of Youth, Mokwugo Okoye, a radical left-wing activist living in what was the Eastern Region in Nigeria. He wrote to say that a Peace Corps volunteer slated to be the principal of a little private boarding secondary school in Mok's village had failed to turn up, and was I interested in coming to Nigeria to fill the post? How could I say no? In early 1961, I drove several hundred kilometres to the Eastern Region, taking up residence in a tiny village between the regional capital, Enugu, and the hub of commercial activity, the chaotic city of Onitsha.

Mok was an astonishing figure. He was a polemicist of raging voice and pen, much admired throughout the country for his intense nationalism and formidable literary power. He was just a few years older than I, and patiently schooled me in the perplexing, often incomprehensible minutiae of Nigerian politics, all of which would serve me well in later life. My sojourn at the school was equally compelling. It had but four classes—two grade nines, two grade tens—with a total student body of about one hundred. I loved those kids: they were so anxious to learn, so excited by the potential reach of knowledge that every class was thrilling, for them and for me. A boarding school allows for a special camaraderie, with teachers and students on a shared site: the sense of family was very real. One of the saddest, most wretched experiences of my life, was to return to the Eastern Region, during the Biafran civil war in the late 1960s, to try to find my former students, only to discover that many of them had died—some from bullets, some from hunger, some from both. It proved to be a premonitory glimpse of things to come.

After several exhilarating months in Nigeria, I asked a Canadian friend to join me, and we drove together across the continent through Chad, the Central African Republic, the Congo, Sudan, Uganda, and, finally, Kenya. (It took us about five weeks; it was not supposed to be possible.) I taught trade unionists in Uganda at the International Confederation of Free Trade Unions' African Labour College in Kampala, and ended up in Nairobi in a job that involved finding university places in North America for African students.

It was in August 1961 that I received a letter from Tommy Douglas, asking me to return to Canada to work for the very recently formed New Democratic Party. I accepted his invitation to leap back into Canada's political fray with abiding reluctance. (You couldn't say no to Tommy, the same Tommy Douglas who that very month in 1961 had become the first leader of the NDP, and was recently chosen in the CBC poll as the greatest Canadian of them all.) On my return to Canada in the fall, I plunged into excited pre-election activity as the first full-time federal organizer for the NDP.

It was, however, incredibly hard to say goodbye to Africa. I travelled there again in the late 1960s, and returned, with regularity, when I was a Canadian diplomat at the United Nations, then with UNICEF, and finally, now, as the HIV/AIDS envoy. I have spent time, at one point or another, in the great majority of the countries on the continent.

It must be understood, without any hint of heady romanticism, that Africa in the 1950s and 1960s, when I was most impressionable, was a continent of vitality, growth, and boundless expectation. It got into your blood, your viscera, your heart. The bonds were not just durable, they were unbreakable. There was something intoxicating about an environment of such hope, anticipation, affection, energy, indomitability. The Africa I knew was poor, but it wasn't staggering under the weight of oppression, disease, and despair; it was absolutely certain that it could triumph over every exigency. There were countless health emergencies—polio, measles, malaria, malnutrition—but it never felt like Armageddon. In fact, life expectancy began to rise in the late 1960s, until the reversal induced by Structural Adjustment Programs on the one hand, and AIDS on the other. And the people, the people everywhere, were so unbelievably kind; I had never encountered cultures so uniformly inclusive, gentle, decent, welcoming.

I was smitten for life.

You can understand, therefore, how painful it is to visit my beloved Africa under present-day circumstances. It's not just the ruinous economic and social decline, the reasons for which I attempted to explain in part in my first lecture. It's the ravaging of the pandemic; it's the way in which a communicable disease called AIDS has taken countries by the throat and reduced them to spectral caricatures of their former selves.

It's impossible to write about the Millennium Development Goals without writing about HIV/AIDS, and that's not simply because defeating the pandemic is one of those goals. It's because every goal, at least in Africa, is put in jeopardy by AIDS. I remember sitting in the General Assembly on June 2, 2005, when there was a Special Session to assess the progress that had been made since the Declaration of Commitment on AIDS was embraced, by consensus, at a more elaborate UN gathering in 2001. Rather mournfully, the Secretary-General told the assembled delegates that progress was minimal, that most countries had defaulted on their commitments, that the pandemic was outpacing the response, and that the MDGs were thus imperiled.

Later that day, at a press conference, Peter Piot, the executive director of UNAIDS, was far less guarded. He said, flatly, that the goals would not be reached.

There is just no way to compare the Africa of forty-five years ago with the Africa of today. It's like comparing Rome with Pompeii. So let me tell you, by way of a procession of anecdotes, what Pompeii looks like. I've deliberately chosen anecdotes as the narrative vehicle, in order to give the pandemic an accessible face, rather than relying on the dehumanizing swamp of numbers. Some of the stories you may have heard before, but all illumine an aspect of Africa's desperation. I don't pretend that every country is similarly afflicted. Southern Africa is the terrifying epicentre, East Africa, including Ethiopia, is in serious straits, central Africa is struggling, and only West Africa seems able to contain the virus. But even there, in countries like Nigeria, Côte d'Ivoire, Cameroon, and Burkina Faso, huge numbers of people are infected or at risk.

It was 2002; I was visiting the Lilongwe Central Hospital in the capital of Malawi. The adult medical wards, male and female, presented a picture right out of Dante. There were two people to every bed, head to foot and foot to head, and in most instances, someone under the bed on the concrete floor, each in an agony of full-blown AIDS. With demonic, rhythmic regularity, another aluminum coffin would be wheeled into the ward to cart away the body of the person who had most recently died.

Every patient was a near cadaver. The wards rumbled with low, almost-inaudible moans, as though those who were ill could not summon the strength to give voice to the pain. The smell was awful: a room of rotting feces and stale urine. And the eyes, so sunken and glazed and pleading.

I talked with the administrator. He told me that on the ten-hour night shift, to care for between sixty and seventy patients—each and every one of whom would have been in intensive care in a Canadian hospital—there would be one nurse. The situation was impossible.

But the situation is impossible in much of southern Africa. The pandemic has taken a decimating toll on nurses, doctors, and clinicians of every variety. There are simply no pharmacists to speak of; incredible though it may seem, I can't remember a hospital or clinic that had a full-time pharmacist. You might well ask: Who, then, dispenses the antiretroviral drugs for the treatment of AIDS? The answer is: Anyone who can be found. The pandemic has also ravaged the ranks of community health workers, teachers, farmers—absolutely every professional discipline, every occupation.

The problem is grievously compounded by the practice of "poaching," and the resulting brain drain from Africa to the outside world. Some of the drain goes to other countries in the region—South Africa or Botswana, for example—but they, too, lose professionals in the predominant flow to the United Kingdom, the United States, Australia, and Canada. It's rancid behaviour on the part of the west.

Please don't misunderstand me. People have the human right to move to better jobs, with better pay, better benefits, better working conditions. But given the situation in Africa, they shouldn't be induced to leave by countries perfectly capable of solving occupational deficits internally. The United Kingdom in particular has a dreadful record; it's said—and not in jest—that there are more Malawian doctors in Manchester than in Malawi, more Zambian doctors in Birmingham than in Zambia. When confronted with these facts, the U.K. government replied by saying that they've passed a law which forbids any public health facility in the United Kingdom from the solicitation of health-care workers in developing countries. And that is indeed the case. What they don't acknowledge, however, is the real problem: personnel agencies advertise for professional people, travelling to countries of southern Africa and interviewing potential candidates, and offering all manner of monetary and related incentives. Until the personnel agencies are barred from such shameless raiding, the protestations of western governments—all of which, to a lesser or greater degree, turn a blind eye—ring hollow.

The other remedy, of course, is to provide significant salary increases for professionals who remain at home, improvements in working conditions, expanded training of health professionals, and even the creation of new career lines—adequate to do the job, but requiring less by way of formal accreditation. The U.K.'s international development agency has a pilot project with exactly those components underway in Malawi; would that it became the pattern across the continent.

The loss of health-care personnel has become a crisis of huge proportions. But it is only one of many crises which turn so many countries on the continent into a quagmire of despair.

In 2003, I had the privilege of travelling in Zambia and Uganda with Graça Machel, a good friend (and hero) of mine with whom I have worked, intermittently, over the last decade. Graça is the former minister of education of Mozambique, the former first lady of Mozambique, now married to Nelson Mandela, and known everywhere in Africa as one of the most charismatic and compelling of personalities. She is also gentle, generous, formidably intelligent, and profoundly knowledgeable about the African continent. Together we wanted to examine the situation of women and children in the face of the pandemic.

In Uganda we experienced two telling episodes. We were taken to ground zero of the pandemic, the district of Rakai, where the first case of HIV was diagnosed in 1982. The local community very much wanted us to see what was happening to the orphans, and in the first instance we were led to a large hut and escorted inside. Immediately to the left of the door as we entered, sat the patriarch of the family, eighty-six years old, clutching a white cane, entirely blind. To the right of the door sat his two wives, one seventy-six, the other seventy-eight. Between them they had given birth to nine children, eight of whom were dead. The ninth was visibly dying in our presence. In the interior of the hut, the orphans had gathered, and sitting on the floor, looking up at us expectantly, were thirty-six orphan children between the ages of two and sixteen.

Graça and I exchanged those wordless glances that occur between adults when there's a feeling of helplessness in the air. Just how the two grandmothers were supposed to cope under the circumstances was nowhere evident. The older kids were out of school because they couldn't afford the school fees, and the younger kids were surviving on one meal a day, or sometimes no food whatsoever on the weekends.

It leads me to want to say a word about grandmothers. They have emerged as the heroes of Africa. The physical ravaging of extended families and the desperate poverty of communities means that grandmothers step in when there's no one else to tread. I wonder if such a situation has ever occurred before in the history of organized society? I wish there were more authoritative information about what happened to orphans during the Black Death of the fourteenth century.

In the instance of Africa today, these old and unimaginably frail women often look after five or ten or fifteen kids, enduring every conceivable hardship for the sake of their grandchildren, alongside additional numbers of other abandoned waifs who wander the landscape of the continent. The trauma of the grandmothers equals that of the orphans; in fact, every normal rhythm of life is violated as grandmothers bury their own children and then look after their orphan grandchildren. I remember, vividly, sitting under the trees, outside the Alex/Tara Children's Clinic in Alexandra Township in Johannesburg, with about twenty grandmothers as they told their heartbreaking stories of personal loss, one by one. I could barely imagine how they were functioning; every one of them had made that heartwrenching trek to the

Stephen Lewis in Africa: What should we do about AIDS? What can we do?
Photo Source: Allafrica.com/Tamela Hultman. Reprinted with permission of the Stephen Lewis Foundation.

graveyard, many more than once, and yet they spoke with a spunk and resilience that was positively supernatural.

Save one. There was one woman, seventy-three years old, sitting slightly apart from the rest, who refused to speak. No amount of encouragement or cajoling would do, until the women collectively, in an incredibly moving show of commiseration, sang a soft song of solidarity and love.

And then Agnes finally spoke. She took no more than a couple of minutes: her story was wrenchingly brief, ghastly in its simplicity. She had buried all five of her adult children between 2001 and 2003—all five—and was left with four orphan grandchildren. That was it. She wept.

I learned as I left that every one of her four grandchildren is HIV-positive. How much can one grandmother endure?

But alas, that's not the end of it. When the grandmothers die, there's no one coming up behind, and so you have the phenomenon of what we call "child-headed households," or "sibling families," where the oldest child is the head of the household, looking after his or her siblings. It's not new: it happened in Rwanda after the genocide. But never have we had a situation involving such large numbers. In Zambia, 23 percent of all children are orphans now, with numbers expected to rise to one in three by 2010; inevitably, a significant number will find themselves in sibling families. In Swaziland, it's expected that up to 15 percent of the entire population will be orphans by 2010. I well remember meeting with several members of the Swaziland cabinet, discussing matters of public policy, when the minister of labour suddenly jumped to his feet, impatient and agitated. "Forget about this policy stuff," he said, his voice rising. "Don't you understand that we're a nation of orphans? That we have hundreds of child-headed households in Swaziland, where the age of the child heading the household is eight?"

Back in Uganda, Graça and I were taken by the local villagers to see one of those sibling families. There were five children in all: three girls, 14, 12 and 10, and two boys, 11 and 8. We entered the modest hut, and sat down with our backs to the wall, Graça with her arm around the three girls on her right and I with my arm around the two boys on my left. Graça then told all the hangers-on to leave—all the media, all the UN staff—except for one community worker and one translator.

I had no idea what was coming. Graça turned to the two older girls, and in a most gentle, reassuring voice aside, "Have you started to menstruate yet?" The two girls, clearly startled, replied in those shy, barely audible whispered voices so characteristics of African children, "Yes." The Graça began to ask a series of questions: "Do you know what it means? Have you talked to anyone about it? Do you talk to the villagers about it—your teachers, your fellow students? Does anyone bring you pads?"

The atmosphere was intense, the little girls, now fully embraced in Graça's arms, seemed to have suspended breathing, and I suddenly understood that I was witness to the first act of "mothering" that these girls had ever received about one of the most transfiguring experiences of a young girl's life.

I've told this story a number of times because the experience had a profound impact on me. At the moment when Graça asked her questions, I thought to myself: That's what's happening right across the continent: the transfer of love and knowledge and values and experience from one generation to the next is gone, and with it goes the confidence and security and sense of place which children normally take for granted. Children, already traumatized by the death of their parents, are left reeling as they confront the void in the aftermath.

As we were leaving, I asked the oldest sister, "Who puts you to bed at night?"

"I put everyone to bed," she replied.

"But bedtime can be pretty scary," I offered. "The nights are dark, the dreams can be upsetting. Don't any of the neighbours come in to help?"

"No," she said, matter-of-factly. "I put them to bed myself. I'm the mother."

I can't emphasize strongly enough the extreme emotional turmoil of children orphaned by AIDS. What the world fails to recognize is that these children don't become orphans when their parents die, they become orphans while their parents are dying, and this is especially true in the case of the death of the mother.

I've now seen innumerable people die, in hospital wards, in clinic corridors, in hospices, and at home. When they die at home, the scene—almost Shakespearean in its sense of tragedy and finality interwoven—is invariably the same. I'm taken to a tiny rural village to see the application of "home-based care." I enter a hut, where the bleakness and gloom are palpable. On the floor of the hut lies a young woman—always young—in her twenties or thirties, so wan and emaciated as to be unable to lift either hand or head. I bend down, painfully inadequate to the circumstance, and touch her brow, uttering some pointless banality which is intended to soothe, and then as I step back, looking around me, I see her children, all her children, standing in the darkened shadows, watching their mother die.

How do they ever recover? The death is long, agonizing, and filled with indignity. The children wash their mother, clean her up when she's incontinent (an experience of excruciating embarrassment for both mother and children), they search everywhere for an aspirin to relieve the pain of some opportunistic infection, and then, horrified, gaping, they stand in the darkened shadows, and watch their mother die.

There is, undoubtedly, some solace to be found in the comfort of relatives, if relatives exist, especially grandmothers, if they're still alive. But as I write, there is no master plan for children orphaned by AIDS. There are to be sure, as there always are, endless studies, and individual projects and frameworks. But nothing is yet taken to scale. The gap between analysis and action yawns like the proverbial chasm, and it's only now, in 2005, a quarter century into the pandemic, that we're beginning to think of a response to the orphans. I shall try to deal with what should be done in my final lecture.

There are certain other aspects of the pandemic that I should like to reconnoitre to demonstrate the contrast between the conditions of today and the conditions of yesteryear.

The first is surprising: it's the monumental crisis of food. I can't remember, when I travelled through the continent forty-five years ago, encountering families, let alone whole communities, who were hungry. I'm sure they existed: I just didn't encounter them. By and large, there was always enough food for everyone; poverty was ubiquitous, but it didn't mean starvation.

Whenever I travel in Africa today, it feels as though everyone is hungry—hungry to the point of starvation. There are, certainly very real areas of famine—Zimbabwe, Zambia, Malawi, Lesotho, Swaziland, Mozambique—they have all suffered terrible droughts over the last several years, and the drought cum pandemic have added up to starvation. But it's more than that. It's hard to go anywhere on the continent without people crying out for food. In fact, if you ask almost anyone what they need most, including people suffering from full-blown AIDS, they will not say drugs; they will say food. It's a universal reply.

I recall visiting with a large group of widows and grandmothers in a rural community hall in Malawi (coincidentally called Canada Hall, with a blurred Canadian flag on the wall because it had been built with Canadian aid money) to chat with them about their lives in the midst of the virus. The conversation was dominated—totally dominated—by pleas for food. It was incomparably sad; I had no food to give them, but that's all they really wanted of me. Sure, I steered things into talk of treatment, and at one point, even tried to raise the issue of condoms, but every voice came back to food. It's so stark and so troubling: even though there was an interpreter present so that no words were lost, the woman constantly pointed at their mouths and stomachs to make absolutely sure that I wouldn't miss what agitated them most.

The question of hunger becomes so much more critical in the presence of AIDS. Treatment is much more difficult, sometimes impossible, if the patient has nothing to eat: the body can't handle the drugs without food. And the further bitter truth is that full-blown AIDS can sometimes be forestalled for a considerable period of time if the body is receiving nutritious foods. When I was in Malawi, I kept repeating the defining mantra: If the body has no food to consume, the virus consumes the body.

I'm not sure there is an answer to this debilitating and systemic plague of hunger, but I shall try to suggest a response as I wind my way to the end of the lectures.

Certainly when I travelled forty-five years ago, death was never a constant companion. But in the presence of the pandemic, it sometimes feels as though death stalks every waking moment. And as the four years of my work have unfolded, more and more it's the death of older children and young adults that is so widespread, stark and unnerving.

I shall inevitably talk a lot about death in these lectures, but let me be intensely personal about it for a moment. I was completely unprepared for the pervasiveness of death. It has shaken me to my core. I must admit that from time to time the enveloping cloak of death, combined with the appalling paucity of response has made me feel futile in the face of the pandemic. I never submit to those momentary lapses because futility leads nowhere, but the way in which death seeps into every crevice of life shifts one's view of the world. I'm not sure I can even find the words to explain it: all of us who live in privileged western societies experience death from time to time, but in much of southern Africa that's all people know. Their lives consist of attending funerals; if I may mangle a phrase, they go on a graveyard crawl every weekend. It's commonplace to say that every family in every country—Kenya, Uganda, Tanzania, Zimbabwe, Zambia, Malawi, Lesotho, Swaziland, South Africa, Namibia, Mozambique, Botswana—has suffered a loss in the carnage of AIDS. But merely to use the words is to rob them of meaning.

One of the moments that lives most ineradicably in my mind, occurred during a visit to the pediatric ward of the University Teaching Hospital in Lusaka, Zambia, in 2003. It was at the height of famine, and every crib had four or five infants and toddlers crushed together between the raised slatted sides, most of them suffering extreme malnutrition or AIDS or both. Their bodies were so thin that it was legitimate to ask, how can they still be alive?

Well, as it happens, not all of them were. Approximately ten minutes into the visit, the walls of the ward vibrated with what can only be called an otherworldly wail—a wail the like of which I had never before heard. I was stunned, and convulsively spun around to find the source. There, kneeling by the side of a bed, embodying anguish and despair, rocking violently back and forth, was a young mother crazed by loss, watching a nurse firmly place a sheet over the body of an infant and take the child away.

Incredible though it may seem, the exact episode was twice more repeated during my forty minutes in the ward. It prompted no brake on the pace of activity; it was commonplace. In the pediatric ward of the University Teaching Hospital in Lusaka, Zambia, throughout 2003, nothing was more commonplace than death.

I remember visiting the wonderful little faith-based organization called Catholic AIDS Action in Windhoek, Namibia. It is a place where people living with AIDS come together to network and seek companionable solace. Sister Raphaele excitedly showed me around, and then asked if I'd go out back to see their income-generating project. I did so, and was greeted by the sight of four young men making miniature papier mâché coffins for infants: tiny, light, plain. As they affixed silver aluminum foil handles to the coffins, they looked at me and said, with an admixture of pride and pain, "We can't keep up with the demand."

I'm reminded of another "income-generating" project, this time in Zambia. It was early in 2005, and I was asked by a district commissioner to visit a fairly remote farming community where a group of village women had a project of which they were greatly proud.

We rode in our Land Rovers over some hideously rocky and tortuous country roads, and then had to get out and walk a fair bit further. Eventually we came to a large cabbage patch, beside which stood a group of fifteen or twenty women holding aloft a large banner reading "PLWA," proclaiming their status as People Living With AIDS.

After several minutes of animated conversation, I asked if the cabbages were the project (not a brilliant hunch on my part). They laughed uproariously and said yes. "You use it to supplement your diet?" Yes again. "Do you have a surplus?"

"Yes," they chorused, "We take whatever we don't use to market."

"And what do you do with the profit?" I asked. It was here that time stood still. They looked at me for ages, as though I were asking a question to which I surely knew the answer, and then they suddenly realized that the question was genuine. "We buy coffins of course," they said, "We never have enough coffins."

My mind ricocheted back to Catholic AIDS Action: "We can't keep up with the demand."

There is just no way to convey the atmosphere of death which hangs like a Damoclean *hammer* over these countries. I have heard the president of Botswana use the word "extermination" to describe what he feels his country is dealing with. I have heard the prime minister of Lesotho use the word "annihilation" to describe what he feels his country is confronting. In my last close conversation with the president of Zambia, he used the word "holocaust" to describe what he feels his country is facing. In June 2005, the new deputy prime minister of Namibia said publicly that her country was "on its knees."

It's heartbreaking to see the Africa I once knew reduced to such desperation.

And death comes with such terrifying speed. When I first travelled to Zambia in the envoy role in 2001, I met the most wonderful group of PLWAs. There must have been twenty, most of them young women—bright, engaging young women; we sat around a large table in a hotel conference room as they laid out their concerns and grievances. They were so smart and so lively, and I loved the conversation. Eight months later I went back to Zambia and met with the group again, and more than half of them were gone. I was afraid to enquire about the absentees because I knew, all too well, why they were absent.

It's actually a pattern. A couple of years back, I met with eighteen representatives of various district and regional groups of PLWAs in Rwanda. They told me that they had met the year previous with UNAIDS Executive Director Peter Piot. Sixteen of the eighteen who had met with Peter were not alive to meet with me.

It's so incredibly painful. You make friends and the friends are gone before you can consummate the friendship. These groups of people living with AIDS are remarkably courageous, coming forward, declaring their status, preaching the message of prevention, sustaining each other in the face of cosmic tragedy. And yet they're scorned and mocked by government, and rarely listened to, rarely given an audience with the powers-that-be. Worse, society heaps endless, often brutal, sometimes even murderous stigma and discrimination upon those who are infected. The antagonism comes from intimate family, from friends, from fellow workers, from teachers, from clerics—no one escapes the barbs and malice. Even the children are targets, mocked and stoned on the way home from school.

It would be wrong, however, and in a sense too easy, to conjure up only the pictures of despair. Let me recount some of the images of hope, because it's the images of hope, however fragile, however intermittent, that keep the countries going.

I was visiting the southern province of Ethiopia in 2004. In the little town of Nazareth, the UN's World Food Programme (WFP), had gathered together a large contingent of truck drivers, two hundred strong, who had undergone a training course on HIV prevention. The idea was smart and it was logical. These were the drivers who encountered commercial sex workers along their delivery routes, the truck drivers whom we regularly list in the high-risk-group category, the truck drivers who return to their homes and partners and spread the virus. So the WFP had conducted workshops on prevention, and I turned out to be the visitor with whom their stories could be shared.

It was memorable and it was hilarious, rather like a robust church service of confessions. One by one these hardy men straggled to the front of the room to give personal testimony. Strangled by unaccustomed shyness, each and every one, they described how they use condoms at every sexual encounter, and would never again venture forth without a supply of condoms (judiciously supplied, free of charge, by the WFP). There was much merriment, much embarrassment, much applause.

And then one of the only two women in the room muscled her way to the front, ostentatiously pushing the men aside. To roars of approval, she announced that it was all true: she knew that the men really did carry condoms, and used them whenever the need arose. She was an itinerant trucker, but also a local organizer, and clearly knew whereof she spoke. It was one of those moments to be cherished. The World Food Programme staff were justly proud of their success.

That reminds me of an encounter involving the other side of the equation. The city of Nairobi, on its outskirts, is home to Kibera, possibly the worst slum in all of East Africa. There are large numbers of commercial sex workers, most of whom are part of a little community-based organization run by Professor Elizabeth Ngugi, who teaches community medicine at the University of Nairobi.

Elizabeth Ngugi is a force of nature. She's a diminutive sixty-seven-year-old, of irrepressible energy and a speaking style reminiscent of the grand orators of yore. She took me to the headquarters of the commercial sex workers' group, where about a hundred had gathered. There she launched into a cascading torrent of speechifying, the like of which I haven't heard anywhere else in Africa. Despite the demagogic quality—or perhaps because of it—the women began to sing in their local language, and to dance, wildly waving unopened condoms above their heads. The song apparently conveyed their unanimous commitment to using condoms for the rest of their lives.

It was a wonderfully raucous scene. And then I asked Elizabeth, *sotto voce,* what percentage of the women she thought were HIV-positive. "About 80 percent," was her unhesitating reply. By now I suspect that most of them will have "passed" (the East African term for "died"), but at least the men with whom they had protected sex will not be infected.

It was so supremely sad and so exhilarating in equal measure.

Let me transport you to Lusaka, Zambia, and a remarkable residential school for girls called Umoyo. The school has sixty students, all between the ages of fifteen and nineteen, all chosen by their respective communities (called "compounds" in Lusaka), and all of them orphaned by AIDS. The school itself has a good teacher–student ratio, and the staff members are uniformly first-rate. The principal is a male feminist of strong conviction. The entire atmosphere is resolute and loving.

The girls spend the first month or two recovering from the trauma of parental death; it's a pretty scary, emotionally volatile time. The next couple of months consist of acclimatizing to each other, with all of the rambunctious swings of mood and behaviour that characterized the teenage years. The final eight months or so are an immersion in academe, and these young women invariably score as high on country-wide tests as any group of young people in any regular school.

I have to say that I have yet to visit any other learning environment in southern Africa that does a better job of girls' empowerment. Somehow, the devotion and affection suffusing the school transmits itself to the girls, and they emerge as an immensely appealing, irrepressible, and bright group of young women. They like each other immensely, and they draw both strength and camaraderie from the intense, shared experience.

I visited Umoyo on two particularly memorable occasions, once with Graça Machel, and once with none other than Oprah Winfrey. Graça was so bowled over by the girls that she vowed to come back for their graduation. Oprah was bowled over, period; she clearly cherished the encounter.

And these encounters are indeed something to behold. The girls burst into song and rhythmic dance at the sight of visitors, their voices meshed in soaring crescendo, so exquisitely musical, so energetic, so joyous that you'd never guess at the tragedy that lurks beneath. And then, when you start to ask questions, as we all did, the self-confidence and brazen candour take your breath away. These are young women who will never automatically submit to any young man; young women who will insist that a condom be worn; young women who will report sexual violence; young women who will stay and work in their own communities. Every one of them learns a trade at Umoyo, sometimes tailoring, sometimes food preparation, sometimes carpentry, sometimes hair-dressing—the nature of the trade matters not. They feel confident that when they leave Umoyo, they'll succeed, and overwhelmingly, they do.

The entire program is a testament to possibilities—possibilities that speak to hope in the face of so much desolation. Fifteen to nineteen is the age group most vulnerable to the virus: Umoyo proves that prevention consists of far more than life skills classes, or cleverly constructed learning modules; it consists of the kind of affirmative action for girls that undoes all the cumulative damage done over time, to their perceptions of themselves, their egos, their self-confidence, their sexuality.

So, too, treatment. There are two anecdotes from Uganda which speak volumes. Graça and I visited the Mulago Hospital in Kampala—specifically, its clinic for pregnant women enrolled in a program called "PMTCT," which stands for "Prevention of Mother-to-Child Transmission." (Do you see how everything, even language, conspires against the woman? How is it that we choose an acronym that avoids the question of who infected the mother?)

It's the unhappy truth that only 5 to 8 percent of pregnant women in sub-Saharan Africa have access to programs of PMTCT. This is a terrible deficiency; there is no excuse for this state of affairs. Because of the low access rates, thousands upon thousands of babies are born HIV-positive who need not be infected; most of them die—helplessly, pathetically—before the age of two. But for those HIV-positive women who have access to PMTCT, the program is a godsend: when infected mothers-to-be take one tablet of the wonder drug nevirapine during the birthing process, and their newborns are given a liquid equivalent within seventy-two hours of birth, the rate of transmission is cut by up to 53 percent.

Of course, if we were to use the practices employed in the western world—that is to say, full antiretroviral therapy for the HIV-positive mother for the final twenty-four weeks of pregnancy—we'd be talking of a transmission rate of 1 or 2 percent! Such is the curse of double standards. It's a true obscenity that all those little lives are lost because the resources aren't available to provide a standard of care routinely offered in industrial countries.

However, the better news is that soon after it was introduced in Africa, PMTCT morphed into PMTCT-*Plus*, where the *Plus* represents treatment of the mother, her partner, and the family.

And therein lies a tale. I vividly remember standing outside a little PMTCT clinic in Kigali, Rwanda, back in 2002, chatting with three pregnant women who had tested HIV-positive and decided to take nevirapine. They were in high good spirits, and put to me quite strongly the following proposition: "Mr. Lewis, we'll do anything to save our children, but what about us?" The question could not have been more apt. It's obviously wonderful to save the child, but why should we then lose the mother?

Enter an innovative consortium of American foundations, led by the Rockefeller Foundation. They collectively decided to initiate a program of PMTCT-*Plus* at a number of facilities across the continent, directed overall by the Columbia School of Public Health. It is now in place, and it is working. And the proof that it's working was exemplified, dramatically, at that little pregnancy clinic at the Mulago hospital.

Some words of medical jargon are now required. In Africa, when the CD4 count of an infected person falls below two hundred, that person requires treatment. The CD4 count is a measure of certain white blood cells. I have seen people with CD4 counts of one hundred, fifty, thirty, even twenty, and when they go on treatment, they experience the Lazarus effect: they're at death's door, and the antiretroviral drugs literally bring them back to life, often in a matter of weeks.

In the waiting-room of the Mulago clinic, Graça and I met a woman whose CD4 count had dropped to *one*. I have no idea how she was still alive. But the doctors had determined they would try treatment, despite so grim a prognosis, and the results were miraculous. So there she was, three months later, smiling exultantly, her HIV-negative baby in her lap, and, playing at her feet, her two other young children.

You see, it can be done. If only the world were to care, Africa can be brought back to the life it once had.

Another evocative excursion within Uganda, this one in 2004, took me to the northwest corner of the country, to the little town of Arua, where Médecins Sans Frontières (MSF, also known as Doctors Without Borders) had set up shop at the local hospital two years earlier. It has to be said that MSF is one of the most impressive NGOs anywhere: principled, effective, radical. They not only do an excellent humanitarian job, saving lives wherever they intervene, but they also brook no nonsense from either national or external governments. On many issues, they are more outspoken than any other leading member of civil society.

On this occasion, I had travelled north in the company of Uganda's minister of health to celebrate the second anniversary of MSF's opening of a treatment program in Arua, where previously treatment had been a pipe dream. As always, MSF had done a remarkable job. There were eleven hundred people in treatment already, twenty-five hundred more on a list for future treatment, and an atmosphere of irrepressible joy cascading through the surrounding community.

Nothing could contain the sense of community exuberance. Across the sprawling grounds of the hospital, one group after another came forward to join in the noisy celebration: women living with AIDS, Muslim women living with AIDS (certainly a first for me), men living with AIDS (also a first for me, as a group separate from women), and a deliciously rowdy contingent of people living with AIDS from across the border in the Democratic Republic of the Congo. There was a boisterous parade through town, accompanied by marching bands, and then everyone—perhaps a couple of thousand—repaired to the hospital for the panorama of speeches, dancing, drama, drums, song, and poetry. It's doubtful that spirits could have soared any higher.

As I stood there drinking it all in, I suddenly realized a startling truth: there was no stigma! The universal availability of free treatment and HIV counseling in Arua meant that the population had nothing to hide. MSF had achieved a near-miracle: keeping people alive on the one hand, and routing stigma and discrimination on the other. It was tremendously inspiring to see so many infected people moving confidently, casually, proudly through the throngs, without the corrosive backlash of prejudice and intolerance.

It will be a long, long time before that experience becomes commonplace in Africa. MSF has only so many professionals, and while the MSF models are exemplary, there are only a relative handful of them across the continent. Stigma is the bane of progress; it savages and ravages, ostracizes and isolates those who are living with the virus. Eradicating stigma will be the last holdout in the epic battle against AIDS.

Still, the little community of Arua gives a glimpse of what might be. I believe to the depths of my being that Africa will one day rejoice in a time when families are whole and funerals are rare. It's just so bitter that such multitudes of lives are being lost along the way. It's hard not to be in a near stupor of anger. And yet I'm sustained, as so many Africans are, by the memories of what the continent used to be, and the conviction that the present will one day reunite with the best of the past.

PERSONAL RESPONSE

Do you think it is the responsibility of developed, or richer, nations to help poorer nations? Why? What do you think are the results of such assistance or lack of assistance?

QUESTIONS FOR CLASS OR SMALL-GROUP DISCUSSION

1. What speaking and writing strategies does Lewis use to convey his message? Do these strategies affect your opinions and sympathies?

2. What reasons does Lewis give for Africa's current situation regarding HIV/AIDS?

3. Given what Lewis says in the piece, discuss the usefulness of the United Nations in making positive changes. What are the strengths and weaknesses of the United Nations and the International Monetary Fund?

4. The world that Lewis moves around in is populated by many confusing non-governmental organizations, governments, policy makers, politicians, and bureaucrats. Select two or three of these organizations or individuals, and try to understand their roles and the source of their power. Discuss their functions and Lewis's attitude toward them.

5. Lewis does not hide his emotions. Point out some of the sentences where his strong emotions leak out. How do these "leakages" affect his credibility? How do they affect your response to the issues? Do they help or hinder his argument?

6. Elsewhere Lewis says, "History will not judge our government kindly." Has Canada met the standard of support that it sets for the rest of the world? Discuss.

EXCERPT: *A JOURNAL OF THE PLAGUE YEAR*

DANIEL DEFOE

Daniel Defoe (1660–1731) is probably best known for his novels Robinson Crusoe *and* Moll Flanders. *Much of* A Journal of the Plague Year *is a description of the 1665 plague that devastated London and parts of the English nation when Defoe was just a child.*

A journalist and novelist, he researched his account thoroughly. Defoe published the Journal *in 1722, when he was 62. In 1720, two years earlier, about 50,000 people had died of the Plague in France, and Londoners feared another full-scale outbreak. The bubonic plague claimed about fifty million lives in Europe between 1345 and 1720.*

I must confess my self to have been very much dejected just before this happen'd; for the prodigious Number that were taken sick the Week or two before, besides those that died, was such, and the Lamentations were so great every where that a Man must have seemed to have acted even against his Reason, if he had so much as expected to escape; and as there was hardly a House, but mine, in all my Neighbourhood, but what was infected; so had it gone on, it would not have been long, that there would have been any more Neighbours to be infected; indeed it is hardly credible, what dreadful Havoc the last three Weeks had made, for if I might believe the Person, whose Calculations I always found very well grounded, there were not less than 30000 People dead, and near 100 thousand fallen sick in the three Weeks I speak of; for the Number that sickened was surprising, indeed it was astonishing, and those whose Courage upheld them all the time before, sunk under it now.

In the Middle of their Distress, when the Condition of the City of *London* was so truly calamitous, just then it pleased God, as it were, by his immediate Hand to disarm this Enemy; the Poyson was taken out of the Sting, it was wonderful, even the Physicians themselves were surprized at it; wherever they visited, the found their Patients better, either they had sweated kindly, or the Tumours were broke, or the Carbuncles went down, and the Inflammations round them chang'd Colour, or the Fever was gone, or the violent Headach was asswag'd, or some good Symptom was in the Case; so that in a few Days, every Body was recovering, whole Families that were infected and down, that had Ministers praying with them, and expected Death every Hour, were revived and healed, and none died at all out of them.

Nor was this by any new Medicine found out, or new Method of Cure discovered, or by any Experience in the Operation, which the Physicians or Surgeons had attain'd to; but it was evidently from the secret invisible hand of him, that had at first sent this Disease as a Judgment upon us; and let the Atheistic part of Mankind call my Saying this what they please, it is no Enthusiasm; it was acknowledg'd at that time by all Mankind; the Disease was enervated, and its Malignity spent, and let it proceed from whencesoever it will, let the Philosophers search for Reasons in nature to account for it by, and labour as much as they will to lessen the Debt they owe to their Maker; those Physicians, who had the least Share of Religion in them, were oblig'd to acknowledge that it was all supernatural, that it was extraordinary, and that no Account could be given of it.

If I should say, that this is a visible Summons to us all to Thankfulness, especially we that were under the Terror of its Increase, perhaps it may be thought by some, after the Sense of the thing was over, an officious canting of religious things, preaching a Sermon instead of writing a History, making my self a Teacher instead of giving my Observations of things, and this restrains me very much from going on here, as I might otherwise do: But if ten Leapers were healed, and but one return'd to give Thanks, I desire to be as that one,[1] and to be thankful for my self.

Nor will I deny, but there were Abundance of People who to all Appearance were very thankful at that time; for their Mouths were stop'd even the Mouths of those, whose Hearts were not extraordinary long affected with it: But the Impression was so strong at that time, that it could not be resisted, no not by the worst of the People.

It was a common thing to meet People in the Street, that were Strangers, and that we knew nothing at all of, expressing their Surprize. Going one Day thro' *Aldgate,* and a pretty many People being passing and repassing, there comes a Man out of the End of the *Minories,* and looking a little up the Street and down, he throws his Hands abroad, *Lord, what an Alteration is here!* Why, last Week I came along here, and hardly any Body was to be seen; another Man, I heard him, adds to his Words, 'tis all wonderful, 'tis all a Dream: Blessed be God, says a third Man, and let us give Thanks to him, for 'tis all his own doing: Human Help and human Skill was at an End. These were all Strangers to one another: But such Salutations as these were frequent in the Street every Day; and in Spight of a loose Behaviour, the very common People went along the Streets, giving God Thanks for their Deliverance.

It was now, as I said before, the People had cast off all Apprehensions, and that too fast; indeed we were no more afraid now to pass by a Man with a white Cap upon his Head, or with a Cloth wrapt round his Neck, or with his Leg limping, occasion'd by the Sores in his Groyn, all which were frightful to the last Degree, but the Week before; but now the Street was full of them, and these poor recovering Creatures, give them their Due, appear'd very sensible of their unexpected Deliverance, and I should wrong them very much, if I should not acknowledge, that I believe many of them were really thankful; but I must own, that for the Generality of the People it might too justly be said of them, as was said of the Children of *Israel,* after their being delivered from the Host of *Pharaoh,* when they passed the *Red-Sea,* and look'd back, and saw the *Egyptians* overwhelmed in the Water, *viz.* That *they sang his Praise, but they soon forgot his Works.*[2]

I can go no farther here. I should be counted censorious, and perhaps unjust, if I should enter into the unpleasant Work of reflecting, whatever Cause there was for it, upon the Unthankfulness and Return of all manner of Wickedness among us, which I was so much an Eye-Witness of my self; I shall conclude the Account of this calamitous Year therefore with a coarse but sincere Stanza of my own, which I plac'd at the End of my ordinary Memorandums, the same Year they were written:

A dreadful Plague in London was,
In the Year of Sixty Five,
Which swept an Hundred Thousand Souls
Away: yet I alive!

                                                                H.F.

FINIS[3]

NOTES

1. Luke 17.12–17; this passage is one of Defoe's favourites, and he compared himself to that one leper several times in his nonfiction prose and in his letters to benefactors.

2. Psalms 106.12–13. Defoe is probably quoting from memory. This psalm would have seemed appropriate to him because it includes a review of Israel's history, deliverance, and repeated lapses into sin and forgetfulness, and it concludes with thanks for God's repeated mercy and forgiveness.

PERSONAL RESPONSE

Does the idea of a plague or epidemic frighten you? In your history classes, have you studied the worldwide flu epidemic at the start of the 20th century that affected Canada? What about contemporary news reports that warn of an impending avian flu epidemic and the economic toll it would take? Do you feel that news reports, such as the reports about the 2003 SARS outbreaks in Toronto and Vancouver, create unnecessary fear?

QUESTIONS FOR CLASS OR SMALL-GROUP DISCUSSION

1. Give an example from this excerpt that demonstrates the belief that the Plague was a visitation or punishment from a divine being.

2. Draw some parallels between the Plague and the AIDS epidemic today, especially in terms of morality. For example, can you find examples of contemporary religious leaders, preachers, or fundamentalists who believe that AIDS is a chastisement or a holy plague from God?

3. It was not until 1894 that the bubonic plague was identified as *Yersinia pestis,* an internal parasite of rodents, especially rats, which is carried by fleas from the dying animals. What were some of the hypotheses as to the origin of the Plague?

4. Is there anything in our time that is like the Plague, and that may have the same impact? Describe what it is and the nature of the impact.

"THIS IS THE END OF THE WORLD": THE BLACK DEATH

Barbara Tuchman

Barbara Tuchman (1912–1989) was a Pulitzer Prize-winning historian who provided insight into the origins of wars and plagues, and who brought the past to life with her popular books.

In October 1347, two months after the fall of Calais,[1] Genoese trading ships put into the harbor of Messina in Sicily with dead and dying men at the oars. The ships had come from the Black Sea port of Caffa (now Feodosiya) in the Crimea, where the Genoese maintained a trading post. The diseased sailors showed strange black swellings about the size of an egg or an apple in the armpits and groin. The swellings oozed blood and pus and were followed by spreading boils and black blotches on the skin from internal bleeding. The sick suffered severe pain and died quickly within five days of the first symptoms. As the disease spread, other symptoms of continuous fever and spitting of blood appeared instead of the swellings or buboes. These victims coughed and sweated heavily and died even more quickly, within three days or less, sometimes in 24 hours. In both types everything that issued from the body—breath, sweat, blood from the buboes and lungs, bloody urine, and blood-blackened excrement—smelled foul. Depression and despair accompanied the physical symptoms, and before the end "death is seen seated on the face."

The disease was bubonic plague, present in two forms: one that infected the bloodstream, causing the buboes and internal bleeding, and was spread by contact; and a second, more virulent pneumonic type that infected the lungs and was spread by respiratory infection. The presence of both at once caused the high mortality and speed of contagion. So lethal was the disease that cases were known of persons going to bed well and dying before they woke, of doctors catching the illness at a bedside and dying before the patient. So rapidly did it spread from one to another that to a French physician, Simon de Covino, it seemed as if one sick person "could infect the whole world." The malignity of the pestilence appeared more terrible because its victims knew no prevention and no remedy.

The physical suffering of the disease and its aspect of evil mystery were expressed in a strange Welsh lament which saw "death coming into our midst like black smoke, a plague which cuts off the young, a rootless phantom which has no mercy for fair countenance. Woe is me of the shilling in the armpit! It is seething, terrible . . . a head that gives pain and causes a loud cry . . . a painful angry knob. . . . Great is its seething like a burning cinder . . . a grievous thing of ashy color." Its eruption is ugly like the "seeds of black peas, broken fragments of brittle sea-coal . . . the early ornaments of black death, cinders of the peelings of the cockle weed, a mixed multitude, a black plague like halfpence, like berries. . . ."

Rumors of a terrible plague supposedly arising in China and spreading through Tartary (Central Asia) to India and Persia, Mesopotamia, Syria, Egypt, and all of Asia Minor had reached Europe in 1346. They told of a death toll so devastating that all of India was said to be depopulated, whole territories covered by dead bodies, other areas with no one left alive. As added up by Pope Clement VI at Avignon, the total of reported dead reached 23,840,000. In the absence of a concept of contagion, no serious alarm was felt in Europe until the trading ships brought their black burden of pestilence into Messina while other infected ships from the Levant carried it to Genoa and Venice.

By January 1348 it penetrated France via Marseille, and North Africa via Tunis. Shipborne along coasts and navigable rivers, it spread westward from Marseille through the ports of Languedoc to Spain and northward up the Rhône to Avignon, where it arrived in March. It reached Narbonne, Montpellier, Carcassonne, and Toulouse between February and May, and at the same time in Italy spread to Rome and Florence and their hinterlands. Between June and August it reached Bordeaux, Lyon, and Paris, spread to Burgundy and Normandy, and crossed the Channel from Normandy into southern England. From Italy during the same summer it crossed the Alps into Switzerland and reached eastward to Hungary.

In a given area the plague accomplished its kill within four to six months and then faded, except in the larger cities, where, rooting into the close-quartered population, it abated during the winter, only to reappear in spring and rage for another six months.

In 1349 it resumed in Paris, spread to Picardy, Flanders, and the new Low Countries, and from England to Scotland and Ireland as well as to Norway, where a ghost ship with a cargo of wool and a dead crew drifted offshore until it ran aground near Bergen. From there the plague passed into Sweden, Denmark, Prussia, Iceland, and as far as Greenland. Leaving a strange pocket of immunity in Bohemia, and Russia unattacked until 1351, it had passed from most of Europe by mid-1350. Although the mortality rate was erratic, ranging from one fifth in some places to nine tenths or almost total elimination in others, the overall estimate of modern demographers has settled—for the area extending from India to Iceland—around the same figure expressed in Froissart's casual words: "a third of the world died." His estimate, the common one at the time, was not an inspired guess but a borrowing of St. John's figure for mortality from plague in Revelation, the favorite guide to human affairs of the Middle Ages.

A third of Europe would have meant about 20 million deaths. No one knows in truth how many died. Contemporary reports were an awed impression, not an accurate count. In crowded Avignon, it was said, 400 died daily; 7,000 houses emptied by death were shut up; a single graveyard received 11,000 corpses in six weeks; half the city's inhabitants reportedly died, including 9 cardinals or one third of the total, and 70 lesser prelates. Watching the endlessly passing death carts, chroniclers let normal exaggeration take wings and put the Avignon death toll at 62,000 and even at 120,000, although the city's total population was probably less than 50,000.

When graveyards filled up, bodies at Avignon were thrown into the Rhône until mass burial pits were dug for dumping the corpses. In London in such pits corpses piled up in layers until they overflowed. Everywhere reports speak of the sick dying too fast for the living to bury. Corpses were dragged out of homes and left in front of doorways. Morning light revealed new piles of bodies. In Florence the dead were gathered up by the Compagnia della Misericordia—founded in 1244 to care for the sick—whose members wore red robes and hoods masking the face except for the eyes. When their efforts failed, the dead lay putrid in the streets for days at a time. When no coffins were to be had, the bodies were laid on boards, two or three at once, to be carried to graveyards or common pits. Families dumped their own relatives into the pits, or buried them so hastily and thinly "that dogs dragged them forth and devoured their bodies."

Amid accumulating death and fear of contagion, people died without last rites and were buried without prayers, a prospect that terrified the last hours of the stricken. A bishop in England gave permission to laymen to make confession to each other as was done by the Apostles, "or if no man is present then even to a woman," and if no priest could be found to administer extreme unction, "then faith must suffice." Clement VI found it necessary to grant remissions of sin to all who died of the plague because so many were unattended by priests. "And no bells tolled," wrote a chronicler of Siena, "and nobody wept no matter what his loss because almost everyone expected death. . . . And people said and believed, 'This is the end of the world.'"

In Paris, where the plague lasted through 1349, the reported death rate was 800 a day, in Pisa 500, in Vienna 500 to 600. The total dead in Paris numbered 50,000 or half the population. Florence, weakened by the famine of 1347, lost three to four fifths of its citizens, Venice two thirds, Hamburg and Bremen, though smaller in size, about the same proportion. Cities, as centers of transportation, were more likely to be affected than villages, although once a village was infected, its death rate was equally high. At Givry, a prosperous village in Burgundy of 1,200 to 1,500 people, the parish register records 615 deaths in the space of fourteen weeks, compared to an average of thirty deaths a year in the previous decade. In three villages of Cambridgeshire, manorial records show a death rate of 47 percent, 57 percent, and in one case 70 percent. When the last survivors, too few to carry on, moved away, a deserted village sank back into the wilderness and disappeared from the map altogether, leaving only a grass-covered ghostly outline to show where mortals once had lived.

In enclosed places such as monasteries and prisons, the infection of one person usually meant that of all, as happened in the Franciscan convents of Carcassonne and Marseille, where every inmate without exception died. Of the 140 Dominicans at Montpellier only seven survived. Petrarch's[2] brother Gherardo, member of a Carthusian monastery, buried the prior and 34 fellow monks one by one, sometimes three a day, until he was left along with his dog and fled to look for a place that would take him in. Watching every comrade die, men in such places could not but wonder whether the strange peril that filled the air had not been sent to exterminate the human race. In Kilkenny, Ireland, Brother John Clyn of the Friars Minor, another monk left alone among dead men, kept a record of what had happened lest "things which should be remembered perish with time and vanish from the memory of those who come after us." Sensing "the whole world, as it were, placed within the grasp of the Evil One," and waiting for death to visit him too, he wrote, "I leave parchment to continue this work, if perchance any man survive and any of the race of Adam escape this pestilence and carry on the work which I have begun." Brother John, as noted by another hand, died of the pestilence, but he foiled oblivion.

The largest cities of Europe, with populations of about 100,000, were Paris and Florence, Venice and Genoa. At the next level, with more than 50,000, were Ghent and Bruges in Flanders, Milan, Bologna, Rome, Naples, and Palermo, and Cologne. London hovered below 50,000, the only city in England except York with more than 10,000. At the level of 20,000 to 50,000 were Bordeaux, Toulouse, Montpellier, Marseille, and Lyon in France, Barcelona, Seville, and Toledo in Spain, Siena, Pisa, and other secondary cities in Italy, and the Hanseatic trading cities of the Empire.

The plague raged through them all, killing anywhere from one third to two thirds of their inhabitants. Italy, with a total population of 10 to 11 million, probably suffered the heaviest toll. Following the Florentine bankruptcies, the crop failures and workers' riots of 1346–47, the revolt of Cola di Rienzi that plunged Rome into anarchy, the plague came as the peak of successive calamities. As if the world were indeed in the grasp of the Evil One, its first appearance on the European mainland in January 1348 coincided with a fearsome earthquake that carved a path of wreckage from Naples up to Venice. Houses collapsed, church towers toppled, villages were crushed, and the destruction reached as far as Germany and Greece. Emotional response, dulled by horrors, underwent a kind of atrophy epitomized by the chronicler who wrote, "And in these days was burying without sorrowe and wedding without friendschippe."

In Siena, where more than half the inhabitants died of the plague, work was abandoned on the great cathedral, planned to be the largest in the world, and never resumed, owing to loss of workers and master masons and "the melancholy and grief" of the survivors. The cathedral's truncated transept still stands in permanent witness to the sweep of death's scythe. Agnolo di Tura, a chronicler of Siena, recorded the fear of contagion that froze every other instinct. "Father abandoned child, wife husband, one brother another," he wrote, "for this plague seemed to strike through the breath and sight. And so they died. And no one could be found to bury the dead for money or friendship. . . . And I, Agnolo di Tura, called the Fat, buried my five children with my own hands, and so did many others likewise."

There were many to echo his account of inhumanity and few to balance it, for the plague was not the kind of calamity that inspired mutual help. Its loathsomeness and deadliness did not herd people together in mutual distress, but only prompted their desire to escape each other. "Magistrates and notaries refused to come and make the wills of the dying," reported a Franciscan friar of Piazza in Sicily; what was worse, "even the priests did not come to hear their confessions." A clerk of the Archbishop of Canterbury reported the same of English priests who "turned away from the care of their benefices from fear of death." Cases of parents deserting children and children their parents were reported across Europe from Scotland to Russia. The calamity chilled the hearts of men, wrote Boccaccio[3] in his famous account of the plague in Florence that serves as introduction to the *Decameron*. "One man shunned another . . . kinsfolk held aloof, brother was forsaken by brother, oftentimes husband by wife; nay, what is more, and scarcely to be believed, fathers and mothers were found to abandon their own children to their fate, untended, unvisited as if they had been strangers." Exaggeration and literary pessimism were common in the 14th century, but the Pope's physician, Guy de Chauliac, was a sober, careful observer who reported the same phenomenon: "A father did not visit his son, nor the son his father. Charity was dead."

Yet not entirely. In Paris, according to the chronicler Jean de Venette, the nuns of the Hôtel Dieu or municipal hospital, "having no fear of death, tended the sick with all sweetness and humility." New nuns repeatedly took the places of those who died, until the majority "many times renewed by death now rest in peace with Christ as we may piously believe."

When the plague entered northern France in July 1348, it settled first in Normandy and, checked by winter, gave Picardy a deceptive interim until the next summer. Either in mourning or warning, black flags were flown from church towers of the worst-stricken villages of Normandy. "And in that time," wrote a monk of the abbey of Fourcarment, "the mortality was so great among the people of Normandy that those of Picardy mocked them." The same unneighborly reaction was reported of the Scots, separated by a winter's immunity from the English. Delighted to hear of the disease that was scouring the "southrons," they gathered forces for an invasion, "laughing at their enemies." Before they could move, the savage mortality fell upon them too, scattering some in death and the rest in panic to spread the infection as they fled.

In Picardy in the summer of 1349 the pestilence penetrated the castle of Coucy to kill Enguerrand's[4] mother, Catherine, and her new husband. Whether her nine-year-old son escaped by chance or was perhaps living elsewhere with one of his guardians is unrecorded. In nearby Amiens, tannery workers, responding quickly to losses in the labor force, combined to bargain for higher wages. In another place villagers were seen dancing to drums and trumpets, and on being asked the reason, answered that, seeing their neighbors die day by day while their village remained immune, they believed they could keep the plague from entering "by the jollity that is in us. That is why we dance." Further north in Tournai on the border of Flanders, Gilles le Muisis, Abbot of St. Martin's, kept one of the epidemic's most vivid accounts. The passing bells rang all day and all night, he recorded, because sextons were anxious to obtain their fees while they could. Filled with the sound of mourning, the city became oppressed by fear, so that the authorities forbade the tolling of bells and the wearing of black and restricted funeral services to two mourners. The silencing of funeral bells and of criers' announcements of deaths was ordained by most cities. Siena imposed a fine on the wearing of mourning clothes by all except widows.

Flight was the chief recourse of those who could afford it or arrange it. The rich fled to their country places like Boccaccio's young patricians of Florence, who settled in a pastoral palace "removed on every side from the roads" with "wells of cool water and vaults of rare wines." The urban poor died in their burrows, "and only the stench of their bodies informed neighbors of their death." That the poor were more heavily afflicted than the rich was clearly remarked at the time, in the north as in the south. A Scottish chronicler, John of Fordun, stated flatly that the pest "attacked especially the meaner sort and common people—seldom the magnates." Simon de Covino of Montpellier made the same observation. He ascribed it to the misery and want and hard lives that made the poor more susceptible, which was half the truth. Close contact and lack of sanitation was the unrecognized other half. It was noticed too that the young died in greater proportion than the old; Simon de Corvino compared the disappearance of youth to the withering of flowers in the field.

In the countryside peasants dropped dead on the roads, in the fields, in their houses. Survivors in growing helplessness fell into apathy, leaving ripe wheat uncut and livestock untended. Oxen and asses, sheep and goats, pigs and chickens ran wild and they too, according to local reports, succumbed to the pest. English sheep, bearers of the precious wool, died throughout the country. The chronicler Henry

Knighton, canon of Leicester Abbey, reported 5,000 dead in one field alone, "their bodies so corrupted by the plague that neither beast nor bird would touch them," and spreading an appalling stench. In the Austrian Alps wolves came down to prey upon sheep and then, "as if alarmed by some invisible warning, turned and fled back into the wilderness." In remote Dalmatia bolder wolves descended upon a plague-stricken city and attacked human survivors. For want of herdsmen, cattle strayed from place to place and died in hedgerows and ditches. Dogs and cats fell like the rest.

The dearth of labor held a fearful prospect because the 14th century lived close to the annual harvest both for food and for next year's seed. "So few servants and laborers were left," wrote Knighton, "that no one knew where to turn for help." The sense of a vanishing future created a kind of dementia of despair. A Bavarian chronicler of Neuberg on the Danube recorded that "Men and women . . . wandered around as if mad" and let their cattle stray "because no one had any inclination to concern themselves about the future." Fields went uncultivated, spring seed unsown. Second growth with nature's awful energy crept back over cleared land, dikes crumbled, salt water reinvaded and soured the lowlands. With so few hands remaining to restore the work of centuries, people felt, in Walsingham's words, that "the world could never again regain its former prosperity."

Though the death rate was higher among the anonymous poor, the known and the great died too. King Alfonso XI of Castile was the only reigning monarch killed by the pest, but his neighbour King Pedro of Aragon lost his wife, Queen Leonora, his daughter Marie, and a niece in the space of six months. John Cantacuzene, Emperor of Byzantium, lost his son. In France the lame Queen Jeanne and her daughter-in-law Bonne de Luxemberg, wife of the Dauphin, both died in 1349 in the same phase that took the life of Enguerrand's mother. Jeanne, Queen of Navarre, daughter of Louis X, was another victim. Edward III's second daughter, Joanna, who was on her way to marry Pedro, the heir of Castile, died in Bordeaux. Women appear to have been more vulnerable than men, perhaps because, being more housebound, they were more exposed to fleas. Boccaccio's mistress Fiammetta, illegitimate daughter of the King of Naples, died, as did Laura, the beloved—whether real or fictional—of Petrarch. Reaching out to us in the future, Petrarch cried, "Oh happy posterity who will not experience such abysmal woe and will look upon our testimony as a fable."

In Florence Giovanni Villani, the great historian of his time, died at 68 in the midst of an unfinished sentence: ". . . *e dure questo pistolenza fino a* . . . (in the midst of this pestilence there came to an end . . .)." Siena's master painters, the brothers Ambrogio and Pietro Lorenzetti, whose names never appear after 1348, presumably perished in the plague, as did Andrea Pisano, architect and sculptor of Florence. William of Ockham and the English mystic Richard Rolle of Hampole both disappear from mention after 1349. Francisco Datini, merchant of Prato, lost both his parents and two siblings. Curious sweeps of mortality afflicted certain bodies of merchants in London. All eight wardens of the Company of Cutters, all six wardens of the Hatters, and four wardens of the Goldsmiths died before July 1350. Sir John Pulteney, master draper and four times Mayor of London, was a victim, likewise Sir John Montgomery, Governor of Calais.

Among the clergy and doctors the mortality was naturally high because of the nature of their professions. Out of 24 physicians in Venice, 20 were said to have lost their lives in the plague, although, according to another account, some were believed to have fled or to have shut themselves up in their houses. At Montpellier, site of the leading medieval medical school, the physician Simon de Corvino reported that, despite the great number of doctors, "hardly one of them escaped." In Avignon, Guy de Chauliac confessed that he performed his medical visits only because he dared not stay away for fear of infamy, but "I was in continual fear." He claimed to have contracted the disease but to have cured himself by his own treatment; if so, he was one of the few who recovered.

Clerical mortality varied with rank. Although the one-third toll of cardinals reflects the same proportion as the whole, this was probably due to their concentration in Avignon. In England, in strange and almost sinister procession, the Archbishop of Canterbury, John Stratford, died in August 1348, his appointed successor died in May 1349, and the next appointee three months later, all three within a year. Despite such weird vagaries, prelates in general managed to sustain a higher survival rate than the lesser clergy. Among bishops the deaths have been estimated at about one in twenty. The loss of priests, even if many avoided their fearful duty of attending the dying, was about the same as among the population as a whole.

Government officials, whose loss contributed to the general chaos, found, on the whole, no special shelter. In Siena four of the nine members of the governing oligarchy died, in France one third of the royal notaries, in Bristol 15 out of the 52 members of the Town Council or almost one third. Tax-collecting obviously suffered, with the result that Philip VI was unable to collect more than a fraction of the subsidy granted him by the Estates in the winter of 1347–48.

Lawlessness and debauchery accompanied the plague as they had during the great plague of Athens of 430 B.C., when according to Thucydides, men grew bold in the indulgence of pleasure: "For seeing how the rich died in a moment and those who had nothing immediately inherited their property, they reflected that life and riches were alike transitory and they resolved to enjoy themselves while they could." Human behaviour is timeless. When St. John had his vision of plague in Revelation, he knew from some experience or race memory that those who survived "repented not of the work of their hands. . . . Neither repented they of their murders, nor of their sorceries, nor of their fornication, nor of their thefts."

Ignorance of the cause augmented the sense of horror. Of the real carriers, rats and fleas, the 14th century had no suspicion, perhaps because they were so familiar. Fleas, though a common household nuisance, are not once mentioned in contemporary plague writings, and rats only incidentally, although folklore commonly associated them with pestilence. The legend of the Pied Piper arose from an outbreak of 1284. The actual plague bacillus, *Pasturella pestis,* remained undiscovered for another 500 years. Living alternately in the stomach of the flea and the bloodstream of the rat who was the flea's host, the bacillus in its bubonic form was transferred to humans and animals by the bite of either rat or flea. It traveled by virtue of *Rattus rattus,* the small medieval black rat that lived on ships, as well as by the heavier brown or sewer rat. What precipitated the turn of the bacillus from innocuous to virulent form is unknown, but the occurrence is now believed to have taken place not in China but somewhere in central Asia and to have spread along the caravan routes. Chinese origin was a mistaken notion of the 14th century based on real but belated reports of huge death tolls in China from drought, famine, and pestilence which have since been traced to the 1330s, too soon to be responsible for the plague that appeared in India in 1346.

The phantom enemy had no name. Called the Black Death only in later recurrences, it was known during the first epidemic simply as the Pestilence or Great Mortality. Reports from the East, swollen by fearful imaginings, told of strange tempests and "sheets of fire" mingled with huge hailstones that "slew almost all," or a "vast rain of fire" that burned up men, beasts, stones, trees, villages, and cities. In another version, "foul blasts of wind" from the fires carried the infection to Europe "and now as some suspect it cometh round the seacoast." Accurate observation in this case could not make the mental jump to ships and rats because no idea of animal- or insect-borne contagion existed.

The earthquake was blamed for releasing sulphurous and foul fumes from the earth's interior, or as evidence of a titanic struggle of planets and oceans causing waters to rise and vaporize until fish died in masses and corrupted the air. All these explanations had in common a factor of poisoned air, of miasmas and thick, stinking mists traced to every kind of natural or imagined agency from stagnant lakes to malign conjunction of the planets, from the hand of the Evil One to the wrath of God. Medical thinking, trapped in the theory of astral influences, stressed air as the communicator of disease, ignoring sanitation or visible carriers. The existence of two carriers confused the trail, the more so because the flea could live and travel independently of the rat for as long as a month and, if infected by the particularly virulent septicemic form of the bacillus, could infect humans without reinfecting itself from the rat. The simultaneous presence of the pneumonic form of the disease, which was indeed communicated through the air, blurred the problem further.

The mystery of the contagion was "the most terrible of all the terrors," as an anonymous Flemish cleric in Avignon wrote to a correspondent in Bruges. Plagues had been known before, from the plague of Athens (believed to have been typhus) to the prolonged epidemic of the 6th century A.D., to the recurrence of sporadic outbreaks in the 12th and 13th centuries, but they had left no accumulated store of understanding. That the infection came from contact with the sick or with their houses, clothes, or corpses was quickly observed but not comprehended. Gentile da Foligno, renowned physician of Perugia and doctor of medicine at the universities of Bologna and Padua, came close to respiratory infection when he surmised that poisonous material was "communicated by means of air breathed out and in." Having no idea of microscopic carriers, he had to assume that the air was corrupted by planetary influences. Planets, however, could not explain the ongoing contagion. The agonized search for an answer gave rise to such theories as transference by sight. People fell ill, wrote Guy de Chauliac, not only by remaining with the sick but "even by looking at them." Three hundred years later Joshua Barnes, the 17th century biographer of Edward III, could write that the power of infection had entered into beams of light and "darted death from the eyes."

Doctors struggling with evidence could not break away from the terms of astrology, to which they believed all human physiology was subject. Medicine was the one aspect of medieval life, perhaps because of its links with the Arabs, not shaped by Christian doctrine. Clerics detested astrology, but could not dislodge its influence. Guy de Chauliac, physician to three popes in succession, practiced in obedience to the zodiac. While his *Cirurgia* was the major treatise on surgery of its time, while he understood the use of anesthesia made from the juice of opium, mandrake, or hemlock, he nevertheless prescribed bleeding and purgatives by the planets and divided chronic from acute diseases on the basis of one being under the rule of the sun and the other of the moon.

In October 1348 Philip VI asked the medical faculty of the University of Paris for a report on the affliction that seemed to threaten human survival. With careful thesis, antithesis, and proofs, the doctors ascribed it to a triple conjunction of Saturn, Jupiter, and Mars in the 40th degree of Aquarius said to have occurred on March 20, 1345. They acknowledged, however, effects "whose cause is hidden from even the most highly trained intellects." The verdict of the masters of Paris became the official version. Borrowed, copied by scribes, carried abroad, translated from Latin into various vernaculars, it was everywhere accepted, even by the Arab physicians of Cordova and Granada, as the scientific if not the popular answer. Because of the terrible interest of the subject, the translations of the plague tracts stimulated use of national languages. In that one respect, life came from death.

To the people at large there could be but one explanation—the wrath of God. Planets might satisfy the learned doctors, but God was closer to the average man. A scourge so sweeping and unsparing without any visible cause could only be seen as Divine punishment upon mankind for its sins. It might even be God's terminal disappointment in his creature. Matteo Villani compared the plague to the Flood in ultimate purpose and believed he was recording "the extermination of mankind." Efforts to appease Divine wrath took many forms, as when the city of Rouen ordered that everything that could anger God, such as gambling, cursing, and drinking, must be stopped. More general were the penitent processions authorized at first by the Pope, some lasting as long as three days, some attended by as many as 2,000, which everywhere accompanied the plague and helped to spread it.

Barefoot in sackcloth, sprinkled with ashes, weeping, praying, tearing their hair, carrying candles and relics, sometimes with ropes around their necks or beating themselves with whips, the penitents wound through the streets, imploring the mercy of the Virgin and saints at their shrines. In a vivid illustration for the *Très Riches Heures* of the Duc de Berry, the Pope is shown in a penitent procession attended by four cardinals in scarlet from hat to hem. He raises both arms in supplication to the angel on top of the Castel Sant'Angelo, while white-robed priests bearing banners and relics in golden cases turn to look as one of their number, stricken by the plague, falls to the ground, his face contorted with anxiety. In the rear, a gray-clad monk falls beside another victim already on the ground as the townspeople gaze in horror. (Nominally the illustration represents a 6th century plague in the time of Pope Gregory the Great, but as medieval artists made no distinction between past and present, the scene is shown as the artist would have seen it in the 14th century.) When it became evident that these processions were sources of infection, Clement VI had to prohibit them.

In Messina, where the plague first appeared, the people begged the Archbishop of neighboring Catania to lend them the relics of St. Agatha. When the Catanians refused to let the relics go, the Archbishop dipped them in holy water and took the water himself to Messina, where he carried it in a procession with prayers and litanies through the streets. The demonic, which shared the medieval cosmos with God, appeared as "demons in the shape of dogs" to terrify the people. "A black dog with a drawn sword in his paws appeared among them, gnashing his teeth and rushing upon them and breaking all the silver vessels and lamps and candlesticks on the altars and casting them hither and thither. . . . So the people of Messina, terrified by this prodigious vision, were all strangely overcome by fear."

The apparent absence of earthly cause gave the plague a supernatural and sinister quality. Scandinavians believed that a Pest Maiden emerged from the mouth of the dead in the form of a blue flame and flew through the air to infect the next house. In Lithuania the Maiden was said to wave a red scarf through the door or window to let in the pest. One brave man, according to legend, deliberately waited at his open window with drawn sword and, at the fluttering of the scarf, chopped off the hand. He died of his deed, but his village was spared and the scarf long preserved as a relic in the local church.

Beyond demons and superstition the final hand was God's. The Pope acknowledged it in a Bull of September 1348, speaking of the "pestilence with which God is afflicting the Christian people." To the Emperor John Cantacuzene it was manifest that a malady of such horrors, stenches, and agonies, and especially one bringing the dismal despair that settled upon its victims before they died, was not a plague "natural" to mankind but "a chastisement from Heaven." To Piers Plowman[5] "these pestilences were for pure sin."

The general acceptance of this view created an expanded sense of guilt, for if the plague were punishment there had to be terrible sin to have occasioned it. What sins were on the 14th century conscience? Primarily greed, the sin of avarice, followed by usury, worldliness, adultery, blasphemy, falsehood, luxury, irreligion. Giovanni Villani, attempting to account for the cascade of calamity that had fallen upon Florence, concluded that it was retribution for the sins of avarice and usury that oppressed the poor. Pity and anger about the condition of the poor, especially victimization of the peasantry in war, was often expressed by writers of the time and was certainly on the conscience of the century. Beneath it all was the daily condition of medieval life, in which hardly an act or thought, sexual, mercantile, or military, did not contravene the dictates of the Church. Mere failure to fast or attend mass was sin. The result was an underground lake of guilt in the soul that the plague now tapped.

That the mortality was accepted as God's punishment may explain in part the vacuum of comment that followed the Black Death. An investigator has noticed that in the archives of Périgord references to the war are innumerable, to the plague few. Froissart mentions the great death but once, Chaucer gives it barely a glance. Divine anger so great that it contemplated the extermination of man did not bear close examination.

NOTES

1. After a year-long siege, the French citizens of Calais surrendered to Edward III, king of England and self-declared king of France.
2. Francesco Petrarch (1303–1374), Italian writer whose sonnets to "my lady Laura" influenced a tradition of European love poetry for centuries.
3. Giovanni Boccaccio (1313–1375), Italian writer best known for his collection of stories, *The Decameron,* in which seven young ladies and three young men flee from Florence to escape the Black Death and tell stories to while away the time.
4. Enguerrand de Coucy, a French nobleman, is the historical figure around whom Tuchman constructs her account of the fourteenth century.
5. The main character (and title) of a fourteenth-century poem by the English poet William Langland (c. 1330–c. 1386).

PERSONAL RESPONSE

Are you frightened by the prospect of a pandemic? List three specific parallels between AIDS and the 14th-century plague, drawing on information from the Tuchman piece or an Internet source. Describe three other modern epidemics, pandemics, or plagues.

QUESTIONS FOR CLASS OR SMALL-GROUP DISCUSSION

1. Plagues have been attributed to the wrath of a divine power. Explain why some people today attribute diseases such as AIDS to God's anger or disappointment. Do you agree or disagree with the view that victims pay for their sins by becoming ill? Discuss.
2. No one surmised in the 14th century that the Black Death could be attributed to fleas or rats. What, today, do we know about the origins of modern diseases?
3. Is there a belief that science or government will take care of us in the event of a plague or pandemic (e.g., avian flu)? Discuss.

FOR FURTHER VIEWING: GLOBAL HEALTH

Twelve Monkeys (1995); *28 Days Later* (2002); *State of Denial* (2003); *A Closer Walk* (2005); *It's My Life* (2001); *The Plague Dogs* (1992); *And the Band Played On* (1993); *ABC Africa* (2001); *3 Needles* (2005); *One Week* (2000); *Absolutely Positive* (2006); *Panic in the Streets* (1959); *Children of Men* (2006); *The Andromeda Strain* (1971).

CHAPTER TWENTY-ONE

ENVIRONMENTAL STUDIES

INTRODUCTION

Here is a fact: Without a properly functioning and reasonably healthy environment, life as we know it on this planet, and especially human life, is going to have a hard time of it. Things, big things, will almost certainly change. We might not even make it, or we certainly won't make it very easily. The equation is hardly complex: We need clean air, clean soil, and clean water—these are finite and fragile—and we don't have a very good history of taking care of these three resources.

There is a superabundance of writings on the environment, ranging from topics such as personal recycling to global warming to the concept that the planet itself may function as a single, complex organism. In fact, we may be overwhelmed by all the competing voices, most of which, though not all, suggest that we'd better do something pretty quickly or we'll be in trouble. Forget all those aliens from outer space that are out to destroy our planet; movies and documentaries such as *The Day After Tomorrow* (2004) and *An Inconvenient Truth* (2006), in their very different ways, point to the destructive forces being here already.

Canada is a big, though ambiguous, player in the environmental scene, and for a few reasons. First of all, Canada reaches into the Far North—the Arctic—where the effects of global warming are claimed by many to be dramatically apparent. Second, Canada's vast wilderness and the idea of the outdoors is precious to national identity. Third, Canadians have been at the front of the environmental movement with organizations such as Greenpeace. Yet recently Canada's policies about environmental issues have become subject to the political whims of individual governments. Canada is actually growing as a producer of greenhouse gases.

The writings in this section reflect a range and history of responses to the changing environment and our attitude toward it. It is one subject that will not go away; after all, when it gets down to it, that's all we have.

IN EPOCH OF MAN, EARTH TAKES A BEATING

MARIANA GOSNELL

Mariana Gosnell, who was a reporter, writer, and associate editor at Newsweek *magazine, is the author of* Zero Three Bravo; Solo across America in a Small Plane *(1993) and* Ice: The Nature, the History and the Uses of an Astonishing Substance *(2004).*

"The whole world is going too fast," an Inuit hunter from Banks Island in the Northwest Territories in Canada told the journalist Elizabeth Kolbert at a bar during a global-warming symposium. A few years before, he and his neighbors had started seeing robins, birds they had no name for. At first the milder weather that drew the robins north seemed a good thing—"warmer winters, you know," he said—but as other changes occurred that affected their traditional way of life, including hunting, it did not seem so good. "Our children may not have a future," the hunter concluded. "I mean, all young people, put it that way. It's not just happening in the Arctic. It's going to happen all over the world."

Field Notes From a Catastrophe: Man, Nature and Climate Change

by Elizabeth Kolbert
210 pages. Bloomsbury.
For "Field Notes From a Catastrophe," Ms. Kolbert went not exactly all over the world to find out what's happening with global warming but to a great many places

in it, and she often heard the same elegiac expressions of foreboding, loss and fear for the next generation. In Shishmaref, Alaska, she met people who were abandoning their tiny island home because, with less sea ice around it as a buffer against storms, their houses and land were being carried away. ("It makes me feel lonely," one woman said of the forced move.) In Iceland, a man monitoring glacial advance and retreat passed on the prediction that by the end of the next century, his country, where glaciers have existed for more than two million years, will be essentially ice-free. On the Greenland ice cap, well away from the coast, researchers gathering meteorological data were surprised to see melt "in areas where liquid water had not been seen for hundreds, perhaps thousands, of years."

And so it went in Fairbanks; Yorkshire; Eugene, Ore. "Such is the impact of global warming," Ms. Kolbert points out, that she could have gone to countless other places, "from Siberia to the Austrian Alps to the Great Barrier Reef to the South African fynbos—to document its effects."

Ms. Kolbert, a former reporter for *The New York Times,* doesn't doubt that human-induced global warming is real and will likely have dire consequences; the title of her book includes the word "catastrophe." The pages are replete with bad news: perennial sea ice, which 25 years ago covered an area of the Arctic the size of the continental United States, has since lost an area "the size of New York, Georgia and Texas combined." Carbon dioxide levels, if emissions go unchecked, could reach three times pre-industrial levels by the end of the century.

Based on a series of articles that appeared in *The New Yorker* magazine, the book is organized around notes Ms. Kolbert took on "field trips," not only to places where climate change is affecting the natural world but also to ones—labs, offices, observatories—where humans are trying to understand the phenomenon of human-induced global warming. Hers is the latest in a large crop of books on the subject— she notes that "entire books have been written just on the history of efforts to draw attention to the problem"—and there are inevitably some places where other authors have trod before.

In language that is clear, if somewhat dry, she examines the major pieces of the story, shedding light on some insider concepts of climatologists, like "dangerous anthropogenic interference," as she goes. The book may make a good handbook; it is both comprehensive and succinct. (If you have ever wondered how a climate model is put together, that's in there, too.)

She visits the Netherlands, where rising sea levels caused by global warming are expected to swallow up large parts of the country. In areas where there are already periodic floods, a construction firm has started building amphibious homes (they resemble toasters, Ms. Kolbert says) as well as "buoyant roads." Another field trip took her to Washington, where she was treated to double-speak by an under secretary charged with explaining the administration's position on climate change. "Astonishingly," she comments in a rare show of heat, "standing in the way" of progress seems to be President Bush's goal. Not only did he reject the Kyoto Protocol, she notes, with its mandatory curbs on emissions, almost killing the treaty in the process, but he also continues to block meaningful follow-up changes to it.

The United States is the largest emitter of carbon in the world, accounting for a quarter of the world's total, with the average American putting out 12,000 pounds of carbon a year, or about 100 times what the average Bangladeshi does. In two decades, the Chinese will surpass Americans in this disheartening achievement, unless they can somehow be persuaded to build their many projected new coal plants using modern, low-emission—and expensive—technology.

Some of the most downbeat (or realistic) observers are climate scientists. "It may be that we're not going to solve global warming," Marty Hoffert, a physics professor at New York University, told Ms. Kolbert, "the earth is going to become an ecological disaster, and, you know, somebody will visit in a few hundred million years and find there were some intelligent beings who lived here for a while, but they just couldn't handle the transition from being hunter-gatherers to high technology."

Mr. Hoffert isn't giving up in despair, though, but turning to high technology for help. He's trying to find carbon-free sources of energy—away from earth. Satellites with photovoltaic arrays could be launched into space, he suggests. Solar collectors could be placed on the moon. Turbines suspended in the jet stream could generate wind power. At least in the long term, "I think we have a shot," he says.

In a final chapter on the "Anthropocene," a newly minted term meaning the geological epoch defined by man, Ms. Kolbert turns from her mostly unbiased field reporting to give her own opinion. She is not optimistic, in large part because it appears that Anthropocene man can't be counted on to do the right thing. "It may seem impossible to imagine that a technologically advanced society could choose, in essence, to destroy itself," she writes, "but that is what we are now in the process of doing."

PERSONAL RESPONSE

What is your belief about global warming and environmental changes brought on by human activity? Is there conclusive evidence for global warming, or just scare tactics that the media likes to take advantage of? Do you feel part of the environmental movement, or outside it? Do you or any people close to you make significant efforts to be environmentally responsible? What do you or those persons actually do, and what impact do these actions have?

QUESTIONS FOR CLASS OR SMALL-GROUP DISCUSSION

1. Summarize what Gosnell thinks about Kolbert's book. What does Gosnell think about global warming?

2. This piece of writing is a review of a book written by Elisabeth Kolbert. What expectations do you have of a book review—what should a book review achieve? Do you find the review critical of views in the book? How does this review communicate what the book is about? How do you distinguish between what the reviewer is saying and what the book is saying?

3. What are the ranges of opinion about global warming that are expressed in the review?

4. Is there a tone of urgency in the review, or is it balanced and objective? What evidence supports your view?

CHAPTER 1 OF *FIELD NOTES FROM A CATASTROPHE: MAN, NATURE, AND CLIMATE CHANGE*

ELIZABETH KOLBERT

Elizabeth Kolbert is a journalist who writes on the impact of climate change. As you will see, her writing is vivid, colourful, and immediate. Perhaps no recent writing has had more impact on the public than the carefully reported scenes of climate devastation around the world, published in The New Yorker. *Her work has been collected in* Field Notes from a Catastrophe: Man, Nature, and Climate Change, *in which she concludes: "It may seem impossible to imagine that a technologically advanced society could choose, in essence, to destroy itself, but that is what we are now in the process of doing."*

The Alaskan village of Shishmaref sits on an island known as Sarichef, five miles off the coast of the Seward Peninsula. Sarichef is a small island—no more than a quarter of a mile across and two and a half miles long—and Shishmaref is basically the only thing on it. To the north is the Chukchi Sea, and in every other direction lies the Bering Land Bridge National Preserve, which probably ranks as one of the least visited national parks in the country. During the last ice age, the land bridge—exposed by a drop in sea levels of more than three hundred feet—grew to be nearly a thousand miles wide. The preserve occupies that part of it which, after more than ten thousand years of warmth, still remains above water.

Shishmaref (population 591) is an Inupiat village, and it has been inhabited, at least on a seasonal basis, for several centuries. As in many native villages in Alaska, life there combines—often disconcertingly—the very ancient and the totally modern. Almost everyone is Shishmaref still lives off subsistence hunting, primarily for bearded seals but also for walrus, moose, rabbits, and migrating birds. When I visited the village one day in April, the spring thaw was under way, and the seal-hunting season was about to begin. (Wandering around, I almost tripped over the remnants of the previous year's catch emerging from storage under the snow.) At noon, the village's transportation planner, Tony Weyiouanna, invited me to his house for lunch. In the living room, an enormous television set tuned to the local public-access station was playing a rock soundtrack. Messages like "Happy Birthday to the following elders . . . " kept scrolling across the screen.

Traditionally, the men in Shishmaref hunted for seals by driving out over the sea ice with dogsleds or, more recently, on snowmobiles. After they hauled the seals back to the village, the women would skin and cure them, a process that takes several weeks. In the early 1990s, the hunters began to notice that the sea ice was changing. (Although the claim that the Eskimos have hundreds of words for snow is an exaggeration, the Inupiat make distinctions among many different types of ice, including sikuliaq, "young ice," sarri, "Pack ice," and tuvaq, "land-locked ice.") The ice was starting to form later in the fall, and also to break up earlier in the spring. Once, it had been possible to drive out twenty miles; now, by the time the seals arrived, the ice was mushy half that distance from shore. Weyiouanna described it as having the consistency of a "slush puppy." When you encounter it, he said, "your hair starts sticking up. Your eyes are wide open. You can't even blink." It became too dangerous to hunt using snowmobiles, and the men switched to boats.

Soon, the changes in the sea ice brought other problems. At its highest point, Shishmaref is only twenty-two feet above sea level, and the houses, most of which were built by the U.S. government, are small, boxy, and not particularly sturdy-looking. When the Chukchi Sea froze early, the layer of ice protected the village, the way a tarp prevents a swimming pool from getting roiled by the wind. When the sea started to freeze later, Shishmaref became more vulnerable to storm surges. A storm in October 1997 scoured away a hundred-and-twenty-five-foot-wide strip from the town's northern edge; several houses were destroyed, and more than a dozen had to be relocated. During another storm, in October 2001, the village was threatened by twelve-foot waves. In the summer of 2002, residents of Shishmaref voted, a hundred and sixty-one to twenty, to move the entire village to the mainland. In 2004, the U.S. Army Corps of Engineers completed a survey of possible sites. Most of the spots that are being considered for a new village are in areas nearly as remote as Sarichef, with no roads or nearby cities or even settlements. It is estimated that a full relocation would cost the U.S. government $180 million.

People I spoke to in Shishmaref expressed divided emotions about the proposed move. Some worried that, by leaving the tiny island, they would give up their connection to the sea and become lost. "It make me feel lonely," one woman said. Others seemed excited by the prospect of gaining certain conveniences, like running water, that Shishmaref lacks. Everyone seemed to agree, though, that the village's situation, already dire, was only going to get worse.

Morris Kiyutelluk, who is sixty-five, has lived in Shishmaref almost all his life. (His last name, he told me, means "without a wooden spoon.") I spoke to him while I was hanging around the basement of the village church, which also serves as the unofficial headquarters for a group called the Shishmaref Erosion and Relocation Coalition. "The first time I heard about global warming, I thought, I don't believe those Japanese," Kiyutelluk told me. "Well, they had some good scientists, and it's become true."

The National Academy of Sciences undertook its first major study of global warming in 1979. At that point, climate modeling was still in its infancy, and only a few groups, one led by Syukuro Manabe at the National Oceanic and Atmospheric Administration and another by James Hansen at NASA's Goddard Institute for Space Studies, had considered in any detail the effects of adding carbon dioxide to the atmosphere. Still, the results of their work were alarming enough that President Jimmy Carter called on the academy to investigate. A nine-member panel was appointed. It was led by the distinguished meteorologist Jule Charney, of MIT, who, in the 1940s, had been the first meteorologist to demonstrate that numerical weather forecasting was feasible.

The Ad Hoc Study Group on Carbon Dioxide and Climate, or the Charney panel, as it became known, met for five days at the National Academy of Sciences' summer study center, in Woods Hole, Massachusetts. Its conclusions were unequivocal. Panel members had looked for flaws in the modelers' work but had been unable to find any. "If carbon dioxide continues to increase, the study group finds no reason to doubt that climate changes will result and no reason to believe that these changes will be negligible," the scientists wrote. For a doubling of CO_2 from preindustrial levels, they put the likely global temperature rise at between two and a half and eight degrees Fahrenheit. The panel members weren't sure how long it would take for changes already set in motion to become manifest, mainly because the climate has a built-in time delay. The effect of adding CO_2 to the atmosphere is to throw the earth out of "energy balance." In order for balance to be restored—as, according to the laws of physics, it eventually must be—the entire planet has to heat up, including the oceans, a process, the Charney panel noted, that could take "several decades." Thus, what might seem like the most conservative approach—waiting for evidence of warming to make sure the models were accurate—actually amounted to the riskiest possible strategy: "We may not be given a warning until the CO_2 loading is such that an appreciable climate change is inevitable."

It is now more than twenty-five years since the Charney panel issued its report, and, in that period, Americans have been alerted to the dangers of global warming so many times that reproducing even a small fraction of these warnings would fill several volumes; indeed, entire books have been written just on the history of efforts to draw attention to the problem. (Since the Charney report, the National Academy of Sciences alone has produced nearly two hundred more studies on the subject, including, to name just a few, "Radiative Forcing of Climate Change," "Understanding Climate Change Feedbacks," and "Policy Implications of Greenhouse Warming.") During this same period, worldwide carbon-dioxide emissions have continued to increase, from five billion to seven billion metric tons a year, and the earth's temperature, much as predicted by Manabe's and Hansen's models, has steadily risen. The year 1990 was the warmest year on record until 1991, which was equally hot. Almost every subsequent year has been warmer still. As of this writing, 1998 ranks as the hottest year since the instrumental temperature record began, but it is closely followed by 2002 and 2003, which are tied for second; 2001, which is third; and 2004, which is fourth. Since climate is innately changeable, it's difficult to say when, exactly, in this sequence natural variation could be ruled out as the sole cause. The American Geophysical Union, one of the nation's largest and most respected scientific organizations, decided in 2003 that the matter had been settled. At the group's annual meeting that year, it issued a consensus statement declaring, "Natural influences cannot explain the rapid increase in global near-surface temperatures." As best as can be determined, the world is now warmer than it has been at any point in the last two millennia, and, if current trends continue, by the end of the century it will likely be hotter than at any point in the last two million years.

In the same way that global warming has gradually ceased to be merely a theory, so, too, its impacts are no longer just hypothetical. Nearly every major glacier in the world is shrinking; those in Glacier National Park are retreating so quickly it has been estimated that they will vanish entirely by 2030. The oceans are becoming not just warmer but more acidic; the difference between daytime and nighttime temperatures is diminishing; animals are shifting their ranges poleward; and plants are blooming days, and in some cases weeks, earlier than they used to. These are the warning signs that the Charney panel cautioned against waiting for, and while in many parts of the globe they are still subtle enough to be overlooked, in others they can no longer be ignored. As it happens, the most dramatic changes are occurring in those places, like Shishmaref, where the fewest people tend to live. This disproportionate effect of global warming in the far north was also predicted by early climate models, which forecast, in column after column of FORTRAN-generated figures, what today can be measured and observed directly: the Arctic is melting.

Most of the land in the Arctic, and nearly a quarter of all the land in the Northern Hemisphere—some five and a half billion acres—is underlaid by zones of permafrost. A few months after I visited Shishmaref, I went back to Alaska to take a trip through the interior of the state with Vladimir Romanovsky, a geophysicist and permafrost expert. I flew into Fairbanks—Romanovsky teaches at the University of Alaska, which has its main campus there—and when I arrived, the whole city was enveloped in a dense haze that looked like fog but smelled like burning rubber. People kept telling me that I was lucky I hadn't come a couple of weeks earlier, when it had been much worse. "Even the dogs were wearing masks," one woman I met said. I must have smiled. "I am not joking," she told me.

Fairbanks, Alaska's second-largest city, is surrounded on all sides by forest, and virtually every summer lightning sets off fires in these forests, which fill the air with smoke for a few days or, in bad years, weeks. In the summer of 2004, the fires started early, in June, and were still burning two and a half months later; by the time of my visit, in late August, a record 6.3 million acres—an area roughly the size of New Hampshire—had been incinerated. The severity of the fires was clearly linked to the weather, which had been exceptionally hot and dry; the average summertime temperature in Fairbanks was the highest on record, and the amount of rainfall was the third lowest.

On my second day in Fairbanks, Romanovsky picked me up at my hotel for an underground tour of the city. Like most permafrost experts, he is from Russia. (The Soviets more or less invented the study of permafrost when they decided to build their gulags in Siberia.) A broad man with shaggy brown hair and a square jaw, Romanovsky as a student had had to choose between playing professional hockey and becoming a geophysicist. He had opted for the latter, he told me, because "I was a little bit better scientist than hockey player." He went on to earn two master's degrees and two Ph.D.s. Romanovsky came to get me at ten A.M.; owing to all the smoke, it looked like dawn.

Any piece of ground that has remained frozen for at least two years is, by defini-tion, permafrost. In some places, like eastern Siberia, permafrost runs nearly a mile deep; in Alaska, it varies from a couple of hundred feet to a couple of thousand feet deep. Fairbanks, which is just below the Arctic Circle, is situated in a region of discontinuous permafrost, meaning that the city is pocked with regions of frozen ground. One of the first stops on Romanovsky's tour was a hole that had opened up in a patch of permafrost not far from his house. It was about six feet wide and five feet deep. Nearby were the outlines of other, even bigger holes, which, Romanovsky told me, had been filled with gravel by the local public-works department. The holes, known as thermokarsts, had appeared suddenly when the permafrost gave way, like a rotting floorboard. (The technical term for thawed permafrost is "talik," from a Russian word meaning "not frozen.") Across the road, Romanovsky pointed out a long trench running into the woods. The trench, he explained, had been formed when a wedge of underground ice had melted. The spruce trees that had been growing next to it, or perhaps on top of it, were now listing at odd angles, as if in a gale. Locally, such trees are called "drunken." A few of the spruces had fallen over. "These are very drunk," Romanovsky said.

In Alaska, the ground is riddled with ice wedges that were created during the last glaciation, when the cold earth cracked and the cracks filled with water. The wedges, which can be dozens or even hundreds of feet deep, tended to form in networks, so when they melt, they leave behind connecting diamond- or hexagon-shaped depressions. A few blocks beyond the drunken forest, we came to a house where the front yard showed clear signs of ice-wedge melt-off. The owner, trying to make the best of things, had turned the yard into a miniature-golf course. Around the corner, Romanovsky pointed out a house—no longer occupied—that basically had split in two; the main part was leaning to the right and the garage to the left. The house had been built in the sixties or early seventies; it had survived until almost a decade ago, when the permafrost under it started to degrade. Romanovsky's mother-in-law used to own two houses on the same block. He had urged her to sell them both. He pointed out one, now under new ownership; its roof had developed an ominous-looking ripple. (When Romanovsky went to buy his own house, he looked only in permafrost-free areas.)

"Ten years ago, nobody cared about permafrost," he told me. "Now everybody want to know." Measurements that Romanovsky and his colleagues at the University of Alaska have made around Fairbanks show that the temperature of the permafrost in many places has risen to the point where it is now less than one degree below freezing. In places where the permafrost has been disturbed, by roads or houses or lawns, much of it is already thawing. Romanovsky has also been monitoring the permafrost on the North Slope and has found that there, too, are regions where the permafrost is very nearly thirty-two degrees Fahrenheit. While thermokarsts in the roadbeds and talik under the basement are the sort of problems that really only affect the people right near—or above—them, warming permafrost is significant in ways that go far beyond local real estate losses. For one thing, permafrost represents a unique record of long-term temperature trends. For another, it acts, in effect, as a repository for green-house gases. As the climate warms, there is a good chance that these gases will be released into the atmosphere, further contributing to global warming. Although the age of permafrost is difficult to determine, Romanovsky estimates that most of it in Alaska probably dates back to the beginning of the last glacial cycle. This means that if it thaws, it will be doing so for the first time in more than a hundred and twenty thousand years. "It's really a very interesting time," Romanovsky told me.

PERSONAL RESPONSE

How does climate change affect you personally? Has it affected the way you travel or the food you buy? Do reports of climate change around the world make you angry or, on the other hand, do they make you skeptical? Why? Do you think some of the relatively recent strange weather patterns are the result of global warming?

QUESTIONS FOR CLASS OR SMALL-GROUP DISCUSSION

1. There is a disconnect between the information available about climate change and the level of public outrage and alarm. Do you agree or disagree?

2. Some critics believe environmentalists are using global warming to further a left-wing agenda: to slow economic progress and to redistribute wealth. Explain why you agree or disagree with those critics.

3. Does climate change have the potential to be geopolitically destabilizing; i.e., to be the next source of violent unrest in the world? Explain your answer and give three reasons to support your viewpoint.

4. Former U.N. Secretary-General Kofi Annan (see his essay on globalization in Chapter 12, pages 178–180) blamed global warming on a lack of leadership. Do you agree? Who is to blame? Annan pointed out that the countries least responsible for climate change may suffer from it the most. For example, Kenya's herders are being displaced from their grasslands by increasing droughts; however, their pollution consists mostly of the smoke from cooking fires and cigarettes. Adding to Africa's woes, an increase in temperatures has contributed to the spread of malaria. So the question is this: Is global warming actually the consequence of climate change, or is it the consequence of politicians who can't, or won't, deal with the issue by reducing emissions or scaling back their economies?

5. What accounts for Canada's massive greenhouse gas emissions?

ROUGHING IT IN THE BUSH: MY PLANS FOR MOOSE HUNTING IN THE CANADIAN WILDERNESS

STEPHEN LEACOCK

Stephen Leacock (1869–1944) was an economics professor at McGill University in Montreal and remains one of Canada's most important humorists. He was born in England, but by age six he had moved with his family to Ontario. Among his numerous books are Sunshine

Sketches of a Little Town *(1912)*, Arcadian Adventures with the Idle Rich *(1914)*, Adventurers of the Far North *(1914), and* Here Are My Lectures *(1937). In his honour, the top award for humour writing in Canada is the Stephen Leacock Memorial Medal for Humour.*

The season is now opening when all those who have a manly streak in them like to get out into the bush and "rough it" for a week or two of hunting and fishing. For myself, I never feel that the autumn has been well spent unless I can get out after the moose. And when I go I like to go right into the bush and "rough it"—get clear away from civilization, out in the open, and take fatigue or hardship just as it comes.

So this year I am making all my plans to get away for a couple of weeks of moose hunting along with my brother George and my friend Tom Gass. We generally go together because we are all of us men who like the rough stuff and are tough enough to stand the hardship of living in the open. The place we go to is right in the heart of the primitive Canadian forest, among big timber, broken with lakes as still as glass, just the very ground for moose.

We have a kind of lodge up there. It's just a rough place that we put up, the three of us, the year before last, built out of tamarack logs faced with a broad axe. The flies, while we were building it, were something awful. Two of the men that we sent in there to build it were so badly bitten that we had to bring them out a hundred miles to a hospital. None of us saw the place while we were building it,—we were all busy at the time,—but the teamsters who took in our stuff said it was the worst season for the black flies that they ever remembered.

Still we hung to it, in spite of the flies, and stuck at it till we got it built. It is, I say, only a plain place but good enough to rough it in. We have one big room with a stone fireplace, and bedrooms round the sides, with a wide verandah, properly screened, all along the front. The verandah has a row of upright tamaracks for its posts and doesn't look altogether bad. In the back part we have quarters where our man sleeps. We had an ice-house knocked up while we were building and water laid on in pipes from a stream. So that on the whole the place has a kind of rough comfort about it,—good enough anyway for fellows hunting moose all day.

The place, nowadays, is not hard to get at. The government has just built a colonization highway, quite all right for motors, that happens to go within a hundred yards of our lodge.

We can get the railway for a hundred miles, and then the highway for forty, and the last hundred yards we can walk. But this season we are going to cut out the railway and go the whole way from the city in George's car with our kit with us.

George has one of those great big cars with a roof and thick glass sides. Personally none of the three of us would have preferred to ride in a luxurious darned thing like that. Tom says that as far as he is concerned he'd much sooner go into the bush over a rough trail in a buckboard, and for my own part a team of oxen would be more the kind of thing that I'd wish.

However, the car is there, so we might as well use the thing especially as the provincial government has built the fool highway right into the wilderness. By taking the big car also we can not only carry all the hunting outfit that we need but we can also, if we like, shove in a couple of small trunks with a few clothes. This may be necessary as it seems that somebody has gone and slapped a great big frame hotel right there in the wilderness, not half a mile from the place we go to. The hotel we find a regular nuisance. It gave us the advantage of electric light for our lodge (a thing none of us care about), but it means more fuss about clothes. Clothes, of course, don't really matter when a fellow is roughing it in the bush, but Tom says that we might find it necessary to go over to the hotel in the evenings to borrow coal oil or a side of bacon or any rough stuff that we need; and they do such a lot of dressing up at these fool hotels now that if we do go over for bacon or anything in the evening we might just as well slip on our evening clothes, as we could chuck them off the minute we get back. George thinks it might not be a bad idea,—just as a way of saving all our energy for getting after the moose,—to dine each evening at the hotel itself. He knew some men who did that last year and they told him that the time saved for moose hunting in that way is extraordinary. George's idea is that we could come in each night with our moose,—such and such a number as the case might be—either bringing them with us or burying them where they die,—change our things, slide over to the hotel and get dinner and then beat it back into the bush by moonlight and fetch in the moose. It seems they have a regular two dollar table d'hôte dinner at the hotel,—just rough stuff of course but after all, as we all admit, we don't propose to go out into the wilds to pamper ourselves with high feeding: a plain hotel meal in a home-like style at two dollars a plate is better than cooking up a lot of rich stuff over a camp fire.

It we do dine at the hotel we could take our choice each evening between going back into the bush by moonlight to fetch in the dead moose from the different caches where we had hidden them, or sticking round the hotel itself for a while. It seems that there is dancing there. Nowadays such a lot of women and girls get the open air craze for the life in the bush that these big wilderness hotels are crowded with them. There is something about living in the open that attracts modern women and they like to get right away from everybody and everything; and of course hotels of this type in the open are nowadays always well closed in with screens so that there are no flies or anything of that sort.

So it seems that there is dancing at the hotel every evening,—nothing on a large scale or pretentious,—just an ordinary hardwood floor,—they may wax it a little for all I know—and some sort of plain, rough Italian orchestra that they fetch up from the city. Not that any of us care for dancing. It's a thing that personally we wouldn't bother with. But it happens that there a couple of young girls that Tom knows that are going to be staying at the hotel and of course naturally he wants to give them a good time. They are only eighteen and twenty (sisters) and that's really younger than we care for, but with young girls like that,—practically kids,—any man wants to give them a good time. So Tom says, and I think quite rightly, that as the kids are going to be there we may as well put in an appearance at the hotel and see that they are having a good time. Their mother is going to be with them too, and of course we want to give her a good time as well; in fact I think I will lend her my moose rifle and let her go out and shoot a moose. One thing we are all agreed upon in the arrangement of our hunting trip, is in not taking along anything to drink. Drinking spoils a trip of that sort. We all remember how in the old days we'd go out into a camp in the bush (I mean before there used to be any highway or any hotel) and carry in rye whiskey in demijohns (two dollars a gallon it was) and sit around the camp fire drinking it in the evenings.

But there's nothing in it. We all agree that the law being what it is, it is better to stick to it. It makes a fellow feel better. So we shall carry nothing in. I don't say that one might not have a flask or something in one's pocket in the car; but only as a precaution against accident or cold. And when we get to our lodge we all feel that we are a darned sight better without it. If we should need anything,—though it isn't likely,—there are still three cases of old Scotch whiskey, kicking around the lodge somewhere; I think they are kicking round in a little cement cellar with a locked door that we had made so as to use it for butter or anything of that sort. Anyway there are three, possibly four, or maybe, five, cases of Scotch there and if we should for any reason want it, there it is. But we are hardly likely to touch it,—unless we hit a cold snap, or a wet spell;—then we might; or if we strike hot dry weather Tom says he thinks there a couple of cases of champagne still in the cellar; some stuff that one of us must have shot in there just before prohibition came in. But we'll hardly use it. When a man is out moose hunting from dawn to dusk he hasn't much use for champagne, not till he gets home anyway. The only thing that Tom says the champagne might come in useful for would be if we cared to ask the two kids over to some sort of dinner; it would be just a rough kind of camp dinner (we could hardly ask their mother to it) but we think we could manage it. The man we keep there used to be a butler in England, or something of the sort, and he could manage some kind of rough meal where the champagne might fit it.

There's only one trouble about our plans for our fall camp that bothers us just a little. The moose are getting damn scarce about that place. There used, so they say, to be any quantity of them. There's an old settler up there that our man buys all our cream from who says that he remembers when the moose were so thick that they would come up and drink whiskey out of his dipper. But somehow they seem to have quit the place. Last year we sent our man out again and again looking for them and he never saw any. Three years ago a boy that works at the hotel said he saw a moose in the cow pasture back of the hotel and there were the tracks of a moose seen last year at the place not ten miles from the hotel where it had come to drink. But apart from these two exceptions the moose hunting has been poor.

Still, what does it matter? What we want is the life, the rough life just as I have described it. If any moose comes to our lodge we'll shoot him, or tell the butler to. But if not,—well, we've got along without for ten years, I don't suppose we shall worry.

PERSONAL RESPONSE

One of the remarkable things about Canada is our vastness—a vastness defined by the wild outdoors: forests, tundra, waters (oceans, lakes, rivers), ice fields, prairies, and, of course, bush. What does that vastness mean to you? Has it influenced your activities, holidays, or interests? Does it affect the way you see the world or think about the environment? Does it make you a different kind of person relative to, say, a person in a small, heavily populated country?

QUESTIONS FOR CLASS OR SMALL-GROUP DISCUSSION

1. At what point when you were reading this did you recognize Leacock was having you on? What was the give-away? How would you describe this kind of humour, and how does it affect your reading of the piece?

2. What is the point that Leacock is trying to make?

3. Leacock wrote this piece more than 80 years ago. Discuss its relevance to today's attitude toward (a) the bush and the environment and (b) masculinity's concept of itself.

4. Examine the connotative relationships among the following words: the bush, the outdoors, the wilderness, the environment, and nature. What do these words suggest to you?

A FABLE FOR TOMORROW

Rachel Carson

*Rachel Carson (1907–1964) was a writer and ecologist who is cred-
ited with starting the modern environmental movement in 1962,
with the publication of her classic bestseller,* Silent Spring. *"A Fable
for Tomorrow" is the first chapter of this book, in which she warned
of the effects of pollution and pesticide use. Although she was attacked
by the chemical industry and by politicians, Carson continued to look
at the world as a place to be cared for, not exploited.* Time *magazine
named Carson one of the 100 most influential people of the twentieth
century.*

There was once a town in the heart of America where all life seemed to live in harmony with its surroundings. The town lay in the midst of a checkerboard of prosperous farms, with fields of grain and hillsides of orchards where, in the spring, white clouds of bloom drifted above the green fields. In autumn, oak and maple and birch set up a blaze of color that flamed and flickered across a backdrop of pines. Then foxes barked in the hills and deer silently crossed the fields, half hidden in the mists of the fall mornings.

Along the roads, laurel, viburnum and alder, great ferns and wildflowers delighted the traveler's eye through much of the year. Even in winter the roadsides were places of beauty, where countless birds came to feed on the berries and on the seed heads of the dried weeds rising above the snow. The countryside was, in fact, famous for the abundance and variety of its bird life, and when the flood of migrants was pouring through in spring and fall people traveled from great distances to observe them. Others came to fish the streams, which flowed clear and cold out of the hills and contained shady pools where trout lay. So it had been from the days many years ago when the first settlers raised their houses, sank their wells, and built their barns.

Then a strange blight crept over the area and everything began to change. Some evil spell had settled on the community: mysterious maladies swept the flocks of chickens; the cattle and sheep sickened and died. Everywhere was a shadow of death. The farmers spoke of much illness among their families. In the town the doctors had become more and more puzzled by new kinds of sickness appearing among their patients. There had been several sudden and unexplained deaths, not only among adults but even among children, who would be stricken suddenly while at play and die within a few hours.

There was a strange stillness. The birds, for example—where had they gone? Many people spoke of them, puzzled and disturbed. The feeding stations in the backyards were deserted. The few birds seen anywhere were moribund; they trembled violently and could not fly. It was a spring without voices. On the mornings that had once throbbed with the dawn chorus of robins, catbirds, doves, jays, wrens, and scores of other bird voices there was now no sound; only silence lay over the fields and woods and marsh.

On the farms the hens brooded, but no chicks hatched. The farmers complained that they were unable to raise any pigs—the litters were small and the young survived only a few days. The apple trees were coming into bloom but no bees droned among the blossoms, so there was no pollination and there would be no fruit.

The roadsides, once so attractive, were now lined with browned and withered vegetation as though swept by fire. These, too, were silent, deserted by all living things. Even the streams were now lifeless. Anglers no longer visited them, for all the fish had died.

In the gutters under the eaves and between the shingles of the roofs, a white granular powder still showed a few patches; some weeks before it had fallen like snow upon the roofs and the lawns, the fields and streams.

No witchcraft, no enemy action had silenced the rebirth of new life in this stricken world. The people had done it themselves.

This town does not actually exist, but it might easily have a thousand counterparts in America and elsewhere in the world. I know of no community that has experienced all the misfortunes I describe. Yet every one of these disasters has actually happened somewhere, and many real communities have already suffered a substantial number of them. A grim specter has crept upon us almost unnoticed, and this imagined tragedy may easily become a stark reality we all shall know.

What has already silenced the voices of spring in countless towns in America? This book is an attempt to explain.

PERSONAL RESPONSE

Describe the progress you think the environmental movement has made since the publication of *Silent Spring*. What, if anything, did you do today to make your environmental footprint as small as possible?

QUESTIONS FOR CLASS OR SMALL-GROUP DISCUSSION

1. Other than joining an organization and paying dues, what can one person do on a local level to help protect the environment?
2. What is the relationship between economic development and environmental health? Can the two co-exist?
3. One purpose of "A Fable for Tomorrow," the first chapter in *Silent Spring*, is to get people to read the rest of the book. The first chapter is a lyrical description of a town that has died. Despite the fact that this town does not exist, do you believe that the opening is effective?
4. Make a list of words in this chapter that evoke an emotional response; e.g., *evil spell*, *witchcraft*, and *enemy action*.
5. As developing nations, or Third World nations, attempt to make economic progress, environmental concerns are sometimes put aside or ignored. Should other nations or corporations have any influence on these particular developmental outcomes?

GREEN WINTER

FRANKE JAMES

Working at the intersection of art, technology, and advertising, Franke James, born in Toronto, in 1956, is a writer and artist committed to bringing awareness to global warming. She has a master's degree in fine arts from the University of Victoria. More about her and her work can be found at http://www.frankejames.com/franke_james.html.

I go to a COCKTAIL party and meet a self-described "ROGUE" ECONOMIST named STEVEN LEVITT. He has a Reputation for TURNING conventional WISDOM upside DOWN, so I ask him, "HOW CAN GLOBAL WARMING BE SOLVED?"

Levitt quips, "Why would you worry about it? GLOBAL WARMING is going to be good for CANADA. Look how much more of the country will be populated if it's WARMER!"

Photo Source: Photographs, illustrations, and writing by Franke James, MFA, *A Green Winter* © 2007 Franke James.

Photo Source: Photographs, illustrations, and writing by Franke James, MFA, *A Green Winter* © 2007 Franke James.

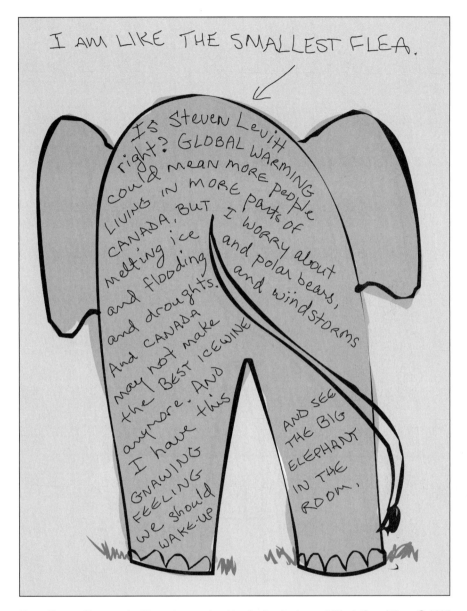

Photo Source: Photographs, illustrations, and writing by Franke James, MFA, *A Green Winter* © 2007 Franke James.

Photo Source: Photographs, illustrations, and writing by Franke James, MFA, *A Green Winter* © 2007 Franke James.

I WEAR MY NEW RED HIKING BOOTS. They were a BOXING DAY BARGAIN and make me FEEL like a kid going on a new adventure. I don't bring ski boots.

Photo Source: Photographs, illustrations, and writing by Franke James, MFA, *A Green Winter* © 2007 Franke James.

Photo Source: Photographs, illustrations, and writing by Franke James, MFA, *A Green Winter* © 2007 Franke James.

The ski lifts are idle.

Usually the hills would be full of skiers, and the snow would be crunching under our feet. Instead we pick our way through the mud.

Photo Source: Photographs, illustrations, and writing by Franke James, MFA, *A Green Winter* © 2007 Franke James.

Photo Source: Photographs, illustrations, and writing by Franke James, MFA, *A Green Winter* © 2007 Franke James.

We hike up the mountain following the Bruce Trail signs. We jump over small streams of trickling water. The FOREST has a wild beauty to it. I want to remember it.

Photo Source: Photographs, illustrations, and writing by Franke James, MFA, *A Green Winter* © 2007 Franke James.

Photo Source: Photographs, illustrations, and writing by Franke James, MFA, *A Green Winter* © 2007 Franke James.

Photo Source: Photographs, illustrations, and writing by Franke James, MFA, *A Green Winter* © 2007 Franke James.

We reach the top and I
am amazed how high up we
are. We gaze out at a vista of
brown and green fields. The
snow is late but soon it
will BLANKET everything.
It will come. It has to
SNOW. This is CANADA.

Photo Source: Photographs, illustrations, and writing by Franke James, MFA, *A Green Winter* © 2007 Franke James.

Photo Source: Photographs, illustrations, and writing by Franke James, MFA, *A Green Winter* © 2007 Franke James.

Photo Source: Photographs, illustrations, and writing by Franke James, MFA, *A Green Winter* © 2007 Franke James.

Photo Source: Photographs, illustrations, and writing by Franke James, MFA, *A Green Winter* © 2007 Franke James.

Photo Source: Photographs, illustrations, and writing by Franke James, MFA, *A Green Winter* © 2007 Franke James.

The INFLATABLE SNOWMEN look ODD + COMICAL on the sickly-green LAWN.   I FEEL SORRY for the kids. How can you be a CANADIAN child and NOT MAKE REAL SNOWMEN?

Photo Source: Photographs, illustrations, and writing by Franke James, MFA, *A Green Winter* © 2007 Franke James.

Photo Source: Photographs, illustrations, and writing by Franke James, MFA, *A Green Winter* © 2007 Franke James.

Photo Source: Photographs, illustrations, and writing by Franke James, MFA, *A Green Winter* © 2007 Franke James.

AND FOR THE FIRST TIME I NOTICE THERE IS A POLAR BEAR ON THE TWOONIE. CANADA'S IDENTITY HAS BEEN JINGLING IN MY POCKET all along. WILL it CHANGE?

Photo Source: Photographs, illustrations, and writing by Franke James, MFA, *A Green Winter* © 2007 Franke James.

Photo Source: Photographs, illustrations, and writing by Franke James, MFA, *A Green Winter* © 2007 Franke James.

Photo Source: Photographs, illustrations, and writing by Franke James, MFA, *A Green Winter* © 2007 Franke James.

I see FRESH FLOWERS for sale on the sidewalk. HOW LOVELY!

Photo Source: Photographs, illustrations, and writing by Franke James, MFA, *A Green Winter* © 2007 Franke James.

I see kids PLAYING HOCKEY OUTDOORS on ICE. YIKES! I think of the ENERGY it takes to make the ice. AND how stubborn CANADIANS are. We'll NEVER LET HOCKEY GO!

Photo Source: Photographs, illustrations, and writing by Franke James, MFA, *A Green Winter* © 2007 Franke James.

Photo Source: Photographs, illustrations, and writing by Franke James, MFA, *A Green Winter* © 2007 Franke James. Tim Hortons is a registered trademark of The TDL Marks Corporation and is used under license by The TDL Group Corp.

Photo Source: Photographs, illustrations, and writing by Franke James, MFA, *A Green Winter* © 2007 Franke James. Tim Hortons is a registered trademark of The TDL Marks Corporation and is used under license by The TDL Group Corp.

Photo Source: Photographs, illustrations, and writing by Franke James, MFA, *A Green Winter* © 2007 Franke James.

PERSONAL RESPONSE

James created this piece after American economist and *Freakonomics* author Steven Levitt remarked to her that global warming would be good for Canada because it would increase the population. Do you think the combination of words and images in her essay is effective? What was your response to the piece as you made your way through it? At what point did you begin to take it seriously?

QUESTIONS FOR CLASS OR SMALL-GROUP DISCUSSION

1. Franke James uses Levitt's unconventional opinion as a springboard to explore questions about complacency, global warming, and Canada's identity. In more formal language, summarize the message of this piece.

2. Describe the strategy used in this piece to comment on the issue of global warming. Is it effective? Discuss. What exactly is global warming?

3. Describe the tone used by the writer.

4. What effect do the pictures, combined with simple handwriting, have on your response to the message?

5. What is the speaker's implicit concept of Canada? What are all the signals that this piece is Canadian? Do you believe this is a typical Canadian response to global warming?

6. Describe the speaker's conflict and whether it becomes resolved.

7. Mainly because of the Alberta oil sands, Canada is becoming one of the largest producers of greenhouse gases. Research and comment on the environmental impact of this massive oil production.

FOR FURTHER VIEWING: ENVIRONMENTAL STUDIES

An Inconvenient Truth (2006); *Manufacturing Landscapes* (2006); *Silkwood* (1983); *The Day After Tomorrow* (2004); *Gorillas in the Mist: The Story of Dian Fossey* (1988); *Soylent Green* (1974); *Silent Running* (1972); *A Civil Action* (1998); *Who Killed the Electric Car?* (2006); *Ilha das Flores* (1989).

FORMATTING GUIDELINES FOR COURSE PAPERS

Your instructor may give you formatting guidelines for your papers, but if not, the following guidelines should serve you well in most cases.

Margins, Spacing, and Page Numbers

Leave a one-inch margin on both sides and at the top and bottom of each page, except for the page number. Double-space all text throughout the paper. Number pages consecutively throughout the paper except for the first page, which does not need a page number. Position the page numbers on the right-hand side, one-half inch from the top of the paper, flush with the right margin. Some instructors request that you include your last name with each page number.

Heading and Title on First Page

If your instructor tells you to use the first page of text for the heading and title rather than a separate title page, drop down one inch from the top of the first page and insert all the information your instructor requires, flush with the left margin. Add your title, centred on the page. Double-space between all lines, including between the date and the title and between the title and the first line of the paper. Do not underline your own title or put it in quotation marks.

```
Salim Rana

Professor Lee

English 102

November 28, 2007

           Trailer Park Boys: Canadian Trash or Canadian Culture?

Trailer Park Boys is a long-running television show that some critics

have derided as a negative portrayal of Canadian culture. However, a

closer look reveals that the show relies on themes of friendship and

camaraderie rather than the violence and sexuality that pervade most TV

shows.
```

Title Page

If your instructor requires a title page, centre your title about halfway down the page. Do not underline your title or add quotation marks around it. Below the title, insert your name. Then drop down the page and insert your instructor's name, the course, and the date.

Trailer Park Boys: Canadian Trash or Canadian Culture?

by

Salim Rana

Professor Lee

English 102

November 28, 2007

DEFINITIONS OF TERMS ASSOCIATED WITH RESEARCH AND WRITING

Abstract. A summary of the essential points of a text. It is usually quite short, no more than a paragraph.

Analysis. A division of a subject into its separate parts for individual study.

Argument/persuasion. An attempt to prove the validity of a position by offering supporting proof. Persuasion takes argument one step further by convincing an audience to adopt a viewpoint or take action.

Book review. A report that summarizes the main ideas of a book and provides critical commentary. You will usually be asked to give your personal response to the book, including both your opinion of the ideas it presents and an evaluation of their worth or credibility.

Case study. A situation or profile of a person or persons, for which you provide a context and background information.

Citation. A reference that provides supporting illustrations or examples for your own ideas; the authority or source of that information is identified.

Comparison. A likeness or strong similarity between two things.

Contrast. A difference or strong dissimilarity between two things.

Debate. A discussion involving opposing points in an argument. In formal debate, opposing teams defend and attack a specific proposition.

Description. The use of words to convey the essential nature of a thing.

Diction. A writer's word choice and level of usage, which vary in informal and formal language; slang, jargon, and regional, nonstandard, and colloquial languages.

Evaluation. A judgment about worth, quality, or credibility.

Forum. An open discussion or exchange of ideas among many people.

Free writing. The act of writing down every idea that occurs to you about your topic without stopping to examine what you are writing.

Hypothesis. A tentative explanation to account for some phenomenon or set of facts. In essence, a theory or an assumption that can be tested by further investigation and is assumed to be true for the purpose of argument or investigation.

Illustration. An explanation or clarification, typically using an example or a comparison.

Journal. A personal record of experiences, thoughts, or responses, usually kept separate from other writings, as in a diary or notebook.

Literature search. A process of locating titles of articles, books, and other material on a specific subject.

Narration. A telling of a story.

Panel discussion. A small group of people (usually between three and six) gathered to discuss a topic. Often each member of a panel is prepared to represent a certain position or point of view on the subject of discussion, with time left after the presentations for questions from audience members.

Paraphrase. A restatement of a passage in your own words. A paraphrase is shorter than the original passage but retains its essential meaning.

Point of view. A writer's perspective on a subject.

Position paper. A detailed report that explains, justifies, or recommends a particular course of action.

Proposition. A statement of a position on a subject, a course of action, or a topic for discussion or debate.

Reflective writing. A process of drawing on personal experience to offer your own response to a topic. This kind of writing uses the first person.

Report. A detailed account.

Subject. A general or broad area of interest.

Summary. A shortened version of a passage, stated in your own words. A summary resembles a paraphrase; both convey the essence of the original, but a summary is shorter than a paraphrase.

Synthesis. Combining the ideas of two or more authors and integrating those ideas into your own discussion.

Thesis. A statement of the specific purpose of a paper. A thesis is essentially a one-sentence summary of what you will argue, explain, illustrate, define, describe, or otherwise develop in the rest of the paper. It is usually stated very early in a paper.

Tone. A writer's attitude toward the subject and the audience, conveyed through word choice and diction.

Topic. A specific, focused, and clearly defined area of interest. A topic is a narrow aspect of a subject.

Workshop. Similar in intent to a forum, a workshop is characterized by exchanges of information, ideas, and opinions, usually among a small group of people. Both workshops and forums involve interaction and exchange of ideas to a greater degree than panel discussions, which typically allot more time to panel members than to audience participants.

Kim Blank's "Marking Grid/Writing Checklist" is designed for students to self-evaluate their work, but more importantly, it was designed to play a role in peer editing and the peer evaluation process. If followed, it forces students to pay attention to the range of particular components both in their writing and the writing of others. In short, it answers the question, "What should I be looking for when I read the work of others?" Following the checklist carefully, and taking responsibility for reading the papers of their peers carefully, is, then, an integral part of the assignment. Instructors can of course fine-tune this checklist given the assignment or what learning outcomes they have.

MARKING GRID AND WRITING CHECKLIST

writer's name _____   course#/assignment#/date _____   marker's name _____

Writing Checklist	Yes/Very Well	Quite Well	Well Enough	No/Not Well	Comments (put corrections directly on to the paper as well)
title page done correctly					
correct Works Cited/documentation style					
presentation/format okay					
word limit stated					
word limit kept to					
every punctuation mark is correct					
grammar handled okay					
usage/lexicon/vocabulary/audience handled okay					
"Quirk List" sheet followed					
methodology and/or point of view and/or critical perspective handled okay					
specific examples used					
close "reading" skills demonstrated					
research materials used appropriately					
specific thesis or clear direction of paper					
all paragraphs point to thesis/are on topic					
conclusion interesting/appropriate/expansive					
assignment followed					
Overall comments and summary:					If applicable to assignment, put mark/assessment in box.

[Use "N/A" if the checklist item is not applicable to the assignment you are assessing.]

Reprinted with permission

APPENDIX FOUR

BLANK'S REALLY ANNOYING QUIRK LIST

Kim Blank's "Quirk List" evolved to rid the world of wordiness, and then went on to include some of the most common writing errors that need to be avoided. The idea is simple: if a phrase or grouping of words seems familiar, then drop those words or find a new way to say what it is you want to say. Get rid of the clutter in your writing.

The Deadly Sins:

DS1) comma splice

DS2) *its/it's* confusion

DS3) sentence fragment

DS4) verb agreement errors

The Quirks:

Q1) Avoid "there is/are/was/were" or "it is/was" or "that is/are/were" or "which is/are."

Q2) Never use "itself" or similar forms in the context of, for example, "the poem itself" or "the king himself."

Q3) Avoid "one" as a pronoun, as in the context "One knows this. . . ." (Too light-in-the-loafers.)

Q4) Avoid "as" when you mean "because" or "since."

Q5) Use an active voice. Write *Foucault states* not *Foucault is stating*. (Get rid of "-ing" everywhere.)

Q6) Always introduce, integrate, and contextualize quotations.

Q7) Do not confuse subject with theme (e.g., subject = cheese; theme = cheese is hell).

Q8) Never use a complex word when a simple one will do.

Q9) Watch out for overuse of *therefore, however, hence, furthermore, consequently, thus,* and *indeed.*

Q10) Avoid beginning sentences with "It." (What does the "It" refer to?)

Q11) Avoid wazzle (waffling/fuzzy) words: *actually, aspects, basically, certainly, essentially, generally, overall, quite, really, simply, situation, truly, ultimately, virtually,* and *very. Could, should,* and *would* are also conspicuous wazzlers.

Q12) **WORDINESS:** When possible and prudent, purge or prune the following—and ALL clichés:

454

NEL

aforementioned = DELETE
a considerable amount of = DELETE OR BE
    SPECIFIC
a lot of = many, much
a majority of = most, much of, many
added bonus = bonus
advance warning = warning
advance planning = planning
after all is said and done = DELETE
all of a sudden = suddenly
all of these = these
along the lines of = like
amongst = among
are/was/were able to = can OR DELETE
as a matter of fact = in fact OR DELETE
as a means to = to
as a whole = DELETE
as being a = as OR DELETE
as it truly is = DELETE
as of the moment = DELETE
as the case may be = DELETE
at all times = always OR DELETE
at first glance = DELETE
at the present time = currently, now
at the same time that = while
at this point in time = now OR DELETE

basic necessity = necessity
basic fundamentals = basics OR
    fundamentals
because of the fact of = because of
being = DELETE
both of these/them/the = both
brings to mind = recalls/suggests
by and large = DELETE
by definition = DELETE
by leaps and bounds = DELETE
by means of = by
by the use of = using
by virtue of [the fact that] = by

came to a realization = realized/recognized
came to an abrupt end = end[ed] abruptly
can be seen as = is OR DELETE
clearly articulate = articulate
close scrutiny = scrutiny
common similarities = similarities
compare and contrast = compare
complete stranger = stranger
completely eliminate = eliminate
concerning the matter of = about/
    regarding
core essence = DELETE
correctional facility = jail

despite the fact that = although
did not succeed = failed
due to the effects = because
due to the fact that = because
during the course of = during

each and every one = each, every
each individual = DELETE OR everyone
each of = each
early on in the = early in the
economically deprived = poor
enter into = enter OR DELETE
erode away = erode
every single one = each one, all, each

final demise/destination/outcome = DELETE
    final
first and foremost = first
for all intents and purposes = DELETE or
    actually
for that which is = for the
for the purpose of = to, for
foreseeable future = [when exactly?]
free gift = gift
future plans/prospects = plans OR prospects

general consensus = consensus
general public = public
grave crisis = crisis

hand-in-hand = together
has/had/have a tendency to = often OR
    DELETE
has/had/have been found to be = is/was/are
has/had/have the ability to/capacity for = can/
    could
has/had/have the effect of = DELETE
has/had/have the opportunity to = can/could

I myself = I
in a situation in which = in
in a very real sense = DELETE
in actuality = DELETE
in all likelihood/probability = likely/probably
in close proximity = near
in connection with = about
in essence = DELETE
in light of the fact that = because
in nature = DELETE
in order to = to
in reality = DELETE
in reference to = about/regarding
in the neighborhood of = about
in spite of = despite
in spite of the fact that = although
in terms of = DELETE
in the area of = in
in the course of = during, while
in the event that = if
in the final analysis = finally OR DELETE
in the light of = considering OR DELETE
in the majority of instances - usually
in the midst of = during, amid
in the nature of = DELETE
in the near future = soon OR DELETE
in the not too distant future = soon OR DELETE

in this day and age = currently, now, today
in today's society = today
in view of the fact that = because
in which = DELETE
inner feelings = feelings
interestingly enough = DELETE
irregardless = DELETE
is able to = can
is aware of the fact that = knows
is found to be = is
is going to = will
is in conflict with = conflicts with/is against
is in contrast to = contrasts with
is of significant importance = is significant OR is important
is scared of = fears
is seen as = is
is when = is OR DELETE
is where = DELETE
is/was more or less = is/was
it can be seen that = DELETE
it could happen that = could/may/might
it goes to show that = DELETE
it is clear/evident/apparent that = DELETE
it is crucial/important that = must/should OR DELETE
it is interesting to note = DELETE
it is necessary that = must/should
it is possible that = DELETE
itself = DELETE

join/gather together = join/gather

last but not least = finally
later on = later

make a decision = decide
make an assumption = assume
make contact with = contact
make reference to = refer to
manner in which = way
mental attitude = attitude
mix together = mix
more or less = DELETE [OR be specific]
more preferable = preferable
mutual agreement = agreement

natural instinct = instinct
necessary prerequisite = prerequisite
new record = record [as in SET A ~~NEW~~ RECORD]

of great importance = DELETE OR is important
off of = off OR from
on a daily basis = daily
on account of the fact that = because
on the basis of = because, based on
on the grounds that = because
on the occasion of = on
on the situation of = about

on the whole = DELETE
on top of all this = moreover OR DELETE
one of the more = DELETE
one of the most interesting = DELETE
only serves to = DELETE
overall goal = goal
overall structure = structure
owing to the fact that = because

particular type of = DELETE
past experience = experience
past history = history
past memories = memories
period of time = period, time
plan ahead = plan
previous/prior to = before
providing that = provided

quite clearly = DELETE

real truth/life = truth/life
reconsider again = reconsider
regardless of the fact that = although
respective/respectively = DELETE
right up to the = up to the OR to the

serve the purpose of = DELETE
serves to explain/show = explain/show
shout loudly = shout
some kind of = DELETE
somewhere in the neighbourhood of – about
sort of = DELETE
study in depth = study
symbolically represents = represents, symbolizes

take action = act
take the time = DELETE
terrible/horrible tragedy = tragedy
that/this being said = DELETE
that exists = DELETE
that exists between/with/among = between/with/among
that is/are = DELETE when possible
that is to say = DELETE
the colour green = green
the end/final result = the result
the fact that = that OR DELETE
the final conclusion = the conclusion
the majority of = most/many
the month of September = September
the overall plan = the plan
the possibility exists for = may/might/could
the reason is because = the reason/because
the reason why = the reason, why, because
the type/use of = DELETE
the way [manner] in which = the way OR DELETE
the whole [any noun] = DELETE "whole"
the world we live in = the world/life OR DELETE

there is a chance that = may/might/could
there is a need = DELETE
to a further extent = further
throughout the course of = throughout the
through the use of = through
total abstinence = abstinence
total annihilation = annihilation
totally obvious = obvious
true facts = facts

united as one = united
until such time as = until
utmost perfection = perfection

valuable asset = asset
various different = various

we are of the opinion that = we believe
well aware of = aware
what is important is = DELETE
when all is said and done = DELETE
whether or not = whether/if OR DELETE
which have been found to be = are OR DELETE
which is = DELETE (when possible)
who are/was/were = DELETE
with regard to = about/regarding
with the exception of = except for
witnessed firsthand = witnessed

CREDITS

This list of credits constitutes an extension of the copyright page. We have made every effort to trace the ownership of all copyrighted material and to secure permission from copyright holders. In the event of any question arising as to the use of any material, we will be pleased to make the necessary corrections in future printings. Thanks are due to the following authors, publishers, and agents for permission to use the material indicated.

Chapter 7
Pages 62–72: Reprinted with the permission of Simon & Schuster Adult Publishing Group, from THE CLOSING OF THE AMERICAN MIND by Allan Bloom. Copyright © 1987 by Allan Bloom. All rights reserved. **Pages 72–77:** Isabelle Leymarie, "Rock 'n' Revolt," reproduced from the *UNESCO Courier*, Feb. 1993, pp. 35–39. **Pages 78–81:** Copyright © 2005 by The New York Times Co. Reprinted with permission.

Chapter 8
Pages 84–89: From *Mayhem: Violence as Public Entertainment* by Sissela Bok, ISBN 0201489791. Copyright © 1998 by Sissela Bok. Reprinted by permission of Da Capo Press, a member of Perseus Books, L.L.C. **Pages 90–93:** P.J. O'Rourke, "I agree with me," *The Atlantic Monthly*, July/August 2004. Reprinted by permission of the author. **Pages 94–97:** Introduction to *Playboy* Interview: "Marshall McLuhan –A Candid Conversation with the High Priest of Popcult and Metaphysician of Media" from *The Essential McLuhan*, edited by Eric McLuhan and Frank Zingrone. Copyright © 1995. Reprinted with the permission of House of Anansi Press, Toronto. **Pages 97–125:** From the *Playboy* Interview: Marshall McLuhan, *Playboy* magazine (March 1969). Copyright © 1969 by Playboy. Reprinted with permission. All rights reserved. **Pages 126–127:** "My name is Joe! And I am Canadian!" reprinted by permission of Molson Canada. All rights reserved.

Chapter 9
Pages 129–131: Doug Beardsley "The Game Is at Canada's Core, and No Labor Dispute Can Dislodge It," *The New York Times,* 27 February 2005, Section 8, page 7. Reprinted with permission of Doug Beardsley. **Pages 132–137:** Reprinted by permission of Ken Dryden. **Pages 138–146:** Reproduced from *Hockey Dreams: Memories of a Man Who Couldn't Play* by David Adams Richards. Copyright © 1996 David Adams Richards. Reprinted by permission of Doubleday Canada.

Chapter 10
Pages 149–150: Copyright © 1990 by Pauline Kael. Reprinted by permission of Curtis Brown, Ltd. **Pages 151–155:** "A Century of Cinema" from WHERE THE STRESS FALLS by Susan Sontag. Copyright © 2001 by Susan Sontag. Reprinted by permission of Farrar, Straus and Giroux, LLC. **Pages 156–159:** Dan Brown *"Trailer Park Boys* Returns," *CBC News Online,* 6 April 2004. Reprinted by permission of CBC.ca.

Chapter 11
Pages 162–165: "Behold the Stone Age," TIME, February 13, 1995. © 2005 Time, Inc. Reprinted by permission. **Pages 166–168:** Northrop Frye "Canadian and Colonial Painting." © Victoria University. Published with permission of Victoria University, Toronto Canada. All rights reserved. **Page 167, photo:** TOM THOMSON Canadian, 1877–1917 Early Snow, 1916 oil on canvas 45.5 × 45.5 cm. Collection of The Winnipeg Art Gallery; acquired with the assistance of a grant from the Canadian Government, approved by the Minister of Canadian Heritage under the terms of the Cultural Property Export and Import Act, and with contributions by The Winnipeg Foundation, The Thomas Sill Foundation Inc., The Winnipeg Art Gallery Foundation Inc., Mr. and Mrs. G. B. Wiswell Fund, DeFehr Foundation Inc., Loch and Mayberry Fine Art Inc., and several anonymous donors Accession # 2000–1. **Pages 169–171:** "Letter to America" from MOVING TARGETS: WRITING WITH INTENT 1982–2004 copyright © 2004 by O.W. Toad Ltd. Reprinted with the permission of House of Anansi Press.

Chapter 12
Pages 176–177: Copyright © 2004 by The New York Times Co. Reprinted with permission. **Pages 178–180:** Kofi Annan "Development Without Borders," HARVARD INTERNATIONAL REVIEW, 23.2 (Summer 2001): 84. Reprinted with permission. **Pages 180–186:** Copyright © 2006 by The New York Times Co. Reprinted with permission.

Chapter 13
Pages 188–194: Jonathan Swift "A Modest Proposal." **Pages 195–198:** "On the meaning of plumbing and poverty" by Melanie Scheller. Reprinted with permission of Melanie Scheller. Originally published in *The Independent Weekly*, Durham, NC. **Pages 198–207:** From TRAVELS WITH LIZBETH by Lars Eighner. Copyright © 1993 by the author and reprinted by permission of St. Martin's Press, LLC.

Chapter 14
Pages 210–215: Gary Kleck, "There Are No Lessons to Be Learned from Littleton," as appeared in CRIMINAL JUSTICE ETHICS, Volume 18, Number 2 (Winter/Spring 1999) pp. 2, 61–63. Reprinted by permission of The Institute for Criminal Justice Ethics, 555 West 57th Street, Suite 607, New York, NY, 10019–1029. **Pages 216–228:** Ch. 3 — Homeboy, from THE AUTOBIOGRAPHY OF MALCOLM X by Malcolm X and Alex Haley, copyright © 1964 by Alex Haley and Malcolm X. Copyright © 1965 by Alex Haley and Betty Shabazz. Used by permission of Random House, Inc. **Pages 229–231:** © Tribune Media Services, Inc. All Rights Reserved. Reprinted with permission. **Pages 232–234:** David Frum, "Reaping What We Sow." Reprinted by permission of the author.

Chapter 15
Pages 237–239: Jane Smiley, "You Can Never Have Too Many." Reprinted by permission of the Molly Friedrich Agency. **Pages 240–244:** Gloria Steinem "Marilyn Monroe: The Woman Who Died Too Soon" *Ms* Magazine, 1972. Reprinted by permission of the author. All rights reserved. **Pages 245–247:** Rebecca Cook Dube "Canada's New PM Worries Gay Couples." USA TODAY. February 15, 2006. Reprinted with permission. **Pages 248–254:** John McMurtry "Kill 'em! Crush 'em! Eat 'em raw!" *Maclean's* Magazine, October 1971. Reprinted by permission of the author. All rights reserved.

Chapter 20
Pages 374–390: "Pandemic: My Country Is on Its Knees" from *Race Against Time* by Stephen Lewis. Copyright © 2005 by Stephen Lewis Associates Ltd. and the Canadian Broadcasting Corporation. Reprinted with the permission of House of Anansi Press. **Pages 390–393:** Daniel Defoe *A Journal of the Plague Year.* **Pages 393–404:** From A DISTANT MIRROR by Barbara W. Tuchman, copyright © 1978 by Barbara W. Tuchman. Used by permission of Alfred A. Knopf, a division of Random House, Inc.

Chapter 21
Pages 406–408: Copyright © 2006 by The New York Times Co. Reprinted with permission. **Pages 409–414:** Reprinted by permission of Bloomsbury USA. **Pages 414–417:** Stephen Leacock "Roughing It in the Bush" from *Over the Footlights.* **Pages 418–419:** "A Fable for Tomorrow," from SILENT SPRING by Rachel Carson. Copyright © 1962 by Rachel L. Carson, renewed 1990 by Roger Christie. Reprinted by permission of Houghton Mifflin Company. All rights reserved.

Appendixes
Pages 453 and 454–457: Reprinted with permission by Kim Blank.

INDEX